Fifth Edition

Math for College Students

Arithmetic with Introductions to Algebra and Geometry

Ronald Staszkow

Ohlone College

KENDALL/HUNT PUBLISHING COMPANY
4050 Westmark Drive Dubuque, Iowa 52002

Contents

Preface

To the Student

The fifth edition of *Math for College Students: Arithmetic with Introductions to Algebra and Geometry* contains the basic math that is the foundation for a college mathematics program. For some of you, the text will provide a review of mathematics you have learned in the past. For others, it will introduce material you may never have learned or may have forgotten. No matter where you find yourself in this continuum, *Math for College Students* will help develop your math skills. It has been written so that you can learn by actually working with mathematics. The text not only shows you how to solve problems, it also attempts to explain the "why" of the solution. Whether you are just out of high school or a reentry student, you will find that the text presents math in a very readable, clear, mature, and positive manner. I am confident that the following features of the text will assist you in learning mathematics.

▶ **Objectives:** A list of the skills you should acquire is given at the beginning of each unit and chapter.
▶ **Pretests:** At the beginning of each chapter, there is a test that you can take and correct. The purpose of the pretest is to help you determine which sections of a chapter you need to study in detail and which ones you can review quickly.
▶ **Explanations and Examples:** The text has readable explanations and detailed examples to show you the "how" and "why" of solving problems.
▶ **Problems:** In addition to explanations and examples, each section contains problems for you to solve. By checking your answers against the solutions given, you can determine your understanding of the concepts and mathematical processes in the section.
▶ **Exercises:** Each section of the text has two sets of exercises to give you practice on the math skills presented in the section.
▶ **Summaries:** At the end of each chapter, you will find a summary of the important concepts and terms used in that chapter.
▶ **Crossword Puzzles:** In each chapter, you will find a crossword puzzle that provides an interesting way to review the material in the chapter.
▶ **Practice Tests:** At the end of each chapter, you will find practice tests to help you evaluate your progress. At the end of each of the four units, you will find a unit exam to test your understanding of the unit. Finally, there is a final exam at the end of the text to check your mastery of all the material contained in the text.

► **Answers and Solutions:** In the Answer Section, you will find all the answers to pretests, exercises, chapter tests, unit exams, and the final exam. You will also find detailed solutions to many of the odd numbered exercises.

► **Humor:** Cartoons that contain some of my classroom humor will hopefully lessen some of the anxiety associated with learning mathematics. A little groan or chuckle in the midst of working on a math problem can be very therapeutic.

► **Recreations:** In each unit you will find a *Brain Buster* and *Math Magic* pages that will both challenge you and provide you with some math recreation.

► **Computer Tutor:** *DEVTUTOR* (computer tutorial program) is packaged with the text. This software, available for IBM and Apple Macintosh personal computers, will give you drill, practice, and tutoring on the major topics contained in the text.

It is my hope that this book will help you develop your math skills. Remember that math is not a spectator sport. You must participate in the solution of its problems in order to learn it. Even if you have experienced difficulty with mathematics in the past, I am confident that you can master the skills covered in the text. If you keep a positive attitude as you progress through the text and work at it earnestly, you can do it! I want to encourage you to develop your math skills and give you best wishes for success.

To the Instructor

This text has been written for college level students who want to acquire a better understanding of and facility with arithmetic and want an introduction to algebra and geometry. The text has enough explanations, examples, solved problems, exercises, tests, and review material to meet the needs of both individualized (lab based) and lecture formats. In this fifth edition, you will find more real-life application problems and exercises than in previous editions. You will also find new sections on the Pythagorean Theorem, properties of algebra, solving equations, translating words to algebra, word problems using algebra, and compound interest and annuities. Further, besides many minor changes, problems that use real data have been updated and the sections that include factoring whole numbers into primes and handling zeros in division have been substantially revised. These changes make the text ideal for pre-algebra courses.

The fifth edition also offers the following:

► a change in the title of the text from *Developmental Mathematics* to **Math for College Students: Arithmetic with Introductions to Algebra and Geometry** that gives a more positive statement about the focus and content of the text.

► a non-threatening format that encourages the student to work in the text itself, but leaves the explanations and examples intact even if the exercise sets are removed.

- ▶ explanations of the "how" and "why" of developmental mathematics that are concise, readable, and contain many examples and solved problems.
- ▶ a good collection of application problems that use real-life data and situations.
- ▶ over 3300 problems contained in exercises, pretests, practice tests, unit exams, and a final exam that have answers and selected solutions in the Answer Section.
- ▶ over 1200 supplementary exercises that have no answers in the text and are ideal for quizzes, homework, or class work.
- ▶ pretests, summaries, crossword puzzles, chapter tests, unit exams and a final exam that give excellent ways for students to review and assess their understanding of the material.
- ▶ a *brain buster* in each unit that will challenge the student, *Math Magic* pages that offer some mathematical recreation, and *cartoons* that provide some humor and hopefully, lessen student's anxiety towards math.

Ancillaries

The fifth edition of *Math for College Students: Arithmetic with Introductions to Algebra and Geometry* comes with an ancillary package that is invaluable to the instructor.

- ▶ **Instructors Resource Book:** This package contains ten forms of chapter, unit, and final exams, answers to supplementary problems, a skills assessment test, and a study guide for using the text in self-paced, individualized programs.
- ▶ *DEVTEST* (test generator): This computer software for IBM and Apple Macintosh computers allows an instructor to quickly generate multiple forms of chapter and unit exams for *Math for College Students.*
- ▶ *DEVTUTOR* (computer tutorial program): This computer software for the IBM and Apple Macintosh interacts with the student giving him/her drill, practice, and tutoring on the major topics contained in *Math for College Students.* The software will be packaged with the text so each student will have access to his/her own computer tutor.

For more information on these ancillary materials contact Kendall/Hunt Publishers.

Acknowledgments

I would like to thank the many students and instructors that used previous editions for their suggestions. I would also like to recognize Bob Bradshaw and Virginia Tebelskis of Ohlone College, and my wife Dianne for their help in making this fifth edition a reality.

Ronald Staszkow

Unit I

Whole Numbers

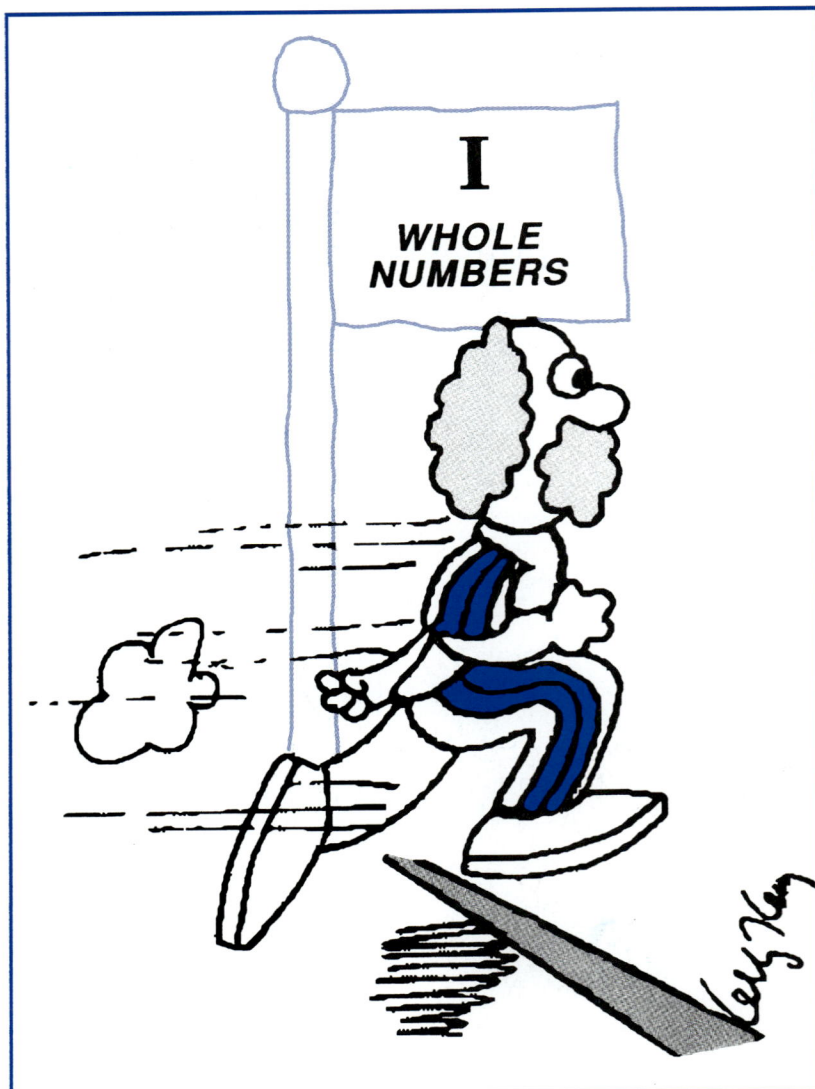

Numbers are all around us. Just take a minute to look back over your day. Try to remember how many times you worked with numbers. Did you do any shopping? Did you pay any sales tax? Did you write a check or balance your checking account? Did you measure ingredients for a recipe or lumber for a bookshelf?

Whether you are at home, in a grocery store, driving along a freeway, using a credit card, or reading the sports page, mathematics is there. In our everyday lives and in many occupations, it is important to understand and be able to work with numbers.

In this unit you will learn to operate with the whole numbers (0, 1, 2, 3, 4, 5, 6, 7, 8, 9, 10, 11, 12, 13, and so on). When you have finished this unit, you should be able to do the following:

1. perform addition, subtraction, multiplication, and division of whole numbers.
2. read, round off, and express whole numbers in expanded exponent form.
3. use the "equals" sign, "greater than" sign, and the "less than" sign.
4. compute simple powers and square roots.
5. use the proper order of computation when different operations are combined in a problem.
6. factor whole numbers into primes.
7. solve word problems that involve operations with whole numbers.

Brain Buster

Your boss offers to pay you according to this scheme:
You get $1 for the first day,
        $2 for the second day,
        $4 for the third day,
        $8 for the fourth day, etc.
        (your daily wage doubles each day).
If you worked 20 days that month,
a. how much would you make on the 20th day?
b. what would your total wages be for the month?
(Hint: You would be a millionaire!)

Chapter 1

Whole Numbers: Addition, Multiplication, Powers, and Square Roots

After finishing the first chapter, you should be able to do the following:

1. read and round off whole numbers.
2. add whole numbers.
3. multiply whole numbers.
4. calculate powers and simple square roots of whole numbers.
5. use the =, >, and < signs.
6. write whole numbers in expanded exponent form.
7. solve word problems using addition and multiplication.

On the next page, you will find a pretest for this chapter. The purpose of the pretest is to help you determine which sections in this chapter you need to study in detail and which sections you can review quickly. By taking and correcting the pretest according to the instructions on the next page, you can better plan your pace through this chapter.

Chapter 1 Pretest

Take and correct this test using the answer section at the end of the book. Those problems that give you difficulty indicate which sections need extra attention. Section numbers are in parentheses before each problem.

(1.1) 1. Write the following using numbers and commas: six hundred two million, sixty-seven thousand, five

1. _____

(1.1) 2. Write the following number in words: 42,107

2. _____

(1.2) In problems 3–4, round off 542,950 to the place indicated.

3. hundreds place

3. _____

4. ten thousands place

4. _____

In problems 5–12, evaluate each expression.

(1.4) 5. $41 + 1278 + 6$

5. _____

(1.4) 6. $5007 + 37 + 4716 + 5 + 87{,}998$

6. _____

(1.6) 7. 356×7

7. _____

(1.7) 8. 6359×486

8. _____

(1.8) 9. $248 \times 95{,}000{,}000$

9. _____

(1.8)   10. $806 \times 4{,}000{,}009$ 10. _____

(1.9)   11. 2^3 11. _____

(1.9)   12. $\sqrt{49}$ 12. _____

(1.9)   13. Write 5,306 in expanded exponent form.   13. _____

(1.9)   In problems 14–15, replace the question mark with >, <, or =.

         14. $0 \times 9 \; ? \; 9 \times 1$ 14. _____

         15. $4^2 \; ? \; \sqrt{64}$ 15. _____

(1.10)   16. How much would a family of 2 adults and 4 children pay to   16. _____
             attend a baseball game, if adults pay $12 and children pay $9?

1.1 Reading Whole Numbers

Number:
The dentist numbed her with novocaine.

All whole numbers can be formed using the **digits** 0, 1, 2, 3, 4, 5, 6, 7, 8, and 9. This can be done since a digit's position in a number gives it a specific meaning called its **place value.**

For example:

In 576,
    the 5 means 5 hundreds (500)
    the 7 means 7 tens (70)
    the 6 means 6 ones (6).

Thus, 576 is read "five hundred seventy-six."

In 4,208,
    the 4 means 4 thousands (4000)
    the 2 means 2 hundreds (200)
    the 0 means 0 tens
    the 8 means 8 ones (8).

Thus, 4,208 is read "four thousand, two hundred, eight."

The following is a chart for the place values in our number system:

Value of Each Group

billions			millions			thousands					
6	7	8	3	1	0	4	5	6	1	2	7
hundred billions	ten billions	billions	hundred millions	ten millions	millions	hundred thousands	ten thousands	thousands	hundreds	tens	ones

In the United States, large numbers are separated into groups of three digits and read according to this place value chart.

For example: In the number 17832536 you would start from the right hand side of the number and mark off every three digits with a comma as follows:

17,832,536

You then read each group of digits that was marked off, followed by the value for that group as noted on the place value chart.

$$1\ \underline{7}\ ,\ \underline{8}\ \ 3\ \ 2\ ,\ \underline{5}\ \ 3\ \ 6$$

millions

thousands

five hundred thirty-six

eight hundred thirty-two *thousand*

seventeen *million*

Thus, the number is read "seventeen million, eight hundred thirty-two thousand, five hundred thirty-six."

Remember: When placing commas to separate the digits, always start from the right hand side of the number and work your way to the left, marking off every three digits.

Note: The word "and" is not used when writing the word equivalent for whole numbers. It is used to indicate the placement of a decimal point, as we shall see later. For example, 5008 is read "five thousand, eight." It is *not* read "five thousand and eight."

Note: Compound numbers from 21 to 99 are written with a hyphen, such as twenty-one or ninety-nine.

Problem 1: Write 10,487 in words.

Answer: ten thousand, four hundred eighty-seven

Problem 2: Write 2,003,500 in words.

Answer: two million, three thousand, five hundred

Problem 3: In the number 325,467 what does the:

5 represent?

4 represent?

2 represent?

Answers:

5 thousands (5000)
4 hundreds (400)
2 ten thousands (20,000)

Problem 4: Write using numbers:

a. four hundred twenty-two million, ten

b. thirty-five billion, twenty-seven million, two thousand, six

Answers:
a. 422,000,010
b. 35,027,002,006

Exercise 1.1   Set A

In problems 1–7, write each number in words.

1. 852

2. 4,256

3. 17,109

4. 3,057,010

5. 14,100,700

6. 946,003

7. 1,357,926,183

1. _____
2. _____
3. _____
4. _____
5. _____
6. _____
7. _____

In problems 8–16, write each expression using numbers and commas.

8. seven hundred forty-five

9. fifty thousand, sixty-eight

10. one hundred five thousand, six

11. forty million, thirty-six

12. five million, seven thousand, two hundred thirty-eight

13. twelve billion, fifteen million

14. eighty-nine billion, eighty-nine

15. three hundred thirteen million, seven hundred ten thousand

16. seven hundred twelve million, four hundred twenty-two

8. _____
9. _____
10. _____
11. _____
12. _____
13. _____
14. _____
15. _____
16. _____

In problems 17–21, consider the number 5,876,492.

17. What does the 5 represent?

18. What does the 9 represent?

19. What does the 8 represent?

20. What does the 6 represent?

21. What does the 7 represent?

17. _____
18. _____
19. _____
20. _____
21. _____

Exercise 1.1   Set B

In problems 1–7, write each number in words.

1. 925

2. 6,172

3. 13,402

4. 6,026,050

5. 17,200,400

6. 196,002

7. 4,307,916,452

1. _____

2. _____

3. _____

4. _____

5. _____

6. _____

7. _____

In problems 8–16, write each expression using numbers and commas.

8. nine hundred sixteen

9. thirty thousand, forty-three

10. two hundred seven thousand, four

11. fifty million, seventy-two thousand, forty

12. four million, six thousand, three hundred eighty-five

13. eighteen billion, twelve million

14. seventy-nine billion, thirty-five

15. one hundred forty-four million, seven hundred thirty thousand

16. nine hundred thirteen million, five hundred fifty-three

8. _____

9. _____

10. _____

11. _____

12. _____

13. _____

14. _____

15. _____

16. _____

In problems 17–21, consider the number 1,827,645.

17. What does the 2 represent?

18. What does the 8 represent?

19. What does the 1 represent?

20. What does the 6 represent?

21. What does the 7 represent?

17. _____

18. _____

19. _____

20. _____

21. _____

1.2   Rounding Off Numbers

Whole Numbers:

The digits in that sign have holes in them. They must be hole-numbers.

If the number of people living in your city were 178,952 ,the road sign would probably read as in the illustration on the left.

The sign gives the approximate population of the city. It is just an estimate of the number of people living there. We say that the population has been rounded off. When you round off a number, it is close to the original number. Rounded numbers are easier to visualize and simpler to work with than the original numbers. Rounded numbers can be used to estimate answers in complicated math problems.

Rounding Off to the Nearest Ten

If you were to count by tens you would say 10, 20, 30, 40, 50, 60, 70, etc. These are called the multiples of ten.

To round off a given number to the nearest ten, you must find the multiple of ten that is closest to the number.

For example: To round off 37 to the nearest ten, the answer would be 40, since 37 is between 30 and 40 but is closer to 40. We say 37 rounds off to 40.

On the other hand, 32 rounds off to 30, since it is closer to 30. We say 32 rounds off to 30.

Now 35 is halfway between 30 and 40. In this case, round it off to the higher multiple of ten. Thus, 35 rounds off to 40.

Problem 1:   Round off 86 to the nearest ten

Answer: 90
86 is between 80 and 90 but is closer to 90.

Problem 2:   Round off 723 to the nearest ten.

Answer: 720
723 is between 720 and 730 but is closer to 720.

Problem 3:   Round off 2695 to the nearest ten.

Answer: 2700
Since 2695 is halfway between 2690 and 2700, round off to the higher multiple, 2700.

Rounding Off to the Nearest Hundred

The multiples of a hundred are 100, 200, 300, 400, 500, 600, and so on.

To round off a given number to the nearest hundred, you must find the multiple of a hundred that is closest to the number.

For example: 768 rounds off to 800 since 768 is between 700 and 800 but is closer to the higher multiple of a hundred, 800.

725 rounds off to 700 since it is closer to the lower multiple of a hundred, 700.

Rounding Off to Other Places

You round off to other places in our number system using the same procedure as was used in rounding off to the nearest ten or hundred. You round off to the lower multiple if a given number is less than half the way between two multiples. You round off to the higher multiple if it isn't. An easy way to decide this is as follows:

> ### Basic Round Off Rule
>
> Look at the digit to the right of the place you are rounding to. If that digit is 5 or more, round off to the higher multiple. Otherwise, round off to the lower multiple.

Example 1

Round off 28,752 to the nearest thousand.

$$28{,}752 \approx 29{,}000 \quad (\approx \text{ means "is approximately equal to."})$$

thousands place $\longrightarrow$ digit to the right is more than 5

Thus, you round off to the higher multiple of a thousand by changing the 8 to a 9, getting 29 thousands (29,000).

Example 2

Round off 413,207,593 to the nearest million.

$$413{,}207{,}593 \approx 413{,}000{,}000$$

millions place $\longrightarrow$ digit to the right is less than 5

Thus, you round off to the lower multiple of a million by leaving the 3 unchanged, getting 413 millions (413,000,000). Notice: All the digits to the left of the millions place are unchanged while those to the right are replaced with zeros.

Problem 4:   Round off 865,000 to the nearest ten thousand.

Answer: 870,000
Since the digit to the right of the ten thousands place is a 5, round off to the higher multiple by adding one to the ten thousands place.

Problem 5:   Round off 96,379 to the nearest thousand.

Answer: 96,000
Since the digit to the right of the thousands place is less than 5, do not increase the 6 in the thousands place. Leave the first two digits as 96 and replace the 379 with zeros.

Exercise 1.2   Set A

In problems 1–7, round off each number to the nearest ten.

1. 53

2. 76

3. 25

4. 506

5. 1473

6. 5895

7. 6997

1. _____

2. _____

3. _____

4. _____

5. _____

6. _____

7. _____

In problems 8–14, round off each number to the nearest hundred.

8. 549

9. 872

10. 650

11. 14,736

12. 27,864

13. 179,950

14. 1,538,276

8. _____

9. _____

10. _____

11. _____

12. _____

13. _____

14. _____

In problems 15–22, round off 215,749,538 to the place indicated.

15. tens place

16. hundreds place

17. thousands place

18. ten thousands place

19. hundred thousands place

20. millions place

21. ten millions place

22. hundred millions place

15. _____

16. _____

17. _____

18. _____

19. _____

20. _____

21. _____

22. _____

Exercise 1.2   Set B

In problems 1–7, round off each number to the nearest ten.

1. 72

2. 48

3. 65

4. 307

5. 2582

6. 4795

7. 3996

1. _____

2. _____

3. _____

4. _____

5. _____

6. _____

7. _____

In problems 8–14, round off each number to the nearest hundred.

8. 748

9. 562

10. 850

11. 25,604

12. 37,589

13. 79,950

14. 4,356,495

8. _____

9. _____

10. _____

11. _____

12. _____

13. _____

14. _____

In problems 15–22, round off 927,563,742 to the place indicated.

15. tens place

16. hundreds place

17. thousands place

18. ten thousands place

19. hundred thousands place

20. millions place

21. ten millions place

22. hundred millions place

15. _____

16. _____

17. _____

18. _____

19. _____

20. _____

21. _____

22. _____

1.3 Addition Facts

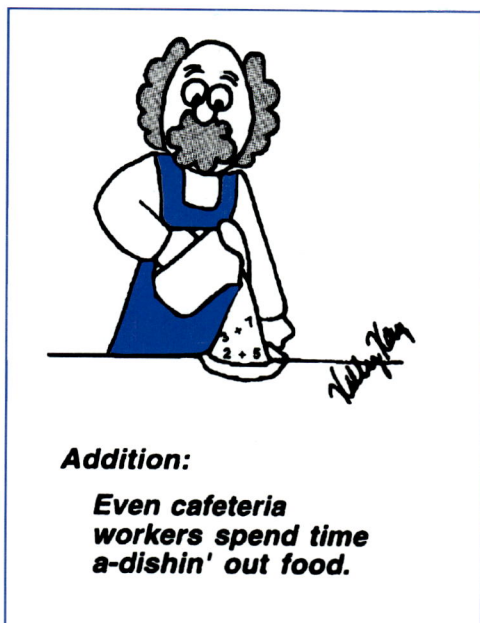

Addition:

Even cafeteria workers spend time a-dishin' out food.

If you drove 5 miles to the store and from there you drove 3 miles to school, how far did you drive? To find the total miles driven you add the two distances and get the answer, 8 miles. We would say:

5 plus 3 equals 8

or 5 + 3   =   8.

The names given to each part of an addition problem such as that are:

addend   addend   sum
↓   ↓   ↓
5   +   3   =   8

This first operation with whole numbers is the basis for the other operations. Addition must be learned well before progress can be made in developing your math skills.

The chart below gives the basic addition facts that you should know.

+	0	1	2	3	4	5	6	7	8	9
0	0	1	2	3	4	5	6	7	8	9
1	1	2	3	4	5	6	7	8	9	10
2	2	3	4	5	6	7	8	9	10	11
3	3	4	5	6	7	8	9	10	11	12
4	4	5	6	7	8	9	10	11	12	13
5	5	6	7	8	9	10	11	12	13	14
6	6	7	8	9	10	11	12	13	14	15
7	7	8	9	10	11	12	13	14	15	16
8	8	9	10	11	12	13	14	14	16	17
9	9	10	11	12	13	14	15	16	17	18

To find the answer to any addition problem, such as 6 + 8, find the 6 on the left hand side and go along that row until you reach the 8 at the top of the chart. That number (14) will be the answer to 6 + 8.

Problem 1:   Find 7 + 9 using the chart.   Answer: 16

Problem 2:   Find 4 + 7 using the chart.   Answer: 11

Since you can not carry that addition chart around with you at all times, you must learn the basic addition facts by working with them. On the next page, you will find rows of problems along with their answers. These rows of problems can help you become better at addition. You might also find the use of "flash cards" helpful in mastering the basic addition facts.

Self Drill in Addition

Directions:

1. Cover the answers for a row.
2. Quickly figure out and write down your answer to each problem.
3. Check your work.
4. Repeat this for each row until you can do each one quickly and correctly.

1 +0 **1**	4 +2 **6**	2 +1 **3**	5 +2 **7**	5 +0 **5**	1 +3 **4**	3 +3 **6**	8 +1 **9**	5 +1 **6**	6 +3 **9**
4 +0 **4**	2 +2 **4**	4 +3 **7**	6 +2 **8**	7 +0 **7**	7 +3 **10**	9 +0 **9**	3 +1 **4**	1 +1 **2**	9 +3 **12**
0 +0 **0**	7 +1 **8**	2 +0 **2**	1 +2 **3**	9 +1 **10**	8 +2 **10**	3 +0 **3**	0 +3 **3**	7 +2 **9**	6 +0 **6**
8 +3 **11**	9 +2 **11**	6 +1 **7**	2 +3 **5**	0 +2 **2**	8 +0 **8**	5 +3 **8**	3 +2 **5**	4 +1 **5**	0 +1 **1**
1 +4 **5**	3 +5 **8**	4 +6 **10**	5 +5 **10**	3 +6 **9**	6 +4 **10**	2 +6 **8**	6 +6 **12**	9 +4 **13**	4 +4 **8**
1 +6 **7**	5 +4 **9**	7 +5 **12**	8 +4 **12**	2 +5 **7**	8 +6 **14**	1 +5 **6**	5 +6 **11**	6 +5 **11**	7 +4 **11**
0 +5 **5**	4 +5 **9**	9 +6 **15**	0 +6 **6**	2 +4 **6**	9 +5 **14**	0 +4 **4**	3 +4 **7**	8 +5 **13**	7 +6 **13**
1 +7 **8**	9 +8 **17**	4 +7 **11**	3 +9 **12**	4 +9 **13**	6 +7 **13**	8 +7 **15**	1 +8 **9**	2 +9 **11**	2 +7 **9**
5 +8 **13**	3 +7 **10**	6 +9 **15**	7 +8 **15**	5 +9 **14**	7 +9 **16**	3 +8 **11**	5 +7 **12**	4 +8 **12**	9 +9 **18**
9 +7 **16**	0 +8 **8**	8 +8 **16**	6 +8 **14**	0 +9 **9**	7 +7 **14**	8 +9 **17**	1 +9 **10**	2 +8 **10**	0 +7 **7**

1.4 Adding Whole Numbers

Once the basic addition facts have been mastered, you can proceed to the addition of larger whole numbers. Let me explain how that is done.

> To add whole numbers you add the digits in the ones place, tens place, hundreds place, etc. of each whole number.

For example: To add 74 and 23 you place the numbers above each other, lining up respective columns.

tens ———⌐ ⌐ — ones
$$74$$
$$+23$$
$$97$$

→ 4 ones + 3 ones = 7 ones

→ 7 tens + 2 tens = 9 tens

Example 1

544 + 32 + 3 = ?

$$544$$
$$32$$
$$+3$$
$$579$$

→ 4 ones + 2 ones + 3 ones = 9 ones

→ 4 tens + 3 tens = 7 tens

→ 5 hundreds

To check your answer, try adding the numbers in a different order.

Problem 1:   1573 + 2312 = ?

Answer: 3885   Check:

$$1573$$ $$2312$$
$$+2312$$ $$+1573$$
$$3885$$ $$3885$$

Problem 2:   641 + 324 + 13 = ?

Answer: 978   Check:

$$641$$ $$13$$
$$324$$ $$641$$
$$+13$$ $$+324$$
$$978$$ $$978$$

If you try to find 47 + 25 in the same manner as the above problems, you will discover that when you add the digits in the ones column, you get 12. Since you can not have a two digit number in the ones place, what do you do?

Example 2

47 + 25 = ?

```
  1 ←————— number carried
 47
+25
 72
```

→ 7 ones + 5 ones = 12 ones (1 ten and 2 ones). Put just the 2 in the ones place and carry the 1 ten to the tens column.

→ 1 ten + 4 tens + 2 tens = 7 tens

Example 3

287 + 158 + 39 = ?

```
  1 2 ←————— numbers carried
287
158
+ 39
484
```

→ 7 ones + 8 ones + 9 ones = 24 ones (2 tens and 4 ones). Put the 4 in the ones place and carry the 2 to the tens column.

→ 2 tens + 8 tens + 5 tens + 3 tens = 18 tens (1 hundred and 8 tens). Put the 8 in the tens place and carry the 1 to the hundreds column.

→ 1 hundred + 2 hundreds + 1 hundred = 4 hundreds

Problem 3:   3576 + 687 = ?

Answer: 4263

```
  111
 3576
+ 687
 4263
```

Problem 4: 1872 + 54 + 137 + 34,567 = ?

Answer: 36,630

```
  122
 1872
   54
  137
+34567
 36630
```

Problem 5: 276 + 89 + 2435 + 9 + 500 = ?

Answer: 3219

```
  122
  276
   89
 2345
    9
+ 500
 3219
```

Exercise 1.4   Set A

1.   45
    +23

2.   76
    +12

3.   356
    + 24

4.   729
    + 46

5. 5072
    + 946

6. 8906
    + 398

7.   426
    5382
    + 90

8.   716
    2053
    + 84

9.   5
     76
    130
    +256

10.   7
      83
    5200
    + 194

11. 76 + 128

12. 405 + 21 + 7

13. 1400 + 7 + 322 + 17

14. 576,276 + 8,006 + 475

15. 52 + 9000 + 876 + 43 + 4

16. 5,000,300 + 852,176 + 3,820

17. 18 + 196 + 45 + 2463 + 757 + 95

1. _____

2. _____

3. _____

4. _____

5. _____

6. _____

7. _____

8. _____

9. _____

10. _____

11. _____

12. _____

13. _____

14. _____

15. _____

16. _____

17. _____

Exercise 1.4   Set B

1.
$$\begin{array}{r} 62 \\ +15 \\ \hline \end{array}$$

2.
$$\begin{array}{r} 34 \\ +25 \\ \hline \end{array}$$

3.
$$\begin{array}{r} 756 \\ + 17 \\ \hline \end{array}$$

4.
$$\begin{array}{r} 243 \\ + 49 \\ \hline \end{array}$$

5.
$$\begin{array}{r} 4706 \\ + 385 \\ \hline \end{array}$$

6.
$$\begin{array}{r} 9821 \\ + 359 \\ \hline \end{array}$$

7.
$$\begin{array}{r} 25 \\ 4186 \\ + 385 \\ \hline \end{array}$$

8.
$$\begin{array}{r} 987 \\ 1063 \\ + 45 \\ \hline \end{array}$$

9.
$$\begin{array}{r} 4 \\ 706 \\ 3819 \\ + 26 \\ \hline \end{array}$$

10.
$$\begin{array}{r} 7 \\ 56 \\ 820 \\ +754 \\ \hline \end{array}$$

11. 84 + 257

12. 809 + 28 + 9

13. 4500 + 296 + 7 + 63

14. 321,506 + 875 + 5,321

15. 94 + 7000 + 326 + 43 + 6

16. 6,000,200 + 763,918 + 3,457

17. 25 + 283 + 76 + 4076 + 656 + 87

1. _____
2. _____
3. _____
4. _____
5. _____
6. _____
7. _____
8. _____
9. _____
10. _____
11. _____
12. _____
13. _____
14. _____
15. _____
16. _____
17. _____

1.5 Multiplication Facts

Factor:
Some wonder if math
is fact or fiction.

If you knocked down 9 pins in six consecutive frames of bowling, how many total pins did you knock down? One way to find the answer is to add 9 for each of the six frames. That is:

$$9 + 9 + 9 + 9 + 9 + 9 = 54$$

There is another way to think through that problem. What you have is six nines. Instead of adding nines together, we say six times nine is 54 ($6 \times 9 = 54$). In mathematics, repeated addition is called multiplication. For example:

$$7 \times 8 \text{ means } 8 + 8 + 8 + 8 + 8 + 8 + 8 = 56$$

$$3 \times 12 \text{ means } 12 + 12 + 12 = 36$$

Each part of such a multiplication problem has a name.

factor		factor		product
↓		↓		↓
6	×	9	=	54

If you were asked to find $637 \times 15{,}218$ by repeated addition, you would have quite a job on your hands. That problem could be done much quicker, if you knew the basic multiplication facts and how to apply them.

The next objective in developing your mathematics skills is to master the basic multiplication facts. They are displayed on the chart below. Since every chapter from here on relies heavily on having these facts memorized, it is extremely important that you take time to learn them well. The self-drill in multiplication on the next page will help make that a little easier. You might also find the use of "flash cards" helpful in mastering the basic multiplication facts.

×	0	1	2	3	4	5	6	7	8	9
0	0	0	0	0	0	0	0	0	0	0
1	0	1	2	3	4	5	6	7	8	9
2	0	2	4	6	8	10	12	14	16	18
3	0	3	6	9	12	15	18	21	24	27
4	0	4	8	12	16	20	24	28	32	36
5	0	5	10	15	20	25	30	35	40	45
6	0	6	12	18	24	30	36	42	48	54
7	0	7	14	21	28	35	42	49	56	63
8	0	8	16	24	32	40	48	56	64	72
9	0	9	18	27	36	45	54	63	72	81

To find the answer to any multiplication problem, such as 6×8, find the 6 on the left hand side and go along that row until you reach the 8 at the top of the chart. That number (48) will be the answer to 6×8.

Self Drill in Multiplication

Directions:

1. Cover the answers for a row.
2. Quickly figure out and write down your answer to each problem.
3. Check your work.
4. Repeat this for each row until you can do each one quickly and correctly.

1	4	2	5	5	1	3	8	5	6
×0	×2	×1	× 2	×0	×3	×3	×1	×5	× 3
0	8	2	10	0	3	9	8	25	18

8	9	6	2	0	8	5	3	4	0
×3	×2	×1	×3	×2	×0	×3	×2	×1	×1
24	18	6	6	0	0	15	6	4	0

1	3	4	5	3	6	2	6	9	4
×4	× 5	× 6	× 5	× 6	× 4	× 6	× 6	× 4	× 4
4	15	24	25	18	24	12	36	36	16

1	5	7	8	2	8	1	5	6	7
×6	×4	×5	×4	×5	×6	×5	×6	×5	×4
6	20	35	32	10	48	5	30	30	28

0	4	9	0	2	9	0	3	8	7
×5	×5	×6	×6	×4	×5	×4	×4	×5	×6
0	20	54	0	8	45	0	12	40	42

1	9	4	3	4	6	8	1	2	2
×7	×8	×7	×9	×9	×7	×7	×8	×9	×7
7	72	28	27	36	42	56	8	18	14

5	3	6	7	5	7	3	5	4	9
×8	×7	×9	×8	×9	×9	×8	×7	×8	×9
40	21	54	56	45	63	24	35	32	81

9	0	8	6	0	7	8	1	2	0
×7	×8	×8	×8	×9	×7	×9	×9	×8	×7
63	0	64	48	0	49	72	9	16	0

6	7	9	8	7	6	9	7	8	8
×7	×8	×8	×6	×9	×9	×7	×8	×9	×8
42	56	72	48	63	54	63	56	72	64

6	6	8	9	7	9	7	8	6	9
×6	×8	×7	×9	×8	×7	×6	×8	×9	×8
36	48	56	81	56	63	42	64	54	72

1.6 Multiplying by One Digit Numbers

Once the basic multiplication facts have been mastered, you can proceed to the multiplication of any whole number by a one digit number. Study the following examples and explanations to understand how that is done.

Example 1

$2 \times 34 = ?$

$$
\begin{array}{r}
34 \\
\times\ 2 \\
\hline
68
\end{array}
$$

First place the numbers above each other and multiply each digit of 34 by the 2.

$\longrightarrow 2 \times 4$ ones = 8 ones

$\longrightarrow 2 \times 3$ tens = 6 tens

Example 2

$4 \times 316 = ?$

$$
\begin{array}{r}
2 \longleftarrow \text{number carried} \\
316 \\
\times\quad 4 \\
\hline
1264
\end{array}
$$

$\longrightarrow 4 \times 6$ ones = 24 (2 tens and 4 ones). Put the 4 in the ones place and carry the 2 to the tens column.

$\longrightarrow 4 \times 1$ ten = 4 tens, plus the 2 tens that were carried is 6 tens.

$\longrightarrow 4 \times 3 = 12$ hundreds

Example 3

$7 \times 6142 = ?$

$$
\begin{array}{r}
21 \longleftarrow \text{numbers carried} \\
6142 \\
\times\qquad 7 \\
\hline
42994
\end{array}
$$

$\longrightarrow 7 \times 2$ ones = 14 (1 ten and 4 ones). Put the 4 in the ones place and carry the 1 to the tens column.

$\longrightarrow 7 \times 4$ tens = 28 tens, plus the 1 ten that we carried equals 29 tens (2 hundreds and 9 tens). Put the 9 in the tens place and carry the 2 to the hundreds column.

$\longrightarrow 7 \times 1$ hundred = 7 hundreds, plus the 2 hundreds that we carried is 9 hundreds.

$\longrightarrow 7 \times 6$ thousands = 42 thousands

By studying the previous examples you can see that to multiply by a one digit number, just multiply each digit of the number by the one digit number. You must, however, remember to carry whenever a product has more than one digit.

Try to apply that principle to the following problems.

Problem 1: $6 \times 371 = ?$

Answer: 2226

$$\begin{array}{r} 4 \\ 371 \\ \times 6 \\ \hline 2226 \end{array}$$

Problem 2: $8 \times 1503 = ?$

Answer: 12,024

$$\begin{array}{r} 42 \\ 1503 \\ \times 8 \\ \hline 12024 \end{array}$$

Problem 3: $5 \times 28,746 = ?$

Answer: 143,730

$$\begin{array}{r} 4323 \\ 28746 \\ \times 5 \\ \hline 143730 \end{array}$$

Problem 4: $7 \times 900,707 = ?$

Answer: 6,304,949

$$\begin{array}{r} 44 \\ 900707 \\ \times 7 \\ \hline 6304949 \end{array}$$

Problem 5: $3 \times 67,127 \times 9 = ?$

Answer: 1,812,429

$$\begin{array}{r} 22 \\ 67127 \\ \times 3 \\ \hline 201381 \end{array} \qquad \begin{array}{r} 137 \\ 201381 \\ \times 9 \\ \hline 1812429 \end{array}$$

Exercise 1.6   Set A

1.   53
      × 4

2.   87
      × 6

3.   78
      × 9

4.   97
      × 8

5.   542
      × 3

6.   715
      × 4

7.   193
      × 5

8.   526
      × 7

9.   5706
      × 2

10. 3904
      × 6

11. 15,326
      × 7

12. 24,185
      × 8

13. 4 × 2576

14. 5 × 195

15. 6 × 23,400

16. 7 × 75,674

17. 8 × 1,238,475

18. 9 × 15,768,207

19. 3 × 4768 × 2

1. _____

2. _____

3. _____

4. _____

5. _____

6. _____

7. _____

8. _____

9. _____

10. _____

11. _____

12. _____

13. _____

14. _____

15. _____

16. _____

17. _____

18. _____

19. _____

Exercise 1.6 Set B

1.   81
   × 3

2.   74
   × 2

3.   67
   × 9

4.   87
   × 8

5.   423
   × 4

6.   614
   × 4

7.   294
   × 5

8.   876
   × 7

9.   5608
   × 2

10.   8706
   × 6

11. 24,376
   × 7

12. 75,149
   × 8

13. 4×1938

14. $5 \times 20{,}756$

15. $6 \times 153{,}282$

16. $7 \times 4{,}000{,}758$

17. $8 \times 56{,}798$

18. $9 \times 4{,}239{,}476$

19. $2 \times 47{,}628 \times 3$

1. _____
2. _____
3. _____
4. _____
5. _____
6. _____
7. _____
8. _____
9. _____
10. _____
11. _____
12. _____
13. _____
14. _____
15. _____
16. _____
17. _____
18. _____
19. _____

1.7 Multiplying by Numbers Having More than One Digit

Using what you have learned about multiplying by one digit numbers, enables you to move on to multiplying by larger whole numbers.

Let me show you how this is done by again working out and explaining some examples.

Example 1

$21 \times 32 = ?$

tens
ones

$\begin{array}{r} 21 \\ \times 32 \\ \hline 42 \\ 63 \\ \hline 672 \end{array}$

2 ones × 21 = 42 ones, so the last digit of 42 is placed in the ones column.

3 tens × 21 = 63 tens, so the last digit of 63 is placed in the tens column.

Now, add those products, making sure the 42 and the 63 are lined up under their respective multipliers: the 42 ends under the 2; the 63 ends under the 3.

Example 2

$516 \times 48 = ?$

$\begin{array}{r} 2 \\ 14 \\ 516 \\ \times\ \ \ 48 \\ \hline 4128 \\ 2064 \\ \hline 24768 \end{array}$

number carried when multiplying by the 4

numbers carried when multiplying by the 8

8 ones × 516 = 4128 ones

4 tens × 516 = 2064 tens

adding those products

Example 3

$327 \times 402 = ?$

$\begin{array}{r} 1\,2 \\ 1 \\ 327 \\ \times 402 \\ \hline 654 \\ 000 \\ 1308 \\ \hline 131454 \end{array}$

numbers carried when multiplying by the 4

number carried when multiplying by the 2

2 ones × 327 = 654 ones

0 tens × 327 = 000 tens

4 hundreds × 327 = 1308 hundreds

adding those products

Notice that the products 654, 000, and 1308 were lined up under their multipliers. The 654 ended under its multiplier 2, the 000 ended under its multiplier 0, and the 1308 ended under its multiplier 4.

To check your answer, try multiplying the numbers in the reverse order.

Problem 1: $571 \times 25 = ?$

Answer: 14,275

Check:

1	2
3	3
571	25
× 25	×571
2855	25
1142	175
14275	125
	14275

Problem 2: $382 \times 560 = ?$

Answer: 213,920

Check:

	1
41	4
41	1
382	560
×560	× 382
000	1120
2292	4480
1910	1680
213920	213920

Problem 3: $15,218 \times 37 = ?$

Answer: 563,066

1   2
3115
15218
× 37
106526
45654
563066

Problem 4: $5036 \times 727 = ?$

Answer: 3,661,172

24
1
24
5036
× 727
35252
10072
35252
3661172

Exercise 1.7   Set A

1.   41
      ×23

2.   34
      ×12

3.   984
     × 67

4.   573
     × 89

5.   407
     × 53

6.   503
     × 84

7.   518
     ×280

8.   473
     ×910

9. 14,256
     ×   568

10. 23,819
     ×   476

11. 5016×58

12. 653×356

13. $74,113 \times 142$

14. $51,763 \times 605$

15. 823×6515

16. $41 \times 816 \times 7556$

1. _____

2. _____

3. _____

4. _____

5. _____

6. _____

7. _____

8. _____

9. _____

10. _____

11. _____

12. _____

13. _____

14. _____

15. _____

16. _____

Exercise 1.7   Set B

1.   43
    ×22

2.   43
    ×31

3.   652
    × 84

4.   539
    × 76

5.   701
    × 85

6.   806
    × 49

7.   624
    ×180

8.   752
    ×920

9. 17,628
    ×   476

10. 34,786
    ×   983

11. 6207 × 47

12. 749 × 394

13. 65,211 × 185

14. 51,487 × 506

15. 945 × 5165

16. 45 × 184 × 6443

1. _____

2. _____

3. _____

4. _____

5. _____

6. _____

7. _____

8. _____

9. _____

10. _____

11. _____

12. _____

13. _____

14. _____

15. _____

16. _____

1.8 Handling Zeros in Multiplying Whole Numbers

Zeros at the End of a Multiplier

If you were to use the process explained in the last section to multiply 21000 by 3000, it would look like this:

$$
\begin{array}{r}
21000 \\
\times\ \ 3000 \\
\hline
00000 \\
00000 \\
00000 \\
63000 \\
\hline
63000000
\end{array}
$$

Multiplying by all those zeros seems to just take space and waste time. There is a more efficient way to do that problem. Since any number times zero is equal to zero, and since the only nonzero answers occurred when you multiplied by the 3, why bother writing all those zeros down? Here is what you can do:

move the multiplier to the right

$$
\begin{array}{r}
21000 \\
\times\ \ 3000
\end{array}
\qquad
\begin{array}{r}
21000\ \vert \\
\times\quad 3\ \vert\ 000 \\
\hline
63000\ \vert\ 000
\end{array}
$$

→ multiplying by the zeros in 3000

→ multiplying by the 3

In either case, you get $21000 \times 3000 = 63{,}000{,}000$.

Observe the similar procedure in the next example.

Example 1

$129 \times 730{,}000{,}000 = ?$

$$
\begin{array}{r}
\overset{26}{}\ \ \ \\
\overset{2}{}\ \ \ \\
129\ \vert \\
\times\ \ 73\ \vert\ 0{,}000{,}000 \\
\hline
387\ \vert\ 0{,}000{,}000 \\
903\ \vert \\
\hline
9417\ \vert\ 0{,}000{,}000
\end{array}
$$

Notice:

zeros placed to the right

→ multiplying by the zeros

→ multiplying 129×73

Thus, $129 \times 730{,}000{,}000 = 94{,}170{,}000{,}000$

Problem 1: $54 \times 780{,}000 = ?$

Answer: 42,120,000

$$
\begin{array}{r}
\overset{2}{}\ \ \ \\
\overset{3}{}\ \ \ \\
54\ \vert \\
78\ \vert\ 0000 \\
\hline
432\ \vert\ 0000 \\
378\ \vert \\
\hline
4212\ \vert\ 0000
\end{array}
$$

Zeros in the Middle of a Multiplier

If you likewise multiply 1312 by 2003 using the process explained in Section 1.7, it would look like this:

$$
\begin{array}{r}
1312 \\
\times 2003 \\
\hline
3936 \\
0000 \\
0000 \\
2624 \\
\hline
2627936
\end{array}
$$

$1312 \times 2003 = 2,627,936$

Those two rows of zeros again take space and waste time. Here is a faster way to do a problem like that:

$$
\begin{array}{r}
1312 \\
\times 2003 \\
\hline
3936 \\
262400 \\
\hline
2627936
\end{array}
$$

multiplying $2 \times 1312 \longleftarrow$ $\longrightarrow 3 \times 1312 = 3936$

$\longrightarrow$ multiplying by the two zeros

Note: You must be careful to line up the products under their respective multipliers. The 3936 was placed under its multiplier 3, the two zeros were placed under their 0 multipliers, and the 2624 was placed under its multiplier 2.

Example 2

$572 \times 60,004 = ?$

$$
\begin{array}{r}
{\scriptstyle 41} \\
{\scriptstyle 2} \\
572 \\
\times 60004 \\
\hline
2288 \\
3432000 \\
\hline
34322288
\end{array}
$$

$\longrightarrow 4 \times 572 = 2288$

$\longrightarrow 6 \times 572 = 3432$, and three zeros $\times 572 = 000$

Problem 2: $4075 \times 2008 = ?$

Answer: 8,182,600

$$
\begin{array}{r}
{\scriptstyle 11} \\
{\scriptstyle 64} \\
4075 \\
\times 2008 \\
\hline
32600 \\
815000 \\
\hline
8182600
\end{array}
$$

Problem 3: $25 \times 100,003 = ?$

Answer: 2,500,075

$$
\begin{array}{r}
{\scriptstyle 1} \\
25 \\
\times 100003 \\
\hline
75 \\
250000 \\
\hline
2500075
\end{array}
$$

Exercise 1.8 Set A

1. 61
    ×70

2. 87
    ×50

3. 64
    ×509

4. 75
    ×807

5. 427
    ×23000

6. 634
    ×19000

7. 700
    ×400

8. 600
    ×500

9. 74000
    × 8000

10. 53000
    × 6000

11. 42
    ×3005

12. 63
    ×3006

13. 2504
    ×4006

14. 6305
    ×3009

15. 185 × 53,000

16. 6,400 × 510,000

17. 30,004 × 2,195

18. 2,009 × 4,000,000

1. _____
2. _____
3. _____
4. _____
5. _____
6. _____
7. _____
8. _____
9. _____
10. _____
11. _____
12. _____
13. _____
14. _____
15. _____
16. _____
17. _____
18. _____

Exercise 1.8 Set B

1. 52
   ×70

2. 49
   ×50

3. 71
   ×309

4. 95
   ×708

5. 398
   ×17000

6. 463
   ×43000

7. 500
   ×600

8. 900
   ×700

9. 45000
   × 3000

10. 76000
   × 7000

11. 23
   ×4005

12. 36
   ×6003

13. 1708
   ×8002

14. 2604
   ×9003

15. 752 × 41,000

16. 8,700 × 230,000

17. 40,003 × 1,921

18. 2,007 × 7,000,000

1. _____
2. _____
3. _____
4. _____
5. _____
6. _____
7. _____
8. _____
9. _____
10. _____
11. _____
12. _____
13. _____
14. _____
15. _____
16. _____
17. _____
18. _____

1.9 Powers, Representing Numbers, Square Roots, Comparing Numbers

If you get $2^3 = 6$, you have experienced power failure

There are a few other concepts that should be learned as you continue to improve your math skills.

Powers

To express a multiplication problem in which a number is repeatedly multiplied by itself, such as $3 \times 3 \times 3 \times 3 \times 3$, instead of writing all those 3's, we write 3^5. The raised number, "5", is the **exponent** or **power** and "3" is the **base.** The expression, 3^5, is read "3 raised to the 5th power."

$$\text{exponent} \searrow$$
$$3^5 = 3 \times 3 \times 3 \times 3 \times 3 = 243$$
$$\text{base} \nearrow$$

The exponent tells you how many times to use the base as a multiplier. For example:

$$7^2 = 7 \times 7 = 49 \qquad\qquad 2^3 = 2 \times 2 \times 2 = 8$$
$$1^8 = 1 \times 1 \times 1 \times 1 \times 1 \times 1 \times 1 \times 1 = 1$$

Example 1

Evaluate 5^4.

5^4 means that the base, 5, is to be used as a multiplier four times. Thus, $5^4 = 5 \times 5 \times 5 \times 5 = 625$.

Example 2

Evaluate 10^3.

10^3 means that the base, 10, is to be used as a multiplier three times. Thus, $10^3 = 10 \times 10 \times 10 = 1000$.

Problem 1: $4^2 = ?$

Answer: 16 (4×4)

Problem 2: $0^7 = ?$

Answer: 0
($0 \times 0 \times 0 \times 0 \times 0 \times 0 \times 0$)

Problem 3: $10^5 = ?$

Answer: 100,000
($10 \times 10 \times 10 \times 10 \times 10$)

Problem 4: $23^3 = ?$

Answer: 12,167 ($23 \times 23 \times 23$)

Representing Whole Numbers

In Section 1.1, we introduced the system used in reading and writing whole numbers. Exponents can be used in this process to emphasize the place value of each digit in a whole number. For example, the number 4265 consists of four digits, each having a different place value.

$$4 \quad 2 \quad 6 \quad 5$$

5 ones	$= 5 \times 1$	$= 5 \times 1$
6 tens	$= 6 \times 10$	$= 6 \times 10^1$
2 hundreds	$= 2 \times 100$	$= 2 \times 10^2$
4 thousands	$= 4 \times 1000$	$= 4 \times 10^3$

$$4265 = 4 \times 10^3 + 2 \times 10^2 + 6 \times 10^1 + 5 \times 1$$

The number 4265 is really the sum of consecutive powers of ten multiplied by the digits of the number. It is these consecutive powers of ten that give each digit its place value. The process of representing a number using the powers of ten is referred to as writing a number in **expanded form.**

Example 3

Write 271,058 in expanded form.

$$2 \quad 7 \quad 1 \quad 0 \quad 5 \quad 8$$

8×1	$= 8 \times 1$
5×10	$= 5 \times 10^1$
0×100	$= 0 \times 10^2$
1×1000	$= 1 \times 10^3$
$7 \times 10,000$	$= 7 \times 10^4$
$2 \times 100,000$	$= 2 \times 10^5$

$$271,058 = 2 \times 10^5 + 7 \times 10^4 + 1 \times 10^3$$
$$+ 0 \times 10^2 + 5 \times 10^1 + 8 \times 1$$

Note: From this example, you can see that if you multiply out a power of ten, it has as many zeros as the exponent. For example, if 10^8 is multiplied out, it will have eight zeros ($10^8 = 100,000,000$).

Problem 5: Write 10,897 in expanded form.

Answer: $1 \times 10^4 + 0 \times 10^3 + 8 \times 10^2$
$+ 9 \times 10^1 + 7 \times 1$

Problem 6: What number is represented by:
$3 \times 10^3 + 6 \times 10^2 + 4 \times 10^1 + 0 \times 1$

Answer: 3640

Problem 7: 10^{11} will contain how many zeros?

Answer: 11 zeros (100,000,000,000)

Square Roots

Raising a number to the second power (using an exponent of 2) is called **squaring** a number. For example, since five raised to the second power gives the area of a 5 by 5 square, it is referred to as 5 squared and its answer is called the square of 5.

$$5^2 = 5 \times 5 = \underline{25}$$

the square of 5

The reverse of squaring a number is called taking the **square root** of a number. In the above example, the number multiplied by itself to get that answer of 25 is the square root of 25, written $\sqrt{25}$. That is,

$$5^2 = 5 \times \underline{5} = 25$$

the square root of 25
($\sqrt{25} = 5$)

> To find a square root of a given number, find a number that, when multiplied by itself, results in the given number.

$\sqrt{9} = 3$, since the number multiplied by itself that gives 9 as an answer is 3. ($3 \times 3 = 9$)

$\sqrt{49} = 7$, since the number multiplied by itself that gives 49 as an answer is 7. ($7 \times 7 = 49$)

$\sqrt{144} = 12$, since the number multiplied by itself that gives 144 as an answer is 12. ($12 \times 12 = 144$)

Note: The square roots shown in this chapter are all whole numbers. However, this is not true for all square roots. For example, $\sqrt{29}$ has a value between 5 and 6, since $5 \times 5 = 25$ and $6 \times 6 = 36$. An approximate answer for $\sqrt{29}$ is the decimal 5.385 (5.385×5.385 is very close to 29). Although we will not be concerned with decimal square roots in this section, we will examine it in Chapter 8.

Example 4:

Between what two whole numbers will you find $\sqrt{88}$?
Since there is no whole number multiplied by itself that gives 88 as an answer, and since $9 \times 9 = 81$ and $10 \times 10 = 100$, you would find $\sqrt{88}$ between 9 and 10.

Problem 8: $\sqrt{64} = ?$ Answer: 8, since $8 \times 8 = 64$.

Problem 9: $\sqrt{121} = ?$ Answer: 11, since $11 \times 11 = 121$.

Problem 10: $\sqrt{0} = ?$ Answer: 0, since $0 \times 0 = 0$.

Problem 11: $\sqrt{10,000} = ?$ Answer: 100, since $100 \times 100 = 10,000$.

Comparing Numbers

There are three basic symbols that are used to compare the size of numbers. They are the **equal** sign ($=$) and the inequality signs, **greater than** ($>$) and **less than** ($<$).

The **equal sign** ($=$) is used to indicate that two numbers are the same or the answers to two problems have the same value. The statement, $7 = 7$, is read "seven is equal to seven." Proper use of the equal sign can be seen in the examples below.

$$105 = 105 \qquad\qquad 4 + 2 = 2 \times 3$$
$$\sqrt{100} = 10 \qquad\qquad 8 \times 7 = 7 \times 8$$

The **greater than sign** ($>$) is used to indicate that the number or answer on the left is greater than the number or answer on the right of the sign. The statement, "$7 > 4$", is read "seven is greater than four." Proper use of the greater than sign can be seen in the examples below.

$$26 > 25 \qquad\qquad 3 + 10 > 5 \times 1$$
$$7^2 > 14 \qquad\qquad 49 > \sqrt{49}$$

The **less than sign** ($<$) is used to indicate that the number or answer on the left is less than the number or answer on the right of the sign. The statement, $0 < 5$, is read "zero is less than five." Proper use of the less than sign can be seen in the examples below.

$$456 < 500 \qquad\qquad 8 \times 2 < 7 + 11$$
$$10^2 < 200 \qquad\qquad 3 < \sqrt{19}$$

Note: If you get confused about which sign, $>$ or $<$, to use in a given situation, just remember that an inequality sign always points to the smaller of the two numbers or answers involved.

Problems: Replace the question mark with $=$, $>$, or $<$ in the following: Answers:

12. $8 \times 0 \, ? \, 8 \times 1$

12. $<$ (0 is less than 8)

13. $15 + 7 + 6 \, ? \, 7 + 15 + 6$

13. $=$ (28 is equal to 28)

14. $9^2 \, ? \, \sqrt{9}$

14. $>$ (81 is greater than 3)

Name _____   Date _____

Exercise 1.9 Set A

In problems 1–15, evaluate each expression.

1. 3^2 2. 7^2 3. 12^2 1. _____   2. _____   3. _____

4. 15^2 5. 4^3 6. 2^3 4. _____   5. _____   6. _____

7. 0^5 8. 0^7 9. 1^4 7. _____   8. _____   9. _____

10. 1^6 11. 2^5 12. 3^5 10. _____   11. _____   12. _____

13. 10^6 14. 10^4 15. 34^2 13. _____   14. _____   15. _____

In problems 16–20, write each number in expanded exponent form.

16. 356   16. _____

17. 6098   17. _____

18. 33,690   18. _____

19. 4,267,983   19. _____

20. 20,607,512   20. _____

In problems 21–32, evaluate each expression.

21. $\sqrt{4}$ 22. $\sqrt{9}$ 23. $\sqrt{25}$ 21. _____   22. _____   23. _____

24. $\sqrt{16}$ 25. $\sqrt{36}$ 26. $\sqrt{49}$ 24. _____   25. _____   26. _____

27. $\sqrt{1}$ 28. $\sqrt{64}$ 29. $\sqrt{0}$ 27. _____   28. _____   29. _____

30. $\sqrt{225}$ 31. $\sqrt{100}$ 32. $\sqrt{81}$ 30. _____   31. _____   32. _____

In problems 33–40, replace the question mark with =, >, or <.

33. 6×4 ? 4×6 34. 0×156 ? 156×1 33. _____   34. _____

35. $757 + 893$? $893 + 757$ 36. 3^2 ? 2^3 35. _____   36. _____

37. $\sqrt{25}$? 5^2 38. 10^4 ? 40 37. _____   38. _____

39. 8^2 ? 4^3 40. $\sqrt{4} \times \sqrt{9}$? $\sqrt{49}$ 39. _____   40. _____

Exercise 1.9 Set B

In problems 1–15, evaluate each expression.

1. 4^2 2. 6^2 3. 13^2

4. 18^2 5. 5^3 6. 3^3

7. 0^4 8. 0^6 9. 1^5

10. 1^7 11. 3^5 12. 2^5

13. 10^5 14. 10^3 15. 43^2

1. _____ 2. _____ 3. _____

4. _____ 5. _____ 6. _____

7. _____ 8. _____ 9. _____

10. _____ 11. _____ 12. _____

13. _____ 14. _____ 15. _____

In problems 16–20, write each number in expanded exponent form.

16. 617

17. 7304

18. 44,275

19. 5,143,879

20. 40,034,126

16. _____

17. _____

18. _____

19. _____

20. _____

In problems 21–32, evaluate each expression.

21. $\sqrt{16}$ 22. $\sqrt{1}$ 23. $\sqrt{36}$

24. $\sqrt{25}$ 25. $\sqrt{49}$ 26. $\sqrt{9}$

27. $\sqrt{0}$ 28. $\sqrt{100}$ 29. $\sqrt{196}$

30. $\sqrt{121}$ 31. $\sqrt{81}$ 32. $\sqrt{4}$

21. _____ 22. _____ 23. _____

24. _____ 25. _____ 26. _____

27. _____ 28. _____ 29. _____

30. _____ 31. _____ 32. _____

In problems 33–40, replace the question mark with =, >, or <.

33. 12×9 ? 9×12 34. 0×986 ? 986×1

35. $793 + 927$? $927 + 793$ 36. 3^4 ? 4^3

37. $\sqrt{100}$? 10^2 38. 5^2 ? 10

39. 3^4 ? 9^2 40. $\sqrt{49}$? $\sqrt{4} \times \sqrt{9}$

33. _____ 34. _____

35. _____ 36. _____

37. _____ 38. _____

39. _____ 40. _____

1.10 Applications Involving Whole Numbers

When math problems are expressed in words, you may have some difficulty deciding what steps should be taken to solve the problem. There is no easy way to tell you what to do in a particular word problem. However, you should be able to apply your knowledge of arithmetic to word problems by thinking carefully and using the steps listed below.

> 1. **Read:** Read the problem slowly and carefully. Determine what is being asked for and what are the facts of the problem.
> 2. **Analyze:** Determine what operations are needed to answer the question presented in the problem.
> 3. **Solve:** Do the necessary computation to obtain the answer to the given problem.

Example 1

If one tire costs $63, how much would four tires cost?

Analyze: 1 tire costs $63, so 4 tires would cost 4 times as much. You must multiply 4 times $63.

$$
\begin{array}{r}
\text{Solve:} \quad \$63 \\
\times \quad 4 \\
\hline
\$252
\end{array}
$$

Example 2

You spend $69 on a sweatsuit, $29 for tennis shoes, and $3 for socks. What is your total bill before sales tax?

Analyze: You want the total of the prices, so add them together.

$$
\begin{array}{r}
\text{Solve:} \quad \$69 \\
29 \\
+ \quad 3 \\
\hline
\$101
\end{array}
$$

Example 3

At a local circus, tickets were priced $5 for adults and $3 for children. How much would a group, consisting of 7 adults and 26 children, pay to go to the circus?

Analyze: To find the total cost, you need to add the cost for the adults ($7 \times \$5$) and the cost for the children ($26 \times \$3$).

Solve: adults: $7 \times \$5 =$ $35
children: $26 \times \$3 =$ $78
total: $=$ $113

Example 4

In October your heating bill was $27. However, your November bill was double your October bill and your December bill was triple your November bill. How much did you pay for heating in those three months?

Analyze: Double means to multiply by 2; triple means to multiply by 3. To find the November bill multiply the October bill by 2. To find the December bill multiply the November bill by 3. Add the amount from each month to get the total.

Solve: October: = $ 27
November: 2 × $27 = $ 54
December: 3 × $54 = $162
Total: = $243

Example 5

A truck is loaded with 7 sacks of cement weighing 90 pounds each, 20 bags of sand weighing 75 pounds each, and 12 posts weighing 24 pounds each. If the truck alone weighs 4500 pounds and the driver weighs 176 pounds, what is the total weight of the loaded truck?

Analyze: To find the total weight, add the weight of the cement, sand, posts, truck, and driver.

Solve: cement: 7 × 90 =   630 lb
sand: 20 × 75 = 1500 lb   (Note: lb is an
posts: 12 × 24 =   288 lb   abbreviation for pounds)
truck: = 4500 lb
driver: =   176 lb
total: = 7094 lb

Problem 1: If an average double-spaced page of typing contains 250 words, how many words would a 15 page term paper contain?

Answer: 3750 words

250 × 15 = 3750

Problem 2: In a football game, 9 touchdowns (6 pts, each), 6 field goals (3 pts. each), and 7 extra points (1 pt each) were scored. How many total points were scored in the football game?

Answer: 79 pts.

9 × 6 = 54
6 × 3 = 18
7 × 1 = 7
total = 79

Problem 3: If you now earn $975 per month, and are guaranteed a $35 raise each month you remain with the company, what is your monthly salary after one year?

Answer: $1395

12 × $35 = $420
+$975
salary: $1395

Exercise 1.10 Set A

1. At the bookstore you spend $35 on a math book, $48 on art books, and $19 on supplies. What is your total cost before sales tax?

1. _____

2. In the first five tournaments of the 1996 Ladies Professional Golf Association, the winners earned $115,000, $67,500, $82,000, $105,000, and $135,000. What was the total prize money given to the winners of those five tournaments?

2. _____

3. Your car gets 39 miles per gallon of gasoline. How many miles can you drive on a full tank of 15 gallons?

3. _____

4. A ream of paper contains 500 sheets of paper. How many sheets of paper are contained in a box of 24 reams of paper?

4. _____

5. If you drink 3 cups of coffee a day and use 2 cubes of sugar in each cup, how many cubes of sugar would you use in one year (365 days)?

5. _____

6. If a box of candy contains 28 pieces of chocolate, how many pieces of chocolate are contained in a dozen boxes of candy?

6. _____

7. A house contains three bedrooms with 144 sq ft of floor space each, a master bedroom with 300 sq ft, two bathrooms with 56 sq ft each, a kitchen with 240 sq ft, a living room with 460 sq ft, and a hallway with 105 sq ft. What is the total floor space of the house?

7. _____

8. During a season, a basketball team made 623 free throws (1 point each), 1742 two-point field goals, and 47 three-point baskets. How many total points did the team score that season?

8. _____

9. Each piece of pipe is 16 ft long and each joint that connects two pieces of pipe adds 2 ft to the length. If 24 sections of pipe and 23 joints are laid end to end in a straight line, find the length of the pipeline.

9. _____

10. A small truck is carrying 25 crates of eggs. If each crate contains 18 dozen eggs, how many eggs is the truck carrying?

10. _____

11. Tickets for a school production cost $5 for general admission and $8 for reserved seats. If 575 general admission and 250 reserved tickets were sold, how much money was collected?

11. _____

12. If there are about 320 beans in one pound of coffee, how many coffee beans are in a 50 pound bag of coffee?

12. _____

13. According to the Boston Globe, in 1991, a pizza served in Mino, Japan, containing matsutake mushrooms, beluga caviar, and fresh abalone had a total cost of $629. Could you buy 35 combination pizzas priced at $16 each with the money spent on that one pizza?

13. _____

14. Would three million dollars be enough to cover the money won by the winning professional golfers in the first ten tournaments in 1996? In six of these tournaments the winner earned $234,000, in three tournaments the winner earned $216,000, and in the other tournament the winner earned $225,000.

14. _____

15. An average adult's heart beats about 72 times per minute, while an infant's heart beats about 120 times per minute. a) How many times does an adult's heart beat in a day? b) How many times does an infant's heart beat in a day?

15. _____

Exercise 1.10 Set B

1. During a shopping trip you wrote checks for $23, $37, $57, $78, and $19. What is the total of the checks you wrote?

1. _____

2. What is the caloric intake for a lunch consisting of an apple (80 cal), a cup of yogurt (230 cal), a hard-boiled egg (80 cal), and tomato juice (45 cal)?

2. _____

3. If a computer prints invoices at a rate of 1256 per hour, how many invoices does it print in 8 hours?

3. _____

4. Due to the stronger force of gravity, objects on earth weigh about 6 times what they weigh on the moon. If an object weighs 28 pounds on the moon, what is its weight on earth?

4. _____

5. If a leaking faucet drips water at a rate of two gallons every hour, how many gallons of water are lost in a week?

5. _____

6. If a bag of peanuts contains 48 peanuts, how many peanuts are contained in two dozen bags?

6. _____

7. If you had three $50 bills, seven $20 bills, nine $10 bills, six $5 bills and seventeen $1 bills, how much cash would you have?

7. _____

8. During a season, a football team scored 39 touchdowns (6 points each), 23 field goals (3 points each), and 35 extra points (1 point each). How many points did the team score that season?

8. _____

9. If you started work earning $375 a week, then received two raises of $35 a week and one raise of $75 a week, how much would you be earning per week?

9. _____

10. A box of pens contains one dozen pens. How many pens would you have if you purchased a dozen boxes of pens?

10. _____

11. A local movie theater charges $7 for adults and $5 for children. How much would a family of two adults and five children pay to see a movie?

11. _____

12. From one cord of wood, 7,500,000 toothpicks can be produced. At that rate, how many toothpicks can be produced from 25 cords of wood?

12. _____

13. If a professional window washer could wash a window in one minute, could all 43,600 windows of the New York Trade Center be washed by one window washer working for 90 days, 8 hours a day?

13. _____

14. If your car travels an average of 28 miles per gallon of gasoline and your gas tank holds 16 gallons, would one full tank of gasoline be enough for a 425 mile trip?

14. _____

15. A woodpecker can peck 20 times a second. At that rate, how many times could a woodpecker peck in 7 minutes?

15. _____

Chapter 1 Summary

Concepts

You may refer to the sections listed below to review how to do the following:

1. read and write whole numbers using the place values of our number system. (1.1)
2. round off whole numbers by changing them to nearest multiples. (1.2)
3. add whole numbers by lining up the digits with corresponding place values. (1.3), (1.4)
4. multiplying whole numbers by placing them above each other and using the carrying process. (1.5), (1.6), (1.7)
5. use short cuts for handling zeros in multiplying whole numbers. (1.8)
6. find powers and square roots of whole numbers. (1.9)
7. use the "equals" (=), "greater than" (>), and "less than" (<) signs. (1.9)
8. write whole numbers in expanded exponent form. (1.9)
9. solve word problems involving whole numbers using the "read, analyze, solve" procedure. (1.10)

Terminology

This chapter's important terms and their page numbers are as follows:

addend: name given to the numbers that are added. (15)
base: the number being raised to a power. (35)
digit: any of the ten numerals 0, 1, 2, 3, 4, 5, 6, 7, 8, 9. (7)
expanded form: representation of a number using powers of ten. (36)
exponent or **power:** raised number that tells how many times to use a number as a factor. (35)
factors: name given to the numbers that are multiplied. (21)
place value: the value assigned to the position of a digit in a number. (7)
product: the answer from multiplication. (21)
square root: a number which, when multiplied by itself, results in the given number. (37)
squaring: the process of raising a number to the second power (multiplying it by itself). (37)
sum: the answer from addition. (15)

Chapter 1 Crossword Puzzle

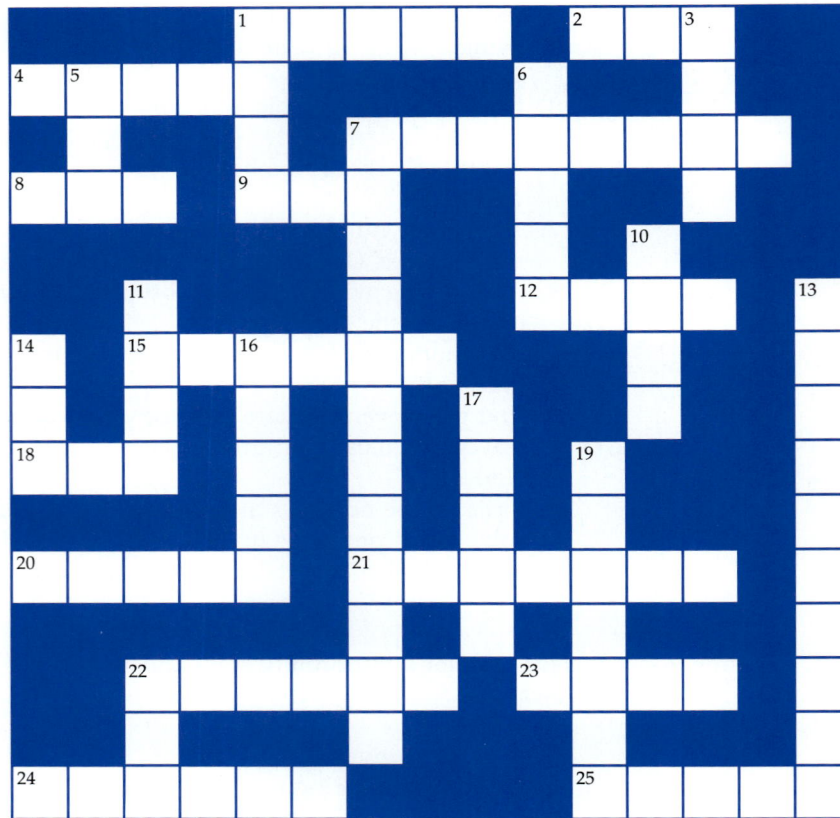

Across

1. Second digit of 5763 + 3552
2. Rounded to the nearest _____, 5649 ≈ 5650.
4. Each digit in 45,614 has a place _____.
7. Power
8. 1, 3, 5, 7, 9, for example
9. Third digit of 459 × 32
12. 6 is the square _____ of 36.
15. That which is added
18. Last digit of 31^2
20. Square root of 64
21. Numbers that are multiplied
22. Something raised to the second power
23. Abbreviation for multiplication
24. Represents a value
25. Digit in the ten thousands place of 1,234,567

Down

1. Place to the left of the ones place
3. Number of zeros in 700 million times 60
5. When you find the sum, you _____.
6. Exponent
7. Expressed using powers of ten (2 wrds)
10. Third digit of 2^{11}
11. That which is raised to a power
13. A digit's position gives it, _____. (2 wrds)
14. First digit of 87,998 + 45,367 + 69,328
16. Each component of a number
17. First word in answer to 13 down
19. Answer to multiplication
22. Answer to addition

Chapter 1 Practice Test A

1. Write the following using numbers and commas: two hundred fifty-four million, thirty thousand, one hundred seven

1. _____

2. Write the following number in words: 3,407,123

2. _____

In problems 3–4, round off 753,250 to the place indicated.

3. thousands place

3. _____

4. hundred thousands place

4. _____

In problems 5–12, evaluate each expression.

5. $234 + 78 + 3804$

5. _____

6. $3456 + 907 + 78,954 + 3012 + 56$

6. _____

7. 769×6

7. _____

8. 5382×879

8. _____

9. $952 \times 41,000,000$

9. _____

10. $365 \times 700,006$

10. _____

11. 3^4

11. _____

12. $\sqrt{9}$

12. _____

13. Write 14,027 in expanded exponent form.

13. _____

In problems 14–15, replace the question mark with >, <, or =.

14. $5 \times 10 \ ? \ 10^5$

14. _____

15. $\sqrt{16} \ ? \ 2^2$

15. _____

16. A delivery van is carrying 12 TV sets weighing 54 pounds each and 25 VCRs weighing 16 pounds each. What is the total weight of the TVs and VCRs in the van?

16. _____

Chapter 1 Practice Test B

1. Write the following using numbers and commas: one billion, twenty-five million, three hundred six thousand, five hundred seventeen

1. _____

2. Write the following number in words: 678,309

2. _____

In problems 3–4, round off 1,257,381 to the place indicated.

3. tens place

3. _____

4. ten thousands place

4. _____

In problems 5–12, evaluate each expression.

5. 347 + 23 + 1067

5. _____

6. 47 + 89,099 + 235 + 9 + 523 + 4128

6. _____

7. 478×8

7. _____

8. 2785×596

8. _____

9. $56 \times 340,000$

9. _____

10. $906 \times 6,000,001$

10. _____

11. 4^3

11. _____

12. $\sqrt{81}$

12. _____

13. Write 259 in expanded exponent form.

13. _____

In problems 14–15, replace the question mark with >, <, or =.

14. 345×67 ? 67×345

14. _____

15. 5^2 ? $\sqrt{25}$

15. _____

16. The low temperature on Monday was 67° F. If there was a 3° increase in the low temperature each day for six consecutive days, what was the low temperature on Sunday?

16. _____

Chapter 1 Supplementary Exercises

Section 1.1

In problems 1–10, write each number in words.

  1. 506   2. 1317   3. 260,000   4. 45,200

  5. 107,070   6. 1,325,006   7. 82,000,090   8. 123,456,789

  9. 1,204,240,000 10. 17,000,987,012

In problems 11–18, write each expression using numbers and commas.

 11. four hundred seven   12. seventeen thousand

 13. five thousand two   14. twenty-one thousand, six hundred

 15. sixty thousand, two hundred eight   16. one million, thirty thousand

 17. fourteen million, five hundred six thousand   18. two billion, two million, two thousand, two

Section 1.2

In problems 1–8, round off each number to the nearest thousand.

  1. 3706   2. 8397   3. 6542   4. 9765

  5. 49,500   6. 126,499   7. 10,179,647   8. 9,989,379

In problems 9–16, round off 36,984,155 to the indicated place.

  9. tens place   10. hundreds place   11. thousands place

 12. ten thousands place   13. hundred thousands place 14. millions place

 15. ones place   16. ten millions place

Section 1.4

 1.   142   2.   7638
     +706   + 297

 3. 3876 + 1849   4. 7500 + 9700

 5. 517 + 6380   6. 276 + 4302

 7. 8976 + 10,385 + 7   8. 46,529 + 9813 + 67

 9. 19 + 126 + 4973   10. 26 + 4198 + 384

 11. 9000 + 287 + 63,509 + 45   12. 400 + 19,876 + 2914 + 198,709

Section 1.6

1.   486
    × 2

2.   4320
    ×   3

3.   487
    × 5

4.   1906
    ×   7

5. 5006 × 8

6. 6008 × 9

7. 8966 × 6

8. 7699 × 6

9. 6 × 27,800

10. 7 × 43,900

11. 5 × 49,457

12. 4 × 76,899

13. 1,256,709 × 9

14. 5 × 45,706,789

Section 1.7

1.   45
    ×31

2.   728
    × 92

3.   96
    ×87

4.   788
    × 96

5. 835 × 496

6. 765 × 537

7. 257 × 4282

8. 536 × 4776

9. 826 × 1418

10. 195 × 6888

11. 43,216 × 128

12. 54,617 × 216

13. 16,736 × 608

14. 14,384 × 907

15. 8769 × 270

16. 7836 × 460

17. 12,548 × 96

18. 3280 × 875

19. 7,607,123 × 345

20. 23,410,811 × 569

Section 1.8

1. 96 × 50

2. 85 × 600

3. 72 × 309

4. 52 × 7001

5. 794 × 8000

6. 5000 × 658

7. 283 × 30,000

8. 918 × 60,000

9. 5019 × 370,000

10. 2097 × 240,000

11. 826 × 5007

12. 766 × 4008

13. 6008 × 436

14. 3009 × 983

15. 40,002 × 78

16. 67 × 30,007

17. 5000 × 420

18. 930 × 6800

19. 700 × 42,000

20. 1200 × 56,000,000

Section 1.9

In problems 1–28, evaluate each expression.

1. 8^2
2. 7^2
3. 6^3
4. 5^4

5. 3^3
6. 11^2
7. 0^6
8. 1^7

9. 4^3
10. 3^4
11. 4^2
12. 2^4

13. 18^2
14. 35^2
15. 10^3
16. 10^4

17. $\sqrt{9}$
18. $\sqrt{25}$
19. $\sqrt{36}$
20. $\sqrt{16}$

21. $\sqrt{64}$
22. $\sqrt{49}$
23. $\sqrt{81}$
24. $\sqrt{121}$

25. $\sqrt{1}$
26. $\sqrt{0}$
27. $\sqrt{225}$
28. $\sqrt{100}$

In problems 29–44, replace the question mark with =, >, or <.

29. $5 + 7$? 5×7
30. $6 + 9$? $9 + 6$
31. 0×89 ? $0 + 89$

32. 96×1 ? $96 + 1$
33. $14 + 9$? $19 + 4$
34. 17×37 ? 37×17

35. 1^5 ? 0^5
36. $\sqrt{49}$? 7^2
37. 78×6 ? 86×7

38. 10^2 ? $\sqrt{100}$
39. 4^2 ? 2^4
40. 3^5 ? 5^2

41. 4^2 ? $\sqrt{4}$
42. $\sqrt{9}$? 9^2
43. 1^4 ? 1^5

44. 10^4 ? 4×10

In problems 45–58, write each number in expanded exponent form.

45. 56
46. 560
47. 5600
48. 3458

49. 12,748
50. 74,053
51. 35,705
52. 568,000

53. 475,120
54. 401,190
55. 1,040,506
56. 1,234,567

57. 23,600,890
58. 145,655,781

In problems 59–65, determine the number represented by each expression.

59. $5 \times 10^4 + 3 \times 10^3 + 2 \times 10^2 + 1 \times 10 + 7 \times 1$

60. $3 \times 10^3 + 0 \times 10^2 + 0 \times 10 + 8 \times 1$

61. $1 \times 10^5 + 2 \times 10^4 + 3 \times 10^3 + 0 \times 10^2 + 7 \times 10 + 9 \times 1$

62. $4 \times 10^6 + 2 \times 10^5 + 0 \times 10^4 + 1 \times 10^3 + 8 \times 10^2 + 6 \times 10 + 4 \times 1$

63. $8 \times 10^2 + 0 \times 10 + 0 \times 1$

64. $9 \times 10^6 + 1 \times 10^5 + 7 \times 10^4 + 0 \times 10^3 + 0 \times 10^2 + 8 \times 10 + 3 \times 1$

65. $9 \times 10^7 + 8 \times 10^6 + 7 \times 10^5 + 6 \times 10^4 + 5 \times 10^3 + 4 \times 10^2 + 3 \times 10 + 2 \times 1$

Section 1.10

1. The attendance at six performances of a local production of "Chorus Line" was 314, 299, 324, 223, 198, and 327. What was the total attendance for the performances?

2. Alice scored 17 points more on the second test of the semester than she did on the first test. If her score on the first test was 76, what was her score on the second test?

3. What is the total cost for a dozen potted plants that sell for $6 each?

4. If a necklace requires 76 pearls, how many pearls would be needed to make 15 necklaces?

5. You rent a car for a week, paying $39 a day and buying your own gas. If the gas costs you $22 a day, how much does it cost to rent the car for the week?

6. If you buy seven cubic yards of gravel at a cost of $49 a cubic yard and pay an additional fee of $35 for delivery, what is the total amount you pay for the gravel?

7. If your regular wage is $6 an hour and you earn $9 an hour for overtime, how much do you earn for working 40 regular hours and 7 overtime hours?

8. If you had one $50 bill, nine $20 bills, and seven $5 bills, how much cash would you have?

9. A history test consists of 10 true–false questions worth 2 points each, 14 multiple choice questions worth 5 points each, and 4 essay questions worth 15 points each. How many total points does the test contain?

10. In a track meet, first place finishers score 5 points, second place finishers score 3 points, and third place finishers score 1 point. If your team took 7 firsts, 12 seconds, and 9 thirds, how many points did your team score?

Math Magic I

Magic Squares

Besides the many practical uses of numbers in our daily lives, numbers can also be a source of recreation. One of these recreational activities is to create a square of whole numbers (1, 2, 3, 4, 5, …) so that each row, column, and diagonal has the same sum. Because such a square displays a unique numerical harmony and, in ancient times, was thought to have mystical powers, it is called a **magic square.** The first evidence of magic squares dates back to the Chinese Emperor Yu the Great (c. 2000 B.C.). It was discovered painted on the back of a tortoise shell and is called the Lo Shu Magic Square.

Lo Shu Magic Square

8	3	4
1	5	9
6	7	2

8	3	4
1	5	9
6	7	2

Each row, column, and diagonal has a sum of 15.

Recreations

1. Verify that the following is a magic square.

16	3	2	13
5	10	11	8
9	6	7	12
4	15	14	1

2. This magic square uses the whole numbers from 1 to 25. Determine the ten missing numbers.

17		1	8	15
23	5	7	14	16
				22
10		19	21	3
	18			

Chapter 2

Whole Numbers: Subtraction, Division, and the Order of Operations

After finishing this chapter, you should be able to do the following:

1. subtract whole numbers.
2. divide whole numbers.
3. perform computations that involve more than one operation.
4. factor whole numbers into primes.
5. solve word problems involving operations with whole numbers.

On the next page, you will find a pretest for this chapter. The purpose of the pretest is to help you determine which sections in this chapter you need to study in detail and which sections you can review quickly. By taking and correcting the pretest according to the instructions on the next page, you can better plan your pace through this chapter.

Name _____   Date _____

Chapter 2 Pretest

Take and correct this test using the answer section at the end of the book.
Those problems that give you difficulty indicate which sections need extra
attention. Section numbers are in parentheses before each problem.

(2.2)   1. 683 − 352   1. _____

(2.2)   2. 77,003 − 10,399   2. _____

(2.2)   3. 8000 − 2947   3. _____

(2.3)   4. 54 ÷ 9   (2.4)   5. 7)‾41‾   4. _____

                                                                 5. _____

(2.4)   6. 36 ÷ 0   (2.5)   7. 318 ÷ 6   6. _____

                                                                 7. _____

(2.6)   8. 8)‾16507‾   (2.6)   9. 692)‾204140‾   8. _____

                                                                 9. _____

(2.7)   10. $57\overline{)34562}$

10. _____

(2.7)   11. $85\overline{)51000}$

11. _____

(2.8)   12. $\sqrt{64} + 9 \times 10^3$

12. _____

(2.8)   13. $5 \times (15 - 3 + 6) + 42 \div 6$

13. _____

(2.9)   14. Factor 140 into primes.

14. _____

(2.10) 15. In your last five math tests, you received scores of 95, 82, 86, 94, and 98. What is the average of your test scores?

15. _____

2.1 Subtraction Facts

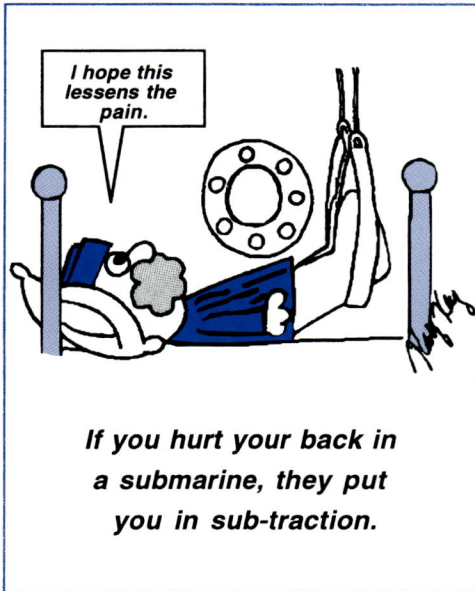

I hope this lessens the pain.

If you hurt your back in a submarine, they put you in sub-traction.

If you had $25 and spent $7 on lunch, how much would you have left? To solve the problem you would take $7 away from the $25 and get the answer, $18. You would have done the opposite of addition. This process is called subtraction. We could write that problem in the following ways:

25 subtract 7 is 18
25 minus 7 equals 18
25 − 7 = 18

The name given to each part of a subtraction problem is as follows:

minuend	subtrahend	difference
↓	↓	↓
25 −	7 =	18

Below is a chart containing the basic subtraction facts that you should know.

To use the chart to find an answer, such as 9 − 6, find the 9 on the left hand side and go along that row until you reach the 6 at the top of the chart. That number (3) will be the answer to 9 − 6.

−	0	1	2	3	4	5	6	7	8	9
0	0	—	—	—	—	—	—	—	—	—
1	1	0	—	—	—	—	—	—	—	—
2	2	1	0	—	—	—	—	—	—	—
3	3	2	1	0	—	—	—	—	—	—
4	4	3	2	1	0	—	—	—	—	—
5	5	4	3	2	1	0	—	—	—	—
6	6	5	4	3	2	1	0	—	—	—
7	7	6	5	4	3	2	1	0	—	—
8	8	7	6	5	4	3	2	1	0	—
9	9	8	7	6	5	4	3	2	1	0
10	10	9	8	7	6	5	4	3	2	1
11	11	10	9	8	7	6	5	4	3	2
12	12	11	10	9	8	7	6	5	4	3
13	13	12	11	10	9	8	7	6	5	4
14	14	13	12	11	10	9	8	7	6	5
15	15	14	13	12	11	10	9	8	7	6
16	16	15	14	13	12	11	10	9	8	7
17	17	16	15	14	13	12	11	10	9	8
18	18	17	16	15	14	13	12	11	10	9

Note: These dashes are there since, at this point, you can not subtract a larger number from a smaller number.

To help you master basic subtraction facts, on the next page you will find a self drill in subtraction. You might also find the use of "flash cards" helpful in learning the basic subtraction facts.

Self Drill in Subtraction

Directions

1. Cover the answers for a row.
2. Quickly figure out and write down your answer to each problem.
3. Check your work.
4. Repeat this for each row until you can do each one quickly and correctly.

2 −0 **2**	5 −1 **4**	3 −3 **0**	9 −2 **7**	9 −0 **9**	6 −3 **3**	2 −1 **1**	3 −2 **1**	1 −0 **1**	10 −3 **7**
10 −2 **8**	7 −0 **7**	4 −3 **1**	3 −1 **2**	5 −3 **2**	8 −2 **6**	4 −0 **4**	8 −1 **7**	2 −2 **0**	9 −1 **8**
8 −0 **8**	4 −2 **2**	9 −3 **6**	3 −0 **3**	11 −3 **8**	1 −1 **0**	8 −3 **5**	4 −1 **3**	7 −3 **4**	6 −2 **4**
6 −1 **5**	5 −2 **3**	6 −0 **6**	7 −1 **6**	10 −1 **9**	0 −0 **0**	11 −2 **9**	7 −2 **5**	12 −3 **9**	5 −0 **5**
4 −4 **0**	6 −5 **1**	10 −6 **4**	8 −4 **4**	13 −6 **7**	11 −5 **6**	10 −4 **6**	7 −5 **2**	7 −6 **1**	10 −5 **5**
15 −6 **9**	14 −6 **8**	6 −4 **2**	5 −5 **0**	12 −6 **6**	13 −4 **9**	13 −5 **8**	9 −6 **3**	11 −4 **7**	14 −5 **9**
12 −5 **7**	5 −4 **1**	11 −6 **5**	9 −5 **4**	8 −6 **2**	7 −4 **3**	9 −4 **5**	8 −5 **3**	6 −6 **0**	12 −4 **8**
9 −7 **2**	11 −9 **2**	8 −8 **0**	11 −8 **3**	7 −7 **0**	12 −9 **3**	16 −9 **7**	14 −7 **7**	8 −7 **1**	14 −9 **5**
9 −9 **0**	15 −8 **7**	9 −8 **1**	10 −7 **3**	13 −7 **6**	10 −8 **2**	13 −9 **4**	11 −7 **4**	17 −9 **8**	12 −8 **4**
18 −9 **9**	16 −8 **8**	12 −7 **5**	16 −7 **9**	14 −8 **6**	13 −8 **5**	15 −9 **6**	15 −7 **8**	17 −8 **9**	10 −9 **1**

2.2 Subtracting Whole Numbers

Using the knowledge of the basic subtraction facts, you can now subtract larger whole numbers. The basic procedure for subtracting is as follows:

> Place the numbers above each other so that the digits with the same place values are lined up. Subtract the digits in the ones, tens, hundreds, etc. places.

By studying the examples, this method will become clear.

Example 1

$7953 - 641 = ?$

$$
\begin{array}{r}
7953 \\
-\ 641 \\
\hline
7312
\end{array}
$$

→ 3 ones − 1 one = 2 ones
→ 5 tens − 4 tens = 1 ten
→ 9 hundreds − 6 hundreds = 3 hundreds
→ 7 thousands − 0 thousands = 7 thousands

If you try to find the answer to $\begin{array}{r}52\\-17\end{array}$ the process in Example 1 fails to work out, since in the ones place you can not subtract a larger number (7) from a smaller number (2).

What do you do to solve that problem? Just as we have carrying in addition, there is a process called borrowing in subtraction. Let me show you what I mean.

Example 2

$52 - 17 = ?$

We borrow 1 ten from the 5 tens, leaving 4 tens.

Adding the 1 ten we borrowed to the 2 ones, we get 12 ones.

$$
\begin{array}{r}
4\ \ 12 \\
\not5\ \not2 \\
-1\ 7 \\
\hline
3\ 5
\end{array}
$$

Now subtract.

→ 12 ones − 7 ones = 5 ones

→ 4 tens − 1 ten = 3 tens

Example 3

$$4628 - 593 = ?$$

Since the 9 is larger than the 2 in the tens column, we borrow 1 hundred from the 6 hundreds, leaving 5 hundreds.

```
    5 12
  4 6̷ 2̷ 8
 −   5 9 3
  4 0 3 5
```

Adding the 1 hundred to the 2 tens we get 12 tens.

→ 8 ones − 3 ones = 5 ones
→ 12 tens − 9 tens = 3 tens
→ 5 hundreds − 5 hundreds = 0 hundreds
→ 4 thousands − 0 thousands = 4 thousands

Example 4

$$603 - 178 = ?$$

Since the 8 is larger than the 3 in the ones column, we must borrow. But there is a zero in the tens place, so we borrow 1 from the 6 hundreds (60 tens) leaving 59 tens. We then have 13 in the ones column.

```
  5 9 13
  6̷ 0̷ 3
 −1 7 8
  4 2 5
```

→ 13 ones − 8 ones = 5 ones
→ 9 tens − 7 tens = 2 tens
→ 5 hundreds − 1 hundred = 4 hundreds

To check your work, add the difference to the subtrahend (the two bottom numbers), and you should get the minuend (the top number).

Problem 1: $5713 - 4975 = ?$

Answer: 738

```
        16 10
    4  6̷  0̷  13
    5̷  7̷  1̷  3̷
  −4  9  7  5
     7  3  8
```

Check:
```
   4975
 +  738
   5713
```

Problem 2: $6003 - 527 = ?$

Answer: 5476

```
  5 9 9 13
  6̷ 0̷ 0̷ 3̷
 −   5 2 7
  5 4 7 6
```

Check:
```
    527
 +5476
   6003
```

Problem 3:   What's wrong with this subtraction problem?

```
  126
 − 48
   82
```

Answer: Subtraction in the ones column was done in the reverse order. Borrowing should have been used.

Name _____ Date _____

Exercise 2.2 Set A

1.   96
   -32

2.   87
   -53

3.   514
  $-\ 13$

4.   816
  $-\ 14$

5. 9876
 -1034

6. 5665
 -1201

7.   83
   -27

8.   94
   -66

9.   329
  $-\ 95$

10.   438
  $-\ 63$

11. 4563
 -2985

12. 3762
 -1974

13.   607
  $-\ 59$

14.   804
  $-\ 75$

15. 4003
 $-\ 758$

16. 5004
 $-\ 639$

17. 5000
 -4638

18. 7000
 -5297

19. 14,625 − 5,073

20. 75,075 − 67,067

21. 1,596,385 − 847,128

1. _____

2. _____

3. _____

4. _____

5. _____

6. _____

7. _____

8. _____

9. _____

10. _____

11. _____

12. _____

13. _____

14. _____

15. _____

16. _____

17. _____

18. _____

19. _____

20. _____

21. _____

Exercise 2.2 Set B

1. $\begin{array}{r} 57 \\ -24 \\ \hline \end{array}$

2. $\begin{array}{r} 65 \\ -42 \\ \hline \end{array}$

3. $\begin{array}{r} 819 \\ -\ 14 \\ \hline \end{array}$

4. $\begin{array}{r} 715 \\ -\ 13 \\ \hline \end{array}$

5. $\begin{array}{r} 6789 \\ -2025 \\ \hline \end{array}$

6. $\begin{array}{r} 5775 \\ -3013 \\ \hline \end{array}$

7. $\begin{array}{r} 92 \\ -57 \\ \hline \end{array}$

8. $\begin{array}{r} 83 \\ -65 \\ \hline \end{array}$

9. $\begin{array}{r} 435 \\ -\ 66 \\ \hline \end{array}$

10. $\begin{array}{r} 548 \\ -\ 79 \\ \hline \end{array}$

11. $\begin{array}{r} 3762 \\ -1375 \\ \hline \end{array}$

12. $\begin{array}{r} 5418 \\ -2329 \\ \hline \end{array}$

13. $\begin{array}{r} 507 \\ -\ 69 \\ \hline \end{array}$

14. $\begin{array}{r} 903 \\ -\ 75 \\ \hline \end{array}$

15. $\begin{array}{r} 3006 \\ -\ 629 \\ \hline \end{array}$

16. $\begin{array}{r} 5005 \\ -\ 738 \\ \hline \end{array}$

17. $\begin{array}{r} 7000 \\ -2561 \\ \hline \end{array}$

18. $\begin{array}{r} 9000 \\ -3275 \\ \hline \end{array}$

19. 13,264 − 4,073

20. 67,067 − 58,058

21. 2,563,871 − 452,076

1. _____
2. _____
3. _____
4. _____
5. _____
6. _____
7. _____
8. _____
9. _____
10. _____
11. _____
12. _____
13. _____
14. _____
15. _____
16. _____
17. _____
18. _____
19. _____
20. _____
21. _____

2.3 Division Facts

Such a report card gives me D-visions.

The last operation to cover is the division of whole numbers. Division occurs in problems such as this:

If you had $28 and you wanted to buy concert tickets that cost $7 each, how many would you buy?

One way to do the problem is to determine how many 7's there are in 28 by subtracting $7 for each ticket, until the money runs out.

$$\begin{array}{cccc} 28 & 21 & 14 & 7 \\ -7 & -7 & -7 & -7 \\ \hline 21 & 14 & 7 & 0 \end{array}$$ There are four 7's in 28.

Thus, we say 28 divided by 7 is 4 and write it:

$$28 \div 7 = 4$$

We can also say 7 divides into 28 four times and write it:

$$7)\overline{28}\,^4$$

Notice the reversal of the order of the 28 and the 7 in these two ways to express division.

Each part of the division problem has a name:

$$\text{divisor} \to 7)\overline{28}\,^{4 \leftarrow \textbf{quotient}} \leftarrow \textbf{dividend}$$

If you had to use repeat subtraction whenever you divided numbers, a problem such as 13,676 ÷ 52 would take much work and many steps. There is another way to consider division. Let's look at that example again.

$$7)\overline{28}\,^4$$

Notice: $4 \times 7 = 28$

$$7)\overline{28}\,^4 \quad \underline{28}$$

That points out the basic fact about division. If you take the answer of a division problem (the quotient) and multiply it by the divisor, you get the number that you are dividing into (the dividend). Let me show you what this means by doing some examples.

Example 1

$$18 \div 6 = ?$$

$$6)\overline{18}\,^? \qquad \text{Think: } ? \times 6 = 18 \qquad 6)\overline{18}\,^? \quad \underline{18}$$

Since $3 \times 6 = 18$, we get $18 \div 6 = 3$.

$$6)\overline{18}\,^3 \quad \underline{18}$$

Example 2

$$72 \div 9 = ?$$

$$9\overline{)72}^{?} \qquad \text{Think: } ? \times 9 = 72 \qquad 9\overline{)72}^{?}$$

Since $8 \times 9 = 72$, we get $72 \div 9 = 8$.

$$9\overline{)72}^{8}$$
$$\underline{72}$$

Using the fact that the quotient times the divisor equals the dividend will make division easier to perform than using repeat subtraction.

Problem 1: Find $32 \div 8$ using repeat subtraction.

Answer: 4

$$\begin{array}{c c c c}
32 & 24 & 16 & 8 \\
\underline{-8} & \underline{-8} & \underline{-8} & \underline{-8} \\
24 & 16 & 8 & 0
\end{array}$$

There are 4 eights in 32.

Problem 2: Find $45 \div 5$ using the multiplication method.

Answer: 9

$$5\overline{)45}^{9}$$
$$45$$

Problem 3: Find $63 \div 9$ using the multiplication method.

Answer: 7

$$9\overline{)63}^{7}$$
$$63$$

Name _____   Date _____

Exercise 2.3 Set A

1. $8 \div 8$

2. $4 \div 4$

3. $7 \div 7$

1. _____ 2. _____ 3. _____

4. $2\overline{)10}$

5. $6\overline{)24}$

6. $7\overline{)28}$

4. _____ 5. _____ 6. _____

7. $9 \div 3$

8. $18 \div 6$

9. $36 \div 9$

7. _____ 8. _____ 9. _____

10. $8\overline{)40}$

11. $4\overline{)20}$

12. $3\overline{)21}$

10. _____ 11. _____ 12. _____

13. $5 \div 1$

14. $12 \div 6$

15. $56 \div 7$

13. _____ 14. _____ 15. _____

16. $9\overline{)45}$

17. $5\overline{)10}$

18. $3\overline{)27}$

16. _____ 17. _____ 18. _____

19. $16 \div 2$

20. $30 \div 5$

21. $32 \div 8$

19. _____ 20. _____ 21. _____

22. $8\overline{)48}$

23. $5\overline{)45}$

24. $3\overline{)15}$

22. _____ 23. _____ 24. _____

25. $9\overline{)72}$

26. $7\overline{)49}$

27. $8\overline{)48}$

25. _____ 26. _____ 27. _____

28. $64 \div 8$

29. $63 \div 7$

30. $81 \div 9$

28. _____ 29. _____ 30. _____

31. $8\overline{)32}$

32. $7\overline{)35}$

33. $8\overline{)24}$

31. _____ 32. _____ 33. _____

34. $30 \div 6$

35. $28 \div 4$

36. $30 \div 5$

34. _____ 35. _____ 36. _____

37. $8\overline{)56}$

38. $9\overline{)54}$

39. $7\overline{)21}$

37. _____ 38. _____ 39. _____

In problems 40–41, use repeat subtraction to show the following are true.

40. $20 \div 4 = 5$

40. _____

41. $3\overline{)18}^{\,6}$

41. _____

Exercise 2.3 Set B

1. $8 \div 2$

2. $10 \div 5$

3. $15 \div 3$

4. $6 \overline{)24}$

5. $4 \overline{)36}$

6. $5 \overline{)30}$

7. $72 \div 8$

8. $14 \div 7$

9. $54 \div 9$

10. $2 \overline{)10}$

11. $3 \overline{)18}$

12. $2 \overline{)12}$

13. $25 \div 5$

14. $16 \div 4$

15. $48 \div 6$

16. $9 \overline{)27}$

17. $7 \overline{)56}$

18. $8 \overline{)32}$

19. $6 \overline{)42}$

20. $8 \overline{)16}$

21. $9 \overline{)72}$

22. $24 \div 3$

23. $10 \div 5$

24. $42 \div 7$

25. $3 \overline{)21}$

26. $5 \overline{)45}$

27. $7 \overline{)35}$

28. $18 \div 3$

29. $40 \div 5$

30. $49 \div 7$

31. $9 \overline{)81}$

32. $8 \overline{)56}$

33. $6 \overline{)42}$

34. $40 \div 8$

35. $63 \div 9$

36. $6 \div 6$

37. $8 \overline{)48}$

38. $54 \div 6$

39. $9 \overline{)54}$

1. _____   2. _____   3. _____

4. _____   5. _____   6. _____

7. _____   8. _____   9. _____

10. _____   11. _____   12. _____

13. _____   14. _____   15. _____

16. _____   17. _____   18. _____

19. _____   20. _____   21. _____

22. _____   23. _____   24. _____

25. _____   26. _____   27. _____

28. _____   29. _____   30. _____

31. _____   32. _____   33. _____

34. _____   35. _____   36. _____

37. _____   38. _____   39. _____

In problems 40–41 use repeat subtraction to show the following are true.

40. $20 \div 5 = 4$

40. _____

41. $6 \overline{)30}^{\,5}$

41. _____

68

2.4 Remainders, Dividing by Zero

**Mission Impossible:
Dividing by zero.**

Now that you have reviewed the basic division facts, you can proceed onto more involved division problems.

For example, what is 26 ÷ 8?
Let's do it by repeat subtraction.

$$
\begin{array}{ccc}
26 & \nearrow 18 & \nearrow 10 \\
-8 & -8 & -8 \\
\hline
18 \nearrow & 10 \nearrow & 2
\end{array}
$$

There are 3 eights in 26 with 2 ones left over. That left over amount is called the **remainder**.

Thus, 26 ÷ 8 = 3 remainder 2 or 3 R2.

If you do that problem using the multiplication method, you would write:

$$
\begin{array}{r}
3 \\
8)\overline{26} \\
24 \\
\hline
2 \end{array} \longleftarrow \text{remainder}
$$

Example 1

57 ÷ 6 = ?

$$
6)\overline{57}^{\,?}
$$
There is no value for the ? × 6 that gives exactly 57.

$$
\begin{array}{r}
9 \\
6)\overline{57} \\
54 \\
\hline
3 \end{array}
$$
The closest we can get to 57, without going over it, is 9 × 6 = 54.

Subtracting the 54 from the 57, we get a remainder of 3.

Example 2

36 ÷ 5 = ?

$$
5)\overline{36}^{\,?}
$$
There is no value for the ? × 5 that gives exactly 36.

$$
\begin{array}{r}
7 \\
5)\overline{36} \\
35 \\
\hline
1 \end{array}
$$
The closest we can get to 36, without going over it, is 7 × 5 = 35.

Subtracting the 35 from the 36, we get a remainder of 1.

We can summarize those examples by saying if a divisor does not divide exactly into a number, find the quotient that gets closest to the number without going over it and subtract to find the remainder.

Problem 1:   23 ÷ 4 = ?

Answer: 5 R3

$$
\begin{array}{r}
5 \\
4\overline{)23} \\
20 \\
\hline
3
\end{array}
$$

Problem 2:   74 ÷ 8 = ?

Answer: 9 R2

$$
\begin{array}{r}
9 \\
8\overline{)74} \\
72 \\
\hline
2
\end{array}
$$

Dividing by Zero

As you have seen, some division problems give exact answers while others have remainders. There are division problems, however, that do not have answers at all. Any division problem that has zero as the divisor can not be done.

YOU CAN NOT DIVIDE BY ZERO.

Problems such as 7 ÷ 0 = ?, $0\overline{)56}$, or 340 ÷ 0 = ? are impossible! Let me explain why this is so. Consider 7 ÷ 0 = ?

1. If you used the first method of division, repeat subtraction, you will never get an answer. Look below:

$$
\begin{array}{cccc}
7 & 7 & 7 & 7 \\
-0 & -0 & -0 & -0 \\
\hline
7 & 7 & 7 & 7
\end{array}
$$

. . . You could subtract zeros forever and still be in the same place.

The repeat subtraction method will not give you an answer for division by zero.

2. If you used the multiplication process for division, no answer can be obtained either. Look below:

$0\overline{)7}$ . . . You simply can not find a value for the ?, since no number times zero equals 7.

The multiplication process for division will also not give an answer for division by zero.

Exercise 2.4 Set A

1. 25 ÷ 4   2. 32 ÷ 6

3. 5)47   4. 4)29

5. 68 ÷ 0   6. 75 ÷ 9

7. 2)13   8. 0)16

9. 49 ÷ 7   10. 81 ÷ 9

11. 8)30   12. 9)50

13. 5)33   14. 9)80

15. 17 ÷ 6   16. 33 ÷ 4

17. 7)58   18. 4)29

19. 53 ÷ 7   20. 19 ÷ 8

21. 75 ÷ 9   22. 46 ÷ 6

23. 9)36   24. 8)64

1. _____
2. _____
3. _____
4. _____
5. _____
6. _____
7. _____
8. _____
9. _____
10. _____
11. _____
12. _____
13. _____
14. _____
15. _____
16. _____
17. _____
18. _____
19. _____
20. _____
21. _____
22. _____
23. _____
24. _____

Exercise 2.4 Set B

1. $17 \div 4$

2. $31 \div 5$

3. $4\overline{)38}$

4. $5\overline{)39}$

5. $15 \div 0$

6. $79 \div 9$

7. $2\overline{)17}$

8. $0\overline{)72}$

9. $36 \div 6$

10. $64 \div 4$

11. $7\overline{)52}$

12. $9\overline{)60}$

13. $6\overline{)57}$

14. $9\overline{)70}$

15. $19 \div 4$

16. $38 \div 7$

17. $7\overline{)66}$

18. $4\overline{)35}$

19. $29 \div 3$

20. $15 \div 2$

21. $8\overline{)70}$

22. $6\overline{)55}$

23. $9\overline{)45}$

24. $6\overline{)48}$

1. _____
2. _____
3. _____
4. _____
5. _____
6. _____
7. _____
8. _____
9. _____
10. _____
11. _____
12. _____
13. _____
14. _____
15. _____
16. _____
17. _____
18. _____
19. _____
20. _____
21. _____
22. _____
23. _____
24. _____

Dividing by One Digit Numbers

In the previous sections, we covered the basic concepts about division. That knowledge will make division of whole numbers much easier. Let's study some examples and their explanations to see how division by a one digit number is accomplished.

Example 1

$693 \div 3 = ?$

If you try to use the concepts of the previous sections to find the answer, you might have some difficulty.

$$\overset{?}{3)\overline{693}}$$
$\hookrightarrow \underline{693}$

. . . It is not obvious what number times 3 gives 693.

I will show you how to break a division problem into steps so that the answer can be obtained.

First: Instead of dividing the 3 into the entire number, divide the 3 into the 6 hundreds, getting:

$$\overset{2}{3)\overline{693}}$$
$\hookrightarrow \underline{6}$

Notice: The 2 is put in the hundreds place above the 6.

Second: Divide the 3 into the 9 in tens place.

(Bring down the 9 as pictured to make it clear that the 3 is dividing into the 9 tens).

$$\overset{23}{3)\overline{693}}$$
$6\downarrow$
$\underline{9}$
$\hookrightarrow 9$

Notice: The answer to the division (3) is put in the tens place above the 9.

Third: Divide the 3 into the 3 in the ones place.

(Bring down the 3 to make it clear that we are dividing into the 3).

$$\overset{231}{3)\overline{693}}$$
$\underline{6}$
9
$\underline{9}\downarrow$
3
$\hookrightarrow 3$

Notice: The answer to that division (1) is put into the ones place above the 3.

Thus, $693 \div 3 = 231$.

Example 2

$$387 \div 4 = ?$$

$$
\begin{array}{r}
9 \\
4\overline{)387} \\
36 \\
\hline
2
\end{array}
$$

The divisor (4) is larger than the first digit of the dividend (3), so divide the 4 into the 38 tens, getting 9 tens and a remainder of 2 tens.

$$
\begin{array}{r}
9 \\
4\overline{)387} \\
36\downarrow \\
\hline
27
\end{array}
$$

Bring down the next digit, the 7 ones, getting 27.

$$
\begin{array}{r}
96 \\
4\overline{)387} \\
36 \\
\hline
27 \\
24 \\
\hline
3
\end{array}
$$

Divide the 4 into the 27, getting 6 with a remainder of 3.

Thus, $387 \div 4 = 96$ R3

Problem 1: $6284 \div 2 = ?$ Answer: 3142

$$
\begin{array}{r}
3142 \\
2\overline{)6284} \\
6 \\
\hline
2 \\
2 \\
\hline
8 \\
8 \\
\hline
4 \\
4 \\
\hline
\end{array}
$$

Problem 2: $897 \div 7 = ?$ Answer: 128 R1

$$
\begin{array}{r}
128 \\
7\overline{)897} \\
7 \\
\hline
19 \\
14 \\
\hline
57 \\
56 \\
\hline
1
\end{array}
$$

Problem 3: $2057 \div 6 = ?$ Answer: 342 R5

$$
\begin{array}{r}
342 \\
6\overline{)2057} \\
18 \\
\hline
25 \\
24 \\
\hline
17 \\
12 \\
\hline
5
\end{array}
$$

Exercise 2.5 Set A

1. 486 ÷ 2

2. 996 ÷ 3

3. 4)96

4. 3)72

5. 441 ÷ 7

6. 342 ÷ 6

7. 5)433

8. 7)591

9. 9)2313

10. 8)5224

11. 3)7372

12. 6)1049

13. 4)19089

14. 4)15638

15. 7)47971

16. 8)19656

17. 9)461241

18. 6)412752

1. _____

2. _____

3. _____

4. _____

5. _____

6. _____

7. _____

8. _____

9. _____

10. _____

11. _____

12. _____

13. _____

14. _____

15. _____

16. _____

17. _____

18. _____

Exercise 2.5 Set B

1. $682 \div 2$

2. $696 \div 3$

3. $5\overline{)65}$

4. $4\overline{)92}$

5. $378 \div 7$

6. $672 \div 8$

7. $9\overline{)551}$

8. $6\overline{)441}$

9. $8\overline{)4338}$

10. $9\overline{)1775}$

11. $6\overline{)1460}$

12. $3\overline{)1972}$

13. $5\overline{)16081}$

14. $4\overline{)11133}$

15. $8\overline{)19968}$

16. $7\overline{)17276}$

17. $6\overline{)147498}$

18. $9\overline{)520578}$

1. _____

2. _____

3. _____

4. _____

5. _____

6. _____

7. _____

8. _____

9. _____

10. _____

11. _____

12. _____

13. _____

14. _____

15. _____

16. _____

17. _____

18. _____

2.6 Dividing by Numbers Having More than One Digit

The process for division that has been explained in the last two sections will enable you to divide even larger numbers. Since those same principles as shown in Section 2.5 are involved in the next examples, I will concentrate on the division method rather than giving detailed explanations.

Example 1

$9065 \div 37 = ?$

$$37)\overline{9065}$$

Step 1: Decide above which digit the quotient will start:
Does the 37 divide into the 9? No.
Does the 37 divide into the 90? Yes.
So the quotient starts above the 0.

$$\begin{array}{r} 2 \\ 37)\overline{9065} \\ 74 \\ \hline 16 \end{array}$$

Step 2: Divide 37 into 90.
37 divides into 90 about 2 times.
The 2 is placed above the 0.
$2 \times 37 = 74$.
The 74 is subtracted from the 90 to get a remainder of 16.

$$\begin{array}{r} 24 \\ 37)\overline{9065} \\ 74 \\ \hline 166 \\ 148 \\ \hline 18 \end{array}$$

Step 3: Bring down the next digit, the 6.
Divide the 37 into the 166.
37 divides into 166 about 4 times.
$4 \times 37 = 148$.
The 148 is subtracted from the 166 to get a remainder of 18.

$$\begin{array}{r} 245 \\ 37)\overline{9065} \\ 74 \\ \hline 166 \\ 148 \\ \hline 185 \\ 185 \end{array}$$

Step 4: Bring down the next digit, the 5.
Divide the 37 into the 185.
37 divides into 185 exactly 5 times.

Example 2

$13678 \div 243 = ?$

$$243)\overline{13678}$$

Step 1: Decide where the quotient should start:
243 divides into the 1367, so the quotient should start above the 7.

$$\begin{array}{r} 5 \\ 243)\overline{13678} \\ 1215 \\ \hline 152 \end{array}$$

Step 2: Divide 243 into 1367.
243 divides into 1367 about 5 times.
$5 \times 243 = 1215$.
The 1215 is subtracted from the 1367 to get a remainder of 152.

$$\begin{array}{r} 56 \\ 243)\overline{13678} \\ 1215 \\ \hline 1528 \\ 1458 \\ \hline 70 \end{array}$$

Step 3: Bring down the next digit, the 8.
Divide 243 into 1528.
243 divides into 1528 about 6 times.
$6 \times 243 = 1458$.
The 1458 is subtracted from the 1528 to get a remainder of 70.

The process of division as described in those two examples is quite involved. There are a few suggestions that I can give to help you arrive at correct answers when doing division problems.

1. Make sure you start the quotient above the correct digit.

For example: $5287\overline{)365425}$

> 5287 will not divide into 3 since 5287 > 3.
> 5287 will not divide into 36 since 5287 > 36.
> 5287 will not divide into 365 since 5287 > 365.
> 5287 will not divide into 3654 since 5287 > 3654.
> 5287 will divide into 36542 since that is the first part of the dividend that 5287 is not larger than.

Thus, the quotient in this example will start above the 2.

2. Every remainder in the division process should be less than the divisor. If you get a remainder that is not less than the divisor, the digit used in the quotient was too small.

For example:

$$\begin{array}{r} 6 \\ 26\overline{)1872} \\ 156 \\ \hline 31 \end{array} \qquad \rightarrow \text{You should use} \rightarrow \qquad \begin{array}{r} 7 \\ 26\overline{)1872} \\ 182 \\ \hline 5 \end{array}$$

a quotient of 7 instead of 6.

Remainder (31) is larger than the divisor (26).

Now remainder is less than the divisor.

3. How do you determine approximately how many times one number will divide into another number? If you round off your divisor, you should be better able to make a good guess about how many times one number divides into another.

For example: $86\overline{)63124}$

> The divisor 86 rounds off to 90.
> Now the 9 in 90 divides into the 63 of 631 about 7 times.
> So 86 should divide into 631 about 7 times.

$$\begin{array}{r} 7 \\ 86\overline{)63124} \\ 602 \\ \hline 29 \end{array}$$

The remainder is less than the divisor so the guess of 7 was correct.

4. How do you check to see if your answer is correct? You could check your work by doing the following:

quotient × divisor + remainder = dividend

Example:

$$
\begin{array}{r}
237 \\
15\overline{)3559} \\
30 \\
\overline{55} \\
45 \\
\overline{109} \\
105 \\
\overline{4}
\end{array}
$$

Check:

$$
\begin{array}{rl}
\text{quotient} \longrightarrow & 237 \\
\times \text{ divisor} \longrightarrow & 15 \\
\hline
& 1185 \\
& 237 \\
\hline
& 3555 \\
+ \text{ remainder} \longrightarrow & +\ 4 \\
= \text{ dividend} \longrightarrow & 3559
\end{array}
$$

Since the quotient times the divisor plus the remainder does equal the dividend (3559), I am sure that the answer, 237 R4, is correct.

Problem 1: In the problem $419\overline{)254670}$, above which digit should the quotient start?

Answer: Start above the 6, since 419 is larger than 2, 25, and 254, but not larger than 2546.

Problem 2: What is wrong with this division problem?

$$
\begin{array}{r}
3 \\
15\overline{)67} \\
45 \\
\overline{22}
\end{array}
$$

Answer: The remainder (22) is larger than the divisor (15). You should use a quotient of 4.

Problem 3: Use rounding off to find about how many times 77 divides into 5035.

Answer: 6 times.
77 rounds off to 80. The 8 in 80 divides into the 50 in 5035 about 6 times.

Problem 4: Use the check method to determine which are correct:

a. $306\overline{)17442}$ with quotient 57

b. $82\overline{)38133}$ with quotient 465 R7

Answers:

a. Correct, since
quotient × divisor = dividend
57 × 306 = 17442

b. Not correct, since
quotient × divisor + remainder = 38137
465 × 82 + 7 = 38137

That result does not equal the dividend, which is 38133.

Problem 5: $1482 \div 26 = ?$ Answer: 57

```
        57
26) 1482
    130
    182
    182
```

Problem 6: $30,378 \div 416 = ?$ Answer: 73 R10

```
          73
416) 30378
     2912
     1258
     1248
       10
```

Problem 7: $5406 \div 17 = ?$ Answer: 318

```
        318
17) 5406
    51
    30
    17
    136
    136
```

Problem 8: $445,588 \div 5,003 = ?$ Answer: 89 R321

```
           89
5003) 445588
      40024
      45348
      45027
        321
```

Problem 9: $1,894,077 \div 783 = ?$ Answer: 2419

```
          2419
783) 1894077
     1566
     3280
     3132
     1487
      783
     7047
     7047
```

Name _____   Date _____

Exercise 2.6 Set A

1. $23\overline{)391}$

2. $41\overline{)943}$

3. $47\overline{)2491}$

4. $58\overline{)2088}$

5. $69\overline{)3249}$

6. $75\overline{)4595}$

7. $232\overline{)15080}$

8. $314\overline{)20410}$

9. $247\overline{)33357}$

10. $643\overline{)55399}$

11. $706\overline{)319818}$

12. $508\overline{)181356}$

13. $4125\overline{)354968}$

14. $3176\overline{)149395}$

15. $5806\overline{)1016050}$

16. $6904\overline{)1346280}$

1. _____

2. _____

3. _____

4. _____

5. _____

6. _____

7. _____

8. _____

9. _____

10. _____

11. _____

12. _____

13. _____

14. _____

15. _____

16. _____

Exercise 2.6 Set B

1. $32 \overline{)832}$

2. $14 \overline{)938}$

3. $57 \overline{)1995}$

4. $48 \overline{)2976}$

5. $86 \overline{)4569}$

6. $79 \overline{)2096}$

7. $322 \overline{)20930}$

8. $414 \overline{)31050}$

9. $536 \overline{)25397}$

10. $463 \overline{)34485}$

11. $506 \overline{)175582}$

12. $706 \overline{)302168}$

13. $5314 \overline{)255396}$

14. $4236 \overline{)305817}$

15. $6908 \overline{)1761540}$

16. $8506 \overline{)2339150}$

1. _____

2. _____

3. _____

4. _____

5. _____

6. _____

7. _____

8. _____

9. _____

10. _____

11. _____

12. _____

13. _____

14. _____

15. _____

16. _____

2.7 Zeros in the Quotient

The number zero quite frequently causes difficulty when it should be part of the quotient in a division problem. Students have a tendency to just leave it out of their answers. If you remember the next suggestion about division, you will be less prone to make errors with zeros in the quotient.

After you place the first digit in the quotient, you should have a digit above each remaining digit in the dividend.

Example 1

$$
\begin{array}{r}
608 \\
3\overline{)1824} \\
\underline{18} \\
2 \\
\underline{0} \\
24 \\
\underline{24}
\end{array}
$$

Notice after we started the quotient above the 8, there is a digit above each digit in the dividend.

Example 2

$$
\begin{array}{r}
32 \\
2\overline{)640} \\
\underline{6} \\
4 \\
\underline{4}
\end{array}
$$

Notice there is no number above the 0 in the dividend. Something must be wrong. The actual answer is 320. The zero at the end of the quotient was left out.

Example 3

$$
\begin{array}{r}
37 \\
4\overline{)1228} \\
\underline{12} \\
28 \\
\underline{28}
\end{array}
$$

Something is wrong again. There is no number above the 8 in the dividend. The actual answer is 307. Again a zero was omitted from the quotient.

Example 4

$$
\begin{array}{r}
3 \\
7\overline{)2100} \\
\underline{21}
\end{array}
$$

⟶ 7 divides into the 21, three times.

$$
\begin{array}{r}
30 \\
7\overline{)2100} \\
\underline{21}\downarrow \\
0 \\
\underline{0}
\end{array}
$$

⟶ Bring the first zero down. 7 divides into zero, 0 times. Thus, 0 was placed in the tens place of the quotient.

$$
\begin{array}{r}
300 \\
7\overline{)2100} \\
\underline{21} \\
0 \\
0\downarrow \\
0 \\
\underline{0}
\end{array}
$$

⟶ Bring down the second zero. 7 divides into zero, 0 times. Thus, 0 was placed in the ones place of the quotient.

Example 5

```
        4  ──────→ 12 divides into 48, four times
12) 4836
    48
```

```
       40
12) 4836
    48↓
```

```
      3  ──────→  Bring down the 3. 12 is larger than 3, so 12 di-
      0             vides into 3, zero times. Thus, 0 is placed above
      3             the 3 in the tens place of the quotient.
```

```
      403
12) 4836
    48 |
     3 |
     0 ↓
    36      Bring down the 6. 12 divides into 36, three times.
    36      Thus, 3 is placed above the 6 in the ones place.
```

Example 6

```
          9 ─────→ 207 divides into 1864, nine times with a remain-
207) 1864256        der of one.
     1863
        1
```

```
         90
207) 1864256
     1863↓
```

```
       12 ──────→ Bring down the 2. 207 is larger than 12, so 207
        0            divides into 12, zero times. Thus, 0 is placed
       12            above the 2.
```

```
        900
207) 1864256
     1863 |
       12 |
        0 ↓
      125 ──────→ Bring down the 5. 207 is larger than 125, so 207
        0            divides into 125, zero times. Thus, 0 is placed
      125            above the 5.
```

```
        9006
207) 1864256
     1863 |
       12 |
        0 |
      125 |
        0 ↓
     1256 →  Bring down the 6. Now 207 divides into 1256, 6
     1242      times with a remainder of 14.
       14
```

Name _____   Date _____

Exercise 2.7 Set A

1. $6\overline{)2400}$ 2. $4\overline{)2800}$

3. $24\overline{)6000}$ 4. $36\overline{)9000}$

5. $70\overline{)28000}$ 6. $90\overline{)45000}$

7. $43\overline{)21629}$ 8. $57\overline{)11742}$

9. $68\overline{)27648}$ 10. $79\overline{)24066}$

11. $23\overline{)23046}$ 12. $34\overline{)34102}$

13. $503\overline{)302856}$ 14. $604\overline{)424652}$

15. $345\overline{)700350}$ 16. $425\overline{)1283500}$

1. _____
2. _____

3. _____
4. _____

5. _____
6. _____

7. _____
8. _____

9. _____
10. _____

11. _____
12. _____

13. _____
14. _____

15. _____
16. _____

Exercise 2.7 Set B

1. $7 \overline{)3500}$

2. $3 \overline{)2400}$

3. $32 \overline{)8000}$

4. $28 \overline{)7000}$

5. $80 \overline{)48000}$

6. $60 \overline{)54000}$

7. $53 \overline{)16271}$

8. $47 \overline{)19176}$

9. $49 \overline{)14835}$

10. $58 \overline{)23573}$

11. $34 \overline{)34238}$

12. $23 \overline{)23207}$

13. $602 \overline{)184834}$

14. $405 \overline{)83045}$

15. $275 \overline{)551100}$

16. $385 \overline{)1157310}$

1. _____

2. _____

3. _____

4. _____

5. _____

6. _____

7. _____

8. _____

9. _____

10. _____

11. _____

12. _____

13. _____

14. _____

15. _____

16. _____

2.8 The Order of Operations

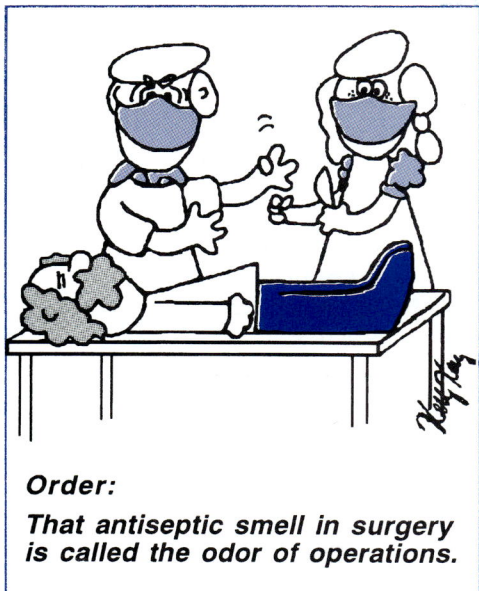

Order:

That antiseptic smell in surgery is called the odor of operations.

Now that you have reviewed the four basic operations, powers, and square roots, you will encounter problems that have combined these operations.

For example: $3 + 7 \times 5 = ?$

Some of you may get an answer of 50 by figuring $3 + 7 = 10$ and $10 \times 5 = 50$. Others may get an answer of 38 by figuring $7 \times 5 = 35$ and $3 + 35 = 38$. Which answer is correct, 50 or 38? Both answers can not be correct. Actually 38 is the correct answer since it is the result of the proper order in which the operations are done.

Computation in mathematics must be done in a standardized order so that everyone could get the same answer for the same pr lem. The order that is agreed upon for doing computation in mathematics is as follows:

The Order of Operations

First: Do operations inside parentheses.
Second: Do powers or square roots.
Third: Do multiplications or divisions from left to right.
Fourth: Do additions or subtractions from left to right.

By "left to right" I mean whichever of the operations you come across first as you move from left to right through the proble

Example 1

$3 \times 5 - (5 + 6) = ?$

$= 3 \times 5 - 11$	Do the parentheses.
$= 15 - 11$	Do the multiplication.
$= 4$	Do the subtraction.

Note: To help assure accuracy, do one step at a time and write down the intermediate results below the computation.

Example 2

$36 \div (3 + 1) \times 6 = ?$

$= 36 \div 4 \times 6$	Do the parentheses.
$= 9 \times 6$	Do the multiplications or divisions from
$= 54$	left to right. (Note: We did the division first since we came across a division first, moving left to right.)

Example 3

$$16 + \sqrt{49} \times 3^2 = ?$$

$= 16 + 7 \times 9$	Do the powers and square roots.
$= 16 + 63$	Do the multiplication.
$= 79$	Do the addition.

Example 4

$$(20 + 25) \div 5 - 2^3 + 1 = ?$$

$= 45 \div 5 - 2^3 + 1$	Do the parentheses
$= 45 \div 5 - 8 + 1$	Do the powers.
$= 9 - 8 + 1$	Do the division.
$= 2$	Do the additions or subtractions from left to right. (Note: We did the subtraction first since we came across it first as we moved left to right.)

Problem 1: $65 - 4 \times 8 = ?$

Answer: 33

$$65 - 4 \times 8 = 65 - 32$$
$$= 33$$

Problem 2: $6 \times (10 - 4) + \sqrt{100} = ?$

Answer: 46

$$6 \times (10 - 4) + \sqrt{100} = 6 \times 6 + \sqrt{100}$$
$$= 6 \times 6 + 10$$
$$= 36 + 10$$
$$= 46$$

Problem 3: $5 \times 3^2 - 9 \div 3 \times 2 = ?$

Answer: 39

$$5 \times 3^2 - 9 \div 3 \times 2 = 5 \times 9 - 9 \div 3 \times 2$$
$$= 45 - 6$$
$$= 39$$

Problem 4: $(7 + 3)^4 \times (2 + 3 \times 4) = ?$

Answer: 140,000

$$(7 + 3)^4 \times (2 + 3 \times 4) = 10^4 \times 14$$
$$= 10000 \times 14$$
$$= 140,000$$

Name _____   Date _____

Exercise 2.8 Set A

1. $5 + 3 \times 4$

2. $7 + 2 \times 6$

3. $(5 + 3) \times 4$

4. $(7 + 2) \times 6$

5. $24 \times 4 \div 6$

6. $20 \times 4 \div 5$

7. $24 \div 4 \times 6$

8. $20 \div 4 \times 5$

9. $4 \times 3^2 - 7 \times 5$

10. $3 \times 2^3 - 2 \times 6$

11. $(2 + 1)^4 \times (12 - 2 \times 5)$

12. $(3 + 2)^2 \times (15 - 3 \times 4)$

13. $\sqrt{100} + 3 \times \sqrt{49}$

14. $\sqrt{81} + 2 \times \sqrt{64}$

15. $(12 + 18) \div 5 + 10$

16. $(15 + 18) \div 3 + 8$

17. $\sqrt{36} \times 10^5 - 3 \times 10^3$

18. $\sqrt{25} \times 10^6 - 3 \times 10^4$

19. $16 - 12 \div 4 \times 3 + 8 \times 2$

20. $28 - 36 \div 9 \times 4 + 6 \times 3$

21. $5 + 3 \times (4^2 + 1)$

22. $(5 + 3) \times (4^2 + 1)$

1. _____
2. _____
3. _____
4. _____
5. _____
6. _____
7. _____
8. _____
9. _____
10. _____
11. _____
12. _____
13. _____
14. _____
15. _____
16. _____
17. _____
18. _____
19. _____
20. _____
21. _____
22. _____

Exercise 2.8 Set B

1. $6 + 2 \times 7$

2. $4 + 5 \times 8$

3. $(6 + 2) \times 7$

4. $(4 + 5) \times 8$

5. $36 \times 4 \div 9$

6. $56 \times 7 \div 8$

7. $36 \div 4 \times 9$

8. $56 \div 7 \times 8$

9. $5 \times 4^2 - 3 \times 6$

10. $4 \times 3^3 - 5 \times 6$

11. $(3 + 2)^2 \times (17 - 3 \times 5)$

12. $(1 + 2)^4 \times (22 - 5 \times 3)$

13. $\sqrt{121} + 2 \times \sqrt{16}$

14. $\sqrt{49} + 3 \times \sqrt{9}$

15. $(18 + 14) \div 8 + 10$

16. $(18 + 18) \div 4 + 8$

17. $\sqrt{16} \times 10^4 - 2 \times 10^2$

18. $\sqrt{64} \times 10^6 - 5 \times 10^3$

19. $29 - 15 \div 3 \times 5 + 6 \times 4$

20. $34 - 16 \div 8 \times 2 + 8 \times 4$

21. $2 + 5 \times (1 + 3^2)$

22. $(2 + 5) \times (1 + 3^2)$

1. _____
2. _____
3. _____
4. _____
5. _____
6. _____
7. _____
8. _____
9. _____
10. _____
11. _____
12. _____
13. _____
14. _____
15. _____
16. _____
17. _____
18. _____
19. _____
20. _____
21. _____
22. _____

2.9 Primes, Divisibility, and Factoring into Primes

Primes

A **prime number** is a whole number greater than 1 that is evenly divisible by only 1 and itself. If a number is evenly divisible by other numbers besides 1 and itself, it is a **composite number.**

2, 3, 5, 7, 11, 13, 17, 19, 23, 29 . . . are prime numbers while
4, 6, 8, 9, 10, 12, 14, 15, 16, 18 . . . are composite numbers.

Examples: Determine whether the following are prime or composite:

31, prime   (divisible by only 1 and 31)
22, composite (divisible by 1 and 22, but also by 2 and 11)
51, composite (divisible by 1 and 51, but also by 3 and 17)

Divisibility

In determining if a given number is prime or composite, you need to decide if any number besides 1 and itself divides evenly into the given number. Below are some facts about divisibility that will hel you figure out what numbers divide evenly into a given number.

Divisibility by 2: If a number ends in 0, 2, 4, 6, or 8, it is an even number. Even numbers are divisible by 2.

96 is divisible by 2, since it is an even number.

Divisibility by 3: Add up the digits of the number. If you can divide the sum evenly by 3, the original number is divisible by 3.

441 is divisible by 3. The sum of its digits is 9 (4 + 4 + 1 = 9), and 9 can be divided by 3.

Divisibility by 5: If a number ends in either 5 or 0, it is divisible by 5.

935 is divisible by 5, since it ends in 5.

Problems: Is 510 divisible by the following:

1. 2 ?
2. 3 ?

3. 5 ?
4. 7 ?

Answers:

1. Yes, it is an even number.
2. Yes, sum of its digits is 6, which is divisible by 3.
3. Yes, it ends in 0.
4. No, dividing by 7 leaves a remainder of 6.

Factoring into Primes

The divisibility rules on the previous page can be helpful in writing a number as the product of other numbers. This process, **factoring,** will be useful in future chapters but will be introduced here. For example, some of the ways the number 12 can be factored using whole numbers are $12 = 1 \times 12$, $12 = 2 \times 6$, $12 = 3 \times 4$, or $12 = 2 \times 2 \times 3$. If all the factors in this process are prime numbers, you have written the number as a product of primes. Thus, $12 = 2 \times 2 \times 3$ gives 12 factored into primes. An effective way to factor a composite number into primes is to find all the prime divisors of the number. The product of these prime divisors will give you the number factored into primes. For example, to factor 60 into primes begin by looking for a prime number that divides evenly into 60. Since 60 is even, 2 is a divisor of 60. Dividing 2 into 60 gives a quotient of 30. Now look for a prime divisor of 30. Continue this process of looking for a prime divisor of resulting quotients until all prime divisors are found. When the last prime divisor is found, the final quotient will be the number 1. The chart below gives an efficient scheme for recording prime divisors and thereby, factoring a number into primes.

$$
\begin{array}{ll}
1 & \longleftarrow \text{(Stop; all prime divisors have been found.)} \\
5\overline{)5} & \longleftarrow \text{(5 is a prime divisor of 5.)} \\
3\overline{)15} & \longleftarrow \text{(3 is a prime divisor of 15.)} \\
2\overline{)30} & \longleftarrow \text{(2 is a prime divisor of 30; 30 is even.)} \\
2\overline{)60} & \longleftarrow \text{(2 is a prime divisor of 60; 60 is even.)} \\
\uparrow &
\end{array}
$$

prime divisors   Thus, $60 = 2 \times 2 \times 3 \times 5 = 2^2 \times 3 \times 5$

Note: When writing the prime factorization of a number, repeated prime factors are written with expone

Example 1

Factor 540 into primes.

$$
\begin{array}{ll}
1 & \longleftarrow \text{(Stop; all prime divisors have been found.)} \\
3\overline{)3} & \longleftarrow \text{(3 is a prime divisor of 3.)} \\
3\overline{)9} & \longleftarrow \text{(3 is a prime divisor of 9.)} \\
3\overline{)27} & \longleftarrow \text{(3 is a prime divisor of 27; sum of the digits is 9.)} \\
5\overline{)135} & \longleftarrow \text{(5 is a prime divisor of 135; 135 ends on 5.)} \\
2\overline{)270} & \longleftarrow \text{(2 is a prime divisor of 270; 270 is even.)} \\
2\overline{)540} & \longleftarrow \text{(2 is a prime divisor of 540; 540 is even.)} \\
\uparrow &
\end{array}
$$

prime divisors   Thus, $540 = 2 \times 2 \times 5 \times 3 \times 3 \times 3 = 2^2 \times 5 \times 3^3$

Example 2

Factor 539 into primes.

(539 is not divisible by 2, 3, or 5, so try larger primes as divisors.)

$$
\begin{array}{ll}
1 & \longleftarrow \text{(Stop; all prime divisors have been found.)} \\
11\overline{)11} & \longleftarrow \text{(11 is a prime divisor of 11.)} \\
7\overline{)77} & \longleftarrow \text{(7 is a prime divisor of 77.)} \\
7\overline{)539} & \longleftarrow \text{(7 is a prime divisor of 539.)} \\
\uparrow &
\end{array}
$$

prime divisors   Thus, $539 = 7 \times 7 \times 11 = 7^2 \times 11$

Problem 5:   Factor 150 into primes.

Answer: $2 \times 3 \times 5^2$

$$
\begin{array}{l}
1 \\
5\overline{)5} \\
3\overline{)15} \\
5\overline{)75} \\
2\overline{)150}
\end{array}
$$

Factor Trees

Another technique used in factoring a whole number into primes involves making a tree-like structure of the factors of the number. For example, to write the number 72 as a product of primes, find any two whole numbers that have a product of 72 and then express those numbers as a product of other whole numbers. If a number is prime it is circled. If it is not, it is factored again. This process gives a diagram called a *factor tree*. The product of all the encircled primes is the prime factorization of 72.

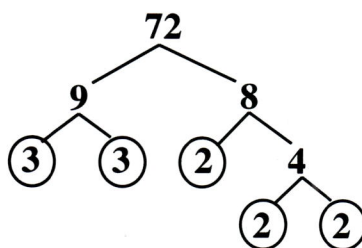

$9 \times 8 = 72$

$3 \times 3 = 9$ and $2 \times 4 = 8$

$2 \times 2 = 4$

Thus, $72 = 3 \times 3 \times 2 \times 2 \times 2 = 3^2 \times 2^3$

In this method, you could start with any two whole numbers that have a product of 72. If you continue factoring until you arrive at prime numbers, you will get the same result. The second factor tree that follows yields the same result for factoring 72 into primes.

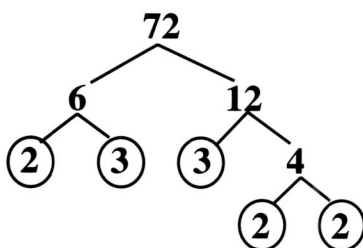

$6 \times 12 = 72$

$2 \times 3 = 6$ and $3 \times 4 = 12$

$2 \times 2 = 4$

Thus, $72 = 2 \times 3 \times 3 \times 2 \times 2 = 3^2 \times 2^3$

Example 3

Factor 1000 into primes.

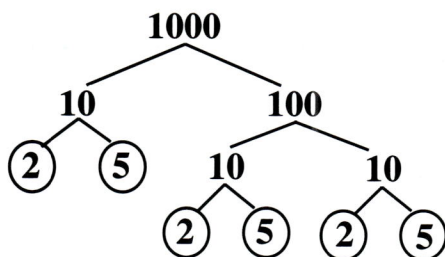

$10 \times 100 = 1000$

$2 \times 5 = 10$

$2 \times 5 = 10$

Thus, $1000 = 2 \times 5 \times 2 \times 5 \times 2 \times 5 = 2^3 \times 5^3$

Example 4

Factor 605 into primes.

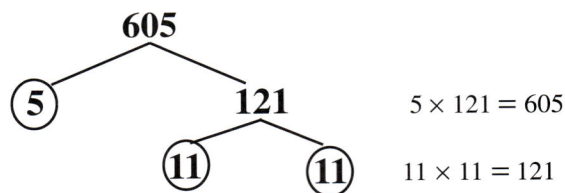

$5 \times 121 = 605$

$11 \times 11 = 121$

Thus, $605 = 5 \times 11 \times 11 = 5 \times 11^2$

Every whole number greater then 1 is either a prime number or can be expressed as a product of prime numbers. Both the division method and factor trees give an efficient way to factor a composi number into primes. You will see that the ability to do this will be useful in finding the least common denominator when adding and subtracting fractions.

Problem 6:   Factor 76 into primes.

Answer: $2^2 \times 19$

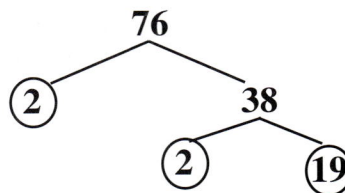

Problem 7:   Factor 1260 into primes.

Answer: $2^2 \times 3^2 \times 5 \times 7$

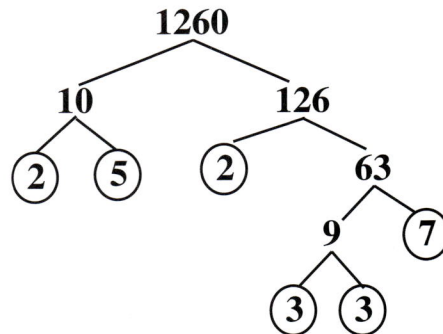

Problem 8:   Factor 137 into primes.

Answer: Not possible.
The number 137 has no divisors other than 1 and itself. Therefore, 137 is a prime number and can not be factored into the product of other primes.

Exercise 2.9 Set A

In problems 1–6, determine if each number is prime or composite.

1. 17   2. 23   3. 21

4. 49   5. 315   6. 441

In problems 7–24 factor each number into primes.

7. 18   8. 24

9. 46   10. 34

11. 42   12. 66

13. 5500   14. 3500

15. 75   16. 245

17. 1375   18. 1625

19. 660   20. 650

21. 222   22. 387

23. 133   24. 143

1. _____

2. _____

3. _____

4. _____

5. _____

6. _____

7. _____

8. _____

9. _____

10. _____

11. _____

12. _____

13. _____

14. _____

15. _____

16. _____

17. _____

18. _____

19. _____

20. _____

21. _____

22. _____

23. _____

24. _____

Exercise 2.9 Set B

In problems 1–6, determine if each number is prime or composite.

1. 35   2. 19   3. 31

4. 501   5. 121   6. 775

In problems 7–24, factor each number into primes.

7. 16   8. 27

9. 58   10. 62

11. 36   12. 40

13. 5000   14. 1250

15. 98   16. 54

17. 1925   18. 525

19. 520   20. 420

21. 234   22. 1722

23. 209   24. 161

1. _____

2. _____

3. _____

4. _____

5. _____

6. _____

7. _____

8. _____

9. _____

10. _____

11. _____

12. _____

13. _____

14. _____

15. _____

16. _____

17. _____

18. _____

19. _____

20. _____

21. _____

22. _____

23. _____

24. _____

2.10 More Applications Involving Whole Numbers

In Section 1.10, the basic steps for solving word problems were covered. You must remember to **read** the problem carefully, **analyze** the problem to determine what operations to use, and **solve** to find the answer to the question asked in the problem. In some problems, you may have difficulty analyzing what operations should be used to calculate the answer. If that happens, you might try substituting very simple numbers for the original numbers in the problem. Decide what should be done with the simpler numbers, then solve the original problem, using the same operations. Study the next example to see what I mean.

Example 1

You drove 637 miles in 13 hours. How many miles did you travel per hour?

Analyze: If you are not sure what to do, try substituting simple numbers for the 637 and the 13. For instance, change the problem to "You drove 10 miles in 2 hours. How many miles did you travel per hour?" The answer (5 miles per hour) is fairly obvious, and was obtained by dividing 2 into 10. So divide the original numbers, 13 into 637.

Solve:
$$
\begin{array}{r}
49 \text{ miles per hour} \\
13\overline{)637} \\
\underline{52} \\
117 \\
\underline{117}
\end{array}
$$

Example 2

The scores on your last four math tests were 96, 88, 83, and 93. What is the average of your scores?

Analyze: To find the **average** of a list of numbers, add the numbers and divide by how many numbers are in the list.

Solve:
$$
\begin{array}{r}
96 \\
88 \\
83 \\
+\ 93 \\
\hline
360
\end{array}
\qquad
\begin{array}{r}
90 \text{ is the average} \\
4\overline{)360} \\
\underline{36} \\
0 \\
\underline{0}
\end{array}
$$

Example 3

The area of the largest state, Alaska, is 589,757 square miles. The smallest state, Rhode Island, has an area of 1,214 square miles. What is the difference in their areas?

Analyze: To find the difference between two numbers you must subtract the two numbers.

Solve: $589,757 - 1,214 = 588,543$ sq. mi.

Example 4

Out of a batch of 450 tennis balls, 21 balls were found to be defective and were discarded. The remaining balls were packed in cans containing 3 balls each. How many cans of tennis balls were packed?

Analyze: Find the number of good balls by subtracting those that were discarded. Since each can contains 3 balls, divide the number of good balls by 3 to find the number of cans.

Solve: good balls: $450 - 21 = 429$
number of cans: $429 \div 3 = 143$

Example 5

The total amount of an auto loan is $11,376. If you pay off the loan with equal monthly payments over four years, how much would you pay each month?

Analyze: Find the number of months over which the payments will be made by multiplying 4 times 12. Divide the total loan by the number of months to get the monthly payment.

Solve: number of months: $4 \times 12 = 48$
monthly payment: $\$11,376 \div 48 = \$237$

Problem 1: The high temperatures during seven consecutive days in May were 75, 68, 80, 83, 77, 72, and 70. What was the average temperature for the week?

Answer: 75
sum of temperatures:
$75 + 68 + 80 + 83 + 77 + 72$
$+ 70 = 525$
average: $525 \div 7 = 75$

Problem 2: If you type at a rate of 45 words per minute, how long would you take to type a nine page report containing 250 words per page?

Answer: 50 min
number of words:
$9 \times 250 = 2250$
amount of time:
$2250 \div 45 = 50$ min.

Problem 3: An amusement park has a family rate of $60 for a family of four. If the regular price is $19 for adults and $16 for children, how much does a family of 2 adults and 2 children save with the family rate?

Answer: $10
regular:
$2 \times \$19 = \$38$
$2 \times \$16 = \underline{\$32}$
$\$70$
savings:
$\$70 - \$60 = \$10$

Exercise 2.10 Set A

1. During their tenth annual sale, an appliance store gave a $250 discount on all appliances with a regular price over $1000. A refrigerator was priced $1199 and a matching freezer was priced $999. What was the cost of the refrigerator after the discount?

1. _____

2. At the start of your vacation, the odometer in your car reads 55743. When you return from your trip, it read 56891. How many miles did you drive on your vacation?

2. _____

3. You want to save $3600 for a trip two years from now. How much should you save each month to have the $3600 by then?

3. _____

4. At a canning factory, a machine seals cans at a rate of 75 cans per minute. At that rate, how long will it take to seal 3000 cans?

4. _____

5. In your last three games of bowling, you bowled 171, 149, and 184. What is your average for those three games?

5. _____

6. The players on a fifth grade basketball team weigh 59 lb, 66 lb, 75 lb, 71 lb, and 84 lb. What is the average weight of the members of the team?

6. _____

7. If you earn $6 per hour and $9 for each hour worked over a regular 40 hour week, how much do you earn if you work 52 hours in one week?

7. _____

8. You borrowed $260 from a friend. After giving him $25 each month for seven months, how much do you still owe him?

8. _____

9. If you earn $19,392 per year, how much do you earn per month?

9. _____

10. Jill is twice as old as her sister Mary. Jill is also 5 years older than her brother Jason. If Jill is 18, how old is Mary? How old is Jason?

10. _____

11. At a garage sale held by four families, $787 was collected. If expenses for advertising the garage sale were $35 and the four families divide the profit equally, how much money would each family receive?

11. _____

12. Iron weighs about 490 pounds per cubic foot, while cork weighs about 15 pounds per cubic foot. How much heavier is 12 cubic feet of iron than 12 cubic feet of cork?

12. _____

13. A fly's heart beats about 90 times per second and a human's heart beats about 72 times per minute. How many more times does a fly's heart beat in an hour than a human's heart?

13. _____

14. If a gross (144 items) of watermelons weighs 2448 pounds and a gross of cantaloupes weighs 288 pounds, what is a) the average weight of a watermelon, b) the average weight of a cantaloupe, and c) the difference between the average weights of each?

14. _____

15. In 1995, the national debt of the United States was about $4,966,000,000,000. If each of the 260 million people in the United States at that time contributed an equal amount to pay off the debt, how much would each person contribute?

15. _____

Exercise 2.10 Set B

1. In 1972, a Holstein-Friesian cow sold for $122,000. If the cow weighed 2000 pounds, how much was it worth per pound?

1. _____

2. Tickets for a concert were priced at $28 and $14. How many $14 concert tickets can you buy with $224?

2. _____

3. In 1994, the Ford Motor Company produced 1,661,350 cars while General Motors produced 2,719,764 cars. How many more cars were produced by General Motors?

3. _____

4. If you earn $678 per week, but have $89 in deductions, how much is your take-home pay?

4. _____

5. In five games, the Renegades football team scored 21 points, 35 points, 17 points, 29 points, and 13 points. What was their scoring average per game?

5. _____

6. The numbers of students enrolled in six basic math classes were 34, 29, 37, 23, 30, and 21. What was the average enrollment in the basic math classes?

6. _____

7. If you earn $6 per hour and $9 for each hour worked over a regular 8 hour day, how much would you earn working 13 hours in one day?

7. _____

8. If a realtor sells $1,865,400 worth of real estate in a year, what is the average amount sold each month?

8. _____

9. If a plane trip of 2215 miles takes 5 hours, how many miles are traveled per hour?

9. _____

10. What do you pay for a $679 stereo after a $99 discount is given and $24 in sales tax is added?

10. _____

11. For a field trip, a school orders three buses which can seat 55 people each. If 192 people show up for the field trip, how many can not be seated on the buses?

11. _____

12. Lead weighs 704 pounds per cubic foot while gold weighs 1202 pounds per cubic foot. How much heavier is 3 cubic feet of gold than 3 cubic feet of lead?

12. _____

13. A bee's wings flap about 250 times per second, while a hummingbird's wings flap 75 times per second. In one hour of flying, how many more times do a bee's wings flap than a hummingbird's wings?

13. _____

14. In horse racing, the unit of distance "furlong" is used. Eight furlongs are equivalent to one mile (1760 yards). Determine a) the number of yards in one furlong and b) the distance in yards of a 6 furlong horse race.

14. _____

15. In July, 1991, White House Budget Director, Richard Daman, announced that a calculation error resulted in a 114 billion dollar under estimate of tax revenues. If each of the 250 million people in the U.S.A. contributed an equal amount to make up for the error, how much should each contribute?

15. _____

Chapter 2 Summary

Concepts

You may refer to the sections listed below to review how to do the following:

1. subtract whole numbers using the borrowing process. (2.1), (2.2)
2. divide whole numbers using the long division process. (2.3), (2.4), (2.5), (2.6)
3. handle zeros in the quotient of division problems. (2.7)
4. solve problems involving more than one operation by using the following order:
   a. operations inside parentheses,
   b. powers and square roots,
   c. multiplication or division from left to right,
   d. addition or subtraction from left to right. (2.8)
5. factor composite numbers into a product of primes. (2.9)
6. find the average of a list of numbers by adding the numbers and dividing by how many numbers are in the list. (2.10)
7. solve word problems involving whole numbers. (2.10)

Terminology

This chapter's important terms and their page numbers are as follows:

average: an estimate obtained by dividing the sum of quantities by the number of quantities. (97)

composite number: a number that is evenly divisible by whole numbers besides 1 and itself. (91)

difference: the answer from subtraction. (59)

dividend: the number in a division problem that is being divided. (65)

divisor: the number by which the dividend is divided. (65)

factoring: the process of writing a number as the product of other numbers. (91)

factor tree: diagram displaying the prime factors of a number. (93)

minuend: the number from which another number is subtracted. (59)

order of operations: the order in which operations of arithmetic are performed. (87)

prime number: a whole number greater than 1 that is evenly divisible by only one and itself. (91)

quotient: the answer from division. (65)

remainder: whole number that is left over in a division problem whose quotient is not exact. (69)

subtrahend: the number that is subtracted from another number. (59)

Chapter 2 Crossword Puzzle

Across

4. Third digit of 5394 − 2527
7. Exponent of $7 \times 7 \times 7 \times 7$
8. To find the difference
10. Number that one divides by
11. _____ of operations
14. Second digit of 207,320 ÷ 568
15. Not the bottom
17. Answer from subtraction
20. Remainder of 39,081 ÷ 96
21. The sum divided by the number of quantities
23. 56,500 ÷ 5650
24. That which is left over in division

Down

1. Answer in division
2. Any digit of 75,998 − 53,776
3. Not no
4. Abbreviation for subtraction
5. Expressing as a product
6. 23 and 29, for example
9. 24 and 27, for example
10. In 36 ÷ 9 = 4, 36 is the _____.
12. Abbreviation for division
13. In 36 − 9 = 27, 36 is the _____.
16. Number of zeros in 18,324 ÷ 36
18. $5 \times 7 − 4 \times (63 \div 9)$
19. Meow creature
22. Random Access Memory (abbr)

Chapter 2 Practice Test A

1. 768 − 543

2. 83,002 − 54,178

3. 37,000 − 6,584

4. 72 ÷ 9

5. 67 ÷ 8

6. 22 ÷ 0

7. 488 ÷ 7

8. $6\overline{)17832}$

9. $384\overline{)252288}$

10. $48\overline{)14837}$

11. $45\overline{)36000}$

12. $5 \times \sqrt{36} + 3 \times 10^4$

13. $56 \div (20 - 14 + 2) \times 7$

14. Factor 750 into primes.

15. In your last four games of bowling, you scored 136, 168, 192, and 156. What is your average bowling score for those games?

1. _____

2. _____

3. _____

4. _____

5. _____

6. _____

7. _____

8. _____

9. _____

10. _____

11. _____

12. _____

13. _____

14. _____

15. _____

Chapter 2 Practice Test B

1. $957 - 436$

2. $74,003 - 6,348$

3. $6000 - 786$

4. $45 \div 9$

5. $57 \div 7$

6. $0\overline{)18}$

7. $469 \div 6$

8. $8\overline{)16504}$

9. $654\overline{)232824}$

10. $53\overline{)21697}$

11. $85\overline{)68000}$

12. $4 \times 10^2 - 3 \times \sqrt{100}$

13. $7 \times (15 - 4 + 5) \div 2$

14. Factor 660 into primes.

15. Out of a batch of 500 light bulbs, 76 were found to be defective and were discarded. The remaining bulbs were shipped in boxes containing four bulbs each. How many boxes of light bulbs were shipped?

1. _____

2. _____

3. _____

4. _____

5. _____

6. _____

7. _____

8. _____

9. _____

10. _____

11. _____

12. _____

13. _____

14. _____

15. _____

Chapter 2 Supplementary Exercises

Section 2.2

1. 86
    −44

2. 95
    −37

3. 367
    −180

4. 5683
    −1392

5. 503 − 185

6. 605 − 387

7. 5683 − 399

8. 4382 − 799

9. 6000 − 5936

10. 4000 − 3761

11. 90,000 − 329

12. 60,000 − 476

13. 70,063 − 19,806

14. 80,019 − 29,671

Section 2.3

1. 63 ÷ 9

2. 24 ÷ 4

3. 56 ÷ 8

4. 72 ÷ 9

5. 72 ÷ 8

6. 54 ÷ 6

7. 56 ÷ 7

8. 32 ÷ 8

9. $5\overline{)45}$

10. $7\overline{)49}$

11. $2\overline{)18}$

12. $9\overline{)36}$

Section 2.4

1. 32 ÷ 5

2. 19 ÷ 2

3. 85 ÷ 9

4. 76 ÷ 7

5. 19 ÷ 7

6. 38 ÷ 5

7. 56 ÷ 9

8. 16 ÷ 6

9. $6\overline{)41}$

10. $8\overline{)61}$

11. $8\overline{)43}$

12. $9\overline{)89}$

Section 2.5

1. 1848 ÷ 4

2. 145 ÷ 5

3. 326 ÷ 2

4. 4113 ÷ 3

5. 2826 ÷ 9

6. 1927 ÷ 7

7. $8\overline{)52715}$

8. $6\overline{)59247}$

9. $6\overline{)64511}$

10. $9\overline{)83801}$

11. $5\overline{)396380}$

12. $7\overline{)41328}$

13. $8\overline{)30123}$

14. $5\overline{)289765}$

15. $7\overline{)34365}$

16. $6\overline{)73694}$

Section 2.6

1. $645 \div 43$
2. $234 \div 39$
3. $351 \div 27$
4. $344 \div 43$
5. $2763 \div 87$
6. $3142 \div 66$
7. $51{,}255 \div 75$
8. $64{,}155 \div 65$
9. $16{,}180 \div 59$
10. $27{,}080 \div 78$
11. $401\overline{)17638}$
12. $305\overline{)17690}$
13. $516\overline{)19608}$
14. $727\overline{)18102}$
15. $368\overline{)458641}$
16. $298\overline{)361552}$
17. $432\overline{)235473}$
18. $365\overline{)239809}$
19. $1853\overline{)237453}$
20. $5216\overline{)281664}$

Section 2.7

1. $4200 \div 7$
2. $3600 \div 4$
3. $40{,}000 \div 8$
4. $30{,}000 \div 6$
5. $584{,}000 \div 73$
6. $667{,}000 \div 29$
7. $100{,}000 \div 25$
8. $300{,}000 \div 75$
9. $5481 \div 27$
10. $7839 \div 39$
11. $43\overline{)4386}$
12. $56\overline{)5836}$
13. $68\overline{)34612}$
14. $38\overline{)7752}$
15. $32\overline{)160128}$
16. $76\overline{)228532}$
17. $701\overline{)216699}$
18. $603\overline{)487296}$
19. $457\overline{)917856}$
20. $238\overline{)714576}$

Section 2.8

1. $6 + 3 \times 2$
2. $3 + 8 \times 2$
3. $17 - 5 \times 3$
4. $28 - 4 \times 5$
5. $36 \div 4 + 8$
6. $50 \div 2 + 8$
7. $18 \times (9 \div 3)$
8. $16 + (8 \times 2)$
9. $5 \times (3 + 8)$
10. $4 \times (8 - 1)$
11. $3^3 - 4 \times \sqrt{25}$
12. $2^3 + 3 \times \sqrt{9}$
13. $6^2 - 28 \div 4 + 8$
14. $5^2 - 36 \div 9 + 6$
15. $19 + 3 \times (\sqrt{16} - 1)$
16. $20 + 2 \times (\sqrt{49} - 2)$
17. $14 \div 2 \times 7 + 14 \times 2 \div 7$
18. $32 \div 2 \times 8 + 32 \times 2 \div 8$
19. $(3 + 4 \times 2) \times (4 \times 2 - 3)$
20. $(16 - 2 \times 3) \times (2 \times 3 + 16)$

Section 2.9

In problems 1–8, determine if the numbers are prime or composite numbers.

1. 9	2. 19	3. 31	4. 18
5. 47	6. 49	7. 23	8. 73

In problems 9–24, factor each number into primes.

9. 14	10. 30	11. 32	12. 65
13. 39	14. 95	15. 57	16. 81
17. 152	18. 184	19. 216	20. 111
21. 312	22. 342	23. 1000	24. 1500

Section 2.10

1. If the cost of seven balcony tickets for an opera is $91, what is the cost of each ticket?

2. The tallest student in a fifth grade class is 62 inches tall. The shortest student is 37 inches tall. What is the difference in their heights?

3. For five performances of "The Christmas Carol," the attendance was 203, 147, 191, 162 and 242. What was the average attendance?

4. The ages of the starting nine for the "Masters" baseball team are 42, 46, 36, 50, 41, 40, 52, 38, and 42. What is the average age of that team?

5. A part-time cook at "McB's Burgers" works a 5 hour shift four days a week. If he frys 92 hamburgers in an hour, how many working days would it take him to fry 13,800 hamburgers?

6. If your pay for the year is $13,500 before deductions, and deductions for the year are $2,400, what is your average monthly salary after deductions?

7. If 12 cubic yards of sand cost $324, what is the cost for one cubic yard?

8. The total amount of a loan for a motor home is $23,640. If you pay off the loan with equal monthly payments over five years, how much would you pay each month?

9. The length of Joan's stride for the last 600 feet of a 3 mile race was 6 feet. If the length of her stride was 5 feet for the rest of the race, how many steps did Joan take in the race? (1 mi = 5280 ft)

10. Suppose a person watches television an average of 2 hours a day, 360 days a year. This is equivalent to how many full days of television watching?

Math Magic II

Magic Crosses

Consider a configuration of squares that form a cross. If the whole numbers (1, 2, 3, 4, 5, . . .) placed in the squares have the same sum vertically and horizontally, it is called a magic cross. A magic cross using the whole numbers from 1 to 5 is shown below.

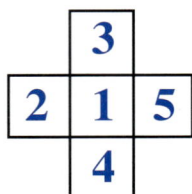

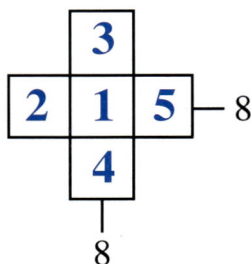

The sum is the same in both directions.

Recreations

1. Complete the following magic crosses using 1, 2, 3, 4, 5.

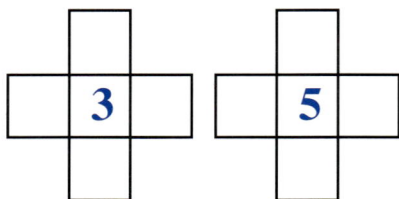

2. Can 2 or 4 be placed in the center of the cross?

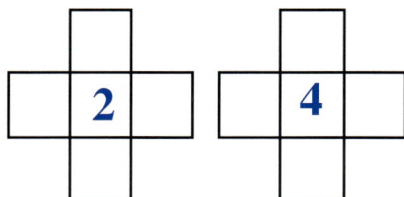

3. Place the whole numbers from 1 to 9 in the squares to make a magic cross. There are five different numbers that can be placed in the center of the cross.

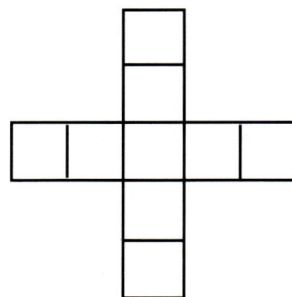

4. Make magic crosses using the whole numbers from 1 to 11, 1 to 13, and 1 to 15. Which numbers could be placed in the center of each cross?

Unit I Exam

Chapters 1 and 2

1. Write 5,000,012,576 in words.

   1. _____

   _____

   _____

2. $37 + 456 + 3215 + 9$ 3. 957×87

   2. _____

   3. _____

4. 875×4003 5. $2179 \times 80,000$

   4. _____

   5. _____

6. $8^2 + \sqrt{81}$ 7. $5209 - 573$

   6. _____

   7. _____

8. $60,000 - 14,357$ 9. $2786 \div 7$

   8. _____

   9. _____

10. $46,989 \div 573$ 11. $111,222 \div 37$

   10. _____

   11. _____

12. $5 \times (8 + 24 \div 2) - 8 \times 3$

   12. _____

13. Factor 680 into primes.

   13. _____

14. A waiter at the end of his shift finds that he has two $20 bills, five $10 bills, seven $5 bills, and thirty-two $1 bills from tips. If he gives the bus boy $17, how much cash does the waiter have left?

   14. _____

15. During the last 5 weeks your grocery bills were $180, $176, $154, $161, and $149. What was the average amount spent on groceries per week?

   15. _____

Unit II

Fractions and Decimals

In Unit I we worked with whole numbers. Even though whole numbers occur very frequently in our daily lives, we also come across other kinds of numbers. Your bill at the bookstore is usually not exactly $10 or $20. It would probably be more like $10.52 or $23.17. The course you jogged was more than 3 miles; it was $3\frac{1}{4}$ miles.

In the grocery, store the sign below the canned peaches reads "5.6¢ per ounce." You hear that $\frac{4}{5}$ of all dentists surveyed recommend ``Best'' toothpaste. Your grade point average was 2.95. All of these give examples of fractional or decimal numbers.

The ability to work with these types of numbers is a necessary step in the development of your math skills. In this unit, you will learn to operate with fractions and decimals. When you have finished this unit, you should be able to do the following:

1. interpret fractions and find equivalent fractions.
2. read and round off decimal numbers.
3. perform the basic operations of fractional and decimal numbers.
4. compare the size of fractions and decimals.
5. do computations involving a combination of fractions and decimals.
6. solve word problems involving operations with fractions and decimals.

Brain Buster

If you had a billion dollar bills, how long would it take you to count them, if you count a dollar each second, 24 hours a day?
(Hint: The answer is in years.)

Chapter 3

Fractions

After finishing this chapter, you should be able to do the following:

1. interpret and find equivalent fractions.
2. multiply fractions.
3. divide fractions.
4. add fractions.
5. subtract fractions.
6. operate with mixed numbers.
7. simplify complex fractions.
8. compare the size of fractions.
9. solve word problems involving fractions.

On the next page, you will find a pretest for this chapter. The purpose of the pretest is to help you determine which sections in this chapter you need to study in detail and which sections you can review quickly. By taking and correcting the pretest according to the instructions on the next page, you can better plan your pace through this chapter.

Chapter 3 Pretest

Take and correct this test using the answer section at the end of the book. Those problems that give you difficutly indicate which sections need extra attention. Section numbers are in parentheses before each problem.

(3.2)   1. Find the number represented by the ?: $\dfrac{7}{8} = \dfrac{?}{56}$

1. _____

(3.3)   2. Express $\dfrac{33}{9}$ as a reduced mixed number.

2. _____

(3.4)   3. $\dfrac{9}{10} \times \dfrac{3}{5}$ (3.5)   4. $\dfrac{6}{10} \div \dfrac{6}{7}$

3. _____

4. _____

(3.6)   5. $3\dfrac{2}{3} \times 1\dfrac{4}{7}$

5. _____

(3.7)   6. A manufacturing company employs 222 people. During the first week of July, one-sixth of the employees are on vacation. How many employees are not on vacation in the first week of July?

6. _____

(3.8)   7. $\dfrac{1}{9} + \dfrac{5}{9}$ (3.9)   8. $\dfrac{3}{8} + \dfrac{1}{4} - \dfrac{3}{16}$

7. _____

8. _____

(3.10) 9. $\dfrac{4}{15} + \dfrac{7}{16} + \dfrac{5}{12}$

9. _____

(3.10) 10. $\dfrac{5}{9} - \dfrac{11}{24}$

10. _____

(3.11) 11. $2\dfrac{1}{3} - 1\dfrac{4}{9}$

11. _____

(3.11) 12. $3\dfrac{2}{3} + 2\dfrac{4}{5}$

12. _____

(3.12) 13. $\dfrac{3 + \dfrac{1}{2}}{3 - \dfrac{4}{5}}$

13. _____

(3.13) 14. Arrange from largest to smallest: $\dfrac{8}{9}, \dfrac{7}{8}, \dfrac{2}{3}$.

14. _____

(3.14) 15. Find the cost per ounce of $6\dfrac{1}{3}$ ounces of juice that sells for 76¢.

15. _____

116

3.1 What Are Fractions?

I am sure you have seen numbers such as $\frac{1}{2}, \frac{5}{8}, \frac{1}{4}, \frac{3}{16}, \frac{2}{7}$, etc. These numbers are called **fractions.** They are not whole numbers since they represent a part or a portion of a whole.

For example, what part of the figure below is shaded?

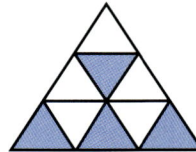

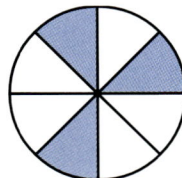

One out of the three equal sections is shaded. So we write $\frac{1}{3}$ (one-third) of the whole figure is shaded.

What part of the figure below is shaded?

Four out of the nine equal sections are shaded. So we write $\frac{4}{9}$ (four-ninths) of the whole figure is shaded.

> Every fraction has three parts. The top number is the numerator, the bottom number is the denominator, and middle line is the fraction line.

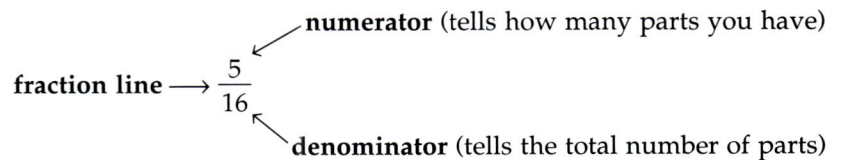

numerator (tells how many parts you have)

fraction line $\longrightarrow \dfrac{5}{16}$

denominator (tells the total number of parts)

I NOMINATE ...

He owes being elected to de-nominator.

Problem 1: What part of the figure is:

shaded?

Answer: $\dfrac{3}{8}$, since 3 out of the 8 sections are shaded.

not shaded?

Answer: $\dfrac{5}{8}$, since 5 out of the 8 sections are not shaded.

Problem 2: If on a 50 question test you get 37 correct, what fraction did you get correct?

Answer: $\dfrac{37}{50}$

Proper Fractions

All the fractions shown so far have displayed a portion of the whole object or a part of one unit. Each of those fractions has a value that is less than 1. We call such fractions **proper fractions.** Proper fractions are easy to recognize since, besides having a value that is less than 1, their numerators are less than their denominators.

For example:

$$\frac{3}{5} \longleftarrow \text{numerator is less than the denominator}$$

Improper Fractions

Besides proper fractions that have a value that is less than 1, there are other fractions which have a value that is either equal to 1 or greater than 1. These are called **improper fractions.** Let me show you some examples:

Example 1

In the figure below, four out of the four sections are shaded. $\frac{4}{4}$ (four-fourths) is shaded.

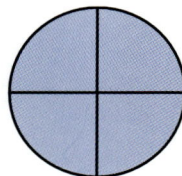

But that represents the whole object. So $\frac{4}{4} = 1$.
Thus, $\frac{4}{4}$ is a fraction whose value is not *part* of a whole; it *is* the whole. It equals 1. Likewise $\frac{8}{8} = 1$, $\frac{10}{10} = 1$, $\frac{327}{327} = 1$, etc.

Example 2

In the figures below, we have $\frac{4}{4}$ of figure A shaded and $\frac{3}{4}$ of figure B shaded. So, a total of $\frac{7}{4}$ is shaded.

A   B

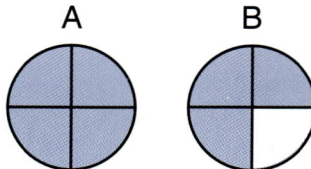

We have one whole object and $\frac{3}{4}$ of another that is shaded.
We have 1 and $\frac{3}{4}$ (written $1\frac{3}{4}$) shaded. So $\frac{7}{4} = 1\frac{3}{4}$.
Thus, $\frac{7}{4}$ is a fraction whose value is greater than 1. Similarly $\frac{13}{5}$, $\frac{110}{17}$, $\frac{9}{2}$, etc., have values that are larger than 1.

Improper fractions such as those are also easily recognized since, besides having a value that is greater than or equal to 1, their numerators are *not* less than their denominators.

For example: $\frac{16}{7} \longleftarrow$ numerators are *not* less $\longrightarrow \frac{14}{14}$
than the denominators.

Name _____ Date _____

Exercise 3.1 Set A

1. What part of the figure to the right is shaded?

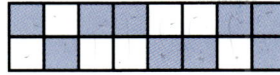

   1. _____

2. What part of the figure to the right is not shaded?

   2. _____

3. What part of the figure to the right is shaded?

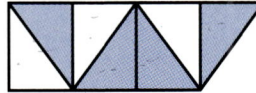

   3. _____

4. What part of the figure to the right is not shaded?

   4. _____

5. What part of the figure to the right is shaded?

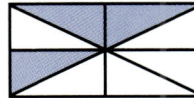

   5. _____

6. What part of the figure to the right is not shaded?

   6. _____

7. If, on a true/false test, you get 17 correct answers out of 20 questions, a) what fraction did you get correct? b) what fraction did you get wrong?

   7. _____

8. If, out of 11 people at a party, three are blondes, a) what fraction are blondes? b) what fraction are not blondes?

   8. _____

9. If, in a class of 30 students, 17 are females, a) what fraction are females? b) what fraction are males?

   9. _____

10. If 37 out of 100 golf balls found in a lake on a golf course are orange, what fraction of the golf balls are not orange?

    10. _____

11. If 4 out of 5 people prefer brand X, what fraction of the people do not prefer brand X?

    11. _____

In problems 12–13, consider the fractions $\frac{1}{2}$, $\frac{3}{5}$, $\frac{7}{7}$, $\frac{9}{6}$, $\frac{8}{1}$, and $\frac{15}{16}$.

12. Which are proper fractions?

    12. _____

13. Which are improper fractions?

    13. _____

In problems 14–15, consider the fractions, $\frac{12}{7}$, $\frac{7}{8}$, $\frac{3}{4}$, $\frac{19}{19}$, $\frac{7}{3}$, and $\frac{10}{1}$.

14. Which are proper fractions?

    14. _____

15. Which are improper fractions?

    15. _____

Exercise 3.1 Set B

1. What part of the figure to the right is shaded?

2. What part of the figure to the right is not shaded?

1. _____

2. _____

3. What part of the figure to the right is shaded?

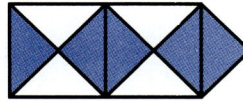

4. What part of the figure to the right is not shaded?

3. _____

4. _____

5. What part of the figure to the right is shaded?

6. What part of the figure to the right is not shaded?

5. _____

6. _____

7. If, on a true/false test, you get 19 correct answers out of 25 questions, a) what fraction did you get correct? b) what fraction did you get wrong?

7. _____

8. If, out of 12 people at a party, five are teachers, a) what fraction are teachers? b) what fraction are not teachers?

8. _____

9. If, in a class of 40 students, 23 are males, a) what fraction are males? b) what fraction are females?

9. _____

10. If 89 out of the 100 coins in a piggy bank are pennies, what fraction of the coins are not pennies?

10. _____

11. If 7 out of 8 people prefer brand X, what fraction of the people do not prefer brand X?

11. _____

In problems 12–13, consider the fractions $\frac{1}{5}, \frac{9}{4}, \frac{2}{3}, \frac{7}{1}, \frac{3}{3},$ and $\frac{5}{8}$.

12. Which are proper fractions?

12. _____

13. Which are improper fractions?

13. _____

In problems 14–15, consider the fractions, $\frac{11}{8}, \frac{17}{32}, \frac{5}{1}, \frac{5}{5}, \frac{3}{5},$ and $\frac{1}{10}$.

14. Which are proper fractions?

14. _____

15. Which are improper fractions?

15. _____

3.2 Equivalent Fractions

Oil reduces fraction.

Consider the two shaded blocks below:

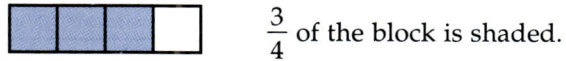

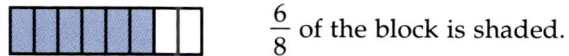

$\frac{3}{4}$ of the block is shaded.

$\frac{6}{8}$ of the block is shaded.

The shaded sections represent the same amount of each block. So those two fractions, $\frac{3}{4}$ and $\frac{6}{8}$, represent the same amount of shaded area. They have the same value.

$\frac{3}{4}$ and $\frac{6}{8}$ are equivalent. $\quad \frac{3}{4} = \frac{6}{8}$

You can change $\frac{3}{4}$ to $\frac{6}{8}$ by multiplying its numerator and denominator by 2. You can change $\frac{6}{8}$ to $\frac{3}{4}$ by dividing its numerator and denominator by 2. Both procedures yield fractions that have the same value.

Raising Fractions to Higher Terms

By multiplying the numerator and denominator of a fraction by the same number, you **raise the fraction to higher terms,** getting an equivalent fraction.

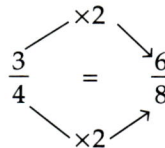

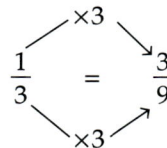

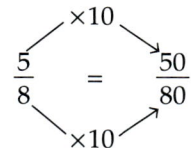

$$\frac{3}{4} \overset{\times 2}{=} \frac{6}{8} \qquad \frac{1}{3} \overset{\times 3}{=} \frac{3}{9} \qquad \frac{5}{8} \overset{\times 10}{=} \frac{50}{80}$$

Example 1

Change $\frac{3}{8}$ to a fraction with a numerator of 12.

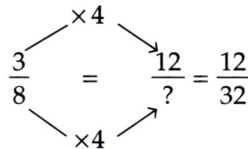

$$\frac{3}{8} \overset{\times 4}{=} \frac{12}{?} = \frac{12}{32}$$

To change the numerator from 3 to 12, you must multiply by 4. So you must also multiply the denominator by 4.

Example 2

Change $\frac{3}{2}$ to a fraction with a denominator of 18.

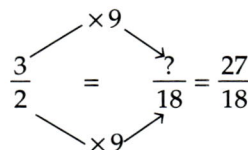

$$\frac{3}{2} \overset{\times 9}{=} \frac{?}{18} = \frac{27}{18}$$

To change the denominator from 2 to 18, you must multiply by 9. So you must also multiply the numerator by 9.

Problem 1: $\dfrac{5}{6} = \dfrac{35}{?}$

Answer: $\dfrac{35}{42}$ (Multiply numerator and denominator by 7.)

Reducing Fractions to Lowest Terms—Method 1

To **reduce a fraction to lower terms,** you must find a number other than 1 that divides evenly into both the numerator and denominator of the fraction. To **reduce to lowest terms,** you must continue to divide both the numerator and the denominator until no whole number except 1 divides evenly into each.

Example 3

Reduce $\dfrac{30}{42}$ to lowest terms.

2 divides evenly into both 30 and 42.

$$\dfrac{30}{42} \overset{\div 2}{\underset{\div 2}{=}} \dfrac{15}{21}$$

Now, 3 divides evenly into both 15 and 21.

$$\dfrac{30}{42} = \dfrac{15}{21} \overset{\div 3}{\underset{\div 3}{=}} \dfrac{5}{7}$$

Example 4

Reduce $\dfrac{140}{910}$ to lowest terms.

Since numbers that end in zero are divisible by 10, 10 divides evenly into both 140 and 910.

$$\dfrac{140}{910} \overset{\div 10}{\underset{\div 10}{=}} \dfrac{14}{91}$$

Now, 7 divides evenly into both 14 and 91.

$$\dfrac{140}{910} = \dfrac{14}{91} \overset{\div 7}{\underset{\div 7}{=}} \dfrac{2}{13}$$

The key to reducing fractions by this method is to find numbers that divide evenly into both the numerator and the denominator of the fraction. Using the divisibility facts covered in Section 2–9 will be very helpful in this process.

Problem 2:   Reduce $\dfrac{12}{24}$ to lowest terms.

Answer: $\dfrac{1}{2}$

$$\dfrac{12}{24} \overset{\div 3}{\underset{\div 3}{=}} \dfrac{4}{8} \overset{\div 2}{\underset{\div 2}{=}} \dfrac{2}{4} \overset{\div 2}{\underset{\div 2}{=}} \dfrac{1}{2}$$

Problem 3:   Reduce $\dfrac{135}{360}$ to lowest terms.

Answer: $\dfrac{3}{8}$

$$\dfrac{135}{360} \overset{\div 5}{\underset{\div 5}{=}} \dfrac{27}{72} \overset{\div 3}{\underset{\div 3}{=}} \dfrac{9}{24} \overset{\div 3}{\underset{\div 3}{=}} \dfrac{3}{8}$$

Reducing Fractions to Lowest Terms—Method 2

Finding numbers that divide evenly into both the numerator and the denominator of a fraction may be troublesome, even with the use of the divisibility facts learned previously. This second method allows you to work separately with the numerator and denominator, instead of searching for a divisor of both.

Example 5

Reduce $\dfrac{28}{210}$ to lowest terms.

1. Factor the numerator into primes: $28 = 2 \times 2 \times 7$
2. Factor the denominator into primes: $210 = 2 \times 3 \times 5 \times 7$
3. Cancel like factors:

$$\frac{28}{210} = \frac{\overset{1}{\cancel{2}} \times 2 \times \overset{1}{\cancel{7}}}{\underset{1}{\cancel{2}} \times 3 \times 5 \times \underset{1}{\cancel{7}}}$$

(If the numerator and denominator have the same factor, divide both by that number, giving the answer of 1 ($\frac{1}{1}$). This process is called **canceling.**)

4. Multiply the resulting factors: $\dfrac{28}{210} = \dfrac{1 \times 2 \times 1}{1 \times 3 \times 5 \times 1} = \dfrac{2}{15}$

By following the steps shown in the above example, you have a second method for reducing fractions to lowest terms. However, you must know how to factor numbers into primes to use this method. See Section 2–9, if you need to review that factoring process.

Example 6

Reduce $\dfrac{52}{78}$ to lowest terms.

$$\frac{52}{78} = \frac{\overset{1}{\cancel{2}} \times 2 \times \overset{1}{\cancel{13}}}{\underset{1}{\cancel{2}} \times 3 \times \underset{1}{\cancel{13}}} = \frac{2}{3}$$

Example 7

Reduce $\dfrac{85}{102}$ to lowest terms.

$$\frac{85}{102} = \frac{5 \times \overset{1}{\cancel{17}}}{2 \times 3 \times \underset{1}{\cancel{17}}} = \frac{5}{6}$$

We can summarize the methods for **reducing fractions** as follows:

> **Method 1**—Divide the numerator and denominator by a whole number (larger than 1) that divides evenly into each. Repeat until no more divisors can be found.
>
> **Method 2**—Factor the numerator and denominator into primes, cancel factors that are the same in both, and multiply the resulting numbers.

Both methods work quite effectively in reducing fractions to lowest terms. Use the method that you find easier to work with.

Problem 4: Reduce $\dfrac{100}{150}$ to lowest terms.

Answer: $\dfrac{2}{3}$

Method 1:

$$\dfrac{100}{150} \overset{\div 10}{\underset{\div 10}{=}} \dfrac{10}{15} \overset{\div 5}{\underset{\div 5}{=}} \dfrac{2}{3}$$

Method 2:

$$\dfrac{100}{150} = \dfrac{\overset{1}{\cancel{2}} \times 2 \times \overset{1}{\cancel{5}} \times \overset{1}{\cancel{5}}}{\underset{1}{\cancel{2}} \times 3 \times \underset{1}{\cancel{5}} \times \underset{1}{\cancel{5}}} = \dfrac{2}{3}$$

Problem 5: Reduce $\dfrac{65}{143}$ to lowest terms.

Answer: $\dfrac{5}{11}$

$$\dfrac{65}{143} = \dfrac{5 \times \overset{1}{\cancel{13}}}{11 \times \underset{1}{\cancel{13}}} = \dfrac{5}{11}$$

Problem 6: Reduce $\dfrac{36}{90}$ to lowest terms.

Answer: $\dfrac{2}{5}$

$$\dfrac{36}{90} = \dfrac{\overset{1}{\cancel{2}} \times 2 \times \overset{1}{\cancel{3}} \times \overset{1}{\cancel{3}}}{\underset{1}{\cancel{2}} \times \underset{1}{\cancel{3}} \times \underset{1}{\cancel{3}} \times 5} = \dfrac{2}{5}$$

Problem 7: Reduce $\dfrac{21}{31}$ to lowest terms.

Answer: $\dfrac{21}{31}$

It is in lowest terms. No number, except 1, divides into both the numerator and denominator.

Name _____   Date _____

Exercise 3.2 Set A

In problems 1–10, raise each fraction to higher terms.

1. $\dfrac{1}{2} = \dfrac{?}{6}$

2. $\dfrac{1}{2} = \dfrac{?}{8}$

3. $\dfrac{2}{3} = \dfrac{?}{9}$

4. $\dfrac{3}{5} = \dfrac{?}{15}$

5. $\dfrac{8}{7} = \dfrac{32}{?}$

6. $\dfrac{9}{8} = \dfrac{36}{?}$

7. $\dfrac{6}{5} = \dfrac{72}{?}$

8. $\dfrac{3}{4} = \dfrac{27}{?}$

9. $\dfrac{1}{6} = \dfrac{?}{180}$

10. $\dfrac{1}{6} = \dfrac{?}{72}$

1. _____

2. _____

3. _____

4. _____

5. _____

6. _____

7. _____

8. _____

9. _____

10. _____

In problems 11–28, reduce each fraction to lowest terms.

11. $\dfrac{3}{15}$

12. $\dfrac{4}{12}$

13. $\dfrac{10}{18}$

14. $\dfrac{6}{9}$

11. _____

12. _____

13. _____

14. _____

15. $\dfrac{21}{33}$

16. $\dfrac{27}{39}$

15. _____

16. _____

17. $\dfrac{80}{120}$

18. $\dfrac{90}{240}$

17. _____

18. _____

19. $\dfrac{75}{180}$

20. $\dfrac{132}{180}$

19. _____

20. _____

21. $\dfrac{78}{441}$

22. $\dfrac{84}{351}$

21. _____

22. _____

23. $\dfrac{108}{144}$

24. $\dfrac{195}{255}$

23. _____

24. _____

25. $\dfrac{34}{85}$

26. $\dfrac{51}{68}$

25. _____

26. _____

27. $\dfrac{52}{91}$

28. $\dfrac{78}{91}$

27. _____

28. _____

Exercise 3.2 Set B

In problems 1–10, raise each fraction to higher terms.

1. $\dfrac{1}{2} = \dfrac{?}{10}$

2. $\dfrac{1}{2} = \dfrac{?}{4}$

3. $\dfrac{4}{5} = \dfrac{?}{15}$

4. $\dfrac{2}{3} = \dfrac{?}{12}$

5. $\dfrac{9}{7} = \dfrac{36}{?}$

6. $\dfrac{7}{6} = \dfrac{28}{?}$

7. $\dfrac{3}{8} = \dfrac{?}{64}$

8. $\dfrac{5}{8} = \dfrac{?}{56}$

9. $\dfrac{7}{20} = \dfrac{?}{180}$

10. $\dfrac{5}{12} = \dfrac{?}{144}$

1. _____

2. _____

3. _____

4. _____

5. _____

6. _____

7. _____

8. _____

9. _____

10. _____

In problems 11–28, reduce each fraction to lowest terms.

11. $\dfrac{3}{12}$

12. $\dfrac{7}{14}$

13. $\dfrac{8}{12}$

14. $\dfrac{6}{10}$

11. _____

12. _____

13. _____

14. _____

15. $\dfrac{27}{33}$

16. $\dfrac{21}{39}$

17. $\dfrac{90}{120}$

18. $\dfrac{60}{150}$

19. $\dfrac{125}{180}$

20. $\dfrac{88}{180}$

21. $\dfrac{96}{315}$

22. $\dfrac{87}{414}$

23. $\dfrac{423}{531}$

24. $\dfrac{148}{188}$

25. $\dfrac{95}{114}$

26. $\dfrac{57}{76}$

27. $\dfrac{78}{104}$

28. $\dfrac{58}{72}$

15. _____

16. _____

17. _____

18. _____

19. _____

20. _____

21. _____

22. _____

23. _____

24. _____

25. _____

26. _____

27. _____

28. _____

3.3 Mixed Numbers

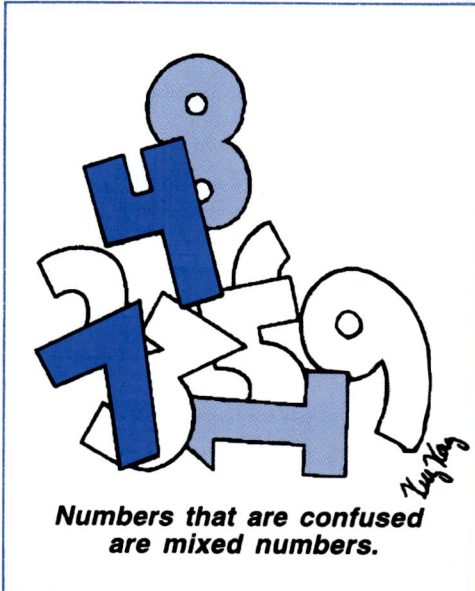

**Numbers that are confused
are mixed numbers.**

Improper fractions have a value that is greater than or equal to 1. For example, in Section 3.1, we showed that $\frac{4}{4} = 1$ and $\frac{7}{4} = 1\frac{3}{4}$. In fact, every improper fraction can be expressed as either a whole number or as the sum of a whole number and a proper fraction (a **mixed number**).

The process for doing this is as follows:

The fraction line not only separates the numerator and the denominator, it also implies a division—the numerator divided by the denominator.

For that reason some improper fractions give whole number results:

$$\frac{4}{4} \quad = \quad 4\overline{)4} = 1$$

$$\frac{15}{3} \quad = \quad 3\overline{)15} = 5$$

$$\frac{120}{12} \quad = \quad 12\overline{)120} = 10$$

Some improper fractions give mixed number results:

$\frac{7}{4} = 4\overline{)7} = 1\ \text{R3} = 1\frac{3}{4}$ Since we are dividing by 4, the remainder is 3 out of 4, or $\frac{3}{4}$. So the mixed number is 1 and $\frac{3}{4}$.

$\frac{19}{5} = 5\overline{)19} = 3\ \text{R4} = 3\frac{4}{5}$ Since we are dividing by 5, the remainder is 4 out of 5, or $\frac{4}{5}$. So the mixed number is 3 and $\frac{4}{5}$.

To simplify an improper fraction all you need to do is to divide the numerator by the denominator and represent any remainder as a proper fraction with the divisor as its denominator. *If you get confused on which number to divide by, you can remember **D** for denominator, down number, and divisor.*

Problem 1:   Simplify $\dfrac{18}{3}$

Answer: 6

$$\frac{18}{3} = 3\overline{)18} = 6$$

Problem 2:   Simplify $\dfrac{39}{7}$

Answer: $5\dfrac{4}{7}$

$$\frac{39}{7} = 7\overline{)39} = 5\ \text{R4} = 5\frac{4}{7}$$

In working with fractions, you will find it sometimes necessary to change whole or mixed numbers into improper fractions. This is the reverse of what we just did in this section.

For example: $\dfrac{2}{1} = 2 \div 1 = 2$

Thus, the whole number 2 is the improper fraction $\frac{2}{1}$.

Similarly, any whole number can be converted into an improper fraction by putting the whole number over a denominator of 1.

That is, $7 = \frac{7}{1}$, $25 = \frac{25}{1}$, $156 = \frac{156}{1}$, and so on.

We can also obtain a method for converting mixed numbers into improper fractions by studying how we changed improper fractions into mixed numbers earlier in this section.

For example: $\dfrac{7}{4} = 1\dfrac{3}{4}$

$$\underset{\text{dividend}}{\dfrac{7}{4}} = 4\overline{)7} = \underset{\text{divisor}}{} \; \underset{\text{quotient}}{1} \; \text{R}\underset{\text{remainder}}{3} = 1\dfrac{3}{4}$$

Thus, if you have a mixed number, you have the quotient, the remainder, and the divisor of a division problem. All you need, to find the improper fraction, is the dividend.

But remember, the dividend = divisor × quotient + remainder.

$$1\dfrac{3}{4} = \dfrac{4 \times 1 + 3}{4} = \dfrac{7}{4}$$

If you understand that process for changing a mixed number into a fraction, the short cut below will make those problems easier to do.

$$5\overset{+3}{\underset{\times 4}{}} \to \dfrac{23}{4} \qquad 10\overset{+1}{\underset{\times 6}{}} \to \dfrac{61}{6} \qquad 122\overset{+2}{\underset{\times 3}{}} \to \dfrac{368}{3}$$

Problem 3: Change $6\dfrac{2}{7}$ to an improper fraction.   Answer: $\dfrac{44}{7}$

$$6\dfrac{2}{7} = \dfrac{7 \times 6 + 2}{7} = \dfrac{44}{7}$$

Problem 4: Change $140\dfrac{1}{2}$ to an improper fraction.   Answer: $\dfrac{281}{2}$

$$140\overset{+1}{\underset{\times 2}{}} \to \dfrac{281}{2}$$

Exercise 3.3 Set A

In problems 1–14, change the fractions to whole or mixed numbers.

1. $\frac{8}{1}$

2. $\frac{7}{1}$

1. _____

2. _____

3. $\frac{15}{3}$

4. $\frac{24}{6}$

3. _____

4. _____

5. $\frac{17}{3}$

6. $\frac{25}{6}$

5. _____

6. _____

7. $\frac{10}{7}$

8. $\frac{11}{8}$

7. _____

8. _____

9. $\frac{37}{5}$

10. $\frac{47}{5}$

9. _____

10. _____

11. $\frac{125}{16}$

12. $\frac{140}{17}$

11. _____

12. _____

13. $\frac{457}{7}$

14. $\frac{396}{7}$

13. _____

14. _____

In problems 15–30, change the whole or mixed numbers to improper fractions.

15. 9

16. 8

15. _____

16. _____

17. $1\frac{1}{2}$

18. $1\frac{3}{5}$

17. _____

18. _____

19. $2\frac{5}{8}$

20. $2\frac{6}{7}$

19. _____

20. _____

21. $9\frac{1}{4}$

22. $8\frac{1}{3}$

21. _____

22. _____

23. $37\frac{1}{2}$

24. $52\frac{1}{6}$

23. _____

24. _____

25. $10\frac{5}{6}$

26. $20\frac{8}{9}$

25. _____

26. _____

27. $124\frac{3}{7}$

28. $209\frac{2}{3}$

27. _____

28. _____

29. $45\frac{15}{17}$

30. $19\frac{19}{32}$

29. _____

30. _____

Exercise 3.3 Set B

In problems 1–14, change the fractions to whole or mixed numbers.

1. $\dfrac{6}{1}$

2. $\dfrac{9}{1}$

3. $\dfrac{18}{3}$

4. $\dfrac{24}{4}$

5. $\dfrac{19}{3}$

6. $\dfrac{25}{4}$

7. $\dfrac{11}{6}$

8. $\dfrac{12}{5}$

9. $\dfrac{37}{7}$

10. $\dfrac{58}{7}$

11. $\dfrac{140}{19}$

12. $\dfrac{150}{13}$

13. $\dfrac{547}{7}$

14. $\dfrac{593}{7}$

1. _____

2. _____

3. _____

4. _____

5. _____

6. _____

7. _____

8. _____

9. _____

10. _____

11. _____

12. _____

13. _____

14. _____

In problems 15–30, change the whole or mixed numbers to improper fractions.

15. 7

16. 6

17. $1\frac{2}{3}$

18. $1\frac{3}{4}$

19. $2\frac{5}{6}$

20. $2\frac{7}{8}$

21. $8\frac{1}{4}$

22. $9\frac{1}{3}$

23. $24\frac{1}{2}$

24. $46\frac{1}{5}$

25. $20\frac{5}{8}$

26. $10\frac{7}{9}$

27. $142\frac{2}{7}$

28. $107\frac{3}{8}$

29. $39\frac{17}{19}$

30. $17\frac{17}{32}$

15. _____

16. _____

17. _____

18. _____

19. _____

20. _____

21. _____

22. _____

23. _____

24. _____

25. _____

26. _____

27. _____

28. _____

29. _____

30. _____

3.4 Multiplying Fractions

The easiest operation with fractions is multiplication, since to multiply fractions you just have to multiply their numerators and multiply their denominators to get the numerator and the denominator of the answer.

For example: $\dfrac{1}{2} \times \dfrac{3}{5} = \dfrac{1 \times 3}{2 \times 5} = \dfrac{3}{10}$

$$\dfrac{4}{7} \times \dfrac{1}{5} \times \dfrac{6}{13} = \dfrac{4 \times 1 \times 6}{7 \times 5 \times 13} = \dfrac{24}{455}$$

The difficulty, however, with working with fractions is that answers should be reduced to lowest terms.

For example: $\dfrac{6}{15} \times \dfrac{42}{63} = \dfrac{6 \times 42}{15 \times 63} = \dfrac{252}{945}$

We must now reduce that answer:

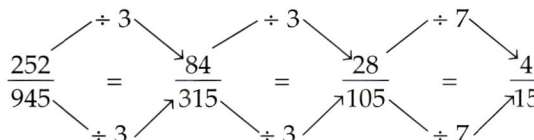

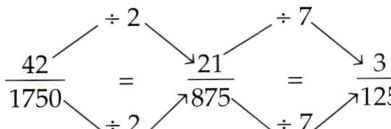

$$\frac{252}{945} = \overset{\div 3}{\underset{\div 3}{\frac{84}{315}}} = \overset{\div 3}{\underset{\div 3}{\frac{28}{105}}} = \overset{\div 7}{\underset{\div 7}{\frac{4}{15}}}$$

The reducing process in that example was quite involved since the numerator and the denominator of the fraction were large numbers. However, if we reduced the fractions before we multiplied, the solution would be a little easier.

Consider $\dfrac{6}{15} \times \dfrac{42}{63}$ again: $\dfrac{6}{15}$ reduces to $\dfrac{2}{5}$ and $\dfrac{42}{63}$ reduces to $\dfrac{2}{3}$.
$$(\div \text{ by } 3) \qquad\qquad\qquad (\div \text{ by } 21)$$

Thus, $\dfrac{6}{15} \times \dfrac{42}{63} = \dfrac{2}{5} \times \dfrac{2}{3} = \dfrac{4}{15}.$

> **Note:** To eliminate some of the writing involved in doing a problem such as that, we would write the problem as shown below:
>
> $$\overset{2}{\cancel{\underset{5}{\cancel{\frac{6}{15}}}}} \times \overset{2}{\cancel{\underset{3}{\cancel{\frac{42}{63}}}}} = \dfrac{2 \times 2}{5 \times 3} = \dfrac{4}{15}$$

Notice that the canceling of numbers is similar to what was previously done.

There is another short cut that can be used when multiplying fractions. Let me show you by another example. Consider:

$$\dfrac{3}{70} \times \dfrac{14}{25} = \dfrac{3 \times 14}{70 \times 25} = \dfrac{42}{1750}$$

We must now reduce that answer:

$$\frac{42}{1750} = \overset{\div 2}{\underset{\div 2}{\frac{21}{875}}} = \overset{\div 7}{\underset{\div 7}{\frac{3}{125}}}$$

Notice that the original fractions $\frac{3}{70}$ and $\frac{14}{25}$ are not reducible. However, the product $\frac{42}{1750}$ is reducible to lower terms. It would be nice if we could reduce before we multiplied, as we did in the previous example. What we could have done is reduce the numerator of the 2nd fraction with the denominator of the 1st fraction.

$$\frac{3}{\overset{}{\underset{5}{\cancel{70}}}} \times \frac{\overset{1}{\cancel{14}}}{25} = \frac{3 \times 1}{5 \times 25} = \frac{3}{125}$$

This process is called cross canceling and can *only* be used when multiplying fractions. The process requires that you divide the same number evenly into any numerator and any denominator. You can do this canceling process in any order, and you should continue until all possible combinations are canceled.

$$2 \times \frac{18}{10} \times \frac{15}{26} = ?$$

$$= \frac{2}{1} \times \frac{\overset{9}{\cancel{18}}}{\underset{5}{\cancel{10}}} \times \frac{15}{26}$$
Change 2 to the fraction $\frac{2}{1}$ and reduce $\frac{18}{10}$ to $\frac{9}{5}$.

$$= \frac{\overset{1}{\cancel{2}}}{1} \times \frac{9}{\underset{1}{\cancel{5}}} \times \frac{\overset{3}{\cancel{15}}}{\underset{13}{\cancel{26}}}$$
Cross cancel the 2 and the 26; cross cancel the 5 and the 15.

$$= \frac{27}{13} = 2\frac{1}{13}$$
Multiply the remaining fractions and change the improper fraction to a mixed number.

Problem 1: $\dfrac{3}{4} \times \dfrac{20}{7} = ?$

Answer: $2\dfrac{1}{7}$

$$\frac{3}{\underset{1}{\cancel{4}}} \times \frac{\overset{5}{\cancel{20}}}{7} = \frac{15}{7} = 2\frac{1}{7}$$

Problem 2: $\dfrac{12}{15} \times \dfrac{8}{25} \times \dfrac{75}{100} = ?$

Answer: $\dfrac{24}{125}$

$$\frac{\overset{4}{\cancel{12}}}{\underset{5}{\cancel{15}}} \times \frac{8}{25} \times \frac{\overset{3}{\cancel{75}}}{\underset{4}{\cancel{100}}} = \frac{4}{5} \times \frac{\overset{2}{\cancel{8}}}{25} \times \frac{3}{\underset{1}{\cancel{4}}} = \frac{24}{125}$$

Exercise 3.4 Set A

Find the reduced answers.

1. $\dfrac{1}{2} \times \dfrac{3}{4}$

2. $\dfrac{1}{3} \times \dfrac{2}{5}$

1. _____

2. _____

3. $\dfrac{7}{8} \times \dfrac{5}{9}$

4. $\dfrac{9}{10} \times \dfrac{7}{8}$

3. _____

4. _____

5. $3 \times \dfrac{1}{5}$

6. $2 \times \dfrac{1}{3}$

5. _____

6. _____

7. $\dfrac{2}{3} \times 5$

8. $\dfrac{3}{7} \times 6$

7. _____

8. _____

9. $\dfrac{3}{7} \times \dfrac{5}{9}$

10. $\dfrac{2}{7} \times \dfrac{5}{6}$

9. _____

10. _____

11. $\dfrac{10}{12} \times \dfrac{11}{7}$

12. $\dfrac{6}{9} \times \dfrac{11}{5}$

11. _____

12. _____

13. $\dfrac{12}{35} \times \dfrac{5}{16}$

14. $\dfrac{10}{27} \times \dfrac{9}{20}$

13. _____

14. _____

15. $3 \times \dfrac{4}{25} \times \dfrac{5}{12}$

16. $2 \times \dfrac{8}{49} \times \dfrac{7}{16}$

17. $\dfrac{13}{35} \times \dfrac{14}{21} \times 5$

18. $\dfrac{11}{42} \times \dfrac{6}{8} \times 6$

19. $\dfrac{1}{3} \times \dfrac{4}{5} \times \dfrac{8}{7}$

20. $\dfrac{1}{4} \times \dfrac{3}{5} \times \dfrac{7}{2}$

21. $\dfrac{1}{3} \times \dfrac{6}{13} \times \dfrac{39}{15}$

22. $\dfrac{1}{4} \times \dfrac{12}{33} \times \dfrac{11}{9}$

23. $\dfrac{20}{21} \times \dfrac{19}{36} \times \dfrac{33}{38}$

24. $\dfrac{22}{13} \times \dfrac{11}{36} \times \dfrac{39}{22}$

25. $\dfrac{150}{320} \times \dfrac{5}{6} \times \dfrac{28}{180}$

26. $\dfrac{108}{320} \times \dfrac{7}{8} \times \dfrac{28}{144}$

15. _____

16. _____

17. _____

18. _____

19. _____

20. _____

21. _____

22. _____

23. _____

24. _____

25. _____

26. _____

Name _____   Date _____

Exercise 3.4 Set B

Find the reduced answers.

1. $\dfrac{1}{4} \times \dfrac{3}{4}$

2. $\dfrac{1}{2} \times \dfrac{1}{3}$

3. $\dfrac{6}{7} \times \dfrac{5}{11}$

4. $\dfrac{7}{10} \times \dfrac{3}{4}$

5. $4 \times \dfrac{1}{5}$

6. $3 \times \dfrac{1}{4}$

7. $\dfrac{3}{4} \times 5$

8. $\dfrac{2}{3} \times 7$

9. $\dfrac{4}{5} \times \dfrac{7}{12}$

10. $\dfrac{3}{7} \times \dfrac{5}{6}$

11. $\dfrac{10}{15} \times \dfrac{13}{3}$

12. $\dfrac{8}{12} \times \dfrac{13}{7}$

13. $\dfrac{24}{35} \times \dfrac{7}{18}$

14. $\dfrac{12}{25} \times \dfrac{35}{36}$

1. _____

2. _____

3. _____

4. _____

5. _____

6. _____

7. _____

8. _____

9. _____

10. _____

11. _____

12. _____

13. _____

14. _____

15. $4 \times \dfrac{6}{25} \times \dfrac{5}{24}$

16. $3 \times \dfrac{6}{49} \times \dfrac{7}{18}$

17. $\dfrac{11}{45} \times \dfrac{8}{12} \times 5$

18. $\dfrac{7}{30} \times \dfrac{6}{9} \times 6$

19. $\dfrac{1}{2} \times \dfrac{10}{18} \times \dfrac{54}{15}$

20. $\dfrac{1}{5} \times \dfrac{12}{27} \times \dfrac{18}{30}$

21. $\dfrac{1}{3} \times \dfrac{2}{5} \times \dfrac{7}{9}$

22. $\dfrac{1}{2} \times \dfrac{3}{4} \times \dfrac{5}{7}$

23. $\dfrac{14}{30} \times \dfrac{11}{36} \times \dfrac{15}{22}$

24. $\dfrac{10}{49} \times \dfrac{19}{36} \times \dfrac{21}{38}$

25. $\dfrac{144}{180} \times \dfrac{7}{3} \times \dfrac{56}{108}$

26. $\dfrac{54}{108} \times \dfrac{4}{9} \times \dfrac{56}{180}$

3.5 Dividing Fractions

Cancel:
A good car salesman can sell.

An understanding of how to multiply fractions is essential in this section. You will learn how division of fractions can be changed into the multiplication of fractions. Look at the problem $12 \div 3$. We can consider dividing a number by 3 the same as taking $\frac{1}{3}$ of it. That is, multiplying it by $\frac{1}{3}$.

$$12 \div 3 = 12 \times \frac{1}{3} = 4$$

Also in a problem such as $\frac{3}{5} \div 2$, we can consider dividing a number by 2 the same as taking a half of it.

$$\frac{3}{5} \div 2 = \frac{3}{5} \times \frac{1}{2} = \frac{3}{10}$$

Let's look closely at those two problems. We know that $3 = \frac{3}{1}$ and $2 = \frac{2}{1}$, so those two problems become:

$$12 \div 3 = 12 \div \frac{3}{1} = 12 \times \frac{1}{3} \qquad \frac{3}{5} \div 2 = \frac{3}{5} \div \frac{2}{1} = \frac{3}{5} \times \frac{1}{2}$$

Those two examples point out a method for dividing fractions.

> ## Dividing Fractions
>
> Invert the divisor (find its **reciprocal**) and change the division into multiplication.

$$12 \div \frac{3}{1} = 12 \times \frac{1}{3} \qquad \frac{3}{5} \div \frac{2}{1} = \frac{3}{5} \times \frac{1}{2}$$

(reciprocal)   (reciprocal)

($\div$ changed to $\times$)   ($\div$ changed to $\times$)

Using that method, problems that involve dividing fractions become multiplication problems with the original divisor inverted. Let's try some examples.

Example 1

$$\frac{2}{3} \div \frac{5}{7} = ?$$

$$= \frac{2}{3} \times \frac{7}{5} \qquad \text{Invert the divisor and multiply.}$$

$$= \frac{14}{15}$$

Example 2

$$\frac{10}{15} \div \frac{7}{27} = ?$$

$$= \frac{10}{15} \div \frac{7}{27} \quad \text{Invert the divisor and multiply.}$$

$$= \frac{\overset{2}{\cancel{10}}}{\underset{3}{\cancel{15}}} \times \frac{27}{7} \quad \text{Reduce.}$$

$$= \frac{2}{\underset{1}{\cancel{3}}} \times \frac{\overset{9}{\cancel{27}}}{7} \quad \text{Cross cancel.}$$

$$= \frac{18}{7} = 2\frac{4}{7} \quad \text{Multiply and change the improper fraction to a mixed number.}$$

Example 3

$$35 \div \frac{28}{6} = ?$$

$$= 35 \times \frac{6}{28} \quad \text{Invert the divisor and multiply.}$$

$$= \frac{35}{1} \times \frac{3}{14} \quad \text{Change 35 to } \frac{35}{1} \text{ and reduce } \frac{6}{28} \text{ to } \frac{3}{14}.$$

$$= \frac{\overset{5}{\cancel{35}}}{1} \times \frac{3}{\underset{2}{\cancel{14}}} \quad \text{Cross cancel.}$$

$$= \frac{15}{2} = 7\frac{1}{2} \quad \text{Multiply and change the improper fraction to a mixed number.}$$

We can summarize **division of fractions** as follows:

> 1. Invert the divisor and change to multiplication.
> 2. Reduce and cross cancel, if possible.
> 3. Multiply the resulting fractions.
> 4. Change any improper fraction into a mixed number.

Problem 1: $\frac{10}{3} \div 45 = ?$ 　　　　　　　　　　Answer: $\frac{2}{27}$

$$\frac{10}{3} \div \frac{45}{1} = \frac{\overset{2}{\cancel{10}}}{3} \times \frac{1}{\underset{9}{\cancel{45}}} = \frac{2}{27}$$

Exercise 3.5 Set A

Find the reduced answers.

1. $\dfrac{1}{3} \div \dfrac{1}{2}$

2. $\dfrac{1}{4} \div \dfrac{1}{3}$

3. $\dfrac{2}{3} \div \dfrac{3}{5}$

4. $\dfrac{5}{6} \div \dfrac{6}{7}$

5. $\dfrac{6}{9} \div \dfrac{7}{5}$

6. $\dfrac{8}{10} \div \dfrac{9}{7}$

7. $\dfrac{5}{6} \div \dfrac{7}{6}$

8. $\dfrac{4}{7} \div \dfrac{3}{7}$

9. $\dfrac{2}{3} \div 4$

10. $\dfrac{3}{5} \div 6$

11. $\dfrac{22}{7} \div \dfrac{22}{21}$

12. $\dfrac{19}{16} \div \dfrac{19}{4}$

13. $18 \div \dfrac{8}{9}$

14. $40 \div \dfrac{25}{7}$

15. $\dfrac{5}{18} \div \dfrac{35}{33}$

16. $\dfrac{4}{21} \div \dfrac{24}{35}$

17. $\dfrac{20}{42} \div \dfrac{15}{28}$

18. $\dfrac{24}{50} \div \dfrac{16}{15}$

19. $\dfrac{32}{30} \div \dfrac{24}{70}$

20. $\dfrac{36}{28} \div \dfrac{30}{35}$

1. _____

2. _____

3. _____

4. _____

5. _____

6. _____

7. _____

8. _____

9. _____

10. _____

11. _____

12. _____

13. _____

14. _____

15. _____

16. _____

17. _____

18. _____

19. _____

20. _____

Exercise 3.5 Set B

Find the reduced answers.

1. $\dfrac{1}{6} \div \dfrac{1}{5}$

2. $\dfrac{1}{5} \div \dfrac{1}{3}$

3. $\dfrac{4}{5} \div \dfrac{5}{7}$

4. $\dfrac{3}{4} \div \dfrac{4}{5}$

5. $\dfrac{9}{12} \div \dfrac{7}{5}$

6. $\dfrac{6}{8} \div \dfrac{11}{7}$

7. $\dfrac{5}{9} \div \dfrac{4}{9}$

8. $\dfrac{3}{8} \div \dfrac{5}{8}$

9. $\dfrac{3}{4} \div 9$

10. $\dfrac{5}{8} \div 10$

11. $\dfrac{18}{7} \div \dfrac{18}{35}$

12. $\dfrac{20}{7} \div \dfrac{20}{21}$

13. $24 \div \dfrac{9}{5}$

14. $36 \div \dfrac{20}{7}$

15. $\dfrac{7}{40} \div \dfrac{21}{25}$

16. $\dfrac{11}{50} \div \dfrac{33}{35}$

17. $\dfrac{28}{30} \div \dfrac{21}{55}$

18. $\dfrac{14}{40} \div \dfrac{21}{25}$

19. $\dfrac{36}{54} \div \dfrac{42}{72}$

20. $\dfrac{32}{40} \div \dfrac{56}{35}$

1. _____
2. _____
3. _____
4. _____
5. _____
6. _____
7. _____
8. _____
9. _____
10. _____
11. _____
12. _____
13. _____
14. _____
15. _____
16. _____
17. _____
18. _____
19. _____
20. _____

3.6 Multiplying and Dividing Mixed Numbers

..., 6, 7, 8, 10, 11, 12, ...
What happened to 9?

Seven ate nine!

In Sections 3.4 and 3.5, you learned how to multiply and divide fractions. If you look over the examples and problems in those sections, you will notice that you operated with both proper and improper fractions. The methods shown worked for both types of fractions. Therefore, the logical way to multiply and divide mixed numbers is to first change them into improper fractions and then use those same methods. Let me show you what I mean.

Multiplying Mixed Numbers

Example 1

$11 \times 5\frac{2}{9} = ?$

$$= \frac{11}{1} \times \frac{47}{9} \quad \text{Change to improper fractions.}$$
$$\left(11 = \frac{11}{1} \text{ and } 5\frac{2}{9} = \frac{47}{9}\right)$$
$$= \frac{517}{9} = 57\frac{4}{9} \quad \text{Multiply across and simplify.}$$

Example 2

$3\frac{3}{4} \times 5\frac{1}{3} = ?$

$$= \frac{15}{4} \times \frac{16}{3} \quad \text{Change the mixed numbers to improper fractions.}$$
$$\left(3\frac{3}{4} = \frac{15}{4} \text{ and } 5\frac{1}{3} = \frac{16}{3}\right)$$
$$= \frac{\overset{5}{\cancel{15}}}{\underset{1}{\cancel{4}}} \times \frac{\overset{4}{\cancel{16}}}{\underset{1}{\cancel{3}}} \quad \text{Cross cancel the 4 and the 16; cross cancel the 15 and the 3.}$$
$$= \frac{20}{1} = 20 \quad \text{Multiply across and simplify.}$$

Problem 1: $7\frac{2}{3} \times 10\frac{1}{2} = ?$ Answer: $80\frac{1}{2}$

$$7\frac{2}{3} \times 10\frac{1}{2} = \frac{23}{\cancel{3}} \times \frac{\overset{7}{\cancel{21}}}{2}$$
$$= \frac{161}{2} = 80\frac{1}{2}$$

Problem 2: $8 \times 2\frac{5}{16} = ?$ Answer: $18\frac{1}{2}$

$$8 \times 2\frac{5}{16} = \frac{\overset{1}{\cancel{8}}}{1} \times \frac{37}{\underset{2}{\cancel{16}}}$$
$$= \frac{37}{2} = 18\frac{1}{2}$$

Dividing Mixed Numbers

When dividing mixed numbers, you will again change the mixed numbers into improper fractions. Remember, however, that when you divide fractions you must invert the divisor and change the division to multiplication.

Example 3

$$10\frac{2}{15} \div 6\frac{2}{5} = ?$$

$$= \frac{152}{15} \div \frac{32}{5}$$ Change the mixed numbers to improper fractions.

$$= \frac{\overset{19}{\cancel{152}}}{\underset{3}{\cancel{15}}} \times \frac{\overset{1}{\cancel{5}}}{\underset{4}{\cancel{32}}}$$ Invert the divisor; change to multiplication; cross cancel the 15 and the 5, and the 152 and the 32.

$$= \frac{19}{12} = 1\frac{7}{12}$$ Multiply across and simplify.

Example 4

$$9\frac{5}{6} \div 12 = ?$$

$$= \frac{59}{6} \div \frac{12}{1}$$ Change the mixed numbers to improper fractions.

$$= \frac{59}{6} \times \frac{1}{12}$$ Invert the divisor and multiply.

$$= \frac{59}{72}$$

Problem 2: $8\frac{1}{3} \div 9\frac{4}{9} = ?$

Answer: $\frac{15}{17}$

$$8\frac{1}{3} \div 9\frac{4}{9} = \frac{25}{3} \div \frac{85}{9}$$

$$= \frac{\overset{5}{\cancel{25}}}{\underset{1}{\cancel{3}}} \times \frac{\overset{3}{\cancel{9}}}{\underset{17}{\cancel{85}}} = \frac{15}{17}$$

Problem 3: $76 \div 2\frac{5}{8} = ?$

Answer: $28\frac{20}{21}$

$$76 \div 2\frac{5}{8} = \frac{76}{1} \div \frac{21}{8}$$

$$= \frac{76}{1} \times \frac{8}{21} = \frac{608}{21} = 28\frac{20}{21}$$

Exercise 3.6 Set A

Find the reduced answers.

1. $2\frac{3}{4} \times 1\frac{2}{3}$

2. $5\frac{1}{4} \times 1\frac{2}{7}$

1. _____

2. _____

3. $5\frac{3}{8} \times 16$

4. $12 \times 7\frac{3}{5}$

3. _____

4. _____

5. $26\frac{2}{3} \times 4\frac{4}{35}$

6. $67\frac{1}{5} \times 7\frac{8}{21}$

5. _____

6. _____

7. $7\frac{3}{5} \div 6\frac{3}{10}$

8. $10\frac{5}{6} \div 12\frac{2}{3}$

7. _____

8. _____

9. $24\frac{5}{8} \div 4$

10. $12\frac{15}{16} \div 6$

9. _____

10. _____

11. $5 \div 7\frac{1}{2}$

12. $22 \div 3\frac{2}{3}$

11. _____

12. _____

Exercise 3.6 Set B

Find the reduced answers.

1. $3\frac{2}{3} \times 1\frac{3}{4}$

2. $4\frac{1}{2} \times 2\frac{5}{6}$

3. $4\frac{3}{8} \times 24$

4. $20 \times 3\frac{5}{16}$

5. $12\frac{6}{7} \times 4\frac{8}{33}$

6. $8\frac{4}{7} \times 11\frac{2}{3}$

7. $5\frac{4}{5} \div 3\frac{7}{10}$

8. $3\frac{3}{4} \div 5\frac{2}{5}$

9. $35\frac{3}{8} \div 4$

10. $40\frac{5}{8} \div 5$

11. $9 \div 10\frac{1}{2}$

12. $33 \div 2\frac{3}{4}$

1. _____

2. _____

3. _____

4. _____

5. _____

6. _____

7. _____

8. _____

9. _____

10. _____

11. _____

12. _____

3.7 Fractional Parts of Numbers

Fractions are often used to find a part of a number or quantity. You might encounter phrases such as "$\frac{4}{5}$ of those surveyed", "$\frac{1}{3}$ off the retail price", or "$\frac{3}{4}$ of the class". In statements such as these, you are finding a part of a total amount. The word "of" in this usage indicates multiplying the fraction and the number.

For example: $\frac{4}{5}$ of 4725 means $\frac{4}{5} \times 4725$

$\frac{1}{3}$ of \$630 means $\frac{1}{3} \times \$630$

$\frac{3}{4}$ of 36 means $\frac{3}{4} \times 36$

When you take a fraction of a number, you simply multiply the fraction and the number and reduce your answer to lowest terms.

Example 1

$\frac{5}{6}$ of 4200 = ?

$\frac{5}{6}$ of 4200 = $\frac{5}{6} \times 4200$

$= \frac{5}{\cancel{6}_1} \times \frac{\cancel{4200}^{700}}{1} = 3500$

Example 2

$\frac{1}{4}$ of $25\frac{3}{8}$ = ?

$\frac{1}{4}$ of $25\frac{3}{8} = \frac{1}{4} \times 25\frac{3}{8}$

$= \frac{1}{4} \times \frac{203}{8} = \frac{203}{32} = 6\frac{11}{32}$

Problem 1: $\frac{2}{3}$ of 951 = ?

Answer: 634

$\frac{2}{\cancel{3}_1} \times \frac{\cancel{951}^{317}}{1} = 634$

Problem 2: $\frac{5}{16}$ of 9 = ?

Answer $2\frac{13}{16}$

$\frac{5}{16} \times \frac{9}{1} = \frac{45}{16} = 2\frac{13}{16}$

Finding the fractional part of a quantity as shown on the previous page is useful in many applications involving fractions. Let's examine some of them.

Example 3

Three fifths of those surveyed preferred "Best" toothpaste. If 100,000 people were surveyed, how many preferred "Best" toothpaste?

Analyze: You need to take a fraction ($\frac{3}{5}$) of the total number of people surveyed (100,000). Multiply $\frac{3}{5}$ times 100,000.

Solve: $\frac{3}{5}$ of $100,000 = \frac{3}{\overset{}{\underset{1}{\cancel{5}}}} \times \frac{\overset{20,000}{\cancel{100,000}}}{1} = 60,000$ people

Example 4

A store is advertising a discount of $\frac{1}{4}$ off all retail prices. What would be the cost of a $304 item after such a discount?

Analyze: 1. Find the amount of the discount ($\frac{1}{4}$ of $304).
2. Subtract the discount from the retail price.

Solve: 1. $\frac{1}{\underset{1}{\cancel{4}}} \times \frac{\overset{76}{\cancel{\$304}}}{1} = \$76$

2. $\$304 - \$76 = \$228$

Problem 3: One-twelfth of the 100,800 runners at a Bay to Breakers Race in San Francisco did not officially register for the race. If $\frac{2}{3}$ of the unregistered runners were males, how many females were not officially registered for the race?

Answer: 2800 females
unregistered: $\frac{1}{12} \times 100,800 = 8400$
unregistered males:
$\frac{2}{3} \times 8400 = 5600$
unregistered females:
$8400 - 5600 = 2800$

Problem 4: What amounts would you use to make half of the amount of Nut Bread given in the recipe below?

Answers:
(Multiply each amount by $\frac{1}{2}$.)

Nut Bread

$\frac{1}{2}$ cup sugar	$3\frac{1}{4}$ cups biscuit mix
2 eggs	$1\frac{1}{2}$ cups chopped nuts
$\frac{1}{8}$ tsp salt	$1\frac{1}{4}$ cups milk

sugar: $\frac{1}{4}$ cup

eggs: 1

salt: $\frac{1}{16}$ tsp

mix: $1\frac{5}{8}$ cups

nuts: $\frac{3}{4}$ cup

milk: $\frac{5}{8}$ cup

Exercise 3.7 Set A

Find the reduced answers.

1. $\frac{1}{2}$ of 537

2. $\frac{1}{3}$ of 441

3. $\frac{2}{5}$ of 4270

4. $\frac{3}{4}$ of 2105

5. $\frac{3}{8}$ of $7\frac{1}{2}$

6. $\frac{5}{7}$ of $4\frac{2}{3}$

7. $\frac{1}{4}$ of $36\frac{5}{8}$

8. $\frac{1}{5}$ of $83\frac{1}{2}$

9. Three-fourths of the club members voted for Jane Adams. If 2452 members voted, how many voted for Jane?

10. Five-eighths of the light bulbs produced at a factory are 60-watt bulbs. If the factory produces 10,000 light bulbs a day, how many of them are 60-watt bulbs?

11. A shoe store is having a $\frac{1}{4}$ off sale. How much would a $52 pair of shoes cost after the discount?

12. During a flu epidemic, $\frac{1}{3}$ of the students were absent on Monday. If the school has an enrollment of 942, how many were in school on that Monday?

13. Three-fourths of the coins in a bank are pennies. $\frac{2}{3}$ of those pennies are dated 1983 or later. If the bank has 876 coins, how many are pennies dated before 1983?

14. An analysis of the 96 member Spartan football team reveals that $\frac{2}{3}$ of them weigh over 200 pounds and that $\frac{1}{4}$ of those over 200 pounds are also over 6'2" tall. How many Spartan football players are both over 200 pounds and over 6'2" tall?

1. _____

2. _____

3. _____

4. _____

5. _____

6. _____

7. _____

8. _____

9. _____

10. _____

11. _____

12. _____

13. _____

14. _____

Exercise 3.7 Set B

Find the reduced answers.

1. $\frac{1}{3}$ of 39

2. $\frac{1}{2}$ of 57

3. $\frac{2}{3}$ of 571

4. $\frac{4}{5}$ of 610

5. $\frac{3}{4}$ of $25\frac{1}{8}$

6. $\frac{5}{8}$ of $16\frac{1}{2}$

7. $\frac{1}{2}$ of $107\frac{5}{16}$

8. $\frac{1}{4}$ of $326\frac{1}{4}$

9. Three-fourths of all entering freshmen at a college live on campus. If the freshman enrollment is 1240, how many live on campus?

10. A 64 ounce jug is $\frac{2}{3}$ full of water. How many ounces of water does the jug contain?

11. One-third of the 5343 students registering for classes paid their fees with cash. How many students did not pay with cash?

12. At a fire sale, items are being sold at $\frac{3}{4}$ off the marked price. What is the sale price of an item which has a marked price of $156?

13. Of the 2310 people polled, $\frac{2}{3}$ favored Proposition A. However, only $\frac{1}{5}$ of those who favored Proposition A also favored Proposition B. How many favored both propositions?

14. A factory has 1710 workers. $\frac{3}{5}$ of the workers are women, and $\frac{1}{6}$ of the women have a college degree. How many of the workers are women with a college degree?

1. _____

2. _____

3. _____

4. _____

5. _____

6. _____

7. _____

8. _____

9. _____

10. _____

11. _____

12. _____

13. _____

14. _____

3.8 Adding and Subtracting Like Fractions

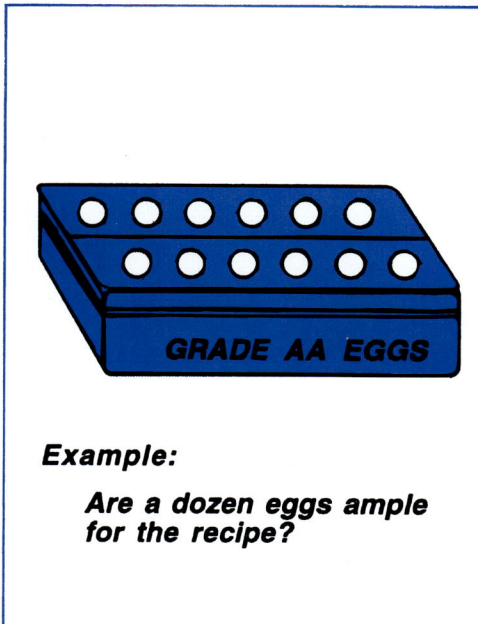

The next step in developing your understanding of fractions is learning how to add and subtract fractions. We will start by adding and subtracting **like fractions,** that is, fractions with the same denominators.

For example:

Example:

Are a dozen eggs ample for the recipe?

$$\frac{2}{5} + \frac{1}{5} = \frac{3}{5}$$

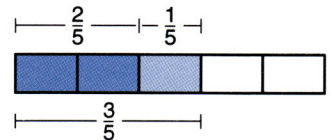

$$\frac{6}{8} - \frac{1}{8} = \frac{5}{8}$$

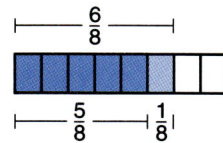

Adding and subtracting like fractions is a straightforward process. If you are adding, the numerator of the answer is the sum of the numerators. If you are subtracting, the numerator is the difference between the numerators. In either case, the denominator of the answer is the same as the like denominators in the problem. Notice, we do not add or subtract the denominators. As with all computations with fractions, you should reduce your final answers.

> When adding or subtracting like fractions, leave the denominator the same as in the problem and add or subtract the numerators.

Example 1

$$\frac{2}{7} + \frac{3}{7} + \frac{1}{7} = ?$$

$$= \frac{2 + 3 + 1}{7} \quad \text{Add numerators.}$$

$$= \frac{6}{7} \quad \text{Leave the denominator the same.}$$

Example 2

$$\frac{5}{6} - \frac{2}{6} = ?$$

$$= \frac{5 - 2}{6} \quad \text{Subtract the numerators.}$$

$$= \frac{3}{6} \quad \text{Leave the denominator the same.}$$

$$= \frac{1}{2} \quad \text{Reduce final answer.}$$

Example 3

$$\frac{5}{8} + \frac{2}{8} + \frac{3}{8} = ?$$

$$= \frac{5 + 2 + 3}{8}$$

$$= \frac{10}{8}$$

$$= \frac{5}{4} \qquad \text{Reduce the answer.}$$

$$= 1\frac{1}{4} \qquad \text{Change the improper fraction to a mixed number.}$$

Example 4

$$\frac{63}{25} - \frac{11}{25} + \frac{8}{25} = ?$$

$$= \frac{63 - 11 + 8}{25}$$

$$= \frac{60}{25}$$

$$= \frac{12}{5} \qquad \text{Reduce the answer.}$$

$$= 2\frac{2}{5} \qquad \text{Change the improper fraction to a mixed number.}$$

Problem 1: $\frac{7}{18} + \frac{3}{18} = ?$

Answer: $\frac{5}{9}$

$$\frac{7}{18} + \frac{3}{18} = \frac{10}{18} = \frac{5}{9}$$

Problem 2: $\frac{11}{30} - \frac{5}{30} = ?$

Answer: $\frac{1}{5}$

$$\frac{11}{30} - \frac{5}{30} = \frac{6}{30} = \frac{1}{5}$$

Problem 3: $\frac{2}{9} + \frac{5}{9} + \frac{7}{9} - \frac{1}{9} = ?$

Answer: $1\frac{4}{9}$

$$\frac{2}{9} + \frac{5}{9} + \frac{7}{9} - \frac{1}{9}$$

$$= \frac{2+5+7-1}{9}$$

$$= \frac{13}{9}$$

$$= 1\frac{4}{9}$$

Exercise 3.8 Set A

Find the reduced answers.

1. $\dfrac{1}{7} + \dfrac{1}{7}$ 2. $\dfrac{1}{3} + \dfrac{1}{3}$

3. $\dfrac{3}{9} - \dfrac{2}{9}$ 4. $\dfrac{4}{7} - \dfrac{2}{7}$

5. $\dfrac{3}{8} + \dfrac{1}{8}$ 6. $\dfrac{5}{12} + \dfrac{1}{12}$

7. $\dfrac{7}{18} - \dfrac{5}{18}$ 8. $\dfrac{8}{15} - \dfrac{2}{15}$

9. $\dfrac{4}{3} + \dfrac{5}{3}$ 10. $\dfrac{5}{2} + \dfrac{7}{2}$

11. $\dfrac{19}{5} - \dfrac{4}{5}$ 12. $\dfrac{17}{6} + \dfrac{5}{6}$

13. $\dfrac{3}{8} + \dfrac{2}{8} + \dfrac{3}{8}$ 14. $\dfrac{3}{9} + \dfrac{4}{9} + \dfrac{2}{9}$

15. $\dfrac{11}{32} + \dfrac{5}{32} - \dfrac{2}{32}$ 16. $\dfrac{13}{32} + \dfrac{8}{32} - \dfrac{3}{32}$

17. $\dfrac{25}{54} + \dfrac{21}{54} + \dfrac{17}{54}$ 18. $\dfrac{27}{64} + \dfrac{15}{64} + \dfrac{18}{64}$

1. _____

2. _____

3. _____

4. _____

5. _____

6. _____

7. _____

8. _____

9. _____

10. _____

11. _____

12. _____

13. _____

14. _____

15. _____

16. _____

17. _____

18. _____

Exercise 3.8 Set B

Find the reduced answers.

1. $\dfrac{1}{9} + \dfrac{1}{9}$

2. $\dfrac{1}{5} + \dfrac{1}{5}$

3. $\dfrac{3}{7} - \dfrac{2}{7}$

4. $\dfrac{4}{9} - \dfrac{2}{9}$

5. $\dfrac{4}{10} + \dfrac{1}{10}$

6. $\dfrac{2}{6} + \dfrac{1}{6}$

7. $\dfrac{7}{15} - \dfrac{2}{15}$

8. $\dfrac{7}{18} - \dfrac{3}{18}$

9. $\dfrac{7}{2} + \dfrac{3}{2}$

10. $\dfrac{7}{3} + \dfrac{5}{3}$

11. $\dfrac{17}{6} - \dfrac{5}{6}$

12. $\dfrac{12}{5} - \dfrac{2}{5}$

13. $\dfrac{4}{7} + \dfrac{2}{7} + \dfrac{1}{7}$

14. $\dfrac{3}{8} + \dfrac{4}{8} + \dfrac{1}{8}$

15. $\dfrac{15}{32} + \dfrac{7}{32} - \dfrac{4}{32}$

16. $\dfrac{17}{32} + \dfrac{10}{32} - \dfrac{3}{32}$

17. $\dfrac{19}{64} + \dfrac{16}{64} + \dfrac{27}{64}$

18. $\dfrac{14}{54} + \dfrac{25}{54} + \dfrac{18}{54}$

1. _____

2. _____

3. _____

4. _____

5. _____

6. _____

7. _____

8. _____

9. _____

10. _____

11. _____

12. _____

13. _____

14. _____

15. _____

16. _____

17. _____

18. _____

3.9 Adding and Subtracting Unlike Fractions

The fractions in the last section were like fractions since the fractions in each problem had the same denominators. We added and subtracted them very easily. In fact, in order to add and subtract any fractions, they *must* be like fractions. In the problem

$$\frac{3}{4} + \frac{1}{5} = ?$$

we must change each fraction to equivalent fractions that have the same denominators before we can add them. *The denominator that we change each fraction into should be the smallest number that is divisible by each denominator. We call it the **least common denominator (LCD).***

In the above problem, the LCD is 20, since 20 is the smallest number that is divisible by both 4 and 5. That means we have to change $\frac{3}{4}$ and $\frac{1}{5}$ into 20ths before we can add them.

$$\frac{3}{4} = \frac{?}{20} \qquad \frac{3}{4} \ \overset{\times 5}{\underset{\times 5}{=}} \ \frac{15}{20}$$

Now add the like fractions.

$$\frac{1}{5} = \frac{?}{20} \qquad +\frac{1}{5} \ \overset{\times 4}{\underset{\times 4}{=}} \ \frac{4}{20}$$

$$= \frac{19}{20}$$

Quite frequently you can determine the LCD by inspection. That is, you look at the denominators in an addition or subtraction problem and think, "What is the smallest number that can be evenly divided by each denominator?"

For example, in these problems:

$$\frac{2}{3} - \frac{1}{2} = ?$$ The LCD is 6, since 6 is the smallest number divisible by 3 and 2.

$$\frac{1}{2} + \frac{2}{5} + \frac{9}{10} = ?$$ The LCD is 10, since 10 is the smallest number divisible by 2, 5, and 10.

$$\frac{3}{4} + \frac{5}{6} + \frac{3}{2} - \frac{2}{3} = ?$$ The LCD is 12, since 12 is the smallest number divisible by 4, 6, 2, and 3.

The method, then, for **adding and subtracting fractions** is as follows:

1. Find the least common denominator.
2. Change each fraction to a fraction with the LCD as its denominator.
3. Add or subtract those like fractions.
4. Reduce your answer and change any improper fraction into a mixed number.

Let's use those steps in doing the three previous examples.

Example 1

$$\frac{2}{3} - \frac{1}{2} = ?$$

$$\frac{2}{3} \xrightarrow{\times 2}{\times 2} = \frac{4}{6}$$

$$-\frac{1}{2} \xrightarrow{\times 3}{\times 3} = \frac{3}{6}$$

$$= \frac{1}{6}$$

The LCD is 6.

Change each fraction to a fraction with a denominator of 6.

Subtract the like fractions.

Example 2

$$\frac{1}{2} + \frac{2}{5} + \frac{9}{10} = ?$$

$$\frac{1}{2} = \frac{5}{10}$$

$$+ \frac{2}{5} = \frac{4}{10}$$

$$+ \frac{9}{10} = \frac{9}{10}$$

$$= \frac{18}{10} = \frac{9}{5} = 1\frac{4}{5}$$

The LCD is 10.

Change each fraction to a fraction with a denominator of 10.

Add the like fractions.

Reduce the answer and change it to a mixed number.

Example 3

$$\frac{3}{4} + \frac{5}{6} + \frac{3}{2} - \frac{2}{3} = ?$$

$$\frac{3}{4} = \frac{9}{12}$$

$$+ \frac{5}{6} = \frac{10}{12}$$

$$+ \frac{3}{2} = \frac{18}{12}$$

$$- \frac{2}{3} = \frac{8}{12}$$

$$= \frac{29}{12} = 2\frac{5}{12}$$

The LCD is 12.

Change each fraction to a fraction with a denominator of 12.

Add and subtract the like fractions.

Change the improper fraction to a mixed number.

Exercise 3.9 Set A

Find the reduced answers.

1. $\dfrac{1}{2} + \dfrac{1}{4}$

2. $\dfrac{2}{3} + \dfrac{1}{6}$

3. $\dfrac{3}{4} - \dfrac{5}{8}$

4. $\dfrac{5}{8} - \dfrac{1}{4}$

5. $\dfrac{3}{4} - \dfrac{1}{3}$

6. $\dfrac{2}{3} - \dfrac{1}{4}$

7. $\dfrac{3}{20} + \dfrac{3}{4}$

8. $\dfrac{13}{20} + \dfrac{1}{4}$

9. $\dfrac{5}{6} - \dfrac{4}{5}$

10. $\dfrac{5}{8} - \dfrac{3}{5}$

11. $\dfrac{7}{10} + \dfrac{5}{2} + \dfrac{4}{5}$

12. $\dfrac{9}{10} + \dfrac{7}{2} + \dfrac{3}{5}$

13. $\dfrac{3}{8} + \dfrac{15}{32} + \dfrac{7}{16}$

14. $\dfrac{1}{8} + \dfrac{13}{32} + \dfrac{5}{16}$

15. $\dfrac{1}{4} + \dfrac{3}{6} + \dfrac{9}{2} - \dfrac{7}{3}$

16. $\dfrac{1}{4} + \dfrac{2}{6} + \dfrac{7}{2} - \dfrac{5}{3}$

1. _____

2. _____

3. _____

4. _____

5. _____

6. _____

7. _____

8. _____

9. _____

10. _____

11. _____

12. _____

13. _____

14. _____

15. _____

16. _____

Exercise 3.9 Set B

Find the reduced answers.

1. $\dfrac{1}{3} + \dfrac{1}{6}$

2. $\dfrac{1}{4} + \dfrac{1}{2}$

3. $\dfrac{3}{4} - \dfrac{3}{8}$

4. $\dfrac{3}{4} - \dfrac{1}{8}$

5. $\dfrac{1}{3} - \dfrac{1}{4}$

6. $\dfrac{3}{4} - \dfrac{2}{3}$

7. $\dfrac{7}{20} + \dfrac{2}{5}$

8. $\dfrac{3}{20} + \dfrac{3}{5}$

9. $\dfrac{4}{5} - \dfrac{3}{4}$

10. $\dfrac{5}{6} - \dfrac{3}{5}$

11. $\dfrac{9}{10} + \dfrac{3}{2} + \dfrac{3}{5}$

12. $\dfrac{7}{10} + \dfrac{5}{2} + \dfrac{4}{5}$

13. $\dfrac{1}{8} + \dfrac{11}{32} + \dfrac{7}{16}$

14. $\dfrac{3}{8} + \dfrac{9}{32} + \dfrac{5}{16}$

15. $\dfrac{1}{4} + \dfrac{5}{6} + \dfrac{3}{2} - \dfrac{4}{3}$

16. $\dfrac{1}{4} + \dfrac{4}{6} + \dfrac{9}{2} - \dfrac{8}{3}$

1. _____

2. _____

3. _____

4. _____

5. _____

6. _____

7. _____

8. _____

9. _____

10. _____

11. _____

12. _____

13. _____

14. _____

15. _____

16. _____

3.10 Finding the Least Common Denominator (LCD)

The first difficulty faced when adding and subtracting unlike fractions is finding the least common denominator (LCD). Sometimes it is difficult to find it by mere inspection. For example, if fractions have denominators of 12, 18, and 10, the LCD is not obvious. To make the process of adding or subtracting such fractions as easy as possible, we need to find the smallest number that is evenly divisible by 12, 18, and 10. But how do you find this number, this LCD?

Since each denominator divides evenly into the LCD, the LCD must contain the prime factors of each denominator. The method illustrated below will enable you to find the LCD when inspection fails you. It requires the use of the factoring process discussed in Section 2.9.

> **Finding the Least Common Denominator (LCD)**
>
> 1. Factor each denominator into primes, using powers to express repeated factors.
> 2. Select each different prime number that appears as a factor in Step 1 and use the highest power of each prime number.
> 3. The product of the numbers found in Step 2 is the LCD.

Example 1

Find the LCD for $\dfrac{5}{12}$ and $\dfrac{3}{8}$.

1. Factor each denominator into primes.

   $12 = 2^2 \times 3$
   $8 = 2^3$

2. Select the different prime factors, using the highest power of each prime.

   The prime factors are 2 and 3. Using the highest power of 2 and 3, we get 2^3 and 3. (note: $3 = 3^1$)

3. Find the product of the results of Step 2.

   $LCD = 2^3 \times 3 = 8 \times 3 = 24$

Example 2

Find the LCD for $\dfrac{1}{12}$, $\dfrac{5}{18}$, and $\dfrac{7}{10}$.

1. Factor each denominator into primes.

   $12 = 2^2 \times 3$
   $18 = 2 \times 3^2$
   $10 = 2 \times 5$

2. Select the different prime factors, using the highest power of each prime.

   The prime factors are 2, 3, and 5. Using the highest power of 2, 3, and 5, we get 2^2, 3^2, and 5.

3. Find the product of the results of Step 2.

   $LCD = 2^2 \times 3^2 \times 5$
   $= 4 \times 9 \times 5 = 180$

Example 3

$$\frac{11}{30} - \frac{7}{25} = ?$$

1. Find the LCD.
   $30 = 2 \times 3 \times 5$
   $25 = 5^2$

   $LCD = 2 \times 3 \times 5^2$
   $= 150$

2. Convert each fraction to a fraction with a denominator of 150.

$$\frac{11}{30} \overset{\times 5}{\underset{\times 5}{=}} \frac{55}{150}$$

$$-\frac{7}{25} \overset{\times 6}{\underset{\times 6}{=}} \frac{42}{150}$$

$$= \frac{13}{150}$$

3. Subtract the like fractions.

Example 4

$$\frac{5}{12} + \frac{11}{15} + \frac{1}{18} = ?$$

1. Find the LCD.
   $12 = 2^2 \times 3$
   $15 = 3 \times 5$
   $18 = 2 \times 3^2$

   $LCD = 2^2 \times 3^2 \times 5$
   $= 180$

2. Convert each fraction to a fraction with a denominator of 180.

$$\frac{5}{12} \overset{\times 15}{\underset{\times 15}{=}} \frac{75}{180}$$

$$+\frac{11}{15} \overset{\times 12}{\underset{\times 12}{=}} \frac{132}{180}$$

$$+\frac{1}{18} \overset{\times 10}{\underset{\times 10}{=}} \frac{10}{180}$$

$$= \frac{217}{180} = 1\frac{37}{180}$$

3. Add the like fractions and simplify.

Problem 1: $\dfrac{5}{28} - \dfrac{1}{24} = ?$

Answer: $\dfrac{23}{168}$

$28 = 2^2 \times 7$
$24 = 2^3 \times 3$

$LCD = 2^3 \times 3 \times 7$
$= 168$

$$\frac{5}{28} = \frac{30}{168}$$

$$-\frac{1}{24} = \frac{7}{168}$$

$$= \frac{23}{168}$$

Exercise 3.10 Set A

Find the reduced answers.

1. $\dfrac{1}{6} + \dfrac{2}{9}$

2. $\dfrac{1}{6} + \dfrac{3}{8}$

3. $\dfrac{11}{20} - \dfrac{7}{15}$

4. $\dfrac{9}{10} - \dfrac{8}{15}$

5. $\dfrac{5}{18} + \dfrac{1}{12}$

6. $\dfrac{7}{16} + \dfrac{1}{12}$

7. $\dfrac{13}{18} - \dfrac{11}{24}$

8. $\dfrac{11}{16} - \dfrac{4}{15}$

9. $\dfrac{5}{42} + \dfrac{7}{36} + \dfrac{1}{21}$

10. $\dfrac{9}{28} + \dfrac{11}{42} + \dfrac{1}{14}$

11. $\dfrac{7}{64} + \dfrac{11}{48} - \dfrac{5}{40}$

12. $\dfrac{19}{72} + \dfrac{11}{63} - \dfrac{7}{56}$

1. _____

2. _____

3. _____

4. _____

5. _____

6. _____

7. _____

8. _____

9. _____

10. _____

11. _____

12. _____

Exercise 3.10 Set B

Find the reduced answers.

1. $\dfrac{1}{6} + \dfrac{5}{8}$

2. $\dfrac{1}{6} + \dfrac{4}{9}$

3. $\dfrac{7}{10} - \dfrac{4}{15}$

4. $\dfrac{11}{20} - \dfrac{7}{15}$

5. $\dfrac{5}{12} + \dfrac{1}{16}$

6. $\dfrac{7}{12} + \dfrac{1}{18}$

7. $\dfrac{13}{16} - \dfrac{7}{15}$

8. $\dfrac{11}{18} - \dfrac{7}{24}$

9. $\dfrac{13}{28} + \dfrac{5}{42}$

10. $\dfrac{13}{42} + \dfrac{7}{36}$

11. $\dfrac{5}{64} + \dfrac{11}{48} - \dfrac{7}{40}$

12. $\dfrac{13}{72} + \dfrac{7}{63} - \dfrac{5}{56}$

1. _____

2. _____

3. _____

4. _____

5. _____

6. _____

7. _____

8. _____

9. _____

10. _____

11. _____

12. _____

3.11 Adding and Subtracting Mixed Numbers

Method 1: Change to Improper Fractions

An effective way to add and subtract mixed numbers is to first change them into improper fractions as you did in previous sections. Let me show you how this is done.

Example 1

$$3\frac{2}{7} + 1\frac{8}{21} = ?$$

$$3\frac{2}{7} = \frac{23}{7} = \frac{69}{21}$$

$$+ 1\frac{8}{21} = \frac{29}{21} = \frac{29}{21}$$

$$= \frac{98}{21} = 4\frac{14}{21} = 4\frac{2}{3}$$

Change the mixed numbers to improper fractions.
The LCD is 21. Change each fraction to a denominator of 21.
Add the like fractions, simplify, and reduce.

Example 2

$$40 - 36\frac{3}{5} = ?$$

$$40 = \frac{40}{1} = \frac{200}{5}$$

$$- 36\frac{3}{5} = \frac{183}{5} = \frac{183}{5}$$

$$= \frac{17}{5} = 3\frac{2}{5}$$

Change the mixed numbers to improper fractions.
The LCD is 5. Change each fraction to a denominator of 5.
Subtract the like fractions and simplify.

Problem 1: $75\frac{1}{2} - 56\frac{4}{5} = ?$

Answer: $18\frac{7}{10}$

$$75\frac{1}{2} = \frac{151}{2} = \frac{755}{10}$$

$$- 56\frac{4}{5} = \frac{284}{5} = \frac{568}{10}$$

$$= \frac{187}{10} = 18\frac{7}{10}$$

Problem 2: $2\frac{1}{12} + 3\frac{2}{3} = ?$

Answer: $5\frac{3}{4}$

$$2\frac{1}{12} = \frac{25}{12} = \frac{25}{12}$$

$$+ 3\frac{2}{3} = \frac{11}{3} = \frac{44}{12}$$

$$= \frac{69}{12} = 5\frac{9}{12} = 5\frac{3}{4}$$

Method 2: Leave as Mixed Numbers

The process described in Method 1 does not require you to learn anything new. However, it may cause you to work with some rather large numbers. You may find it easier to operate separately with the fractional and whole number parts of the mixed numbers.

Example 3

$$182\frac{2}{3} + 48\frac{3}{4} = ?$$

$$182\frac{2}{3} = 182\frac{8}{12}$$
$$+ 48\frac{3}{4} = 48\frac{9}{12}$$
$$= 230\frac{17}{12}$$

Change the fractional parts to an LCD of 12; leave the whole numbers alone.
Add the fractional parts. Add the whole number parts.

$$= 230 + 1\frac{5}{12} = 231\frac{5}{12}$$

Convert the improper fraction to a mixed number and add the whole numbers together.

Example 4

$$37\frac{4}{7} - 12\frac{6}{7} = ?$$

Since the fractional part being subtracted ($\frac{6}{7}$) is larger than the $\frac{4}{7}$, you must borrow 1 (in the form $\frac{7}{7}$) from 37 and add it to the $\frac{4}{7}$ (making $\frac{11}{7}$).

$$\overset{37}{37\frac{4}{7}} = 36\frac{7}{7} + \frac{4}{7} = 36\frac{11}{7}$$
$$-12\frac{6}{7} = 12\frac{6}{7} \qquad = 12\frac{6}{7}$$
$$= 24\frac{5}{7}$$

Borrow $1 = \frac{7}{7}$ and add it to $\frac{4}{7}$.

Subtract the fractional parts.
Subtract the whole number parts.

Problem 3: $26\frac{4}{9} - 17\frac{3}{4} = ?$

Answer: $8\frac{25}{36}$

$$26\frac{4}{9} = 26\frac{16}{36} = 25\frac{36}{36} + \frac{16}{36} = 25\frac{52}{36}$$
$$-17\frac{3}{4} = 17\frac{27}{36} = 17\frac{27}{36} \qquad = 17\frac{27}{36}$$
$$= 8\frac{25}{36}$$

Exercise 3.11 Set A

Find the reduced answers.

1. $4\dfrac{5}{6} + 2\dfrac{1}{6}$

2. $8\dfrac{5}{32} + 3\dfrac{7}{32}$

3. $9\dfrac{13}{16} + 6\dfrac{5}{8}$

4. $7\dfrac{11}{24} + 15\dfrac{7}{12}$

5. $76\dfrac{3}{8} + 52\dfrac{7}{12}$

6. $84\dfrac{7}{15} + 57\dfrac{5}{18}$

7. $8\dfrac{5}{8} - 5\dfrac{7}{8}$

8. $9\dfrac{1}{4} - 4\dfrac{3}{4}$

9. $94\dfrac{5}{14} - 21\dfrac{11}{21}$

10. $86\dfrac{11}{15} - 32\dfrac{3}{10}$

11. $9 - 4\dfrac{5}{9}$

12. $13 - 7\dfrac{4}{7}$

1. _____

2. _____

3. _____

4. _____

5. _____

6. _____

7. _____

8. _____

9. _____

10. _____

11. _____

12. _____

Exercise 3.11 Set B

Find the reduced answers.

1. $5\frac{3}{5} + 2\frac{2}{5}$

2. $9\frac{5}{8} + 4\frac{7}{8}$

3. $7\frac{11}{16} + 8\frac{3}{4}$

4. $4\frac{5}{18} + 9\frac{7}{9}$

5. $62\frac{5}{8} + 43\frac{5}{12}$

6. $75\frac{3}{14} + 61\frac{11}{21}$

7. $9\frac{3}{8} - 6\frac{5}{8}$

8. $8\frac{2}{7} - 5\frac{5}{7}$

9. $95\frac{3}{10} - 32\frac{7}{15}$

10. $132\frac{1}{18} - 17\frac{11}{27}$

11. $8 - 5\frac{3}{9}$

12. $10 - 6\frac{7}{11}$

1. _____

2. _____

3. _____

4. _____

5. _____

6. _____

7. _____

8. _____

9. _____

10. _____

11. _____

12. _____

3.12 Complex Fractions

This section is concerned with complex fractions. A **complex fraction** is a fraction that contains more than one fraction line. The objective for this section is to learn to simplify complex fractions and express them as a single fraction. Let me show you how this is done by simplifying the three examples below.

Example 1

$$\frac{\frac{2}{3}}{\frac{3}{4}} = ?$$

The fraction line indicates that you are to divide the fraction above the line by the fraction below the line.

$$\frac{\frac{2}{3}}{\frac{3}{4}} = \frac{2}{3} \div \frac{3}{4}$$

$$= \frac{2}{3} \times \frac{4}{3} = \frac{8}{9}$$

Invert divisor and multiply.

Example 2

$$\frac{\frac{5}{6} + \frac{2}{6}}{4 - \frac{2}{3}} = ?$$

The procedure for simplifying a complex fraction is to get an answer for the fractions above the fraction line and divide it by the answer from the fractions below the line.

$$\frac{\frac{5}{6} + \frac{2}{6} = \frac{7}{6}}{4 - \frac{2}{3} = \frac{4}{1} - \frac{2}{3} = \frac{12}{3} - \frac{2}{3} = \frac{10}{3}}$$

Add the fractions above the line.
Subtract the fractions below the line.

$$\frac{\frac{5}{6} + \frac{2}{6}}{4 - \frac{2}{3}} = \frac{\frac{7}{6}}{\frac{10}{3}} = \frac{7}{6} \div \frac{10}{3}$$

Now divide those two results.

$$= \frac{7}{\cancel{6}_{2}} \times \frac{\cancel{3}^{1}}{10} = \frac{7}{20}$$

Invert divisor and multiply.

Example 3

$$\frac{2\frac{2}{3} + 1\frac{3}{8}}{\frac{7}{12} + \frac{11}{30}} = ?$$

$$\begin{aligned} 2\frac{2}{3} &= \frac{8}{3} = \frac{64}{24} \\ + 1\frac{3}{8} &= \frac{11}{8} = \frac{33}{24} \\ \hline &= \frac{97}{24} \end{aligned}$$

Add the fractions above the fraction line. (Change mixed numbers to improper fractions and use an LCD of 24.)

$$\begin{aligned} \frac{7}{12} &= \frac{35}{60} \\ + \frac{11}{30} &= \frac{22}{60} \\ \hline &= \frac{57}{60} = \frac{19}{20} \end{aligned}$$

Add the fractions below the fraction line. (Change to an LCD of 60.)

Reduce the answer (by dividing by 3).

$$\frac{2\frac{2}{3} + 1\frac{3}{8}}{\frac{7}{12} + \frac{11}{30}} = \frac{\frac{97}{24}}{\frac{19}{20}} = \frac{97}{24} \div \frac{19}{20}$$

Now divide those results.

$$= \frac{97}{\overset{}{\underset{6}{24}}} \times \frac{\overset{5}{20}}{19}$$

Invert divisor and multiply.

$$= \frac{485}{114} = 4\frac{29}{114}$$

Problem 1: $\dfrac{\frac{4}{5}}{3\frac{1}{2}} = ?$

Answer: $\dfrac{8}{35}$

$$\frac{\frac{4}{5}}{\frac{7}{2}} = \frac{4}{5} \div \frac{7}{2} = \frac{4}{5} \times \frac{2}{7} = \frac{8}{35}$$

Problem 2: $\dfrac{\frac{2}{3} - \frac{5}{12}}{5 + \frac{1}{2}} = ?$

Answer: $\dfrac{1}{22}$

$$\frac{\frac{8}{12} - \frac{5}{12}}{\frac{5}{1} + \frac{1}{2}} = \frac{\frac{3}{12}}{\frac{10}{2} + \frac{1}{2}} = \frac{\frac{1}{4}}{\frac{11}{2}}$$

$$= \frac{1}{4} \div \frac{11}{2} = \frac{1}{\underset{2}{4}} \times \frac{\overset{1}{2}}{11} = \frac{1}{22}$$

Exercise 3.12 Set A

Find the reduced answers.

1. $\dfrac{\frac{3}{4}}{\frac{2}{3}}$

2. $\dfrac{\frac{5}{7}}{\frac{3}{4}}$

3. $\dfrac{\frac{7}{8}}{\frac{3}{4}}$

4. $\dfrac{\frac{5}{6}}{\frac{2}{3}}$

5. $\dfrac{3\frac{7}{10}}{4\frac{1}{15}}$

6. $\dfrac{2\frac{5}{12}}{3\frac{7}{30}}$

7. $\dfrac{5+\frac{1}{2}}{4-\frac{1}{2}}$

8. $\dfrac{6+\frac{2}{3}}{5-\frac{2}{3}}$

9. $\dfrac{\frac{3}{8}+\frac{5}{8}}{\frac{2}{3}+\frac{3}{4}}$

10. $\dfrac{\frac{7}{10}+\frac{3}{10}}{\frac{4}{5}+\frac{2}{3}}$

11. $\dfrac{1\frac{5}{16}+2\frac{1}{2}}{24}$

12. $\dfrac{5\frac{7}{12}-2\frac{1}{6}}{24}$

13. $\dfrac{\frac{1}{4}+\frac{5}{9}}{\frac{7}{18}-\frac{2}{27}}$

14. $\dfrac{\frac{3}{7}+\frac{1}{3}}{\frac{8}{15}-\frac{4}{21}}$

1. _____

2. _____

3. _____

4. _____

5. _____

6. _____

7. _____

8. _____

9. _____

10. _____

11. _____

12. _____

13. _____

14. _____

Exercise 3.12 Set B

Find the reduced answers.

1. $\dfrac{\frac{3}{5}}{\frac{2}{3}}$

2. $\dfrac{\frac{3}{4}}{\frac{5}{7}}$

3. $\dfrac{\frac{5}{6}}{\frac{1}{3}}$

4. $\dfrac{\frac{5}{8}}{\frac{3}{4}}$

5. $\dfrac{2\frac{5}{12}}{4\frac{1}{16}}$

6. $\dfrac{3\frac{7}{20}}{5\frac{2}{15}}$

7. $\dfrac{6+\frac{1}{3}}{5-\frac{1}{3}}$

8. $\dfrac{5+\frac{3}{4}}{2-\frac{3}{4}}$

9. $\dfrac{\frac{5}{6}+\frac{1}{6}}{\frac{2}{3}+\frac{3}{4}}$

10. $\dfrac{\frac{3}{5}+\frac{2}{5}}{\frac{4}{5}+\frac{2}{3}}$

11. $\dfrac{1\frac{3}{10}+2\frac{1}{2}}{18}$

12. $\dfrac{4\frac{1}{8}+2\frac{3}{4}}{18}$

13. $\dfrac{\frac{3}{5}+\frac{5}{6}}{\frac{8}{15}-\frac{5}{12}}$

14. $\dfrac{\frac{4}{9}+\frac{1}{4}}{\frac{9}{16}-\frac{5}{12}}$

1. _____

2. _____

3. _____

4. _____

5. _____

6. _____

7. _____

8. _____

9. _____

10. _____

11. _____

12. _____

13. _____

14. _____

3.13 Comparing Fractions

In a certain survey, $\frac{3}{8}$ of the people questioned preferred the color red, while $\frac{4}{11}$ like the color blue. According to the survey, which color had the greater preference? To solve this problem we must determine if $\frac{3}{8} > \frac{4}{11}$ or if $\frac{4}{11} > \frac{3}{8}$. Those two fractions are very close in value so you can not simply get the answer by inspection. What you must do is change each fraction to fractions with the same denominator, by either reducing them to lower terms or raising them to higher terms. Once the fractions have the same denominator, you can compare them. In the problem above, $\frac{3}{8}$ and $\frac{4}{11}$ can't be reduced, so we must raise them to higher terms. In this case the LCD is 88.

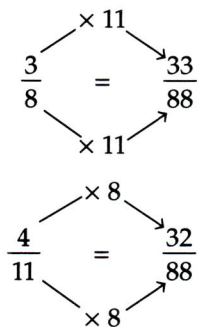

$$\overset{\times 11}{\underset{\times 11}{\frac{3}{8} = \frac{33}{88}}}$$

$$\overset{\times 8}{\underset{\times 8}{\frac{4}{11} = \frac{32}{88}}}$$

Changing each fraction to the LCD we notice that $\frac{33}{88} > \frac{32}{88}$.

$$\text{Thus, } \frac{3}{8} > \frac{4}{11}.$$

> To **compare fractions** convert the fractions into fractions with the same denominator before deciding if they are equal or not equal.

Example 1

Compare the fractions $\frac{4}{5}$ and $\frac{5}{6}$.

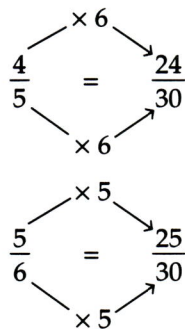

$$\overset{\times 6}{\underset{\times 6}{\frac{4}{5} = \frac{24}{30}}}$$

$$\overset{\times 5}{\underset{\times 5}{\frac{5}{6} = \frac{25}{30}}}$$

$$\frac{25}{30} > \frac{24}{30}$$

$$\text{Thus, } \frac{5}{6} > \frac{4}{5}.$$

Since the fractions are not reducible, we must raise them to higher terms. The LCD is 30 in this case.

Change each fraction to a denominator of 30.

Determine which fraction is larger by looking at the like fractions.

Example 2

Compare the fractions $\frac{14}{16}$ and $\frac{21}{24}$.

Both fractions are reducible.

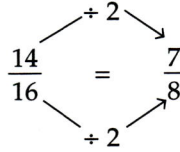

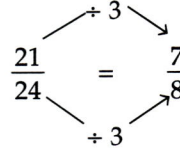

$$\frac{14}{16} \xrightarrow{\div 2}{\div 2} = \frac{7}{8} \qquad \frac{21}{24} \xrightarrow{\div 3}{\div 3} = \frac{7}{8}$$

But $\frac{7}{8} = \frac{7}{8}$.

Thus, $\frac{14}{16} = \frac{21}{24}$.

Example 3

Arrange the following in order from largest to smallest: $\frac{7}{8}, \frac{3}{4}, \frac{11}{12}, \frac{5}{6}$

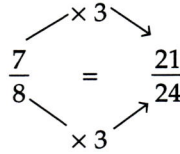

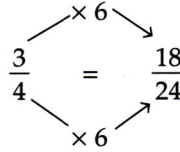

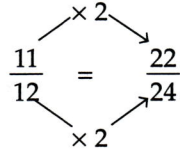

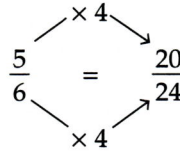

$$\frac{7}{8} \xrightarrow{\times 3}{\times 3} = \frac{21}{24}$$

The fractions are not reducible, so raise them to higher terms. The LCD is 24 in this case.

$$\frac{3}{4} \xrightarrow{\times 6}{\times 6} = \frac{18}{24}$$

$$\frac{11}{12} \xrightarrow{\times 2}{\times 2} = \frac{22}{24}$$

Change each fraction to fractions with denominators of 24.

$$\frac{5}{6} \xrightarrow{\times 4}{\times 4} = \frac{20}{24}$$

Determine the order by comparing the like fractions.

$$= \frac{22}{24} > \frac{21}{24} > \frac{20}{24} > \frac{18}{24}.$$

Thus, $\frac{11}{12} > \frac{7}{8} > \frac{5}{6} > \frac{3}{4}$.

Problem 1: Compare these fractions: $\frac{10}{15}$ and $\frac{14}{21}$

Answer: They are equal.

$\frac{10}{15}$ reduces to $\frac{2}{3}$ (÷ by 5)

$\frac{14}{21}$ reduces to $\frac{2}{3}$ (÷ by 7)

Problem 2: Arrange $\frac{5}{9}, \frac{2}{3}, \frac{11}{18}$ in order from largest to smallest:

Answer: $\frac{2}{3}, \frac{11}{18}, \frac{5}{9}$

The LCD is 18.

$\frac{5}{9} = \frac{10}{18}, \quad \frac{2}{3} = \frac{12}{18}, \quad \frac{11}{18} = \frac{11}{18}$

Exercise 3.13 Set A

In problems 1–8, replace the question mark with =, >, or <.

1. $\dfrac{1}{2}$? $\dfrac{3}{6}$

2. $\dfrac{2}{3}$? $\dfrac{4}{6}$

3. $\dfrac{5}{6}$? $\dfrac{3}{6}$

4. $\dfrac{4}{7}$? $\dfrac{3}{7}$

5. $\dfrac{5}{6}$? $\dfrac{6}{7}$

6. $\dfrac{7}{8}$? $\dfrac{8}{9}$

7. $\dfrac{5}{4}$? $\dfrac{4}{3}$

8. $\dfrac{6}{5}$? $\dfrac{7}{6}$

1. _____

2. _____

3. _____

4. _____

5. _____

6. _____

7. _____

8. _____

In problems 9–13, arrange the numbers in order from largest to smallest.

9. $\dfrac{1}{2}, \dfrac{3}{8}, \dfrac{9}{16}$

9. _____

10. $1\dfrac{3}{5}, 1\dfrac{1}{2}, 1\dfrac{2}{3}$

10. _____

11. $\dfrac{5}{4}, \dfrac{3}{2}, \dfrac{4}{5}, \dfrac{2}{3}$

11. _____

12. $2, \dfrac{9}{4}, \dfrac{15}{7}, \dfrac{11}{6}$

12. _____

13. $\dfrac{11}{12}, \dfrac{13}{15}, \dfrac{11}{18}$

13. _____

Exercise 3.13 Set B

In problems 1–8, replace the question mark with =, >, or <.

1. $\dfrac{1}{2}$? $\dfrac{4}{8}$

2. $\dfrac{2}{5}$? $\dfrac{4}{10}$

3. $\dfrac{5}{8}$? $\dfrac{3}{8}$

4. $\dfrac{5}{6}$? $\dfrac{4}{6}$

5. $\dfrac{6}{7}$? $\dfrac{7}{8}$

6. $\dfrac{4}{5}$? $\dfrac{6}{7}$

7. $\dfrac{4}{3}$? $\dfrac{5}{4}$

8. $\dfrac{6}{5}$? $\dfrac{5}{4}$

1. _____

2. _____

3. _____

4. _____

5. _____

6. _____

7. _____

8. _____

In problems 9–13, arrange the numbers in order from largest to smallest.

9. $\dfrac{5}{8}, \dfrac{7}{16}, \dfrac{1}{2}$

10. $1\dfrac{2}{5}, 1\dfrac{2}{3}, 1\dfrac{3}{4}$

11. $\dfrac{4}{3}, \dfrac{4}{5}, \dfrac{3}{2}, \dfrac{3}{4}$

12. $2, \dfrac{7}{3}, \dfrac{15}{7}, \dfrac{11}{6}$

13. $\dfrac{5}{12}, \dfrac{7}{15}, \dfrac{7}{18}$

9. _____

10. _____

11. _____

12. _____

13. _____

3.14 Applications Involving Fractions

Too many fifths hurt his math skills.

In this section, you will encounter word problems that involve operations with fractions and mixed numbers. Again, you should read each problem carefully, analyze the problem to decide what operations should be used, and solve for the answer.

Example 1

At a convention of 252 delegates, 168 of them favored the new charter. What fraction of the delegates were in favor of the new charter?

Analyze: You need to find what part 168 is of the total of 252 delegates.

Solve: $\dfrac{168}{252} = \dfrac{2 \times \overset{1}{\cancel{2}} \times \overset{1}{\cancel{2}} \times \overset{1}{\cancel{3}} \times \overset{1}{\cancel{7}}}{3 \times \underset{1}{\cancel{2}} \times \underset{1}{\cancel{2}} \times \underset{1}{\cancel{2}} \times \underset{1}{\cancel{7}}} = \dfrac{2}{3}$

Example 2

How many encyclopedias that are $1\frac{1}{4}$ inches thick can you place on a shelf that is 40 inches long?

Analyze: What do you do with the $1\frac{1}{4}$ and the 40? If you are stumped, try using simpler numbers. Use a whole number such as 2 for the $1\frac{1}{4}$. With a 40 inch shelf and 2 inch books, you would get an answer of 20 by dividing the 2 into the 40. So you would divide the $1\frac{1}{4}$ into the 40 to solve the original problem. (Note: $1\frac{1}{4}$ divided into 40 is the same as $40 \div 1\frac{1}{4}$.)

Solve: $40 \div 1\dfrac{1}{4} = 40 \div \dfrac{5}{4} = \overset{8}{\cancel{40}} \times \dfrac{4}{\underset{1}{\cancel{5}}} = 32$

Example 3

You buy $\frac{1}{2}$ lb of fudge, $\frac{3}{4}$ lb of taffy, and $\frac{1}{8}$ lb of caramels. What is the total amount purchased?

Analyze: To find the total weight, you must add the amounts.

Solve: $\dfrac{1}{2} + \dfrac{3}{4} + \dfrac{1}{8} = \dfrac{4}{8} + \dfrac{6}{8} + \dfrac{1}{8} = \dfrac{11}{8} = 1\dfrac{3}{8}$ lb

Example 4

How much larger is a $\frac{5}{8}$ inch socket than a $\frac{17}{32}$ inch socket?

Analyze: You need to find the difference between the two measurements, so you must subtract the two.

Solve: $\dfrac{5}{8} - \dfrac{17}{32} = \dfrac{20}{32} - \dfrac{17}{32} = \dfrac{3}{32}$

Example 5

John ate $\frac{1}{4}$ of a pie. Mike ate $\frac{1}{2}$ of what was left. How much of the pie remained uneaten?

Analyze: John ate $\frac{1}{4}$, so $\frac{3}{4}$ was left. Mike ate $\frac{1}{2}$ of what was left. "Of" indicates "times," so you have to multiply $\frac{1}{2}$ times $\frac{3}{4}$ to get the amount Mike ate. Then, you must subtract that answer from the $\frac{3}{4}$ to get the amount that was uneaten. (Hint: It may help to draw a picture.)

Solve: $1 - \dfrac{1}{4} = \dfrac{3}{4}$ (amount left after John ate)

$\dfrac{1}{2} \times \dfrac{3}{4} = \dfrac{3}{8}$ (amount Mike ate)

$\dfrac{3}{4} - \dfrac{3}{8} = \dfrac{6}{8} - \dfrac{3}{8} = \dfrac{3}{8}$ (amount that was uneaten)

Problem 1: Robert Matern ate 83 hamburgers in $2\frac{1}{2}$ hours during a contest in May of 1973. How many hamburgers did he eat per hour?

Answer: $33\dfrac{1}{5}$

(Note: "Per" means to divide.)

burgers per hour
$\downarrow \qquad \downarrow \qquad \downarrow$
$83 \qquad \div \qquad 2\frac{1}{2}$

$= 83 \div \dfrac{5}{2} = 83 \times \dfrac{2}{5}$

$= \dfrac{166}{5} = 33\dfrac{1}{5}$

Problem 2: You purchased 80 shares of stock at $40\frac{7}{8}$ dollars per share. A year later you sold all the shares for $51\frac{3}{8}$ dollars per share. How much profit did you make on the sale?

Answer: $840

paid:

$80 \times 40\dfrac{7}{8} = 80 \times \dfrac{327}{8}$

$= \$3270$

received:

$80 \times 51\dfrac{3}{8} = 80 \times \dfrac{411}{8}$

$= \$4110$

profit:

$\$4110 - \$3270 = \$840$

Exercise 3.14 Set A

1. If a gum drop weighs $\frac{1}{97}$ of a pound, how many gum drops are in one pound?

1. _____

2. Which makes the smallest hole: a $\frac{5}{16}$ inch, $\frac{1}{4}$ inch, or $\frac{9}{32}$ inch drill bit?

2. _____

3. All 26,000 tickets were sold for a football game. What fraction of the fans were "no-shows," if because of bad weather only 20,800 actually attend the game?

3. _____

4. If 18 people are coming for dinner and you plan to allow $\frac{3}{4}$ lb of meat per person, how many pounds of meat do you need to buy?

4. _____

5. How many $3\frac{1}{2}$ ft pieces of rope can be cut from a 49 ft coil of rope?

5. _____

6. A pole is 32 feet long. If $\frac{3}{8}$ of the pole is underground, how many feet are above ground?

6. _____

7. Jim weighed $134\frac{3}{4}$ pounds at age 14 and $236\frac{1}{2}$ pounds at age 18. How much weight did he gain in the 4 years?

7. _____

8. At a recent fill-up, your car took $18\frac{7}{10}$ gallons of gas. If your gas tank holds $20\frac{1}{2}$ gallons, how much gas was in the tank before you filled it up?

8. _____

9. If the three sections of a book shelf are $18\frac{3}{8}$ inches, $28\frac{3}{4}$ inches, and $30\frac{1}{2}$ inches long, how long is the entire shelf?

9. _____

10. If a bottle holds 28 ounces of liquid, how many ounces of liquid will $2\frac{3}{4}$ bottles contain?

10. _____

11. On a trip of 1830 miles, you filled up your gas tank four times with $14\frac{1}{2}$, $15\frac{1}{5}$, $14\frac{1}{10}$, and $16\frac{1}{5}$ gallons of gas. How many miles did your car travel per gallon of gas?

11. _____

12. A package of hot dogs weighs 16 ounces and contains 12 hot dogs. What is the weight of each hot dog?

12. _____

13. How many minutes is $\frac{3}{5}$ of an hour?

13. _____

14. A share of INCEL stock sells for $49\frac{3}{8}$ dollars. How much would 160 shares of that stock cost?

14. _____

15. If the cost for advertising in a school paper is $8 per column inch, how much more would you pay for a $6\frac{3}{4}$ inch ad than a $4\frac{1}{2}$ inch ad?

15. _____

16. Twenty-four boxes of candy, weighing $1\frac{3}{4}$ lb each, are shipped in a special crate. If the total weight of the candy and the crate is $44\frac{5}{8}$ lb, what is the weight of the crate that holds the boxes of candy?

16. _____

17. Using the road sign below, find the distance from the Church St. exit to a) the Main St. exit and b) the Park St. exit.

17. _____

Church St.	$1\frac{1}{2}$ mi
Main St.	$3\frac{1}{4}$ mi
Park St.	$5\frac{3}{4}$ mi

18. Of the 2,300,000,000 acres of land in America, native American Indians own $\frac{1}{50}$ of it. How many acres of land are owned by American Indians?

18. _____

19. Human brains range in weight from $2\frac{1}{4}$ pounds to $3\frac{1}{4}$ pounds. If about $\frac{4}{5}$ of the human brain is water, find the range of the amount of water in the human brain.

19. _____

20. The force of gravity on other planets differs from that of the earth. For example, the force of gravity on Mercury is about $\frac{1}{4}$ that of the earth. Using this approximation, what would a 140 pound astronaut weigh on Mercury?

20. _____

Exercise 3.14 Set B

1. If you sleep $\frac{1}{3}$ of the day and work $\frac{5}{12}$ of the day, what fraction of the day is left for other activities?

1. _____

2. If 2800 of the 3500 voters favored Proposition D, what fraction of the voters favored the proposition?

2. _____

3. If you ride your bike at $12\frac{1}{2}$ miles per hour, how far would you ride in $2\frac{3}{4}$ hours?

3. _____

4. A finished 2" by 4" board has a width of $3\frac{1}{2}$ inches. How many 2" by 4" boards would you need for a deck that is 14 ft (168 in.) wide?

4. _____

5. How many $\frac{1}{4}$ pound hamburger patties can be made from $38\frac{1}{2}$ pounds of hamburger?

5. _____

6. If $\frac{3}{4}$ of a pie is divided evenly among six people, how much of the pie does each person get?

6. _____

7. After you trim $\frac{5}{8}$ pounds of fat off a $4\frac{3}{4}$ pound pork roast, how much of the roast is left?

7. _____

8. During a two hour tennis match, Wendy's weight went from $112\frac{1}{2}$ pounds to $109\frac{1}{4}$ pounds. How much weight did she lose?

8. _____

9. Bob was $62\frac{3}{4}$ inches tall and weighed 120 pounds on his 13th birthday. He grew $3\frac{1}{2}$ inches and weighed $16\frac{1}{2}$ pounds more the next year. The year after that he grew $2\frac{7}{8}$ inches and weighed 20 pounds more. How tall was Bob on his 15th birthday?

9. _____

10. What is the cost of $7\frac{2}{3}$ pounds of apples at 51¢ per pound?

10. _____

11. A recipe for a wedding punch calls for 12 quarts of champagne. If the champagne comes in bottles that are $\frac{4}{5}$ of a quart, how many bottles of champagne would be needed?

11. _____

12. How many pieces of material that are $6\frac{1}{4}$ yards long can be cut from a bolt of material that is $43\frac{3}{4}$ yards long?

12. _____

13. How many minutes is $\frac{2}{3}$ of an hour?

13. _____

14. You buy 32 shares of ACME stock at $29\frac{3}{8}$ dollars per share, and 760 shares of COMTEC stock at $33\frac{1}{8}$ dollars per share. What is the total cost of these stock purchases?

14. _____

15. During an 8 hour work day, you take three coffee breaks of $\frac{1}{4}$ hour each and a lunch break of $\frac{3}{4}$ hour. How many hours are you actually working in a five day week?

15. _____

16. A full section of pipe is $18\frac{1}{4}$ feet long. If 22 full sections and one-half of another section are laid end to end in a straight line, what is the total length of the pipeline?

16. _____

17. Using the road sign below, find the distance from the Church St. exit to a) the Main St. exit and b) the Park St. exit.

17. _____

Church St.	$2\frac{1}{2}$ mi
Main St.	$6\frac{3}{4}$ mi
Park St.	$9\frac{1}{3}$ mi

18. Approximately seven out of one hundred men are color blind. At that rate, how many color blind men would you expect at a baseball game with 37,500 men in attendance?

18. _____

19. In a 60 minute football game, there is about 14 minutes of actual "action" time. a) What fraction of a football game is the "action" time? b) If you attend 12 of these games, how many minutes of actually "action" takes place?

19. _____

20. The force of gravity on the planets differ from that of the earth. For example, the force of gravity on Mars is about $\frac{2}{5}$ that of the earth. Using this approximation, what would a 3500 pound rhinoceros weigh on Mars?

20. _____

Chapter 3 Summary

Concepts   You may refer to the sections listed below to review how to do the following:

1. define proper and improper fractions. (3.1)
2. raise fractions to higher terms by multiplying the numerator and the denominator, by the same number. (3.2)
3. reduce fractions by finding divisors of both the numerator and the denominator or by using factoring. (3.2)
4. convert between improper fractions and mixed numbers. (3.3)
5. multiply fractions by reducing, cross canceling, and multiplying the resulting numerators and denominators. (3.4)
6. divide fractions by inverting the divisor and changing to multiplication. (3.5)
7. multiply and divide mixed numbers by first changing them into improper fractions. (3.6)
8. find fractional parts of a number by using the word "of" as an indication of multiplication. (3.7)
9. add or subtract fractions with the same denominators. (3.8)
10. find the least common denominator by factoring each denominator. (3.10)
11. add or subtract unlike fractions by converting each to a fraction with the LCD as its denominator. (3.9), (3.10)
12. add or subtract mixed numbers by either changing them to improper fractions or by operating separately with the fractional and whole parts. (3.11)
13. simplify complex fractions by dividing the answer of the fractions above the middle fraction line by the answer of those below that line. (3.12)
14. compare the size of fractions by changing them into fractions with the same denominators. (3.13)
15. solve word problems involving operations with fractions. (3.14)

Terminology   This chapter's important terms and their page numbers are as follows:

canceling: the process of dividing a numerator and denominator by the same number. (123)
complex fraction: a fraction with more than one fraction line. (169)
denominator: the part of the fraction written below the fraction line. (117)
fraction: a portion of a whole, indicated by the quotient of whole numbers. (117)
fraction line: the line in the middle of a fraction. (117)
improper fraction: a fraction with a value that is not less than one. (118)
least common denominator: the smallest whole number that is evenly divisible by the denominators of other fractions. (157)
like fractions: fractions that have the same denominators. (155)
mixed number: the sum of a whole number and a proper fraction. (129)
numerator: the part of a fraction written above the function line. (117)
proper fraction: a fraction with a value that is less than one. (118)
raise a fraction to higher terms: the process of multiplying the numerator and the denominator of a fraction by the same number. (121)
reciprocal: the fraction formed by interchanging the numerator and denominator of a given fraction. (141)
reduce a fraction to lower terms: the process of dividing the numerator and denominator of a fraction by a number that divides into both evenly. (122)
reduce to lowest terms: the process of reducing a fraction until no whole number except 1 divides evenly into both its numerator and denominator. (122)

Chapter 3 Crossword Puzzle

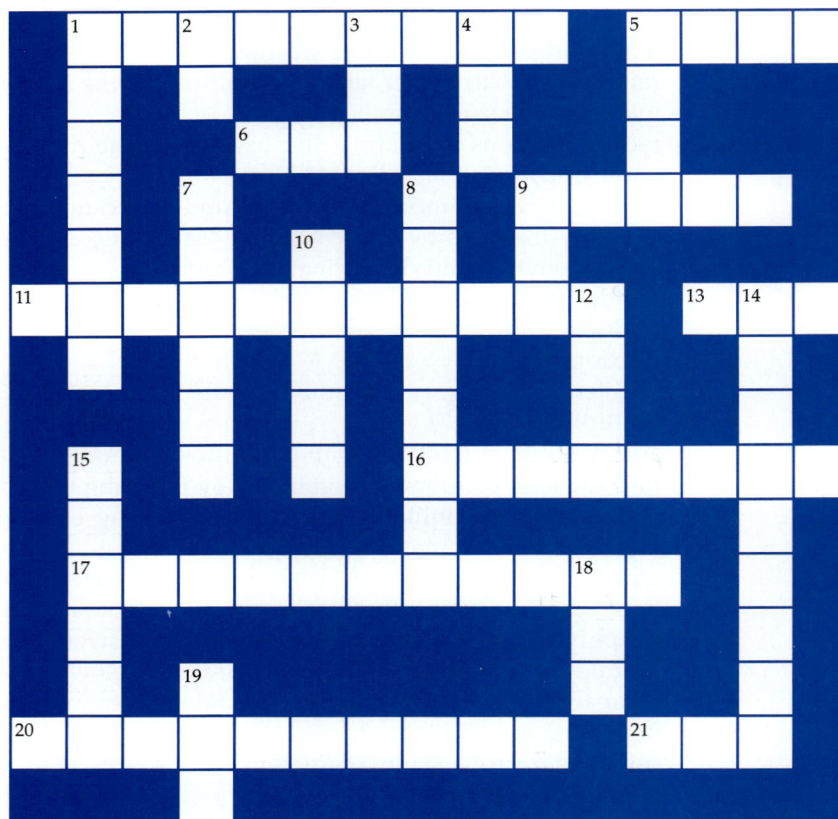

Across

1. Cross reducing
5. Numerator of $\frac{3}{8} + \frac{2}{8}$
6. 5 across is an example of this.
9. Numerator of $\frac{3}{4} - \frac{3}{20}$
11. Bottom of a fraction
13. Denominator of the reciprocal of $\frac{1}{3}$
16. $\frac{4}{3}$ and $\frac{6}{2}$ are _____ fractions.
17. The D in LCD
20. Used when dividing fractions
21. An indicator for division in application problems

Down

1. Fraction within a fraction
2. Not yes
3. Needed when adding fractions
4. Not old
5. Whole number part of $\frac{4}{9} \times \frac{21}{2}$
7. $\frac{1}{6}$ and $\frac{3}{4}$ are _____ fractions.
8. Less than a whole
9. Denominator of the fractional form of $5\frac{1}{2}$
10. $5\frac{1}{2}$ is an example of this type of number.
12. Back
14. Top of a fraction
15. If you _____, $\frac{91}{117}$ you get $\frac{7}{9}$.
18. Any number divided by itself
19. The LCD for 2 and 3

Name _____ Date _____

Chapter 3 Practice Test A

1. Find the number represented by the ?: $\dfrac{6}{7} = \dfrac{?}{63}$

   1. _____

2. Express $17\dfrac{5}{6}$ as an improper fraction.

   2. _____

3. $\dfrac{5}{6} \times \dfrac{2}{3}$ 4. $\dfrac{5}{9} \div \dfrac{4}{9}$

   3. _____

   4. _____

5. $2\dfrac{3}{4} \times 1\dfrac{5}{6}$ 6. $\dfrac{1}{8} + \dfrac{5}{8}$

   5. _____

   6. _____

7. $\dfrac{2}{3} + \dfrac{5}{12} - \dfrac{3}{4}$ 8. $\dfrac{7}{15} + \dfrac{11}{18} + \dfrac{3}{10}$

   7. _____

   8. _____

9. $\dfrac{4}{15} - \dfrac{5}{27}$ 10. $3\dfrac{2}{3} - 2\dfrac{5}{6}$

   9. _____

   10. _____

11. $4\dfrac{5}{6} + 1\dfrac{4}{5}$ 12. $\dfrac{4 + \dfrac{1}{3}}{4 - \dfrac{3}{4}}$

   11. _____

   12. _____

13. Arrange in order from largest to smallest: $\dfrac{4}{3}, \dfrac{8}{7}, \dfrac{7}{6}$

   13. _____

14. A team won three-fourths of its games during the season. If the team played 28 games, how many games did it win?

   14. _____

15. Find the cost per ounce of $3\dfrac{1}{3}$ ounces of cheese that sells for 90¢.

   15. _____

Chapter 3 Practice Test B

1. Find the number represented by the ?: $\dfrac{78}{123} = \dfrac{26}{?}$

    1. _____

2. Express $\dfrac{55}{15}$ as a reduced mixed number.

    2. _____

3. $\dfrac{5}{8} \times \dfrac{3}{7}$

4. $\dfrac{3}{7} \div \dfrac{4}{7}$

    3. _____

    4. _____

5. $3\dfrac{5}{6} \times 2\dfrac{5}{9}$

6. $\dfrac{3}{10} + \dfrac{1}{10}$

    5. _____

    6. _____

7. $\dfrac{3}{10} + \dfrac{1}{2} + \dfrac{2}{5}$

8. $\dfrac{7}{18} + \dfrac{5}{14} + \dfrac{8}{21}$

    7. _____

    8. _____

9. $\dfrac{7}{12} - \dfrac{3}{20}$

10. $2\dfrac{1}{2} - 1\dfrac{5}{8}$

    9. _____

    10. _____

11. $3\dfrac{1}{7} + 4\dfrac{2}{3}$

12. $\dfrac{5 + \dfrac{1}{4}}{5 - \dfrac{2}{3}}$

    11. _____

    12. _____

13. Arrange in order from largest to smallest: $\dfrac{7}{9}, \dfrac{9}{11}, \dfrac{2}{3}$

    13. _____

14. Seven-eighths of those registered at a resort were senior citizens. If a total of 616 people were registered, how many were senior citizens?

    14. _____

15. Find the cost per ounce of $5\frac{2}{3}$ ounces of syrup that sells for 68¢.

    15. _____

Chapter 3 Supplementary Exercises

Section 3.1

Classify the following as proper or improper fractions.

1. $\dfrac{7}{8}$

2. $\dfrac{8}{7}$

3. $\dfrac{8}{1}$

4. $\dfrac{12}{5}$

5. $\dfrac{9}{3}$

6. $\dfrac{1}{3}$

Section 3.2

Reduce the following completely.

1. $\dfrac{3}{6}$

2. $\dfrac{3}{15}$

3. $\dfrac{10}{16}$

4. $\dfrac{12}{18}$

5. $\dfrac{45}{75}$

6. $\dfrac{24}{30}$

7. $\dfrac{70}{84}$

8. $\dfrac{42}{96}$

9. $\dfrac{120}{168}$

10. $\dfrac{294}{336}$

11. $\dfrac{52}{65}$

12. $\dfrac{51}{85}$

Section 3.3

Change problems 1–3 to mixed numbers.

1. $\dfrac{11}{5}$

2. $\dfrac{19}{2}$

3. $\dfrac{13}{6}$

Change problems 4–6 to improper fractions.

4. 6

5. $1\dfrac{3}{4}$

6. $3\dfrac{2}{3}$

Section 3.4

1. $\dfrac{2}{3} \times \dfrac{5}{7}$

2. $\dfrac{1}{4} \times 7$

3. $\dfrac{3}{8} \times \dfrac{2}{5}$

4. $9 \times \dfrac{2}{3}$

5. $\dfrac{5}{30} \times \dfrac{7}{8}$

6. $\dfrac{2}{3} \times \dfrac{1}{7} \times \dfrac{5}{9}$

7. $\dfrac{14}{10} \times \dfrac{5}{21} \times \dfrac{15}{65}$

8. $\dfrac{10}{7} \times \dfrac{21}{30} \times \dfrac{6}{11}$

9. $\dfrac{60}{80} \times 16 \times \dfrac{144}{192}$

Section 3.5

1. $\dfrac{3}{5} \div \dfrac{1}{2}$

2. $\dfrac{10}{11} \div \dfrac{2}{3}$

3. $\dfrac{6}{8} \div \dfrac{2}{3}$

4. $\dfrac{5}{8} \div 3$

5. $15 \div \dfrac{5}{6}$

6. $\dfrac{6}{7} \div \dfrac{24}{21}$

7. $\dfrac{14}{21} \div \dfrac{16}{27}$

8. $\dfrac{28}{42} \div \dfrac{35}{30}$

9. $\dfrac{18}{20} \div \dfrac{54}{45}$

Section 3.6

1. $2\dfrac{1}{2} \times 5\dfrac{2}{3}$

2. $10 \times 4\dfrac{1}{5}$

3. $6\dfrac{3}{4} \times 2\dfrac{5}{32}$

4. $12\dfrac{5}{8} \div 13\dfrac{1}{4}$

5. $18\dfrac{7}{16} \div 6$

6. $30 \div 5\dfrac{5}{6}$

Section 3.7

1. $\dfrac{3}{5}$ of 170

2. $\dfrac{1}{6}$ of 2274

3. $\dfrac{3}{8}$ of 37

4. $\dfrac{5}{6}$ of $49\dfrac{1}{2}$

5. $\dfrac{1}{3}$ of $8\dfrac{1}{4}$

6. $\dfrac{3}{4}$ of $17\dfrac{2}{3}$

7. In a recent experiment, $\frac{5}{6}$ of those tasting coffee preferred Brand X. If 1632 people participated in the experiment, how many preferred Brand X?

8. In a $\frac{1}{3}$ off sale, what would be the sale price for a refrigerator that regularly sells for $915?

9. A drum holds $47\frac{1}{2}$ gallons of oil. If the drum is $\frac{3}{4}$ full, how much oil does the drum contain?

10. Five-eighths of the animals in a pet shop are fish and $\frac{1}{2}$ of the fish are guppies. If the pet shop has a total of 1600 animals, how many are guppies?

Section 3.8

1. $\dfrac{5}{16} + \dfrac{2}{16}$

2. $\dfrac{1}{8} + \dfrac{3}{8}$

3. $\dfrac{7}{20} + \dfrac{7}{20}$

4. $\dfrac{5}{8} - \dfrac{2}{8}$

5. $\dfrac{35}{17} - \dfrac{8}{17}$

6. $\dfrac{11}{48} + \dfrac{31}{48} - \dfrac{9}{48}$

Section 3.9

1. $\dfrac{1}{5} + \dfrac{3}{10}$

2. $\dfrac{1}{2} + \dfrac{2}{3}$

3. $\dfrac{3}{4} + \dfrac{7}{8}$

4. $\dfrac{3}{4} - \dfrac{2}{3}$

5. $\dfrac{7}{5} - \dfrac{2}{3}$

6. $\dfrac{5}{8} - \dfrac{3}{16}$

7. $\dfrac{3}{4} - \dfrac{2}{5} - \dfrac{1}{10}$

8. $\dfrac{1}{2} + \dfrac{1}{3} + \dfrac{1}{4} + \dfrac{1}{5}$

9. $\dfrac{7}{24} + \dfrac{5}{6} - \dfrac{1}{12}$

Section 3.10

1. $\dfrac{7}{15} + \dfrac{5}{12}$

2. $\dfrac{5}{8} + \dfrac{3}{28}$

3. $\dfrac{7}{10} + \dfrac{11}{25}$

4. $\dfrac{23}{24} - \dfrac{13}{60}$

5. $\dfrac{37}{75} - \dfrac{11}{60}$

6. $\dfrac{1}{12} + \dfrac{7}{8} - \dfrac{11}{30}$

Section 3.11

1. $4\dfrac{3}{4} + 6\dfrac{1}{2}$

2. $38\dfrac{17}{32} + 29\dfrac{9}{16}$

3. $12 + 8\dfrac{7}{18}$

4. $5\dfrac{2}{3} - 2\dfrac{1}{4}$

5. $13 - 5\dfrac{7}{8}$

6. $119\dfrac{4}{15} - 95\dfrac{3}{10}$

Section 3.12

1. $\dfrac{\frac{2}{7}}{\frac{4}{7}}$

2. $\dfrac{4\frac{3}{5}}{6\frac{7}{15}}$

3. $\dfrac{\frac{3}{7} + \frac{2}{7}}{\frac{5}{6} - \frac{4}{15}}$

4. $\dfrac{3 + \frac{1}{3}}{2 - \frac{1}{3}}$

5. $\dfrac{\frac{3}{8} + 7\frac{1}{10}}{12}$

6. $\dfrac{\frac{2}{3} + \frac{3}{4}}{\frac{5}{6} - \frac{7}{18}}$

Section 3.13

Arrange in order from largest to smallest.

1. $\dfrac{11}{21}, \dfrac{4}{9}, \dfrac{5}{12}$

2. $\dfrac{7}{10}, \dfrac{11}{15}, \dfrac{13}{18}$

3. $\dfrac{15}{8}, \dfrac{11}{6}, \dfrac{13}{7}$

Section 3.14

1. What fraction of a quart is 24 ounces? (1 qt = 32 oz)

2. In a recent trip, Anne spent $2\frac{1}{2}$ hours driving to the airport, 5 hours flying, $\frac{3}{4}$ of an hour waiting for her baggage, and $1\frac{1}{3}$ hours riding a taxi to her destination. How many hours did Anne's trip take?

3. Because of traffic problems, the trip to work on Monday took $3\frac{1}{2}$ hours. However, on Tuesday, the same trip took only $1\frac{2}{3}$ hours. How much more time was spent driving on Monday than on Tuesday?

4. The roasting time for a 16 to 20 pound turkey is $\frac{1}{4}$ hour per pound. How long will it take to roast an 18 pound turkey?

5. Henry practices the violin $\frac{3}{4}$ of an hour a day. If he practices 6 days a week, how many hours will he have practiced in four weeks?

6. A recipe for 4 people requires $2\frac{1}{2}$ pounds of hamburger. If you plan to have 10 people for dinner, how many pounds of hamburger should you use?

7. How many $\frac{3}{4}$ quart cans of grape juice must be used to completely fill a 6 quart punch bowl?

8. A pole that is 50 feet long is driven vertically into the bottom of a lake to act as a support for a pier. If $\frac{2}{3}$ of the pole is below the water level, how many feet are above the water?

9. The Leaning Tower of Pisa in Italy tilts another $\frac{1}{4}$ inch from center each year. At this rate, how much further will it be leaning in 25 years?

10. Frank, Mike, and 93,998 other golfers each own one share in the Poppy Hills Golf Course. If Mike sells his share to Frank, what fraction of the total shares does Frank own?

11. Suppose a small airplane consumes gasoline at a rate of $8\frac{1}{4}$ gallons per minute. At that rate, how long will 22 gallons of gasoline last?

12. Three $7\frac{3}{8}$ inch lengths of tubing were cut from a 36" piece of tubing. If each cut was $\frac{1}{16}$", what is left from the 36" piece of tubing?

Math Magic III

Magic Polygons

Consider a polygon that has the whole numbers (1, 2, 3, 4, 5, . . .) placed at each corner and at the midpoint of each side. If the sum of the three numbers on each side of the polygon is the same, it is a **magic polygon.** A three-sided magic polygon is shown below.

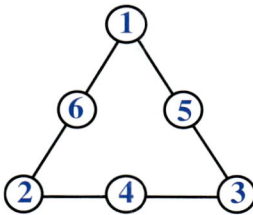

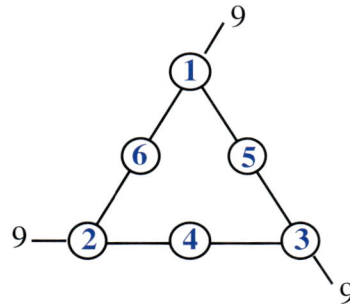

The sum of the numbers on each side of the triangle is 9.

Recreations

1. Verify that the following four-sided figure is a magic polygon.

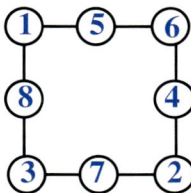

2. Place the whole numbers from 1 to 6 in the circles to make a magic polygon with a sum of 12.

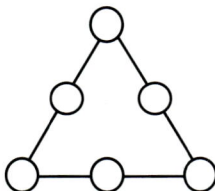

3. This five-sided magic polygon uses whole numbers from 1 to 10. Find the missing numbers.

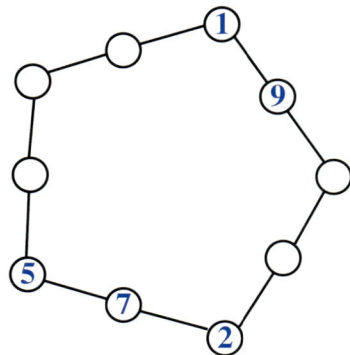

Chapter 4

Decimals

After finishing Chapter 4, you should be able to do the following:

1. read and write decimal numbers.
2. add, subtract, multiply, and divide decimal numbers.
3. round off decimal numbers.
4. convert fractions to decimals and vice versa.
5. compare the size of decimals.
6. solve problems that involve both fractions and decimals.
7. solve word problems involving decimals.

On the next page, you will find a pretest for this chapter. The purpose of the pretest is to help you determine which sections in this chapter you need to study in detail and which sections you can review quickly. By taking and correcting the pretest according to the instructions on the next page, you can better plan your pace through this chapter.

Note: Unless otherwise indicated, application problems with answers that have more than three decimal digits will be rounded off to the nearest hundredth.

Name _____   Date _____

Chapter 4 Pretest

Take and correct this test using the answer section at the end of the book. Those problems that give you difficulty indicate which sections need extra attention. Section numbers are in parentheses before each problem.

(4.1)   1. Write 27.016 in words.   1. _____

(4.2)   2. Round off 3,907.6197 to the nearest thousandth.   2. _____

(4.3)   3. $16.7 + 14 + 0.017 + 3.0065 + 674.6$ 3. _____

(4.4)   4. $843.4 - 78.687$ 4. _____

(4.5)   5. 91.23×67.5 5. _____

(4.6)   6. $34.19 \div 5.26$ 6. _____

(4.7)   7. Find $23 \div 7.351$ rounded to the nearest tenth.   7. _____

(4.8)   8. $5.274 \times 5,000,000$ 8. _____

(4.8)   9. $436.4 \div 200,000$ 9. _____

(4.9)   10. Express 0.62 as a reduced fraction.

10. _____

(4.9)   11. Express $3\frac{1}{16}$ as an exact decimal.

11. _____

(4.10) 12. Arrange in order from largest to smallest: 0.05, 0.049, 0.005, 0.5

12. _____

(4.11) 13. $\left(\frac{1}{3}\right)^2 + 5.4 \times 2\frac{2}{3}$

13. _____

(4.12) 14. You are working part time at a shoe store and earn $5.96 per hour plus time-and-a-half for overtime. If during one week you work 20 regular hours and 4 overtime hours, what do you earn for the week?

14. _____

(4.12) 15. You plan to carpet a room and determine that you need 20 yards of carpet and pad. If the carpet sells for $26.95 a yard, the pad sells for $4.99 a yard, the sales tax is $44.72, and installation costs are $100.00, what is the total cost of carpeting the room?

15. _____

4.1 Reading and Writing Decimals

I'm really 10.7

Decimal numbers:

Numbers that are gloomy and miserable are dismal numbers

I am sure you have seen numbers such as 15.32, .5, 0.638, 127.009. These kinds of numbers are called **decimal numbers** and the dot used in them is called the **decimal point.** Decimal numbers give another way to express proper fractions and mixed numbers. Let me explain.

In our number system, we have learned place values for whole numbers. The place values get smaller as we go from left to right. Each place value is equal to the previous value divided by 10. So any digit to the right of the ones place must have a value that is less than one—a fraction.

millions	hundred thousands	ten thousands	thousands	hundreds	tens	ones	tenths	hundredths	thousandths	ten-thousandths	hundred-thousandths	millionths
2	5	1	7	4	0	6	3	4	1	0	1	9

For example, in 0.576,

the 5 means 5 tenths $\left(\dfrac{5}{10}\right)$,

the 7 means 7 hundredths $\left(\dfrac{7}{100}\right)$,

the 6 means 6 thousandths $\left(\dfrac{6}{1000}\right)$.

Numbers to the right of the decimal point are read like whole numbers and are given a value according to the position of the last digit.

0.7   is read "seven tenths." $\left(\dfrac{7}{10}\right)$

0.2 3   is read "twenty-three hundredths." $\left(\dfrac{23}{100}\right)$

0.1 7 7   is read "one hundred seventy-seven thousandths." $\left(\dfrac{177}{1000}\right)$

0.0 0 4 8   is read "forty-eight ten-thousandths." $\left(\dfrac{48}{10,000}\right)$

Notice that place values to the right of the decimal point end in "ths."

If we have numbers to the right and left of the decimal point, we really have a mixed number. For example,

5.3 is read "five and three tenths."

whole number

decimal point

fractional part

16.08 is read "sixteen and eight hundredths."

172.056 is read "one hundred seventy-two and fifty-six thousandths."

We can summarize **reading numbers** that contain a decimal point as follows:

> 1. Read the whole number part before the decimal point.
> 2. Read an "and" for the decimal point.
> 3. Read the number to the right of the decimal point along with the place value determined by the last digit of that number.

Note: Decimal numbers that have no whole number part, such as .6, .37, or .0063, are often written with a zero in the ones place—0.6, 0.37, or 0.0063. The zero in the ones place does two things: it calls attention to the decimal point and it emphasizes that the number is less than one; it has zero ones.

Example 1

Represent 20,056.0073 in words.

twenty thousand, fifty-six and seventy-three ten-thousandths

Example 2

Write one thousand, five and seven hundredths using numbers.

1,005.07

Example 3

In the number 23.75 what does the:

7 represent?	7 tenths $\left(\dfrac{7}{10}\right)$
5 represent?	5 hundredths $\left(\dfrac{5}{100}\right)$
3 represent?	3 ones (3)
2 represent?	2 tens (20)

Problem 1: Write 215.0705 in words.

Answer: two hundred fifteen and seven hundred five ten-thousandths

Problem 2: Write using numbers:

two thousand fifty-five and twelve hundredths.

Answer: 2,055.12

Exercise 4.1 Set A

In problems 1–7, write each number in words.

1. 0.5

2. 0.17

3. 0.039

4. 5.0007

5. 16.35

6. 426.9

7. 6.1236

1. _____

2. _____

3. _____

4. _____

5. _____

6. _____

7. _____

In problems 8–15, write each expression using numbers.

8. seven tenths

9. twelve hundredths

10. nine and three thousandths

11. forty-five and six ten-thousandths

12. one hundred and sixteen hundredths

13. three hundred fifty-six and two hundred seven thousandths

14. five thousand, twenty-three and three thousand, five hundred seventeen ten-thousandths

15. two million, eighty thousand and one thousand eighty-six millionths

8. _____

9. _____

10. _____

11. _____

12. _____

13. _____

14. _____

15. _____

In the number 167.2354,

16. What does the 2 represent?

17. What does the 5 represent?

18. What does the 4 represent?

19. What does the 6 represent?

20. What does the 7 represent?

21. What does the 3 represent?

16. _____

17. _____

18. _____

19. _____

20. _____

21. _____

Exercise 4.1 Set B

In problems 1–7, write each number in words.

1. 0.7

2. 0.29

3. 0.076

4. 6.0007

5. 17.82

6. 429.7

7. 5.2174

1. _____

2. _____

3. _____

4. _____

5. _____

6. _____

7. _____

In problems 8–15, write each expression using numbers.

8. five tenths

9. sixteen hundredths

10. four and nine thousandths

11. sixty-one and four ten-thousandths

12. one thousand and five hundredths

13. nine hundred ninety-nine and six hundred nine thousandths

14. eight thousand, eleven and one thousand, four hundred, eighteen ten-thousandths

15. three million, four thousand and one hundred two millionths.

8. _____

9. _____

10. _____

11. _____

12. _____

13. _____

14. _____

15. _____

In the number 5,128.3467,

16. What does the 4 represent?

17. What does the 6 represent?

18. What does the 1 represent?

19. What does the 7 represent?

20. What does the 2 represent?

21. What does the 3 represent?

16. _____

17. _____

18. _____

19. _____

20. _____

21. _____

4.2 Rounding Off Decimals

The more digits there are after the decimal point in a number, the more difficult it is to read and work with that number. In many situations, an approximate or rounded off number would suffice. Rounded off decimal numbers have a value that is close to the original number.

Decimal numbers are rounded off using a similar procedure to the one we used to round off whole numbers in Chapter 1.

> ### Rounding Off Decimal Numbers
>
> 1. Look at the digit to the right of the place that you are rounding off to.
> 2. If that digit is 5 or more, round off by increasing the digit in the place you are rounding to by one, and discarding all the digits to the right of that place.
> 3. If that digit is less than 5, round off by discarding all the digits to the right of the place you are rounding to.

Let me make that clear by explaining some examples.

Example 1

Round off 3.47 to the nearest tenth (to one **decimal place**).

$$3.47 \approx 3.5$$

tenths place ⟶ digit to the right is more than 5

Round off by increasing the tenths place by 1 (changing the 4 to a 5), and discarding the digits to its right.

Example 2

Round off 17.4236 to two decimal places.

$$17.4236 \approx 17.42$$

second decimal place ⟶ digit to the right is less than 5

Round off by discarding the digits to the right of the second decimal place.

Example 3

Round off 0.5895 to the nearest thousandth.

$$0.5895 \approx 0.590$$

thousandths place ⟶ digit to the right is 5

Round off by increasing the thousandths place by one and discarding the digits to the right of the thousandths place.

$0.5895 \approx 0.590$ (Note: The zero is left at the end of the answer. Since the problem asks you to round off to the thousandths place, there should be a digit in the thousandths place.)

Problems: Round off to the nearest:

	whole number	tenth	hundredth	thousandth
1. 4.7658	_____	_____	_____	_____
2. 15.0313	_____	_____	_____	_____
3. 105.47532	_____	_____	_____	_____
4. 68.599512	_____	_____	_____	_____
5. 0.60051	_____	_____	_____	_____

Answers: 1. 5, 4.8, 4.77 4.766
            2. 15, 15.0 15.03 15.031
            3. 105, 105.5, 105.48 105.475
            4. 69, 68.6, 68.60, 68.600
            5. 1, 0.6, 0.60, 0.601

Problems: Round off 5672.418 to the following:

6. nearest ten.

7. nearest hundred.

8. nearest thousand.

Answers: 6. 5670
           7. 5700
           8. 6000

Exercise 4.2 Set A

In problems 1–6, round off each number to the nearest tenth.

1. 36.72

2. 4.65

3. 125.482

4. 89.971

5. 8.95

6. 0.149

1. _____

2. _____

3. _____

4. _____

5. _____

6. _____

In problems 7–12, round off each number to the nearest hundredth.

7. 18.724

8. 5.475

9. 792.038218

10. 0.8964

11. 7.195

12. 1.0249

7. _____

8. _____

9. _____

10. _____

11. _____

12. _____

In problems 13–16, round off 562.01846 to the indicated place.

13. thousandth

14. ten-thousandth

15. ten

16. hundred

13. _____

14. _____

15. _____

16. _____

In problems 17–19, round off 46.96352 to the indicated place.

17. 2 decimal places.

18. 3 decimal places.

19. 4 decimal places.

17. _____

18. _____

19. _____

Exercise 4.2 Set B

In problems 1–6, round off each number to the nearest tenth.

1. 43.84

2. 116.75

3. 3.271

4. 9.973

5. 37.95

6. 0.349

1. _____

2. _____

3. _____

4. _____

5. _____

6. _____

In problems 7–12, round off each number to the nearest hundredth.

7. 95.623

8. 0.365

9. 706.019216

10. 7.6973

11. 24.295

12. 100.0349

7. _____

8. _____

9. _____

10. _____

11. _____

12. _____

In problems 13–16, round off 382.01937 to the indicated place.

13. thousandths place

14. ten-thousandths place

15. hundreds place

16. tens place

13. _____

14. _____

15. _____

16. _____

In problems 17–19, round off 52.69524 to the indicated place.

17. 2 decimal places.

18. 3 decimal places.

19. 4 decimal places.

17. _____

18. _____

19. _____

4.3 Adding Decimals

The method for adding decimal numbers is very similar to adding whole numbers. You want to make sure that you add the digits with the same place value.

> **Adding Decimals**
>
> 1. Place the numbers in a column so that their decimal points are lined up.
> 2. Add the digits that have the same place value.
> 3. Place the decimal point in the answer below the other decimal points.

For example, to add 5.3 + .076 + 12.21:

┌─── Line up the decimal points.
↓

```
  5.3
   .076      Add the digits in each column and place the decimal
+12.21       point in the answer below the other decimal points.
─────
17.586
```

If any of the numbers you are trying to add are whole numbers without a decimal point, you can simply place a decimal point at the end of the whole number.

For example: $26 = 26.$
$5 = 5.$
$37{,}612 = 37{,}612.$

Let us look at a few examples.

Example 1

$52 + 3.01 + 0.035 + 1.58 = ?$

┌─── Line up the decimal points.
↓

```
 52.
  3.01      (Notice a decimal point was placed at the end of 52
   .035     before adding.)
+ 1.58      Add each column and place the decimal point in the
──────
56.625      answer below the other decimal points.
```

Example 2

$307.52 + 136 + .65 + 28 + 1.17 + 0.2 = ?$

```
307.52
136.
   .65
 28.
  1.17
+  0.2
──────
473.54
```

Problem 1: $56 + 354.89 + 7.98 + 0.02 = ?$ Answer: 418.89

$$
\begin{array}{r}
56. \\
354.89 \\
7.98 \\
+\quad 0.02 \\
\hline
418.89
\end{array}
$$

Problem 2: $0.01 + 0.002 + 0.0003 + 0.00004 = ?$ Answer: 0.01234

$$
\begin{array}{r}
0.01 \\
0.002 \\
0.0003 \\
+\,0.00004 \\
\hline
0.01234
\end{array}
$$

Problem 3: $465.9087 + 7.8001 + 1235.2 + 45 + 3.2 = ?$ Answer: 1757.1088

$$
\begin{array}{r}
465.9087 \\
7.8001 \\
1235.2 \\
45. \\
+\quad 3.2 \\
\hline
1757.1088
\end{array}
$$

Problem 4:   What is wrong with the solution below?

$2.345 + 90.8 + 1234.009 + 0.823 + .2 = ?$

$$
\begin{array}{r}
2.345 \\
90.8 \\
1234.009 \\
0.823 \\
+\qquad .2 \\
\hline
1237.187
\end{array}
$$

Answer:
The decimal points were not lined up in a vertical column.

Problem 5:   What is wrong with the solution below?

$307 + 47.6 = ?$

$$
\begin{array}{r}
.307 \\
+47.6 \\
\hline
47.907
\end{array}
$$

Answer:
The decimal point for 307 was placed at the beginning of the number instead of at the end.

Exercise 4.3 Set A

1. 287.04
    4.5
    + 29.

2. 436.09
    7.6
    + 80.

3.   0.05
     0.096
    +0.1

4.   0.056
     0.7
    +0.48

5. 81.26
    43.99
    16.57
    + 4.06

6. 19.05
    30.26
    12.47
    + 6.98

7. 586.94 + 306.87

8. 0.25 + 0.016 + 0.9

9. 12.6 + 14 + 126.423

10. 307.0007 + 16.25 + 526 + 18.04

11. 809 + 3.65 + 19.0702 + 76.43

12. 1287.52 + 4700.072 + 29.1103 + 6.5 + 81

13. 123 + 86.057 + 1283.001 + 4.7 + 68.0119

1. _____

2. _____

3. _____

4. _____

5. _____

6. _____

7. _____

8. _____

9. _____

10. _____

11. _____

12. _____

13. _____

Exercise 4.3 Set B

1. 173.07
      3.5
  + 45.

2. 180.03
      2.6
  + 11.

1. _____

2. _____

3. 0.072
    0.01
  +0.0036

4. 0.012
    0.07
  +0.0058

3. _____

4. _____

5. 14.52
    17.21
    23.65
  +10.08

6. 24.27
    18.06
    30.29
  +16.84

5. _____

6. _____

7. 425.63 + 174.52

7. _____

8. 0.57 + 0.4 + 0.085

8. _____

9. 43 + 17.4 + 485.207

9. _____

10. 301.0005 + 19.76 + 443 + 6.99

10. _____

11. 8.0123 + 46.78 + 94 + 0.091

11. _____

12. 1706.58 + 4.217 + 89 + 316.4 + 15.0103

12. _____

13. 62.019 + 4.302 + 8256 + 9000.5 + 7.3

13. _____

4.4 Subtracting Decimals

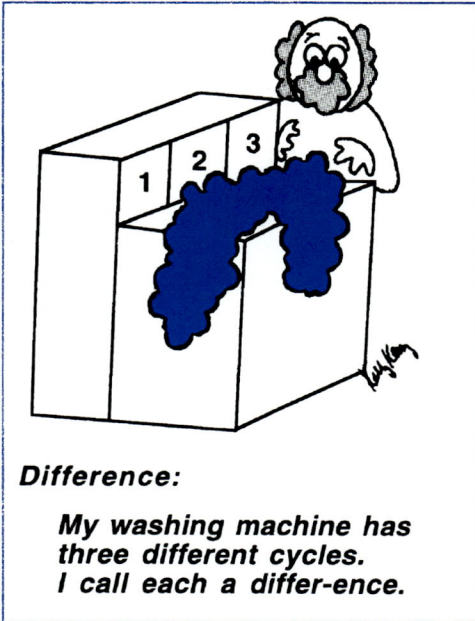

Difference:

My washing machine has three different cycles. I call each a differ-ence.

Subtracting or finding the difference between decimal numbers is similar to adding decimal numbers in that you want to operate on digits with the same place value. To do this you must line up the decimal points before you do the subtraction.

For example: $27.973 - 2.241 = ?$

1. Line up the decimal points.

$$\begin{array}{r} 27.973 \\ -\ 2.241 \\ \hline 25.732 \end{array}$$

2. Subtract and place the decimal point in the answer below the other points.

In that example, both numbers had 3 decimal digits. Subtraction is easier when both numbers have the same number of decimal digits. In order to have that happen with other subtraction problems, we sometimes have to give an alternate representation for a decimal number.

Let me show you what I mean.

The number 0.7 can be written in many different ways:

$$\begin{aligned} &0.7 \\ =\ &0.70 \\ =\ &0.700 \\ =\ &0.7000 \\ =\ &0.70000 \end{aligned}$$
etc.

This is true since $0.70 = \frac{70}{100}$, which reduces to $\frac{7}{10}$; and $.700 = \frac{700}{1000}$, which also reduces to $\frac{7}{10}$. Similarly all the other representations reduce to $\frac{7}{10}$.

Those zeros that are attached after the decimal point do not change the value of the decimal number; they simply give other equivalent numbers. By attaching zeros, we likewise get:

52	1.89
= 52.	= 1.890
= 52.0	= 1.8900
= 52.00	= 1.89000
= 52.000	= 1.890000
etc.	etc.

Example 1

$.5762 - .34 = ?$

Line up the decimal points.

$$\begin{array}{r} .5762 \\ -.3400 \\ \hline .2362 \end{array}$$

Change the .34 to .3400 to get the same number of digits after the decimal point.

Example 2

56.4 − 3.27 = ?

$$
\begin{array}{r}
56.40 \\
-\ \ 3.27 \\
\hline
53.13
\end{array}
$$

Change the 56.4 to 56.40 to get the same number of digits after the decimal point.

Example 3

189 − 13.567 = ?

$$
\begin{array}{r}
189.000 \\
-\ \ 13.567 \\
\hline
175.433
\end{array}
$$

Change the 189 to 189.000 to get the same number of digits after the decimal point.

This then is a summary of subtracting decimal numbers.

Subtracting Decimals

1. Get the same number of digits after the decimal point in both numbers by attaching zeros after the decimal point.
2. Line up the decimal points of both numbers.
3. Subtract as usual.
4. Place the decimal point in the answer below the other decimal points.

Problem 1: 23.62 − 19.048 = ?

Answer: 4.572

$$
\begin{array}{r}
23.620 \\
-\ \ 19.048 \\
\hline
4.572
\end{array}
$$

Problem 2: 57.2457 − 20.7 = ?

Answer: 36.5457

$$
\begin{array}{r}
57.2457 \\
-\ \ 20.7000 \\
\hline
36.5457
\end{array}
$$

Problem 3: 901 − 23.452 = ?

Answer: 877.548

$$
\begin{array}{r}
901.000 \\
-\ \ 23.452 \\
\hline
877.548
\end{array}
$$

Name _____   Date _____

Exercise 4.4 Set A

1.　8.647
　　− 5.216

2.　17.65
　　−　8.41

3.　47.7
　　− 26.25

4.　84.3
　　− 72.16

5.　316
　　− 158.017

6.　485
　　− 206.035

7.　52.093
　　− 18.4

8.　60.082
　　− 41.7

9.　785.1852
　　−　97

10.　643.1926
　　−　195

11.　750 − 32.5

12.　420 − 14.7

13.　89.2876 − 71.6

14.　806.1 − 392.0753

15.　1532 − 27.6

16.　4275 − 186.7284

1. _____

2. _____

3. _____

4. _____

5. _____

6. _____

7. _____

8. _____

9. _____

10. _____

11. _____

12. _____

13. _____

14. _____

15. _____

16. _____

Exercise 4.4 Set B

1.   5.789
    −2.356

2.   36.86
   − 5.23

3.   85.6
   −37.24

4.   66.4
   −28.17

5.   175
   −143.128

6.   294
   −189.317

7.   48.086
   −15.1

8.   49.067
   −18.2

9.   386.1972
   − 57

10.   820.0751
    −639

11. 870 − 46.8

12. 526 − 120.76

13. 43.2765 − 24.4

14. 976.5 − 288.0176

15. 1716 − 3.14159

16. 1287 − 32.4

1. _____

2. _____

3. _____

4. _____

5. _____

6. _____

7. _____

8. _____

9. _____

10. _____

11. _____

12. _____

13. _____

14. _____

15. _____

16. _____

4.5 Multiplying Decimals

4095 × 8795 = 36,015,525

Even rabbits can multiply quickly.

To understand how to multiply decimal numbers, we must look at the fractions which the decimal numbers represent.

For example: $0.3 \times 0.71 = ?$

$$0.3 = \frac{3}{10} \text{ and } 0.71 = \frac{71}{100}$$

$$\text{So, } 0.3 \times 0.71 = \frac{3}{10} \times \frac{71}{100}$$

$$= \frac{213}{1000}$$

$$= 0.213$$

If every time you wanted to multiply decimal numbers you had to change them to fractions, it could become a very involved process. So as we have done previously, we will use that example to obtain a shorter way to multiply decimals.

Let us look at that example again.

$$0.3 \times 0.71 = 0.213$$

0.3	has 1 decimal digit.
0.71	has 2 decimal digits.
0.213	has 3 decimal digits.

The number of decimal digits in the product is the total of the number of decimal digits in the numbers being multiplied.

We can now do the above example as follows:

Write the numbers above each other, ignoring the decimal points, and multiply the numbers as if they were whole numbers.

0.71	has 2 decimal digits.
× 0.3	has 1 decimal digit.
.213	The answer has a total of 3 decimal digits.

Example 1

$15.31 \times 0.07 = ?$

15.31	has 2 decimal digits.
× 0.07	has 2 decimal digits.
1.0717	The answer has a total of 4 decimal digits.

Example 2

$$19.86 \times 0.089 = ?$$

1 9.8 6	has 2 decimal digits.
× 0.0 8 9	has 3 decimal digits.
1 7 8 7 4	
1 5 8 8 8	
1.7 6 7 5 4	The answer has a total of 5 decimal digits. (Note: To place the decimal in the answer, start from the right and move 5 places to the left.)

Example 3

$$0.0002 \times 0.007 = ?$$

0.0 0 0 2 ⟵	has 4 decimal digits.
× 0.0 0 7 ⟵	has 3 decimal digits.
.0 0 0 0 0 1 4 ⟵	The answer has a total of 7 decimal digits. (Note: 5 zeros are used as place holders in front of the 14 to give the 7 decimal digits.)

Problem 1: $43.6 \times 2.7 = ?$

Answer: 117.72

```
      4 3.6
    × 2.7
    3 0 5 2
      8 7 2
    1 1 7.7 2
```

Problem 2: $6.075 \times 3.14 = ?$

Answer: 19.0755

```
      6.0 7 5
    × 3.1 4
    2 4 3 0 0
      6 0 7 5
    1 8 2 2 5
    1 9.0 7 5 5 0
```

Problem 3: $5.3 \times 0.006 = ?$

Answer: 0.0318

```
        5.3
    × 0.0 0 6
    .0 3 1 8
```

Problem 4:   What is wrong with the solution below?

```
      43
    ×  .05
    21.5
```

Answer:

The decimal point should be placed two digits from the *right* of the number.

Exercise 4.5 Set A

1. 14.37
    ×   3

2. 21.75
    ×   5

1. _____

2. _____

3. 8.08
    × 7.1

4. 6.06
    × 5.1

3. _____

4. _____

5. 694.4
    ×   2.6

6. 503.7
    ×   4.8

5. _____

6. _____

7. 2.0014
    ×   .025

8. 4.0042
    ×   .035

7. _____

8. _____

9. 16.34 × 4

9. _____

10. 26.5 × 0.0008

10. _____

11. 7.019 × .04

11. _____

12. 50.48 × 5.25

12. _____

13. 148.34 × 2.017

13. _____

14. 609.24 × .0125

14. _____

Exercise 4.5 Set B

1. 16.36
    ×   4

2. 17.25
    ×   3

3. 7.07
    × 8.1

4. 9.09
    × 6.1

5. 185.6
    × 3.7

6. 294.5
    × 4.9

7. 5.0028
    × .015

8. 7.0016
    × .045

9. 20.15 × 3

10. 15.5 × 0.0006

11. 9.096 × .07

12. 43.28 × 7.15

13. 34.26 × 3.016

14. 507.23 × .0175

1. _____

2. _____

3. _____

4. _____

5. _____

6. _____

7. _____

8. _____

9. _____

10. _____

11. _____

12. _____

13. _____

14. _____

4.6 Dividing Decimals

Dividing decimals is done using similar methods as used in dividing whole numbers. The only difference is in placing the decimal point in the answer. *If the divisor is a whole number, the decimal point is simply placed in the answer above its position in the dividend and the division is done ignoring the decimal point.* The reasoning here is that the divisor is dividing into the whole number part and the fractional part with the decimal point used to separate both parts in the answer.

Example 1

52.8 ÷ 4 = ?

Place the decimal point above the decimal point in the dividend. That separates the whole and fractional parts of the answer.

$$
\begin{array}{r}
13.2 \\
4\overline{)52.8} \\
\underline{4} \\
12 \\
\underline{12} \\
8 \\
\underline{8}
\end{array}
$$

whole number divisor →

If the divisor is not a whole number, you can make it a whole number by moving its decimal point to the right. You must, however, also move the decimal point the same number of places to the right in the dividend.

Example 2

2.38 ÷ .7 = ?

$$
\begin{array}{r}
3.4 \\
.7\overline{)2.3\,8} \\
\underline{2\,1} \\
2\,8 \\
\underline{2\,8}
\end{array}
$$

1. Move the decimal point to change the divisor into a whole number.
2. Move the point the same in the dividend.
3. Place the decimal point in the answer above the moved decimal point.
4. Do the division ignoring the decimal points.

What you are really doing when you move the decimal point one place to the right is multiplying the divisor and the dividend by 10.

$$
2.38 \div .7 = \frac{2.38}{.7} \quad \xrightarrow{\times 10} \quad = \quad \frac{23.8}{.7} = 23.8 \div 7 \quad \xleftarrow{\times 10}
$$

You have transformed the original problem into an equivalent problem, using the same methods as raising fractions to higher terms. Similar reasoning can be used to justify movement of the decimal point in other division problems.

Example 3

$$1.30647 \div 4.07 = ?$$

```
            .3 2 1
   4.0 7 ) 1 .3 0 6 4 7
           1 2 2 1
             8 5 4
             8 1 4
               4 0 7
               4 0 7
```

1. Move the decimal point to change the divisor into a whole number.
2. Move the point the same in the dividend.
3. Place the decimal point in the answer above the moved decimal point.
4. Do the division ignoring the decimal points.

Example 4

$$21 \div .0028 = ?$$

```
             7 5 0 0.
   .0 0 2 8 ) 2 1 .0 0 0 0
             1 9 6
               1 4 0
               1 4 0
                   0
                   0
                   0
                   0
```

1. Move the decimal point to change the divisor into a whole number.
2. Move the point the same in the dividend. (Notice that four zeros were attached.)
3. Place the decimal point in the answer above the moved decimal point.
4. Do the division ignoring the decimal points.

Example 5

Find the exact answer for .23 ÷ 18.4.

(Finding the exact answer means to continue dividing until there is no remainder. The answer is not to be rounded off.)

```
           .0 1 2 5
   1 8 .4 ) .2 3 0 0 0
            1 8 4
              4 6 0
              3 6 8
                9 2 0
                9 2 0
```

Zeros were attached one at a time until there was no remainder in the division.

To find the exact answer in a division problem, it may be necessary to attach zeros after the decimal point as we did that last example.

Problem 1: $510.17 \div 6.002 = ?$ Answer: 85

```
                            8 5.
               6.0 0 2 ) 5 1 0.1 7 0
                         4 8 0 1 6
                           3 0 0 1 0
                           3 0 0 1 0
```

Name _____ Date _____

Exercise 4.6 Set A

Find the exact answer in each division problem that follows.

1. $4\overline{)50.4}$

2. $6\overline{)82.2}$

3. $7.2\overline{)58.608}$

4. $3.7\overline{)34.447}$

5. $0.65\overline{)48.1}$

6. $0.54\overline{)51.3}$

7. $84\overline{)1.554}$

8. $66\overline{)1.155}$

9. $0.01636 \div 4.09$

10. $0.02807 \div 8.02$

11. $21.08 \div .0034$

12. $21.84 \div .0026$

13. $243.36 \div 6.24$

14. $488.36 \div 8.42$

15. $1.1 \div 3.2$

16. $1.4 \div 6.4$

1. _____

2. _____

3. _____

4. _____

5. _____

6. _____

7. _____

8. _____

9. _____

10. _____

11. _____

12. _____

13. _____

14. _____

15. _____

16. _____

Exercise 4.6 Set B

Find the exact answer in each division problem that follows.

1. $3\overline{)50.7}$

2. $5\overline{)68.5}$

3. $6.4\overline{)46.272}$

4. $8.3\overline{)76.028}$

5. $0.74\overline{)18.5}$

6. $0.62\overline{)27.9}$

7. $58\overline{)3.741}$

8. $72\overline{)1.044}$

9. $0.06018 \div 7.08$

10. $0.05134 \div 6.04$

11. $13.16 \div .0028$

12. $35.28 \div .0036$

13. $206.64 \div 3.28$

14. $355.68 \div 4.56$

15. $1.3 \div 3.2$

16. $2.8 \div 6.4$

1. _____

2. _____

3. _____

4. _____

5. _____

6. _____

7. _____

8. _____

9. _____

10. _____

11. _____

12. _____

13. _____

14. _____

15. _____

16. _____

4.7 Dividing Decimals—Rounding Off Answers

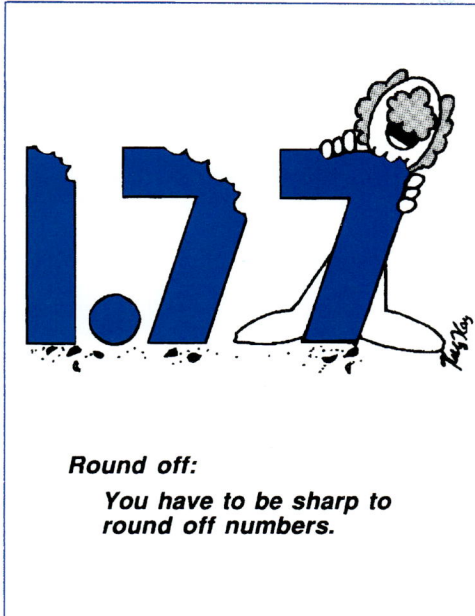

Round off:

You have to be sharp to round off numbers.

Frequently when dividing decimal numbers, the answer seems to go on and on. Consider the problem:

$$\begin{array}{r} 1.7\,7\,7\ \ldots = 1.\overline{7} \\ 9)\overline{1\,6.0\,0\,0} \\ \underline{9} \\ 7\,0 \\ \underline{6\,3} \\ 7\,0 \\ \underline{6\,3} \\ 7\,0 \\ \underline{6\,3} \end{array}$$

(The dash over the 7 indicates that it repeats forever in the decimal.)

You could attach zeros forever and never get an exact answer. Because of this and because long decimal answers are difficult to work with, the answers to division problems are frequently rounded off to a number that is close to the exact answer.

So $16 \div 9 = 1.7777\ \ldots$, but rounded off to the nearest

tenth it equals 1.8,
hundredth it equals 1.78,
thousandth it equals 1.778.

Depending on the degree of accuracy asked for, the answers will vary. Yet each answer is close to the actual answer of $1.\overline{7}$.

Example 1

Rounded off to the nearest hundredth, $4.29 \div .045 = ?$

In order to round off the answer to the nearest hundredth, you must carry out the division one digit past the hundredths place. Zeros were attached so that the division could be done.

$$\begin{array}{r} 9\,5.3\,3\,3 \approx 95.33 \text{ (rounded to the hundredths place)} \\ .0\,4\,5)\overline{4.2\,9\,0,0\,0\,0} \\ \underline{4\,0\,5} \\ 2\,4\,0 \\ \underline{2\,2\,5} \\ 1\,5\,0 \\ \underline{1\,3\,5} \\ 1\,5\,0 \\ \underline{1\,3\,5} \\ 1\,5\,0 \\ \underline{1\,3\,5} \end{array}$$

Example 2

Find $7.8 \div 5.06$ rounded off to three decimal places.

Perform the division one digit past the third decimal place.

$$
\begin{array}{r}
1.5\,4\,1\,5 \approx 1.542 \text{ (rounded to the third decimal place)} \\
5.0\,6\,\overline{)\,7.8\,0\,0\,0\,0\,0} \\
5\,0\,6 \\
\overline{2\,7\,4\,0} \\
2\,5\,3\,0 \\
\overline{2\,1\,0\,0} \\
2\,0\,2\,4 \\
\overline{7\,6\,0} \\
5\,0\,6 \\
\overline{2\,5\,4\,0} \\
2\,5\,3\,0
\end{array}
$$

Example 3

Find $16.302 \div 7.6$ accurate to the nearest tenth.

Carry out the division one digit past the tenths place.

$$
\begin{array}{r}
2.1\,4 \approx 2.1 \quad \text{(correct to the nearest tenth)} \\
7.6\,\overline{)\,1\,6.3\,0\,2} \\
1\,5\,2 \\
\overline{1\,1\,0} \\
7\,6 \\
\overline{3\,4\,2} \\
3\,0\,4
\end{array}
$$

In order to round off the answer correctly when dividing, remember to carry out the division process one place past the degree of accuracy asked for.

Problem 1:   Find $1.54 \div 4.27$ correct to two decimal places.   Answer: 0.36

$$
\begin{array}{r}
.3\,6\,0 \\
4.2\,7\,\overline{)\,1.5\,4\,0\,0\,0} \\
1\,2\,8\,1 \\
\overline{2\,5\,9\,0} \\
2\,5\,6\,2 \\
\overline{2\,8\,0} \\
0
\end{array}
$$

Problem 2:   Find $0.175 \div 3.023$ accurate to the nearest thousandth.   Answer: .058

$$
\begin{array}{r}
.0\,5\,7\,8 \\
3.0\,2\,3\,\overline{)\,.1\,7\,5\,0\,0\,0\,0} \\
1\,5\,1\,1\,5 \\
\overline{2\,3\,8\,5\,0} \\
2\,1\,1\,6\,1 \\
\overline{2\,6\,8\,9\,0} \\
2\,4\,1\,8\,4
\end{array}
$$

Exercise 4.7 Set A

In problems 1–6, find quotients rounded to the nearest tenth.

1. $8.5 \div 7$

2. $8.4 \div 9$

3. $3.006 \div 0.36$

4. $3.096 \div 0.48$

5. $608 \div 2.4$

6. $854 \div 4.2$

1. _____

2. _____

3. _____

4. _____

5. _____

6. _____

In problems 7–10, find quotients rounded to 2 decimal places.

7. $8.43 \div 6$

8. $7.24 \div 5$

9. $9.1 \div 0.289$

10. $6.3 \div 0.361$

7. _____

8. _____

9. _____

10. _____

In problems 11–14, find quotients accurate to the thousandths place.

11. $11 \div 66$

12. $49 \div 81$

13. $28.89 \div 7.205$

14. $31.6 \div 6.308$

11. _____

12. _____

13. _____

14. _____

Exercise 4.7 Set B

In problems 1–6, find quotients rounded to the nearest tenth.

1. $7.6 \div 9$

2. $9.6 \div 5$

3. $2.511 \div 0.54$

4. $3.706 \div 0.68$

5. $798 \div 1.8$

6. $728 \div 2.1$

1. _____

2. _____

3. _____

4. _____

5. _____

6. _____

In problems 7–10, find quotients rounded to 2 decimal places.

7. $2.56 \div 7$

8. $6.79 \div 9$

9. $5.2 \div 0.169$

10. $8.6 \div 0.121$

7. _____

8. _____

9. _____

10. _____

In problems 11–14, find quotients accurate to the thousandths place.

11. $21 \div 36$

12. $35 \div 75$

13. $24.7 \div 8.206$

14. $26.49 \div 4.408$

11. _____

12. _____

13. _____

14. _____

4.8 Multiplying and Dividing by Numbers that End in Zeros

If you multiply and divide numbers that end in zeros using the methods explained so far in this chapter, you will find yourself spending much of the time placing zeros in the right columns. The following examples are worked out using those methods.

Example 1

$5.37 \times 20{,}000 = ?$

```
          5.3 7
     × 2 0 0 0 0
          0 0 0
        0 0 0
      0 0 0
    0 0 0
    1 0 7 4
    1 0 7 4 0 0.0 0
```
Thus, $5.37 \times 20{,}000 = 107{,}400.$

Example 2

$83.4 \div 200{,}000 = ?$

```
                0.0 0 0 4 1 7
    2 0 0 0 0 ) 8 3.4 0 0 0 0 0
                8 0 0 0 0 0
                  3 4 0 0 0 0
                  2 0 0 0 0 0
                  1 4 0 0 0 0 0
                  1 4 0 0 0 0 0
```
Thus, $83.4 \div 200{,}000 \div 0.000417.$

Most of the effort in these examples involved positioning zeros. There are shorter and more efficient ways to handle these zeros.

Multiplying by Numbers that End in Zeros

Let's look at Example 1 again. You can move the multiplier to the right as we did in Section 1.8. Since there are four zeros in the multiplier, we move it four places to the right.

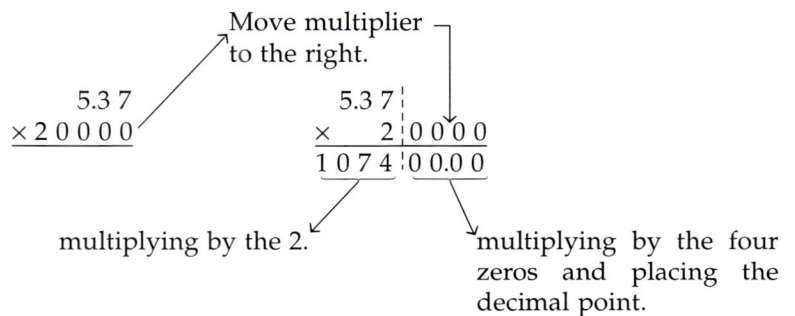

Move multiplier to the right.

```
    5.3 7              5.3 7
 × 2 0 0 0 0        ×     2 0 0 0 0
                   1 0 7 4 0 0.0 0
```

multiplying by the 2.   multiplying by the four zeros and placing the decimal point.

Use this technique to find the product in the next example.

Example 3

$0.764 \times 46{,}000 = ?$

$$
\begin{array}{r}
0.7\,6\,4 \\
\times \quad 4\,6\,0\,0\,0 \\
\hline
4\,5\,8\,4\,0\,0\,0 \\
3\,0\,5\,6 \\
\hline
3\,5\,1\,4\,4.0\,0\,0
\end{array}
$$

The multiplier is moved three places to the right so that the zeros can be handled more efficiently.

The answer has three decimal places. Thus, $0.764 \times 46{,}000 = 35{,}144$.

Problem 1: $53.5 \times 10^5 = ?$

Answer: 5,350,000

$$10^5 = 10 \times 10 \times 10 \times 10 \times 10$$
$$= 100{,}000$$

Moving multiplier five places to the right, we get:

$$
\begin{array}{r}
5\,3.5 \\
\times \quad 1\,0\,0\,0\,0\,0 \\
\hline
5\,3\,5\,0\,0\,0\,0.0
\end{array}
$$

Problem 2: $74.66 \times 7000 = ?$

Answer: 522,620

Moving multiplier three places to the right, we get:

$$
\begin{array}{r}
7\,4.6\,6 \\
7\,0\,0\,0 \\
\hline
5\,2\,2\,6\,2\,0.0\,0
\end{array}
$$

Problem 3: $3.671 \times 2400 = ?$

Answer: 8810.4

Moving multiplier two places to the right, we get:

$$
\begin{array}{r}
3.6\,7\,1 \\
\times \quad 2\,4\,0\,0 \\
\hline
1\,4\,6\,8\,4\,0\,0 \\
7\,3\,4\,2 \\
\hline
8\,8\,1\,0.4\,0\,0
\end{array}
$$

Dividing by Numbers that End in Zeros

When dividing numbers, the division process becomes more involved if the divisor has many digits. When the divisor contains many zeros (as in Example 2), the zeros seem to make the problem more difficult. There is, however, a technique which simplifies a problem in which the divisor ends in zeros. It involves moving the decimal points to get an equivalent problem. Let's take another look at Example 2.

$$83.4 \div 200{,}000 = \frac{83.4}{200{,}000}$$

A division problem can be changed into a fraction.

$$= \frac{.00083.4}{2.00{,}00}$$

The numerator and denominator can both be divided by 100,000 resulting in moving the decimal points five places to the left.

$$= \frac{.000834}{2}$$

$$= 0.000417$$

The decimal point is moved five places in order to eliminate the zeros at the end of the divisor. The result is an easier division problem.

This example gives us a technique for simplifying a division problem in which the divisor ends in zeros. We can eliminate the zeros in the divisor by moving the decimal point to the left and then moving the decimal point the same number of places to the left in the dividend. The following examples will clarify this technique.

Example 4

$91{,}945 \div 3500 = ?$

$$3500\overline{)919.45}$$

To eliminate the zeros in the divisor, move the decimal point two places to the left. Do the same with the decimal point in the dividend. Now find $919.45 \div 35$.

$$
\begin{array}{r}
26.27 \\
35\overline{)919.45} \\
\underline{70} \\
219 \\
\underline{210} \\
94 \\
\underline{70} \\
245 \\
\underline{245}
\end{array}
$$

Thus, $91{,}945 \div 3500 = 26.27$.

Example 5

$174.34 \div 460{,}000 = ?$

$$460000\overline{)174.34}$$

To eliminate the zeros in the divisor, move the decimal point four places to the left. Do the same with the decimal point in the dividend. Notice that it is necessary to put a zero place holder to the left of the dividend. Now find $.017434 \div 46$.

$$
\begin{array}{r}
.000379 \\
46\overline{).017434} \\
\underline{138} \\
363 \\
\underline{322} \\
414 \\
\underline{414}
\end{array}
$$

Thus, $174.34 \div 460{,}000 = 0.000379$.

Problem 4: $23{,}720 \div 800 = ?$

Answer: 29.65

Move decimal points in the divisor and dividend.

$$800\overline{)237.20}$$

$$\begin{array}{r} 29.65 \\ 8\overline{)237.20} \\ \underline{16} \\ 77 \\ \underline{72} \\ 52 \\ \underline{48} \\ 40 \\ \underline{40} \end{array}$$

Problem 5: $57.6 \div 10^4 = ?$

Answer: 0.00576

$10^4 = 10 \times 10 \times 10 \times 10$
$ = 10{,}000$

Move decimal points in the divisor and dividend.

$$10000\overline{)57.6}$$

$$\begin{array}{r} .00576 \\ 1\overline{).00576} \end{array}$$

Problem 6:   Find $711{,}124 \div 376{,}000$ rounded to two decimal places.

Answer: ≈ 1.89

Move decimal points in the divisor and dividend.

$$376000\overline{)711124}$$

$$\begin{array}{r} 1.891 \approx 1.89 \\ 376\overline{)711.124} \\ \underline{376} \\ 3351 \\ \underline{3008} \\ 3432 \\ \underline{3384} \\ 484 \\ \underline{376} \\ 108 \end{array}$$

The techniques explained in this section will increase accuracy when multiplying and dividing by numbers that end in zeros. The exercise sets that follow will give you practice in using these techniques.

Exercise 4.8 Set A

In problems 1–8, find the indicated products.

1. 4.36×1000 2. $5.23 \times 10{,}000$

3. $47.617 \times 20{,}000$ 4. 53.109×4000

5. $0.093 \times 42{,}000$ 6. $0.072 \times 63{,}000$

7. 3.127×10^5 8. 4.173×10^6

1. _____

2. _____

3. _____

4. _____

5. _____

6. _____

7. _____

8. _____

In problems 9–16, find the exact quotients.

9. $54.3 \div 100$ 10. $75.6 \div 100$

11. $700 \div 2000$ 12. $1200 \div 3000$

13. $1957.3 \div 370{,}000$ 14. $1939.6 \div 260{,}000$

15. $376.5 \div 10^5$ 16. $408.7 \div 10^6$

9. _____

10. _____

11. _____

12. _____

13. _____

14. _____

15. _____

16. _____

Exercise 4.8 Set B

In problems 1–8, find the indicated products.

1. $8.17 \times 100{,}000$

2. 6.04×1000

1. _____

2. _____

3. 92.575×3000

4. $84.019 \times 200{,}000$

3. _____

4. _____

5. $0.072 \times 54{,}000$

6. $0.051 \times 76{,}000$

5. _____

6. _____

7. 7.263×10^6

8. 6.108×10^5

7. _____

8. _____

In problems 9–16, find the exact quotients.

9. $82.3 \div 100$

10. $64.5 \div 100$

9. _____

10. _____

11. $2400 \div 6000$

12. $2100 \div 7000$

11. _____

12. _____

13. $1982.4 \div 420{,}000$

14. $1263.6 \div 360{,}000$

13. _____

14. _____

15. $510.3 \div 10^6$

16. $827.4 \div 10^5$

15. _____

16. _____

4.9 Converting Fractions and Decimals

To convert a fraction to a decimal you must remember that the fraction line indicates that you divide the numerator by the denominator.

Example 1

Express $\dfrac{3}{4}$ as an exact decimal.

$$\dfrac{3}{4} = \begin{array}{r} .75 \\ 4\overline{)3.00} \\ \underline{2\,8} \\ 20 \\ \underline{20} \end{array}$$

divisor

Thus, $\dfrac{3}{4}$ is the decimal 0.75.

Example 2

Express $\dfrac{8}{12}$ as a decimal rounded to two decimal places.

$$\dfrac{8}{12} = \begin{array}{r} .666\;\ldots = 0.\overline{6} \approx 0.67 \\ 12\overline{)8.000} \\ \underline{7\,2} \\ 80 \\ \underline{72} \\ 80 \\ \underline{72} \end{array}$$

divisor

Thus, $\dfrac{8}{12} \approx 0.67$.

Example 3

Express $2\dfrac{3}{5}$ as a decimal number.

$$2\dfrac{3}{5} = \dfrac{13}{5} = \begin{array}{r} 2.6 \\ 5\overline{)13.0} \\ \underline{10} \\ 3\,0 \\ \underline{3\,0} \end{array}$$

Thus, $\dfrac{23}{5} = 2.6$.

Problem 1:   Express $\dfrac{7}{8}$ as an exact decimal.

Answer: 0.875

$$\begin{array}{r} .875 \\ 8\overline{)7.000} \\ \underline{6\,4} \\ 60 \\ \underline{56} \\ 40 \\ \underline{40} \end{array}$$

Problem 2:   Express $4\frac{3}{17}$ as a decimal accurate to the tenths place.   Answer: 4.2

$$4\frac{3}{17}=\frac{71}{17}= \begin{array}{r} 4.17 \\ 17\overline{)71.00} \\ \underline{68} \\ 3\,0 \\ \underline{1\,7} \\ 1\,30 \\ \underline{1\,19} \end{array}$$

Some commonly used relationships between fractions and decimals are listed in the chart below.

> ### Fraction—Decimal Equivalents
>
> $\dfrac{1}{2}=.5$ $\dfrac{1}{4}=.25$ $\dfrac{3}{4}=.75$ $\dfrac{1}{3}=.\overline{3}\approx.33$ $\dfrac{2}{3}=.\overline{6}\approx.67$

Changing Decimals to Fractions

To convert a decimal number to a fraction you must remember the place values of digits to the right of the decimal point. As you go to the right from the decimal point, they are tenths, hundredths, thousandths, ten-thousandths, etc. Using those place values and the way you read decimal numbers in our number system, you can easily convert decimals to fractions.

For example: 0.9 reads "nine tenths": $=\dfrac{9}{10}$

0.35 reads "thirty-five hundredths" $=\dfrac{35}{100}=\dfrac{7}{20}$

0.052 reads "fifty-two thousandths" $=\dfrac{52}{1000}=\dfrac{13}{250}$

If there is a whole number before the decimal point, you really have a mixed number.

For example: 5.3 reads "five and three tenths" $=5\dfrac{3}{10}$

18.07 reads "eighteen and seven hundredths" $=18\dfrac{7}{100}$

Problems: Convert the following to reduced fractions or mixed numbers: Answers:

3. 0.25

4. 0.172

5. 3.7

6. 45.02

7. 100.003

3. $0.25=\dfrac{25}{100}=\dfrac{1}{4}$

4. $0.172=\dfrac{172}{1000}=\dfrac{43}{250}$

5. $3.7=3\dfrac{7}{10}$

6. $45.02=45\dfrac{2}{100}=45\dfrac{1}{50}$

7. $100.003=100\dfrac{3}{1000}$

Exercise 4.9 Set A

In problems 1–6, convert each fraction to exact decimals.

1. $\dfrac{3}{5}$

2. $\dfrac{7}{14}$

3. $\dfrac{5}{8}$

4. $\dfrac{1}{16}$

5. $\dfrac{41}{32}$

6. $\dfrac{37}{32}$

1. _____

2. _____

3. _____

4. _____

5. _____

6. _____

In problems 7–12, convert each fraction to 3 digit decimals.

7. $\dfrac{6}{11}$

8. $\dfrac{5}{6}$

9. $1\dfrac{6}{7}$

10. $2\dfrac{4}{9}$

11. $23\dfrac{2}{3}$

12. $37\dfrac{7}{9}$

7. _____

8. _____

9. _____

10. _____

11. _____

12. _____

In problems 13–20, convert each to reduced fractions or mixed numbers.

13. 0.6

14. 0.4

15. 0.62

16. 0.74

17. 0.0425

18. 0.0475

19. 4.001

20. 3.009

13. _____

14. _____

15. _____

16. _____

17. _____

18. _____

19. _____

20. _____

Exercise 4.9 Set B

In problems 1–6, convert each fraction to exact decimals.

1. $\dfrac{4}{5}$ 2. $\dfrac{9}{12}$

3. $\dfrac{3}{8}$ 4. $\dfrac{5}{16}$

5. $\dfrac{39}{32}$ 6. $\dfrac{35}{32}$

1. _____

2. _____

3. _____

4. _____

5. _____

6. _____

In problems 7–12, convert each fraction to 3 digit decimals.

7. $\dfrac{5}{9}$ 8. $\dfrac{4}{7}$

9. $2\dfrac{3}{13}$ 10. $3\dfrac{5}{11}$

11. $44\dfrac{1}{6}$ 12. $32\dfrac{1}{7}$

7. _____

8. _____

9. _____

10. _____

11. _____

12. _____

In problems 13–20, convert each to reduced fractions or mixed numbers.

13. 0.2   14. 0.6

15. 0.86   16. 0.98

17. 0.0375   18. 0.0275

19. 1.007   20. 2.003

13. _____

14. _____

15. _____

16. _____

17. _____

18. _____

19. _____

20. _____

4.10 Comparing Decimals

507
50.7
5.07
0.0507
?

If deciding which number is the largest gives you trouble, you missed the point of the section.

In Section 3.13, you learned to compare the size of fractions by changing them to fractions with common denominators. Decimal numbers that have the same number of decimal places have the same place value. They actually represent fractions with a common denominator.

For example, consider the decimals 0.34,   0.07,   0.18,   0.91:

$$0.34 = \frac{34}{100}$$

$$0.07 = \frac{7}{100}$$

$$0.18 = \frac{18}{100}$$

$$0.91 = \frac{91}{100}$$

They have the same number of decimal places and represent fractions with common denominators.

The method, then, for comparing the size of decimal numbers is to represent each with the same number of decimal places. Those with a larger number after the decimal point will have a larger fractional part.

Example 1

Which is larger: 0.370 or 0.307?

They both have the same number of decimal places, and since 370 > 307, 0.370 is larger than 0.307.

Example 2

Arrange in order from largest to smallest: 0.1,   0.0195,   0.019,   0.109,   0.19

Since the greatest number of decimal places is four places in the number 0.0195, we want to get four decimal places in each number by attaching zeros after the decimal points. Then, since 1900 > 1090 > 1000 > 195 > 190, the order from largest (on top) to smallest is:

$$0.19 = .1900$$
$$0.109 = .1090$$
$$0.1 = .1000$$
$$0.0195 = .0195$$
$$0.019 = .0190$$

Example 3

Arrange in order from largest to smallest: 1.23,   1.203,   1,   1.3,   1.2

Since the greatest number of decimal places is three places in the number 1.203, we can get three decimal places in each number by attaching zeros after the decimal points. Then, since 1.300 > 1.230 > 1.203 > 1.200 > 1.000, the order from largest (on top) to smallest is:

$$1.3 = 1.300$$
$$1.23 = 1.230$$
$$1.203 = 1.203$$
$$1.2 = 1.200$$
$$1 = 1.000$$

Problem 1:   Which is larger: 0.078 or 0.08?

Answer: 0.08

$$0.078 = 0.078$$
$$0.08 = 0.080$$

Since 80 is greater than 78, then 0.08 is larger.

Problem 2:   Arrange in order from largest to smallest: 3.4, 4.3, 4.03, 4.003, 3.0004

Answer: (largest on top)

$$4.3 = 4.3000$$
$$4.03 = 4.0300$$
$$4.003 = 4.0030$$
$$3.4 = 3.4000$$
$$3.0004 = 3.0004$$

Problem 3:   Which is the largest: $\frac{5}{8}$, 0.8, $\frac{5}{6}$, or 0.75?

Answer: $\frac{5}{6}$

Change each to a decimal.

$$\frac{5}{6} = .8\overline{3}$$

$$.8 = .800$$

$$.75 = .750$$

$$\frac{5}{8} = .625$$

$.8\overline{3}$ is the largest decimal number.

Name _____   Date _____

Exercise 4.10 Set A

In problems 1–10, which quantity is larger?

1. 0.5 or 0.6?   1. _____

2. 0.57 or 0.75?   2. _____

3. 2.076 or 1.067?   3. _____

4. 5.092 or 5.009?   4. _____

5. 0.6 or 0.06?   5. _____

6. 0.162 or 0.1062?   6. _____

7. 3.4002 or 3.402?   7. _____

8. 76.125 or 76.1025?   8. _____

9. $\frac{2}{3}$ or .66?   9. _____

10. $3\frac{1}{4}$ or 3.125?   10. _____

In problems 11–15, arrange the numbers in order from largest to smallest.

11. 0.7, 0.76, 0.076, 0.706, 0.6   11. _____

12. 0.54, 0.4, 0.5, 0.504, 0.054   12. _____

13. 3.12, 2.13, 2, 3.102, 2.3   13. _____

14. $\frac{3}{4}$, $\frac{3}{5}$, .7, .65, .076   14. _____

15. $1\frac{1}{3}$, 1.8, $1\frac{1}{2}$, 1.258, 1.625   15. _____

Exercise 4.10 Set B

In problems 1–10, which quantity is larger?

1. 0.9 or 0.8?

1. _____

2. 0.89 or 0.98?

2. _____

3. 3.1205 or 3.0125?

3. _____

4. 12.076 or 12.706?

4. _____

5. 0.07 or 0.7?

5. _____

6. 0.129 or 0.1029?

6. _____

7. 3.5007 or 3.507?

7. _____

8. 84.306 or 84?

8. _____

9. $\frac{3}{8}$ or .4?

9. _____

10. $4\frac{1}{3}$ or 4.033?

10. _____

In problems 11–15, arrange the numbers in order from largest to smallest.

11. 0.37,   0.037,   0.07,   0.3, 0.307

11. _____

12. 0.9,   0.901,   0.091,   0.9001,   0.19

12. _____

13. 4.3,   4.03,   3.4,   3.04,   3.4003

13. _____

14. $\frac{4}{5}$,   .755,   .82, $\frac{5}{8}$,   .5

14. _____

15. 2.66, $2\frac{2}{3}$,   2.7, $2\frac{7}{8}$,   2.78

15. _____

4.11 Operating with Both Fractions and Decimals

The last skill to develop in this unit involves problems that combine both fractional and decimal numbers. When doing problems of this type, you must first remember to use the proper order of operations as covered in Section 2.8.

> ## Order of Operations
>
> 1. Do any operations inside parentheses.
> 2. Do the powers and square roots.
> 3. Do the multiplications and divisions from left to right.
> 4. Do the additions and subtractions from left to right.

Secondly, you must decide whether to do the problem using only fractions, only decimals, or a combination of fractions and decimals. Consider the problem: $5\frac{3}{4} \times 18.8$; it can be done in three different ways.

1. Using only fractions:

$$5\frac{3}{4} \times 18.8 = 5\frac{3}{4} \times 18\frac{8}{10}$$

$$= 5\frac{3}{4} \times 18\frac{4}{5}$$

$$= \frac{23}{\overset{}{\underset{2}{\cancel{4}}}} \times \frac{\overset{47}{\cancel{94}}}{5}$$

$$= \frac{1081}{10}$$

$$= 108\frac{1}{10}$$

2. Using only decimals:

$$5\frac{3}{4} \times 18.8 = 5.75 \times 18.8$$

$$
\begin{array}{r}
5.7\,5 \\
\times 1\,8.8 \\
\hline
4\,6\,0\,0 \\
4\,6\,0\,0 \\
5\,7\,5 \\
\hline
1\,0\,8.1\,0\,0 = 108.1
\end{array}
$$

3. Using both fractions and decimals:

$$5\frac{3}{4} \times 18.8 = \frac{23}{4} \times \frac{18.8}{1}$$

$$= \frac{23}{\underset{1}{\cancel{4}}} \times \frac{\overset{4.7}{\cancel{18.8}}}{1}$$

$$= \frac{108.1}{1} = 108.1$$

As you can see, we obtained the same answer no matter which way we did the problem. In deciding which method to use, the following suggestions may be helpful.

Operating with Both Fractions and Decimals

1. If the fractions can be converted into exact decimals, work the problem using decimal numbers.
2. If the fractions can not be converted into exact decimals, work the problem using fractions.

Example 1

$$(1.5)^2 + 4\frac{3}{5} \times 6 = ?$$

Note: $\frac{3}{5}$ is the exact decimal 0.6:

$$\begin{array}{r} .6 \\ 5\overline{)3.0} \\ \underline{3\,0} \end{array}$$

$$(1.5)^2 + 4\frac{3}{5} \times 6 = (1.5)^2 + 4.6 \times 6$$
$$= 2.25 + 4.6 \times 6$$
$$= 2.25 + 27.6$$
$$= 29.85$$

Example 2

$$3 - 6\frac{2}{3} \div 2.4 = ?$$

Note: $\frac{2}{3} = .\overline{6}$ is not an exact decimal, work with fractions.

$$3 - 6\frac{2}{3} \div 2.4 = 3 - \frac{20}{3} \div 2\frac{4}{10}$$
$$= 3 - \frac{20}{3} \div 2\frac{2}{5}$$
$$= 3 - \frac{20}{3} \div \frac{12}{5}$$
$$= 3 - \frac{\overset{5}{\cancel{20}}}{\cancel{3}} \times \frac{5}{\underset{3}{\cancel{12}}}$$
$$= 3 - \frac{25}{9}$$
$$= \frac{27}{9} - \frac{25}{9} = \frac{2}{9}$$

Even with those suggestions some trial and error might be necessary to determine the easiest way to do a particular problem.

Problem 1: $32.2 \times \left(3\frac{1}{2} - 2\frac{3}{7}\right) = ?$

Answer: 34.5

$$32.2 \times \left(\frac{7}{2} - \frac{17}{7}\right) =$$
$$32.2 \times \left(\frac{49}{14} - \frac{34}{14}\right) =$$
$$\overset{2.3}{\cancel{32.2}} \times \frac{15}{\underset{1}{\cancel{14}}} = 34.5$$

Exercise 4.11 Set A

1. $14.4 \div 4\frac{1}{2}$

2. $19.2 \div 1\frac{3}{5}$

3. $3\frac{3}{4} \times 5.6$

4. $1\frac{5}{8} \times 7.2$

5. $\left(1\frac{1}{2}\right)^2 + 2\frac{2}{3} \times 1.2$

6. $\left(2\frac{1}{3}\right)^2 + 3\frac{1}{3} \times 3.1$

7. $0.25 \times (2 + 4 \div 12)$

8. $0.75 \times (2 + 3 \div 15)$

9. $\frac{1}{2} \times 3^3 - 5.3 \times .031$

10. $\frac{1}{4} \times 5^2 - 7.2 \times .15$

11. $80 \times \frac{1}{4} \div 5 + 8.25$

12. $80 \div \frac{1}{4} \times 5 + 8.25$

13. $\frac{1}{3} \times \sqrt{16} + 10 \div 2.5$

14. $\frac{1}{6} \times \sqrt{49} + 21 \div 3.5$

15. $\frac{3}{5} \times 10^3 \div (1.25 \times 10^2)$

16. $\frac{3}{4} \times 10^4 \div (0.8 \times 10^2)$

17. $6 \times 3\frac{2}{3} + 12 \times 4\frac{1}{2}$

18. $6\frac{1}{2} \times (5 - 3.25)$

1. _____

2. _____

3. _____

4. _____

5. _____

6. _____

7. _____

8. _____

9. _____

10. _____

11. _____

12. _____

13. _____

14. _____

15. _____

16. _____

17. _____

18. _____

Exercise 4.11 Set B

1. $22.4 \div 3\frac{1}{2}$

2. $36 \div 2\frac{2}{5}$

3. $4\frac{3}{5} \times 6.5$

4. $2\frac{1}{4} \times 5.2$

5. $\left(1\frac{1}{5}\right)^2 + 1\frac{1}{6} \times 4.8$

6. $\left(3\frac{1}{2}\right)^2 + 2\frac{1}{2} \times 3.7$

7. $0.5 \times (3 + 2 \div 6)$

8. $0.75 \times (4 + 4 \div 16)$

9. $\frac{3}{4} \times 8^2 - 4.2 \times 0.35$

10. $\frac{1}{2} \times 7^2 - 8.5 \times 0.46$

11. $100 \times \frac{1}{5} \div 4 + 6.35$

12. $100 \div \frac{1}{5} \times 4 + 6.35$

13. $\frac{2}{3} \times \sqrt{25} + 36 \div 4.5$

14. $\frac{5}{6} \times \sqrt{4} + 39 \div 6.5$

15. $\frac{3}{4} \times 10^3 \div (0.6 \times 10^2)$

16. $\frac{1}{2} \times 10^2 \div (0.008 \times 10^4)$

17. $16 \times 4\frac{1}{8} + 6 \times 3\frac{1}{2}$

18. $3\frac{1}{4} \times (7 - 4.5)$

1. _____

2. _____

3. _____

4. _____

5. _____

6. _____

7. _____

8. _____

9. _____

10. _____

11. _____

12. _____

13. _____

14. _____

15. _____

16. _____

17. _____

18. _____

4.12 Applications Involving Decimals

"*Balancing my checkbook is fun.*"

Word problems involving decimals can also be solved using the read, analyze, and solve procedure. When working with decimals, you may have to round off answers, especially when working with dollars and cents.

Example 1

Johnny Salo in 1929 ran 3665 miles from New York to Los Angeles in 79 days. How many miles did he average per day?

Analyze: Miles *per* day means miles *divided* by days.

Solve:
$$
\begin{array}{r}
46.392 \approx 46.39 \text{ miles} \\
79\overline{)3665.000} \\
\underline{316} \\
505 \\
\underline{474} \\
31\,0 \\
\underline{23\,7} \\
7\,30 \\
\underline{7\,11} \\
190 \\
\underline{158}
\end{array}
$$

Example 2

At the start of the month you had a checking account balance of $25.36. During the month you made a deposit of $245.08 and wrote checks for $12.75, $25.00, $132.50, $18.64, and $5.76. What was the balance in your account at the end of the month?

Analyze: You must add the checks and subtract that amount from the total of the balance and deposits.

Solve:

checks:	$ 12.75	initial balance:	$25.36
	25.00	deposit:	+ 245.08
	132.50		$270.44
	18.64	checks:	−194.65
+	5.76	final balance:	$ 75.79
	$194.65		

Thus, the checking account balance was $75.79.

Example 3

Hurts Car Rental charges $16.75 a day and 16.5¢ a mile. How much would you pay for one day if you drove 225 miles?

Analyze: Find the cost for the miles driven by multiplying 16.5¢ times 225 miles. Add that result to $16.75.

Solve: 16.5¢ = $.165 (changing the cents to dollars)

mileage
$$
\begin{array}{r}
\$.1\,6\,5 \\
\times\,2\,2\,5 \\
\hline
8\,2\,5 \\
3\,3\,0 \\
3\,3\,0 \\
\hline
\$3\,7\,.1\,2\,5 \approx \$37.13
\end{array}
$$

total cost:
$$
\begin{array}{r}
\$16.75 \\
+\ 37.13 \\
\hline
53.88
\end{array}
$$

$ 3 7 .1 2 5 ≈ $37.13 (rounded off to the nearest cent—two decimal places)

Example 4

You work for a department store and earn $5.56 per hour and time-and-a-half for overtime. If during one week you work 40 regular hours and 12 overtime hours, what are your earnings for the week?

Analyze:	Solve:
1. Get regular earnings by multiplying 40 × $5.56.	1. 40 × $5.56 = $222.40
2. Determine hourly overtime wage. Time-and-a-half means your hourly wage plus $\frac{1}{2}$ of that wage. You can find that overtime wage by multiplying the regular wage by 1.5.	2. 1.5 × $5.56 = $8.34 per hour
3. Get overtime earnings by multiplying 12 × $6.84.	3. 12 × $8.34 = $100.08
4. Add the regular and overtime earnings together.	4. $222.40 + $100.08 = $322.48

Example 5

At the beginning of the week when you filled up your gas tank your odometer read 52,756.8. At the end of the week you filled up again. Your odometer then read 53,172.1 and you put in 18.2 gallons of gas. To the nearest tenth of a mile, how many miles did you travel per gallon of gas?

Analyze:	Solve:

1. Determine the number of miles driven by subtracting the odometer readings.	1. 53172.1
	  −52756.8
	  —————
	   415.3

2. Miles for each gallon implies that you divide the number of miles by the number of gallons.	2. 415.3 ÷ 18.2 ≈ 22.8

Problem 1: To carpet a room you need 16 square yards of carpet and 16 square yards of padding. If the carpet costs $18.95 a sq yd, the pad costs $4.50 a sq yd, installation fees are $100.00, and sales tax is $23.35, find the total cost to carpet the room.

Answer: $498.55

Carpet: 16 × $18.95	=	$303.20
Pad: 16 × $4.50	=	72.00
Sales tax:	=	23.35
Installation:	=	100.00
Total:	=	$498.55

Name _____   Date _____

Exercise 4.12 Set A

1. You started the week with $22.56 balance in your checking account. During the week you made a deposit of $415.25 and wrote checks of $47.35, $10.00, $239.50, and $22.98. What was your balance at the end of the week?

1. _____

2. What is the balance in your savings account, if you started with $256.37; made deposits of $67.89, $45.00, $20.50, $176.67, and $80.00; withdrew $95.00; and received interest of $17.65?

2. _____

3. By comparing the cost per 1000 miles of warranty, determine which is the better buy: a $62.95 tire with a 50,000 mile warranty or a tire with the same ratings that costs $57.50 and has a 40,000 mile warranty?

3. _____

4. Which is the better buy: 7 ounces of toothpaste priced at $1.37 or 5.5 ounces of the same brand priced at $1.04?

4. _____

5. The odometer reading in your car when you filled it with gas was 39247.1. The next time you filled up your car, it read 39762.4 and you put 18.3 gallons of gas in the tank. How many miles did your car travel per gallon of gas?

5. _____

6. A car uses about 1.6 ounces of gasoline when it idles for one minute. How much gasoline does a car use while idling for 45 minutes?

6. _____

7. During a week you work 40 regular hours and 7 overtime hours. If your regular wage is $5.96 per hour and you get time-and-a-half for overtime, what is your gross income for the week?

7. _____

8. The amounts you spend for lunch at school during the week are as follows: Mon., $2.79; Tue., $3.05; Wed., $2.56; Thu., $3.89; and Fri., $3.58. What is the average amount spent on lunch during the week?

8. _____

9. If a long distance phone call costs 85¢ for the first 3 minutes and 17¢ for each additional minute, how much does a 30 minute call cost?

9. _____

10. On your utility bill, you are charged 10.95¢ per kilowatt-hour of electricity and 50.4¢ for each thermal unit of natural gas. If you use 250 kilowatt-hours of electricity and 180 thermal units of natural gas in a month, how much are you billed for utilities?

10. _____

11. In 1995, a pack of cigarettes cost about $2.15 and a pack of gum cost $0.59. If a person smokes 2 packs of cigarettes a day, how much will be spent on cigarettes in a year (365 days)?

11. _____

12. If term life insurance costs $6.78 per $1000 of coverage each year, how much would a $25,000 policy cost a year?

12. _____

13. According to the Network Television Association, each hour of television programming for ABC, CBS, and NBC contains 9.75 minutes of commercials. At that rate, how many minutes of commercials do you view in 24 hours of watching these networks?

13. _____

14. A pound is approximately 454 grams. At that rate, how much would a pound of gold chain cost if it sells for $14.54 per gram?

14. _____

15. A meter that records the number of cubic feet of water used reads 36491. Fifty-five days later it reads 37654. a) Find the number of cubic feet of water used. b) Find the number of gallons of water used. (Note: 1 cu ft ≈ 7.48 gal)

15. _____

16. According to the United States Mint, the cost to make a nickel is 3.42¢. At that price, how much does it cost to make $1000 in nickels?

16. _____

17. In 1991, a meal of a cheeseburger, fries, and a soft drink was purchased in New York for $4.63 while in Paris the same meal was $7.97. How many more of these meals could you buy for $100 in New York than in Paris?

17. _____

18. How much heavier is a gross (144) of baseballs (5.25 oz each) than a gross of ping-pong balls (0.0944 oz each)?

18. _____

19. According to the U.S. Energy Information Administration, petroleum consumption in 1993 for the United States was 6,299,900,000 barrels. Find the amount of petroleum used per person, if the U.S. population in 1993 was 258 million people.

19. _____

20. About 4.4 billion pieces of liter are discarded in California each year. If the population of California is 27,000,000, find the number of pieces of litter discarded per person.

20. _____

21. "Why pay $100 a year for a cellular phone, when you pay only $9.95 per month with us." What is wrong with this advertisement?

21. _____

Exercise 4.12 Set B

1. What was the balance in your checking account, after beginning with $65.45; depositing $285.88; and writing checks for $30.00, $23.67, $122.75, $7.50, $8.99, and $17.36?

   1. _____

2. At a drug store you buy the following: 2 bottles of vitamins at $3.95 a bottle, 3 toothbrushes at $1.07 each, and 4 boxes of cough drops at $0.49 each. If the sales tax on the purchase is $0.91, what is the total cost of the purchase?

   2. _____

3. By comparing the cost per ounce, determine which is the better buy: a 12.5 oz can of soup priced at 63¢ or a 10.75 oz can of the same soup priced at 55¢?

   3. _____

4. If gasoline costs $1.17 per gallon and you use an average of 42 gallons a month, how much do you spend on gasoline in a year?

   4. _____

5. Find the miles you travel per gallon of gasoline, if odometer readings of two fill-ups were 24476.5 and 24977.8 and your car used 20.9 gallons of gasoline.

   5. _____

6. During one year you spent the following on your car: gas and oil, $1490.26; repairs, $295.47; insurance and licence fees $650; and tires, $275.75. If you drove 19,500 miles that year, what was the cost per mile for driving your car?

   6. _____

7. If you earn $5.38 per hour and time-and-half for overtime, what would you earn in a week in which you work 25 regular and 6 overtime hours?

   7. _____

8. The rainfall measured in inches in the San Francisco Bay Area is typically Jan.–4.4, Feb.–3.0, Mar.–2.5, Apr.–1.6, May–0.4, June–0.1, July–0.0, Aug.–0.0, Sept.–0.2, Oct.–1.0, Nov.–2.3, Dec.–4.0. What is the average monthly rainfall in the San Francisco Bay Area?

   8. _____

9. If a long distance call costs $1.25 for the first 3 minutes and 32¢ for each additional minute, how much does a 45 minute call cost?

   9. _____

10. If your family drinks a gallon of milk a week and milk costs $2.65 a gallon, how much do you spend on milk in a year?

   10. _____

11. If the yearly cost for $1000 of term life insurance is $7.16, how much would a $35,000 policy cost a year?

11. _____

12. You buy $2\frac{3}{4}$ yards of material at $4.80 per yard and pay $0.87 sales tax. How much change do you get from a $20 bill?

12. _____

13. According to the Network Television Association, each hour of television programming for independent stations contains 11.75 minutes of commercials. At that rate, how many minutes of commercials do you view in 8 hours of watching independent TV stations?

13. _____

14. A pound is approximately 454 grams. At that range, how much would a pound of 14 carat gold chain cost, if it sells for $23.52 per gram?

14. _____

15. A meter that records the number of cubic feet of water used reads 63546. Thirty-two days later it reads 64875. a) Find the number of cubic feet of water used. b) Find the number of gallons of water used. (Note: 1 cu ft ≈ 7.48 gal)

15. _____

16. According to the United States Mint, the cost to make a dime is 1.71¢. At that price, how much does it cost to make $1000 in dimes?

16. _____

17. In 1991, a meal of a cheeseburger, fries, and a soft drink was purchased in Los Angeles for $3.68 while in Denmark the same meal was $11.25. How many more of these meals could you buy for $100 in Los Angeles than in Denmark?

17. _____

18. How much heavier is a gross (144) of basketballs (22.9 oz each) than a gross of golf balls (1.62 oz each)?

18. _____

19. According to the U.S. Energy Information Administration, the oil consumption in 1993 in Japan was 1,963,700,000 barrels. Find the amount of oil used per person in Japan, if its population in 1993 was 124 million people.

19. _____

20. According to the National Center for Education Statistics, in 1992, the total enrollment in grades K–12 was 48,109,000 and the total number of classroom teachers was 2,821,000. Rounded to the nearest tenth, what was the number of pupils per teacher in 1992?

20. _____

21. "Why pay $300 for a year to join a health club, when you pay only $29 a month with us." What is wrong with this advertisement?

21. _____

Chapter 4 Summary

Concepts

You may refer to the sections listed below to review how to do the following:

1. read and write decimal numbers using the place values to the right of the decimal point. (4.1)
2. round off decimal numbers using the "five or more" rule. (4.2)
3. add and subtract decimals by first lining up their decimal points. (4.3), (4.4)
4. multiply decimal numbers by positioning the decimal point in the product according to the total number of decimal digits in the numbers being multiplied. (4.5)
5. divide decimal numbers by first moving the decimal point to make the divisor a whole number. (4.6), (4.7)
6. use short-cuts for multiplying and dividing numbers that end in zeros. (4.8)
7. convert fractions to decimals by dividing the numerator by the denominator. (4.9)
8. convert decimals to fractions by making use of the place values of our number system. (4.9)
9. compare the size of decimal numbers by writing them with the same number of decimal digits. (4.10)
10. solve problems involving operations on both fractions and decimals by working the problems using only fractions, only decimals, or a combination of the two. (4.11)
11. solve word problems involving decimals. (4.12)

Terminology

This chapter's important terms and their page number are as follows:

decimal digit: a digit to the right of the decimal point. (211)
decimal number: a number containing a decimal point. (195)
decimal place: the position of a digit to the right of the decimal point. (199)
decimal point: a dot (.) used in a number to separate the whole part from the fractional part of the number. (195)

Chapter 4 Crossword Puzzle

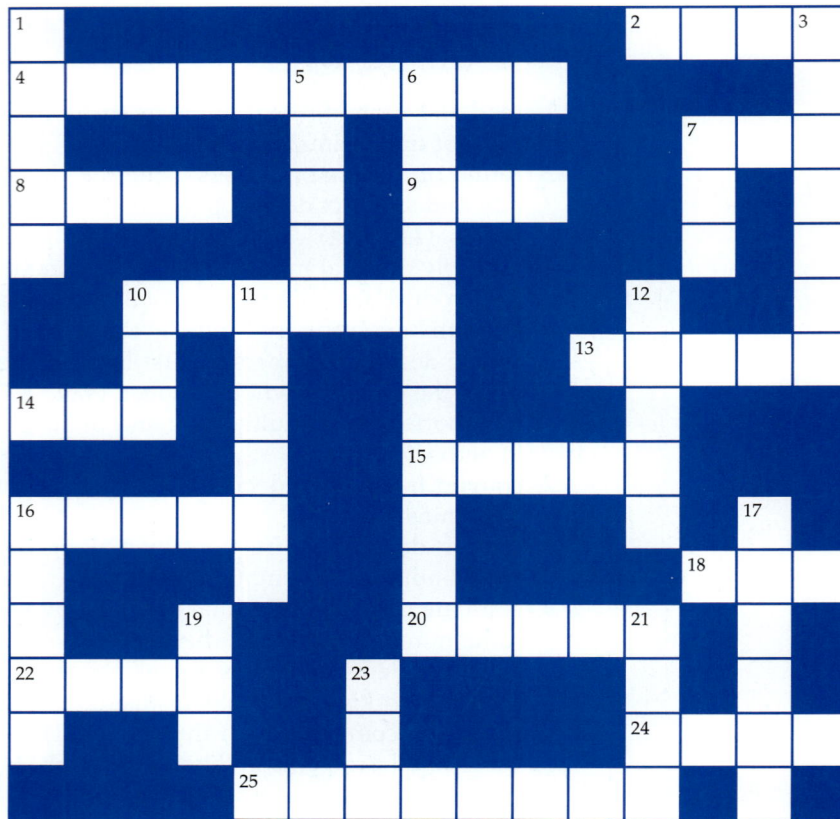

Across

2. You spend money when you do this.
4. Money is rounded to the _____ place.
7. First digit of 575 × 0.43
8. 2, 4, 6, 8, 10, 12, for example
9. Last digit of 1.25 + 3. 4 + 43.23 + 123.63
10. 19.8 is read nineteen and eight _____ .
13. 188.4 ÷ 23.55
14. Second digit of 45.76 − 2.9
15. Each component of a number
16. Round off money to the hundredths _____.
18. Rounded to the nearest _____ , 757.65 ≈ 760.
20. All digits of 899.77 − 122
22. Digit in tenths place of 114.95 ÷ 2.5
24. Third digit of 0.365 × 1396.6
25. 2.3 is read, _____ and _____ tenths.

Down

1. 36 months is _____ years.
3. Result of multiplication
5. 50 × 0.064 × 2.5
6. Third digit to the right of the decimal point
7. Digit in hundredths place of 5/8 as a decimal
10. Last digit of 576 − 0.25 × 576
11. Indicates an amount
12. $22.47 ÷ 37.45 = _____¢
16. The dot is the decimal _____.
17. 10.1 is read _____ and _____ tenth.
19. 467 ÷ _____ = 46.7
21. At $144 per pound, what's the cost per ounce.
23. Thousandths place in 0.23 ÷ 18.4

Chapter 4 Practice Test A

1. Write the following using numbers: four hundred seven and seven thousandths.

    1. _____

2. Round off 746.325 to the nearest hundredth.

    2. _____

3. $45.6 + 0.0017 + 75 + 197.7 + 3.12$

    3. _____

4. $65.3 - 27.296$

    4. _____

5. 45.07×17.96

    5. _____

6. $341.22 \div 4.84$

    6. _____

7. Find $59 \div 5.293$ rounded to the nearest hundredth.

    7. _____

8. $4.862 \times 500,000$

    8. _____

9. $573.3 \div 3,000,000$

    9. _____

10. Express 0.026 as a reduced fraction.

    10. _____

11. Express $2\frac{5}{16}$ as an exact decimal.

    11. _____

12. Arrange in order from largest to smallest; 1.27, 1.0127, 1.1027, 1.2

    12. _____

13. $5\frac{5}{6} \times 4.2 + \left(3\frac{2}{3}\right)^2$

    13. _____

14. You started the week with a $58.23 balance in your checking account. During the week you wrote checks for $10.25, $115.16, $74.00, $3.95, and $8.99, and deposited $215.66. What was your balance at the end of the week?

    14. _____

15. In a 1991 California Lottery, $117.1 million was divided among ten winning tickets. However, one of the winning tickets was to be shared equally by 31 hospital workers. If the winnings are paid to the hospital workers over a twenty year period, how much did each worker receive a year?

    15. _____

Chapter 4 Practice Test B

1. Write 84.56 in words.

1. _____

2. Round off 56.374 to the nearest tenth.

2. _____

3. $1.25 + 756 + 0.0018 + 34.76 + 152.5$

3. _____

4. $57.5 - 19.458$

4. _____

5. 87.6×14.5

5. _____

6. $15.264 \div 5.76$

6. _____

7. Find $45 \div 6.237$ rounded to the nearest hundredth.

7. _____

8. $9.2165 \times 4,000,000$

8. _____

9. $476.5 \div 500,000$

9. _____

10. Express 0.38 as a reduced fraction.

10. _____

11. Express $5\frac{3}{8}$ as an exact decimal.

11. _____

12. Arrange in order from largest to smallest: 0.306, 0.3, 0.036, 0.0306

12. _____

13. $\left(2\frac{1}{3}\right)^3 + 4\frac{1}{6} \times 9.6$

13. _____

14. How much would a 24 minute long-distance phone call cost, if you pay $1.27 for the first 3 minutes and $.26 for each additional minute?

14. _____

15. Two lottery players had the winning tickets for a $3.65 million payoff. If their share of the winnings is paid off monthly over a twenty year period and the IRS withholds $1950 in taxes each month, how much will each winner receive each month?

15. _____

Chapter 4 Supplementary Exercises

Section 4.1

In problems 1–10, write the numbers in words.

1. 0.7

2. 5.4

3. 0.03

4. 16.01

5. 0.12

6. 3.035

7. 0.006

8. 122.07

9. 0.123

10. 2.0031

In problems 11–15, write each expression using numbers.

11. six tenths

12. seven hundredths

13. five and two thousandths

14. sixty-four and sixteen thousandths

15. nine and eighty ten thousandths

Section 4.2

Round off the following to the nearest hundredth.

1. 5.732

2. 5.735

3. 5.738

4. 16.405

5. 16.403

6. 16.407

7. 141.9531

8. 0.7675

9. 452.1234

10. 67.095

11. 89.997

12. 89.993

Section 4.3

1. $4.3 + 7.6$

2. $0.21 + 8.7$

3. $6.38 + 75$

4. $89 + 1.003$

5. $7.65 + 13.74$

6. $8.07 + 3.025$

7. $1.0134 + 12 + 0.276$

8. $17.6 + 18 + 19.007$

9. $3.2 + 0.0012 + 23 + 570$

10. $327 + 9.876 + 5.6 + 4.32$

11. $47 + 8.06 + 2.763 + 4.5$

12. $12.32 + 4.57 + 10.9 + 865$

Section 4.4

1. 9.79 − 4.35
2. 6.878 − 5.193
3. 45.75 − 17.6
4. 124.127 − 79.07
5. 56.318 − 27.5
6. 6.007 − 2.03
7. 720.24 − 46.518
8. 6.5 − 3.824
9. 16.72 − 12.0231
10. 826 − 176.285
11. 42 − 21.76
12. 1763 − 1.763
13. 150.008 − 37.0992
14. 17 − 0.0329
15. 500.5 − 50.095

Section 4.5

1. 9.5 × 6
2. 8.75 × 3
3. 4.5 × 6.8
4. 42.13 × 5.06
5. 7.18 × 3.2
6. 20.24 × 0.765
7. 173.5 × 57.22
8. 5327.8 × 1.015
9. 47.8 × .0487
10. 423.001 × 6.07
11. 56.4 × 83.005
12. 64.73 × 42.75
13. 1624 × 0.0005
14. 99 × 0.065
15. 0.0132 × 7000

Section 4.6

Find the exact quotients in the following problems.

1. 105 ÷ 6
2. 7 ÷ 8
3. 32.93 ÷ 3.7
4. 52 ÷ 1.3
5. 75.6 ÷ 0.0012
6. 107.6 ÷ 2.152
7. 45.7 ÷ 0.032
8. 6.9408 ÷ 5.76
9. 1.1016 ÷ 0.017
10. 172.89 ÷ 3.06
11. 1003.703 ÷ 20.05
12. 0.5535 ÷ 12.3

Section 4.7

In problems 1–9, round off quotients to the nearest tenth.

1. 15.7 ÷ 9
2. 23 ÷ 91
3. 6.293 ÷ 4.37
4. 459 ÷ 3.7
5. 12 ÷ 1.093
6. 43.5 ÷ 2.39
7. 47.9 ÷ 0.19
8. 4139.6 ÷ 24.5
9. 98.123 ÷ 23

In problems 10–18, round off quotients to the nearest hundredth.

10. 21.91 ÷ 2.017
11. 6.4352 ÷ 8.6
12. 178 ÷ 36.91
13. 9000 ÷ 5.5
14. 778 ÷ 99
15. 35,000 ÷ 24.04
16. 1991 ÷ 52
17. 0.347 ÷ 0.219
18. 5.6 ÷ 9.9

Section 4.8

Find exact answers in the following problems.

1. 5.7×100
2. $37.86 \times 30{,}000$
3. 13.8×10^5
4. $0.098 \times 73{,}000$
5. $463.187 \times 21{,}000$
6. $0.707 \times 4{,}000{,}000$
7. $57 \div 100$
8. $29{,}746.2 \div 3000$
9. $948.5 \div 35{,}000$
10. $161 \div 23{,}000$
11. $28.9 \div 10^3$
12. $76{,}586 \div 200{,}000$

Section 4.9

In problems 1–9, convert each fraction to an exact decimal.

1. $3/4$
2. $3/10$
3. $7/8$
4. $14/5$
5. $5/32$
6. $27/16$
7. $49/50$
8. $3/25$
9. $17/64$

In problems 10–18, change each decimal to a reduced fraction or mixed number.

10. 0.25
11. 0.8
12. 0.015
13. 0.228
14. 0.0002
15. 0.0075
16. 2.24
17. 10.015
18. 34.64

Section 4.10

Arrange the following quantities in order from largest to smallest.

1. $0.5, 0.505, 0.55, 0.5055$
2. $1.7, 1.701, 1.07, 1.7001$
3. $3.3, 3.33, 3.13, 3\frac{1}{3}$
4. $\dfrac{3}{4}, \dfrac{19}{25}, 0.756, 0.0765$
5. $\dfrac{1}{8}, 0.0125, 0.152, 0.0152, 0.215$
6. $56.5, 55.6, 65.6, 56.05, 55.006$

Section 4.11

1. $12.7 \times 3\frac{1}{4}$
2. $14\frac{1}{2} \div 3.7$
3. $7^2 \times 2\frac{1}{4} + 8.7$
4. $4.6 \times \left(2\frac{1}{3} - \frac{5}{6}\right)$
5. $15\frac{1}{2} \times 0.89 - 3$
6. $\left(1\frac{5}{6}\right)^2 + 4 \times 8.6$
7. $8\frac{2}{3} + 4.25 \div 3.4$
8. $47.75 + 8\frac{3}{4} \times 7\frac{1}{5}$
9. $156 - 15\frac{7}{8} - 3.125$

Section 4.12

1. What is the balance in your checking account, if you start with a balance of $147.62, and write checks for $5.76, $13.85, and $124.99?

2. What is the cost per ounce of cheese that costs $2.90 for 7.6 oz?

3. Art's Rent-a-Heap charges $24.99 a day and 27¢ a mile to rent a car. What would you pay if you rented a car for two days and drove 317 miles?

4. If soft drinks cost $2.19 a six-pack and you drink 18 cans a month, how much would you spend on soft drinks a year?

5. At the start of a trip, your car odometer reads 65176.6 and at the end of the trip it reads 66098.3. If you use 46 gallons of gasoline during the trip, how many miles did your car average per gallon of gasoline?

6. Working at Benny's Burgers you earn $5.90 per hour plus time-and-a-half for overtime. If during one week you work 40 regular hours and 5 overtime hours, what do you earn for the week?

7. The Alcat Company's budget shows that 34¢ out of each dollar is spent on wages. How much is spent on wages in a $997,000 budget?

8. The price for the same product at four different stories is $1.17, $1.58, $1.46, and $1.07. What is the average price charged for the item?

9. Which is the better buy: four ounces of instant coffee selling for $3.39 or six ounces of the same coffee selling for $4.99?

10. Which is the better buy: A six ounce container of mushrooms selling for $0.89 or loose mushrooms of the same quality selling for $2.19 a pound?

Name _____   Date _____

Unit II Exam

Chapters 3 and 4

1. Express $\dfrac{196}{42}$ as a reduced mixed number.

2. Write 152.037 in words.

3. Express $\dfrac{45}{77}$ as a decimal rounded to the nearest hundredth.

4. $\dfrac{5}{8} \times \dfrac{14}{45}$ 5. $6\dfrac{3}{4} \div 4\dfrac{1}{2}$

6. $\dfrac{3}{8} - \dfrac{1}{10} + \dfrac{5}{6}$ 7. $27\dfrac{2}{3} - 19\dfrac{4}{5}$

8. $\dfrac{6 - \dfrac{3}{4}}{5\dfrac{1}{3} + \dfrac{1}{2}}$ 9. $8.75 + 84 + 107.3 - 3.674$

10. $17.36 \times 15{,}000$ 11. $1.3314 \div 0.015$

12. Three-fifths of the students in a math class did all the assignments during the semester. If 35 students are in the class, how many did not do all the assignments?

13. A board, $11\frac{1}{2}$ feet long, is cut into 3 equal pieces. How long is each piece?

14. The balance owed on a loan is $6356.16. After 12 payments of $176.56, how much is still owed on the loan?

15. A pad of scratch paper contains 225 sheets of paper with 23.375 square inches of writing surface on each side of a sheet. If you use both sides of each sheet, how much writing area does the scratch pad provide?

1. _____

2. _____

3. _____

4. _____

5. _____

6. _____

7. _____

8. _____

9. _____

10. _____

11. _____

12. _____

13. _____

14. _____

15. _____

Unit III

Ratio, Percent, Measurement, and Statistics

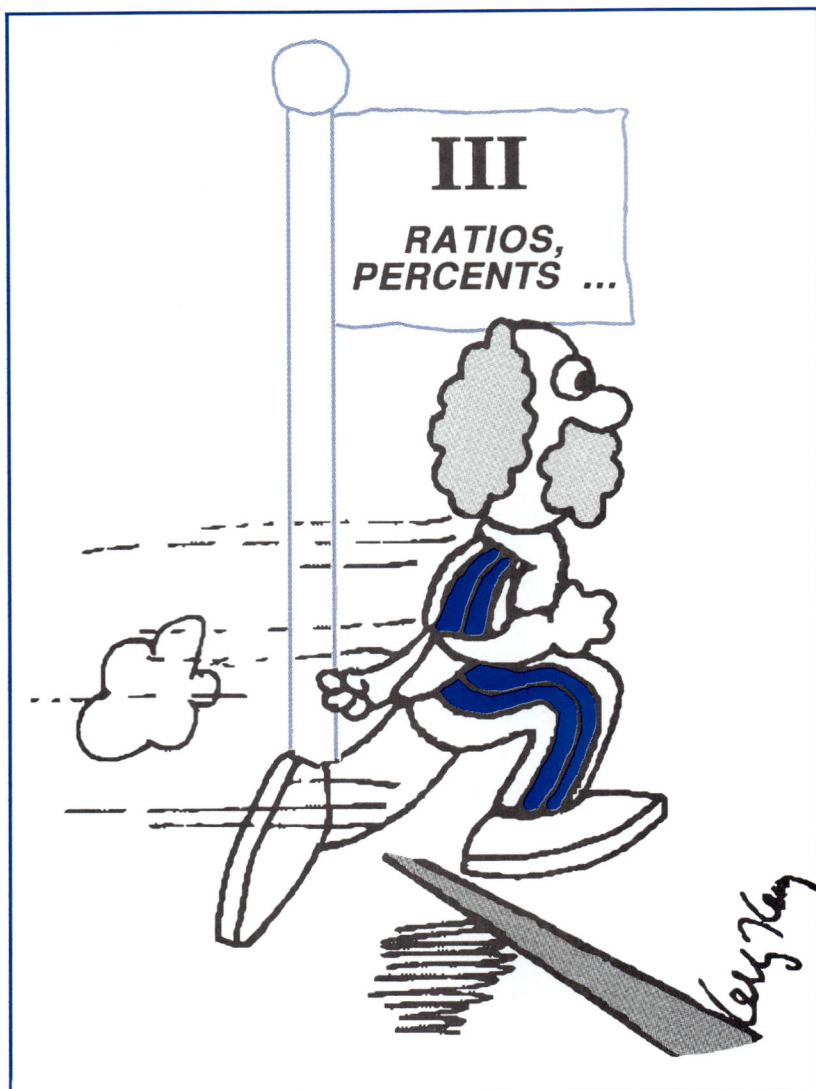

In the previous two units, you have learned the essentials of arithmetic. You have learned how to do computations that involve whole numbers, fractions, and decimals. You have also applied that knowledge to the solution of various kinds of real life problems.

In this unit, you will discover there are many other everyday problems which can be solved with further knowledge of arithmetic. You will learn to work with ratios, proportions, and percents. You will learn how to read measuring devices and convert between U.S. and metric units. You will learn how to read and analyze statistical graphs. After finishing this unit, you should be able to do the following:

1. set up ratios and solve proportions.
2. solve percentage problems.
3. apply percents and proportions to real life problems.
4. work with the U.S. and metric systems of measurement.
5. analyze measuring devices and statistical graphs.
6. find the mean and median of a set of data.
7. solve word problems involving measurement and statistics.

Note

Unless otherwise indicated in this unit, when the answers have more than three decimal digits, they will be rounded off to the nearest hundredth.

Brain Buster

Consider a very large piece of paper that is 0.01 inches thick. If you could continue to fold that piece of paper in half, how high will the stack be after 25 such folds? Express the answer to the nearest tenth of a mile.

(Yes! The height of the stack would be more than a mile.)

Chapter 5

Ratio, Proportion, and Percent

After completing this chapter, you should be able to do the following:

1. set up and reduce ratios.
2. solve proportions.
3. express percents as fractions or decimals.
4. convert decimals and fractions to percents.
5. solve percentage problems.
6. solve word problems involving percents and proportions.

On the next page, you will find a pretest for this chapter. The purpose of the pretest is to help you determine which sections in this chapter you need to study in detail and which sections you can review quickly. By taking and correcting the pretest according to the instructions on the next page, you can better plan your pace through this chapter.

Note

Unless otherwise indicated in this chapter, when the answers have more than three decimal digits, they will be rounded off to the nearest hundredth.

Name _____ Date _____

Chapter 5 Pretest

Take and correct this test using the answer section at the end of the book. Those problems that give you difficulty indicate which sections need extra attention. Section numbers are in parentheses before each problem.

(5.1)   1. Express a ratio of 63 to 105 as a reduced fraction.   1. _____

(5.2)   2. Solve for N. $\dfrac{N}{30} = \dfrac{28}{35}$ 2. _____

(5.2)   3. Solve for A. $\dfrac{39}{9} = \dfrac{A}{45}$ 3. _____

(5.3)   4. Solve for P. $\dfrac{16}{7} = \dfrac{9}{P}$ 4. _____

(5.3)   5. Solve for Y. $\dfrac{0.83}{Y} = \dfrac{2.52}{26.6}$ 5. _____

(5.5)   6. Express 4.5% as a decimal and as a reduced fraction.   6. _____

(5.6)   7. Express 0.114 as a reduced fraction and as a percent.   7. _____

(5.7)   8. Find 14.9% of 300.   8. _____

(5.7)   9. How much sales tax would be added to the cost of a $79.99 watch, if the sales tax rate is 6.5%? Find the tax accurate to the nearest cent.   9. _____

(5.8)   10. 4 is what percent of 25?   10. _____

(5.8)   11. 9 is 12% of what number?   11. _____

(5.8)   12. What is $32\frac{2}{3}\%$ of $520.80?   12. _____

(5.4)   13. If $3\frac{1}{4}$ pounds of oranges cost $1.18, how much should 5   13. _____
             pounds cost, to the nearest cent?

(5.9)   14. If the price of a ring drops from $176 to $97, what is the per-   14. _____
             cent decrease in price, to the nearest tenth?

(5.10)   15. What monthly payments are needed to pay off a $2400 loan   15. _____
             with an annual interest rate of 11.7% for 42 months? Find the
             payments rounded to the nearest cent.

5.1 Ratios

Ratio:

After Anna's song, get ready for the laser demonstration. It's an awesome ray show!

If there were 18 males and 12 females in a class, you could compare the number of men to women by saying there is a ratio of 18 men to 12 women. You could represent that comparison in three different ways:

$$18 \text{ to } 12$$

$$18 : 12$$

$$\frac{18}{12}$$

The ratio of 18 to 12 is another way to represent the fraction $\frac{18}{12}$. The three representations above are equal.

$$18 \text{ to } 12 = 18 : 12 = \frac{18}{12}$$

Depending on the situation, any of those three forms can be used. *A ratio, then, is simply a comparison of numbers that can be expressed as a fraction.*

The first operation to perform on ratios is reducing them to lowest terms. The above ratio, 18 : 12, can be reduced to lower terms just as we reduced fractions.

$$18 : 12 = \frac{18}{12} \xrightarrow[\div 6]{\div 6} = \frac{3}{2}$$

$$18 : 12 = \frac{3}{2} = 3 : 2$$

By reducing the ratio you can get a better understanding of the original ratio. The ratio of 18 males to 12 females reduces to a ratio of 3 males to 2 females. This means that for every 3 males in the class there are 2 females.

Example 1

Express the ratio of the value of 4 dimes to 3 quarters.

You must first find the value of each by changing them to the same unit (cents).

$$4 \text{ dimes} = 40¢ \text{ and } 3 \text{ quarters} = 75¢$$

Thus, the ratio of the respective values is:

$$40 : 75 = \frac{40}{75} = \frac{8}{15}$$

Example 2

A basketball team wins 16 games and loses 14 games. Find the reduced ratio of:

wins to losses. $16 : 14 = \dfrac{16}{14} = \dfrac{8}{7}$

losses to wins. $14 : 16 = \dfrac{14}{16} = \dfrac{7}{8}$

wins to total games played. $16 : 30 = \dfrac{16}{30} = \dfrac{8}{15}$

Notice that the order of the numbers is critical.

Example 3

Find the reduced ratio of $5\dfrac{2}{3}$ to 2.5.

$$5\dfrac{2}{3} : 2.5 = \dfrac{5\dfrac{2}{3}}{2.5} = \dfrac{5\dfrac{2}{3}}{2\dfrac{1}{2}}$$

$$= \dfrac{\dfrac{17}{3}}{\dfrac{5}{2}} = \dfrac{17}{3} \div \dfrac{5}{2}$$

$$= \dfrac{17}{3} \times \dfrac{2}{5} = \dfrac{34}{15}$$

If you keep in mind that a ratio is simply a comparison of quantities expressible as a fraction, you should be able to do the following problems.

Problem 1: What is the reduced ratio $3\dfrac{1}{4}$ inches to 3 feet?

Answer: 13:144
(Note: 3 ft = 36 in.)

$$3\dfrac{1}{4} : 36 = \dfrac{3\dfrac{1}{4}}{36} = 3\dfrac{1}{4} \div 36$$

$$= \dfrac{13}{4} \div \dfrac{36}{1}$$

$$= \dfrac{13}{4} \times \dfrac{1}{36} = \dfrac{13}{144}$$

Exercise 5.1 Set A

A team wins 8 games out of 12 games played.
What is the reduced ratio of the following:

1. wins to games played?

2. wins to losses?

3. losses to games played?

A jar contains 12 white, 10 red, and 18 blue balls.
What is the reduced ratio of the following:

4. white balls to blue balls?

5. red balls to the total number of balls?

6. blue balls to balls that are not blue?

A bank contains 7 dimes, 20 nickels, and 9 quarters.
What is the reduced ratio of the value of the following:

7. nickels to dimes?

8. dimes to nickels?

9. dimes to quarters?

10. quarters to total money in the bank?

In problems 11–17, what is the reduced ratio of the distances:

11. 18 inches to 45 inches?

12. 5 inches to 5 feet?

13. 8 feet to 10 yards?

14. $11\frac{3}{8}$ inches to $8\frac{1}{2}$ inches?

15. $3\frac{3}{4}$ inches to $10\frac{1}{2}$ inches?

16. 9 feet to $3\frac{3}{8}$ inches?

17. $20\frac{1}{4}$ inches to 3 yards?

1. _____

2. _____

3. _____

4. _____

5. _____

6. _____

7. _____

8. _____

9. _____

10. _____

11. _____

12. _____

13. _____

14. _____

15. _____

16. _____

17. _____

Exercise 5.1 Set B

A class of 40 contains 18 females.
What is the reduced ratio of the following:

1. females to the total in the class?

1. _____

2. females to males?

2. _____

3. males to the total in the class

3. _____

A jar contains 8 white, 16 red, and 6 blue balls.
What is the reduced ratio of the following:

4. white balls to red balls?

4. _____

5. red balls to the total number of balls?

5. _____

6. blue balls to balls that are not blue?

6. _____

A wallet contains twelve $1 bills, four $5 bills, and three $20 bills.
What is the reduced ratio of the value of the following:

7. $1 bills to $5 bills?

7. _____

8. $5 bills to $1 bills?

8. _____

9. $5 bills to $20 bills?

9. _____

10. $20 bills to the total money in the wallet?

10. _____

In problems 11–17, what is the reduced ratio of the distances:

11. 14 inches to 35 inches?

11. _____

12. 3 inches to 3 feet?

12. _____

13. 9 feet to 12 yards?

13. _____

14. $12\frac{1}{2}$ inches to $9\frac{3}{8}$ inches?

14. _____

15. $5\frac{1}{4}$ inches to $9\frac{7}{8}$ inches?

15. _____

16. 2 feet to $2\frac{5}{8}$ inches?

16. _____

17. $13\frac{1}{2}$ inches to 3 yards?

17. _____

5.2 Proportions

A **proportion** is a statement that one ratio is equal to another ratio.

For example, a ratio of 4 : 8 is equal to a ratio of 3 : 6.

$$4 : 8 = \frac{4}{8} = \frac{1}{2} \text{ and } 3 : 6 = \frac{3}{6} = \frac{1}{2}$$

$$4 : 8 = 3 : 6$$

$$\frac{4}{8} = \frac{3}{6}$$

Those ratios form a proportion since they are equal to each other. In a proportion, you will notice that if you **cross multiply** the terms of a proportion as shown below, those **cross-products** are equal.

$$\frac{4}{8} \overset{=}{\rightleftarrows} \frac{3}{6} \qquad 4 \times 6 = 8 \times 3 \text{ (both equal 24)}$$

$$\frac{3}{2} \overset{=}{\rightleftarrows} \frac{18}{12} \qquad 3 \times 12 = 2 \times 18 \text{ (both equal 36)}$$

This, then, is the **fundamental principle** for working with proportions:

> If you cross multiply in a proportion, both answers are equal.

Example 1

Do $\frac{4}{7}$ and $\frac{36}{63}$ form a proportion?

Cross multiply the ratios. $\frac{4}{7} \overset{=}{\rightleftarrows} \frac{36}{63}$ $4 \times 63 = 252$
     $7 \times 36 = 252$

The cross-products are equal, so the ratios form a proportion.

That fundamental principle of proportions enables you to solve problems in which one number of the proportion is not known. For example, if N represents the number that is unknown in the proportion below, we can find its value.

$$\frac{N}{12} = \frac{3}{4}$$

$4 \times N = 12 \times 3$ Cross multiply the proportion.

$4 \times N = 36$ We know that N = 9 since $4 \times 9 = 36$. However, other problems may not be so easy. You should learn this method for finding the value for N:

$\dfrac{4 \times N}{4} = \dfrac{36}{4}$ *Divide the terms on both sides of the equals sign by the number next to the unknown letter.*

$1 \times N = 9$ In this problem, we would divide both sides by 4.

$N = 9$ That will leave the N on the left side and the answer (9) on the right side.

Example 2

Solve for N. $\dfrac{2}{5} = \dfrac{N}{35}$

$5 \times N = 2 \times 35$ Cross multiply.

$5 \times N = 70$

$\dfrac{5 \times N}{5} = \dfrac{70}{5}$ Divide by the number next to the unknown letter; divide by 5.

$N = 14$

Example 3

Solve for N. $\dfrac{15}{N} = \dfrac{3}{13}$

$3 \times N = 15 \times 13$ Cross multiply.

$3 \times N = 195$

$\dfrac{3 \times N}{3} = \dfrac{195}{3}$ Divide by the number next to the unknown letter; divide by 3.

$N = 65$

Problem 1:   Solve for N. $\dfrac{6}{7} = \dfrac{102}{N}$

Answer: N = 119

$$\dfrac{6}{7} = \dfrac{102}{N}$$

$$\dfrac{6 \times N}{6} = \dfrac{714}{6}$$

$$N = 119$$

Problem 2:   Solve for N. $\dfrac{4}{N} = \dfrac{6}{27}$

Answer: N = 18

$$\dfrac{4}{N} = \dfrac{6}{27}$$

$$\dfrac{6 \times N}{6} = \dfrac{108}{6}$$

$$N = 18$$

Exercise 5.2 Set A

In problems 1–6, determine if the ratios form a proportion.

1. $\dfrac{12}{21}$ and $\dfrac{8}{14}$

2. $\dfrac{24}{20}$ and $\dfrac{12}{10}$

3. $\dfrac{57}{38}$ and $\dfrac{114}{76}$

4. $\dfrac{138}{184}$ and $\dfrac{69}{92}$

5. $\dfrac{73}{53}$ and $\dfrac{53}{33}$

6. $\dfrac{34}{62}$ and $\dfrac{26}{43}$

In problems 7–18, solve for N.

7. $\dfrac{N}{4} = \dfrac{6}{8}$

8. $\dfrac{N}{3} = \dfrac{12}{9}$

9. $\dfrac{20}{N} = \dfrac{4}{7}$

10. $\dfrac{21}{N} = \dfrac{3}{8}$

11. $\dfrac{18}{15} = \dfrac{N}{100}$

12. $\dfrac{27}{6} = \dfrac{N}{100}$

13. $\dfrac{65}{52} = \dfrac{5}{N}$

14. $\dfrac{49}{91} = \dfrac{7}{N}$

15. $\dfrac{N}{18} = \dfrac{63}{27}$

16. $\dfrac{N}{12} = \dfrac{35}{15}$

17. $\dfrac{9}{14} = \dfrac{N}{266}$

18. $\dfrac{8}{57} = \dfrac{N}{285}$

1. _____

2. _____

3. _____

4. _____

5. _____

6. _____

7. _____

8. _____

9. _____

10. _____

11. _____

12. _____

13. _____

14. _____

15. _____

16. _____

17. _____

18. _____

Exercise 5.2 Set B

In problems 1–6, determine if the ratios form a proportion.

1. $\dfrac{10}{35}$ and $\dfrac{14}{21}$

2. $\dfrac{12}{33}$ and $\dfrac{8}{22}$

3. $\dfrac{78}{234}$ and $\dfrac{39}{117}$

4. $\dfrac{228}{266}$ and $\dfrac{114}{133}$

5. $\dfrac{56}{85}$ and $\dfrac{58}{65}$

6. $\dfrac{96}{78}$ and $\dfrac{78}{69}$

In problems 7–18, solve for N.

7. $\dfrac{N}{3} = \dfrac{6}{9}$

8. $\dfrac{N}{2} = \dfrac{12}{8}$

9. $\dfrac{42}{N} = \dfrac{7}{8}$

10. $\dfrac{27}{N} = \dfrac{3}{7}$

11. $\dfrac{27}{30} = \dfrac{N}{100}$

12. $\dfrac{9}{15} = \dfrac{N}{100}$

13. $\dfrac{6}{114} = \dfrac{5}{N}$

14. $\dfrac{9}{117} = \dfrac{7}{N}$

15. $\dfrac{N}{21} = \dfrac{24}{9}$

16. $\dfrac{N}{24} = \dfrac{15}{18}$

17. $\dfrac{9}{14} = \dfrac{N}{238}$

18. $\dfrac{3}{38} = \dfrac{N}{494}$

1. _____

2. _____

3. _____

4. _____

5. _____

6. _____

7. _____

8. _____

9. _____

10. _____

11. _____

12. _____

13. _____

14. _____

15. _____

16. _____

17. _____

18. _____

5.3 More on Solving Proportions

Proportion:
The N. F. L. scores are in the pro-portion of the radio sports program.

In Section 5.2, we covered the basic steps for solving a proportion. By using those methods and your knowledge of fractions and decimals, you can now attempt problems that are more difficult.

Example 1

Do $1\frac{3}{4} : \frac{2}{5}$ and $2\frac{11}{12} : \frac{2}{3}$ form a proportion?

$$\frac{1\frac{3}{4}}{\frac{2}{5}} \stackrel{?}{=} \frac{2\frac{11}{12}}{\frac{2}{3}}$$

$$1\frac{3}{4} \times \frac{2}{3} \stackrel{?}{=} \frac{2}{5} \times 2\frac{11}{12} \qquad \text{Cross multiply.}$$

$$\frac{7}{\underset{2}{\cancel{4}}} \times \frac{\overset{1}{\cancel{2}}}{3} \stackrel{?}{=} \frac{2}{\underset{1}{\cancel{5}}} \times \frac{\overset{7}{\cancel{35}}}{\underset{6}{\cancel{12}}}$$

$$\frac{7}{6} = \frac{7}{6}$$

Yes, they do form a proportion.

Example 2

Solve for P. $\frac{2}{3} = \frac{P}{100}$

$$3 \times P = 200 \qquad \text{Cross multiply.}$$

$$\frac{3 \times P}{3} = \frac{200}{3} \qquad \text{Divide by the number next to the unknown letter; divide by 3.}$$

$$P \approx 66.67$$

Example 3

Solve for N. $\frac{4.6}{3.75} = \frac{N}{7.875}$

$$3.75 \times N = 4.6 \times 7.875 \qquad \text{Cross multiply.}$$

$$\frac{3.75 \times N}{3.75} = \frac{36.225}{3.75} \qquad \text{Divide by 3.75.}$$

$$N = 9.66$$

Example 4

Solve for B. $\dfrac{\frac{1}{2}}{B} = \dfrac{\frac{1}{4}}{100}$

$\dfrac{1}{4} \times B = \dfrac{1}{2} \times 100$ Cross multiply.

$\dfrac{\frac{1}{4} \times B}{\frac{1}{4}} = \dfrac{50}{\frac{1}{4}}$ Divide by $\dfrac{1}{4}$.

$B = 50 \div \dfrac{1}{4}$

$B = 50 \times 4$

$B = 200$

Problem 1:   Do 16.4 : 5.6 and 18.4 : 7.6 form a proportion?

Answer: No.

The cross products are not equal.

$\dfrac{16.4}{5.6} \overset{\longleftrightarrow}{=} \dfrac{18.4}{7.6}$

$16.4 \times 7.6 = 124.64$
$5.6 \times 18.4 = 103.04$

Problem 2:   Solve for A. $\dfrac{A}{\frac{17}{3}} = \dfrac{21}{100}$

Answer: A = 1.19

$100 \times A = \dfrac{17}{\cancel{3}} \times \cancel{21}^{7}$
$\phantom{100 \times A = \dfrac{17}{3} \times 21}_{1}$

$\dfrac{100 \times A}{100} = \dfrac{119}{100}$

$A = 1.19$

Problem 3:   Solve for B. $\dfrac{1.6}{B} = \dfrac{3.5}{6.39}$

Answer: B ≈ 2.92

$3.5 \times B = 1.6 \times 6.39$

$\dfrac{3.5 \times B}{3.5} = \dfrac{10.224}{3.5}$

$B \approx 2.92$

Name _____   Date _____

Exercise 5.3 Set A

In problems 1–4, determine if the ratios form a proportion.

1. $2\dfrac{2}{3} : 1\dfrac{1}{5}$ and $1\dfrac{2}{3} : \dfrac{3}{4}$

2. $1\dfrac{1}{4} : 3\dfrac{1}{3}$ and $1\dfrac{1}{2} : 4$

3. 1.4 to 5.6 and 0.4 to 1.6

4. 0.3 to 3.8 and 0.9 to 11.4

In problems 5–18, solve for the unknown.

5. $\dfrac{A}{16} = \dfrac{7}{100}$

6. $\dfrac{A}{15} = \dfrac{9}{100}$

7. $\dfrac{5}{8} = \dfrac{7}{N}$

8. $\dfrac{4}{9} = \dfrac{7}{N}$

9. $\dfrac{Y}{.35} = \dfrac{1.2}{.17}$

10. $\dfrac{Y}{.12} = \dfrac{1.8}{.71}$

11. $\dfrac{5.3}{B} = \dfrac{9}{100}$

12. $\dfrac{4.6}{B} = \dfrac{7}{100}$

13. $\dfrac{F}{\frac{1}{2}} = \dfrac{38}{\frac{1}{4}}$

14. $\dfrac{F}{\frac{1}{4}} = \dfrac{36}{\frac{1}{2}}$

15. $\dfrac{17}{2.5} = \dfrac{P}{100}$

16. $\dfrac{28}{3.9} = \dfrac{P}{100}$

17. $\dfrac{1\frac{3}{4}}{D} = \dfrac{\frac{7}{8}}{1\frac{1}{4}}$

18. $\dfrac{2\frac{1}{2}}{D} = \dfrac{\frac{5}{6}}{1\frac{1}{6}}$

1. _____

2. _____

3. _____

4. _____

5. _____

6. _____

7. _____

8. _____

9. _____

10. _____

11. _____

12. _____

13. _____

14. _____

15. _____

16. _____

17. _____

18. _____

Exercise 5.3 Set B

In problems 1–4, determine if the ratios form a proportion.

1. $3\frac{1}{3} : 1\frac{1}{5}$ and $\frac{5}{9} : \frac{1}{5}$

2. $1\frac{2}{5} : \frac{3}{4}$ and $\frac{2}{3} : \frac{5}{14}$

3. 4 to 28.5 and 0.8 to 5.7

4. 4.2 to 1.8 and 6.3 to 2.7

1. _____

2. _____

3. _____

4. _____

In problems 5–18, solve for the unknown.

5. $\dfrac{A}{18} = \dfrac{3}{100}$

6. $\dfrac{A}{21} = \dfrac{11}{100}$

7. $\dfrac{7}{8} = \dfrac{6}{N}$

8. $\dfrac{6}{7} = \dfrac{5}{N}$

9. $\dfrac{Y}{.56} = \dfrac{3.4}{.23}$

10. $\dfrac{Y}{.49} = \dfrac{5.6}{.19}$

11. $\dfrac{4.2}{B} = \dfrac{11}{100}$

12. $\dfrac{5.3}{B} = \dfrac{13}{100}$

13. $\dfrac{F}{\frac{1}{4}} = \dfrac{56}{\frac{1}{2}}$

14. $\dfrac{F}{\frac{1}{2}} = \dfrac{72}{\frac{1}{4}}$

15. $\dfrac{13}{5.7} = \dfrac{P}{100}$

16. $\dfrac{19}{8.6} = \dfrac{P}{100}$

17. $\dfrac{1\frac{1}{3}}{D} = \dfrac{9\frac{1}{3}}{1\frac{2}{5}}$

18. $\dfrac{2\frac{1}{2}}{D} = \dfrac{1\frac{2}{7}}{\frac{1}{7}}$

5. _____

6. _____

7. _____

8. _____

9. _____

10. _____

11. _____

12. _____

13. _____

14. _____

15. _____

16. _____

17. _____

18. _____

5.4 Applications Involving Proportions

Distance:

"May I have dis-dance?"

In Sections 5.2 and 5.3, we discussed how to solve for an unknown quantity in a proportion. In this section, we will use that knowledge to solve real-life problems in which two ratios or rates are equal.

Example 1

At 2 P.M. on a sunny day, a 5 ft woman had a 2 ft shadow, while a church steeple had a 27 ft shadow. Use this information to find the height of the steeple.

Analyze: Since both shadows were measured at 2 P.M., the ratio of the height of the woman to her shadow must equal the ratio of the height of the steeple to its shadow. If H represents the height of the steeple, we get the proportion 5 : 2 = H : 27.

Solve: $\dfrac{5}{2} = \dfrac{H}{27}$ $\left[\dfrac{\text{height}}{\text{shadow}} = \dfrac{\text{height}}{\text{shadow}}\right]$

$2 \times H = 5 \times 27$
$2 \times H = 135$
$H = 67.5 \text{ ft}$

Many problems can be solved using proportions to show that two ratios or rates are the same. You must be careful to place the same quantities in corresponding positions in the proportion. In example 1, we placed the heights of the objects in the numerator of each ratio and the lengths of the shadows in the denominator of each ratio. It would not be logical to let the ratio of a height to its shadow equal the ratio of a shadow to the height of the object. The quantities in the numerator and denominator of the left of the equal sign must be in the same logical order as the quantities in the ratio on the right of the equal sign.

Example 2

During 15 minutes of television watching, you noticed that there were 2 minutes of commercials. If the amount of commercials continued at the same rate, how many minutes of commercials can you expect in 65 minutes of television watching?

Analyze: Since we are assuming that the commercials will continue at the same rate, we can set up a proportion in which the ratios of commercial time to time watching TV are equal. If N represents the number of minutes of commercials in 65 minutes of TV watching, we get the proportion 2 : 15 = N : 65.

Solve: $\dfrac{2}{15} = \dfrac{N}{65}$ $\left[\dfrac{\text{commercial time}}{\text{time watching TV}} = \dfrac{\text{commercial time}}{\text{time watching TV}}\right]$

$15 \times N = 2 \times 65$
$15 \times N = 130$

$\dfrac{15 \times N}{15} = \dfrac{130}{15}$

$N = 8\dfrac{2}{3} \text{ minutes}$

Example 3

Suppose $4\frac{3}{4}$ pounds of apples cost $1.79. At that rate, how much should 10 pounds of apples cost?

Analyze: The ratio of cost to weight should be the same for $4\frac{3}{4}$ pounds of apples and 10 pounds of apples. Since we do not know the cost of the 10 pounds of apples, let's use A to represent it. Thus, the proportion comparing cost to weight is $1.79 : $4\frac{3}{4} = A : 10$.

Solve: $$\frac{\$1.79}{4\frac{3}{4}} = \frac{A}{10} \qquad \left[\frac{cost}{weight} = \frac{cost}{weight}\right]$$

$4.75 \times A = 10 \times \$1.79$
$4.75 \times A = \$17.90$
$\qquad A \approx \$3.77$ (rounded to the nearest cent)

Example 4

A brass alloy contains only copper and zinc in the ratio of 4 parts of copper to 3 parts zinc. If a total of 140 grams of brass is made, how much copper is used?

Analyze: Since the total amount of alloy (140 g) is known and the amount of copper is unknown, we need to set up a proportion of copper to the total material. The ratio of copper to zinc is 4 : 3, so there are 4 parts copper out of 7 parts of copper and zinc combined. Thus, the ratio of copper to total material is 4 : 7. If N represent the amount of copper in the 140 grams of alloy, the proportion of copper to the total amount is $4 : 7 = N : 140$.

Solve: $$\frac{4}{7} = \frac{N}{140} \qquad \left[\frac{copper}{total} = \frac{copper}{total}\right]$$

$7 \times N = 4 \times 140$
$7 \times N = 560$
$\qquad N = 80$ grams

Problem 1:   At a 4-H Junior Livestock Sale, the advertised hoof-to-freezer ratio for a hog was 220 to 119. That is, if a hog weighed 220 lbs, it should yield 119 lbs of pork after being butchered. At that rate, how many pounds of pork can be expected from a hog that weighs 275 lbs?

Answer: 148.75 pounds

$$\left[\frac{weight}{yield} = \frac{weight}{yield}\right]$$

$$\frac{220}{119} = \frac{275}{Y}$$

$220 \times Y = 32{,}725$
$\qquad Y = 148.75$ lbs

Exercise 5.4 Set A

1. If a man who is 6 feet tall has a shadow that is 5 feet long, how tall is a pine tree that has a shadow of 37 feet?

1. _____

2. If a $2\frac{1}{2}$ foot shrub has a 6 foot shadow, how tall is a pole that has an 84 foot shadow?

2. _____

3. On a scale drawing, a 27 mile stretch of freeway is represented by a 7 inch line. How long would a street be that is represented by a $5\frac{1}{4}$ inch line?

3. _____

4. If the scale on a map reads, *1.5 in. = 2 mi*, how long is a river that measures 7 inches on the map?

4. _____

5. If 6 pounds of fertilizer are required for 1400 sq ft of lawn, how many pounds of fertilizer should be used on a 2000 sq ft lawn?

5. _____

6. If 5 gallons of paint covers 1800 sq ft of stucco, how many gallons of paint would you need to paint a home with 6120 sq ft of stucco?

6. _____

7. The real estate tax is $688.00 for a $40,000 condominium. If a condominium taxed at the same rate pays $834.20 in real estate tax, what is the value of the condominium?

7. _____

8. If you drive 175 miles in 3 hours, how many miles can you expect to drive in $5\frac{3}{4}$ hours traveling at the same average speed?

8. _____

9. You run 6.2 miles in 40 minutes. If you could keep the same pace, how long would it take you to run 7.5 miles?

9. _____

10. If a $2.00 bet on the winning horse returns $2.80, how much money would a $5.00 bet have returned?

10. _____

11. If 12.5 ounces of a cough syrup cost $3.95, at that rate how much should 16.76 ounces of the cough syrup cost?

11. _____

12. If a dozen apples cost $1.29, how much should 50 apples cost at that rate?

12. _____

13. In 1995, it was estimated that there were 27 personal computers for every 100 people in the U.S.A. At that rate, how many PC's would there be in the state of Illinois (population 11,817,000)?

13. _____

14. On the Fourth of July, a local store is selling banana splits that usually cost $1.79 for only 50¢. If they sold their 99¢ hot dogs at the same proportional rate, what would the special price be?

14. _____

15. The school you graduated from has a total of 800 students. You graduated with the 27th highest grade point average in your class of 213 students. At that rate, in what position would you expect to graduate in a school that has 1200 graduates?

15. _____

16. In an indoor running track, there are 11 laps to a mile. How many laps do you need to run for the quarter-mile race?

16. _____

17. If a punch mix calls for 2 parts mix to 5 parts water, how much mix should be used to fill a 128 ounce punch bowl?

17. _____

18. Suppose for every 5 games a team wins, it loses 3 games. At that rate, how many games should the team win in a 32 game season?

18. _____

19. If you wanted to divide 6300 acres in a ratio of 2 to 7, how many acres would each part contain?

19. _____

20. With every purchase at a local fast food restaurant, a ticket with the chance of winning free food is being given away. The restaurant claims that there are seven winning tickets for every three losing tickets. At that rate, if 3500 tickets are given away, how many of them are winning tickets?

20. _____

Name _____   Date _____

Exercise 5.4 Set B

1. If a vertical yardstick casts a shadow of 2 feet, how tall is a building that casts a shadow of 82 feet?

1. _____

2. The ratio of men to women in a large lecture class is 5 to 7. If there are 45 men in the class, how many women are in the class?

2. _____

3. If a $5\frac{1}{4}$ inch line on a map represents a 9 mile road, how many miles would be represented by a $3\frac{1}{2}$ inch line?

3. _____

4. The scale on an atlas reads, *1 in. = 97 mi.* In the atlas, how far would San Francisco be from Hawaii, if the distance between those states is 2076 miles?

4. _____

5. If an 8 oz bottle of weed-killer is used on 1200 sq ft of lawn, how many ounces should you use on a 700 sq ft lawn?

5. _____

6. A cassette player's counter goes from 0 to 316 after 40 minutes of playing. At that rate, what should the counter read after playing a 60 minute cassette?

6. _____

7. If the interest paid by a bank for one day on an account of $8650 is $2.16, how large is a similar account that earns $5.20 interest on the same day?

7. _____

8. If it takes 16 quart jars to can 44 pounds of peaches, how many quart jars should it take to can 121 pounds of peaches?

8. _____

9. Your car uses $25\frac{1}{4}$ gallons of gasoline in 510 miles of driving. At that rate, to the nearest tenth of a gallon, how many gallons of gasoline will it use in 750 miles of driving?

9. _____

10. If 4.875 pounds of meat cost $12.84, how much should 3.26 pounds of meat cost?

10. _____

11. If a dozen donuts cost $3.98, at that rate, what should 15 donuts cost?

11. _____

12. Sound travels at about 1100 feet per second. At that rate, how far would sound travel in 12 minutes?

12. _____

13. If the odometer on your car registers 2.9 miles when you have actually gone 3 miles, how far did you actually travel when the odometer reads 65000.0?

13. _____

14. It is estimated that in India there are 35 TV sets for every 1000 people. If the population of India is 936,546,000, how many TV sets are in India?

14. _____

15. In a local 10K run, you placed 23rd out of 275 runners. At that rate, in what position would you expect to finish in a San Francisco Bay to Breakers Race that has 105,000 runners?

15. _____

16. If a car completes 7 laps in a midget car race it has traveled 2 miles. On that track, how long is the 50 lap feature event?

16. _____

17. If 5290 pounds of wheat is to be divided between two silos in the ratio of 3 to 7, how many pounds of wheat should be put into each silo?

17. _____

18. For every ten people that complete a certain class three do not finish. At that rate, out of 39 enrolled in the class how many will not finish?

18. _____

19. If a softball team's ratio of wins to losses over the last five years is 7 to 4, how many wins did it have out of the 121 games played?

19. _____

20. The ratio of red jelly beans to green jelly beans in a Christmas jar is 5 to 4. If there is a total of 4500 jelly beans in the jar, how many are green?

20. _____

21. An old jingle states, "Shave and a haircut, 2 bits (25¢)." At that rate, how many bits would a $12.00 haircut cost?

21. _____

5.5 Percents

Percent:
The odor of a purse.

A common standard of measurement is the **percent (%).** "Percent" means "out of a hundred." An 85% test score means that out of 100 points you got 85 points. If the sales tax in your state is 7%, it means that for every 100¢ (dollar), there is 7¢ sales tax.

Remember: *"Percent" means "out of a hundred."*

So, 25% means 25 out of 100.

$$25\% = \frac{25}{100} = 0.25$$

137% means 137 out of 100.

$$137\% = \frac{137}{100} = 1.37$$

6.5% means 6.5 out of 100.

$$6.5\% = \frac{6.5}{100} = 0.065$$

From those examples, you can see that a percent can be easily expressed as a fraction or a decimal.

Converting Percents to Fractions

To convert a percent to a fraction, drop the % sign, put the number over 100, and reduce if possible.

Converting Percents to Decimals

To convert a percent to a decimal, drop the % sign and move the decimal point two places to the left.

Example 1

Express 30% as a fraction and as a decimal.

$$30\% = \frac{30}{100} = \frac{3}{10} \text{ (a reduced fraction)}$$

$$30\% = .30 \text{ (a decimal)}$$

Example 2

Express 125% as a mixed number and as a decimal.

$$125\% = \frac{125}{100} = \frac{5}{4} = 1\frac{1}{4} \text{ (a reduced mixed number)}$$

$$125\% = 1.25 \text{ (a decimal)}$$

Example 3

Express 9.4% as a decimal.

$9.4\% = .094$

Example 4

Express $3\frac{1}{3}\%$ as a fraction.

$$3\frac{1}{3}\% = \frac{3\frac{1}{3}}{100} = 3\frac{1}{3} \div 100$$

$$= \frac{10}{3} \div \frac{100}{1}$$

$$= \frac{\overset{1}{\cancel{10}}}{3} \times \frac{1}{\underset{10}{\cancel{100}}} = \frac{1}{30}$$

You may sometimes find it easier to express a percent as a fraction by converting the percent to a decimal, then converting the decimal to a fraction.

Example 5

Express $18\frac{1}{2}\%$ as a fraction.

Since $\frac{1}{2}$ is easily expressed as the exact decimal .5,

$18\frac{1}{2}\% = 18.5\% = .185$ (a decimal)

$.185 = \frac{185}{1000} = \frac{37}{200}$ (a reduced fraction)

Problem 1: Express 5.3% as a decimal and as a fraction.

Answers: .053 and 53/1000

decimal: $5.3\% = .053$

fraction: $0.053 = \frac{53}{1000}$

Problem 2: Express $166\frac{2}{3}\%$ as a mixed number.

Answer: $1\frac{2}{3}$

$$= 166\frac{2}{3}\% = \frac{166\frac{2}{3}}{100}$$

$$= 166\frac{2}{3} \div 100 = \frac{500}{3} \div \frac{100}{1}$$

$$= \frac{\overset{5}{\cancel{500}}}{3} \times \frac{1}{\underset{1}{\cancel{100}}} = \frac{5}{3} = 1\frac{2}{3}$$

Exercise 5.5 Set A

In problems 1–12, convert each percent to a reduced fraction
or mixed number.

1. 17%   2. 23%   1. _____

                                                         2. _____

3. 5%   4. 6%   3. _____

                                                         4. _____

5. 8.4%   6. 6.2%   5. _____

                                                         6. _____

7. $9\frac{2}{3}\%$ 8. $7\frac{5}{6}\%$ 7. _____

                                                         8. _____

9. 136%   10. 215%   9. _____

                                                         10. _____

11. $43\frac{3}{4}\%$ 12. $27\frac{1}{4}\%$ 11. _____

                                                         12. _____

In problems 13–22, convert each percent to a decimal.

13. 45%   14. 58%   13. _____

                                                         14. _____

15. 5%   16. 8%   15. _____

                                                         16. _____

17. 236%   18. 189%   17. _____

                                                         18. _____

19. 26.5%   20. 20.4%   19. _____

                                                         20. _____

21. $8\frac{1}{4}\%$ 22. $9\frac{3}{4}\%$ 21. _____

                                                         22. _____

Exercise 5.5 Set B

In problems 1–12, convert each percent to a reduced fraction
or mixed number.

1. 19%

2. 31%

3. 8%

4. 2%

5. 7.6%

6. 4.8%

7. $6\frac{1}{3}\%$

8. $9\frac{1}{6}\%$

9. 212%

10. 152%

11. $57\frac{1}{4}\%$

12. $87\frac{3}{4}\%$

In problems 13–22, convert each percent to a decimal.

13. 36%

14. 45%

15. 4%

16. 3%

17. 157%

18. 139%

19. 15.8%

20. 16.3%

21. $4\frac{3}{4}\%$

22. $6\frac{1}{4}\%$

1. _____

2. _____

3. _____

4. _____

5. _____

6. _____

7. _____

8. _____

9. _____

10. _____

11. _____

12. _____

13. _____

14. _____

15. _____

16. _____

17. _____

18. _____

19. _____

20. _____

21. _____

22. _____

5.6 Converting Decimals and Fractions to Percents

In the previous section, you learned how to change percents to either decimals or fractions. In this section you will learn to do the reverse process, that is, change decimals or fractions to percents.

Remember that "percent" means "out of a hundred." So reading how many hundredths are in a decimal number tells the percent.

$$0.07 = \frac{7}{100} \quad \text{so} \quad 0.07 = 7\%.$$

$$0.9 = .90 = \frac{90}{100} \quad \text{so} \quad 0.9 = 90\%.$$

$$1.23 = 1\frac{23}{100} = \frac{123}{100} \quad \text{so} \quad 1.23 = 123\%.$$

Those examples point out a nice way to convert a decimal to a percent.

> ## Converting Decimals to Percents
>
> To convert a decimal to a percent, move the decimal point two places to the right and attach a % sign.

For example:

$$0.34 = 34\% \qquad 0.01 = 1\%$$
$$0.005 = .5\% \qquad 0.0625 = 6.25\%$$
$$2.75 = 275\% \qquad 1.146 = 114.6\%$$

In Section 4.9, you learned to change a fraction to a decimal by dividing the denominator into the numerator of the fraction. Since the above shows how to change a decimal to a percent, putting the two steps together will convert a fraction to a percent.

> ## Converting Fractions to Percents
>
> To convert a fraction to a percent, divide the denominator of the fraction into the numerator to get a decimal number, then convert the decimal to a percent.

For example:

$$\frac{3}{4} = 4)\overline{3.00}^{\,.75} = 75\% \qquad \frac{2}{5} = 5)\overline{2.0}^{\,.4} = 40\%$$

$$\frac{37}{500} = 500)\overline{37.000}^{\,.074} = 7.4\% \qquad \frac{8}{12} \approx 12)\overline{8.00000}^{\,.66666} \approx 66.67\%$$

$$\frac{5}{7} \approx 7)\overline{5.00000}^{\,.71428} \approx 71.43\% \qquad \frac{13}{11} \approx 11)\overline{13.00000}^{\,1.18181} \approx 118.18\%$$

Since the decimal form of some of those examples had many decimal digits, they were rounded off to the nearest hundredth of a percent. You may likewise have to round off the answers to some of the problems and exercises in this section.

Problem 1: On a test you got 63 out of 75 possible points. What percent did you get correct?

Answer: 84%

$$63 \text{ out of } 75 = \frac{63}{75}$$

$$\begin{array}{r} .84 \\ 75)\overline{63.00} \\ \underline{60\ 0} \\ 3\ 00 \\ \underline{3\ 00} \end{array}$$

$$.84 = 84\%$$

Problem 2: Express a ratio of 5 to 6 as a fraction, as a decimal, and as a percent.

Answers:

$$\text{fraction: } 5 \text{ to } 6 = \frac{5}{6}$$

$$\text{decimal: } 6)\overline{5.00000}^{.83333}$$

$$\text{percent: } .83333 \approx 83.33\%$$

Problem 3: Express 0.063 as a fraction and as a percent.

Answers:

$$\text{fraction: } \frac{63}{1000}$$

$$\text{percent: } 0.063 = 6.3\%$$

Problem 4: Express $\frac{4}{5}$ as a decimal and as a percent.

Answers:

$$\text{decimal: } 5)\overline{4.0}^{.8}$$
$$\underline{4.0}$$

$$\text{percent: } .8 = 80\%$$

Problem 5: Express $2\frac{3}{8}$ as a percent.

Answer: 237.5%

$$2\frac{3}{8} = \frac{19}{8} = 8)\overline{19.000}^{2.375}$$

$$2.375 = 237.5\%$$

Name _____   Date _____

Exercise 5.6 Set A

Determine the missing forms in each problem.

Mixed Number or Fraction	Decimal	Percent
1. $\dfrac{37}{50}$	.74	74%
2. $\dfrac{3}{25}$	.12	12%
3.	.02	2%
4.	.08	8%
5. $\dfrac{57}{1000}$	.057	5.7%
6.		1.9%
7. $\dfrac{1}{5}$		
8. $\dfrac{7}{10}$		
9.	.4675	
10.	.4425	
11. $2\dfrac{1}{6}$		
12. $1\dfrac{5}{6}$		
13.	2.375	
14.	1.025	
15.		$6\dfrac{5}{8}\%$

Handwritten work in problems 3 and 4 column: $\frac{2}{100} = \frac{1}{50}$ $\frac{8}{100} \stackrel{4}{=} \frac{2}{25}$

Exercise 5.6 Set B

Determine the missing forms below in each problem.

Mixed Number or Fraction	Decimal	Percent
1. $\dfrac{13}{50}$	_____	_____
2. $\dfrac{2}{25}$	_____	_____
3. _____	.04	_____
4. _____	.06	_____
5. _____	_____	6.1%
6. _____	_____	4.3%
7. $\dfrac{3}{5}$	_____	_____
8. $\dfrac{2}{5}$	_____	_____
9. _____	.2375	_____
10. _____	.2425	_____
11. $1\dfrac{2}{3}$	_____	_____
12. $2\dfrac{1}{3}$	_____	_____
13. _____	1.125	_____
14. _____	2.075	_____
15. _____	_____	$5\dfrac{3}{8}\%$

5.7 Percent of a Number

Percents are often used to find a part of a number or quantity. For example, you may encounter statements such as "60% of those surveyed", "35% discount", or "5.5% sales tax." In statements such as those, you are finding a part of a total amount. Again the word "of" indicates multiplication, just as it did in finding a fraction of a number in Section 3.7.

For example:

60% of 5690	means	$60\% \times 5690$
35% of \$236	means	$35\% \times \$236$
5.5% of \$179.99	means	$5.5\% \times \$179.99$

Remember to change the percent into either a fraction or a decimal before you use it in multiplication.

Example 1

Find 25% of 76.

Method 1 (as a decimal)

$25\% = .25$

25% of $76 = .25 \times 76 = 19$

Method 2 (as a fraction)

$25\% = \dfrac{25}{100} = \dfrac{1}{4}$

25% of $76 = \dfrac{1}{4} \times 76 = 19$

Example 2

Find 6.5% of \$275.44.

$6.5\% = 0.065$

6.5% of $\$275.44 = 0.065 \times \$275.44$

$= \$17.9036 \approx \$17.90$
(rounded to the hundredths)

Problem 1: Find 60% of 3420.

Answer: 2052

60% of $3420 =$
$0.6 \times 3420 = 2052$

Problem 2: Find $43\frac{1}{4}\%$ of \$54.72.

Answer: \$23.67

$43\dfrac{1}{4}\% = 43.25\% = 0.4325$

$43\dfrac{1}{4}\%$ of $\$54.72 =$

$0.4325 \times \$54.72 =$
$\$23.6664 \approx \$23.67$

Matters such as taxes, commissions, discounts, down payments, bonuses, raises, deductions, etc., are often calculated as a percent of a certain number. The word **"of"** in this situation again means **"times"**; it indicates that you must multiply the percent times the number.

Example 3

If your state has a 5% sales tax, what would your tax be, to the nearest cent, on a $178.99 purchase?

Analyze: The sales tax is 5% of the price. That is, 5% × $178.99.

Solve: 5% × $178.99 =
$0.05 \times \$178.99 = \$8.9495$
$\approx \$8.95$

Example 4

If you now earn $295.50 per week, a 9.2% raise would increase your earnings by how much?

Analyze: The raise is 9.2% of your present salary.
That is, 9.2% × $295.50.

Solve: 9.2% × $295.50 =
$0.092 \times \$295.50 = \$27.186$
$\approx \$27.19$

Example 5

A local department store is giving a 30% discount on all merchandise. How much of a discount would you receive on a VCR that regularly sells for $489.99?

Analyze: The discount is 30% of the regular price.
That is, 30% × $489.99.

Solve: 30% of $489.99 =
$0.3 \times \$489.99 = \$146.997$
$\approx \$147.00$

Problem 3:   A realtor's commission is 3% of the sale price of a house. If a house sells for $98,000, what is the realtor's commission?

Answer: $2940

3% of $98,000 =
$0.03 \times \$98,000 = \$2940$

Problem 4:   How much would you need for the down payment on a $9,984 car, if the dealer requires 15% down?

Answer: $1497.60

15% of $9,984 =
$0.15 \times \$9,984 = \$1497.60$

Problem 5:   5.2% of the students withdrew from school during a semester. If the beginning enrollment was 4250, how many students withdrew?

Answer: 221 students

5.2% of 4250 =
$0.052 \times 4250 = 221$

Exercise 5.7 Set A

Round off dollar amounts to the nearest cent.

1. 30% of 50

2. 60% of 65

3. 5% of 18.7

4. 6% of 17.7

5. 0.8% of $1476.59

6. 0.3% of $5,700,259

7. 16.4% of 600

8. 19.3% of 700

9. 78.32% of $76.99

10. 67.58% of $992.86

11. $5\frac{3}{4}$% of 82

12. $4\frac{1}{4}$% of 91

1. _____

2. _____

3. _____

4. _____

5. _____

6. _____

7. _____

8. _____

9. _____

10. _____

11. _____

12. _____

13. If the sales tax rate is 7.5%, what is the sales tax on a bike priced at $189.95?

14. How much would a 33% discount amount to on a $159.99 suit?

15. How much would you make from selling $980 worth of books, if you receive $8\frac{1}{4}$% commission on the sale?

16. How much would you make on the sale of a $125,000 house, if you receive $3\frac{1}{4}$% commission on the sale?

17. If a car dealer requires a 15% down payment, how much would you have to put down when purchasing a $6957 car?

18. The Newark School District plans to increase budget amounts by 5.8% next year. If $85,200 is now spent on the library, how much will be budgeted for next year?

13. _____

14. _____

15. _____

16. _____

17. _____

18. _____

Exercise 5.7 Set B

Round off dollar amounts to the nearest cent.

1. 20% of 55

2. 40% of 65

3. 4% of 27.6

4. 3% of 18.4

5. 0.12% of $49,600,740

6. 6.9% of $376.36

7. 14.6% of 500

8. 16.7% of 700

9. 86.23% of $612.75

10. 74.32% of $82.59

11. $3\frac{1}{4}$% of 58

12. $6\frac{3}{4}$% of 84

13. What is the sales tax on a $345.62 rug, if the sales tax rate is 4.5%?

14. What would a 40% discount amount to on the purchase of a $89.75 radio?

15. How much would you make from selling $850 worth of tickets, if you receive an $11\frac{1}{4}$% commission on the sales?

16. If you receive $2\frac{1}{4}$% commission on sales you make, how much would you make on sales of $650,790?

17. How much is the 25% down payment on a truck that sells for $5789?

18. ZETCO stocks experienced a 12.6% decrease during a week. If the stock sold for $35.00 a share at the start of the week, how much did it sell for at the end of the week?

1. _____

2. _____

3. _____

4. _____

5. _____

6. _____

7. _____

8. _____

9. _____

10. _____

11. _____

12. _____

13. _____

14. _____

15. _____

16. _____

17. _____

18. _____

5.8 Percentage Problems

Consider this problem again: "On a test you got 63 out of 75 possible points. What percent did you get correct?" Since "percent" means "out of a hundred," we can consider this problem as a proportion: 63 out of 75 is what number out of 100? That is,

$$\frac{63}{75} = \frac{P}{100}$$ (Note: P is used to represent the percent or part out of 100.)

We can get the answer for the percent (P) by solving that proportion.

$$\frac{63}{75} = \frac{P}{100}$$

$$\frac{75 \times P}{75} = \frac{6300}{75}$$

$$P = 84$$

The amount you got correct was 63, the test was based on 75 points, and we discovered that the percent was 84. That relationship can be expressed by the **percent proportion:**

$$\frac{A}{B} = \frac{P}{100}$$

A is the amount

B is the base

P is the percent

The percent proportion can be used to solve different types of percentage problems. If you can identify the amount (A), the base (B), and the percent (P), you can utilize the percent proportion.

Here is how you can identify the **amount (A),** the **base (B),** and the **percent (P):**

1. The percent (P) is written with the word "percent" or the % sign.
2. The base (B) follows the word "of."
3. The amount (A) is the remaining number.

By correctly identifying the percent, base, and amount, you can set up a proportion that will enable you to efficiently solve percentage problems. The examples and problems that follow will show you how this is done.

Example 1

15 is what percent of 50?

1. Identify the A, B, P:

$$\underset{\underset{A}{\downarrow}}{15} \text{ is } \underset{\underset{P}{\downarrow}}{\underline{\text{what percent}}} \text{ of } \underset{\underset{B}{\downarrow}}{\underline{50}}?$$
(unknown)   (follows "of")

2. Set up the percent proportion:

$$\frac{A}{B} = \frac{P}{100}$$

$$\frac{15}{50} = \frac{P}{100} \quad \text{(Leave the unknown with its letter.)}$$

3. Solve the proportion:

$$\frac{50 \times P}{50} = \frac{1500}{50}$$

$$P = 30$$

Note: When using the percent proportion, you do *not* move the decimal point to express the percent. The answer to Example 1 is simply 30%

Example 2

16 is 22% of what number?

1. Identify the A, B, P:

$$\underset{\underset{A}{\downarrow}}{16} \text{ is } \underset{\underset{P}{\downarrow}}{22\%} \text{ of } \underset{\underset{B}{\downarrow}}{\underline{\text{what number}}}?$$
(unknown)

2. Set up the percent proportion:

$$\frac{A}{B} = \frac{P}{100}$$

$$\frac{16}{B} = \frac{22}{100}$$

3. Solve the proportion:

$$22 \times B = 16 \times 100$$

$$\frac{22 \times B}{22} = \frac{1600}{22}$$

$$B \approx 72.73$$

Example 3

9.35% of 259.9 is how much?

1. Identify the A, B, P:

$$\underset{\underset{P}{\downarrow}}{\underline{9.35\%}} \text{ of } \underset{\underset{B}{\downarrow}}{\underline{259.9}} \text{ is } \underset{\underset{\substack{A \\ (\text{unknown})}}{\downarrow}}{\underline{\text{how much?}}}$$

2. Set up the percent proportion:

$$\frac{A}{B} = \frac{P}{100}$$

$$\frac{A}{259.9} = \frac{9.35}{100}$$

3. Solve the proportion:

$$\frac{100 \times A}{100} = \frac{2430.065}{100}$$

$$A \approx 24.30$$

Problem 1: 91 is what percent of 364?

Answer: 25%

Percent: P unknown
Base: $B = 364$
Amount: $A = 91$

$$\frac{A}{B} = \frac{P}{100}$$

$$\frac{91}{364} = \frac{P}{100}$$

$$\frac{364 \times P}{364} = \frac{9100}{364}$$

$$P = 25$$

Problem 2: 84.3 is 15% of what number?

Answer: 562

Percent: $P = 15$
Base: B unknown
Amount: $A = 84.3$

$$\frac{A}{B} = \frac{P}{100}$$

$$\frac{84.3}{B} = \frac{15}{100}$$

$$\frac{15 \times B}{15} = \frac{8430}{15}$$

$$B = 562$$

Problem 3:   What is 9.5% of 75,000?

Answer: 7125

Percent: $P = 9.5$
Base: $B = 75,000$
Amount: A unknown

$$\frac{A}{75,000} = \frac{9.5}{100}$$

$$\frac{100 \times A}{100} = \frac{712,500}{100}$$

$$A = 7125$$

Problem 4: $41\frac{1}{4}$ is what percent of 30?

Answer: 137.5

Percent: P unknown
Base: $B = 30$
Amount: $A = 41\frac{1}{4} = 41.25$

$$\frac{A}{B} = \frac{P}{100}$$

$$\frac{41.25}{30} = \frac{P}{100}$$

$$\frac{30 \times P}{30} = \frac{4125}{30}$$

$$P = 137.5$$

Problem 5:   19.8 is $7\frac{1}{3}$% of what number?

Answer: 25%

Percent: $P = 7\frac{1}{3}$
Base: B unknown
Amount: $A = 19.8$

$$= \frac{P}{100}$$

$$\frac{19.8}{B} = \frac{7\frac{1}{3}}{100}$$

$$\frac{7\frac{1}{3} \times B}{7\frac{1}{3}} = \frac{1980}{7\frac{1}{3}}$$

$$B = 1980 \div 7\frac{1}{3}$$

$$B = 1980 \div \frac{22}{3}$$

$$B = 1980 \times \frac{3}{22}$$

$$B = 270$$

Exercise 5.8 Set A

1. 9 is what percent of 15?

2. 28 is what percent of 35?

3. 20 is 60% of what number?

4. 18 is 40% of what number?

5. What is 6% of 50?

6. What is 5% of 70?

7. 3.38 is what percent of 13?

8. 4.2 is what percent of 20?

9. 18 is 8% of what number?

10. 15 is 8% of what number?

11. 32% of 148 is how much?

12. 43% of 291 is how much?

13. 63 is what percent of 17.5?

14. 15 is what percent of 2.5?

15. 24 is $5\frac{2}{3}$% of what number?

16. 18 is $4\frac{2}{3}$% of what number?

17. What is 17.6% of 45.6?

18. What is 15.3% of 20.7?

19. $\frac{3}{4}$ is what percent of $\frac{5}{8}$?

1. _____

2. _____

3. _____

4. _____

5. _____

6. _____

7. _____

8. _____

9. _____

10. _____

11. _____

12. _____

13. _____

14. _____

15. _____

16. _____

17. _____

18. _____

19. _____

Exercise 5.8 Set B

1. 12 is what percent of 40?

2. 10 is what percent of 25?

3. 60 is 75% of what number?

4. 18 is 40% of what number?

5. What is 4% of 80?

6. What is 7% of 60?

7. 19.8 is what percent of 90?

8. 13.2 is what percent of 55?

9. 17 is 3% of what number?

10. 24 is 4% of what number?

11. 82% of 176 is how much?

12. 53% of 247 is how much?

13. 27.5 is what percent of 11?

14. 76.8 is what percent of 12?

15. 42 is $7\frac{2}{3}$% of what number?

16. 36 is $8\frac{2}{3}$% of what number?

17. What is 14.8% of 21.8?

18. What is 12.7% of 43.6?

19. $\frac{3}{8}$ is what percent of $\frac{3}{4}$?

1. _____

2. _____

3. _____

4. _____

5. _____

6. _____

7. _____

8. _____

9. _____

10. _____

11. _____

12. _____

13. _____

14. _____

15. _____

16. _____

17. _____

18. _____

19. _____

5.9 Applications Involving Percents

In Section 5.7, you saw how percents can be used to determine sales tax, down payments, raises, commissions, discounts, and the like. In this section, you will apply those principles along with your other arithmetic skills to solve other problems that involve the use of percents.

Example 1

68% of those polled were in favor of the Park Initiative. If 6,275 people were polled, how many were in favor of the initiative? How many were not in favor of the initiative?

Analyze: 1. The number in favor is 68% of the 6,275 polled.
2. Subtract those in favor from the total polled to get the number not in favor.

Solve: 1. 68% of 6,275 =
.68 × 6275 = 4267
2.   6275
−4267
2008

Example 2

According to Schedule X (single filing status) of the 1995 Federal Tax Booklet, if your taxable income is over $117,950 but not over $256,500, your tax is $31,832.50 plus 36% of the amount over $117,950. If your taxable income for 1995 was $152,000, how much tax did you owe the government?

Analyze: 1. Determine the amount earned over $117,950.
2. Find 36% of that amount.
3. Find total tax by adding the result of step 2 to $31,832.50.

Solve: 1. $152,000 − $117,950 = $34,050
2. 36% of $34,050 = 0.36 × $34,050
= $12,258
3. $31,832.50
+12,258.00
$44,090.50

Example 3

A stereo has a regular price of $598.00. If you receive a 25% discount, how much would the stereo cost?

Analyze: 1. The discount is 25% of the regular price.
2. Get the cost by subtracting the discount from the regular price.

Solve: 1. 25% of $598.00 =
.25 × $598.00 = $149.50
2. $598.00
−149.50
$448.50

Problem 1: What is the final cost of a $28.75 item, after 6.5% sales tax has been added?

Answer: $30.62
tax: 065 × $28.75 ≈ $1.87
cost: $28.75 + $1.87 = $30.62

Using the Percent Proportion

In other types of percent problems, you may have to use the percent proportion that was discussed in Section 5.8:

$$\frac{A}{B} = \frac{P}{100} \quad \text{where} \quad \begin{matrix} A = \text{the amount} \\ B = \text{the base} \\ P = \text{the percent} \end{matrix}$$

You will find it easier to use the percent proportion if you first translate the percent word problem into a condensed phrase of the form ___ is ___% of ___. By doing that, you can readily identity the A, P, and B.

Example 4

During the last 3 years the Stuffers won 75% of their basketball games. If they won 69 games, how many games did they play?

Analyze: 1. Restate the problem in a condensed form:
69 is 75% of ? .
2. $P = 75$, $B = $ unknown, $A = 69$

Solve:

$$\frac{A}{B} = \frac{P}{100}$$

$$\frac{69}{B} = \frac{75}{100}$$

$$75 \times \frac{B}{75} = \frac{6900}{75}$$

$$B = 92$$

Example 5

A microwave oven was reduced from $450 to $390. To the nearest tenth, what percent was the oven reduced?

(Note: In a percent decrease or increase problem, the base is always the *original price*, the "base price.")

Analyze: 1. The reduction is 60 (450 − 390).
2. Restate the problem in a condensed form:
60 is ? % of 450.
3. $P = $ unknown, $B = 450$, $A = 60$

Solve:

$$\frac{A}{B} = \frac{P}{100}$$

$$\frac{60}{450} = \frac{P}{100}$$

$$450 \times \frac{P}{450} = \frac{6000}{450}$$

$$P \approx 13.3$$

Name _____ Date _____

Exercise 5.9 Set A

1. What is the final price of a $679.79 typewriter, if $6\frac{1}{2}\%$ sales tax is charged?

1. _____

2. How much should a $179.99 ring cost after a 40% discount?

2. _____

3. How much would a $763.45 item cost after a 12% discount?

3. _____

4. What is the final price of a $1397 computer system, if 7% sales tax is charged?

4. _____

5. Using the tax facts from Example 2 on page 297, what would the tax be for a 1995 taxable income of $180,000?

5. _____

6. After making a 25% down payment on a $3450 boat, how much do you still owe on the boat?

6. _____

7. Of the 46,550 registered voters in a precinct, 32% voted on election day. How many registered voters actually voted?

7. _____

8. If you earn $27,890 a year but a change in jobs causes a 6.2% cut in pay, how much do you now earn per year?

8. _____

9. If you earn $652 a month and get a 12.5% raise, what will your new monthly salary be?

9. _____

10. If you get 68 points out of a possible 80 points on a test, what is your percent score on the test?

10. _____

11. What is the net pay on $400 after deductions of 7.65% for insurance, 10% for federal income tax, and 1.62% for state taxes?

11. _____

12. If a team wins 84 out of 120 games, what percent of their games did they win?

12. _____

13. If a $200 dress sells for $140, what is the percent decrease in price?

13. _____

14. If your hourly wage increases from $5.60 to $6.44, what is the percent increase in your hourly wage?

14. _____

15. In a school election 52% voted for Jason Chen. If 325 voted for Jason, how many voted in the election?

15. _____

16. In a survey of TV viewers, 526 people were watching the *Night Show.* If that is 20% of those surveyed, how many were surveyed?

16. _____

17. If within a month after purchasing a $16,000 car it is worth $15,000, what is the percent decrease in its value?

17. _____

18. In 1990, Pro Rodeo All-Around Champion, Ty Murray, won $213,772 and in 1994, he won $246,170. What was the percent increase in his earnings?

18. _____

19. According to the U.S. Bureau of Statistics, in 1983, the unemployment rate was 9.6% and in 1993 the rate was 6.8%. If the U.S. work force in 1983 was 112 million and in 1993 was 128 million, in which year was there more unemployed workers?

19. _____

20. According to the Bureau of Labor Statistics, in 1985 the number of men, aged 25 to 54, who were out of the paid labor force to do house-keeping and/or care for children was 148,000. In 1990, that amount jumped to 257,000. What is the percent increase the number of these stay-at-home dads?

20. _____

21. According to the California Milk Advisory Board, nonfat milk contains 0.25% fat. How much fat is contained in a half-gallon (128 ounces) of milk?

21. _____

Exercise 5.9 Set B

1. What is the final price of a $978.88 sofa, if $6\frac{1}{2}$% sales tax is charged?

1. _____

2. How much would a $678.99 T.V. set cost after a 30% discount?

2. _____

3. How much would an $89.75 radio cost after a 25% discount?

3. _____

4. If $7\frac{1}{2}$% sales tax is charged, what is the final price of a $2367.59 motor-cycle?

4. _____

5. Using the tax facts from Example 2 on page 297, what would the tax be for a 1995 taxable income of $250,000?

5. _____

6. After making a 15% down payment on a $19,450 van, how much do you still owe on the van?

6. _____

7. Of the 16,500 registered voters in a precinct, 47% cast a ballot on election day. How many registered voters actually voted?

7. _____

8. If you earn $1700 a month but a change in jobs causes a 4.3% cut in pay, how much do you now earn per year after the cut?

8. _____

9. If you earn $12,790 a year and get a 13.7% raise, what will your new yearly salary be?

9. _____

10. If you picked 6 of the winners out of 15 horse races, what percent did you pick correctly?

10. _____

11. What is the net pay on $560 after deductions of 7.65% for insurance, 10% for federal income tax, and 1.62% for state taxes?

11. _____

12. If a quarterback completes 27 out of 40 passes, what is the quarterback's percent completion?

12. _____

13. If a painting that is marked $350 is sold for $287, what is the percent decrease in price?

13. _____

14. If your hourly wage increases from $7.00 to $7.48, what is the percent increase in your hourly wage?

14. _____

15. Sixty percent of the students in a class get grades above a "C." If 27 people get above a "C" grade, how many were in the class?

15. _____

16. Suppose 1.5% of the light bulbs shipped from a factory are defective. If there are 18 defective light bulbs in a shipment, how many light bulbs were shipped?

16. _____

17. If the price of a share of stock drops from $175 to $154 in one day, what is the percent decrease in price?

17. _____

18. The U.S. Bureau of Statistics estimates that there will be a 74.4% increase in special education teachers by the year 2005. In 1992, there were 358,000 special ed teachers. How many are estimated for 2005?

18. _____

19. From 1991 to 1994, Ford Taurus sales in the U.S. went from 299,659 to 397,031, while Honda Accord sales went from 397,297 to 367,615. Find the percent increase in Ford sales and percent decrease in Honda sales.

19. _____

20. A world class sprinter can run a 100 meters at an average speed of 22.6 mph, while a world class swimmer can swim a 100 meters at an average of 4.6 mph. What is the percent decrease between a sprinter's and a swimmer's speed?

20. _____

5.10 Applications Involving Simple Interest

These problems really pique my interest.

$I = P \times R \times T$

If you borrow money, you must pay back more than you borrowed. That extra amount that you pay back is called **interest.** The amount of interest you are charged is determined by taking a percent of the amount borrowed times the length of time of the loan. The amount borrowed is called the **principal** (P). The percent used is called the **rate** (R). The length of time for the loan is called the **time** (T). Interest on a loan can be determined using this formula:

$$\text{Interest} = \text{Principal} \times \text{Rate} \times \text{Time}$$

$$I = P \times R \times T$$

Interest calculated using that formula is called **simple interest,** since it is computed on only the original principal during the time period. Banks, however, compute interest on previously earned interest, called compound interest, and use principles of compound interest in amortizing loans. Compound interest and amortization techniques are beyond the scope of this chapter but will be examined in chapter 7.

Example 1

How much interest is charged on a $500 loan for one year using a 12% yearly interest rate?

Analyze: Use the interest formula with:

$P = \$500$
$R = 12\% = 0.12$ per year
$T = 1$ year

Solve: $I = P \times R \times T$
$= \$500 \times 0.12 \times 1$
$= \$60$

In interest problems you must make sure that the rate and the time are expressed in the same units. If the rate (R) is a *yearly* rate, then the time (T) must be expressed in *years*. If the rate (R) is a *monthly* rate, then the time (T) must be expressed in *months*.

Example 2

What is the interest on $3200 at 1.5% per month for 2 years?

Analyze: Use the interest formula with:

$P = \$3200$
$R = 1.5\% = 0.015$ per month
$T = 2$ years $= 24$ months

Solve: $I = P \times R \times T$
$= \$3200 \times 0.015 \times 24$
$= \$1152$

Once you know how to calculate the interest on a loan, you can determine how much you must pay each month to pay off the loan. Keep in mind that when you pay off a loan you must pay back the principal *and* the interest.

Example 3

Determine the monthly payments necessary to pay off a $6300 loan for 3 years at an annual rate of 13%.

Analyze: 1. Determine the interest using the interest formula.
2. Determine the total to be paid back by adding the principal and the interest.
3. Determine the monthly payments by dividing the total by the number of months. (3 yr = 36 mo)

Solve: 1. $I = P \times R \times T$
$= \$6300 \times 0.13 \times 3$
$= \$2457$
2. total = $6300 + $2457 = $8757
3. payments = $8757 ÷ 36 = $243.25

Example 4

You are purchasing a new car with a total price of $9500. The dealer gives you a 10% discount and a $1500 trade-in on your old car. To pay off the balance you take out a loan with a 12.6% yearly rate for 42 months. To the nearest cent, what should your monthly payments be to pay off the loan?

Analyze: 1. Determine the balance by subtracting the 10% discount and the $1500 trade-in from the total price of $9500.
2. Determine the interest. P = $7050, R = 12.6% = 0.126 per yr., T = 42 months = 3.5 yrs.
3. Get the total to be repaid by adding principal and interest.
4. Get monthly payments by dividing the total by the number of months.

Solve: 1. discount = 0.10 × 9500
$= \$950$
balance = 9500 − 950 − 1500 = $7050
2. $I = P \times R \times T$
$= \$7050 \times 0.126 \times 3.5$
$= \$3109.05$
3. total = 7050 + 3109.05 = $10,159.05
4. payments = $10,159.05 ÷ 42 ≈ $241.88

Problem 1: Determine to the nearest cent the monthly payment needed to pay off a loan of $700 at 9.5% per year in two years.

Answer: $34.71

$I = 700 \times 0.095 \times 2$
$= \$133$
total = 700 + 133
$= \$833$
payments = 833 ÷ 24
$\approx \$34.71$

Name _____   Date _____

Exercise 5.10 Set A

In problems 1–10, find the simple interest to the nearest cent for loans with the following principal (P), rate (R), and time (T).

1. P = $500, R = 15% per year, T = 2 years

1. _____

2. P = $700, R = 16% per year, T = 3 years

2. _____

3. P = $2000, R = 9% per year, T = 3.5 years

3. _____

4. P = $5000, R = 8% per year, T = 2.5 years

4. _____

5. P = $7500, R = 12.76% per year, T = 4 years

5. _____

6. P = $9600, R = 14.75% per year, T = 5 years

6. _____

7. P = $4655, R = 13.83% per year, T = 42 months

7. _____

8. P = $5994, R = $14\frac{1}{4}$% per year, T = 30 months

8. _____

9. P = $10,800, R = 1.5% per month, T = 5 years

9. _____

10. P = $12,700, R = 1.2% per month, T = 6 years

10. _____

In problems 11–15, round off answers to the nearest cent.

11. You borrow $700 from "Insta-loan" at a yearly interest rate of 17.5% for 4 years. What will your monthly payment be to repay the loan?

11. _____

12. You borrow $8900 from the "Easy-Out" Loan Company at a yearly interest rate of 16.9% for 5 years. What will your monthly payment be to repay the loan?

12. _____

13. "John's T.V." gives you a 25% discount on a $987.48 T.V. and you pay $6\frac{1}{2}$% sales tax on the balance. If you take out a 2 year loan with an annual interest rate of 15.6%, what will your monthly payment be?

13. _____

14. What is the monthly payment needed to pay off a $7325.66 loan for 30 months with a yearly interest rate of $16\frac{1}{4}$%?

14. _____

15. After trading in your old car, you still owe $6200 on a new car. You pay 7% sales tax on that balance and the dealer adds $355 for license and dealer preparation fees. If you take out a 5 year loan for the balance after those fees, with a yearly interest rate of 19.2% on the loan, what is your monthly payment?

15. _____

Exercise 5.10 Set B

In problems 1–10, find the simple interest to the nearest cent for loans with the following principal (P), rate (R), and time (T).

1. P = $800, R = 16% per year, T = 2 years

1. _____

2. P = $400, R = 13% per year, T = 3 years

2. _____

3. P = $4000, R = 11% per year, T = 4.5 years

3. _____

4. P = $600, R = 12% per year, T = 1.5 years

4. _____

5. P = $6700, R = 13.26% per year, T = 4 years

5. _____

6. P = $7900, R = 15.46% per year, T = 5 years

6. _____

7. P = $3467, R = 19.2% per year, T = 18 months

7. _____

8. P = $7899, R = 17.6% per year, T = 42 months

8. _____

9. P = $10,700, R = 1.3% per month, T = 5 years

9. _____

10. P = $11,600, R = 1.4% per month, T = 6 years

10. _____

In problems 11–15, round off answers to the nearest cent.

11. You borrow $900 from "Man at Atlantic Plan" for 3 years at a yearly interest rate of 14.5%. What is the monthly payment needed to pay off the loan?

11. _____

12. You borrow $8900 from the "Speed-Cash" Loan Company for 5 years at a yearly interest rate of 15.6%. What is the monthly payment needed to pay off the loan?

12. _____

13. "Atlantic Stereo" gives you $\frac{1}{3}$ off on a $1653.99 stereo system and you pay $5\frac{1}{2}$% sales tax on the balance. What is the monthly payment, if you take out a 2 year loan with an annual interest rate of 14.8%?

13. _____

14. What is the monthly payment needed to pay off a $6987.45 loan for 42 months with a yearly interest rate of $14\frac{1}{4}$%?

14. _____

15. After trading in your old car, you still owe $5800 on a new car. You pay 6% sales tax on that balance and the dealer adds $285 for license and dealer preparation fees. If you take out a 4 year loan for the balance after those fees, with a yearly interest rate of 17.4% on the loan, what is your monthly payment?

15. _____

Chapter 5 Summary

Concepts

You may refer to the sections listed below to review how to do the following:

1. set up and reduce ratios by expressing them as fractions. (5.1)
2. solve proportions by using cross multiplication. (5.2), (5.3)
3. solve word problems involving proportions. (5.4)
4. convert a percent to a fraction by dropping the percent sign, placing the number over 100, and reducing if possible. (5.5)
5. convert a percent to a decimal by dropping the percent sign and moving the decimal point two places to the left. (5.5)
6. convert a decimal to a percent by moving the decimal point two places to the right and attaching a percent sign. (5.6)
7. convert a fraction to a percent by first changing the fraction to a decimal. (5.6)
8. find a percent of a number by using the word "of" as an indication of multiplication. (5.7)
9. solve percentage problems by using the percent proportion:

$$\frac{\mathbf{A}}{\mathbf{B}} = \frac{\mathbf{P}}{\mathbf{100}} \qquad \text{where } A \text{ is the amount, } B \text{ is the base,}$$
and P is the percent. (5.8)

10. solve word problems involving percents. (5.9)
11. calculate simple interest using the formula: $\mathbf{I = P \times R \times T}$

Interest = Principal × Rate × Time (5.10)

Terminology

This chapter's important terms and their page numbers are as follows:

cross multiplying: in a proportion, the process of multiplying the numerator of the first ratio by the denominator of the second ratio, and multiplying the denominator of the first ratio by the numerator of the second ratio. (265)

cross products: the answers from cross multiplying. (265)

interest: profit derived from money that has been loaned. (303)

percent: amount expressed as a part out of one hundred. (279)

percent proportion: the proportion, $\dfrac{A}{B} = \dfrac{P}{100}$, used in percentage problems. (291)

principal: amount of money being loaned. (303)

proportion: a statement that two ratios are equal. (265)

ratio: a comparison of two quantities that can be expressed as a fraction. (261)

simple interest: the interest calculated on the original principal during the time period of the loan. (303)

Chapter 5 Crossword Puzzle

Across

4. P × R × T
6. Not high
8. The ratio, 4 to 12, is equivalent to _____ to 3.
9. First digit of 47% of 1256.
10. Out of 100.
11. 20 : 45 is equivalent to _____ : 9
13. Percent of interest
14. The units place is called the _____ place.
15. 40% discount on a $5 item
17. A fraction
19. 17.85 is what percent of $255?
20. Results of cross multiplying
22. Not odd
23. Third digit of 36.5% of $1388.36

Down

1. The T in I = P × R × T
2. Amount deposited
3. Last digit of $576 after a 25% discount
5. Digit to the right of the decimal point
6. To change % to decimal, move decimal _____.
7. 56.3% as a decimal has 5 in the _____ place.
10. Two equal ratios form a _____.
12. Money is rounded to the _____ place.
16. Third digit of $5\frac{3}{4}$% of 82
18. Simple interest on $15 at 5% for 4 years
21. 600% as a decimal

Name _____   Date _____

Chapter 5 Practice Test A

1. Express a ratio of 84 to 315 as a reduced fraction.

   1. _____

2. Solve for N. $\dfrac{N}{21} = \dfrac{24}{9}$ 3. Solve for B. $\dfrac{91}{B} = \dfrac{13}{100}$

   2. _____

   3. _____

4. Solve for Y. $\dfrac{5.5}{Y} = \dfrac{9.6}{18.7}$ 5. Solve for P. $\dfrac{5}{8} = \dfrac{P}{100}$

   4. _____

   5. _____

6. Express 6.4% as a decimal and as a reduced fraction.

   6. _____

7. Express 0.132 as a reduced fraction and as a percent.

   7. _____

8. What is 16.8% of 420?   9. 72 is what percent of 120?

   8. _____

   9. _____

10. 19 is 7% of what number?   11. What is $47\frac{1}{3}$% of $150.60?

   10. _____

   11. _____

12. To the nearest cent, what is the final price of clothing totaling $64.25, after 6% sales tax is added?

   12. _____

13. On a sunny day a 5 ft boy casts a 6 ft shadow. At the same time, a pole casts a shadow of 32 ft. How tall is the pole?

   13. _____

14. How much would you still owe on a $3620 bill after paying 15% of the bill?

   14. _____

15. From the "Easy-Out Finance Company" you borrow $2140 with a simple interest loan of 14.6% per year and plan to pay it back in 42 months. To the nearest cent, how much will your monthly payments be?

   15. _____

Chapter 5 Practice Test B

1. Express a ratio of 130 to 273 as a reduced fraction.

1. _____

2. Solve for N. $\dfrac{N}{21} = \dfrac{15}{9}$ 3. Solve for B. $\dfrac{77}{B} = \dfrac{14}{100}$

2. _____

3. _____

4. Solve for Y. $\dfrac{6.5}{Y} = \dfrac{7.6}{12.3}$ 5. Solve for P. $\dfrac{7}{16} = \dfrac{P}{100}$

4. _____

5. _____

6. Express 8.2% as a decimal and as a reduced fraction.

6. _____

7. Express 0.146 as a reduced fraction and as a percent.

7. _____

8. What is 17.3% of 120?   9. 63 is what percent of 175?

8. _____

9. _____

10. 17 is 9% of what number?   11. What is $54\dfrac{2}{3}$% of $91.20?

10. _____

11. _____

12. To the nearest cent, what is the final price of tools costing $84.16, after 7% sales tax is added?

12. _____

13. If the ratio of chemical to water in a plant spray is 2 to 9, how much water should be added to 8.6 ounces of the chemical?

13. _____

14. If you earn $525 a month and receive a 7.6% raise, how much will you then earn per month?

14. _____

15. From the "Fast Finance Company" you borrow $3040 with a simple interest loan of 15.2% per year and plan to pay it back in 30 months. To the nearest cent, how much will your monthly payments be?

15. _____

Chapter 5 Supplementary Exercises

Section 5.1

A soccer team won 20 games, lost 16, and tied 4. Find the reduced ratio for the following:

1. wins to losses
2. wins to ties
3. wins to total games
4. ties to total games
5. ties to losses
6. losses to total games
7. losses to wins
8. ties to wins

Section 5.2

In problems 1–6, determine if the ratios form a proportion.

1. $\dfrac{4}{6}$ and $\dfrac{24}{36}$

2. $\dfrac{16}{21}$ and $\dfrac{39}{52}$

3. $\dfrac{7}{12}$ and $\dfrac{35}{60}$

4. $\dfrac{10}{17}$ and $\dfrac{20}{27}$

5. $\dfrac{12}{18}$ and $\dfrac{18}{27}$

6. $\dfrac{56}{85}$ and $\dfrac{36}{65}$

In problems 7–21, solve for N.

7. $\dfrac{N}{5} = \dfrac{21}{15}$

8. $\dfrac{14}{N} = \dfrac{7}{4}$

9. $\dfrac{9}{14} = \dfrac{N}{84}$

10. $\dfrac{25}{60} = \dfrac{N}{24}$

11. $\dfrac{N}{48} = \dfrac{35}{20}$

12. $\dfrac{28}{12} = \dfrac{N}{18}$

13. $\dfrac{24}{45} = \dfrac{56}{N}$

14. $\dfrac{78}{52} = \dfrac{6}{N}$

15. $\dfrac{N}{56} = \dfrac{7}{8}$

16. $\dfrac{12}{19} = \dfrac{N}{114}$

17. $\dfrac{132}{N} = \dfrac{11}{4}$

18. $\dfrac{N}{45} = \dfrac{133}{35}$

19. $\dfrac{N}{12} = \dfrac{84}{112}$

20. $\dfrac{21}{N} = \dfrac{99}{165}$

21. $\dfrac{25}{70} = \dfrac{N}{84}$

Section 5.3

Solve for N in each of the following:

1. $\dfrac{N}{9} = \dfrac{7}{12}$

2. $\dfrac{16}{N} = \dfrac{17}{100}$

3. $\dfrac{6}{7} = \dfrac{N}{4}$

4. $\dfrac{14}{N} = \dfrac{4}{9}$

5. $\dfrac{21}{17} = \dfrac{6}{N}$

6. $\dfrac{4.7}{9.3} = \dfrac{N}{6.5}$

7. $\dfrac{19}{2.75} = \dfrac{13.4}{N}$

8. $\dfrac{N}{5.6} = \dfrac{.43}{2.15}$

9. $\dfrac{6.5}{N} = \dfrac{11}{3.7}$

10. $\dfrac{\frac{1}{2}}{6} = \dfrac{N}{\frac{1}{4}}$

11. $\dfrac{N}{6\frac{1}{4}} = \dfrac{8}{\frac{1}{2}}$

12. $\dfrac{5\frac{1}{3}}{N} = \dfrac{1\frac{1}{6}}{6\frac{2}{3}}$

Section 5.4

1. If 9 baseball tickets cost $47.97, how much would 37 tickets cost?

2. If you spend $445 on gasoline for five months, what would you expect to spend on gasoline for the year?

3. If a 3″ line appears as a 7″ line on an enlargement, how long would a $16\frac{1}{2}$″ line appear on the same enlargement?

4. If the ratio of males to females in a class of 35 students is 3 to 4, how many females are in the class?

Section 5.5

In problems 1–12, express each percent as a reduced fraction or mixed number.

1. 28%

2. 76%

3. 4%

4. 9%

5. 13.6%

6. 28.8%

7. 6.2%

8. 5.4%

9. 147%

10. 225%

11. $62\frac{1}{2}\%$

12. $42\frac{1}{4}\%$

In problems 13–24, express each percent as a decimal.

13. 36%

14. 47%

15. 8%

16. 7%

17. 14.3%

18. 16.2%

19. 8.25%

20. 6.75%

21. $9\frac{1}{2}\%$

22. $8\frac{1}{4}\%$

23. 156%

24. 207%

Section 5.6

Express each of the following as percents.

1. $\dfrac{3}{5}$

2. $\dfrac{1}{4}$

3. $\dfrac{9}{10}$

4. $\dfrac{7}{8}$

5. $2\dfrac{4}{5}$

6. 0.07

7. 0.24

8. 0.155

9. 2.13

10. 3.175

11. 0.0625

12. 0.1775

Section 5.7

1. 25% of 77

2. 6% of 83.7

3. 19.2% of 505

4. 7.6% of 85.53

5. 0.75% of 2375

6. $8\dfrac{1}{4}$% of 60

7. 143% of 500

8. 126.7% of 447.6

9. $5\dfrac{2}{3}$% of 911

10. 0.0124% of $456.77

11. 34.6% of $509.55

12. 0.325% of $4000

13. If the sales tax rate is 4.25%, what is the tax on a $500.00 item?

14. A 20% discount on a $799.95 TV would give you how much off the original price.

15. How much would you make on $75,600 in sales, if you receive 1.275% commission on the sales?

16. 76% of the students in an elementary school preferred peanut butter and jelly sandwiches. If the school has 800 students, how many preferred peanut butter and jelly sandwiches?

Section 5.8

1. 12 is what percent of 25?

2. 42 is 40% of what number?

3. 83% of 176 is how much?

4. 64 is what percent of 70?

5. 26 is 18% of what number?

6. 6% of 120 is how much?

7. 16.5 is what percent of 376.8?

8. 94 is 60% of what number?

9. 46.8 is 5.6% of what number?

10. 6.25% of 225 is how much?

11. What is 19.8% of 72.5?

12. 403 is $19\dfrac{1}{4}$% of what number?

13. 20.5 is 137% of what number?

14. 806.3 is what percent of 523?

15. 0.05 is what percent of 0.005?

16. 0.003 is 6% of what number?

Section 5.9

1. What is the final price of a $375.99 TV after $7\frac{1}{4}\%$ sales tax is charged?

2. If you earn $275.65 a week and get a 5.8% raise, how much would you earn each month?

3. What would you still owe on an $8,595 car if you make a 25% down payment?

4. What is your take home pay if you earn $1740 a month and have deductions that total 19.65%?

5. If a $399.99 vacuum cleaner is on sale for $299.99, what is the percent decrease in price?

According to Schedule Z (head of household) of the 1995 Federal Tax Booklet, if your taxable income is over $130,800 but not over $256,500, your tax is $34,063 plus 36% of the amount over $130,800.

6. What is the tax on a 1995 taxable income of $151,950?

7. What is the tax on a 1995 taxable income of $197,000?

8. What is the tax on a 1995 taxable income of $250,000?

Section 5.10

1. Find the simple interest on $6000 at 14.7% per year for 4 years.

2. Find the simple interest on $4750 at 1.6% per month for 3 years.

3. Find the simple interest on $9763.85 at 15.7% per year for 30 months.

4. What is the monthly payment needed to pay off a $9,276.27 loan in 54 months with a yearly interest rate of $16\frac{1}{4}\%$?

5. You purchase a $627.99 stereo and $6\frac{1}{4}\%$ sales tax is added. What would your monthly payment be if you take out a 2 year loan at 13.9% per year?

6. You are buying a microwave oven costing $479.99. If 7% sales tax is added and you take out a 2 year loan with an annual interest rate of 14.9% for the total amount, what is your monthly payment?

Math Magic IV

Magic Wheels

Consider a wheel with whole numbers (1, 2, 3, 4, 5, . . .) placed at the center of the wheel and at the end of the spokes of the wheel. If the three numbers on each spoke have the same sum, it is called a **magic wheel.** A magic wheel using the whole numbers from 1 to 7 is shown below.

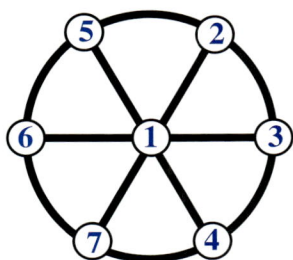

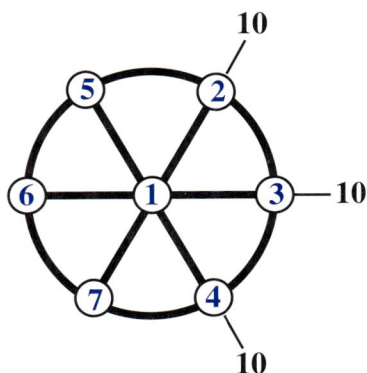

The sum of the three numbers on each spoke is 10.

Recreations

1. Find two other ways to create a magic wheel using the whole numbers from 1 to 7. Each wheel has a different sum for the numbers on each spoke.

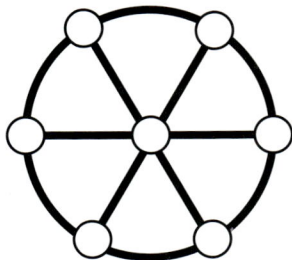

2. In the figures that follow, find all possible magic wheels using whole numbers starting with 1.

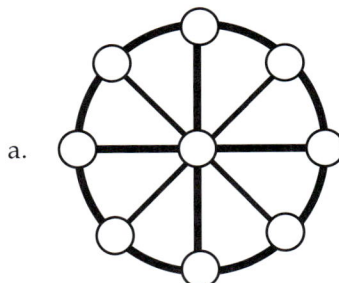

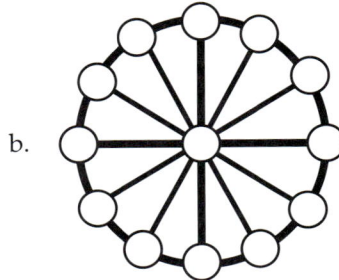

a.

b.

Chapter 6

Measurement and Statistics

After finishing this chapter, you should be able to do the following:

1. read measuring devices.
2. use the units of measurement and make conversions in the U.S. system.
3. use the units of measurement and make conversions in the metric system.
4. make conversions between the U.S. and the metric systems of measurement.
5. analyze statistical graphs.
6. find the mean and median of a set of data.
7. solve word problems involving measurement and statistics.

On the next page, you will find a pretest for this chapter. The purpose of the pretest is to help you determine which sections in this chapter you need to study in detail and which sections you can review quickly. By taking and correcting the pretest according to the instructions on the next page, you can better plan your pace through this chapter.

Note:

Unless otherwise indicated in this chapter, when the answers have more than three decimal digits, they will be rounded off to the nearest hundredth.

Name _____   Date _____

Chapter 6 Pretest

Take and correct this test using the answer section at the end of the book.
Those problems that give you difficulty indicate which sections need extra
attention. Section numbers are in parentheses before each problem.

(6.1)   1. What amount is indicated by the arrow below?   1. _____

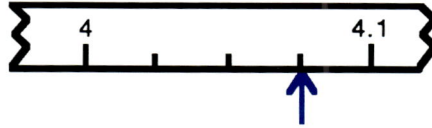

(6.2)   2. 2.7 mi = _?_ ft   2. _____

(6.2)   3. 100 fl oz = _?_ cups   3. _____

(6.2)   4. $1\frac{3}{4}$ tons = _?_ oz   4. _____

(6.3)   5. 1 kl = _?_ liters   5. _____

(6.3)   6. 1 g = _?_ cg   6. _____

(6.4)   7. 9 m = _?_ cm   7. _____

(6.4)   8. 1159 mm = _?_ m   8. _____

(6.4)   9. 5.76 cg = _?_ mg   9. _____

(6.5)   10. 50 in. = _?_ cm   10. _____

(6.5)   11. 147.4 lb = _?_ kg   11. _____

(6.5)   12. 3200 cl = _?_ gal   12. _____

(6.6)   13. What Celsius temperature corresponds to 150° Fahrenheit?   13. _____

(6.7)   14. Using the line graph on page 348, find the mean and median   14. _____
            enrollment at Old Timers College from 1930 to 1936.

(6.9)   15. Which is longer: 120 yd or 100 m?   15. _____

6.1 Reading Measuring Devices

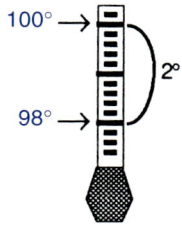

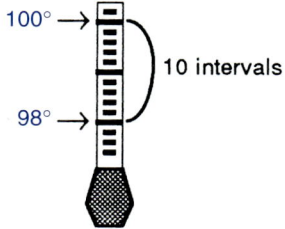

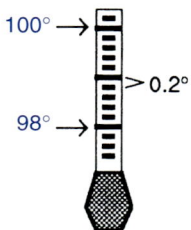

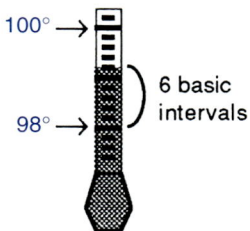

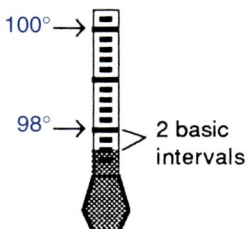

We are always concerned with measurement. We frequently determine time, length, volume, weight, temperature, voltage, speed, etc. Each measurement includes a number followed by some kind of a unit, such as 52 seconds, 6.4 centimeters, $3\frac{1}{2}$ quarts, 98.6 degrees, 9 volts, 55 miles per hour, etc. To measure quantities such as these, we use devices such as watches, measuring cups, scales, rulers, thermometers, etc. Before we study different units of measurement, let's examine some measuring devices and learn how to read them. I will use a thermometer to establish the principles needed to read various kinds of measuring devices.

To read a measuring device, you need to determine the value of the basic interval measured between adjacent marks of its scale.

1. Find the amount measured between two labeled values of the scale. (Subtract the two labeled values.)

$$100° - 98° = 2°$$

2. Find the number of equal intervals between the two labeled values. (Count the number of spaces.)

There are 10 in this example.

3. Calculate the basic interval of the measuring device. (Divide the result of step 1 by the result of step 2.)

$$\text{basic interval} = 2° \div 10 = 0.2°$$

Once the basic interval of the scale has been established, you can now read the amounts measured by the thermometer.

What temperature is indicated on the left?
The temperature is 6 basic intervals above 98°.

$$\begin{aligned} \text{The temperature} &= 98° + 6 \times 0.2° \\ &= 98° + 1.2° \\ &= 99.2° \end{aligned}$$

What temperature is indicated on the left?
The temperature is 2 basic intervals below 98°.

$$\begin{aligned} \text{The temperature} &= 98° - 2 \times 0.2° \\ &= 98° - 0.4° \\ &= 97.6° \end{aligned}$$

Example 1

Find the measurements indicated by the arrows at A, B, and C on the ruler shown below.

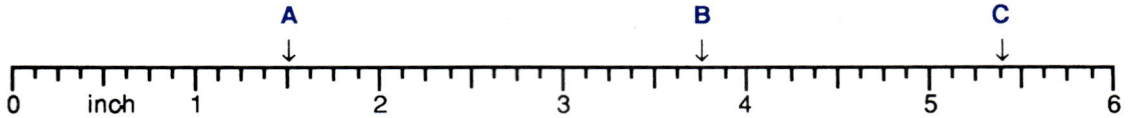

Find the length measured by a basic interval on the ruler. Between 1 and 2 there are 8 equal intervals.

$$\text{The basic interval} = 1 \div 8 = \frac{1}{8} \text{ inch}$$

A measures $1\frac{1}{2}$ in. It is 4 basic intervals above 1 inch.

$$1 + \frac{4}{8} = 1\frac{1}{2} \text{ in.}$$

B measures $3\frac{3}{4}$ in. It is 6 basic intervals above 3 inches.

$$3 + \frac{6}{8} = 3\frac{3}{4} \text{ in.}$$

C measures $5\frac{3}{8}$ in. It is 3 basic intervals above 5 inches.

$$5 + \frac{3}{8} = 5\frac{3}{8} \text{ in.}$$

Example 2

Find the measurements indicated by the arrows at A, B, and C on the voltmeter shown below.

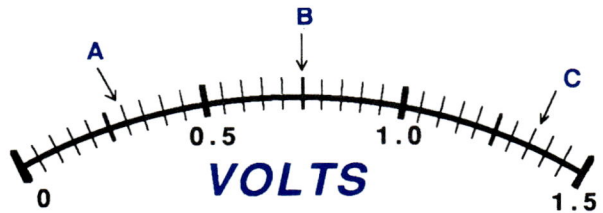

Find the amount measured by a basic interval on the volt-meter. Between 0 and 0.5 volts, there are 10 equal intervals.

$$\text{The basic interval} = 0.5 \div 10 = 0.05 \text{ volts}$$

A measures 0.3 volts. It is 6 basic intervals above 0.

$$0 + 6 \times 0.05 = 0 + 0.3 = 0.3 \text{ volts}$$

B measures 0.75 volts. It is 5 basic intervals above 0.5.

$$0.5 + 5 \times 0.05 = 0.5 + 0.25 = 0.75 \text{ volts}$$

C measures 1.35 volts. It is 7 basic intervals above 1.0.

$$1.0 + 7 \times 0.05 = 1.0 + 0.35 = 1.35 \text{ volts}$$

Exercise 6.1 Set A

In problems 1–5, determine the length in centimeters (cm) indicated by the letters.

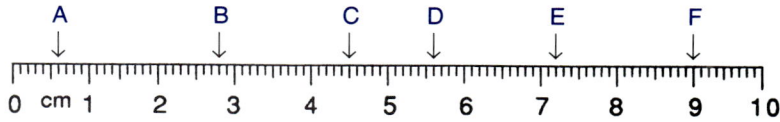

| A | B | C | D | E | F |

0 cm 1   2   3   4   5   6   7   8   9   10

1. A   2. B   1. _____

                                                                      2. _____

3. C   4. D   3. _____

                                                                      4. _____

5. E   6. F   5. _____

                                                                      6. _____

In problems 7–10, determine the speed in miles per hour (mph) indicated by the letters.

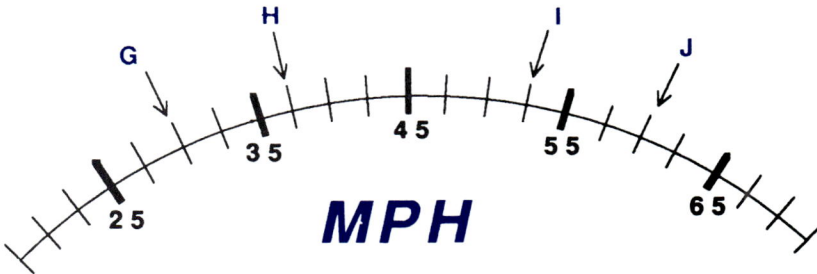

MPH

7. G   8. H   7. _____

                                                                      8. _____

9. I   10. J   9. _____

                                                                      10. _____

In problems 11–14, determine the volume in milliliters (ml) indicated by the letters.

11. K   11. _____

12. L   12. _____

13. M   13. _____

14. N   14. _____

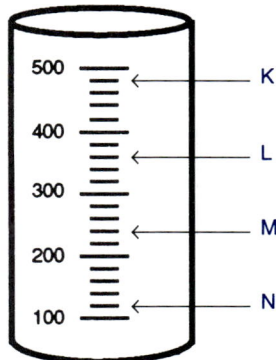

Exercise 6.1 Set B

In problems 1–6, determine the length in inches (in.) indicated by the letters.

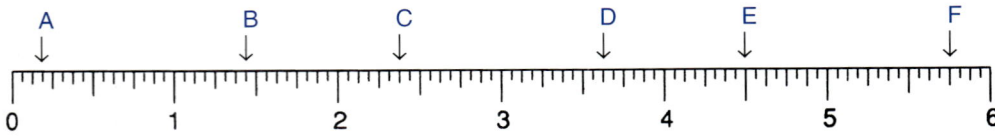

1. A   2. B

3. C   4. D

5. E   6. F

| 1. _____ |
| 2. _____ |
| 3. _____ |
| 4. _____ |
| 5. _____ |
| 6. _____ |

In problems 7–10, determine the weight in pounds (lb) indicated by the letters.

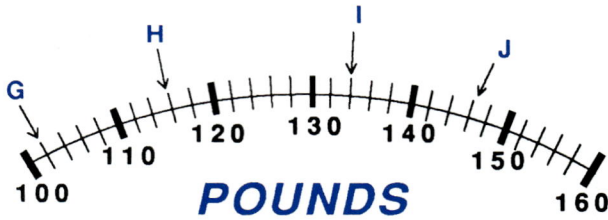

7. G   8. H

9. I   10. J

| 7. _____ |
| 8. _____ |
| 9. _____ |
| 10. _____ |

In problems 11–14, determine the Centigrade temperature indicated by the letters.

11. K

12. L

13. M

14. N

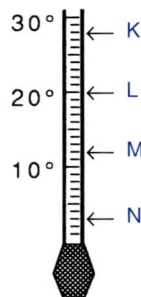

| 11. _____ |
| 12. _____ |
| 13. _____ |
| 14. _____ |

6.2 The U.S. Customary System of Measurement

In the United States, we measure length with units such as inches, feet, yards, and miles; weight with units such as ounces, pounds, and tons; volume with units such as fluid ounces, pints, quarts, and gallons. These are the common units of the U.S. Customary System of Measurement. The relationship between these units are given in the chart below.

Length	**Weight**
1 foot (ft) = 12 inches (in.)	1 pound (lb) = 16 ounces (oz)
1 yard (yd) = 3 feet (ft)	1 ton (T) = 2000 pounds (lb)
1 mile (mi) = 5280 feet (ft)	

Volume

1 cup (c) = 8 fluid ounces (fl oz)
1 pint (pt) = 2 cups (c)
1 quart (qt) = 2 pints (pt) = 32 fl oz
1 gallon (gal) = 4 quarts (qt)

You will find that it is often necessary to change a measurement in one unit into another unit. The method that I will use to explain how to do this is called the **unit-fraction** method.

The Unit-Fraction Method of Conversion

The unit-fraction method of converting units of measurement is based on the fact that multiplying a number by 1 does not change the value of the number. Consider this problem:

$$23 \text{ qt} = \underline{\ ?\ } \text{ gal}$$

The fraction $\dfrac{1 \text{ gal}}{4 \text{ qt}}$ has a value that is equal to 1, since 1 gal = 4 qt.

Such a fraction is called a unit-fraction and it can be used as follows:

$$23 \text{ qt} = 23 \text{ qt} \times 1$$

$$= 23 \text{ qt} \times \frac{1 \text{ gal}}{4 \text{ qt}}$$

We are now multiplying fractions, and can cancel units just as we did numbers.

$$23 \text{ qt} = 23 \text{ qt} \times \frac{1 \text{ gal}}{4 \text{ qt}} = \frac{23 \times 1 \text{ gal}}{4} = 5.75 \text{ gal}$$

Notice that since you wanted to eliminate "qt," it was put in the denominator of the unit fraction. Thus, quarts (qt) canceled, leaving gallons (gal).

The unit-fraction method of changing units of measurement requires that you multiply by a fraction that has:

> 1. a value equal to 1. (Top measures the same as the bottom.)
> 2. a denominator using the given unit, so that it will cancel.
> 3. a numerator using the unit wanted in the answer.

Example 1

40 lb = _?_ oz

$$40 \text{ lb} = 40 \text{ lb} \times 1$$

$$= 40 \text{ lb} \times \frac{16 \text{ oz}}{1 \text{ lb}}$$

$$= \frac{40 \times 16 \text{ oz}}{1}$$

$$= 640 \text{ oz}$$

Since we want to eliminate pounds (lb), that unit must be in the denominator of the unit-fraction, while its equivalent in ounces (oz) is placed in the numerator.

Example 2

40 oz = _?_ lb

$$40 \text{ oz} = 40 \text{ oz} \times 1$$

$$= 40 \text{ oz} \times \frac{1 \text{ lb}}{16 \text{ oz}}$$

$$= \frac{40 \times 1 \text{ lb}}{16}$$

$$= 2.5 \text{ lb}$$

The unit-fraction has ounces (oz) on the bottom so that ounces (oz) cancel, leaving pounds (lb).

Problem 1:   6.2 mi = _?_ ft

Answer: 32,736 ft

$$6.2 \text{ mi} \times \frac{5280 \text{ ft}}{1 \text{ mi}} = \frac{6.2 \times 5280 \text{ ft}}{1}$$

$$= 32{,}736 \text{ ft}$$

Problem 2:   30.46 pt = _?_ gal

Answer: ≈ 3.81 gal

a. change pints to quarts

$$30.46 \text{ pt} \times \frac{1 \text{ qt}}{2 \text{ pt}} = 15.23 \text{ qt}$$

b. change quarts to gallons

$$15.23 \text{ qt} \times \frac{1 \text{ gal}}{4 \text{ qt}} \approx 3.81 \text{ gal}$$

Exercise 6.2 Set A

Determine the equivalent for each measurement.

1. 9 ft = _?_ in.

2. 15 lb = _?_ oz

3. 48 pt = _?_ qt

4. 72 fl oz = _?_ c

5. 12.6 yd = _?_ ft

6. 4.8 gal = _?_ qt

7. 9516.8 lb = _?_ T

8. 139.2 in. = _?_ ft

9. $4\frac{1}{6}$ mi = _?_ ft

10. $15\frac{1}{3}$ pt = _?_ c

11. $17\frac{1}{3}$ oz = _?_ lb

12. $18\frac{3}{8}$ in. = _?_ ft

13. 75 qt = _?_ c

14. 51,200 oz = _?_ T

15. $3\frac{1}{2}$ T = _?_ oz

16. $84\frac{3}{5}$ c = _?_ qt

17. 3.1 mi = _?_ yd

18. 4241.6 yd = _?_ mi

1. _____

2. _____

3. _____

4. _____

5. _____

6. _____

7. _____

8. _____

9. _____

10. _____

11. _____

12. _____

13. _____

14. _____

15. _____

16. _____

17. _____

18. _____

Exercise 6.2 Set B

Determine the equivalent for each measurement.

1. 5 cups = _?_ fl oz

2. 7 qt = _?_ pt

3. 81 in. = _?_ ft

4. 96 oz = _?_ lb

5. 4.75 tons = _?_ lb

6. 448.8 ft = _?_ in.

7. 50.7 ft = _?_ yd

8. 37.5 qt = _?_ gal

9. $18\frac{3}{8}$ lb = _?_ oz

10. $27\frac{2}{3}$ ft = _?_ in.

11. $9\frac{3}{4}$ ft = _?_ yd

12. $6\frac{3}{4}$ c = _?_ pt

13. 73,600 oz = _?_ T

14. 23 qt = _?_ c

15. $7\frac{5}{8}$ gal = _?_ fl oz

16. $131\frac{1}{5}$ fl oz = _?_ gal

17. 36.5 c = _?_ qt

18. 2.7 T = _?_ oz

1. _____

2. _____

3. _____

4. _____

5. _____

6. _____

7. _____

8. _____

9. _____

10. _____

11. _____

12. _____

13. _____

14. _____

15. _____

16. _____

17. _____

18. _____

6.3 The Metric System

Unit:

"Ms. Gram, did you knit that dress?"

The system of measurement used in most countries throughout the world, and used along with the U.S. Customary system in America is the metric system. In the metric system, there are basic units for length, weight, and volume.

Basic Units in the Metric System

1. For Length: **meter (m)**—a little longer than a yard
2. For Weight: **gram (g)**—about the weight of a paper clip
3. For Volume: **liter (l)**—a little more than a quart

Larger or smaller units in the system are obtained by multiplying or dividing those basic units by powers of 10. Prefixes are used to signify the change from one of the basic units.

Prefixes in the Metric System

*kilo (k)—means a thousand (1000)
hecto (h)—means a hundred (100)
deca (da)—means ten (10)

deci (d)—means a tenth $\left(\dfrac{1}{10} \text{ or } 0.1\right)$

*centi (c)—means a hundredth $\left(\dfrac{1}{100} \text{ or } 0.01\right)$

*milli (m)—means a thousandth $\left(\dfrac{1}{1000} \text{ or } 0.001\right)$

Those with asterisks are the prefixes that are most commonly used, so we will concentrate on those in this chapter. *Putting a prefix together with a basic unit gives the other units in the metric system.* For example:

$$\text{kilogram means 1000 grams (1 kg = 1000 g)}$$

$$\text{centimeter means } \frac{1}{100} \text{ meter (1 cm = 0.01 m)}$$

$$\text{milliliter means } \frac{1}{1000} \text{ liter (1 ml = 0.001 liter)}$$

When the prefix kilo is used, you have a unit that is larger than the basic unit. When centi or milli is used, you have a unit that is smaller than the basic unit. The first step in understanding the metric system is to become familiar with its units and to have a feel for the relative size of each unit. The chart below shows the metric units and their relative size.

Larger Units			Basic Units	Smaller Units		
kilo (1000)	hecto (100)	deca (10)	1	deci (.1)	centi (.01)	milli (.001)
km	hm	dam	meter	dm	cm	mm
kg	hg	dag	gram	dg	cg	mg
kl	hl	dal	liter	dl	cl	ml

Example 1

What is a mg?

mg means milligram. It is used to measure weight.

$$mg = \frac{1}{1000} \text{ g} = 0.001 \text{ g}$$

A milligram is much lighter than a gram. It would take 1000 mg to make a gram (1000 mg = 1 g).

Example 2

What is a km?

km means kilometer. It is used to measure length or distance.

$$km = 1000 \text{ m}$$

A kilometer is much larger than a meter. It is 1000 meters.

Example 3

What is a cl?

cl means centiliter. It is used to measure volume.

$$cl = \frac{1}{100} \text{ liter} = 0.01 \text{ liter}$$

A cl is less than a liter. It would take 100 cl to make a liter (100 cl = 1 liter).

Problem 1:   Arrange in order from largest to smallest: g, kg, mg, cg

Answer: kg, g, cg, mg

kg = 1000 g
cg = 0.01 g
mg = 0.001 g

Problem 2:   1 kl = _?_ liters

Answer: 1000

kilo means 1000.

Problem 3:   1 cm = _?_ meters

Answer: $\frac{1}{100}$ or 0.01

centi means $\frac{1}{100}$ or 0.01.

Name _____   Date _____

Exercise 6.3 Set A

In problems 1–6, determine the meaning of each abbreviation.

1. km   2. kl   1. _____

                                                             2. _____

3. cg   4. cm   3. _____

                                                             4. _____

5. ml   6. mg   5. _____

                                                             6. _____

In problems 7–16, determine the equivalent of each measurement.

7. 1 km = _?_ m   8. 1 kg = _?_ g   7. _____

                                                             8. _____

9. 1 cl = _?_ liter   10. 1 cm = _?_ m   9. _____

                                                             10. _____

11. 1 mg = _?_ g   12. 1 ml = _?_ liter   11. _____

                                                             12. _____

13. 1 m = _?_ cm   14. 1 g = _?_ cg   13. _____

                                                             14. _____

15. 1 liter = _?_ ml   16. 1 m = _?_ mm   15. _____

                                                             16. _____

In problems 17–20, arrange the measurements from largest to smallest.

17. kg, cg, g   18. cm, m, mm   17. _____

                                                             18. _____

19. mm, km, cm   20. cl, ml, kl   19. _____

                                                             20. _____

Exercise 6.3 Set B

In problems 1–6, determine the meaning of each abbreviation.

1. kg   2. km   1. _____

                                                  2. _____

3. cl   4. cg   3. _____

                                                  4. _____

5. mm   6. ml   5. _____

                                                  6. _____

In problems 7–16, determine the equivalent of each measurement.

7. 1 kl = _?_ liters   8. 1 km = _?_ m   7. _____

                                                  8. _____

9. 1 cg = _?_ g   10. 1 cl = _?_ liter   9. _____

                                                  10. _____

11. 1 mm = _?_ m   12. 1 mg = _?_ g   11. _____

                                                  12. _____

13. 1 liter = _?_ cl   14. 1 m = _?_ cm   13. _____

                                                  14. _____

15. 1 g = _?_ mg   16. 1 liter = _?_ ml   15. _____

                                                  16. _____

In problems 17–20, arrange the measurements from largest to smallest.

17. mg, g, cg   18. cm, m, km   17. _____

                                                  18. _____

19. kl, ml, cl   20. mg, kg, cg   19. _____

                                                  20. _____

6.4 Conversions within the Metric System

Now that you know the units of the metric system, you can learn to change a measurement using one unit into the same measurement using a different unit. I will first review how to do this using the unit-fraction method as covered in Section 6.2, and then using a short cut.

The Unit-Fraction Method

The unit-fraction method requires that you multiply a given measurement by a fraction that has the following:

1. a value equal to 1. (The top measures the same as the bottom.)
2. a denominator using the given unit, so that it will cancel.
3. a numerator using the unit wanted in the answer.

Example 1

$5 \text{ kg} = \underline{\ ?\ } \text{ g}$

$5 \text{ kg} = 5 \text{ kg} \times 1$

(Note: 1 kg = 1000 g)

$= 5 \, \cancel{\text{kg}} \times \dfrac{1000 \text{ g}}{1 \, \cancel{\text{kg}}}$

The unit-fraction should have kilograms (kg) on the bottom, so that kilograms (kg) cancel, leaving grams (g).

$= 5 \times \dfrac{1000 \text{ g}}{1}$

$= 5000 \text{ g}$

Example 2

$3450 \text{ mm} = \underline{\ ?\ } \text{ m}$

$3450 \text{ mm} = 3450 \text{ mm} \times 1$

(Note: 1 mm = .001 m)

$= 3450 \, \cancel{\text{mm}} \times \dfrac{.001 \text{ m}}{1 \, \cancel{\text{mm}}}$

The unit-fraction should have millimeters (mm) on the bottom, so that millimeters (mm) cancel, leaving meters (m).

$= \dfrac{3450 \times .001 \text{ m}}{1}$

$= 3.45 \text{ m}$

Example 3

$65.4 \text{ cl} = \underline{\ ?\ } \text{ liters}$

$65.4 \text{ cl} = 65.4 \text{ cl} \times 1$

(Note: 1 cl = .01 liter)

$= 65.4 \, \cancel{\text{cl}} \times \dfrac{.01 \text{ liter}}{1 \, \cancel{\text{cl}}}$

The unit-fraction should have centiliters (cl) on the bottom, so that centiliters (cl) cancel, leaving liters (l).

$= \dfrac{65.4 \times .01 \text{ liter}}{1}$

$= .654 \text{ liters}$

A Short Cut

Look at the results of the last three examples.

$$5 \text{ kg} = 5000 \text{ g}$$
$$3450 \text{ mm} = 3.45 \text{ m}$$
$$65.4 \text{ cl} = .654 \text{ liters}$$

In each conversion, the difference between the two forms is merely the position of the decimal point. In fact, *that is the beauty of the metric system—units can be changed by a simple movement of the decimal point.*

5 kg = 5000 g   (decimal point moved 3 places right)

3450 mm = 3.450 m   (decimal point moved 3 places left)

65.4 cl = .654 liters   (decimal point moved 2 places left)

All you need to do to change units in the metric system is to learn which direction to move the decimal point and how many places it should be moved.

1. How do you determine which way to move the decimal point?

   If you study those examples, you will see the following:

   a. When changing a larger unit to a smaller unit, move the decimal point to the right. (We need a larger number of the smaller units to express the same quantity; to make a number larger, we move the decimal point right.)
   b. When changing a smaller unit to a larger unit, move the decimal point to the left. (We need a smaller number of the larger units to express the same quantity; to make a number smaller, we move the decimal point left.)

2. How do you determine how many places to move the decimal point?

   The prefixes used tell you how many places to move the decimal point. If you consider the basic unit as the reference point, then:

   a. kilo represents a 3 place movement from the basic unit. (kilo = 1000, and 1000 has three zeros)
   b. centi represents a 2 place movement from the basic unit. (centi = $\frac{1}{100}$, and 100 has two zeros)
   c. milli represents a 3 place movement from the basic unit. (milli = $\frac{1}{1000}$, and 1000 has three zeros)

Metric System: Movement of Decimal Place

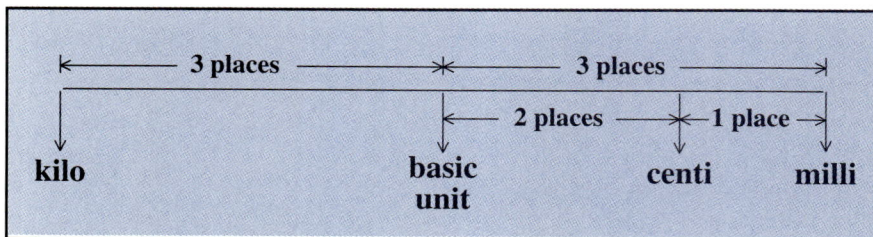

Using that short cut method just explained, try the following examples:

Example 4

5.3 g = _?_ cg

Centigrams are smaller than grams, so we need more of them to express the same quantity. To make the number larger, move the decimal point to the right.

Gram to centigram is a 2 place movement.

5.3 g = 530‿ cg (decimal moved 2 places right)

= 530 cg

Example 5

7500 ml = _?_ liters

Liters are larger than milliliters, so we need fewer of them to express the same quantity. To make the number smaller, move the decimal point to the left.

Milliliter to liter is a 3 place movement.

7500 ml = 7.‿500 liters (decimal moved 3 places left)

= 7.5 liters

Example 6

642 mm = _?_ cm

Centimeters are larger than millimeters, so we need fewer of them to express the same amount. To make the number smaller, move the decimal point to the left.

Millimeter to centimeter is a 1 place movement. (0.001 to 0.01 is a 1 decimal place difference.)

642 mm = 64.2‿ cm (decimal moved 1 place left)

= 64.2 cm

Example 7

A bubbly punch recipe calls for 5 bottles of sparkling water and 2 bottles of punch mix. If the sparkling water comes in 750 ml bottles and the mix comes in 360 ml bottles, how many liters of punch will the recipe make?

Analyze:	Solve:
1. Find the total number of milliliters called for.	1. 5×750 ml = 3750 ml 2×360 ml = 720 ml total = 4470 ml
2. Change ml to liters.	2. 4470 ml = 4.‿470 liters

When making conversions in the metric system, you can use either the unit-fraction method or the decimal movement short cut just explained. Try the following problems using one of the methods.

Problem 1:   2.65 km = _?_ m

Answer: 2650 m

$$2.65 \ \cancel{km} \times \frac{1000 \text{ m}}{1 \ \cancel{km}}$$

$$= \frac{2.65 \times 1000 \text{ m}}{1}$$

$$= 2650 \text{ m}$$

Problem 2:   56 mg = _?_ g

Answer: 0.056 g
G is larger, so move the decimal to the left. Mg to g moves it 3 places.

$$56 \text{ mg} = .056 \text{ g}$$

Problem 3:   35.6 cm = _?_ mm

Answer: 356 mm
Mm is smaller, so move the decimal to the right. Cm to mm moves it 1 place.

$$35.6 \text{ cm} = 356 \text{ mm}$$

Problem 4:   7 kg = _?_ cg

Answer: 700,000 cg
Cg is smaller, so move the decimal to the right. Kg to cg is a 5 place movement (3 from kg to g and 2 from g to cg).

$$7 \text{ kg} = 700000 \text{ cg}$$

Problem 5:   A doctor's prescription calls for three 250 mg tablets four times a day. How many grams of medicine is taken each day?

Answer: 3 g

$$3 \text{ tablets} = 3 \times 250 \text{ mg}$$
$$= 750 \text{ mg}$$

$$4 \text{ times a day} = 4 \times 750$$
$$= 3000 \text{ mg}$$

$$3000 \text{ mg} = 3.000 \text{ g}$$

Exercise 6.4 Set A

Determine the equivalent for each measurement.

1. 3 kg = _?_ g

2. 8 kl = _?_ liters

3. 5200 cl = _?_ liters

4. 7100 cm = _?_ m

5. 5 m = _?_ cm

6. 7 g = _?_ cg

7. 5000 ml = _?_ liters

8. 7000 mg = _?_ g

9. 4.6 liters = _?_ ml

10. 7.3 m = _?_ mm

11. 1697 mm = _?_ m

12. 1555 mg = _?_ g

13. 8.9 g = _?_ mg

14. 7.6 liters = _?_ ml

15. 570 liters = _?_ kl

16. 860 m = _?_ km

17. 40 cm = _?_ mm

18. 50 cl = _?_ ml

19. 7.6 ml = _?_ cl

20. 8.3 mg = _?_ cg

21. 4.2 kg = _?_ cg

22. 3.7 km = _?_ cm

23. 16.5 ml = _?_ liters

24. 180 cm = _?_ m

1. _____

2. _____

3. _____

4. _____

5. _____

6. _____

7. _____

8. _____

9. _____

10. _____

11. _____

12. _____

13. _____

14. _____

15. _____

16. _____

17. _____

18. _____

19. _____

20. _____

21. _____

22. _____

23. _____

24. _____

Exercise 6.4 Set B

Determine the equivalent for each measurement.

1. 4 kl = ? liters

2. 9 kg = ? g

3. 5300 cm = ? m

4. 4100 cl = ? liters

5. 9 g = ? cg

6. 2 m = ? cm

7. 3000 mg = ? g

8. 2000 ml = ? liters

9. 5.9 m = ? mm

10. 2.8 liters = ? ml

11. 3127 mg = ? g

12. 2095 mm = ? m

13. 4.3 liters = ? ml

14. 5.9 g = ? mg

15. 610 m = ? km

16. 230 liters = ? kl

17. 70 cl = ? ml

18. 60 cm = ? mm

19. 2.9 mg = ? cg

20. 3.2 ml = ? cl

21. 4.1 km = ? cm

22. 6.4 kg = ? cg

23. 280 mg = ? g

24. 140 mm = ? m

1. _____

2. _____

3. _____

4. _____

5. _____

6. _____

7. _____

8. _____

9. _____

10. _____

11. _____

12. _____

13. _____

14. _____

15. _____

16. _____

17. _____

18. _____

19. _____

20. _____

21. _____

22. _____

23. _____

24. _____

6.5 Conversions between the Metric and U.S. Systems

Conversion: A prisoner's explanation of a problem.

Since both the U.S. and the metric systems are used in America, it is important that you are able to find relationships between the two systems. In this section, we will use the unit-fraction method to make conversions between the two systems. The following is a chart of the commonly used conversions between the two systems.

Length:	1 in. ≈ 2.54 cm
	39.4 in. ≈ 1 m
	0.621 mi ≈ 1 km
Weight:	1 oz ≈ 28.35 g
	1 lb ≈ 454 g
	2.2 lb ≈ 1 kg
Volume:	1.06 qt ≈ 1 liter

Applying the unit-fraction method of conversion and the values in that chart, we can convert metric measurements to U.S. units and vice versa.

Example 1

12 in. = _?_ cm

$$12 \text{ in.} = 12 \text{ in.} \times 1$$

$$= 12 \text{ in.} \times \frac{2.54 \text{ cm}}{1 \text{ in.}}$$

$$= \frac{12 \times 2.54 \text{ cm}}{1}$$

$$= 30.48 \text{ cm}$$

(Note: 1 in. ≈ 2.54 cm)

The unit-fraction should have inches (in.) on the bottom, so that inches (in.) cancel, leaving centimeters (cm).

Example 2

33 lb = _?_ kg

$$33 \text{ lb} = 33 \text{ lb} \times 1$$

$$= 33 \text{ lb} \times \frac{1 \text{ kg}}{2.2 \text{ lb}}$$

$$= \frac{33 \times 1 \text{ kg}}{2.2}$$

$$= 15 \text{ kg}$$

(Note: 2.2 lb ≈ 1 kg)

The unit-fraction should have pounds (lb) on the bottom, so that pounds (lb) cancel, leaving kilograms (kg).

Example 3

13.25 qt = __?__ liters

13.25 qt = 13.25 qt × 1   (Note: 1.06 qt ≈ 1 liter)

$$= 13.25 \cancel{qt} = \frac{1 \text{ liter}}{1.06 \cancel{qt}}$$

The unit-fraction should have quarts (qt) on the bottom, so that quarts (qt) cancel, leaving liters.

$$= \frac{13.25 \times 1 \text{ liter}}{1.06}$$

$$= 12.5 \text{ liters}$$

Example 4

1589 g = __?__ lb

1589 g = 1589 g × 1   (Note: 1 lb ≈ 454 g)

$$= 1589 \cancel{g} \times \frac{1 \text{ lb}}{454 \cancel{g}}$$

The unit-fraction should have grams (g) on the bottom, so that grams (g) cancel, leaving pounds (lb).

$$= \frac{1589 \times 1 \text{ lb}}{454}$$

$$= 3.5 \text{ lb}$$

Example 5

5 km = __?__ mi

5 km = 5 km × 1   (Note: .621 mi ≈ 1 km)

$$= 5 \cancel{km} \times \frac{.621 \text{ mi}}{1 \cancel{km}}$$

The unit-fraction should have kilometers (km) on the bottom, so that kilometers (km) cancel, leaving miles (mi).

$$= \frac{5 \times .621 \text{ mi}}{1}$$

$$= 3.105 \text{ mi}$$

If you set up the unit-fraction correctly, there should be no confusion as to whether you multiply or divide to make the conversion from one system to the other. Let us now consider some problems that involve more than one conversion.

Example 6

7 gal = __?__ liters

Analyze: The conversion chart has the conversion between quarts and liters, so we must first change the gallons to quarts and then change the quarts to liters.

Solve: Convert gal to qt.   Convert qt to liters.
(1 gal = 4 qt)   (1.06 qt ≈ 1 liter)

7 gal = 7 gal × 1   28 qt = 28 qt × 1

$$= 7 \cancel{gal} \times \frac{4 \text{ qt}}{1 \cancel{gal}} \qquad\qquad = 28 \cancel{qt} \times \frac{1 \text{ liter}}{1.06 \cancel{qt}}$$

$$= \frac{7 \times 4 \text{ qt}}{1} \qquad\qquad\qquad = \frac{28 \times 1 \text{ liter}}{1.06}$$

$$= 28 \text{ qt} \qquad\qquad\qquad\qquad = 26.42 \text{ liters}$$

Example 7

$$3000 \text{ kg} = \underline{\ ?\ } \text{ T}$$

Analyze: Convert kg to lb.   Convert lb to T.
    (2.2 lb ≈ 1 kg)   (1 T = 2000 lb)

Solve: 3000 kg = 3000 kg × 1   6600 lb = 6600 lb × 1

$$= 3000 \ \cancel{kg} \times \frac{2.2 \text{ lb}}{1 \ \cancel{kg}} \qquad\qquad = 6600 \ \cancel{lb} \times \frac{1 \text{ T}}{2000 \ \cancel{lb}}$$

$$= 6600 \text{ lb} \qquad\qquad\qquad = 3.3 \text{ T}$$

Example 8

Which is longer, the 1600 m or the U.S. mile?

Analyze: The U.S. mile is 5280 ft, so convert 1600 m into feet and then
        compare.

Solve: Convert m to in.   Convert in. to ft.
    (1 m ≈ 39.4 in.)   (12 in. = 1 ft)

1600 m = 1600 m × 1   63,040 in. = 63,040 in. × 1

$$= 1600 \ \cancel{m} \times \frac{39.4 \text{ in.}}{1 \ \cancel{m}} \qquad\qquad = 63,040 \ \cancel{\text{in.}} \times \frac{1 \text{ ft}}{12 \ \cancel{\text{in.}}}$$

$$= 63,040 \text{ in.} \qquad\qquad\qquad ≈ 5253.33 \text{ ft}$$

Answer: The U.S. mile (5280 ft) is longer than 1600 m (5253.33 ft).

Example 9

Which holds more: a fifth ($\frac{4}{5}$ of a quart), or a 750 ml bottle?

Analyze: $\frac{4}{5}$ = 0.8, so a fifth is 0.8 qt. Convert the 0.8 qt to ml, and then
        compare.

Solve: Convert qt to liters.   Convert liters to ml.
(1.06 qt ≈ 1 liter)   (1 ml = .001 liter)

.8 qt = .8 qt × 1   .7547 liter = .7547 liter × 1

$$= .8 \ \cancel{qt} \times \frac{1 \text{ liter}}{1.06 \ \cancel{qt}} \qquad\qquad = .7547 \ \cancel{\text{liter}} \times \frac{1 \text{ ml}}{.001 \ \cancel{\text{liter}}}$$

$$= .7547 \text{ liter} \qquad\qquad\qquad = 754.7 \text{ ml}$$

Answer: A fifth (754.7 ml) holds more than a 750 ml bottle.

After studying those examples on the last three pages, you should be ready to do some conversions by yourself. Refer to the conversion chart at the bottom of the page as you work through these problems.

Problem 1:   36 in. = _?_ cm

Answer: 91.44 cm

$$36 \text{ in.} \times \frac{2.54 \text{ cm}}{1 \text{ in.}}$$

$$= \frac{36 \times 2.54 \text{ cm}}{1}$$

$$= 91.44 \text{ cm}$$

Problem 2:   26.2 mi = _?_ km

Answer: 42.19 km

$$26.2 \text{ mi} \times \frac{1 \text{ km}}{.621 \text{ mi}}$$

$$= \frac{26.2 \times 1 \text{ km}}{.621}$$

$$\approx 42.19 \text{ km}$$

Problem 3:   8 liters = _?_ gal

Answer: 2.12 gal

$$8 \text{ liters} \times \frac{1.06 \text{ qt}}{1 \text{ liter}}$$

$$= \frac{8 \times 1.06 \text{ qt}}{1} = 8.48 \text{ qt}$$

$$= 8.48 \text{ qt} \times \frac{1 \text{ gal}}{4 \text{ qt}}$$

$$= \frac{8.48 \text{ gal}}{4} = 2.12 \text{ gal}$$

U.S.—Metric Conversions

Length	Volume	Weight
1 in. ≈ 2.54 cm	1.06 qt ≈ 1 liter	1 oz ≈ 28.35 g
39.4 in. ≈ 1 m		1 lb ≈ 454 g
0.621 mi ≈ 1 km		2.2 lb ≈ 1 kg

Exercise 6.5 Set A

Answers may vary slightly depending on conversions used.

1. 9 in. = _?_ cm

2. 8 liters = _?_ qt

3. 33 lb = _?_ kg

4. 197 in. = _?_ m

5. 4 m = _?_ in.

6. 7 lb = _?_ g

7. 170.1 g = _?_ oz

8. 18.63 mi = _?_ km

9. 24.75 m = _?_ in.

10. 58.95 kg = _?_ lb

11. 147.4 lb = _?_ kg

12. 62.73 cm = _?_ in.

13. 0.05 kg = _?_ oz

14. 10 ft = _?_ m

15. 560 fl oz = _?_ ml

16. 0.001 oz = _?_ cg

17. 50 gal = _?_ liters

18. 50 liters = _?_ gal

19. 3000 m = _?_ mi

20. 3000 mi = _?_ m

21. 40 c = _?_ liters

22. 4 liters = _?_ c

1. _____

2. _____

3. _____

4. _____

5. _____

6. _____

7. _____

8. _____

9. _____

10. _____

11. _____

12. _____

13. _____

14. _____

15. _____

16. _____

17. _____

18. _____

19. _____

20. _____

21. _____

22. _____

Exercise 6.5 Set B

Answers may vary slightly depending on conversions used.

1. 5 oz = _?_ g

2. 9 kg = _?_ lb

3. 591 in. = _?_ m

4. 66 lb = _?_ kg

5. 80 km = _?_ mi

6. 5 liters = _?_ qt

7. 1657.1 g = _?_ lb

8. 3.657 qt = _?_ liters

9. 53.25 in. = _?_ cm

10. 76.45 kg = _?_ lb

11. 84.6 in. = _?_ m

12. 319.6 g = _?_ oz

13. 60 yd = _?_ m

14. 15.5 c = _?_ liters

15. 32 liters = _?_ gal

16. $\frac{4}{5}$ pt = _?_ ml

17. 100 m = _?_ ft

18. 100 ft = _?_ m

19. $\frac{7}{16}$ in. = _?_ mm

20. 12 mm = _?_ in.

21. 2.5 km = _?_ in.

22. 1600 yds = _?_ km

1. _____
2. _____
3. _____
4. _____
5. _____
6. _____
7. _____
8. _____
9. _____
10. _____
11. _____
12. _____
13. _____
14. _____
15. _____
16. _____
17. _____
18. _____
19. _____
20. _____
21. _____
22. _____

6.6 U.S. and Metric Temperatures

In the last four sections, we discussed ways of measuring length, weight, and volume. Another quantity that is commonly measured is temperature. We are always concerned about how hot or cold the day is going to be. When we feel sick, we wonder if we are running a ``temperature.'' In the U.S. system, we measure temperature using the Fahrenheit scale. In the metric system, temperature is measured using the Celsius scale. A comparison of the two scales is listed below:

Celsius		**Fahrenheit**
100°	water boils	212°
37°	normal body temperature	98.6°
30°	a hot day	86°
20°	room temperature	68°
10°	a cool day	50°
0°	water freezes	32°

This clever rhyme, courtesy of the Newhouse News Service, gives an easy way to relate to the temperatures on the Celsius scale:

"Celsius: 30 is hot, 20 is nice, 10 is cool, and 0 is ice."

To convert a temperature in one scale to a temperature in the other scale, we will use one of the formulas below:

To Find the Celsius Temperature

$$C = \frac{5}{9} \times (F - 32)$$

In other words, to find the Celsius temperature, you should subtract 32 from the Fahrenheit temperature, then multiply that results by $\frac{5}{9}$.

To Find the Fahrenheit Temperature

$$F = \frac{9}{5} \times C + 32$$

In other words, to find the Fahrenheit temperature, you should multiply the Celsius temperature by $\frac{9}{5}$, then add 32 to that result.

Example 1

$$95° \text{ F} = \underline{}° \text{ C}$$

Since we want to find the Celsius temperature, we will use the first formula.

$$C = \frac{5}{9} \times (F - 32)$$

$$= \frac{5}{9} \times (95 - 32) \qquad \text{Replace the F in the formula with 95°.}$$

$$= \frac{5}{\cancel{9}} \times \cancel{63}^{7} \qquad \text{Work inside the parentheses first, then cross cancel.}$$

$$= 35° \qquad \text{Do the multiplication.}$$

Example 2

$$66° \text{ C} = \underline{}° \text{ F}$$

Since we want to find the Fahrenheit temperature, we will use the second formula.

$$F = \frac{9}{5} \times C + 32$$

$$= \frac{9}{5} \times 66 + 32 \qquad \text{Replace the C in the formula with 66°.}$$

$$= 118.8 + 32 \qquad \text{Do the multiplication first.}$$

$$= 150.8° \qquad \text{Do the addition.}$$

Example 3

On July 13, 1913, the temperature in Death Valley reached a temperature of 134° F in the shade. To the nearest tenth of a degree, what temperature would that be on the Celsius scale?

$$C = \frac{5}{9} \times (F - 32)$$

$$= \frac{5}{9} \times (134 - 32) = \frac{5}{\cancel{9}_{3}} \times \cancel{102}^{34} = \frac{170}{3} \approx 56.7°$$

Problem 1: In Browning, Montana, on January 23, 1916, the temperature changed 37.8° C in a 24 hour period. To the nearest degree, how much is that change on the Fahrenheit scale?

Answer: 100° F

$$F = \frac{9}{5} \times 37.8 + 32$$

$$= 68.04 + 32$$

$$= 100.04$$

$$\approx 100°$$

Exercise 6.6 Set A

In problems 1–10, use $F = \dfrac{9}{5} \times C + 32$ and $C = \dfrac{5}{9} \times (F - 32)$ to determine the equivalent temperatures.

1. $70°$ C = $\underline{\;?\;}°$ F

2. $45°$ C = $\underline{\;?\;}°$ F

1. _____

2. _____

3. $104°$ F = $\underline{\;?\;}°$ C

4. $50°$ F = $\underline{\;?\;}°$ C

3. _____

4. _____

5. $52°$ C = $\underline{\;?\;}°$ F

6. $82°$ C = $\underline{\;?\;}°$ F

5. _____

6. _____

7. $350°$ F = $\underline{\;?\;}°$ C

8. $100°$ F = $\underline{\;?\;}°$ C

7. _____

8. _____

9. $72.6°$ C = $\underline{\;?\;}°$ F

10. $82.7°$ C = $\underline{\;?\;}°$ F

9. _____

10. _____

In problems 11–13, determine which temperature is hotter.

11. $200°$ C or $390°$ F?

11. _____

12. $25°$ C or $77°$ F?

12. _____

13. $39°$ F or $4°$ C?

13. _____

Exercise 6.6 Set B

In problems 1–10, use $F = \dfrac{9}{5} \times C + 32$ and $C = \dfrac{5}{9} \times (F - 32)$ to determine the equivalent temperatures.

1. $60°\ C = \underline{\ ?\ }°\ F$ 2. $85°\ C = \underline{\ ?\ }°\ F$

1. _____

2. _____

3. $68°\ F = \underline{\ ?\ }°\ C$ 4. $95°\ F = \underline{\ ?\ }°\ C$

3. _____

4. _____

5. $43°\ C = \underline{\ ?\ }°\ F$ 6. $73°\ C = \underline{\ ?\ }°\ F$

5. _____

6. _____

7. $400°\ F = \underline{\ ?\ }°\ C$ 8. $275°\ F = \underline{\ ?\ }°\ C$

7. _____

8. _____

9. $93.4°\ C = \underline{\ ?\ }°\ F$ 10. $75.3°\ C = \underline{\ ?\ }°\ F$

9. _____

10. _____

In problems 11–13, determine which temperature is hotter.

11. 300° C or 570° F?

11. _____

12. 15° C or 59° F?

12. _____

13. 2° C or 36° F?

13. _____

6.7 Statistical Graphs

In order to present statistical information in a more visual and understandable manner, we often use bar, line, and circle graphs. These **graphs** are diagrams that display numerical facts in a way that aids us in interpreting and comparing those facts.

Bar Graphs

Bar graphs use parallel bars to represent numerical information. The bar graph on the left compares five retail stores and the amounts of sales each made during the year. Along the horizontal axis are the names of the stores. Along the vertical axis are the sales in millions of dollars. By studying the graph, you can quickly make comparisons and conclusions about the five stores.

RETAIL SALES

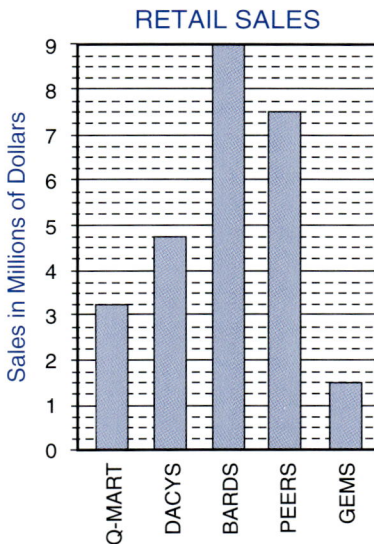

Example 1

Which store had the most sales and how much did it sell?

Bards had the most sales, which was $9,000,000. (Its bar is the longest and reaches to the 9 on the vertical axis.)

Example 2

How much in sales did Dacys have?

Dacys sold $4,750,000, since the bar for Dacys reaches 3/4 of the way between 4 and 5 million, and 3/4 of $1,000,000 is $750,000.

Example 3

How much more did Q-Mart sell than Gems?

Q-Mart sold $1,750,000 more than Gems.

Q-Mart:	$3,250,000
Gems:	−$1,500,000
difference:	$1,750,000

Example 4

What is the average of the sales for the five stores?

To find the average, add up the sales of the five stores and divide by five.

$26,000,000 ÷ 5 = $5,200,000$

The average is $5,200,000.

Q-Mart:	$3,250,000
Dacys:	$4,750,000
Bards:	$9,000,000
Peers:	$7,500,000
Gems:	$1,500,000
Total:	$26,000,000

Line Graphs

A graph that uses line segments to represent numerical information is called a **line graph.** Line graphs are used primarily when one of the axes measures time or distance. In the line graph on the left, you can quicly see that when the line rises, enrollment increases; when the line falls, enrollment decreases; when the line is level, enrollment is unchanged. By studying the graph, you can make various comparisons and conclusions about the enrollment at Old-Timers College.

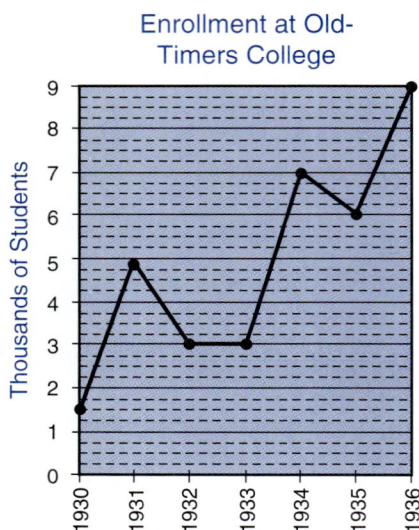

Enrollment at Old-Timers College

Thousands of Students

Example 5

During what year was the enrollment lowest, and what was that enrollment?

The year of lowest enrollment was 1930, since in that year the graph reaches its lowest value of 1500.

Example 6

Between what two years was there the largest increase in enrollment, and what was that increase?

The largest increase in enrollment was between 1933 and 1934. The graph rises the most between those two years.

1934:	7000 students
1933:	−3000 students
increase:	4000 students

Example 7

What percent did the enrollment decrease between 1931 and 1932?

1931:	4750 students
1932:	−3000 students
decrease:	1750 students

To find the percent decrease, you can restate the problem as follows: "1750 is what percent of 4750?" Using the percent proportion, $A = 1750$, $B = 4750$, and P is unknown.

$$\frac{A}{B} = \frac{P}{100} \qquad \frac{1750}{4750} = \frac{P}{100}$$

$$\frac{4750 \times P}{4750} = \frac{175{,}000}{4750}$$

$$P \approx 36.84$$

Circle Graphs

Circle graphs are used to show the division of a whole into parts. In the circle graph on the left, the whole represents the Smiths' yearly income and the parts represent the portion of that income spent on various items. By studying the size of the sectors of the circle, you can readily make conclusions about the Smiths' annual budget.

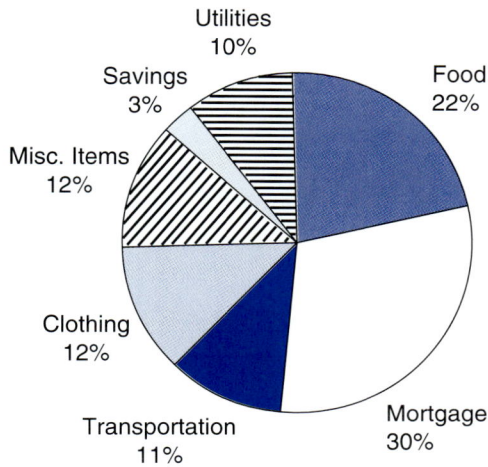

The Smith's Annual Budget

Utilities
10%

Savings
3%

Food
22%

Misc. Items
12%

Clothing
12%

Transportation
11%

Mortgage
30%

Example 8

If the Smiths earn $19,500 per year, how much would they spend on food each year?

22% is spent on food each year
22% of $19,500 = 0.22 × $19,500
= $4290

Example 9

If the Smiths earn $24,000 per year, how much would they spend on clothing each month?

12% of the income is spent on clothing each year
12% of $24,000 = 0.12 × $24,000
= $2880 each year

To find the amount spent each month, divide by 12.

$2880 ÷ 12 = $240

Example 10

If the Smiths spend $1980 a year on transportation, what is their yearly income?

Since the Smiths spend 11% of their income on transportation, you can restate the problem as follows: "$1980 is 11% of what income?"

Using the percent proportion with $A = 1980$, $P = 11$, and B the unknown.

$$\frac{A}{B} = \frac{P}{100} \qquad \frac{1980}{B} = \frac{11}{100}$$

$$\frac{11 \times B}{11} = \frac{198,000}{11}$$

$$B = \$18,000$$

When an object is dropped from above the earth, it accelerates to earth because of gravity. The graph on the right gives the distance a dropped object falls after a given number of seconds.

Problem 1: How far did the object fall after 6 seconds?

Answer: ≈ 580 ft

Problem 2: How far did the object fall from the 5th to the 10th seconds?

Answer: 1200 ft

after 10 sec:	1600
after 5 sec:	−400
difference:	1200

Distance Travelled by Falling Objects

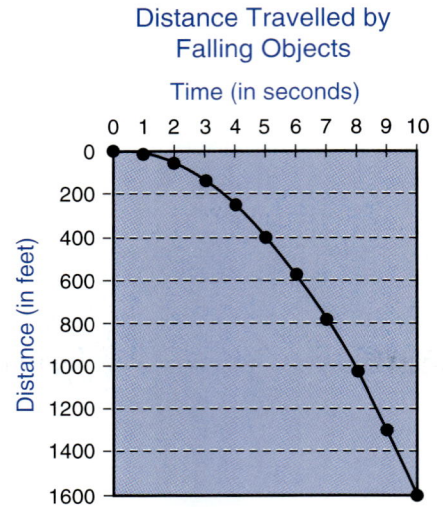

Wind-chill temperature represents the combined effect of temperature and wind upon the body. That means the wind makes it feel colder than it really is. The graph on the right shows the effect the wind has when the temperature is actually 35° Fahrenheit.

Problem 3: A wind of 15 mph makes a 35° temperature feel equivalent to what temperature?

Answer: 16°

Problem 4: Between what two wind speeds is there the greatest decrease in wind-chill temperature?

Answer: Between 5 and 10 mph

Wind-Chill Temperatures at 35°F

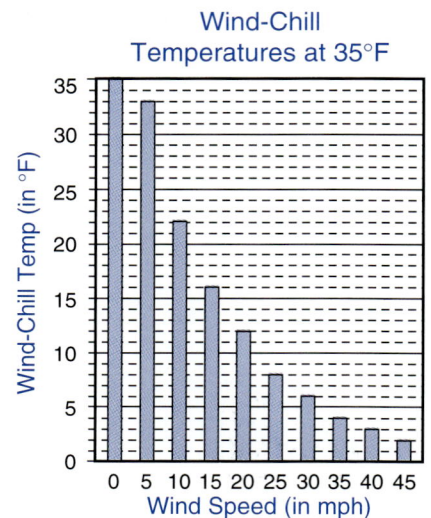

Exercise 6.7 Set A

Average Monthly Temperatures in Fresno, California

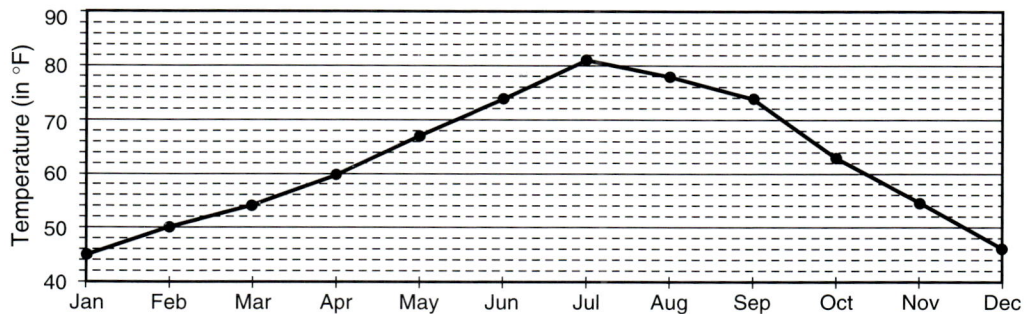

1. What is the highest average monthly temperature in Fresno?   1. _____

2. What is the lowest average monthly temperature in Fresno?   2. _____

3. What is the average temperature for the year?   3. _____

4. What is the percent increase in temperature from Jan. to May? 4. _____

5. What is the percent decrease in temperature from May to Dec.? 5. _____

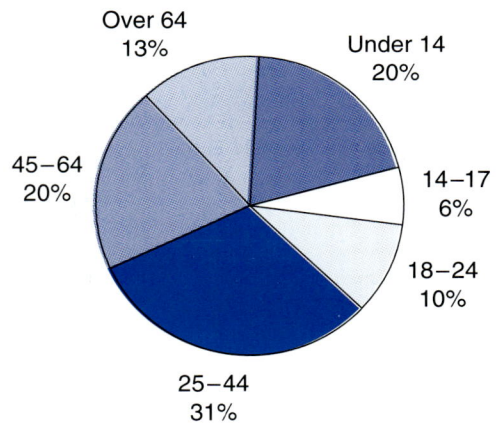

1995 United States Population by Age Groups

If the population of the United States is 260,000,000,

6. What age group has the largest number of people?   6. _____

7. What age group has the smallest number of people?   7. _____

8. How many people live in the U.S. who are over 17?   8. _____

9. How many people live in the U.S. who are under 45?   9. _____

10. How many more people are under 18 than over 64?   10. _____

Exercise 6.7 Set B

Winning Long Jumps: Local Olympics 1976–1996

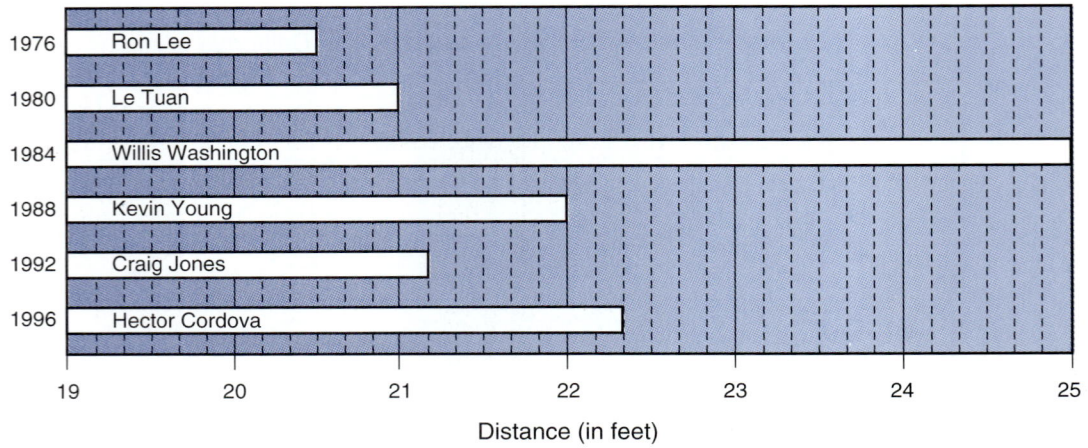

Year	Name
1976	Ron Lee
1980	Le Tuan
1984	Willis Washington
1988	Kevin Young
1992	Craig Jones
1996	Hector Cordova

Distance (in feet)

1. How long was the longest jump in feet and inches? 1. _____

2. How long was the shortest jump in feet and inches? 2. _____

3. What was the average distance jumped from 1976 to 1996? 3. _____

4. What is the percent decrease in distance from 1984 to 1988? 4. _____

5. What is the percent increase in distance from 1980 to 1984? 5. _____

Land Area of the Earth by Continents

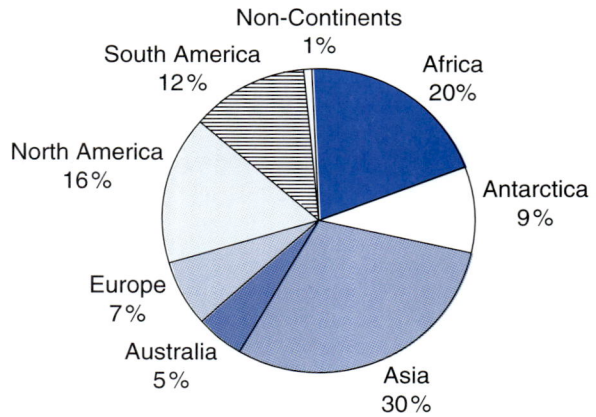

Non-Continents 1%
South America 12%
Africa 20%
North America 16%
Antarctica 9%
Europe 7%
Australia 5%
Asia 30%

Since the land area of the earth is about 57,500,000 sq. miles,

6. What is the largest continent and what is its area? 6. _____

7. What is the smallest continent and what is its area? 7. _____

8. How much larger is Africa than Europe in sq. miles? 8. _____

9. How much larger is North America than South America? 9. _____

10. What is the total land area of North and South America? 10. _____

6.8 The Mean and Median

"Really, I'm average but I'm not mean!"

The statistical graphs studied in the previous section give us a visual presentation of numerical information or data. However, to analyze the data, it is often necessary to find a value that summarizes all of the information. In this section, we will introduce two common measures that are used as a summary of numerical information. These measures, mean and median, are used to describe the "average" of the data.

The Mean

The **mean** is commonly known as the average as discussed in Section 2.10. The mean is found by adding up all the data and dividing this sum by the number of data values. For example, if on five 10-point quizzes, you had scores of 7, 9, 5, 10, and 9, the mean of the scores would be 8.

$$\text{mean} = \frac{7 + 9 + 5 + 10 + 9}{5} = \frac{40}{5} = 8$$

Although you did not have a score of 8, a mean of 8 indicates that your scores on the five quizzes are equivalent to having a score of 8 on all five quizzes.

The procedure to determine the mean of a set of data is shown below.

$$\text{Mean} = \frac{\text{sum of the data}}{\text{number of data values}}$$

The Median

The second measure used to summarize a set of data is the median. If the set of data is placed in increasing order, the **median** is the score that is in the middle of the data. There are the same number of data values above and below the median.

For example, if on five 10-point quizzes, you had scores of 7, 9, 5, 10, and 9, the median would be 9. If we list the scores in increasing order (5, 7, 9, 9, 10), the middle value is 9. If there is an even number of values, the median is the average of the two middle values. For example, if on the sixth quiz, you received a score of 8, the median would be 8.5. If we list the scores in increasing order (5, 7, 8, 9, 9, 10), there is no single value in the middle of the data. There is a pair of values in the middle (8, 9). To find the median, take the average of this pair (median = $\frac{8+9}{2} = \frac{17}{2} = 8.5$).

The procedure to determine the median of a set of data is outlined on the next page.

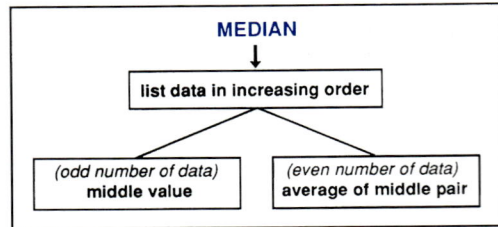

```
                          ┌─────────────────────────────────────────┐
                          │              MEDIAN                       │
                          │                ↓                          │
                          │   ┌───────────────────────────┐          │
                          │   │ list data in increasing order │       │
                          │   └───────────────────────────┘          │
                          │        ╱              ╲                    │
                          │  ┌──────────────┐  ┌──────────────────┐   │
                          │  │(odd number of data)│ │(even number of data)│ │
                          │  │  middle value │  │average of middle pair│  │
                          │  └──────────────┘  └──────────────────┘   │
                          └─────────────────────────────────────────┘
```

Example 1

The yearly salaries of the nine full-time employees at Park Press are $18,000, $16,000, $12,000, $13,000, $48,000, $15,000, $12,000, $25,000, and $12,000. Find the mean and median yearly salaries.

$$\text{mean} = \frac{18{,}000 + 16{,}000 + 12{,}000 + 13{,}000 + 48{,}000 + 15{,}000 + 12{,}000 + 25{,}000 + 12{,}000}{9}$$

$$= \frac{171{,}000}{9} = \$19{,}000$$

median: Listing the salaries in increasing order we get: $12,000, $12,000, $12,000, $13,000, $15,000, $16,000, $18,000, $25,000, $48,000. The middle value is $15,000. This is the median salary.

Both the mean and the median are used in analyzing a set of data. The mean is affected by extremely high or low scores while the median lessens the affect of such scores. From Example 1, the mean salary and median salary can give different interpretations of the data. The owners of Park Press would probably emphasize the mean salary ($19,000) while the union would stress the median salary ($15,000) in arbitration over a new contract.

Problem 1: According to the Department of the Treasury, the average number of years U.S. currency lasts in circulation is as follows: $1 bill—1.5 years, $2 bill—36 years, $5 bill—2 years, $10 bill—3 years, $20 bill—4 years, $50 bill—9 years, $100 bill—9 years. Find the mean and median of this data.

Answers:
mean ≈ 9.2 years
$$\left(\frac{1.5 + 36 + 2 + 3 + 4 + 9 + 9}{7}\right)$$
median = 4 years
(In increasing order, 4 is the middle value.)

Problem 2: Find the median and mean for the daily household water use of these eight neighboring California communities: Pleasanton—330 gal, Livermore—326 gal, Manteca—544 gal, Danville—545 gal, Blackhawk—935 gal, Dublin—308 gal, San Ramon—339 gal, Tracy—403 gal.

Answers:
median = 371 gal
Average of middle pair in increasing order.
(339 + 403) ÷ 2

mean = 466.25 gal
(Sum of all the amounts divided by 8.)

Exercise 6.8 Set A

In problems 1–4, find the mean and median of the data.

1. 80, 68, 30, 67, 70, 21, 62

   1. _____

   _____

2. 11, 93, 65, 80, 56, 51, 94, 72, 81

   2. _____

   _____

3. 68.5%, 78.6%, 62.1%, 68.6%, 89.2%, 90.0%, 97.3%, 89.2%

   3. _____

   _____

4. 169.1, 127.9, 151.7, 139.4, 151.7, 160.4

   4. _____

   _____

5. According to the Cellular Telecommunications Industry Association, the number of cellular telephone subscribers from 1987 to 1994 are as follows:

1987	1,232,000	1991	7,557,000
1988	2,069,000	1992	11,033,000
1989	3,509,000	1993	12,805,000
1990	5,283,000	1994	17,920,000

   What are the mean and median number of subscribers during this time period?

   5. _____

   _____

6. According to Nielsen Media Research, in 1995 the amount of hours and minutes spent viewing television Monday to Sunday from 8–11 P.M. are:

Women 18$^+$	7:59	Children 6–11	5:13
Men 18$^+$	8:27	Children 2–5	4:08
Teens 12–17	6:14		

   What are the mean and median time spent viewing TV?

   6. _____

   _____

7. In 1995, the salaries paid to the governors in the states that have borders on the Pacific Ocean are as follows:

Alaska	$87,643	California	$120,000
Hawaii	$94,780	Oregon	$80,000
Washington	$121,000		

   What are the mean and median salaries of these "far west" governors?

   7. _____

   _____

Exercise 6.8 Set B

In problems 1–4, find the mean and median of the data.

1. 51, 49, 27, 48, 40, 26, 72

    1. _____

    _____

2. 46, 98, 76, 82, 98

    2. _____

    _____

3. 30.5, 40.2, 83.1, 53.7, 30.5, 65.9

    3. _____

    _____

4. 4.1, 5.2, 8.8, 2.2, 5.4, 6.8, 2.2, 1.9

    4. _____

    _____

5. According to the College Entrance Examination Board, the average Scholastic Aptitude Test (SAT) scores for college bound seniors in math from 1986 to 1995 are as follows:

    5. _____

    _____

1986	475	1991	474
1987	476	1992	476
1988	476	1993	478
1989	476	1994	497
1990	476	1995	482

What are the mean and median SAT scores during those years?

6. During a day in July, the high temperatures from representative cities throughout California were as follows: Eureka—68°, Red Bluff—90°, Tahoe Valley—76°, Sacramento—87°, San Francisco—65°, Monterey—65°, Fresno—95°, Bakersfield—97°, Los Angeles—79°, Palm Springs—109°, and San Diego—70°. What are the mean and median high temperatures?

    6. _____

    _____

7. The number of Americans that died in wars are as follows:

    7. _____

    _____

1) Civil War	497,000	7) Revolutionary War	4,000
2) World War I	406,000	8) Spanish-American	2,400
3) World War II	116,000	9) War of 1812	2,000
4) Vietnam	58,000	10) Indian Wars	1,000
5) Korea	54,000	11) Persian Gulf	141
6) Mexican War	13,000		

To the nearest whole number, what are the mean and median number of American war deaths?

6.9 Applications Involving Statistics and Measurement

"That girl is sure nice. I'd like to meter."

In this section, we will encounter applications that utilize our knowledge of measurement conversions and statistics.

Example 1

Which is longer, the metric mile (1500 m) or the English mile (5280 ft)?

Analyze: If we represent both miles in the same unit, we could easily compare them. Using conversion factors, we can convert 1500 meters to feet.

Solve: Convert m to in.   Convert in. to ft
         (1 m ≈ 39.4 in.)   (12 in. = 1 ft)

$$1500 \text{ m} = 1500 \text{ m} \times \frac{39.4 \text{ in.}}{1 \text{ m}} \qquad 59{,}100 \text{ in.} = 59{,}100 \text{ in.} \times \frac{1 \text{ ft}}{12 \text{ in.}}$$

$$= 59{,}100 \text{ in.} \qquad\qquad = 4925 \text{ ft}$$

The metric mile, 1500 m, equals 4925 ft. Thus, the English mile of 5280 ft is longer than the metric mile.

Example 2

The bar graph on the left shows the average amount refunded on tax returns by the Internal Revenue Service from 1970 to 1990. Use the graph to answer the following questions:

a)   What are the mean and median amounts refunded by the IRS from 1970 to 1990?

b)   What is the percent increase in refunds from 1970 to 1990?

a)   Analyze: To find the mean find the sum of the refunds for each year and divide by five. Since the refunds are in increasing order, the median is the amount in the middle.

Solve: $$\text{mean} = \frac{241 + 410 + 614 + 866 + 878}{5} = \frac{3009}{5}$$
$$= \$601.80$$

median = \$614, the middle value in increasing order.

b)   Analyze: To find the percent increase, we find the amount refunds increased from the base year, 1970, to 1990. With that information, we can use the percent proportion, $\frac{A}{B} = \frac{P}{100}$.

Solve: $A = 878 - 241 = 637$, $\frac{637}{241} = \frac{P}{100}$
$B = 241$, P is unknown.

$$241 \times P = 63{,}700$$
$$P \approx 264.3\%$$

Average Amount Refunded by IRS

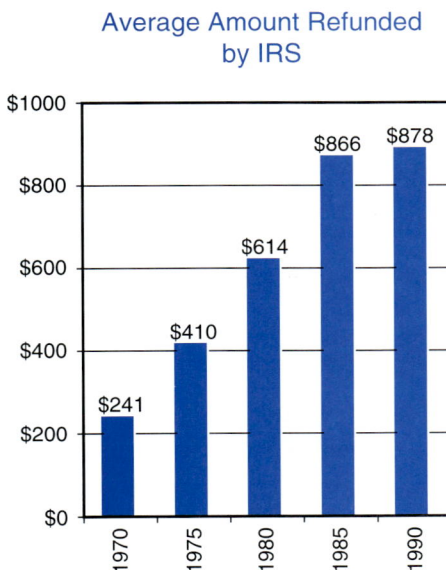

Example 3

A race car can reach a speed of 270 mph on a straight quarter mile track. How fast is the race car traveling in feet per second?

Analyze: 270 mph (270 miles per hour) means that the car can travel 270 miles in one hour. That is equivalent to the ratio $\frac{270 \text{ mi}}{1 \text{ hr.}}$. If we convert the 270 mi to feet and the 1 hr to seconds and substitute those answers into the ratio of $\frac{270 \text{ mi}}{1 \text{ hr}}$, we will get the ratio of feet to seconds.

Solve:

Convert 270 mi to ft
(1 mi = 5280 ft)

$$270 \text{ mi} = 270 \text{ mi} \times \frac{5280 \text{ ft.}}{1 \text{ mi}}$$

$$= 1{,}425{,}600 \text{ ft}$$

Convert 1 hr to sec
1 hr = 60 min
60 min = 3600 sec

Thus, $\dfrac{270 \text{ mi}}{1 \text{ hr}} = \dfrac{1{,}425{,}600 \text{ ft}}{3600 \text{ sec}} = 396 \text{ ft/sec.}$

Problem 1: The bar graph below shows the number of minutes Ron takes to get to work in a typical week. a) What is the average time spent getting to work each day? b) If Ron works 230 days per year, how many hours does he spend getting to work?

Ron's Drive Time to Work (in minutes)

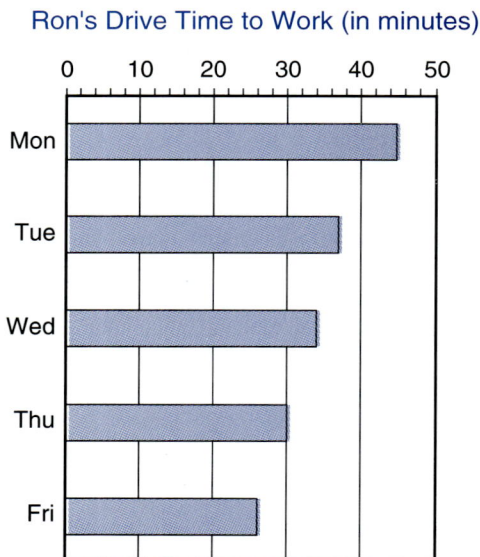

Answers: a) 34.6 min
b) 132.63 hrs

To find the average, get the sum of the number of minutes spent each day and divide by 5.

$$\text{mean} = \frac{45 + 37 + 35 + 30 + 26}{5}$$

$$= \frac{173}{5} = 34.6 \text{ min}$$

To find the number of hours spent a year, find the number of hours in 230 days at an average of 35 minutes a day.

$$\text{hrs} = \frac{230 \times 34.6}{60} \approx 132.63 \text{ hr}$$

Problem 2: A speed limit sign in a foreign country reads "80" which means 80 kilometers per hour (80 km/hr). What is the corresponding speed in miles per hour?

Answer: 49.68 mph
Convert km to mi

$$80 \text{ km} = 80 \text{ km} \times \frac{0.621 \text{ mi}}{1 \text{ km}}$$

$$= 49.68 \text{ mi}$$

Thus, 80 km/hr = 49.68 mph.

Exercise 6.9 Set A

1. A road sign along Highway I-80 in California reads *"Reno 113 mi 182 km."* These distances are not exactly the same. Which one is longer?

   1. _____

2. Which makes a smaller hole: a $\frac{7}{16}$ inch drill bit or a 12 mm drill bit?

   2. _____

3. A cheetah can reach a speed of 70 miles per hour. What is its speed in feet per second?

   3. _____

4. Which is heavier: a metric ton (1000 kg) or a U.S. Customary ton (2000 lb)?

   4. _____

5. A snail would take about 115 days to travel one mile. What is the snail's speed in yards per day?

   5. _____

6. When a ping-pong ball is hit, it can leave the paddle at a speed of 105.6 miles per hour. What is that speed in inches per second?

   6. _____

7. A dollar bill is $6\frac{3}{16}$ inches long. If a billion dollar bills were laid lengthwise end to end, how far in miles would they reach?

   7. _____

8. According to the U.S. Department of Agriculture, the amount of land utilized for farming on the east coast of the U.S. in 1994, measured in millions of acres, is:

8. _____

1) Georgia	12.1	8) Maine	1.4
2) Florida	10.3	9) New Jersey	0.9
3) North Carolina	9.3	10) Delaware	0.7
4) Virginia	8.6	11) Massachusetts	0.6
5) New York	8.0	12) New Hampshire	0.5
6) South Carolina	5.1	13) Connecticut	0.4
7) Maryland	2.3	14) Rhode Island	0.1

What are the mean and median amount of land utilized for farming on the east coast? Give answers accurate to the nearest tenth of a million.

9. The circle graph below shows and percent breakdown of beverage consumption in the U.S. in 1993.

9. _____

1993 U.S. Beverage Consumption

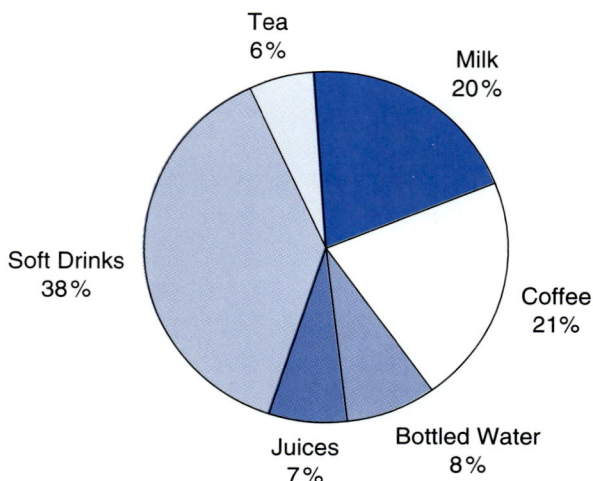

Tea 6%
Milk 20%
Soft Drinks 38%
Coffee 21%
Juices 7%
Bottled Water 8%

According to the U.S. Department of Agriculture, the average beverage consumption per person in 1993 was 122.1 gallons. How many more gallons of soft drinks did the average person consume than milk?

10. Chicken eggs are classified by the weight per dozen eggs. Large eggs weigh 24 ounces a dozen, while medium eggs weigh 21 ounces a dozen.
   a) If you do not include the shell, which is 12% of the egg, how many ounces of egg do you get from a dozen of large eggs? From a dozen medium eggs?
   b) At a local store large eggs sell for $1.29 a dozen and medium eggs sell for $1.09 a dozen. If you do not include the shell, which is the better buy: the large or medium eggs?
   c) If large eggs sell for $1.29 a dozen, find the cost per pound for large eggs when the shell is included.
   d) If large eggs sell for $1.29 a dozen, find the cost per pound for large eggs when the shell is not included.

10. a) _____

b) _____

c) _____

d) _____

Name _____   Date _____

Exercise 6.9 Set B

1. A road sign along Highway I-80 in California reads *"Reno 85 mi 137 km."* These distances are not exactly the same. Which one is longer?

1. _____

2. Which holds more: a 50 gallon drum or a 200 liter drum?

2. _____

3. In a 300 mile homing pigeon race, the first place finisher won with a speed of 1596.2 yards per minute. How fast did the pigeon fly in miles per hour?

3. _____

4. Who is taller: a woman who is 5 ft tall or a woman who is 150 cm tall?

4. _____

5. A jogger completed 8 miles in 75 minutes. What is the jogger's speed in miles per hour?

5. _____

6. If the cost of gasoline is 30.9¢ per liter, what is its cost per gallon?

6. _____

7. The width of a dollar bill is $2\frac{5}{8}$ inches. If a million dollar bills were laid side by side, how far in miles would they reach?

7. _____

8. According to the U.S. Department of Agriculture, the acreage per farm in the states west of the Rocky Mountains in 1994, is as follows:

1) Arizona	4,557	5) Oregon	467
2) Nevada	3,708	6) Washington	445
3) Utah	854	7) California	388
4) Idaho	659		

8. _____

What are the mean and median acreage per farm in these states? Give answers accurate to the nearest acre.

9. The bar graph below gives the electricity cost for a rural California home in 1995.

9. a) _____

b) _____

c) _____

1995 Electricity Costs for Rural California Home

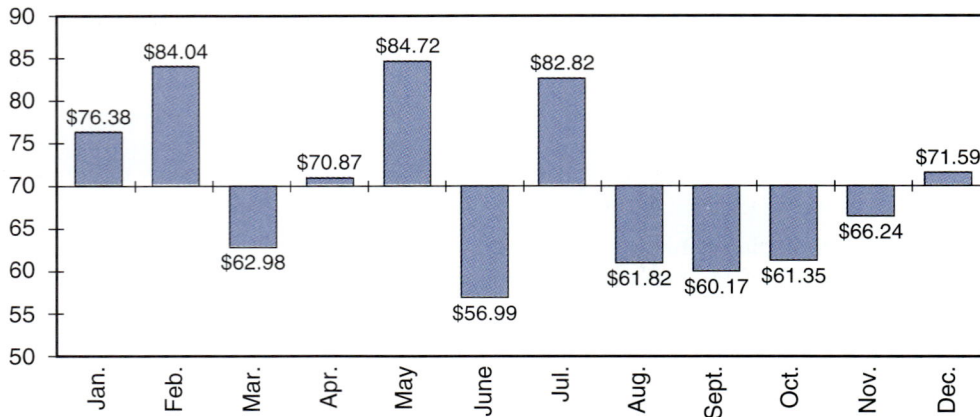

a) The design of the graph gives the mean electricity cost without doing any computation. What is this mean? Verify your answer by actually computing the mean.
b) What is the median electricity cost?
c) Between which two months was there the greatest increase in electricity costs? What is the increase?

10. Chicken eggs are classified by the weight per dozen eggs. Jumbo eggs weigh 30 ounces a dozen, while extra large eggs weigh 27 ounces a dozen.
   a) If you do not include the shell, which is 12% of the egg, how many ounces of egg do you get from a dozen jumbo eggs? From a dozen extra large eggs?
   b) At a local store jumbo eggs sell for $1.69 a dozen and extra large eggs sell for $1.59 a dozen. If you do not include the shell, which is the better buy: the jumbo or extra large eggs?
   c) If jumbo eggs sell for $1.69 a dozen, what is the cost per pound for jumbo eggs when the shell is included?
   d) If jumbo eggs sell for $1.69 a dozen, what is the cost per pound for jumbo eggs when the shell is not included?

10. a) _____

b) _____

c) _____

d) _____

Chapter 6 Summary

Concepts

You may refer to the sections listed below to review how to:

1. read measuring devices. (6.1)
2. change units of measurement in the U.S. system using the unit-fraction method. (6.2)
3. represent the units of measurement in the metric system by using a combination of a prefix and a basic unit. (6.3)
4. change units of measurement in the metric system by using either the unit-fraction method or movement of the decimal point. (6.4)
5. make conversions between measurements in the U.S. and the metric systems utilizing the unit-fraction method. (6.5)
6. make conversions between Celsius and Fahrenheit temperatures using the formulas:

$$C = \frac{5}{9} \times (F - 32) \quad \text{or} \quad F = \frac{9}{5} \times C + 32 \qquad (6.6)$$

7. analyze bar, line, and circle graphs. (6.7)
8. find the mean and median of a set of data. (6.8)
9. solve word problem involving measurement and statistics. (6.9)

Terminology

This chapter's important terms and their corresponding page numbers are:

bar graph: a graph that uses parallel bars to represent numerical information. (347)
centi: prefix meaning hundredth. (327)
circle graph: a graph that uses sectors of a circle to show the division of a whole into parts. (349)
deca: prefix meaning ten. (327)
gram: the basic unit of weight in the metric system. (327)
hecto: prefix meaning hundred. (327)
kilo: prefix meaning thousand. (327)
line graph: a graph that uses line segments to represent numerical information. (348)
liter: the basic unit for volume in the metric system. (327)
mean: the average of a list of data. (353)
median: the middle data value when data is placed in increasing order. (353)
meter: the basic unit for length in the metric system. (327)
milli: prefix meaning thousandth. (327)
unit-fraction: a fraction with equivalent measurements in its numerator and its denominator, giving it a value of 1. (323)

U.S. Conversions

Length

1 foot (ft) = 12 inches (in.)
1 yard (yd) = 3 feet (ft)
1 mile (mi) = 5280 feet (ft)

Weight

1 pound (lb) = 16 ounces (oz)
1 ton (T) = 2000 pounds (lb)

Volume

cup (c) = 8 fluid ounces (fl oz)
1 pint (pt) = 2 cups (c)
1 quart (qt) = 2 pints (pt) = 32 fl oz
1 gallon (gal) = 4 quarts (qt)

U.S.—Metric Conversions

Length

1 in. ≈ 2.54 cm
39.4 in. ≈ 1 m
0.621 mi ≈ 1 km

Volume

1.06 qt ≈ 1 liter

Weight

1 oz ≈ 28.35 g
1 lb ≈ 454 g
2.2 lb ≈ 1 kg

Fahrenheit—Centigrade Conversions

$$F = \frac{9}{5} \times C + 32 \qquad C = \frac{5}{9} \times (F - 32)$$

Chapter 6 Crossword Puzzle

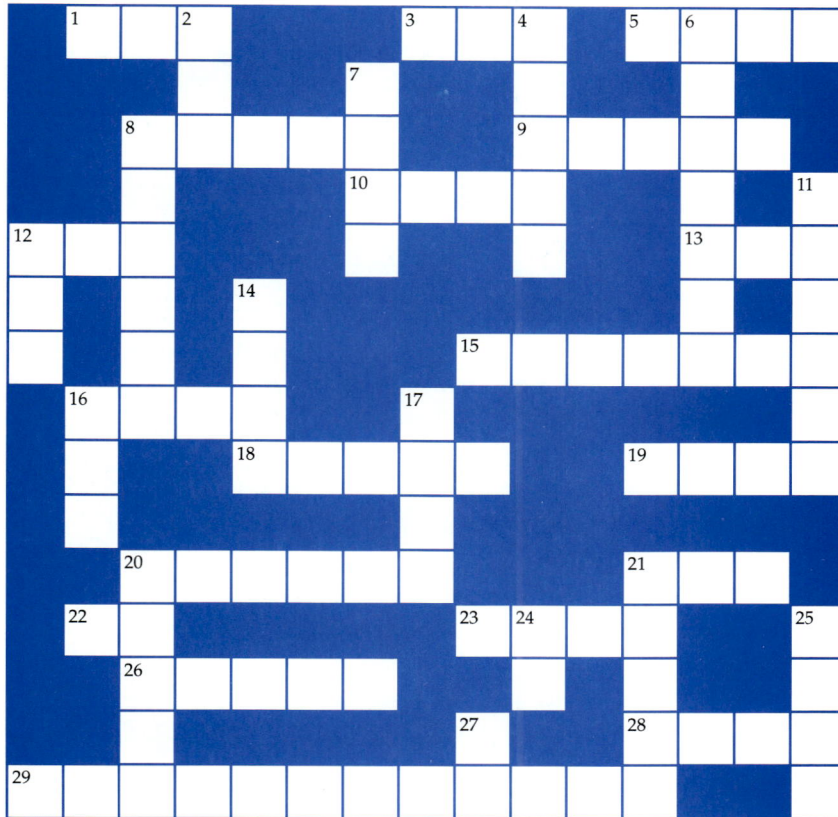

Across
1. 2000 mg = _____ g
3. Four quarts (abbr)
5. Thirty-six inches
8. Prefix meaning $\frac{1}{100}$
9. 7.62 cm = _____ inches
10. Graph using segments
12. Graph using vertical or horizontal strips
13. Abbreviation for average
15. Out of 100
16. Prefix meaning 10
18. Standard metric length
19. Smaller than
20. Middle value
21. Mean of 5.5, 3.6, 4.4, 2.5, 14
22. 5280 feet (abbr)
23. Median of 1, 3, 3, 4, 6, 8, 12, 13
26. Smallest
28. Not odd
29. Has a value of one (2 wrds)

Down
2. 26.2 mi = _____ km (3rd digit)
4. Standard metric measure of volume
6. mean
7. Prefix meaning 1000
8. Round graph
11. One place to the right of the decimal point
12. Not good
14. Standard metric measure of weight
16. The loan payment is _____ .
17. The average
20. Prefix meaning 0.001
21. 44.6° F = _____ ° C
24. Abbreviation for $\frac{1}{12}$ of a foot
25. 9.8 qt = _____ liters (first digit)
27. Four of these make a gallon (abbr)

MATH MAGIC V

Magic Stars

A **magic star** is formed by placing whole numbers at the intersection points of the lines of a star so that the sum of the numbers on each line is the same. In a magic star no number may be used twice, however, it is not limited to the consecutive whole numbers (1, 2, 3, 4, 5, . . .). Because of this, there are many solutions for each type of star.

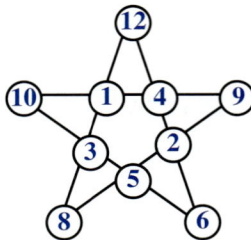

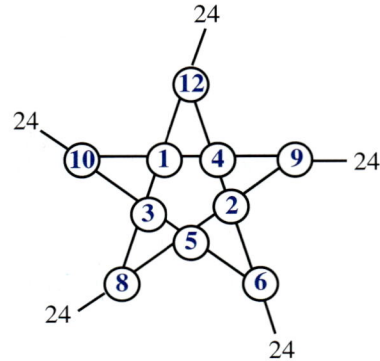

The sum of the four numbers on each line of the star is 24.

Recreations

1. Verify that the following is a five-point magic star.

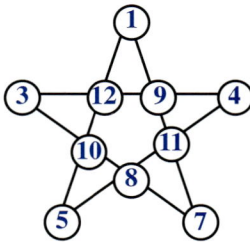

2. What would happen if you added the same amount to each number in a magic star? Give some examples of the result.

3. Find the missing numbers in this six-point magic star.

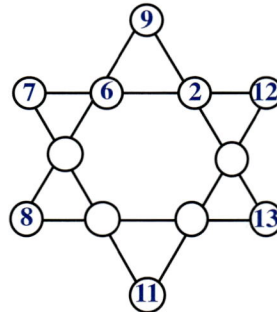

4. Create two other six-point magic stars.

Chapter 6 Practice Test A

1. What amount is indicated by the arrow below?

    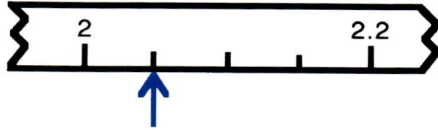

2. 8.7 tons = _?_ lb   3. 162 in. = _?_ ft

4. 24 pt = _?_ gal   5. 1 kg = _?_ g

6. 1 m = _?_ cm   7. 8 g = _?_ mg

8. 1697 ml = _?_ liters   9. 8.24 cm = _?_ mm

10. 5 km = _?_ mi   11. 101.6 cm = _?_ in.

12. 0.04 kg = _?_ oz   13. Which is longer: 400 m or 440 yd?

14. What Celsius temperature corresponds to 104° Fahrenheit?

15. In the line graph on page 352, find the mean and median winning long jump in Local Olympics 1976–1996.

1. _____

2. _____

3. _____

4. _____

5. _____

6. _____

7. _____

8. _____

9. _____

10. _____

11. _____

12. _____

13. _____

14. _____

15. _____

Chapter 6 Practice Test B

1. What amount is indicated by the arrow below?

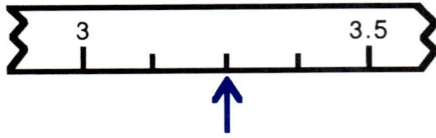

$$\boxed{3 \qquad\qquad 3.5}$$
↑

2. 12.5 ft = _?_ in.

3. 36 lb = _?_ oz

2. _____

3. _____

4. $8\frac{3}{4}$ pt = _?_ fl oz

5. 1 km = _?_ m

4. _____

5. _____

6. 1 liter = _?_ ml

7. 5 m = _?_ cm

6. _____

7. _____

8. 1555 mg = _?_ g

9. 6.23 mm = _?_ cm

8. _____

9. _____

10. 50 m = _?_ in.

11. 4.968 mi = _?_ km

10. _____

11. _____

12. 324 fl oz = _?_ liters

13. Which is heavier: 1 ton or 1000 kg?

12. _____

13. _____

14. What Fahrenheit temperature corresponds to 45° Celsius?

14. _____

15. In the line graph on page 351, find the mean and median temperature in Fresno, California.

15. _____

Chapter 6 Supplementary Exercises

Section 6.1

In problems 1–10, determine the length in inches indicated by each letter.

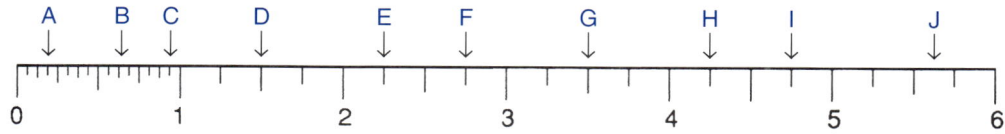

1. A	2. B
3. C	4. D
5. E	6. F
7. G	8. H
9. I	10. J

In problems 11–20, determine the weight in kilograms (kg) indicated by each letter.

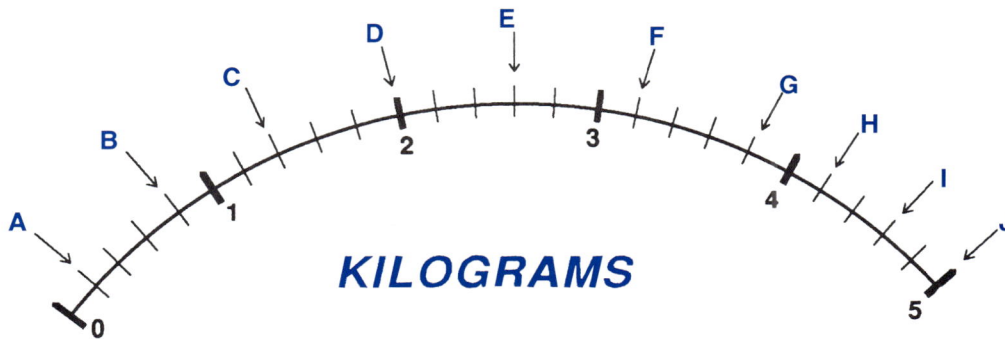

11. A	12. B
13. C	14. D
15. E	16. F
17. G	18. H
19. I	20. J

Section 6.2

1. 4 ft = _?_ in.
2. 18 ft = _?_ yd
3. 5 c = _?_ fl oz
4. 56 fl oz = _?_ c
5. 20 qt = _?_ gal
6. 50 gal = _?_ qt
7. 7920 ft = _?_ mi
8. 3.5 mi = _?_ ft
9. $4\frac{1}{2}$ yd = _?_ in.
10. 51 in. = _?_ ft
11. 7500 lb = _?_ T
12. 5.43 T = _?_ lb
13. 729.6 oz = _?_ lb
14. 3.125 lb = _?_ oz
15. 31,680 in. = _?_ mi
16. 0.62 mi = _?_ in.
17. 37,676 oz = _?_ T
18. 1.225 T = _?_ oz
19. 3.1 mi = _?_ yd
20. 1320 yd = _?_ mi

Section 6.3

In problems 1–8, determine the measurement given by each abbreviation.

1. cm
2. kl
3. mg
4. mm
5. kg
6. cl
7. km
8. ml

In problems 9–14, determine the equivalent measurement.

9. 1 kg = _?_ g
10. 1 g = _?_ kg
11. 1 m = _?_ mm
12. 1 mm = _?_ m
13. 1 cl = _?_ liter
14. 1 liter = _?_ cl

Section 6.4

1. 6000 g = _?_ kg
2. 3 km = _?_ m
3. 7 liter = _?_ ml
4. 5 g = _?_ cg
5. 3250 mg = _?_ g
6. 5.6 kg = _?_ g
7. 6.85 m = _?_ cm
8. 12 ml = _?_ cl
9. 53 cl = _?_ ml
10. 16.25 g = _?_ mg
11. 328.8 cg = _?_ g
12. 72.6 mm = _?_ cm
13. 4.75 km = _?_ m
14. 0.85 m = _?_ mm
15. 12,500 mm = _?_ m
16. 1.06 liters = _?_ cl
17. 2.5 g = _?_ mg
18. 63.8 g = _?_ kg
19. 14 cl = _?_ ml
20. 9.4 liters = _?_ ml

Section 6.5

1. 17.78 cm = _?_ in.
2. 12 in. = _?_ cm
3. 13.2 lb = _?_ kg
4. 5 kg = _?_ lb
5. 8 m = _?_ in.
6. 157.6 in. = _?_ m
7. 170.1 g = _?_ oz
8. 5 oz = _?_ g
9. 15.9 qt = _?_ liters
10. 4.3 liters = _?_ qt
11. 5000 km = _?_ mi
12. 6.21 mi = _?_ km
13. 0.75 lb = _?_ g
14. 1021.5 g = _?_ lb
15. 3.5 ft = _?_ cm
16. 76.2 cm = _?_ ft

Section 6.6

1. 41° F = _?_ ° C
2. 20° C = _?_ ° F
3. 45° C = _?_ ° F
4. 86° F = _?_ ° C
5. 185° F = _?_ ° C
6. 155° C = _?_ ° F
7. 37.6° C = _?_ ° F
8. 80.3° F = _?_ ° C
9. 74.9° F = _?_ ° C
10. 95° C = _?_ ° F
11. 242.5° C = _?_ ° F
12. 110.2° F = _?_ ° C
13. 82.76° F = _?_ ° C
14. 1000° C = _?_ ° F
15. 88.25° C = _?_ ° F
16. 91.85° F = _?_ ° C
17. 212° F = _?_ ° C
18. 7.75° C = _?_ ° F
19. 64° C = _?_ ° F
20. 109.76° F = _?_ ° C

Section 6.7

Accidental Deaths in the U.S.A.

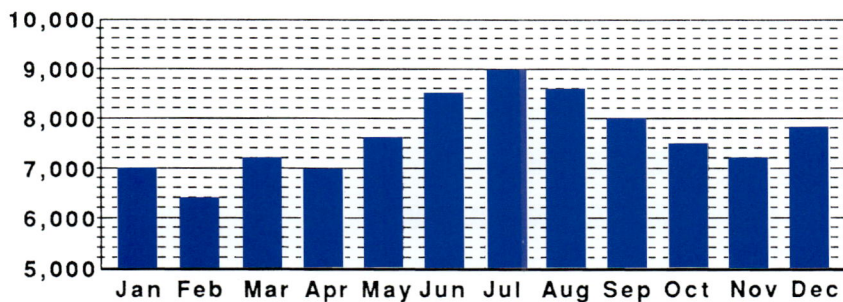

1. How many accidental deaths were recorded in March?

2. How many accidental deaths were recorded in June?

3. During what month were there 7500 accidental deaths?

4. During what month were there 7600 accidental deaths?

5. What is the percent increase in accidental deaths from February to July?

6. What is the percent decrease in accidental deaths from July to November?

7. What is the average number of accidental deaths occurring during the summer months of June, July, and August?

8. What is the average number of accidental deaths occurring during the winter months of December, January, and February?

Section 6.8

Find the mean and median of the following sets of data:

1. 76, 89, 89, 65, 93, 95, 72

2. 3.25, 3.6, 2.97, 2.55, 3.92

3. 155.6, 123.9, 140.0, 110.5, 107.2, 110.5

4. 0.12, 0.34, 0.29, 0.41, 0.34, 0.56, 0.89, 0.43

Solve the following application problems:

5. The batting champions and their batting averages for the National League in the 1980's were:

1980 Bill Buckner	.324		1985 Willie McGee	.353
1981 Bill Madlock	.341		1986 Tim Raines	.334
1982 Al Oliver	.331		1987 Tony Gwynn	.369
1983 Bill Madlock	.323		1988 Tony Gwynn	.313
1984 Tony Gwynn	.351		1989 Tony Gwynn	.336

 Find the mean and median batting average for the National League champions of the 1980's.

6. According to the Population Division of the United Nations, the population of the countries of Northern Europe in the year 2000 is projected as follows: Denmark—5.1 million, Finland—5.0 million, Ireland—4.2 million, Norway—4.2 million, Sweden—8.1 million, and United Kingdom—56.2 million. Find the projected mean and median population for Northern Europe.

Section 6.9

1. Which is heavier: 1000 pounds or 500 kilograms?

2. Who is taller: Hazel, who is 6 ft tall, or Alicia, who is 180 cm tall?

3. A road sign in Canada reads *"Jasper 8.5 km."* How far is that in miles?

4. The 1993 U.S. median income for persons 25 years and older based on educational attainment is displayed below. (Source: U.S. Bureau of the Census)

U.S. Median Income (by Education) for Persons 25 Years and Older in 1993

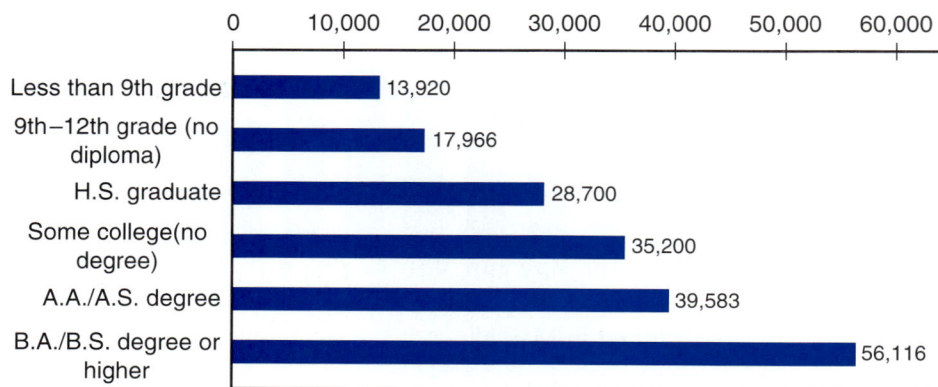

Education	Income
Less than 9th grade	13,920
9th–12th grade (no diploma)	17,966
H.S. graduate	28,700
Some college (no degree)	35,200
A.A./A.S. degree	39,583
B.A./B.S. degree or higher	56,116

 a) How much more money does a holder of a Bachelor's degree make than a person with less than a 9th grade education?

 b) What is the percent increase from the income of a person with less than a 9th grade education to the income of a holder of a Bachelor's degree?

 c) What is the average income for persons 25 years and older in 1993?

5. The price for cable television service over the seven year period from 1985 to 1991 in a small town is as follows: 1985—$9.95, 1986—$12.95, 1987—$14.45, 1988—$15.60, 1989—$16.75, 1990—$17.50, and 1991—$19.80. a) Find the mean and median cost for cable TV service in that time period. b) Find the percent increase in cable TV service from 1985 to 1991.

Unit III Exam

Chapters 5 and 6

In problems 1–2, solve each proportion.

1. $\dfrac{7}{15} = \dfrac{N}{105}$

2. $\dfrac{13.5}{7.6} = \dfrac{2.25}{Y}$

3. Express 45% as a decimal and reduced fraction.

4. 54 is what percent of 72?

5. 22% of what number is 19.03?

6. 2.5 mi = _?_ in.

7. 5600 mg = _?_ g

8. 1.5 qt = _?_ ml

9. 60° C = _?_ ° F

10. Which is heavier: 600 g or 30 oz?

11. On a drafting ruler each inch is divided into 32 equal parts. What distance is indicated by the mark just before the mark at 5 inches?

12. On a circle graph showing the budget for a company, the sector representing advertising is 12% of the graph. If the company's total budget is $256,000, how much is spent on advertising?

13. The scale on a road map is 1.5 inches equals 90 miles. What is the actual distance between two cities that are 7 inches apart on that map?

14. After one year the resale value of an $8000 truck was only $5,500. That drop in price represents what percent decrease in the value of the truck?

15. How much simple interest is charged on a $876 loan for 2 years with a yearly interest rate of 11%?

1. _____

2. _____

3. _____

4. _____

5. _____

6. _____

7. _____

8. _____

9. _____

10. _____

11. _____

12. _____

13. _____

14. _____

15. _____

Unit IV

Introductions to Algebra and Geometry

In the first three units, you covered basic arithmetic. The next step on the path of math development is algebra and geometry. You are probably thinking to yourself, "What are algebra and geometry? They sound very difficult." You shouldn't be too worried, because people seem to put an unwarranted mystique around these subjects.

To understand what algebra is all about, you must realize that, in algebra, letters are used to stand for numbers. Just as you operated with numbers in arithmetic, in algebra you simply replace those numbers with letters and work with them. In geometry, you learn about the shapes you see in the world around you, and how the arithmetic you learned applies to those shapes.

In this unit, you will see that algebra goes beyond the computations of arithmetic and gives you a system to solve problems of increased difficulty. You will also see how a knowledge of geometry will help you classify and measure the shapes you see each day. After finishing this unit, you should be able to do the following:

1. work with algebraic variables.
2. operate with positive and negative numbers.
3. solve equations containing one variable.
4. define basic geometric shapes.
5. classify common geometric shapes.
6. find perimeters and areas of common plane figures.
7. find surface areas and volumes of common 3-dimensional objects.
8. identify properties of quadrilaterals.
9. find angles of polygons.
10. solve word problems involving algebra and geometry.

Brain Buster

How many different triangles are contained in the figure below?

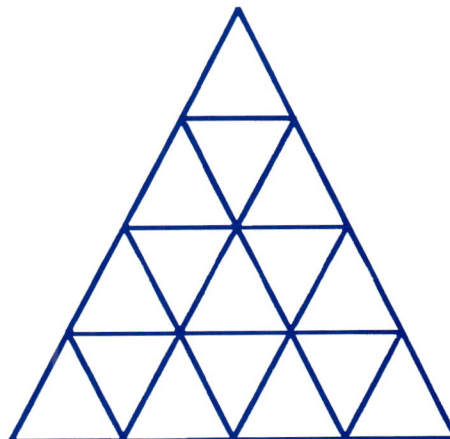

Chapter 7

Introduction to Algebra

After completing this chapter, you should be able to do the following:

1. evaluate algebraic expressions.
2. compare the size of signed numbers.
3. operate with positive and negative numbers.
4. solve equations using the addition property.
5. solve equations using the multiplication and division properties.
6. apply the properties of algebra in combining like terms.
7. translate phrases and statements into algebraic expressions and equations.
8. solve word problems using algebra.
9. apply algebraic techniques to compound interest and annuity problems.

On the next page, you will find a pretest for this chapter. The purpose of the pretest is to help you determine which sections in this chapter you need to study in detail and which sections you can review quickly. By taking and correcting the pretest according to the instructions on the next page, you can better plan your pace through this chapter.

Name _____   Date _____

Chapter 7 Pretest

Take and correct this test using the answer section at the end of the book.
Those problems that give you difficulty indicate which sections need extra
attention. Section numbers are in parentheses before each problem.

(7.1)   1. If A = 5, B = 4, and C = 1, then 3A − 2B + C = ?   1. _____

In problems 2–3, replace the question mark with > or <.

(7.2)   2. 0 ? −9   3. −7 ? −5   2. _____

                                                                       3. _____

In problems 4–10, perform the indicated operations.

(7.3)   4. −16 + 9   4. _____

(7.3)   5. −14 + (−17)   5. _____

(7.4)   6. 5 − 17   6. _____

(7.4)   7. −8 − (−6)   7. _____

(7.5)   8. 7(−6)   8. _____

(7.5)   9. (−5)(−9)   9. _____

(7.6)   10. $\dfrac{-2 + 10(3 - 16)}{-5 - 7}$ 10. _____

In Problems 11–14, solve for x in each equation.

(7.7)   11. $x + 6 = 15$ (7.8)   12. $x - 14 = -36$

11. _____

12. _____

(7.9)   13. $152 = 4x$ (7.10)   14. $\dfrac{x}{7} + 30 = 3$

13. _____

14. _____

(7.11)   15. Simplify by combining like terms:

$2(4x - 5) + 3(x + 7)$

15. _____

(7.12)   16. Solve for x:

$2(3x - 5) = 4x - 18$

16. _____

(7.13)   17. Translate the following into an algebraic expression or equation.
a) Twice the sum of a number and three
b) Four less than a number is the same as the product of the number and three.

17a) _____

17b) _____

(7.14)   18. The sum of three consecutive whole numbers is 84. What are the numbers?

18. _____

(7.15)   19. If $500 is left in an account that pays 6% annual interest, compounded monthly, how much will be in the account after 4 years?

19. _____

(7.15)   20. Suppose an annuity pays 8.4% annual interest. How much would you have to deposit in the annuity each month to have $50,000 at the end of 8 years?

20. _____

7.1 From Numbers to Letters

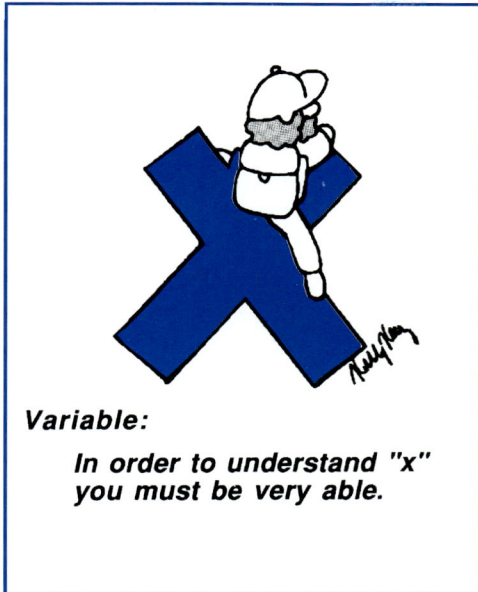

Variable:

In order to understand "x" you must be very able.

The basis of algebra is its use of letters to stand for numbers. The letters used are called **variables.** The first thing that you have to accept and understand in algebra is that letters can be used in the same ways as numbers. Consider the basic operations:

Addition

$A + B$ means that two numbers are being added; A and B represent the two addends.

Subtraction

$p - q$ means that two numbers are being subtracted; p and q represent those numbers.

Division

$f \div R$ or $\dfrac{f}{R}$ means that two numbers are being divided; f and R represent those numbers.

Multiplication

$X \cdot Y$ or $(X)(Y)$ or XY means that two numbers are being multiplied; X and Y represent the two factors.

Note: We do not use the letter "x" to signify multiplication, since in algebra the "x" can represent a number. Multiplication can be displayed in three other ways:

1. using a dot: $5 \cdot K$
2. using parentheses: $5(k)$
3. using no sign between factors: $5k$

Combined Operations

$4x + 3y$ means 4 times a number (x) plus 3 times a number (y).

$\dfrac{P}{RT}$ means a number (P) is divided by the product of two numbers (R and T).

Do not be confused by those letters in algebra. Just keep telling yourself that letters are used just like numbers, since they simply represent numbers.

A fundamental problem in algebra involves finding the value of **algebraic expressions**—expressions that have numbers, variables, and operations. We can find the value of an algebraic expression, if we know the value of each variable and use the proper order of operations as discussed in Section 2.8.

Example 1

If $x = 5$, and $y = 2$, then $4x + 3y = ?$

$4x + 3y = 4 \cdot 5 + 3 \cdot 2$ Replace each variable with its value.

$= 20 + 6$

$= 26$ Do the computation using the proper order of operations.

Example 2

If $P = 10$ and $q = \dfrac{1}{2}$, then $3(P - 2q) = ?$

$3(P - 2q) = 3\left(10 - 2 \cdot \dfrac{1}{2}\right)$ Replace each variable with its value.

$\qquad = 3(10 - 1)$
$\qquad = 3(9)$ Do the computation using the proper
$\qquad = 27$ order of operations.

Example 3

If $S = P + PRT$ and $P = 5200$, $R = 12\%$, and $T = 3$, find the value of S.

$S = P + PRT$ Replace the P, R, and T with the
$\quad = 5200 + 5200(.12)(3)$ given values.

$\quad = 5200 + 1872$

$\quad = 7072$ Do the computation using the proper order of operations.

Problem 1:   If $H = .6$, $Z = 36$, and $W = 1$, then $ZH - W + \dfrac{Z}{H} = ?$ Answer: 80.6

$\qquad\qquad = 36(.6) - 1 + \dfrac{36}{.6}$

$\qquad\qquad = 21.6 - 1 + 60$

$\qquad\qquad = 80.6$

Problem 2:   If $A = \dfrac{3}{4}$ and $B = 6$, then $A(20 - 2B + 8) = ?$ Answer: 12

$\qquad\qquad = \dfrac{3}{4}(20 - 2 \cdot 6 + 8)$

$\qquad\qquad = \dfrac{3}{4}(20 - 12 + 8)$

$\qquad\qquad = \dfrac{3}{4}(16) = 12$

Name _____   Date _____

Exercise 7.1 Set A

In problems 1–8, if $A = 2$, $B = 7$, and $C = 1$, evaluate each expression.

1. $A + B - C$ 2. $B + C - A$ 1. _____

                                                          2. _____

3. $\dfrac{4B}{A}$ 4. $\dfrac{7A}{B}$ 3. _____

                                                          4. _____

5. $2BC - 7A$ 6. $14AC - 4B$ 5. _____

                                                          6. _____

7. $A(3B + 5A)$ 8. $A(9C + 2B)$ 7. _____

                                                          8. _____

In problems 9–13, evaluate each expression.

9. If $x = 1.2$, $y = 5$, and $z = 24$, then $xy + \dfrac{z}{x} - \dfrac{y}{2} = ?$ 9. _____

10. If $p = 5.8$, $q = 6$, and $r = 29$, then $pq - \dfrac{q}{5} + \dfrac{r}{p} = ?$ 10. _____

11. If $M = \dfrac{3}{4}$ and $N = 5\dfrac{1}{2}$, then $M(3N - 2M) = ?$ 11. _____

12. If $R = \dfrac{5}{8}$ and $S = 3\dfrac{1}{5}$, then $R\,(2S + 8) = ?$ 12. _____

13. If $f = \dfrac{2}{5}$, $g = .65$, and $h = 15$, then $3hf + h\left(\dfrac{h}{f} - 6g\right) = ?$ 13. _____

Exercise 7.1 Set B

In problems 1–8, if $A = 3$, $B = 6$, and $C = 1$, evaluate each expression.

1. $C + B - A$ 2. $A + B - C$

3. $\dfrac{2B}{A}$ 4. $\dfrac{8A}{B}$

5. $4AC - 2B$ 6. $2BC - 4A$

7. $A(2C + 3B)$ 8. $B(2A + 4C)$

In problems 9–13, evaluate each expression.

9. If $h = 3.5$, $j = 6$, and $k = 7$, then $jk + \dfrac{h}{k} + \dfrac{h}{2} = ?$

10. If $q = 2.8$, $r = 5$, and $s = 20$, then $rq - \dfrac{r}{4} + \dfrac{r}{s} = ?$

11. If $U = \dfrac{2}{3}$ and $V = 1\dfrac{1}{4}$, then $U(3V - 3) = ?$

12. If $p = \dfrac{7}{8}$ and $q = 2\dfrac{4}{5}$, then $q(8p - 2) = ?$

13. If $d = \dfrac{4}{5}$, $e = .45$, and $f = 25$, then $2df + f\left(\dfrac{f}{5} - 8e\right) = ?$

1. _____

2. _____

3. _____

4. _____

5. _____

6. _____

7. _____

8. _____

9. _____

10. _____

11. _____

12. _____

13. _____

7.2 Signed Numbers

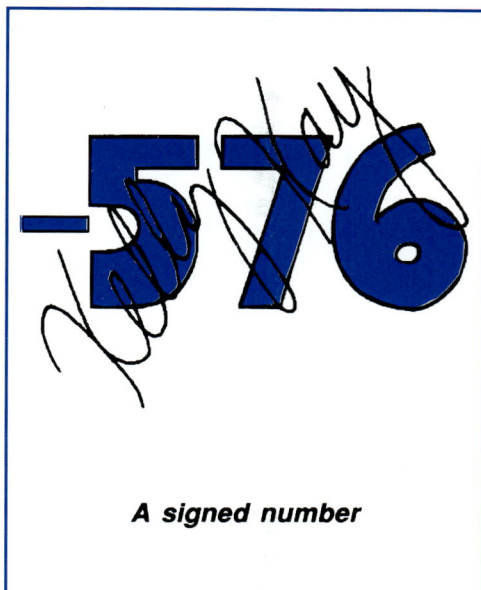

A signed number

Through our study of arithmetic, we worked with numbers that were larger than zero. These numbers are called positive numbers. They are sometimes written with a "+" sign, such as +5 instead of just 5. Here the "+" sign is not used to signify the operation of addition. It is used to indicate that the number is larger than zero—a positive number.

Before we can proceed into an introduction of algebra, we must learn about another group of numbers called negative numbers. You have probably encountered these numbers before.

If the temperature is 12° below zero, we say it is minus twelve degrees (−12°). If you write a check for $50.75, when you have only $20.00 in your checking account, you would be overdrawn and have a balance of −$30.75.

These numbers that have values less than zero are the negative numbers. They are the opposite of positive numbers. The "−" sign used with these numbers does not signify the operation of subtraction. It means you have a number that is less than zero. These two types of numbers, positive and negative numbers, are called **signed numbers,** since they are written with either a positive sign (+) or a negative sign (−).

The number zero separates the positive numbers and the negative numbers. It is neither positive nor negative. It is the only neutral number in our number system. We can show the relative values of signed numbers by placing them along a line called a **number line.**

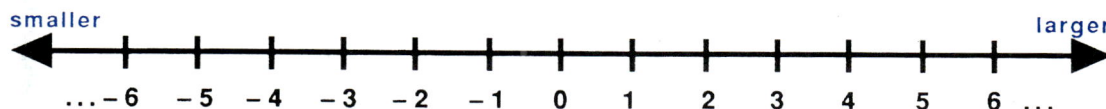

smaller   larger

$$\dots -6 \quad -5 \quad -4 \quad -3 \quad -2 \quad -1 \quad 0 \quad 1 \quad 2 \quad 3 \quad 4 \quad 5 \quad 6 \dots$$

You can use the number line to compare signed numbers. *As you go to the right along the number line, the numbers get larger; and as you go to the left along the number line, the numbers get smaller.*

For example: $3 > -2$ 3 is greater than −2, since 3 is farther to the right on the number line than −2.

$-4 < 0$ −4 is less than 0, since −4 is farther to the left on the number line than 0.

$-6 > -10$ −6 is greater than −10, since −6 is farther to the right on the number line than −10.

$-12 < -7$ −12 is less than −7, since −12 is farther to the left on the number line than −7.

Fractional and decimal numbers can also be placed on the number line by placing them between the positive and negative whole numbers.

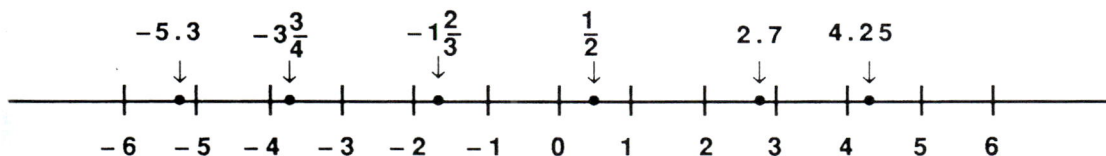

$$-5.3 \quad -3\tfrac{3}{4} \quad -1\tfrac{2}{3} \quad \tfrac{1}{2} \quad 2.7 \quad 4.25$$

$$-6 \quad -5 \quad -4 \quad -3 \quad -2 \quad -1 \quad 0 \quad 1 \quad 2 \quad 3 \quad 4 \quad 5 \quad 6$$

Problem 1: Place the following numbers in the correct position on the number line:

Answer:

2, −3, 1/4, 3.6, −.2, −1 1/2

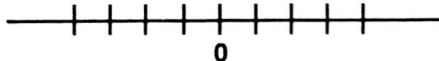

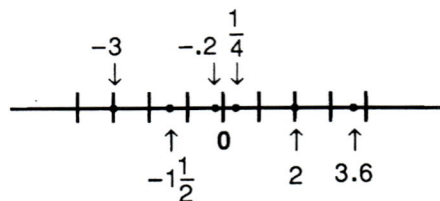

Problems: Replace the ? with > or <:

Answers:

2. 0 ? −7

2. >

3. −400 ? −506

3. >

4. −4.5 ? $2\frac{1}{3}$

4. <

5. +45.67 ? +45.607

5. >

6. $-6\frac{2}{3}$? $-6\frac{1}{2}$

6. <

Problems: Which number is further to the right on a number line?

Answers:

7. −3 or 3

7. 3

8. −3 or −5

8. −3

9. −0.17 or −0.2

9. −0.17

10. $5\frac{3}{4}$ or $5\frac{2}{3}$

10. $5\frac{3}{4}$

Exercise 7.2 Set A

In problems 1–5, locate each number on the number line in the answer column.

1. −2, 2, 3, −4

2. −3, 3, −1, 4

3. $\frac{3}{4}$, $-2\frac{1}{2}$, $3\frac{2}{3}$, $-3\frac{1}{3}$

4. $-\frac{1}{2}$, $1\frac{2}{3}$, $-3\frac{3}{4}$, $4\frac{1}{2}$

5. 3.5, −2.25, 0.6, −1.9

1.

2.

3.

4.

5.

In problems 6–19, replace the question mark with > or <.

6. 5 ? 3

7. 4 ? 2

8. 0 ? −3

9. 0 ? −2

10. −6 ? 3

11. −7 ? 2

12. −7 ? −4

13. −6 ? −2

14. $-5\frac{1}{2}$? $-5\frac{3}{4}$

15. $-7\frac{1}{2}$? $-7\frac{3}{4}$

16. −1.6 ? −1.5

17. −2.7 ? −2.6

18. $-50\frac{1}{2}$? −50.6

19. −37.5 ? 3.75

6. _____

7. _____

8. _____

9. _____

10. _____

11. _____

12. _____

13. _____

14. _____

15. _____

16. _____

17. _____

18. _____

19. _____

Exercise 7.2 Set B

In problems 1–5, locate each number on the number line in the answer column.

1. −1, 1, −2, 4

2. −3, 3, 4, −4

3. $\frac{1}{2}$, $-\frac{3}{4}$, $1\frac{2}{3}$, $-2\frac{1}{3}$

4. $-\frac{1}{3}$, $2\frac{1}{2}$, $-3\frac{3}{4}$, $3\frac{1}{4}$

5. −2.6, 0.5, 3.5, −3.75

1.

2.

3.

4.

5.

In problems 6–19, replace the question mark with > or <.

6. 7 ? 4

7. 8 ? 3

8. 0 ? −4

9. 0 ? −1

10. −7 ? 5

11. −8 ? 4

12. −9 ? −4

13. −7 ? −3

14. $-1\frac{1}{2}$? $-1\frac{2}{3}$

15. $-3\frac{1}{2}$? $-3\frac{2}{3}$

16. −4.7 ? −4.4

17. −5.5 ? −5.4

18. −40.6 ? $-40\frac{1}{2}$

19. −34.5 ? 3.45

6. _____

7. _____

8. _____

9. _____

10. _____

11. _____

12. _____

13. _____

14. _____

15. _____

16. _____

17. _____

18. _____

19. _____

7.3 Adding Signed Numbers

Now that you understand what is meant by signed numbers, you can learn to perform the basic operations on these numbers. The first operation is the addition of signed numbers. To help explain how this is done, we will use a number line. **Adding signed numbers** can be illustrated on a number line as follows:

> 1. Adding a positive number is the same as moving that many units in the positive direction.
> 2. Adding a negative number is the same as moving that many units in the negative direction.

Example 1

$5 + (-3) = ?$

That problem suggests that you start at 5 on a number line and go 3 units in the negative direction.

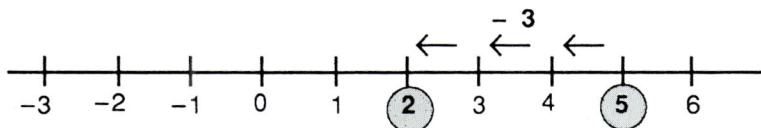

So, $5 + (-3) = 2$

Example 2

$-7 + 4 = ?$

Start at -7 on a number line and go 4 units in the positive direction.

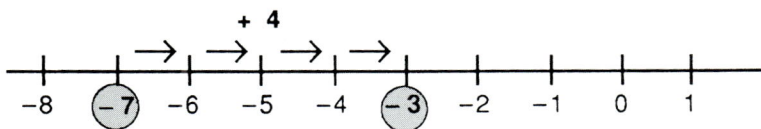

So, $-7 + 4 = -3$

Example 3

$-2 + (-6) = ?$

Start at -2 on a number line and go 6 units in the negative direction.

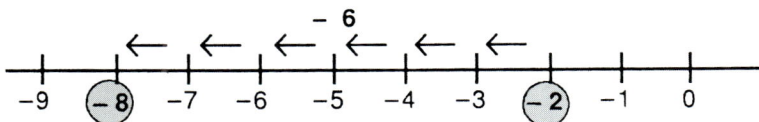

So, $-2 + (-6) = -8$

If the numbers to be added had many digits, such as −576 + 329, using a number line to find the answer would really be impractical. Because of that difficulty, let us consider a method that will enable us to add signed numbers more quickly than using a number line.

Every number has two parts: a "+" or "−" sign, and a number part.

number
sign ⌐ ⌐part
−8

number
sign ⌐ ⌐part
+9

If a number has no sign, it is understood to be a positive number.

$$16 = +16$$

Rules for Adding Signed Numbers

1. If the numbers have the same signs, add their number parts and use that same sign as the sign of the answer.
2. If the numbers have different signs, subtract their number parts and use the sign of the larger number part.

Example 4

$$-5 + (-8) = ?$$

The numbers have the same signs.

Add the number parts.

$$\begin{array}{r} 5 \\ 8 \\ \hline 13 \end{array}$$

Since both are negative, the answer is negative.

So, −5 + (−8) = −13.

Example 5

$$-5 + 8 = ?$$

The numbers have different signs. Subtract the number parts. Subtract the smaller number part (5) from the larger (8).

$$\begin{array}{r} 8 \\ 5 \\ \hline 3 \end{array}$$

Since the larger number part (8) is positive, the answer is positive.

So, −5 + 8 = 3.

You could also obtain the answer by picturing movement on a number line. If you start at −5 and move 8 units in the positive direction you will end up at +3.

Example 6

$-75 + (-46) = ?$

The numbers have the same signs.

Add the number parts.

$$\begin{array}{r} 75 \\ \underline{46} \\ 121 \end{array}$$

Since both are negative, the answer is negative.

So, $-75 + (-46) = -121$

Example 7

$27 + (-52) = ?$

The numbers have different signs. Subtract the number parts.

Subtract the smaller number part (27) from the larger (52).

$$\begin{array}{r} 52 \\ \underline{27} \\ 25 \end{array}$$

Since the larger number part (52) is negative, the answer is negative.

So, $27 + (-52) = -25$.

Example 8

$-35 + 19 = ?$

The numbers have different signs. Subtract the number parts.

Subtract the smaller number part (19) from the larger (35).

$$\begin{array}{r} 35 \\ \underline{19} \\ 16 \end{array}$$

Since the larger number part (35) is negative, the answer is negative.

So, $-35 + 19 = -16$.

Problem 1: $-12 + 5 = ?$

Answer: -7

> Since the numbers have different signs, subtract the number parts.
>
> $$\begin{array}{r} 12 \\ \underline{5} \\ 7 \end{array}$$
>
> Since the larger number part (12) has a negative sign, the answer is negative. $-12 + 5 = -7$

Problem 2: $167 + (-88) = ?$

Answer: 79

> Since the numbers have different signs, subtract the number parts.
>
> $$\begin{array}{r} 167 \\ \underline{88} \\ 79 \end{array}$$
>
> Since the larger number part (167) has a positive sign, the answer is positive. $167 + (-88) = 79$

Problem 3: $-45 + (-79) = ?$

Answer: -124

> Since the numbers have the same sign, add the number parts and use the negative sign in the answer.
>
> $$\begin{array}{r} 45 \\ \underline{79} \\ 124 \end{array}$$
>
> $-45 + (-79) = -124$

Problem 4: $-76 + 29 = ?$

Answer: -47

> Since the numbers have different signs, subtract the number parts.
>
> $$\begin{array}{r} 76 \\ \underline{29} \\ 47 \end{array}$$
>
> Since the larger number part (76) has a negative sign, the answer is negative. $-76 + 29 = -47$

Name _____   Date _____

Exercise 7.3 Set A

Perform the indicated additions.

1. $7 + 5$

2. $6 + 8$

3. $8 + (-5)$

4. $9 + (-7)$

5. $-12 + 8$

6. $-13 + 7$

7. $-6 + (-4)$

8. $-7 + (-5)$

9. $-7 + 9$

10. $-9 + 12$

11. $-3 + (-15)$

12. $-2 + (-16)$

13. $12 + (-17) + (-4)$

14. $16 + (-3) + (-9)$

15. $-20 + 9 + 11$

16. $-30 + 8 + 22$

17. $75 + (-37)$

18. $84 + (-49)$

19. $-124 + 76$

20. $-145 + 95$

21. $-83 + (-156)$

22. $-92 + (-189)$

23. $274 + (-406)$

24. $316 + (-578)$

1. _____
2. _____
3. _____
4. _____
5. _____
6. _____
7. _____
8. _____
9. _____
10. _____
11. _____
12. _____
13. _____
14. _____
15. _____
16. _____
17. _____
18. _____
19. _____
20. _____
21. _____
22. _____
23. _____
24. _____

Exercise 7.3 Set B

Perform the indicated additions.

1. 8 + 4

2. 5 + 9

3. 7 + (−4)

4. 6 + (−5)

5. −11 + 5

6. −17 + 9

7. −7 + (−8)

8. −6 + (−8)

9. −5 + 12

10. −7 + 18

11. −4 + (−12)

12. −1 + (−16)

13. 13 + (−15) + (−9)

14. 15 + (−17) + (−8)

15. −24 + 11 + 13

16. −34 + 9 + 25

17. 87 + (−49)

18. 92 + (−38)

19. −150 + 77

20. −127 + 89

21. −65 + (−146)

22. −98 + (−216)

23. 329 + (−417)

24. 546 + (−679)

1. _____

2. _____

3. _____

4. _____

5. _____

6. _____

7. _____

8. _____

9. _____

10. _____

11. _____

12. _____

13. _____

14. _____

15. _____

16. _____

17. _____

18. _____

19. _____

20. _____

21. _____

22. _____

23. _____

24. _____

7.4 Subtracting Signed Numbers

In the previous section, we learned to add signed numbers by using either a number line or the rules for adding signed numbers. In order to perform subtraction on signed numbers, we will learn to change a subtraction problem into an addition problem. Consider the problems $5 - 2 = ?$ and $5 + (-2) = ?$.

$$5 - 2 = 3 \quad \text{and} \quad 5 + (-2) = 3$$

Those examples are different ways to represent the same problem. The first one, $5 - 2$, is a subtraction problem, and the second one, $5 + (-2)$, is an addition problem. This points out how to subtract signed numbers.

Rules for Subtracting Signed Numbers

1. Change the sign of the number being subtracted.
2. Change the subtraction to addition.

That is, for any numbers represented by A and B:

$$A - B = A + (-B)$$

For example:
$$13 - 7 = 13 + (-7) = 6$$
$$6 - 9 = 6 + (-9) = -3$$
$$-4 - 6 = -4 + (-6) = -10$$
$$75 - 97 = 75 + (-97) = -22$$
$$-37 - 21 = -37 + (-21) = -58$$

Notice that each subtraction was changed into addition of signed numbers, then the rules for addition were applied.

Problem 1: $15 - 23 = ?$

Answer: -8
$$15 - 23 = 15 + (-23) = -8$$

Problem 2: $-30 - 12 = ?$

Answer: -42
$$-30 - 12 = -30 + (-12)$$
$$= -42$$

You will notice that the "$-$" sign is used in different ways.

1. To represent subtraction. $12 - 8$ means 12 subtract 8.
2. To signify a negative number. -7 indicates a number that is less than zero—a negative number.

There is yet another way to use the "$-$" sign. It is sometimes used to indicate the inverse or opposite of a number.

$-(+8)$ indicates the opposite of a $+8$, which is -8.

$$-(+8) = -8$$

$-(-3)$ indicates the opposite of a -3, which is $+3$.

$$-(-3) = +3 = 3$$

This usage of the "−" sign gives us a way to determine the result of a number that has two negative signs in front of it.

$$-(-7) = +7 = 7$$
$$-(-35) = +35 = 35$$
$$-(-103) = +103 = 103$$

That property of signed numbers should be familiar to us, since, even in everyday English, two negatives give a positive statement.

For example: "I'm *not mis*behaving!" implies the positive meaning that you are behaving.

So $5 - (-2)$ becomes $5 + 2$, which equals 7.

Similarly,

$$8 - (-7) = 8 + 7$$
$$= 15$$

$$-17 - (-8) = -17 + 8$$
$$= -9$$

$$-67 - (-67) = -67 + 67$$
$$= 0$$

You will notice that this is consistent with the rules for subtracting signed numbers as stated on the previous page.

Problem 3: $28 - (-12) = ?$ Answer: 40

$$28 - (-12) = 28 + 12 = 40$$

Problem 4: $-8 - (-15) = ?$ Answer: 7

$$-8 - (-15) = -8 + 15 = 7$$

Problem 5: $-20 - 11 = ?$ Answer: −31

$$-20 - 11 = -20 + (-11)$$
$$= -31$$

Problem 6: $-43 - (-31) = ?$ Answer: −12

$$-43 - (-31) = -43 + 31$$
$$= -12$$

Exercise 7.4 Set A

Perform the indicated subtractions.

1. 9 – 6

2. 10 – 5

3. 6 – 10

4. 4 – 9

5. –7 – 3

6. –4 – 8

7. 5 – (–3)

8. 6 – (–4)

9. –7 – (–5)

10. –8 – (–3)

11. –7 – (–7)

12. –4 – (–4)

13. 52 – 6 – 19

14. 34 – 5 – 15

15. 20 – 11 – 17

16. 24 – 9 – 17

17. 53 – 143

18. 72 – 165

19. 72 – (–94)

20. 83 – (–77)

21. –51 – (–38)

22. –27 – (–96)

23. –125 – (–72)

24. –146 – (–61)

1. _____

2. _____

3. _____

4. _____

5. _____

6. _____

7. _____

8. _____

9. _____

10. _____

11. _____

12. _____

13. _____

14. _____

15. _____

16. _____

17. _____

18. _____

19. _____

20. _____

21. _____

22. _____

23. _____

24. _____

Exercise 7.4 Set B

Perform the indicated subtractions.

1. $8 - 5$

2. $9 - 4$

3. $3 - 9$

4. $5 - 11$

5. $-4 - 9$

6. $-6 - 8$

7. $7 - (-2)$

8. $8 - (-3)$

9. $-5 - (-3)$

10. $-7 - (-5)$

11. $-3 - (-3)$

12. $-5 - (-5)$

13. $42 - 6 - 20$

14. $41 - 8 - 19$

15. $27 - 16 - 15$

16. $25 - 18 - 15$

17. $84 - 176$

18. $93 - 157$

19. $63 - (-82)$

20. $75 - (-56)$

21. $-43 - (-39)$

22. $-27 - (-95)$

23. $-175 - (-82)$

24. $-163 - (-17)$

1. _____

2. _____

3. _____

4. _____

5. _____

6. _____

7. _____

8. _____

9. _____

10. _____

11. _____

12. _____

13. _____

14. _____

15. _____

16. _____

17. _____

18. _____

19. _____

20. _____

21. _____

22. _____

23. _____

24. _____

7.5 Multiplying and Dividing Signed Numbers

Multiplying Signed Numbers

To arrive at a method for multiplying signed numbers, we must consider four possibilities.

1. **A positive number times a positive number.**

$$(+3) \cdot (+4) = ?$$

The answer will be a positive number, 12.

2. **A positive number times a negative number.**

$$(3) \cdot (-4) = ?$$

In our first discussion of multiplication in Section 1.5, we saw that multiplication is actually a way to represent repeated addition. $3 \cdot (-4)$ means that you have three -4's; that is, $(-4) + (-4) + (-4)$. The answer to that is -12.

$$\text{So, } 3 \cdot (-4) = -12$$

The result of multiplying a positive times a negative number is a negative number.

3. **A negative number times a positive number.**

$$-3 \cdot 4 = ?$$

By similar reasoning, the result of a negative number times a positive number is a negative number.

$$-3 \cdot 4 = -12$$

4. **A negative number times a negative number.**

$$-3 \cdot (-4) = ?$$

Consider the list below:

$-3 \cdot 3 = -9$	As we proceed down the list, each new answer can be obtained by adding 3 to a previous answer.
$\quad\quad\quad\quad)\ +3$	
$-3 \cdot 2 = -6$	
$\quad\quad\quad\quad)\ +3$	
$-3 \cdot 1 = -3$	If you continue the pattern, you will find that:
$\quad\quad\quad\quad)\ +3$	
$-3 \cdot 0 = 0$	
$\quad\quad\quad\quad)\ +3$	
$-3 \cdot (-1) = ?$	
$\quad\quad\quad\quad)\ +3$	$-3 \cdot (-4) = 12$
$-3 \cdot (-2) = ?$	
$\quad\quad\quad\quad)\ +3$	
$-3 \cdot (-3) = ?$	
$\quad\quad\quad\quad)\ +3$	
$-3 \cdot (-4) = ?$	

A negative number times a negative number is a positive number.

The results can be summarized as follows:

$$(+) \cdot (+) = (+)$$
$$(-) \cdot (-) = (+)$$
$$(+) \cdot (-) = (-)$$
$$(-) \cdot (+) = (-)$$

Notice, if the numbers being multiplied have the same signs, the answer will be positive. If they have different signs, the answer will be negative.

Dividing Signed Numbers

You will be pleased to know that there are no new rules for dividing signed numbers. As we showed in Section 3.5, dividing by a number will give the same result as multiplying by an appropriate fraction. For example,

$$8 \div 2 = 8 \cdot \frac{1}{2} = 4 \quad \text{and} \quad 12 \div 3 = 12 \cdot \frac{1}{3} = 4$$

Since division can be changed into multiplication, the rules to obtain the sign of the answer in division are the same as those in multiplication.

> ### Rules for Multiplying and Dividing Signed Numbers
>
> 1. Multiply or divide the number parts.
> 2. If the numbers have the same signs, the answer will be positive.
> 3. If the numbers have different signs, the answer will be negative.

Problems: Perform the indicated operations: Answers:

1. $-7 \cdot 5 = ?$ 1. -35

2. $-9 \cdot (-6) = ?$ 2. 54

3. $40 \div (-8) = ?$ 3. -5

4. $+27 \div 3 = ?$ 4. 9

5. $4 \cdot (-7) = ?$ 5. -28

6. $-45 \div (-15) = ?$ 6. 3

7. $-12 \cdot 1 = ?$ 7. -12

8. $24 \div (-4) = ?$ 8. -6

Exercise 7.5 Set A

Perform the indicated operations.

1. $5 \cdot (+3)$

2. $6 \cdot (+4)$

3. $3(-7)$

4. $2(-9)$

5. $-4 \cdot 8$

6. $-5 \cdot 6$

7. $(-8)(-6)$

8. $(-7)(-5)$

9. $-9 \cdot (-8)$

10. $-7 \cdot (-9)$

11. $\dfrac{+36}{9}$

12. $\dfrac{+27}{3}$

13. $\dfrac{-40}{5}$

14. $\dfrac{-42}{7}$

15. $\dfrac{56}{-8}$

16. $\dfrac{63}{-9}$

17. $\dfrac{-72}{-9}$

18. $\dfrac{-32}{-8}$

19. $\dfrac{-25}{-5}$

20. $\dfrac{-36}{-6}$

21. $\dfrac{143}{-11}$

22. $\dfrac{144}{-12}$

1. _____

2. _____

3. _____

4. _____

5. _____

6. _____

7. _____

8. _____

9. _____

10. _____

11. _____

12. _____

13. _____

14. _____

15. _____

16. _____

17. _____

18. _____

19. _____

20. _____

21. _____

22. _____

Exercise 7.5 Set B

Perform the indicated operations.

1. $3 \cdot (+7)$

2. $8 \cdot (+3)$

3. $5(-8)$

4. $3(-9)$

5. $-6 \cdot 7$

6. $-9 \cdot 7$

7. $(-8)(-7)$

8. $(-6)(-6)$

9. $-5 \cdot (-9)$

10. $-8 \cdot (-4)$

11. $\dfrac{+45}{9}$

12. $\dfrac{+32}{8}$

13. $\dfrac{-24}{6}$

14. $\dfrac{-35}{7}$

15. $\dfrac{63}{-9}$

16. $\dfrac{48}{-8}$

17. $\dfrac{-36}{-4}$

18. $\dfrac{-30}{-5}$

19. $\dfrac{-81}{-9}$

20. $\dfrac{-49}{-7}$

21. $\dfrac{156}{-13}$

22. $\dfrac{180}{-12}$

1. _____

2. _____

3. _____

4. _____

5. _____

6. _____

7. _____

8. _____

9. _____

10. _____

11. _____

12. _____

13. _____

14. _____

15. _____

16. _____

17. _____

18. _____

19. _____

20. _____

21. _____

22. _____

7.6 The Order of Operations—Signed Numbers

In Section 2.8, you encountered problems that had a combination of operations with whole numbers. In this section, you will combine operations with signed numbers. The order in which the operations are done is still the same.

> ## The Order of Operations
>
> First: Do operations inside parentheses ( ) or brackets [ ].
> Second: Do powers or square roots.
> Third: Do multiplications or divisions from left to right.
> Fourth: Do additions or subtractions from left to right.

Note: If a problem contains a fraction line, do the operations above and below the fraction line separately before simplifying the fraction. Inside the parentheses and brackets, you must again do multiplications and divisions before you do additions and subtractions.

Example 1

$6^2 + (5)(-2) = ?$

$= 36 + (5)(-2)$	Do the powers.
$= 36 + (-10)$	Do the multiplication.
$= 26$	Do the addition.

Example 2

$4 - \dfrac{15}{3} - 10(2) = ?$

$= 4 - 5 - 20$	Do the multiplication and division.
$= 4 + (-5) + (-20)$	Change subtractions to adding the opposite of the number.
$= -21$	Do the additions.

Example 3

$\dfrac{5(-3 + 7)}{4 + (-2)(-3)} = ?$

$= \dfrac{5(4)}{4 + (6)}$	Do the addition inside the parentheses above the fraction line. Do the multiplication below the fraction line.
$= \dfrac{20}{10}$	Do the multiplication above the fraction line. Do the addition below the fraction line.
$= 2$	Simplify the fraction (divide 20 by 10).

Example 4

$$-7[5 + 4(-2)] = ?$$

$= -7[5 + (-8)]$	Do the multiplication inside the brackets.
$= -7[-3]$	Do the addition inside the brackets.
$= 21$	Do the multiplication.

Example 5

$$-8 - (4 - 11) + 5 = ?$$

$= -8 - (-7) + 5$	Do the subtraction inside the brackets.
$= -8 + 7 + 5$	Change subtraction to adding the opposite of the number.
$= 4$	Do the additions.

Example 6

$$\frac{15[-4 + (-2)]}{(-4 - 1)(-9 + 8)} = ?$$

$= \dfrac{15[-6]}{(-5)(-1)}$	Do the operations inside the parentheses and brackets above and below the fraction line.
$= \dfrac{-90}{5}$	Do the multiplication above the fraction line. Do the multiplication below the fraction line.
$= -18$	Simplify the fraction (divide -90 by 5).

Problem 1: $3 - 7 + 4(-2) = ?$

Answer: -12

$$= 3 - 7 + (-8)$$
$$= -4 + (-8)$$
$$= -12$$

Problem 2: $3^2 + [-5 + (4 - 9)] = ?$

Answer: -1

$$= 9 + [-5 + (-5)]$$
$$= 9 + [-10]$$
$$= -1$$

Problem 3: $\dfrac{2(7 - 4)}{5 - 9} = ?$

Answer: $-\dfrac{3}{2}$

$$= \frac{2(3)}{-4}$$

$$= \frac{6}{-4} = -\frac{3}{2}$$

Exercise 7.6 Set A

Perform the indicated operations.

1. $4^2 + (2)(-3)$

2. $6^2 + (5)(-2)$

3. $(-2)(6) - 3 \cdot 5$

4. $(4)(-3) - 2 \cdot 7$

5. $-5(-3 + 7)$

6. $6(-5 + 8)$

7. $8 - \dfrac{8}{2} - 5 \cdot 3$

8. $-4 + \dfrac{9}{3} - 6 \cdot 2$

9. $-3 - (4 - 6)$

10. $5 - (6 - 7)$

11. $(-5 + 2 \cdot 2)(7 - 9)$

12. $(3 \cdot 2 - 9)(-4 + 1)$

13. $5 + 2[3 - (-4)]$

14. $17 - 3[2 - (-3)]$

15. $\dfrac{-4 - 2(8 - 5)}{5}$

16. $\dfrac{6 + 3(5 - 3)}{3}$

17. $\dfrac{8 + (-6)}{5 - (-3)}$

18. $\dfrac{3 - (-2)}{-7 + (-3)}$

19. $\dfrac{-9[3 + 2(-4)]}{3(4 - 1)}$

20. $\dfrac{2(7 - 1)}{3[5 + (-3)]}$

1. _____
2. _____
3. _____
4. _____
5. _____
6. _____
7. _____
8. _____
9. _____
10. _____
11. _____
12. _____
13. _____
14. _____
15. _____
16. _____
17. _____
18. _____
19. _____
20. _____

Exercise 7.6 Set B

Perform the indicated operations.

1. $3^2 + (3)(-5)$

2. $5^2 + (-4)(6)$

3. $(-2)(5) - 3 \cdot 6$

4. $(4)(-2) - 5 \cdot 2$

5. $7(-8 + 10)$

6. $-4(-2 + 8)$

7. $-6 + \dfrac{6}{3} - 3 \cdot 2$

8. $4 - \dfrac{8}{4} - 2 \cdot 5$

9. $4 - (3 - 7)$

10. $-6 - (2 - 9)$

11. $(2 - 6)(-6 + 2 \cdot 3)$

12. $(-8 + 3 \cdot 4)(3 - 8)$

13. $[2 - (-5)] \cdot 3 - 4$

14. $[6 - (-8)] \cdot 2 + 9$

15. $\dfrac{-8 + 2(7 - 6)}{2}$

16. $\dfrac{15 - 3(6 - 5)}{3}$

17. $\dfrac{2 - (-2)}{-6 - 4}$

18. $\dfrac{1 - (-3)}{-2 - 4}$

19. $\dfrac{3(5 - 1)}{2[8 + 2(-3)]}$

20. $\dfrac{4[-5 + 2(-1)]}{-2(3 - 4)}$

1. _____

2. _____

3. _____

4. _____

5. _____

6. _____

7. _____

8. _____

9. _____

10. _____

11. _____

12. _____

13. _____

14. _____

15. _____

16. _____

17. _____

18. _____

19. _____

20. _____

7.7 What Are Equations?

Now that we have covered the operations with signed numbers, we can return to the use of variables in algebra. In Section 7.1, you learned what a variable is and how to find the value of an algebraic expression. The next and probably the most important process in elementary algebra is learning how to solve algebraic equations.

An **equation** is a statement that two quantities are equal. The value of the terms on the left of the equals sign (the left side) is equal to the value of the terms on the right of the equals sign (the right side). The following are examples of equations:

$$y - 5 = 2$$

$$X + 7 = -3$$

$$21 = 4P + 1$$

$$-\frac{1}{2}R = 8$$

In each of the above equations, a variable is used. We know that a variable is simply a letter that represents a number. In an equation, our objective is to determine what number the variable represents.

Let's try to determine what number the variable represents in each of the above equations.

1. $y - 5 = 2$ What value for y will make $y - 5$ equal 2?
   $y = 7$ since $7 - 5$ gives an answer of 2.

2. $X + 7 = -3$ What value for X will make $X + 7$ equal -3?
   $X = -10$ since $-10 + 7$ gives an answer of -3.

3. $21 = 4p + 1$ What value for p will make $4p + 1$ equal 21?
   $5 = p$ since $4 \cdot 5 + 1$ gives an answer of 21.

4. $-\frac{1}{2}R = 8$ What value for R will make $-\frac{1}{2}$ times R equal 8?

   $R = -16$ since $-\frac{1}{2}$ times -16 gives an answer of 8.

What we have done in the previous examples is solve for the variable in each equation. We determined the value for the variable that made the left side equal to the right side of each equation, without using any specific method to find the answers. We looked at each equation and mentally figured out the answers. We solved them by inspection. See if you can determine the solutions to the following equations in the same manner.

Problem 1: Solve for X.

$X + 6 = 17$

Answer: $X = 11$

since $11 + 6 = 17$

Problem 2: Solve for S.

$-4 = S - 7$

Answer: $S = 3$

since $-4 = 3 - 7$

Problem 3: Solve for z.

$6z = -42$

Answer: $z = -7$

since $6 \cdot (-7) = -42$

Problem 4: Solve for T.

$3T - 4 = 5$

Answer: $T = 3$

since $3 \cdot 3 - 4 = 5$

Problem 5: Is $X = -1$ a solution of this equation?

$$\frac{3}{4}X + \frac{1}{2} = \frac{1}{4}$$

Answer: No

$$\frac{3}{4} \cdot (-1) + \frac{1}{2} = -\frac{3}{4} + \frac{2}{4}$$

$$= -\frac{1}{4}$$

Problem 6: Is $Y = 9$ a solution of this equation?

$0.5(Y + 3) = 6$

Answer: Yes

$$0.5(9 + 3) = 0.5(12)$$

$$= 6$$

Exercise 7.7 Set A

In problems 1–16, solve for the variable by inspection.

1. $A + 3 = 5$

2. $B + 2 = 6$

3. $X - 4 = 7$

4. $Y - 3 = 8$

5. $3P = 12$

6. $5z = 15$

7. $\dfrac{r}{5} = 4$

8. $\dfrac{S}{6} = 3$

9. $-5 = t + 4$

10. $-3 = v + 5$

11. $-16 = -8T$

12. $-15 = -3N$

13. $3y + 2 = 8$

14. $2k + 1 = 7$

15. $5 = 5 - 2m$

16. $7 = 7 - 3n$

1. _____

2. _____

3. _____

4. _____

5. _____

6. _____

7. _____

8. _____

9. _____

10. _____

11. _____

12. _____

13. _____

14. _____

15. _____

16. _____

In problems 17–20, determine if $x = -2$ is a solution of the equation.

17. $-\dfrac{3x}{2} - 6 = -9$

18. $\dfrac{6x}{9} - 1 = -1$

19. $5x + (-7) = -17$

20. $8 + 7x = -6$

17. _____

18. _____

19. _____

20. _____

Exercise 7.7 Set B

In problems 1–16, solve for the variable by inspection.

1. $X + 2 = 6$

2. $Y + 3 = 8$

3. $C - 5 = 2$

4. $D - 7 = 3$

5. $4r = 24$

6. $3s = 18$

7. $\dfrac{t}{5} = 3$

8. $\dfrac{v}{4} = 2$

9. $-1 = A + 3$

10. $-2 = B + 4$

11. $-8 = -2R$

12. $-24 = -8T$

13. $2n + 6 = 10$

14. $3m + 2 = 11$

15. $8 = 8 - 5Z$

16. $6 = 6 - 3r$

In problems 17–20, determine if $x = -3$ is a solution of the equation.

17. $\dfrac{-6x}{9} - 1 = 3$

18. $\dfrac{4x}{3} - 1 = -3$

19. $2x + 5 = -1$

20. $6 + 3x = -9$

1. _____

2. _____

3. _____

4. _____

5. _____

6. _____

7. _____

8. _____

9. _____

10. _____

11. _____

12. _____

13. _____

14. _____

15. _____

16. _____

17. _____

18. _____

19. _____

20. _____

7.8 Solving Equations Using the Addition Property

Property:

A sophisticated English drink.

The inspection method for solving equations as seen in the previous section works as long as you can mentally determine the correct value for the variable in the equation. As the problems get more involved, it will be very difficult to solve the equation just by mental inspection. In this and in the next two sections, we will develop a method for solving equations that have one variable.

An equation is like a balance. If you add the same amount to both sides of the balance, it will still be in balance.

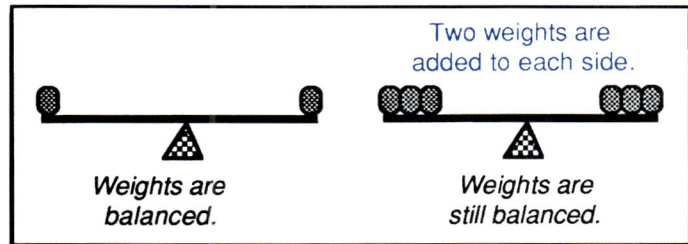

Two weights are
added to each side.

Weights are
balanced.

Weights are
still balanced.

What this means is that in an equation you can add the same amount to both sides of the equation and the results will be equal. That fact is known as:

The Addition Property of Equality

For any numbers A, B, and C, if $A = B$, then $A + C = B + C$.

You can use this property to help solve equations.

Example 1

Solve for P.

$$
\begin{array}{r}
P - 7 = 19 \\
+7 \quad +7 \\
\hline
P + 0 = 26 \\
P = 26
\end{array}
$$

If you add 7 to both sides of the equation, you get P on the left hand side and the answer for the variable (26) on the right.

(Note: $-7 + 7 = 0$ and $P + 0 = P$ on the left side of the equation.)

Example 2

Solve for X.

$$
\begin{array}{r}
X + 5 = -3 \\
-5 \quad -5 \\
\hline
X \quad = -8
\end{array}
$$

If you add -5 to both sides, you will have X on the left side and the answer (-8) on the right.

The method, then, for solving equations is to go through a series of steps so that the variable is alone on one side of the equals sign and a number is on the other side. That number will be the solution for the variable in the equation. Adding the same quantity to both sides of an equation is sometimes all you need to do to find the number which the variable represents.

Example 3

Solve for g.

$$-5.3 + g = 12.8$$
$$\underline{+5.3 \qquad\quad +5.3}$$
$$g = 18.1$$

Add 5.3 to both sides, get g on the left, and the answer (18.1) on the right.

Example 4

Solve for R.

$$-37 = R + 16$$
$$\underline{-16 \qquad -16}$$
$$-53 = R$$

Add -16 to both sides, get R on the right, and the answer (-53) on the left.

Problem 1: Solve for B.

$$B + \frac{1}{2} = \frac{1}{4}$$

Answer: $B = -\dfrac{1}{4}$

$$B + \frac{1}{2} = \frac{1}{4}$$
$$\underline{\qquad -\frac{1}{2} \qquad -\frac{1}{2}}$$
$$B = -\frac{1}{4}$$

Problem 2: Solve for k.

$$187 = 79 + k$$

Answer: $K = 108$

$$187 = \quad 79 + k$$
$$\underline{-79 \qquad -79}$$
$$108 = \quad k$$

Problem 3: Solve for T.

$$-67 + T = -19$$

Answer: $T = 48$

$$-67 + T = \quad -19$$
$$\underline{+\,67 \qquad\qquad +67}$$
$$T = \quad 48$$

Note: *You can always check your answer by replacing the variable with the answer you obtained to see if it, in fact, makes the left side equal to the right side of the equation.*

Exercise 7.8 Set A

Solve for the variable in each equation.

1. $S + 7 = 9$

2. $S + 4 = 10$

3. $t - 7 = 5$

4. $t - 2 = 7$

5. $1 = y + 5$

6. $2 = y + 7$

7. $-6 = x - 4$

8. $-7 = x - 6$

9. $x + 9 = 22$

10. $X + 7 = 36$

11. $K - 15 = 17$

12. $K - 17 = 25$

13. $12 = Z + 15$

14. $13 = Z + 17$

15. $-2.5 + p = -1.7$

16. $-4.6 + p = -2.5$

17. $R - (-8) = 20$

18. $R - (-9) = 30$

19. $A + \dfrac{2}{3} = \dfrac{4}{5}$

20. $x - \dfrac{2}{3} = \dfrac{4}{5}$

1. _____

2. _____

3. _____

4. _____

5. _____

6. _____

7. _____

8. _____

9. _____

10. _____

11. _____

12. _____

13. _____

14. _____

15. _____

16. _____

17. _____

18. _____

19. _____

20. _____

Exercise 7.8 Set B

Solve for the variable in each equation.

1. $Z + 3 = 12$

2. $X + 7 = 15$

3. $K - 5 = 7$

4. $K - 8 = 2$

5. $-3 = X + 1$

6. $-2 = Z + 2$

7. $-8 = R - 5$

8. $-9 = R - 3$

9. $S + 7 = 26$

10. $S + 8 = 34$

11. $t - 17 = 14$

12. $t - 12 = 29$

13. $10 = y + 13$

14. $7 = y + 16$

15. $-4.6 + N = -2.7$

16. $-3.9 + N = -1.8$

17. $M - (-9) = 17$

18. $M - (-4) = 19$

19. $B + \dfrac{3}{4} = \dfrac{2}{3}$

20. $x - \dfrac{3}{4} = \dfrac{2}{3}$

1. _____

2. _____

3. _____

4. _____

5. _____

6. _____

7. _____

8. _____

9. _____

10. _____

11. _____

12. _____

13. _____

14. _____

15. _____

16. _____

17. _____

18. _____

19. _____

20. _____

7.9 Solving Equations Using Multiplication/Division Properties

Not all equations can be solved by adding a number to both sides of the equals sign. The Addition Property only works in an equation that has a number added to or subtracted from the variable. There are other equations where you have to multiply or divide both sides of the equation by a number in order to obtain the variable on one side and the answer on the other side.

If you multiply or divide both sides of an equation by the same number, both sides are still equal. These properties can be stated as follows:

The Multiplication Property of Equality

For any numbers A, B, and C, if $A = B$, then $A \cdot C = B \cdot C$.

The Division Property of Equality

For any numbers A, B, and C, if $A = B$, then $\dfrac{A}{C} = \dfrac{B}{C}$

Note: $\dfrac{A}{C}$ is another way to write $A \div C$. C can not be equal to zero since we can not divide by zero

Here is how those properties are used to solve equations:

Example 1

Solve for y.

$$6y = -30$$

$$\frac{6y}{6} = \frac{-30}{6}$$

$$y = -5$$

Divide both sides by 6, leaving y on the left side, and the answer (-5) on the right.

(Note: $\dfrac{6y}{6} = 1y = y$)

Example 2

Solve for x.

$$\frac{1}{3}x = 9$$

$$3 \cdot \frac{1}{3}x = 9 \cdot 3$$

$$x = 27$$

Multiply both sides by 3, leaving the x on the left, and the answer (27) on the right.

(Note: $3 \cdot \dfrac{1}{3}x = 1x = x$)

Example 3

Solve for V.

$$-24 = -4V$$

$$\frac{-24}{-4} = \frac{-4V}{-4}$$

Divide both sides by −4, leaving V on the right, and the answer (6) on the left.

$$6 = V$$

Example 4

Solve for m.

$$\frac{m}{7} = 8$$

$$7 \cdot \frac{m}{7} = 8 \cdot 7$$

Multiply both sides by 7, leaving m on the left, and the answer (56) on the right.

$$m = 56$$

The Multiplication and Division Properties enable you to solve equations where the variable is divided or multiplied by a number. You must remember that you want to get the variable alone on one side of the equation. If you have a number *times* the variable, you must *divide* both sides by the number. If you have the variable *divided* by a number, you must *multiply* both sides by that divisor.

Problem 1: Solve for k.
$$-8k = 19$$

Answer: $k = -2\frac{3}{8}$

$$\frac{-8k}{-8} = \frac{19}{-8}$$

$$k = -2\frac{3}{8}$$

Problem 2: Solve for d.
$$\frac{d}{6} = -3$$

Answer: $d = -18$

$$6 \cdot \frac{d}{6} = -3 \cdot 6$$

$$d = -18$$

Problem 3: Solve for R.
$$-9 = -2R$$

Answer: $R = 4\frac{1}{2}$

$$\frac{-9}{-2} = \frac{-2R}{-2}$$

$$4\frac{1}{2} = R$$

Problem 4: Solve for H.
$$\frac{1}{5}H = 17$$

Answer: $H = 85$

$$5 \cdot \frac{1}{5}H = 17 \cdot 5$$

$$H = 85$$

Exercise 7.9 Set A

Solve for the variable in each equation.

1. $5m = 45$

2. $7m = 49$

3. $-8Z = 64$

4. $-6X = 72$

5. $\dfrac{n}{5} = 7$

6. $\dfrac{n}{6} = 4$

7. $\dfrac{R}{-9} = -72$

8. $\dfrac{R}{-4} = -52$

9. $-48 = 6K$

10. $-32 = 4K$

11. $-8 = \dfrac{1}{4}t$

12. $-12 = \dfrac{1}{3}t$

13. $-90 = -6y$

14. $-98 = -7y$

15. $85v = 595$

16. $76v = 456$

17. $-3.2m = 20.8$

18. $-4.4m = 15.4$

19. $78 = \dfrac{T}{-12}$

20. $\dfrac{x}{-5} = -6.2$

1. _____

2. _____

3. _____

4. _____

5. _____

6. _____

7. _____

8. _____

9. _____

10. _____

11. _____

12. _____

13. _____

14. _____

15. _____

16. _____

17. _____

18. _____

19. _____

20. _____

Exercise 7.9 Set B

Solve for the variable in each equation.

1. $3m = 24$

2. $6m = 42$

3. $-9X = 72$

4. $-8X = 56$

5. $\dfrac{N}{3} = 7$

6. $\dfrac{N}{4} = 9$

7. $\dfrac{R}{-7} = -9$

8. $\dfrac{R}{-6} = -8$

9. $-54 = 9K$

10. $-72 = 8K$

11. $-9 = \dfrac{1}{3}t$

12. $-11 = \dfrac{1}{5}t$

13. $-104 = -8y$

14. $-126 = -9y$

15. $57r = 513$

16. $69r = 552$

17. $-5.8m = 14.5$

18. $-6.2m = 27.9$

19. $69 = \dfrac{T}{-13}$

20. $\dfrac{x}{-6} = -5.2$

1. _____

2. _____

3. _____

4. _____

5. _____

6. _____

7. _____

8. _____

9. _____

10. _____

11. _____

12. _____

13. _____

14. _____

15. _____

16. _____

17. _____

18. _____

19. _____

20. _____

7.10 More on Solving Equations

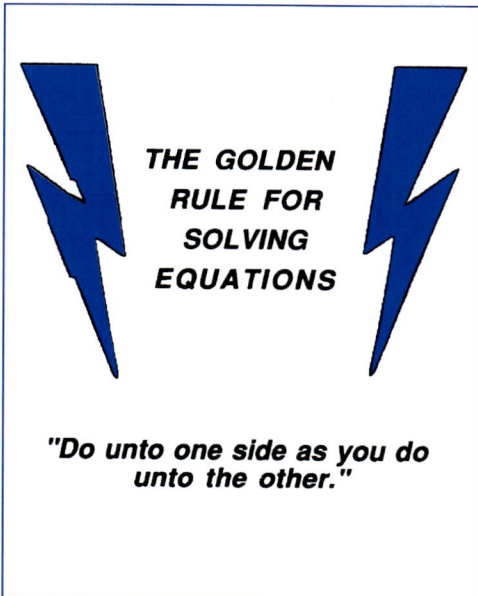

THE GOLDEN
RULE FOR
SOLVING
EQUATIONS

*"Do unto one side as you do
unto the other."*

In the last two sections, we covered the basic properties that are needed to solve equations with one variable. In those sections, we used just one of the properties to obtain the answer for each equation. Some equations, however, require more than one property to get its solution. The most efficient order to apply those properties is:

First: If a number is added to or subtracted from a variable term, use the Addition Property to get that variable term alone on one side of the equation.

Second: If a variable is divided or multiplied by a number, use the Multiplication or Division Property to get the variable equal to its answer.

Example 1

Solve for x.

$$5x - 4 = 31$$

$$\begin{array}{rcl} 5x - 4 &=& 31 \\ +4 && +4 \\ \hline 5x &=& 35 \end{array}$$

Add 4 to both sides, leaving the variable term ($5x$) on the left side.

$$\frac{5x}{5} = \frac{35}{5}$$

Divide both sides by 5, leaving x on the left, and the answer (7) on the right.

$$x = 7$$

Example 2

Solve for n.

$$6 - 3n = 18$$

$$\begin{array}{rcl} 6 - 3n &=& 18 \\ -6 && -6 \\ \hline -3n &=& 12 \end{array}$$

Add -6 to both sides, to get the variable term ($-3n$) on one side.

$$\frac{-3n}{-3} = \frac{12}{-3}$$

Divide both sides by -3, leaving n on the left, and the answer (-4) on the right.

$$n = -4$$

Example 3

Solve for S.

$$\frac{S}{4} + 7 = 10$$

$$\frac{S}{4} + 7 = 10$$

$$\underline{\quad -7 \quad\quad -7 \quad}$$

$$\frac{S}{4} = 3$$

Add -7 to both sides, leaving the variable term $(S/4)$ on the left side.

$$4 \cdot \frac{S}{4} = 3 \cdot 4$$

Multiply both sides by 4, leaving S on the left, and the answer (12) on the right.

$$S = 12$$

Example 4

Solve for n.

$$-4 = \frac{n}{2} - 7$$

$$-4 = \frac{n}{2} - 7$$

$$\underline{\quad +7 \quad\quad\quad +7 \quad}$$

$$3 = \frac{n}{2}$$

Add 7 to both sides, to get the variable term $(n/2)$ on one side.

$$2 \cdot 3 = \frac{n}{2} \cdot 2$$

Multiply both sides by 2, leaving n on the right, and the answer (6) on the left.

$$6 = n$$

Problem 1: Solve for z.
$$2z - 2 = 13$$

Answer: $z = 7\frac{1}{2}$

$$2z - 2 = 13$$
$$\underline{\quad +2 \quad\quad +2 \quad}$$
$$\frac{2z}{2} = \frac{15}{2}$$
$$z = 7\frac{1}{2}$$

Problem 2: Solve for N.
$$-1 = \frac{N}{-3} + 5$$

Answer: $N = 18$

$$-1 = \frac{N}{-3} + 5$$
$$\underline{\quad -5 \quad\quad\quad -5 \quad}$$
$$-6 = \frac{N}{-3}$$
$$(-3)(-6) = \frac{N}{-3}(-3)$$
$$18 = N$$

Exercise 7.10 Set A

Solve for the variable in each equation

1. $2x + 5 = 9$

2. $3x + 1 = 13$

3. $40 = -8y + 8$

4. $27 = -3y + 9$

5. $-3 + 5z = 12$

6. $-6 + 4z = 14$

7. $-18 = -3K - 6$

8. $-7 = -2K - 1$

9. $\dfrac{n}{3} + 6 = 10$

10. $\dfrac{n}{2} + 5 = 13$

11. $\dfrac{1}{6}m - 4 = 3$

12. $\dfrac{1}{4}m - 5 = 2$

13. $-12 = \dfrac{R}{5} - 8$

14. $-16 = \dfrac{R}{6} - 7$

15. $4 + \dfrac{t}{-7} = -8$

16. $5 + \dfrac{t}{-3} = -7$

17. $\dfrac{3x}{4} = 27$

18. $\dfrac{2x}{3} = 18$

19. $5.6 = \dfrac{1}{7}N + 4.5$

20. $\dfrac{-3x}{4} = 27$

1. _____

2. _____

3. _____

4. _____

5. _____

6. _____

7. _____

8. _____

9. _____

10. _____

11. _____

12. _____

13. _____

14. _____

15. _____

16. _____

17. _____

18. _____

19. _____

20. _____

Exercise 7.10 Set B

Solve the following equations

1. $2x + 1 = 13$

2. $3x + 2 = 17$

3. $33 = -5y + 3$

4. $37 = -4y + 5$

5. $-5 + 7z = 9$

6. $-3 + 8z = 21$

7. $-10 = -2k - 6$

8. $-8 = -3k - 5$

9. $\dfrac{N}{4} + 5 = 7$

10. $\dfrac{N}{5} + 3 = 8$

11. $\dfrac{1}{2}m - 7 = 5$

12. $\dfrac{1}{3}m - 6 = 2$

13. $-15 = \dfrac{R}{6} - 12$

14. $-18 = \dfrac{R}{7} - 13$

15. $3 + \dfrac{t}{-8} = -7$

16. $9 + \dfrac{t}{-3} = -6$

17. $\dfrac{5x}{8} = 30$

18. $\dfrac{4x}{5} = 16$

19. $8.7 = \dfrac{1}{5}N + 7.4$

20. $\dfrac{-5x}{8} = 30$

1. _____

2. _____

3. _____

4. _____

5. _____

6. _____

7. _____

8. _____

9. _____

10. _____

11. _____

12. _____

13. _____

14. _____

15. _____

16. _____

17. _____

18. _____

19. _____

20. _____

7.11 Properties of Algebra

So far in our introduction to algebra we have examined variables, signed numbers, equations, and word problems. However, in order to progress farther, we need to discuss some of the other properties of mathematics. These properties will enable you to add and subtract expressions that contain numbers and variables. The properties we will examine are the commutative, associative, and distributive properties.

The Commutative Property

I am sure you have noticed that the order in which you add or multiply two numbers has no effect on the answer. For example,

$$3 + 5 = 5 + 3$$
$$(3)(5) = (5)(3)$$

This property of mathematics is called the **commutative property.** It allows you to interchange the numbers when you are adding or multiplying. Beware, however, this property does not apply when subtracting or dividing. That is, $5 - 3 \neq 3 - 5$ and $5 \div 3 \neq 3 \div 5$. However, for any numbers a and b,

> **Commutative Property**
>
> $$a + b = b + a$$
> $$a \cdot b = b \cdot a$$

Example 1

The following show how the commutative property can be used to find equivalent algebraic expressions.

a) $8 + x = $ ___?___   a) $8 + x = x + 8$
b) $x\, 8 = $ ___?___   b) $x\, 8 = 8x$
c) $-4 + 3y = $ ___?___   c) $-4 + 3y = 3y + (-4)$
                                                          $= 3y - 4$

The Associative Property

Suppose you wanted to find the sum of 2, 6, and 4. You could add the 2 and 6 first and then add the 4 or you could add the 6 and 4 first and then add the 2.

$$(2 + 6) + 4 = 2 + (6 + 4) = 12$$

If you wanted to find the product of 2, 6, and 4, you could multiply the 2 and 6 first and then multiply by the 4 or you could multiply the 6 and 4 first and then multiply by the 2.

$$(2 \cdot 6) \cdot 4 = 2 \cdot (6 \cdot 4) = 48$$

In those examples, the order of the numbers did not change. The grouping of numbers changed but the final sum or product is equal. This property of mathematics is called the **associative property.** As with the commutative property, the associative property does not work with subtraction and division. However, for any numbers a, b, and c,

> ## Associative Property
>
> $(a + b) + c = a + (b + c)$
> $(a \cdot b) \cdot c = a \cdot (b \cdot c)$

Example 2

The following show how the associative property can be used to find equivalent algebraic expressions.

a) $7 + (8 + x) = $ ___?___

b) $3(2h) = $ ___?___

a) $7 + (8 + x) = (7 + 8) + x$
$= 15 + x$

b) $3(2h) = (3 \cdot 2)h$
$= 6h$

The Distributive Property

Suppose you wanted to find the value of $5(8 + 6)$. If you use the order of operations that was previously discussed in this text, you would get:

$$5(8 + 6) = 5(14)$$
$$= 70$$

This is the correct answer. There is, however, another way that you could arrive at the same answer. You could find the 5 times 8 and 5 times 6 and then add those products.

$$5(8 + 6) = 5(8) + 5(6)$$
$$= 40 + 30$$
$$= 70$$

This property of mathematics is called the **distributive property.** It allows us to multiply a sum or difference by a number. In general, for numbers a, b, and c,

> ## Distributive Property
>
> $a(b + c) = ab + ac$
> $a(b - c) = ab - ac$

Example 3

The following show how the distributive property can be used to find equivalent algebraic expressions.

a) $3(8 + x) =$ _____?_____   a) $3(8 + x) = (3)(8) + (3)x$

$= 24 + 3x$

b) $2(y - 7) =$ _____?_____   b) $2(y - 7) = 2(y) - 2(7)$

$= 2y - 14$

c) $2k + 6z =$ _____?_____   c) $2k + 6z = 2(k + 3z)$

The commutative and distributive properties are important in algebra because they allow us to add and subtract expressions with the same variables in them. For example, the properties can be used to simplify the following.

$5x + 3x =$ _____?_____

$5x + 3x = x(5 + 3)$	by the distributive property.
$= x(8)$	by adding 5 and 3.
$= 8x$	by the commutative property.

$7y - 12y =$ _____?_____

$7y - 12y = y(7 - 12)$	by the distributive property.
$= y(-5)$	by subtracting 12 from 7.
$= -5y$	by the commutative property.

The associative property, in combination with the distributive and commutative properties, is also used in simplifying expressions.

Example 4

Simplify $(7x + 5) + 4x$ using the properties of algebra.

$(7x + 5) + 4x = (5 + 7x) + 4x$	by the commutative property.
$= 5 + (7x + 4x)$	by the associative property.
$= 5 + x(7 + 4)$	by the distributive property.
$= 5 + x(11)$	by adding 7 and 4.
$= 5 + 11x$	by the commutative property.

Combining Like Terms

A **term** in algebra is a number, a variable, or the product of a number and variable(s). Terms that are similar, that is, are numbers or have the same variable are called *like terms.* Examples of *like terms* are 5 and 7, $3x$ and $9x$, $4y$ and y, or $-6p$, $3p$ and $-p$. The commutative, associative, and distributive properties enable us to simplify algebraic expressions by combining (adding or subtracting) these *like terms.*

Simplifying Expressions

1. Use the distributive property if it applies.
2. Use the commutative property to move like terms next to each other.
3. Combine the *like* terms using addition and subtraction.

Note: Unlike terms can not be combined. For example, you cannot simplify the following: $5x + 6$, $3p - 2q$, or $-h + 4z$.

In the examples that follow, we will simplify expressions using the above steps. Even though we will not indicate when each property is being used, the results are a direct result of the properties.

Example 5

Simplify: $5x + 8 + 4x - 5$

$$5x + 8 + 4x - 5 = 5x + 4x + 8 - 5 \quad \text{by the commutative property.}$$
$$= \quad 9x \quad + \quad 3 \qquad \text{by combining like terms.}$$

Note: Since multiplying by 1 does not affect a product, variable expressions without a number such as x, $-y$, $-(2p + 5)$ or $-(k - 3)$ can be written with a factor of one.

$$x = 1x$$
$$-y = 1y$$
$$-(2p + 5) = -1(2p + 5) = (-1)(2p) + (-1)(5) = -2p - 5$$
$$-(k - 3) = -1(k - 3) = (-1)k - (-1)(3) = -k + 3$$

Example 6

Simplify: $-3(2x + 6) - (x - 7)$

$$-3(2x + 6) - (x - 7) = -3(2x + 6) - 1(x - 7)$$
$$= -6x + (-18) - 1x + 7 \qquad \text{by the distributive property.}$$
$$= -6x - 1x + (-18) + 7 \qquad \text{by the commutative property.}$$
$$= -7x - 11 \qquad \text{by combining like terms.}$$

Problems:

1. Using the distributive property, $5(x + 3) =$ ___?___

    Answer: $5x + 15$

2. Using the associative property, $5(3x) =$ ___?___

    Answer: $(5 \cdot 3)x$

3. Using the commutative property, $x \cdot 5 \cdot y =$ ___?___

    Answer: $5xy$ or $xy \cdot 5$

In problems 4–6, simplify each expression.

4. $4x + 3y - 7 + 2x - 5y - x$

    Answer: $5x - 2y - 7$
    $= 4x + 2x - x + 3y - 5y - 7$
    $= 5x - 2y - 7$

5. $5 + 7(6p - 1)$

    Answer: $42p - 2$
    $5 + 7(6p - 1) = 5 + 42p - 7$
    $= 42p - 7 + 5$
    $= 42p - 2$

6. $3(2x + 6) - 5(7 - 3x)$

    Answer: $21x - 17$
    $= 6x + 18 - 35 + 15x$
    $= 6x + 15x + 18 - 35$
    $= 21x - 17$

Exercise 7.11 Set A

In problems 1–5, state what property is used to obtain the expression on the right of the equal sign from the one on the left.

1. $[4 + (-9)] + (-7) = 4 + [(-9) + (-7)]$

    1. _____

2. $3x + 6 + x = 3x + x + 6$

    2. _____

3. $3(2x - 6) = 6x - 18$

    3. _____

4. $-(5 - 3s) = -5 + 3s$

    4. _____

5. $(x + 6) \cdot 3 = 3(x + 6)$

    5. _____

In problems 6–16, simplify each expression by combining like terms.

6. $5x + 9x - 3x$

    6. _____

7. $-4y + 3y + 5y$

    7. _____

8. $3m + 6 + 4m - 10 + m$

    8. _____

9. $-5p - 7 + 6p + 9 - p$

    9. _____

10. $3(2x - 6) + 4(7 - 3x)$

    10. _____

11. $-4(x - 4) + 2(3x - 5)$

    11. _____

12. $-(2q - 5) + 3(q - 7) + 12$

    12. _____

13. $4(f - 5) - (3f - 1) + f$

    13. _____

14. $-5(x + 2y) - 3x + 8y + 5$

    14. _____

15. $4y - 3x + 5(2x + y) - 9$

    15. _____

16. $a + b - 2c + 3(a - b) + c$

    16. _____

Exercise 7.11 Set B

In problems 1–5, state what property is used to obtain the expression on the right of the equal sign from the one on the left.

1. $[4(-9)](-7) = 4[(-9)(-7)]$

1. _____

2. $3(6 + x) = 18 + 3x$

2. _____

3. $-(5 + 7s) = -5 - 7s$

3. _____

4. $3x(6) = 3(6)x$

4. _____

5. $5p + 3 + 6p = 5p + 6p + 3$

5. _____

In problems 6–16, simplify each expression by combining like terms.

6. $7x + 3x - 5x$

6. _____

7. $-4y + 6y + 7y$

7. _____

8. $5m + 1 + 2m - 10 - m$

8. _____

9. $-3p - 4 + 4p + 9 - p$

9. _____

10. $2(3x - 5) + 4(2 - 4x)$

10. _____

11. $-3(x - 5) + 2(3x - 4)$

11. _____

12. $-(3q - 5) + 5(q - 7) + 24$

12. _____

13. $3(f - 5) - (2f - 1) + f$

13. _____

14. $-5(2x + y) - 6x + 7y + 2$

14. _____

15. $7y - 5x + 4(2x + y) - 7$

15. _____

16. $a - b + 2c + 3(a - b) - c$

16. _____

7.12 More Equations

The ability to simplify algebraic expressions will enable you to find solutions to a wider range of equations. In an equation that contains expressions that look complicated, we can combine like terms, simplify expressions, and then solve the resulting equation.

Example 1

Solve for x: $2(3x + 5) - 4x = 16$

$$2(3x + 5) - 4x = 16$$

$6x + 10 - 4x = 16$ by the distributive property.

$6x - 4x + 10 = 16$ by the commutative property.

$2x + 10 = 16$ by combining like terms.

$\underline{-10 \quad -10}$

$2x = 6$ by subtracting 10 from both sides.

$x = 3$ by dividing both sides by 2.

Since we know how to add and subtract like terms, this technique can be used to solve equations that have variable terms on both sides of the equal sign.

Example 2

Solve for x: $x + 9 = -2x + 21$

$$x + 9 = -2x + 21$$

$\underline{+2x \qquad\quad +2x}$ Put the variables on one side by adding $2x$

$3x + 9 = \quad 0 \;\; + 21$ to both sides.

$3x + 9 = 21$

$\underline{-9 \quad -9}$ Put the numbers on the other side by sub-

$3x \quad\;\; = 12$ tracting 9 from both sides.

$x = 4$ Obtain answer by dividing both sides by 3.

Combining the techniques used in the two previous examples we get the following strategy for solving equations with one variable.

> ## Solving Equations
>
> 1. Simplify each side of the equation.
> 2. Put the variable terms on one side of the equation by using the addition or subtraction property.
> 3. Put the numbers on the other side of the equation by using the addition or subtraction property.
> 4. Obtain the answer for the variable by using the multiplication or division property.

While using this strategy, it is important to do one step at a time and to make sure your computations with signed numbers are correct. Let's show you how this strategy works by solving a few more equations.

Example 3

Solve for x: $5x - 3x = 9 + x - 4$

$$5x - 3x = 9 + x - 4$$
$$2x = 9 - 4 + x$$ Simplify the left and right side.
$$2x = 5 + x$$
$$\underline{-x \qquad -x}$$ Put the variables on one side by sub-
$$x = 5$$ tracting x from both sides.

Example 4

Solve for x: $4(x - 3) + 7 = 6x + 9$

$$4(x - 3) + 7 = 6x + 9$$
$$4x - 12 + 7 = 6x + 9$$ Simplify the left side.
$$4x - 5 = 6x + 9$$
$$\underline{-6x \qquad -6x}$$ Put the variables on one side by sub-
$$-2x - 5 = \qquad 9$$ tracting $6x$ from both sides.
$$\underline{+5 \qquad +5}$$ Put the numbers on the other side by
$$-2x \quad = \quad 14$$ adding 5 to both sides.
$$x = \quad -7$$ Obtain answer by dividing by -2.

The value we have found for the variable in each equation will make the right side of the equation equal the left side of the equation. There is little chance that we could have obtained those answers by guessing. The strategy described in this section gives an efficient means of arriving at the solution to an equation.

Problem 1:   Solve for x: $2(3x - 5) = -10$

Answer: $x = 0$
$$2(3x - 5) = -10$$
$$6x - 10 = -10$$
$$\underline{+ 10 \quad + 10}$$
$$6x = 0$$
$$x = 0$$

Problem 2:   Solve for x: $5x - 7 = 4x - 8$

Answer: $x = -1$
$$5x - 7 = 4x - 8$$
$$\underline{-4x \qquad - 4x}$$
$$x - 7 = -8$$
$$\underline{+7 \qquad +7}$$
$$x = -1$$

Problem 3:   Solve for x: $6 + 2x + 3x = 16 - (2 - x)$

Answer: $x = 2$
$$6 + 2x + 3x = 16 - 2 + x$$
$$6 + 5x = 14 + x$$
$$\underline{-x \qquad -x}$$
$$6 + 4x = 14$$
$$\underline{-6 \qquad -6}$$
$$4x = 8$$
$$x = 2$$

Exercise 7.12 Set A

Solve for x in each equation.

1. $3x + 2x = 7 + 8$ 1. _____

2. $5x - 3x = 3 - 9$ 2. _____

3. $4(2x - 1) = -20$ 3. _____

4. $2(3x + 5) = -2$ 4. _____

5. $6x = 4x - (-10)$ 5. _____

6. $8x = 5x - 12$ 6. _____

7. $5 - 2x = 4x + 11$ 7. _____

8. $7x + 5 = -9 + 5x$ 8. _____

9. $5(x + 3) = 2(3x - 4)$ 9. _____

10. $3(x + 2) = 2(x - 5)$ 10. _____

11. $-6(2x + 1) + 8 = 4x + 2$ 11. _____

12. $-5x + 7 = -2(x + 2) + 11$ 12. _____

13. $9 + 8x - 5x = 4(2x + 3) - 8$ 13. _____

14. $3(2x - 3) = 4x - 6 + 5x$ 14. _____

15. $7 - (3x - 5) = 3(x + 1) - 3x$ 15. _____

Exercise 7.12 Set B

Solve for x in each equation.

1. $x - 4x = 3 + 7$

1. _____

2. $8x - 6x = -7 + 13$

2. _____

3. $3(2x - 7) = -3$

3. _____

4. $2(7 - 3x) = 20$

4. _____

5. $9x = 5x - (-28)$

5. _____

6. $8x = 3x - 45$

6. _____

7. $4 - x = 3x + 12$

7. _____

8. $5x + 9 = 2x - 12$

8. _____

9. $2(3x + 4) = 5(x + 7)$

9. _____

10. $4(x + 3) = 3(x - 2)$

10. _____

11. $-5(2x + 3) = 2x - 15 + 4x$

11. _____

12. $-4x - 3 = 2(3x + 1) - 5$

12. _____

13. $6 + 9x - 4x = 3(x + 2) - 2$

13. _____

14. $-3(x - 5) = 4x - 1 + 9x$

14. _____

15. $5 - (3 - 2x) = 2(x - 6) - 2x$

15. _____

7.13 From Words to Algebra

In the next two sections, we will look at problems stated in words and determine how to translate them into algebraic statements. After being able to do this, you will see how algebra can be used to solve problems that you may find difficult to solve with just arithmetic.

In order to translate worded statements into algebraic ones, it is important to learn how key words can be translated. In the phrases and statements in the following list, you could use any letter to represent an unknown number or quantity. However, to keep things simple we will use the letter x.

Concept	Key Word(s)	Phrase or Statement	Algebraic Translation
Addition:	plus	six *plus* a number	$6 + x$
	add	*add* seven to a number	$x + 7$
	sum	the *sum* of a number and two	$x + 2$
	added to	a number *added* to thirteen	$13 + x$
	more than	five *more than* a number	$x + 5$
	increased by	a quantity *increased by* nine	$x + 9$
	total of	the *total of* forty and a number	$40 + x$
	longer than	ten inches *longer than* a quantity	$x + 10$
Subtraction:	minus	a number *minus* six	$x - 6$
	subtract . . .from	*subtract* three *from* a number	$x - 3$
	difference	the *difference* between x and two	$x - 2$
	fewer than	ten *fewer than* a quantity	$x - 10$
	less than	seven *less than* a number	$x - 7$
	decrease by	nine *decreased by* a number	$9 - x$
	shorter than	five feet *shorter than* a length	$x - 5$
Multiplication:	times	six *times* a number	$6x$
	multiplied by	a number *multiplied by* three	$3x$
	product	the *product* of eight and a number	$8x$
	twice	*twice* a number	$2x$
	doubled	a length is *doubled*	$2x$
	tripled	an amount is *tripled*	$3x$
	of	three-fourths *of* a number	$\frac{3}{4}x$
Division:	divided by	a number *divided by* four	$\frac{x}{4}$
	quotient	the *quotient* of a number and -9	$\frac{x}{-9}$
	ratio	a *ratio* of a number and five	$\frac{x}{5}$
Equality:	is equal to	Twice a number *is equal to* 36.	$2x = 36$
	is	The sum of a number and six *is* nine.	$x + 6 = 9$
	result . . . is	The *result* of a number tripled *is* 42.	$3x = 42$
	same result as	Increasing a number by six gives the *same result as* doubling the number.	$x + 6 = 2x$
	is the same as	The quotient of a number and five *is the same as* the product of 3 and 2.	$\frac{x}{5} = (3)(2)$

Example 1

Write the following phrases as algebraic expressions. Use x for an unknown number.

Word Phrase	Algebraic Expression
a. the sum of seven and a number	a. $7 + x$
b. the product of −5 and a number	b. $-5x$
c. the difference between twice a number and nineteen	c. $2x - 19$
d. five more than the quotient of a number and eight	d. $\dfrac{x}{8} + 5$
e. twice the sum of a number and five	e. $2(x + 5)$

Example 2

Write the following statements as algebraic equations using x for an unknown number or amount.

Word Statement	Algebraic Equation
a. Three less than twice a number is 15.	a. $2x - 3 = 15$
b. The product of a number and five is the same as the number increased by eight.	b. $5x = x + 8$
c. The result of a number tripled is twelve less than the number.	c. $3x = x - 12$
d. The sum of an amount and twice the amount is equal to fifty-seven.	d. $x + 2x = 57$

Problems: Translate the following into algebraic expressions or equations. Use x for the unknown number.

Answers:

1. Three times a number decreased by eight.

    1. $3x - 8$

2. The product of a number and six is the same as the sum of the number and fifteen.

    2. $6x = x + 15$

3. Seven less than twice a number.

    3. $2x - 7$

4. The difference between five times a number and six is fifty-four.

    4. $5x - 6 = 54$

Exercise 7.13 Set A

Write each of the following as an algebraic expression or equation. Use *x* for the unknown number.

1. The sum of a number and six

2. The sum of three and a number

3. Five fewer than twice a number

4. Six less than twice a number

5. The product of a number and six

6. The product of a number and nine

7. Four more than three times a number

8. Two more than five times a number

9. The quotient of a number and seven

10. The quotient of a number and four

11. The sum of twice a number and six is twenty-four.

12. The difference between a number and two is sixteen.

13. Twice the sum of a number and six is twenty-four.

14. Four times a number, increased by seven, is −13.

15. The product of −7 and a number, decreased by five, is 86.

16. Ten less than a number tripled gives the same result as the total of the number and six.

17. The sum of twice a number, three times the number, and four times the number is ninety.

18. Three times the difference between a number and five is equal to −25 increased by four.

19. If the sum of a number and three is multiplied by four, the result is forty-eight.

20. If twice the sum of a number and three is increased by the number, the result is equal to the sum of the number and eighteen.

1. _____

2. _____

3. _____

4. _____

5. _____

6. _____

7. _____

8. _____

9. _____

10. _____

11. _____

12. _____

13. _____

14. _____

15. _____

16. _____

17. _____

18. _____

19. _____

20. _____

Exercise 7.13 Set B

Write each of the following as an algebraic expression or equation. Use x for the unknown number.

1. The sum of a number and two

2. The sum of eight and a number

3. Seven less than twice a number

4. Four fewer than twice a number

5. The product of a number and five

6. The product of three and a number

7. Six more than four times a number

8. One more than three times a number

9. The quotient of a number and nine

10. The quotient of a number and two

11. The sum of twice a number and four is eighteen.

12. The difference between a number and five is twelve.

13. Twice the sum of a number and three is thirty-two.

14. Five times a number, increased by nine, is 39.

15. The product of −6 and a number, decreased by five, is 67.

16. Four less than a number tripled gives the same result as the total of the number and twelve.

17. The sum of twice a number, three times the number, and five times the number is ninety.

18. Four times the difference between a number and six is equal to −21 increased by five.

19. If the sum of a number and four is multiplied by three, the result is eighteen.

20. If twice the sum of a number and five is increased by the number, the result is equal to the sum of the number and sixteen.

1. _____

2. _____

3. _____

4. _____

5. _____

6. _____

7. _____

8. _____

9. _____

10. _____

11. _____

12. _____

13. _____

14. _____

15. _____

16. _____

17. _____

18. _____

19. _____

20. _____

7.14 Word Problems

Translate:

Commuters hate it when the train's late.

The ability to translate statements into equations and solve those equations can help solve many problems. In this section, you will discover that using algebra to solve problems is far superior to guessing the answer. For example, it would be difficult to simply guess the solution to this problem.

Twice a number increased by nine gives the same result as the sum of the number and three. What is the number?

An effective strategy to solve word problems such as this one is:

> 1. **Read:** Read the problem slowly and carefully making note of key words used in the problem.
> 2. **Represent the Unknowns:** Use a variable to represent the unknown quantities in the problem.
> 3. **Translate:** Translate the words of the problem into an equation using the variable.
> 4. **Solve:** Solve the equation.
> 5. **Check:** Check your answer using the words of the problem. Does your answer make sense?

Let's approach the problem stated above using this strategy.

Example 1

Twice a number increased by nine gives the same result as the sum of the number and three. What is the number?

Represent the unknown: x = the number

Translate: $2x + 9 = x + 3$

Solve:
$$2x + 9 = x + 3$$
$$\underline{-x \qquad -x}$$
$$x + 9 = 3$$
$$\underline{-9 \quad -9}$$
$$x \qquad = -6$$

Check: $2(-6) + 9 = -3$ and $-6 + 3 = -3$

Many of the problems you will see in this section will ask you, "What is the number?" Each problem is like a mini-mystery where the value of the number is not known and it is your job to find it. If you let x represent an unknown number, then you can express other numbers based on x. Suppose x = a whole number, other numbers can be represented using the variable x.

$x + 9 \rightarrow$ nine more than the number

$x - 5 \rightarrow$ five less than the number

$2x \rightarrow$ twice the number

$$\left.\begin{array}{l} x + 1 \\ x + 2 \\ x + 3 \\ \quad\vdots \end{array}\right\} \rightarrow \text{consecutive whole numbers larger than } x$$

Example 2

The sum of three consecutive whole numbers is 114. What are the three numbers?

Represent the unknowns: $x =$ the first whole number
$x + 1 =$ the second whole number
$x + 2 =$ the third whole number

Translate: $x + (x + 1) + (x + 2) = 114$

Solve:
$$x + (x + 1) + (x + 2) = 114$$
$$x + x + x + 1 + 2 = 114$$
$$3x + 3 = 114$$
$$\underline{\quad -3 \quad -3}$$
$$3x = 111$$
$$x = 37$$
$$x + 1 = 38$$
$$x + 2 = 39$$

Check: 37, 38, 39 are consecutive whole numbers and $37 + 38 + 39 = 114$.

Example 3

The sum of a number and sixteen is three times the number. What is the number?

Represent the unknowns: $x =$ the number
$3x =$ three times the number

Translate: $x + 16 = 3x$

Solve:
$$x + 16 = 3x$$
$$\underline{-x \qquad\quad -x}$$
$$\frac{16}{2} = \frac{2x}{2}$$
$$8 = x$$

Check: $8 + 16 = 24$ and $3(8) = 24$

Example 4

If the sum of a number and three is doubled, the result is ten more than the number. Find the number.

Represent the unknowns: $x =$ the number
$x + 3 =$ sum of a number and three

Translate: $2(x + 3) = x + 10$

Solve:
$$2(x + 3) = x + 10$$
$$2x + 6 = x + 10$$
$$\underline{-x \qquad\quad -x}$$
$$x + 6 = 10$$
$$\underline{\quad -6 \quad -6}$$
$$x = 4$$

Check: $2(4 + 3) = 14$ and $4 + 10 = 14$

Example 5

In an NBA basketball game, the Bulls scored 27 more points than the Warriors. If a total points scored in the game was 221 points, how points did each team score?

Represent the unknowns: x = number of points for Warriors
$x + 27$ = number of points for Bulls

Translate: $x + (x + 27) = 221$

Solve:
$$x + (x + 27) = 221$$
$$2x + 27 = 221$$
$$\underline{-27 \quad\quad -27}$$
$$2x \quad\;\; = 194$$
$$x = 97$$
$$x + 27 = 124$$

The Warriors scored 97 points and the Bulls scored 124 points.

Check: $97 + 124 = 221$

Example 6

Kisha had three math tests. The score on her second test was nine points more than her first test and the score on her third test was two points less than her first test. If she had a total of 262 points on the three tests, what was her score on the first test?

Represent the unknowns: x = score on first test
$x + 9$ = score on second test
$x - 2$ = score on third test

Translate: $x + (x + 9) + (x - 2) = 262$

Solve:
$$x + (x + 9) + (x - 2) = 262$$
$$x + x + x + 9 - 2 = 262$$
$$3x + 7 = 262$$
$$\underline{-7 \quad\quad -7}$$
$$\frac{3x}{3} = \frac{255}{3}$$
$$x = 85$$

She scored 85 points on her first test.

Check: $85 + (85 + 9) + (85 - 2) = 262$

The previous examples demonstrate how the ability to translate statements into equations and solve those equations can improve problem solving skills. Use the same strategy on the following problems.

Problem 1: Three times a number, decreased by seven, is fourteen. What is the number?

Answer: 7

x = the number

$$3x - 7 = 14$$
$$\underline{+7 \quad +7}$$
$$3x = 21$$
$$x = 7$$

Problem 2: Twice the sum of a number and six gives the same result as the product of four and fifteen. Find the number.

Answer: 24

x = the number

$$2(x + 6) = (4)(15)$$
$$2x + 12 = 60$$
$$\underline{-12 \ -12}$$
$$2x = 48$$
$$x = 24$$

Problem 3: My age plus four times my age gives the same result as subtracting my age from 300. How old am I?

Answer: 50

x = my age

$$x + 4x = 300 - x$$
$$5x = 300 - x$$
$$\underline{+x \qquad\quad +x}$$
$$6x = 300$$
$$x = 50$$

Problem 4: Find two consecutive whole numbers such that three times the smaller number is 25 more than the larger one.

Answer: 13, 14

x = the smaller number
$x + 1$ = the larger number

$$3x = (x + 1) + 25$$
$$3x = x + 26$$
$$\underline{-x \ -x}$$
$$2x = 26$$
$$x = 13, x + 1 = 14$$

Problem 5: Lee has $27 more than twice the amount of money Ed has. If together they had $78, how much money does each have?

Answer: Ed: $17, Lee: $61

x = amount Ed has
$2x + 27$ = amount Lee has

$$x + 2x + 27 = 78$$
$$3x + 27 = 78$$
$$\underline{-27 \ -27}$$
$$\frac{3x}{3} = \frac{51}{3}$$

$$x = 17$$
$$2x + 27 = 61$$

Exercise 7.14 Set A

Solve each problem using the five step strategy explained in this section.

1. The sum of twice a number and six is twenty-four. Find the number.

    1. _____

2. The difference between a number and two is sixteen. Find the number.

    2. _____

3. Twice the sum of a number and six is twenty-four. What is the number?

    3. _____

4. Four times a number, increased by seven, is −13. Find the number.

    4. _____

5. The product of −7 and a number, decreased by five, is 86. Find the number.

    5. _____

6. Ten less than a number tripled gives the same result as as the total of the number and six. What is the number?

    6. _____

7. The sum of twice a number, three times the number, and four times the number is ninety. What is the number?

    7. _____

8. Three times the difference between a number and five is equal to −25 increased by four. Find the number.

    8. _____

9. If the sum of a number and three is multiplied by four, the result is forty-eight. Find the number.

    9. _____

10. If twice the sum of a number and three is increased by the number, the result is equal to the sum of the number and eighteen. What is the number?

    10. _____

11. The sum of three consecutive whole numbers is 306. Find the numbers.

    11. _____

12. The sum of four consecutive whole numbers is 174. What are the whole numbers?

    12. _____

13. In an election runoff, Tom Mercer received 570 more votes than Ken Pico. If 4586 votes were cast, how many votes did each candidate get?

    13. _____

14. The center on an NFL football team weighed 137 pounds more than his wife. If their total weight was 395 pounds, how much does each weigh?

    14. _____

15. Three times my age increased by twice my age gives the same result as 38 years less than seven times my age. How old am I?

    15. _____

Exercise 7.14 Set B

Solve each problem using the five step strategy explained in this section.

1. The sum of twice a number and four is eighteen. What is the number?

1. _____

2. The difference between a number and five is twelve. Find the number.

2. _____

3. Twice the sum of a number and three is thirty-two. Find the number.

3. _____

4. Five times a number, increased by nine, is 39. What is the number?

4. _____

5. The product of −6 and a number, decreased by five, is 67. What is the number?

5. _____

6. Four less than a number tripled gives the same result as the total of the number and twelve. Find the number.

6. _____

7. The sum of twice a number, three times the number, and five times the number is ninety. Find the number.

7. _____

8. Four times the difference between a number and six is equal to −21 increased by five. Find the number.

8. _____

9. If the sum of a number and four is multiplied by three, the result is eighteen. What is the number?

9. _____

10. If twice the sum of a number and five is increased by the number, the result is equal to the sum of the number and sixteen. What is the number?

10. _____

11. The sum of three consecutive whole numbers is 201. Find the numbers.

11. _____

12. The sum of four consecutive whole numbers is 222. What are the whole numbers?

12. _____

13. In a push-up contest, Alan Lau did 56 more push-ups than Ed Silva. If between the both of them they did 580 push-ups, how many did each one do?

13. _____

14. The center on an NBA basketball team is 25 inches taller than his wife. If the total of their heights is 151 inches, how tall is each of them?

14. _____

15. Six times my age decreased by twice my age gives the same result as 69 years more than my age. How old am I?

15. _____

440

7.15 Algebra and Finance (Optional)

A knowledge of algebra gives you a problem solving tool that can be used in many other areas. My goal is to show you that variables and equations can actually be used for something important—saving money. In Section 5.10, we examined problems involving the simple interest (interest added to the principal of an account only once). In the real world, however, most financial institutions do not use simple interest. They pay interest on both the principal and previously earned interest at regular time periods. This type of interest is called **compound interest**. The formula used to determine the amount in an account with compound interest is as follows.

Compound Interest

$A = P(1 + r)^n$ where

A = amount in the account after n time periods

P = principal (amount deposited)

r = rate per period (annual rate ÷ number of periods per year)

n = number of periods (number of years × number of periods per year)

Example 1

Suppose you deposit $700 into an account that pays 6% annual interest, compounded monthly. How much would you have in the account after 4 years?

According to the information given in the problem,

A, the amount in the account, is not known.
$P = \$700$ (That is the amount of the deposit.)
$r = 0.005$ (The annual rate divided by the number of periods (months) in a year is $0.06 \div 12 = 0.005$.)
$n = 48$ (The number of periods (months) in 4 years is $4 \times 12 = 48$.)

Substituting those values into the compound interest formula, will allow us to find the amount in the account (A).

$A = P(1 + r)^n$
$A = 700(1 + 0.005)^{48}$
$A = 700(1.005)^{48}$ → (A calculator is necessary here.)
$A = 700(1.270489)$
$A \approx \$889.34$ → (Answer rounded to the nearest cent.)

Example 2

Suppose you wanted to set up a college fund for your new baby. How much would you have to deposit today to have $9,000 in 18 years, if the account that pays 4.38% annual interest compounded daily?

According to the information given in the problem,

P, the amount deposited, is not known.

$A = \$9000$ (This is the amount we want in the account.)

$r = 0.00012$ (The annual rate divided by the number of periods (days) in a year is $0.0438 \div 365 = 0.00012$.)

$n = 6570$ (The number of periods (days) in 18 years is $18 \times 365 = 6570$.)

Substituting those values into the compound interest formula, will allow us to solve for the amount to deposit (P).

$$A = P(1 + r)^n$$
$$9000 = P(1 + 0.00012)^{6570}$$
$$9000 = P(1.00012)^{6570} \qquad \rightarrow \text{(A calculator is necessary here.)}$$
$$\frac{9000}{2.19977} = \frac{P(2.19977)}{2.19977}$$
$$\$4091.34 \approx P \qquad \rightarrow \text{(Answer rounded to the nearest cent.)}$$

Annuities

Most people do not have $4091.34 to place into a savings account. Instead, they may save a little each month in the hopes of building a college fund for their baby. An account in which money is deposited at the end of each month is called an ordinary **annuity.** Each month the account grows because of new payments and interest earned on previous payments. The formula to determine the amount in an annuity (S) is a follows.

$$S = PMT\left[\frac{(1 + r)^n - 1}{r}\right] \text{ where } \begin{cases} S = \text{amount in the annuity after } n \text{ payments} \\ PMT = \text{amount of each deposit} \\ r = \text{rate per period (annual rate} \div \text{ number of payments per year)} \\ n = \text{number of payments (number of years} \times \text{number of payments per year)} \end{cases}$$

Example 3

Suppose you deposit $100 a month into an annuity earning 6%, compounded monthly. How much will you have in the account after 18 years?

According to the information given in the problem,

S, the amount in the annuity, is not known.

$PMT = \$100$ (That is the amount of each deposit.)

$r = 0.005$ (The annual rate divided by the number of payments in a year is $0.06 \div 12 = 0.005$.)

$n = 216$ (The number of payments in 18 years is $18 \times 12 = 216$.)

$$S = PMT\left[\frac{(1+r)^n - 1}{r}\right]$$

$$S = 100\left[\frac{(1+0.005)^{216} - 1}{0.005}\right]$$

$$S = 100\left[\frac{2.93677 - 1}{0.005}\right]$$

$$S = 100[387.35319]$$

$$S \approx \$38{,}735.32$$

Many people dream about becoming a millionaire. Let's use some algebra to determine if, through a regular savings plan, you could become a millionaire.

Example 4

How much would you have to deposit each month into an annuity that earns 7.2% annual interest, compounded monthly, to become a millionaire by the time you retire in 45 years?

According to the information given in the problem,

PMT, the amount of each deposit, is not known.

$S = \$1{,}000{,}000$ (That is the amount you want in the account.)

$r = 0.006$ (The annual rate divided by the number of payments in a year is $0.072 \div 12 = 0.006$.)

$n = 540$ (The number of payments in 45 years is $45 \times 12 = 540$.)

$$S = PMT\left[\frac{(1+r)^n - 1}{r}\right]$$

$$1{,}000{,}000 = PMT\left[\frac{(1+0.006)^{540} - 1}{0.006}\right]$$

$$1{,}000{,}000 = PMT\left[\frac{25.28772 - 1}{0.006}\right]$$

$$\frac{1{,}000{,}000}{4047.9525} = \frac{PMT[4047.9525]}{4047.9525}$$

$$\$247.04 \approx PMT$$

The mathematics shows us that if you make regular monthly deposits of $247.04 for 45 years with an annual interest rate of 7.2%, you will become a millionaire.

This section has attempted to show you that a knowledge of variables and equations can be very helpful in financial matters like saving money. As you learn more about mathematics, you will become more aware of its usefulness and power. The problems that follow will give you more practice in working with compound interest and annuities.

Problem 1: If you deposit $1000 into an account that pays 4.5% annual interest, compounded monthly, much would be in the account after 10 years?

Answer: $1566.99

A is unknown, $P = 1000$,
$r = 0.045 \div 12 = 0.00375$,
$n = 10(12) = 120$

$$A = P(1 + r)^n$$
$$A = 1000(1 + 0.00375)^{120}$$
$$A = 1000(1.00375)^{120}$$
$$A = 1000(1.56699)$$
$$A \approx \$1566.99$$

Problem 2: How much would you have to deposit now into an account that pays 7.3% annual interest, compounded daily, to have $40,000 fifteen years later?

Answer: $13,383.05

P unknown, $A = 40{,}000$,
$r = 0.073 \div 365 = 0.0002$,
$n = 15(365) = 5475$

$$A = P(1 + r)^n$$
$$40{,}000 = P(1.0002)^{5475}$$

$$\frac{40{,}000}{2.98886} = \frac{P(2.98886)}{2.98886}$$

$$\$13{,}383.05 \approx P$$

Problem 3: After making $50 monthly payments in an annuity for 20 years that earns 8.4% annual interest, what is the amount in the annuity?

Answer: $30,958.89

S is unknown, $PMT = 50$,
$r = 0.084 \div 12 = 0.007$,
$n = 12(20) = 240$

$$S = PMT\left[\frac{1 + r)^n - 1}{r}\right]$$

$$S = 50\left[\frac{(1 + 0.007)^{240} - 1}{0.007}\right]$$

$$S = 50[619.17781]$$
$$S \approx \$30{,}958.89$$

Problem 4: How much would you have to deposit monthly in an annuity that earns 6% annual interest to have a $9,000 college fund in 18 years?

Answer: $23.23

PMT is unknown, $S = 9000$,
$n = 12(18) = 216$,
$r = 0.06 \div 12 = 0.005$

$$S = PMT\left[\frac{(1 + r)^n - 1}{r}\right]$$

$$9{,}000 = PMT\left[\frac{(1 + 0.005)^{216} - 1}{0.005}\right]$$

$$\frac{9{,}000}{387.35319} = \frac{PMT[387.35319]}{387.35319}$$

$$\$23.23 \approx PMT$$

Name _____   Date _____

Exercise 7.15 Set A

1. If $750 is deposited into an account that earns 4.8% annual interest, compounded monthly, how much is in the account after 8 years?

1. _____

2. If $750 is deposited into an account that earns 7.3% annual interest, compounded daily, how much is in the account after 8 years?

2. _____

3. How much must you deposit into an account that earns 5.84% annual interest, compounded daily, to have $1250 in two years?

3. _____

4. How much must you deposit into an account that earns 8.76% annual interest, compounded monthly, to have $1250 in two years?

4. _____

5. If you make regular monthly payments of $75 into an annuity that earns 8.4%, compounded monthly, for 9 years, how much will you have in the annuity?

5. _____

6. If you make regular monthly payments of $125 into an annuity that earns 10.8%, compounded monthly, for 12 years, how much will you have in the annuity?

6. _____

7. An annuity claims to pay an annual rate of 15.6%, compounded monthly. How much would you have to deposit each month in this annuity to have $7500 at the end of three years?

7. _____

8. An annuity claims to pay an annual rate of 18% compounded monthly. How much would you have to deposit each month in this annuity to have 3 million dollars at the end of 25 years?

8. _____

Exercise 7.15 Set B

1. If $950 is deposited into an account that earns 6% annual interest, compounded monthly, how much is in the account after 8 years?

1. _____

2. If $950 is deposited into an account that earns 7.3% annual interest, compounded daily, how much is in the account after 10 years?

2. _____

3. How much must you deposit into an account that earns 3.65% annual interest, compounded daily, to have $2300 in two years?

3. _____

4. How much must you deposit into an account that earns 7.2% annual interest, compounded monthly, to have $4000 in two years?

4. _____

5. If you make regular monthly payments of $95 into an annuity that earns 7.2%, compounded monthly, for 12 years, how much will you have in the annuity?

5. _____

6. If you make regular monthly payments of $340 into an annuity that earns 9.6%, compounded monthly, for 30 years, how much will you have in the annuity?

6. _____

7. An annuity claims to pay an annual rate of 12%, compounded monthly. How much would you have to deposit each month in this annuity to have 5 million dollars at the end of 30 years?

7. _____

8. An annuity claims to pay an annual rate of 19.2%, compounded monthly. How much would you have to deposit each month in this annuity to have $75,000 at the end of six years

8. _____

Chapter 7 Summary

Concepts

You may refer to the sections listed below to review how to:

1. evaluate algebraic expressions by replacing each variable with the number that it represents. (7.1)
2. compare signed numbers by understanding that numbers get larger proceeding to the right along a number line and smaller proceeding to the left. (7.2)
3. add signed numbers using either movement on a number line or the following rule: if the numbers have the same signs, add their number parts and use that same sign as the sign of the answer; if the numbers have different signs, subtract their number parts and use the sign of the larger number part. (7.3)
4. subtract signed numbers by changing the sign of the number being subtracted and converting the subtraction to addition. (7.4)
5. multiply and divide signed numbers by multiplying or dividing their number parts and using the fact that same signs give positive answers and different signs give negative answers. (7.5)
6. use the order of operations on signed numbers. (7.6)
7. solve simple equations by mentally determining what number the variable represents. (7.7)
8. simplify expressions and solve equations using the properties of algebra. (7.8), (7.9), (7.10), (7.11), (7.12)
9. translate phrases and statements into algebraic expressions and equations. (7.13)
10. solve word problems by reading, representing the unknown, translating, solving, and checking. (7.14)
11. solve problems involving compound interest and annuities. (7.15)

Terminology

This chapter's important terms and their corresponding page numbers are:

algebraic expression: a quantity containing numbers, variables, and operations. (379)

annuity: an account in which money is deposited at the end of each month. (442)

associative property: for numbers a, b, and c, $(a + b) + c = a + (b + c)$ and $(a \cdot b) \cdot c = a \cdot (b \cdot c)$ (421)

commutative property: for numbers a, b, and c, $a + b = b + a$ and $a \cdot b = b \cdot a$ (421)

compound interest: interest earned on both the principal and previously earned interest. (441)

distributive property: for numbers a, b, and c, $a(b + c) = a \cdot b + a \cdot c$ or $a(b - c) = a \cdot b - a \cdot c$ (422)

equation: a statement that two quantities are equal. (405)

number line: a straight line whose points are associated with numbers. (383)

signed number: a positive or negative number. (383)

variable: a letter used to represent a number. (379)

Chapter 7 Crossword Puzzle

Across

3. If $x + 6 = 77$, then $x =$ _____.
6. Negative numbers are _____ than zero.
8. If $4x = 20$, then $x =$ _____ .
9. Statement that two quantities are equal
12. A meaning of the symbol, $>$.
14. Street
15. 8 oz.
18. Symbol that represents numbers
20. 12 inches (abbr)
22. Numbers less than zero
23. $12 - (-28)$
25. $-7(-3) + (10 - 12)$
26. Separates positive and negative numbers

Down

1. Expression containing variables
2. Indicator of equality
4. If $-15 = x - 16$, then $x =$ _____ .
5. Not odd
7. Numbers with $+$ or $-$
8. $(-24) \div (-6)$
10. Plus
11. Holds . . . 1, 2, 3, . . . , not clothes (2 wrds)
13. Zero is _____ than any negative number.
15. $\frac{1}{100}$ of a meter (abbr)
16. To the right of zero on number line
17. Used for variables
19. $\frac{1}{12}$ of a foot (abbr)
21. 1000 grams (abbr)
24. If $2x - 8 = 12$, then $x =$ _____ .

Chapter 7 Practice Test A

1. If $x = 6$, $y = 2$, and $z = 5$, then $\dfrac{x}{y} + 2y - z = ?$ 1. _____

In problems 2–3, replace the question mark with $>$ or $<$.

2. $-7 \; ? \; 0$ 3. $-17 \; ? \; -18$ 2. _____

3. _____

In problems 4–10, perform the indicated operations.

4. $-12 + 8$ 5. $-24 + (-18)$ 4. _____

5. _____

6. $16 - 27$ 7. $-4 - (-10)$ 6. _____

7. _____

8. $5(-8)$ 9. $\dfrac{63}{-9}$ 8. _____

9. _____

10. $\dfrac{6[3 - (-8)]}{-5 + 2(-3)}$ 10. _____

In problems 11–14, solve each equation.

11. $x + 37 = 61$ 12. $28 = x - 8$ 11. _____

12. _____

13. $342 = 9x$ 14. $\dfrac{x}{-3} + 22 = 3$ 13. _____

14. _____

15. Simplify by combining like terms: $3(2x - 4) + 3(x - 1)$ 15. _____

16. Solve for x: $5x - 8 = 3(x - 4)$ 16. _____

17. Translate into an algebraic equation and solve: 17. _____

    The product of four and a certain number gives the same result as the sum of the number and twelve. What is the number?

18. How much must you deposit in an account paying 4.8% annual interest, compounded monthly, to have $7000 after 5 years?   18. _____

Chapter 7 Practice Test B

1. If $r = 6$, $s = 1$, and $t = 2$, then $\dfrac{r}{t} + 3r - 2s = ?$

1. _____

In problems 2–3, replace the question mark with $>$ or $<$.

2. $0 \; ? \; -6$

3. $-24 \; ? \; -25$

2. _____

3. _____

In problems 4–10, perform the indicated operations.

4. $17 + (-14)$

5. $-36 + (-17)$

4. _____

5. _____

6. $14 - 29$

7. $8 - (-6)$

6. _____

7. _____

8. $(-6) \cdot 9$

9. $(-4)(-8)$

8. _____

9. _____

10. $\dfrac{(7 - 11)(2 - 3 \cdot 6)}{-5 - (-3)}$

10. _____

In problems 11–14, solve each equation.

11. $70 = x + 44$

12. $x - 9 = 27$

11. _____

12. _____

13. $273 = 7x$

14. $-2x + 7 = 23$

13. _____

14. _____

15. Simplify by combining like terms: $2(3x - 5) + 4(x - 3)$

15. _____

16. Solve for x: $8(x - 1) = 6x - 4$

16. _____

17. Translate into an algebraic equation and solve:

    Six less than a number is four more than twice the number. What is the number?

17. _____

18. How much money will you have in an annuity that pays 8.4% annual interest, if you deposit $150 a month for 10 years?

18. _____

Chapter 7 Supplementary Exercises

Section 7.1

If $P = 3$, $Q = 5$, and $R = 1$, evaluate the following:

1. $Q + P - R$
2. $4Q + 2P$
3. $3PQR$
4. $5(2P - 3R)$
5. $RQ - RP$
6. $4(Q + 6 - R)$
7. $\frac{1}{2}Q + \frac{1}{4}R$
8. $\frac{1}{4}\left(Q - \frac{1}{2}P\right)$
9. $2Q + 2P - 2(R + P)$
10. $\frac{6Q}{P}$
11. $\frac{5P + R}{2}$
12. $\frac{9Q - P}{R + 2}$

Section 7.2

Replace the ? with > or <.

1. 8 ? 0
2. $\frac{1}{2}$? $\frac{1}{4}$
3. -41 ? -81
4. -8 ? 0
5. $-\frac{1}{2}$? $-\frac{1}{4}$
6. 0 ? -0.5
7. -5 ? 4
8. -5 ? -56
9. $-6\frac{1}{2}$? $-6\frac{1}{4}$
10. -5 ? -4
11. 2.7 ? -2.6
12. -3.8 ? -3.9

Section 7.3

Perform the indicated operations.

1. $7 + 5$
2. $-7 + 5$
3. $7 + (-5)$
4. $-7 + (-5)$
5. $-15 + 18$
6. $15 + (-18)$
7. $-15 + (-18)$
8. $-6 + (-35)$
9. $-40 + 18$
10. $14 + (-33)$
11. $56 + (-87)$
12. $44 + (-29)$
13. $-4 + 6 + (-7)$
14. $8 + (-9) + (-13)$
15. $-15 + 9 + (-7)$
16. $-77 + 18 + 9$
17. $14 + (-32) + (-12)$
18. $54 + (-77) + 5$

Section 7.4

Perform the indicated operations.

1. $12 - 7$	2. $7 - 12$	3. $13 - 25$
4. $-7 - 9$	5. $-9 - 7$	6. $-6 - 4$
7. $-38 - 56$	8. $18 - 6$	9. $-18 - 6$
10. $9 - (-3)$	11. $5 - (-2)$	12. $12 - (-7)$
13. $-18 - (-6)$	14. $-7 - (-14)$	15. $-3 - (-17)$
16. $25 - 10 - (-6)$	17. $35 - 6 - 27$	18. $-5 - 5 - (-5)$
19. $-12 + 32 - (-7)$	20. $-56 - 7 + 23$	21. $-22 + 17 - (-9)$
22. $-23 - (-55) + 17$	23. $34 - (-21) + 9$	24. $1 - 9 + 8 - 6$

Section 7.5

Perform the indicated operations.

1. $5 \cdot (7)$	2. $6 \cdot (-3)$	3. $-4(7)$
4. $-5 \cdot 3$	5. $(-9)(-6)$	6. $-3(-5)$
7. $(-1)(-27)$	8. $-8(12)$	9. $5(-31)$
10. $8 \cdot (-3)(-2)$	11. $-7(-3) \cdot 9$	12. $-6 \cdot 8 \cdot (-3)$
13. $-2(-4)(-7)$	14. $-3(-3)(-3)$	15. $(-2)(-8)(-1)(5)$
16. $\dfrac{-45}{9}$	17. $\dfrac{-36}{4}$	18. $\dfrac{-72}{-8}$
19. $\dfrac{-52}{-4}$	20. $\dfrac{-81}{-9}$	21. $\dfrac{52}{-4}$
22. $-\dfrac{225}{5}$	23. $\dfrac{441}{-3}$	24. $\dfrac{-700}{-25}$

Section 7.6

Perform the indicated operations.

1. $5 - 2 \cdot 7$	2. $-6 + 3 \cdot 2$	3. $-6 - (3 + 8)$
4. $9 - (8 - 5)$	5. $3(-2) + 2(-3)$	6. $(-4)(6) + 8 \cdot 3$
7. $(-5)(-2) + 3(-6)$	8. $4(-9) + (-5)(-4)$	9. $3[-2 + 4(8 - 1)]$
10. $-2[7 - 5(3 - 9)]$	11. $25 - [4 - (3{-}10)]$	12. $-34 + [2(4 - 12) + (-5)]$
13. $4^2 - (2)(-5)$	14. $2^3 - (-5)(6)$	15. $(-7 + 10)^3 - (-4)$
16. $(-6 + 9)^2 - (-8)$	17. $\dfrac{4 - 2 \cdot 7}{-3 + (-7)}$	18. $\dfrac{-8 - 1}{5 + 3(-2)}$
19. $\dfrac{-5 + 13}{2(7 - 9)}$	20. $\dfrac{-4(6 + 8)}{-7 + 5}$	21. $\dfrac{-6(4) - (8)(-3)}{(-7 - 5)(8 - 3)}$
22. $\dfrac{(-6)(-6) + 4(-9)}{3(2 - 8) - (-4)}$	23. $\dfrac{7 - 3(-4) - 4}{3[8 - (-5)]}$	24. $\dfrac{8 + 2(-3) - (-4)}{-5[-6 + (-4)]}$

Section 7.7

Solve for x in each equation.

1. $x + 3 = 5$
2. $2 + x = 8$
3. $-1 = x + 9$
4. $x - 4 = 10$
5. $7 - x = -2$
6. $3 = x - 5$
7. $3x = 12$
8. $-5x = -30$
9. $56 = -7x$
10. $\dfrac{x}{5} = 2$
11. $-3 = \dfrac{x}{7}$
12. $3x + 1 = 13$
13. $2x + 1 = 9$
14. $2x - 1 = 9$
15. $12 = 2x + 2$

Section 7.8

Solve for n in each equation.

1. $n + 7 = 19$
2. $-4 = n + 3$
3. $18 = n + 47$
4. $n - 23 = 14$
5. $25 = n - 7$
6. $12 = n - 12$
7. $n - 43 = -43$
8. $5.6 + n = 8.7$
9. $n - 5.3 = -2.4$
10. $-(-9) + n = 6$
11. $n - (-8) = -4$
12. $-16 = n - (-16)$
13. $7 + n = 4$
14. $-8 + n = -3$
15. $5 + n = 5$
16. $n + \dfrac{1}{6} = \dfrac{5}{6}$
17. $\dfrac{3}{4} + n = \dfrac{1}{4}$
18. $\dfrac{2}{3} = n + \dfrac{1}{2}$
19. $n - \dfrac{1}{6} = \dfrac{5}{6}$
20. $-\dfrac{3}{4} + n = \dfrac{1}{4}$
21. $\dfrac{2}{3} = n - \dfrac{1}{2}$

Section 7.9

Solve for p in each equation.

1. $4p = 32$
2. $-5p = 35$
3. $-36 = 9p$
4. $-120 = -6p$
5. $15p = -45$
6. $-16p = -64$
7. $\dfrac{1}{2}p = -18$
8. $9 = -\dfrac{1}{4}p$
9. $-\dfrac{1}{2}p = -7$
10. $\dfrac{p}{7} = 4$
11. $\dfrac{p}{-3} = 12$
12. $-6 = \dfrac{p}{8}$
13. $144 = -6p$
14. $-144 = 8p$
15. $-144 = -9p$
16. $\dfrac{p}{5} = -15$
17. $\dfrac{p}{-5} = 15$
18. $\dfrac{p}{-5} = -15$

Section 7.10

Solve for x in each equation.

1. $3x + 1 = 16$

2. $2x - 3 = 15$

3. $7 - 2x = -11$

4. $-18 = -5x - 3$

5. $5x + 8 = 49$

6. $81 = 6 + 3x$

7. $6x - 8 = 34$

8. $-2x + 3 = 7$

9. $46 + 8x = 6$

10. $3.5x + 6 = 13$

11. $50 = -4x + 6$

12. $-7x - 3 = -24$

13. $\dfrac{x}{2} + 6 = 8$

14. $\dfrac{x}{4} - 4 = 15$

15. $-15 = \dfrac{x}{2} - 6$

16. $\dfrac{1}{5}x + 3 = 9$

17. $-3 + \dfrac{1}{5}x = 4$

18. $3 = \dfrac{1}{5}x - 2$

19. $8 - 2x = 22$

20. $8 + 2x = -21$

21. $8 - 2x = -22$

Section 7.11

Simplify each expression by combining like terms.

1. $4x + 6x - 9x$

2. $-6y + 7y - 8y$

3. $5m + 9 + m - 7$

4. $-4 + 2h - 5h + 6 - h$

5. $x - 3y + 4x - 7y + y$

6. $3(x + 4) + 5(x - 3)$

7. $2(4x - 6) + 3(5 - 2x)$

8. $-3(x + 5) - 2(3x - 1) + 2x$

9. $a - b + c + 4(-a + b - 2c)$

10. $a + b - 3c + 4(a - b + 2c) + 7$

Section 7.12

Solve for x in each equation.

1. $3x + x = 7 - 11$

2. $5x - 2x = 16 + (-1)$

3. $6(x - 7) = x + 13$

4. $16 = 2(5 - x)$

5. $7x = 5x - 8$

6. $5x + 9 = 2x - 6$

7. $-5(3x + 4) = -7(2x - 1)$

8. $3(2x + 1) - 2 = 7 + x - 6$

9. $6(x + 1) - 5 + x = x - 5$

10. $4 - (5 - 2x) = 4(x + 3) - 1$

Section 7.13

Write each of the following as an algebraic expression or equation. Use x as the variable.

1. The sum of a number and 9.

2. The quotient of a number and 9.

3. The product of a number and 9.

4. The difference between a number and 9.

5. The sum of twice a number and five is −37.

6. Six less than a number results in the product of the number and four.

7. Three times the difference between a number and six gives the same result as the sum of the number and 14.

8. If a number is tripled and that result is decreased 7, the result is the product of 2 and −8.

9. If three times the sum of twice a number and four is increased by 5, the result is eleven.

Section 7.14

1. The sum of twice a number and five is −37. What is the number?

2. Six less than a number results in the product of the number and four. What is the number?

3. Three times the difference between a number and six gives the same result as the sum of the number and 14. What is the number?

4. If a number is tripled and that result is decreased 7, the result is the product of 2 and −8. What is the number?

5. If three times the sum of twice a number and four is increased by 5, the result is eleven. What is the number?

6. The sum of four consecutive whole numbers is 110. What are the numbers?

7. In a basketball game Jordan scored 29 more points than Pippen. If the total points they scored was 47, how many did each score?

8. Five times my age decreased by twice my age gives the same result as the sum of my age and 38. How old am I?

Section 7.15

1. How much would a savings account contain after 20 years if $1000 was deposited and it earned 7.3% annual interest, compounded daily, for the entire time?

2. How much would a savings account contain after 20 years if $1000 was deposited and it earned 7.2% annual interest, compounded monthly, for the entire time?

3. Suppose an account pays 6% annual interest, compounded monthly. What should you deposit now to have $15,000 in the account after 12 years?

4. An annuity pays 7.2% annual interest, compounded monthly. How much would you have in the annuity after depositing $350 a month for 12 years?

5. An annuity pays 7.2% annual interest, compounded monthly. How much would you have to deposit every month to have $950,000 after 20 years?

Chapter 8

Introduction to Geometry

After completing this chapter, you should be able to do the following:

1. define basic geometric terms.
2. distinguish between different kinds of angles.
3. classify different types of triangles.
4. identify various kinds of plane figures.
5. draw common geometric shapes.
6. find perimeters and areas of common plane figures.
7. find angles of polygons.
8. find surface areas and volumes of common 3-dimensional solids.
9. solve for sides of right triangles using the Pythagorean Theorem.
10. solve word problems involving geometry.

On the next page, you will find a pretest for this chapter. The purpose of the pretest is to help you determine which sections in this chapter you need to study in detail and which sections you can review quickly. By taking and correcting the pretest according to the instructions on the next page you, can better plan your pace through this chapter.

Note: Unless otherwise indicated in this chapter, when the answers have more than three decimal digits, they will be rounded off to the nearest hundredth.

Name _____   Date _____

Chapter 8 Pretest

Take and correct this test using the answer section at the end of the book.
Those problems that give you difficulty indicate which sections need extra
attention. Section numbers are in the parentheses before each problem.

(8.1)   1. List all the line segments in the figure on the right.   1. _____

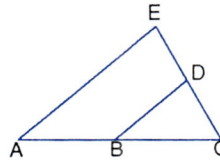

(8.1)   2. In the figure on the right, if B is the mid-   2. _____
         point of $\overline{AC}$, and AC = 25, then how long
         is AB?

(8.2)   3. What kind of an angle is ∠E, if it measures 75°?   3. _____

(8.2)   4. Find the complement and supplement of a 46° angle.   4. _____

(8.3)   5. Sketch and label isosceles triangle, △DEF.   5. _____

(8.3)   6. Sketch and label right triangle, △ABC, with ∠A the right   6. _____
         angle.

(8.4)   7. Sketch and label parallelogram MNOP, with ∠N an obtuse   7. _____
         angle.

(8.5)   8. Sketch a regular pentagon and find the measure of each of its angles.

8. _____

(8.6)   9. Find the circumference and area of a circle with a diameter of 25 cm.

9. _____

(8.6)   10. Find the perimeter and area of the parallelogram on the right.

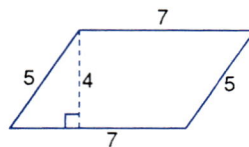

10. _____

(8.7)   11. Find the surface area and volume of a cylinder with a height of 10 cm and a diameter of 6 cm.

11. _____

(8.8)   12. The two legs of a right triangle are 10 in. and 24 in. How long is its hypotenuse?

12. _____

(8.9)   13. A cubic tank with 5 ft edges is filled with water. Find the weight of the water in the tank. (Note: water weighs 62.4 lbs per cu ft.)

13. _____

8.1 Basic Geometric Objects

As you look around the world we live in, you see many different objects, each having its own size and shape. Since early times, man has measured the earth and classified the shapes around him. This study we call geometry. To begin an introduction to geometry, we will consider the most basic objects—the point, line, and plane.

Geometry:
What do little acorns say when they grow up? "Gee, I'm a tree!"

Point

A point is a location. It has no size; it has only position. For example, there is a point on the upper right-hand corner of this page. Even though you can not see it, the location is there. A point is represented by a dot and named by a letter placed next to it. Shown below are three points—A, B, and C.

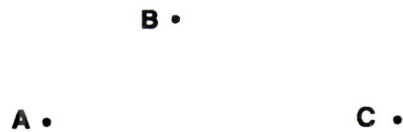

B •

A •   C •

Line

A line is made up of points. It is straight and extends forever in opposite directions. Only one line can be drawn connecting two points. A line is represented by a double-headed arrow and is named by a single lower-case letter or by two points that are on the line. Shown below is line w or line $\overleftrightarrow{AB}$.

←————————•————————————•————————→ w
              A   B

Plane

A plane is a flat surface that has no thickness and extends indefinitely in every direction. A thin plate of glass that stretches forever in all directions is a good model of a plane. A plane is represented by a parallelogram as pictured below and is named by a single letter.

plane E (The letter E may be placed in any corner.)

Problem 1:   Draw and label plane K containing point P and $\overleftrightarrow{AB}$.

Answer: (One of many possible sketches.)

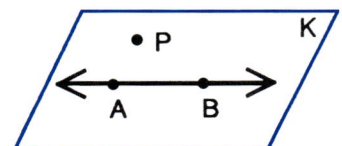

Intersecting and Parallel Lines

Lines that cross each other at one point are called *intersecting lines.* Lines in the same plane that never intersect are called *parallel lines.*

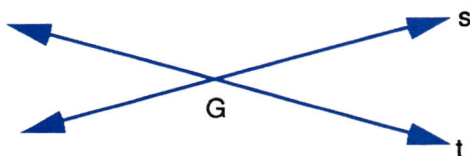

Line s intersecting line t at point G.

Line p is parallel to line q, written p ∥ q.

Line Segment

A **line segment** is the part of a line that consists of two points and all the points in between those two points.

The line segment connecting points D and F is written $\overline{DF}$ or $\overline{FD}$.

Note: The order of the letters does not make a difference.

Length of a Line Segment

Every line segment has a length, a distance from one end point to the other end point. The line segment above is 2 inches long. We write DF = 2" or FD = 2". In the length of a line segment, the dash is not written above the letters. $\overline{DF}$ is the line segment while DF represents the length of the line segment.

Midpoint of a Line Segment

A point that divides a line segment into two equal parts is called the **midpoint** of the line segment.

X is the midpoint of the line segment $\overline{RS}$ since RX = XS.

Problem 2:   List all the different line segments on $\overleftrightarrow{DB}$.

Answer:
$\overline{DA}$, $\overline{AB}$, $\overline{DB}$

Problem 3:   In the line above, if DB = 12 and A is the midpoint of $\overline{DB}$, how long is $\overline{DA}$?

Answer: 6

Problem 4:   Draw and label k ∥ j with $\overleftrightarrow{MN}$ intersecting both k and j.

Answer:

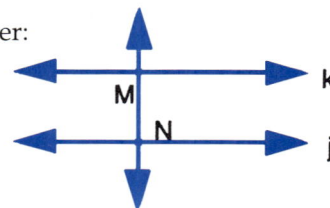

Name _____   Date _____

Exercise 8.1 Set A

In problems 1–8, draw and label a figure for each description.

1. Line w containing points Y, P, and F.

2. $\overleftrightarrow{JK}$ passing through points C and X.

3. Plane G containing points J and V.

4. Plane W containing line d.

5. Lines g and h with g ∥ h.

6. $\overleftrightarrow{FE}$ ∥ $\overrightarrow{GH}$

7. $\overleftrightarrow{QP}$ intersecting line segment $\overline{CD}$ at point Y.

8. Line r intersecting line segment $\overline{AB}$ at point F.

In problems 9–10, list all the line segments in each figure.

9.

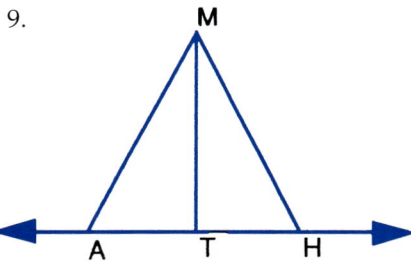

10.

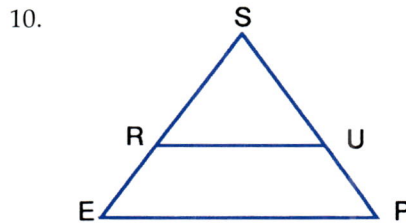

9. _____

10. _____

In problems 11–12, determine the indicated lengths.

11. If ES = 10, A is the midpoint of $\overline{ES}$, and S is the midpoint of $\overline{AY}$, find the lengths of $\overline{EA}$, $\overline{AS}$, and $\overline{AY}$.

11. _____

12. If IE = 24, C is the midpoint of $\overline{IE}$, and NI = IE, find the lengths of $\overline{NI}$, $\overline{IC}$, and $\overline{CE}$.

12. _____

461

Exercise 8.1 Set B

In problems 1–8, draw and label a figure for each description.

1. Line v passing through points A, R, T, and S.

2. $\overleftrightarrow{MN}$ containing points B and E.

3. Plane R containing intersecting lines p and q.

4. Plane Q containing point A and line segment $\overline{LT}$.

5. Lines a, b, c with a ∥ b ∥ c.

6. $\overleftrightarrow{GH}$ ∥ $\overrightarrow{LD}$.

7. Line segment $\overline{AB}$ intersecting line segment $\overline{XZ}$ at point T.

8. Line segment $\overline{TQ}$ intersecting line b at point R.

In problems 9–10, list all the line segments in each figure.

9. 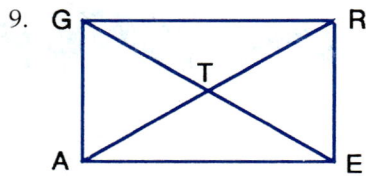   10.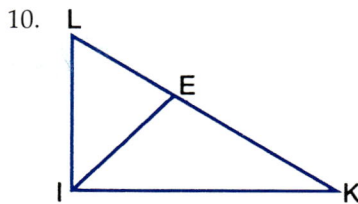

9. _____

10. _____

In problems 11–12, determine the indicated lengths.

11. If HP = 6, O is the midpoint of $\overline{HP}$, and HP = PE, find the lengths of $\overline{HO}$, $\overline{OP}$, and $\overline{PE}$.

11. _____

12. If LC = 14, U is the midpoint of $\overline{LC}$, and C is the midpoint of $\overline{UK}$, find the lengths of $\overline{LU}$, $\overline{UC}$, and $\overline{CK}$.

12. _____

8.2 Angles

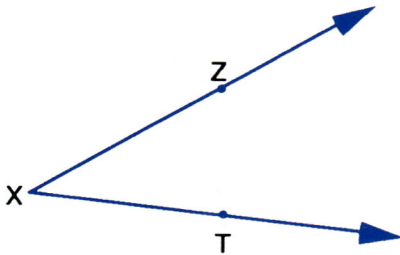

A **ray** is part of a line that has one end point and extends indefinitely in only one direction. When two rays meet at the same end point, they form an **angle.** The two rays are called the sides of the angle and the common end point is the vertex of the angle. In the angle below, ray $\overleftrightarrow{XZ}$ and ray $\overrightarrow{XT}$ are the sides of the angle, and point X is its vertex. An angle is named using the angle symbol ∠. This angle can be named:

$$\angle X \text{ or } \angle ZXT \text{ or } \angle TXZ.$$

Note: When using a three-letter name for an angle, the vertex is always the middle letter.

Example 1

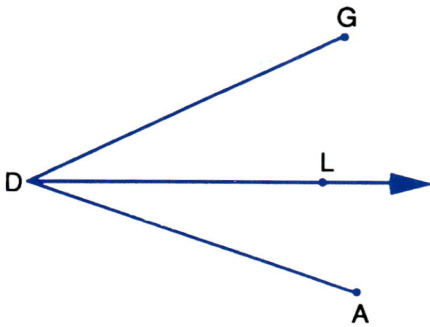

Name the three angles at point D in the figure below:

The three angles at point D are:

$$\angle GDL \text{ (or } \angle LDG)$$
$$\angle LDA \text{ (or } \angle ADL)$$
$$\angle GDA \text{ (or } \angle ADG).$$

Note: None of these angles may be named D because there is more than one angle having a vertex at D.

Measuring Angles

Angles have a measurement determined by the amount of rotation needed to swing one side of the angle around to the other side of the angle. That amount of rotation is measured in degrees. A complete rotation is 360 degrees (360°) and 1/360 of a full rotation is one degree (1°).

Problem 1: What are the five different angles in the figure below?

Answers: $\angle A$, $\angle D$, $\angle ABD$, $\angle DBE$, and $\angle ABE$

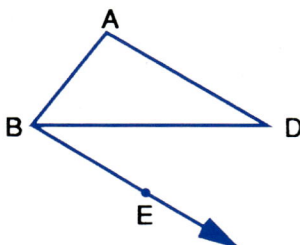

Types of Angles

Half of a complete rotation forms a 180° angle, called a **straight angle.** One-fourth of a complete rotation forms a 90° angle, called a **right angle.**

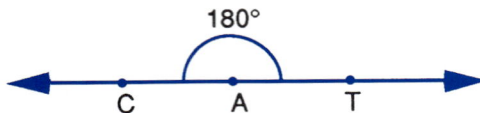

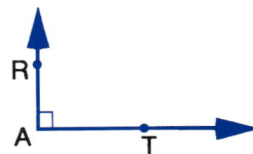

∠CAT is a straight angle.   ∠RAT is a right angle.
                                   (The box in the angle means 90°)

If an angle measures between 0° and 90°, it is called an **acute angle.** If an angle measures between 90° and 180°, it is called an **obtuse angle.**

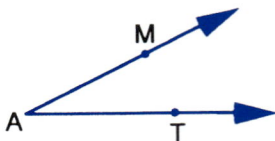

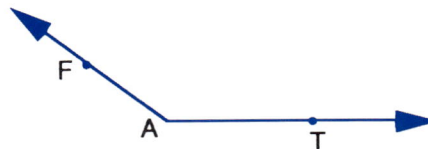

∠MAT is acute.   ∠FAT is obtuse.

If the measures of two angles add up to 90°, they are called **complementary angles.** If the measures of two angles add up to 180°, they are called **supplementary angles.**

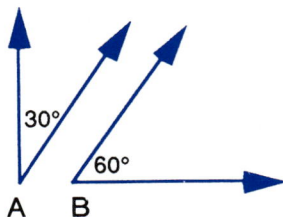

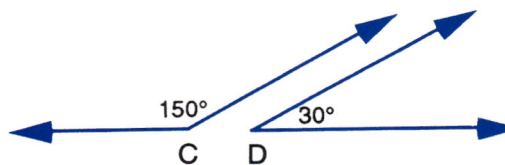

∠A and ∠B are complementary.   ∠C and ∠D are supplementary.
(∠A is the complement of ∠B.)   (∠C is the supplement of ∠D.)

Example 2

a) Draw obtuse angle ∠TAN and its supplement ∠RAN.
b) Draw acute angle ∠TAN and its complement ∠RAN.

Point A must be at the vertex of each angle and side $\overrightarrow{AN}$ is common to both angles.

a)   b)

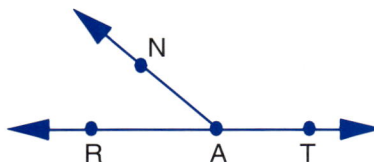

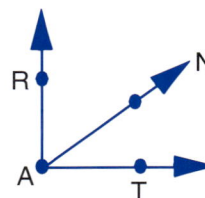

Example 3

For the given times, determine if the angle between the hour and minute hands of a clock form an acute, obtuse, straight, or right angle.   a) 3:00   b) 10:00   c) 6:00   d) 7:00

By examining the hands of a clock you will see that at:
a) 3:00 there is a right angle.   b) 10:00 there is an acute angle.

   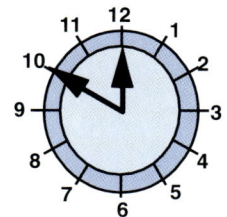

c) 6:00 there is a straight angle.   d) 7:00 there is an obtuse angle.

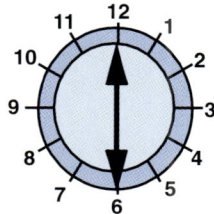   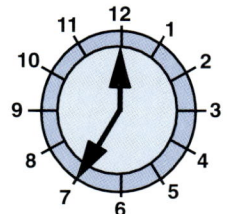

Problems: Refer to ∠A below to answer each question.

Answers:

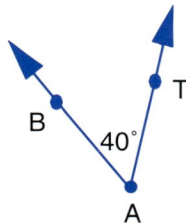

2. What type of angle is ∠A?

3. What is the complement of ∠A?

4. What is the supplement of ∠A?

5. Draw line f through point B, making a right angle with $\overrightarrow{AB}$.

2. acute angle (less than 90°)

3. 50° (40° + 50° = 90°)

4. 140° (40° + 140° = 180°)

5.

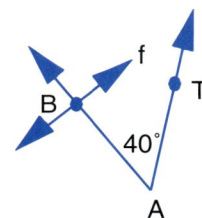

Problem 6:   For each time given below,

1) 2:00   2) 8:00   3) 9:00   4) 12:30

    a) make a sketch of the angle formed by the hands of a clock.
    b) determine the number of degrees in the angle.
    c) determine if the angle is acute, obtuse, right, or straight.

Answers:

1)
a)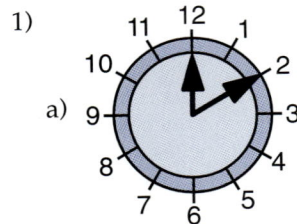

b) 60° (There is a 30° angle between two adjacent hour marks on a clock.)
c) acute angle

2)
a)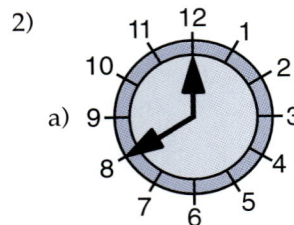

b) 120°
c) obtuse angle

3)
a)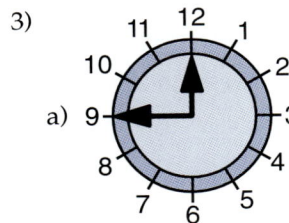

b) 90°
c) right angle

4)
a)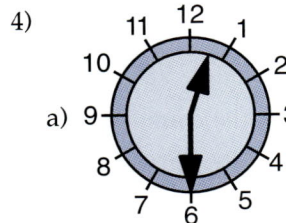

b) 165°
c) obtuse angle

Exercise 8.2 Set A

In problems 1–8, draw and label a figure for each description.

1. Right angle, ∠BIT.

2. Acute angle, ∠FIT.

3. Obtuse angle, ∠HIT.

4. Straight angle, ∠KIT.

5. Plane F containing an acute angle, ∠LIT.

6. Plane G containing a right angle, ∠MIT.

7. Plane H containing a straight angle, ∠NIT.

8. Plane J containing an obtuse angle, ∠PIT.

In problems 9–12, classify ∠SIT as a right angle, straight angle, acute angle, or obtuse angle.

9. ∠SIT = 65°

10. ∠SIT = 117°

11. ∠SIT = 180°

12. ∠SIT = 90°

9. _____

10. _____

11. _____

12. _____

In problems 13–16, find the number of degrees in both the complement and supplement of ∠WIT.

13. ∠WIT = 45°

14. ∠WIT = 60°

15. ∠WIT = $22\frac{1}{2}°$

16. ∠WIT = 15.5°

13. _____

14. _____

15. _____

16. _____

In problems 17–18, find the angle between the minute and hour hands of a clock at:

17. 5:00

18. 11:00

17. _____

18. _____

Exercise 8.2 Set B

In problems 1–8, draw and label a figure for each description.

1. Right angle, ∠BAD.

2. Acute angle, ∠CAD.

3. Obtuse angle, ∠FAD.

4. Straight angle, ∠HAD.

5. Plane H containing an acute angle, ∠LAD.

6. Plane I containing a right angle, ∠MAD.

7. Plane J containing a straight angle, ∠PAD.

8. Plane K containing an obtuse angle, ∠RAD.

In problems 9–12, classify ∠SAD as a right angle, straight angle, acute angle, or obtuse angle.

9. ∠SAD = 43°

10. ∠SAD = 105°

11. ∠SAD = 90°

12. ∠SAD = 180°

9. _____

10. _____

11. _____

12. _____

In problems 13–16, find the number of degrees in both the complement and supplement of ∠TAD.

13. ∠TAD = 15°

14. ∠TAD = 30°

15. ∠TAD = $17\frac{1}{2}$°

16. ∠TAD = 30.5°

13. _____

14. _____

15. _____

16. _____

In problems 17–18, find the angle between the minute and hour hands of a clock at:

17. 11:30

18. 1:00

17. _____

18. _____

8.3 Triangles

A **triangle** is a figure that has three sides. A triangle is named by using the triangle symbol, △, followed by the letters of its three vertex points written in any order.

For example, △ABC or △BAC

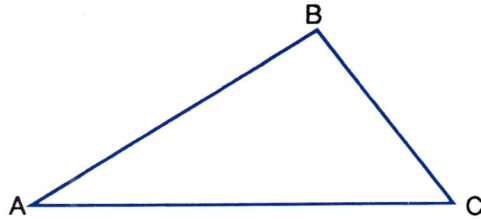

Its three vertices are A, B, C. Its three sides are AB, BC, CA. Its three angles are ∠A, ∠B, ∠C.

A cute triangle

Types of Triangles

One way to classify triangles is by the lengths of the sides, as shown below.

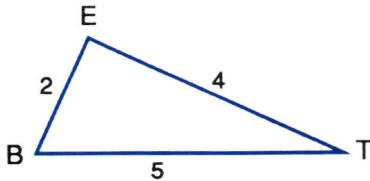

A **scalene triangle** is a triangle in which each side has a different length.

In △BET, no two sides are equal.
△BET is a scalene triangle.

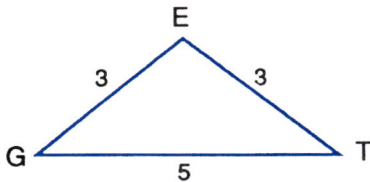

An **isosceles triangle** is a triangle that has two sides of equal length.

In △GET, two sides are equal: EG = ET.
△GET is an isosceles triangle.

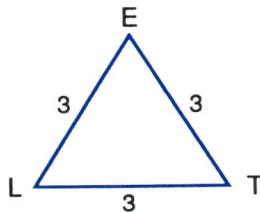

An **equilateral triangle** is a triangle with all three sides equal.

In △LET, all sides are equal: LE = ET = LT.
△LET is an equilateral triangle.

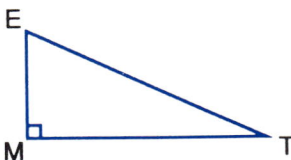

Triangles are also classified by the size of their angles. A **right triangle** is a triangle that has one right angle.

In △MET, ∠M = 90°
△MET is a right triangle.

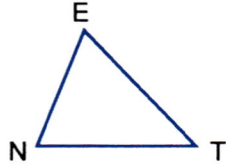

An **acute triangle** is a triangle in which each angle measures less than 90°.

In △NET, ∠N, ∠E, and ∠T are all less than 90°.
△NET is an acute triangle.

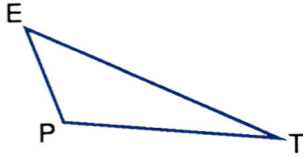

An **obtuse triangle** is a triangle in which one angle measures more than 90°.

In △PET, ∠P is larger than 90°.
△PET is an obtuse triangle.

Problem 1:   Name the three triangles in the figure below.

Answers:
△BAD, △BDC, △BAC

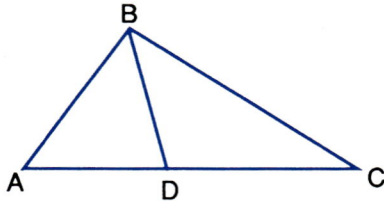

Problem 2:   Classify the triangles below as acute, right, or obtuse.

Answers:
△SET—obtuse
△VET—right
△WET—acute

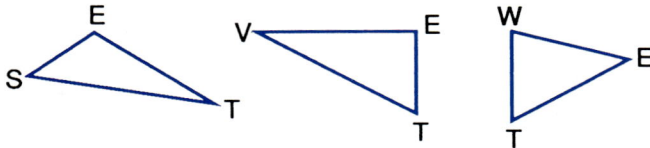

Problem 3:   Classify the triangles below as scalene, isosceles, or equilateral.

Answers:
△XET—isosceles
△YET—scalene
△ZET—equilateral

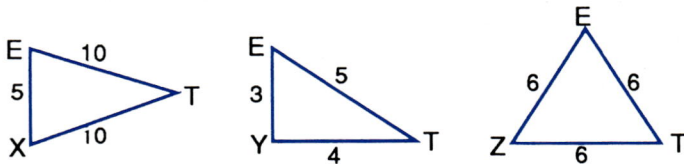

Name _____   Date _____

Exercise 8.3 Set A

In problems 1–4, draw and label a figure for each description.

1. Right triangle, △LAW, with ∠W the right angle.   2. Obtuse triangle, △SON, with ∠S the obtuse angle.

3. Isosceles triangle, △FUN, with side UN the unequal side.   4. Equilateral triangle, △MUT.

In problems 5–6, name all the different triangles in each figure.

5. 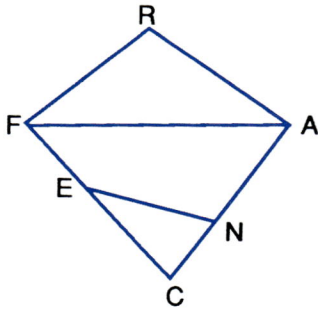   6.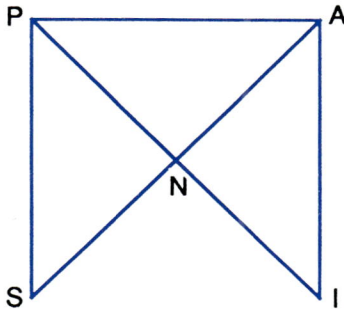

5. _____

6. _____

In problems 7–10, classify the following triangles as acute, right, or obtuse.

7.    8.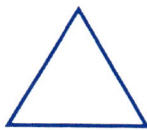

9.    10.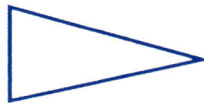

7. _____

8. _____

9. _____

10. _____

In problems 11–14, classify the following triangles as scalene, isosceles, or equilateral.

11. 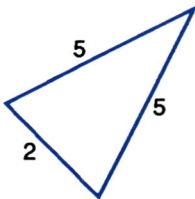   12.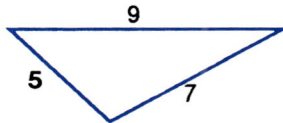

13. 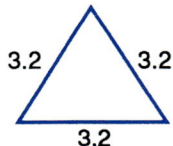   14.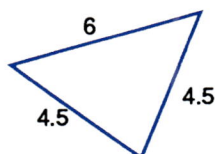

11. _____

12. _____

13. _____

14. _____

Exercise 8.3 Set B

In problems 1–4, draw and label a figure for each description.

1. Acute triangle, △POT.

2. Equilateral triangle, △CUP.

3. Right triangle, △PAN, with ∠P the right angle.

4. Isosceles triangle, △LID, with side $\overline{ID}$ the unequal side.

In problems 5–6, name all the different triangles in each figure.

5.

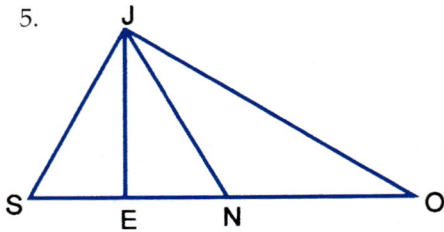

6.

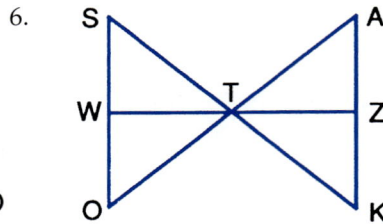

5. _____

6. _____

In problems 7–10, classify the following triangles as acute, right, or obtuse.

7.

8.

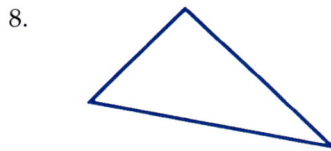

9.

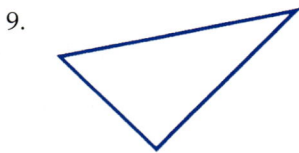

10.

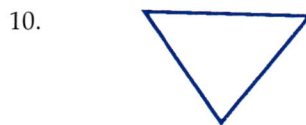

7. _____

8. _____

9. _____

10. _____

In problems 11–14, classify the following triangles as scalene, isosceles, or equilateral.

11.

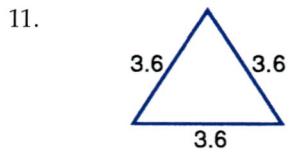

12.

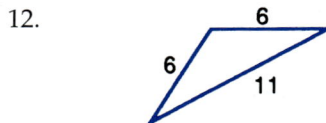

13.

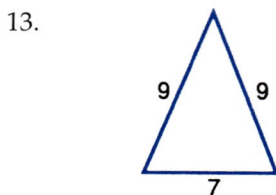

14.

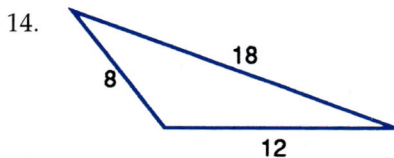

11. _____

12. _____

13. _____

14. _____

8.4 Quadrilaterals and Circles

There are many other geometric shapes besides those discussed in the first three sections of this chapter. In this section, we will limit our investigation to some very common ones: quadrilaterals and circles. Quadrilaterals and circles are examples of **plane figures**, 2-dimensional objects that can be contained in a plane.

Quadrilaterals

Quadrilaterals are four-sided plane figures. Its sides are line segments that meet at four vertices forming four angles. A quadrilateral is named by placing upper-case letters at its vertices and writing these letters as they appear in either a clockwise or counter clockwise direction. Four types of quadrilaterals are displayed below. A **rectangle** is a quadrilateral with four right angles. A **square** is a quadrilateral with four right angles and four equal sides. A **trapezoid** is a quadrilateral that has one pair of parallel sides. A **parallelogram** is a quadrilateral that has both pairs of sides parallel.

Rectangle	**Square**	**Trapezoid**	**Parallelogram**

In rectangle IJKL, $\angle I = \angle J = \angle K = \angle L = 90°$

In square MNOP, $\angle M = \angle N = \angle O = \angle P = 90°$ and MN = NO = OP = PM

In trapezoid QRST, $\overline{QR} \parallel \overline{TS}$

In parallelogram UVWX, $\overline{UV} \parallel \overline{XW}$ and $\overline{UX} \parallel \overline{VW}$

Properties of Quadrilaterals

Some of the properties which these quadrilaterals possess are listed below.

1. Opposite sides of rectangles and parallelograms have the same length.

AB = DC
AD = BC

2. **Diagonals** (line segments connecting nonadjacent vertices) of rectangles and squares have the same length.

AC = DB

3. Opposite angles of a parallelogram have the same measure.

$\angle$**A** = $\angle$**C**
$\angle$**D** = $\angle$**B**

Example 1

Draw parallelogram EFGH so that its shape makes it clear that the diagonals are not equal in length.

In parallelogram EFGH, the diagonals are not equal: EG > FH.

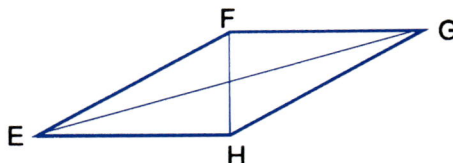

Circles

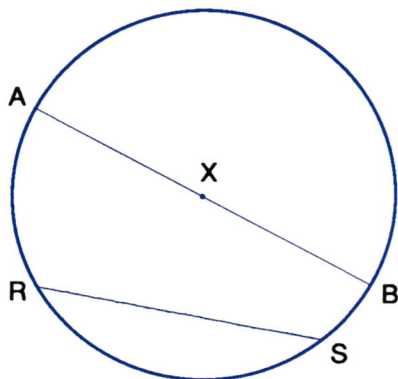

Another very common geometric shape is the circle. A **circle** is a plane figure that consists of all points that are the same distance away from a center point. Any line segment with one endpoint at the center and the other endpoint on the circle is a **radius** of the circle. A line segment that has both of its endpoints on the circle is a **chord** of the circle. If a chord passes through the center of the circle, it is a **diameter** of the circle.

In the circle on the left,
  X is its center,
  $\overline{XA}$ and $\overline{XB}$ are radii,
  $\overline{AB}$ and $\overline{RS}$ are chords,
  $\overline{AB}$ is a diameter.

A diameter actually consists of two radii. We can express this fact in two ways. The diameter (**D**) of the circle is twice the radius (**r**) or the radius is one-half the diameter of the circle.

$$D = 2r \text{ or } r = \frac{D}{2}$$

Problems: Using the circle below with O its center,

1. List all radii and diameters.

2. List all chords.

3. If OA = 7, how long is $\overline{OY}$?

4. If PA = 17, how long is $\overline{OP}$?

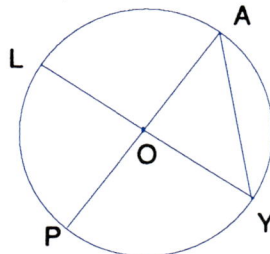

Answers:

1. radii: $\overline{OP}, \overline{OL}, \overline{OA}, \overline{OY}$
   diameters: $\overline{PA}, \overline{LY}$
2. Chords: $\overline{PA}, \overline{LY}, \overline{AY}$

3. OY = 7
   (All radii of a circle are equal.)
4. OP = 8.5
   (A radius is half the diameter.)

Exercise 8.4 Set A

In problems 1–10, sketch and label each plane figure described.

1. Rectangle FDIC.

2. Square FICA.

3. Trapezoid USMC with $\overline{US} \parallel \overline{CM}$.

4. Quadrilateral USAF with no two sides having equal lengths.

5. Parallelogram YMCA with $\angle Y$ acute.

6. Parallelogram YWCA with $\angle Y$ obtuse.

7. Trapezoid NYSE with no two sides having equal lengths.

8. Trapezoid DISN with unequal diagonals.

9. Circle with center T, radius $\overline{TV}$, and chord $\overline{VC}$.

10. Circle with center M, diameter $\overline{RX}$, and chord $\overline{VP}$.

For problems 11–16, use the circle below with center at E.

11. List all radii.

12. List all diameters.

13. List all chords.

14. If ED = 4, find EA.

15. If EN = 5, find DN.

16. If DN = 13, find EI.

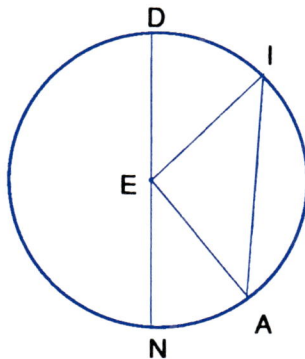

11. _____

12. _____

13. _____

14. _____

15. _____

16. _____

Exercise 8.4 Set B

In problems 1–10, sketch and label each plane figure described.

1. Square OPEC.

2. Rectangle NATO.

3. Trapezoid UCLA with ∠U a right angle.

4. Quadrilateral USAF with two adjacent sides of equal length.

5. Quadrilateral UNLV that has no parallel sides.

6. Parallelogram YWCA with diagonal $\overline{YC}$ longer than diagonal $\overline{WA}$.

7. Trapezoid ESPN with diagonals having equal lengths.

8. Trapezoid AMEX with a pair of opposite sides having equal lengths.

9. Circle with center Y and diameters $\overline{DA}$ and $\overline{US}$.

10. Circle with center F, radius $\overline{FT}$, and diameter $\overline{DT}$.

For problems 11–16, use the circle below with center at A.

11. List all radii.

12. List all diameters.

13. List all chords.

14. If AE = 5, find AD.

15. If AE = 4, find FE.

16. If FE = 25, find AD.

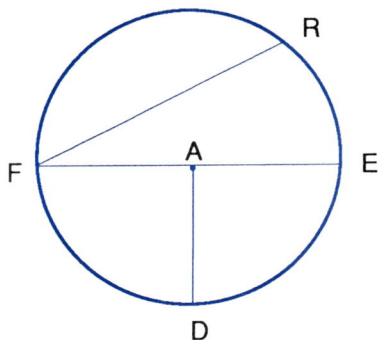

11. _____

12. _____

13. _____

14. _____

15. _____

16. _____

8.5 Polygons and Their Angles

Polygon

The triangles and quadrilaterals studied in previous sections are examples of a class of geometric figures called polygons. A **polygon** is a closed plane figure formed by line segments that intersect each other only at their endpoints. Some common polygons are shown in the chart below:

Sides	Name	A	B
3	triangle		
4	quadrilateral		
5	pentagon		
6	hexagon		
8	octagon		

A polygon is classified by the number of sides it has. Further, if all the sides of a polygon have the same length and all its angles have the same measure, it is a **regular polygon**. In the chart above, column B shows some common regular polygons.

Example 1

Stop signs are examples of what type of polygon?

Since stop signs have eight sides of equal length and eight angles that have the same measure, they are examples of regular octagons.

Example 2

What special name is given to a regular triangle?

A triangle with equal angles and equal sides is called an equilateral triangle.

The Angles of Polygons

The angles of polygons have a unique property. The sum of the angles for each type of polygon is always the same. For example, if you add up the measures of the three angles of any triangle, the result is always 180°. No matter what shape the triangle has, the sum of its angles is always 180°.

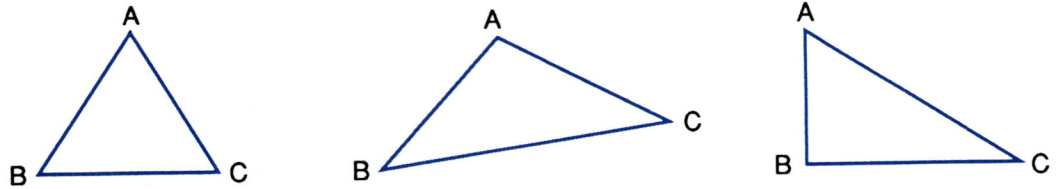

In each triangle, ∠A + ∠B + ∠C = 180°.

The fact that the sum of the angles of a triangle equals 180° can be visually verified by examining the figures below. If you fold sections of ΔABC on the left along the dotted lines in the direction of the given arrows, you get the figure on the right.

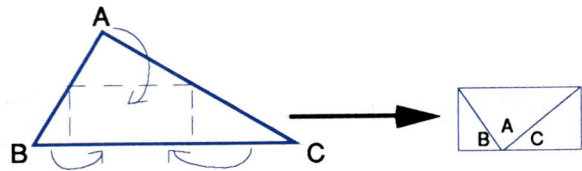

In the figure on the right, you will notice that together ∠A, ∠B, and ∠C form a straight angle. Since straight angles measure 180°, it follows that ∠A + ∠B + ∠C = 180°. We can use this fact to determine the sum of the angles for other polygons. Any polygon can be covered with non-overlapping triangles and the number of triangles can be used to calculate the sum of its angles.

Sides		Triangles	Sum of Angles
4		2	180°(2) = 360°
5		3	180°(3) = 540°
6		4	180°(4) = 720°

If you study the information above, you will notice that there is a relationship between the number of sides and the number of triangles that cover each polygon. The number of triangles is 2 less than the number of sides. Thus, if we have n-sides, we have $(n - 2)$ triangles and the sum of the angles of the polygon (S) can be determined by the formula $S = 180°(n - 2)$.

Further, if the polygon is a regular polygon, all of its angles have the same measure. Therefore, to find the measure of each angle of a regular polygon, you can simply divide the sum of its angles by the number of angles (sides) in the polygon. The following boxes highlight the formulas needed to determine angles of polygons.

Sum of the Angles of a Polygon

$$S = 180°(n - 2) \quad \text{where} \quad \begin{cases} S = \text{sum of its angles} \\ n = \text{number of sides} \end{cases}$$

Each Angle of a Regular Polygon

$$E.A. = \frac{S}{n} \quad \text{where} \quad \begin{cases} E.A. = \text{each angle} \\ S = \text{sum of its angles} \\ n = \text{number of sides} \end{cases}$$

Example 3

Find the sum of the angles of an octagon by a) showing non-overlapping triangles covering the polygon and b) using the formula.

a) There are 6 non-overlapping triangles that cover an eight-sided polygon. So, the sum of its angles = $180°(6) = 1080°$.

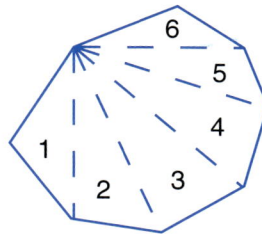

b) Since $n = 8$, using the sum of the angles formula, we get
$S = 180°(n - 2)$
$\quad = 180°(8 - 2)$
$\quad = 180°(6)$
$\quad = 1080°$

Example 4

If the octagon in Example 3 is a regular polygon (the shape of a STOP sign), what is the measure of each angle?

Each angle is 135°.

$$E.A. = \frac{S}{n} = \frac{1080°}{8} = 135°$$

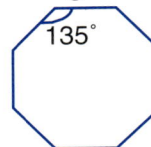

135°

Problem 1: Make a sketch of a regular pentagon, determine the sum of its angles, and find the measure of each of its angles.

Answers:

$$S = 180°(n - 2)$$
$$= 180°(5 - 2)$$
$$= 180°(3) = 540°$$

$$E.A. = \frac{S}{n} = \frac{540}{5}$$

$$= 108°$$

Problem 2: Determine the measure of each angle of a regular 20-sided polygon.

Answer:

$$S = 180°(n - 2)$$
$$= 180°(20 - 2)$$
$$= 180°(18)$$
$$= 3240°$$

$$E.A. = \frac{S}{n} = \frac{3240°}{20}$$

$$= 162°$$

Problem 3: What shape do bees create in making their honey combs? What is the sum the angles and each angle of that shape?

Answers: Regular hexagons

$$S = 180°(n - 2)$$
$$= 180°(6-2)$$
$$= 180°(4) = 720°$$

$$E.A. = \frac{S}{n} = \frac{720°}{6} = 120°$$

8.6 Plane Figures: Perimeters and Areas

The famous English knight: Sir Cumference

The plane figures studied in the previous sections can be measured in two ways. In this section, we will investigate how to find perimeters and areas of some common plane figures.

Perimeter

A **perimeter** gives the measure around an object. To find the perimeter of a plane figure, you must find the length of the boundary of the figure. If a figure has line segments as sides, you add up the lengths of the sides to find the perimeter (*P*).

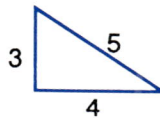

$P = 3+4+5$
$= 12$

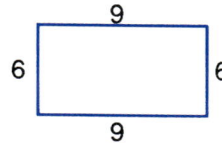

$P = 6+9+6+9$
$= 30$

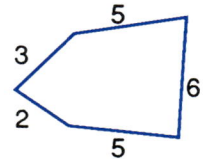

$P = 2+3+5+6+5$
$= 21$

Even though the perimeter of many plane figures can be found by simply adding up the lengths of segments, formulas are frequently used to find the perimeters. In figures that are not made up of line segments, such as circles, you can not find the distance around the object by simply adding the lengths of segments. To find the distance around a circle, its **circumference,** we introduce the number **pi,** π. Pi is approximately equal to 3.14 and is obtained by dividing the circumference (*C*) of a circle by its diameter (*D*) ($\pi = C/D \approx 3.14$). Using pi, the formula for the circumference of a circle with a radius *r* is $C = 2\pi r$. Further, for triangles with sides *a*, *b*, and *c*, rectangles with length (*l*) and width (*w*), and squares with sides (*s*), their perimeter (*P*) formulas are as follows:

Triangle

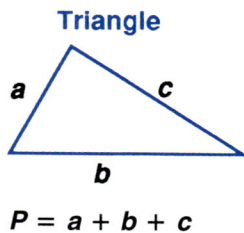

$P = a + b + c$

Rectangle

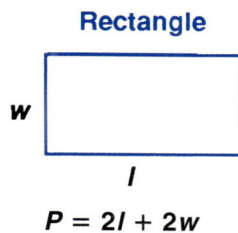

$P = 2l + 2w$

Square

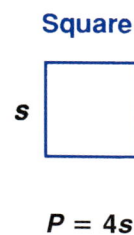

$P = 4s$

Circle

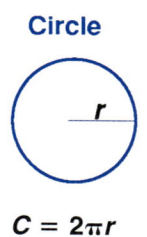

$C = 2\pi r$

Area

The **area** of a plane figure gives a measure of the interior of the figure. The area tells us how many non-overlapping squares of a given size are needed to completely fill the interior of a plane figure. Areas are measured in square units such as square inches (sq in.), square feet (sq ft), square meters (sq m), or square centimeters (sq cm). If you count the number of 1 cm by 1 cm squares covering the 2 cm by 6 cm rectangle below, you will see that it has an area of 12 sq cm.

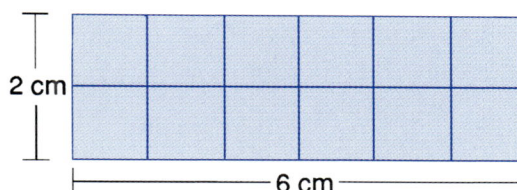

Area = 12 sq cm

To find areas of plane figures, you could simply cover the interior with squares and count the number of squares. There are, however, some formulas that can be used to determine the area of common plane figures. These formulas use length (l), width (w), side (s), base (b), height (h), and radius (r).

Rectangle	Square	Triangle	Parallelogram	Circle
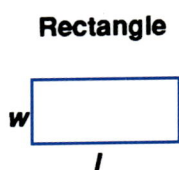	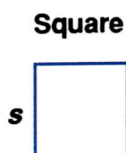	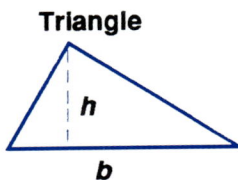	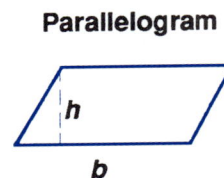	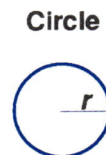
$A = lw$	$A = s^2$	$A = \dfrac{1}{2}bh$	$A = bh$	$A = \pi r^2$

Note: The base of a triangle or parallelogram can be any side of the triangle or parallelogram. However, the height of a triangle is the shortest distance from the vertex that is not on the base to the line containing the base. The height of a parallelogram is the shortest distance between the base and the side parallel to the base.

Example 1

Find the perimeter and area of the square.

Perimeter: $P = 4s$
$\qquad = 4(3) = 12$ m

Area: $A = s^2$
$\qquad = 3^2 = 9$ sq m

3 m

Example 2

Find the perimeter and area of the triangle.

Perimeter: $P = a + b + c$
$\qquad = 5 + 6 + 5 = 16$ in.

Area: $A = \dfrac{1}{2}bh$

$\qquad = \dfrac{1}{2}(6)(4) = 12$ sq in.

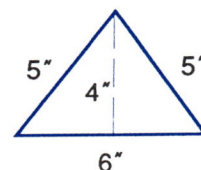

Example 3

Find the circumference and area of the circle shown below.

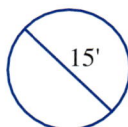

To find the circumference and area, we need the radius of the circle. Since the radius is one-half the diameter, $r = \dfrac{15}{2} = 7.5$.

Circumference: $C = 2\pi r$
$\qquad = 2(3.14)(7.5) = 47.1$ ft

Area: $A = \pi r^2$
$\qquad = (3.14)(7.5)^2$
$\qquad = (3.14)(56.25) = 176.625$ sq ft

Example 4

A circle is inscribed in a square. Find a) the perimeter of the square and b) the area of the shaded region between the square and the circle.

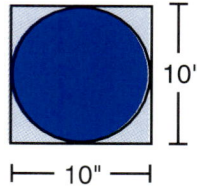

Perimeter: The square has sides of 10″ each.
$$P = 4s = 4(10) = 40 \text{ in.}$$

Area of shaded region: To find this area, determine the area of the square and subtract the area of the circle. The square has sides (s) of 10″. The circle has a diameter of 10″, so its radius (r) is 5″.

Square: $A = s^2$
$$= 10^2 = 100 \text{ sq in.}$$

Circle: $A = \pi r^2$
$$= 3.14(5)^2 = 78.5 \text{ sq in.}$$

Shaded region : $A = 100 - 78.5 = 21.5$ sq in.

Problem 1: A Norman window consists of a rectangle and a semi-circle (half-circle). What is the perimeter and area of the Norman Window shown below?

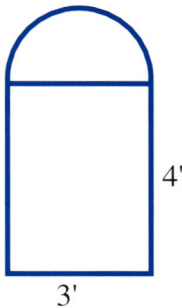

Answers: $P = 15.51$ ft
$A = 15.53$ sq ft

Rectangle:
$$P = 4 + 3 + 4 = 11 \text{ ft}$$
$$A = lw = 4(3) = 12 \text{ sq ft}$$

Circle:

$$C = \tfrac{1}{2}(2\pi r)$$
$$= \tfrac{1}{2}(2(3.14)(1.5))$$
$$= 4.71$$
$$A = \tfrac{1}{2}(\pi r^2)$$
$$= \tfrac{1}{2}(3.14(1.5)^2)$$
$$\approx 3.53$$

Totals:
$$P = 11 + 4.71 = 15.71 \text{ ft}$$
$$A = 12 + 3.53$$
$$= 15.53 \text{ sq ft}$$

Problem 2:   The sails on a yacht are shown below. How many square feet of sail does the yacht have?

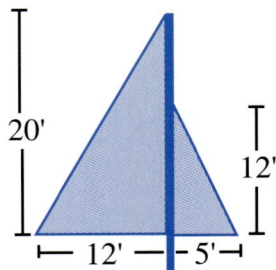

Answer: A = 150 sq ft

For each triangle:

$A = \frac{1}{2}bh$

$= \frac{1}{2}(12)(20)$

$= 120$ sq ft

$A = \frac{1}{2}bh$

$= \frac{1}{2}(5)(12)$

$= 30$ sq ft

Total: $120 + 30 = 150$ sq ft

Problem 3:   The front of a cabin is picture below. If the windows and the door are not included, how many square feet does it contain?

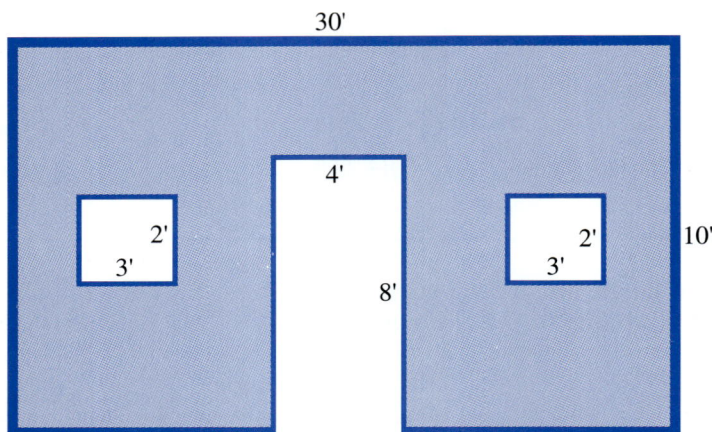

Answer: 256 sq ft

Windows/door: $A = lw$

$A = 3(2) + 3(2) + 8(4)$
$= 44$ sq ft

Entire Front: $A = lw$

$A = 30(10)$
$= 300$ sq ft

Answer:

$300 - 44 = 256$ sq ft

Problem 4:   In the front of the above cabin, find the amount of molding needed to frame the windows and the door.

Answer: 40 ft

Each window:

$P = 2l + 2w$
$= 2(3) + 2(2) = 10$

Door: (molding on only three sides

$P = 2l + w$
$= 2(8) + 4 = 20$

Total: $10 + 10 + 20 = 40$ ft

Name _____   Date _____

Exercise 8.6 Set A

Find the perimeters and areas of the following:

1. A rectangle with 5′ and 9′ sides. 2. A rectangle with 4′ and 7′ sides.

    1. _____

    2. _____

3. A square with $8\frac{1}{2}$ inch sides. 4. A square with $11\frac{1}{2}$ inch sides.

    3. _____

    4. _____

5. A circle with a 6.7 cm radius. 6. A circle with an 8.3 cm radius.

    5. _____

    6. _____

7. The triangle below. 8. The triangle below.

    7. _____

    8. _____

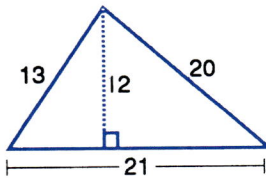
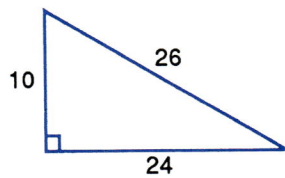

9. The parallelogram below. 10. The parallelogram below.

    9. _____

    10. _____

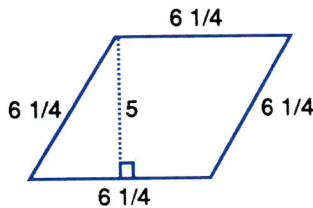
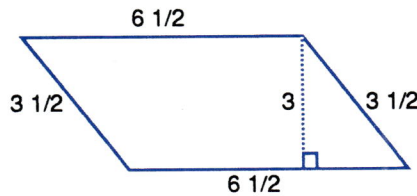

11. The half-circle below. 12. The half-circle below.

    11. _____

    12. _____

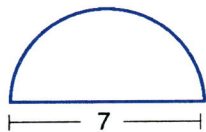

13. The trapezoid below. 14. The trapezoid below.

    13. _____

    14. _____

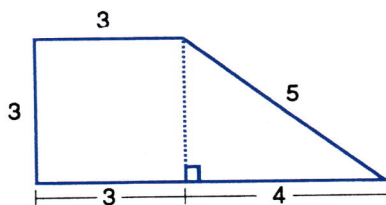
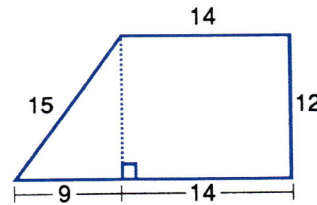

Exercise 8.6 Set B

Find the perimeters and areas of the following:

1. A rectangle with 5 cm and 8 cm sides.

2. A rectangle with 6 cm and 9 cm sides.

3. A square with $6\frac{1}{4}$ inch sides.

4. A square with $11\frac{1}{4}$ inch sides.

5. A circle with a 12.7 m radius.

6. A circle with a 15.6 m radius.

7. The triangle below.

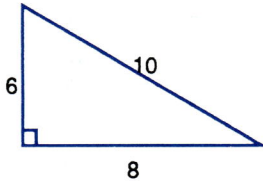

8. The triangle below.

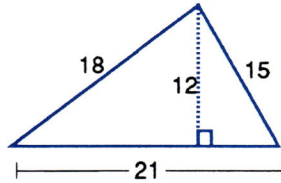

9. The parallelogram below.

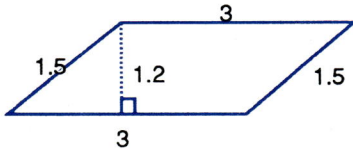

10. The parallelogram below.

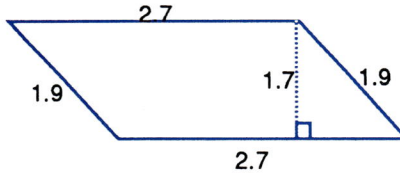

11. The quarter-circle below.

12. The quarter-circle below.

13. The pentagon below.

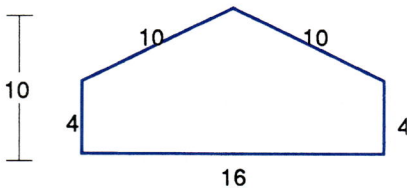

14. The pentagon below.

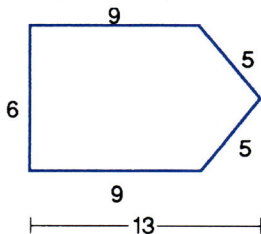

1. _____

2. _____

3. _____

4. _____

5. _____

6. _____

7. _____

8. _____

9. _____

10. _____

11. _____

12. _____

13. _____

14. _____

8.7 Three Dimensional Objects: Surface Areas and Volumes

Dragging this sphere is no ball!

In addition to geometric objects that can be drawn in a plane, there are objects that are three-dimensional. They occupy space and can not be contained in a plane. Some of these common three-dimensional (3-D) objects are cubes, boxes, cylinders, and spheres.

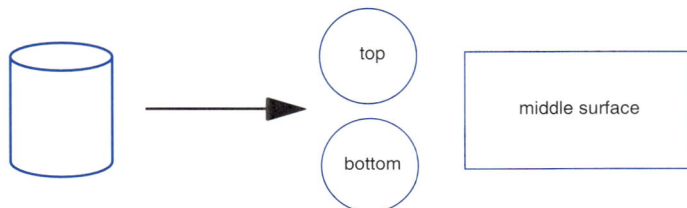

CUBE   **BOX**   **CYLINDER**   **SPHERE**

Each of these 3-dimensional objects has unique geometric properties. The **cube** has 8 corner points (vertices) and 6 equal square faces. The line segments that join its vertices form the cube's 12 edges.

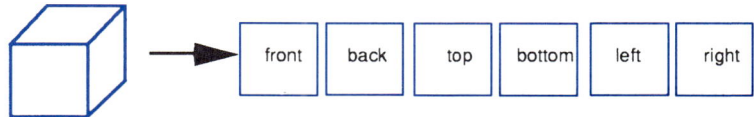

| front | back | top | bottom | left | right |

The **box** also has 8 vertices, 6 faces, and 12 edges, but its faces consist of 6 rectangles where the front is the same as the back, the top is the same as the bottom, and the face on the left side is the same as the one on the right.

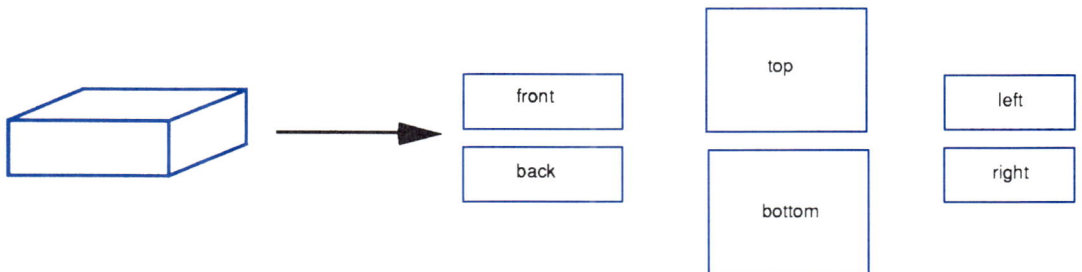

The **right cylinder** has equal circles on the top and the bottom. The middle surface makes a right angle with the top and bottom of the right cylinder. If the right cylinder is unrolled, the surface in the middle would form a rectangle.

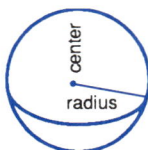

Each point on a **sphere** is the same distance from the point in the center of the sphere. Any line segment connecting a point on the sphere to this center point is a radius of the sphere.

In this section, we will investigate ways to measure these objects. We will find their surface areas and volumes.

Surface Area

The **surface area** of a 3-dimensional object gives a measure of the outside of the object. The surface area tells us how many non overlapping squares of a given size are needed to cover the object. A surface area of a 3-dimensional object is determined by finding the sum of the areas of each face or surface of the object. As with areas of other objects studied in this chapter, surface areas are measured in square units.

$S = 6e^2$

The **cube:** The surface area of a cube can be determined by finding the sum of the areas of its six square faces. Thus, if the length of an edge of the cube is e, the area of each of its square faces is $e \times e$ or e^2 and the surface area of the cube is $S = 6e^2$.

Example 1

Find the surface area of a cube that has 6.5 cm edges.

Using the formula for the surface area of a cube ($S = 6e^2$) with $e = 6.5$ cm, we get the following:

$$S = 6e^2$$
$$= 6(6.5)^2$$
$$= 6(42.25)$$
$$= 253.5 \text{ sq cm}$$

h $S = 2lw + 2lh + 2wh$ l w

The **box:** To determine the surface area of a box, find the sum of the areas of the six rectangular faces of the box. Since the top equals the bottom, front equals the back, and left equals the right side, the formula for the surface area of a box is $S = 2lw + 2lh + 2wh$.

Example 2

Find the surface area of a storage box that measures 13 ft by 7 ft by 4 ft.

When dimensions of a box are given, the width and the length are usually given first and the height is given last. Thus, in this box, we can use $l = 13$, $w = 7$, and $h = 4$. Its surface area is as follows:

$$S = 2lw + 2lh + 2wh$$
$$= 2(13)(7) + 2(13)(4) + 2(7)(4)$$
$$= 182 + 104 + 56$$
$$= 342 \text{ sq ft}$$

h $S = 2\pi r^2 + 2\pi rh$

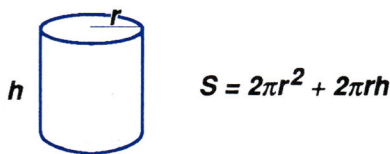

The **right cylinder:** To determine the surface area of a right cylinder, find the areas of the circles on its top and bottom and the rectangle created by the surface in the middle of the right cylinder. If a right cylinder has circles with radius (r), the area of each circle is $A = \pi r^2$. If the right cylinder has a height (h), the rectangle from the middle section will have a height (h) and a length equal to the circumference of the top or bottom circle, $C = 2\pi r$.

Thus, the surface area of a right cylinder is $S = 2\pi r^2 + 2\pi rh$.

Example 3

A soft drink can is about 12 cm tall and the top of the can has a diameter of 6.5 cm. Find the approximate surface area of the can.

Since a can is a right cylinder, we can use $h = 12$ and $r = 3.25$ (one-half of the diameter) in the formula for the surface area of a right cylinder and get the following:

$$S = 2\pi r^2 + 2\pi rh$$
$$= 2(3.14)(3.25)^2 + 2(3.14)(3.25)(12)$$
$$= 2(3.14)(10.5625) + 2(3.14)(3.25)(12)$$
$$= 66.3325 + 244.92$$
$$= 311.2525 \approx 311.25 \text{ sq cm}$$

$S = 4\pi r^2$

The **sphere:** The formula to determine the surface area of a sphere is given by $S = 4\pi r^2$ where r is the radius of the sphere.

Example 4

The earth has the approximate shape of a sphere with an average radius of 3959 miles. Find the surface area of the earth.

Using $r = 3959$ in the surface area formula for a sphere, we get

$$S = 4\pi r^2$$
$$S = 4(3.14)(3959)^2$$
$$S = 4(3.14)(15,673,681)$$
$$S = 196,861,433.36 \text{ sq mi}$$

Formulas for Surface Areas

Cube: $S = 6e^2$ Box: $S = 2lw + 2lh + 2wh$

Right Cylinder: $S = 2\pi r^2 + 2\pi rh$ Sphere: $S = 4\pi r^2$

Volume

The volume of a 3-dimensional object gives us a measure of the inside of the object. The volume tells us how many cubes of a given size are needed to completely fill the object. Volume is measured in cubic units. For example, the box below has a volume of 6 cubic centimeters (6 cu cm), since it can be filled by six cubes with an edge of one centimeter.

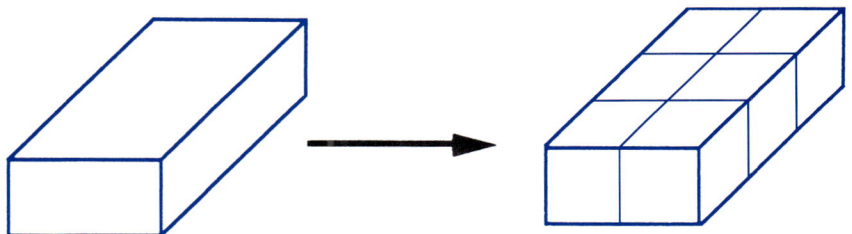

Just as there are formulas to calculate the surface areas of 3-dimensional objects, there are formulas to determine the volumes of cubes, boxes, right cylinders, and spheres. The formulas and examples of how to use them are given below.

The volume (V) formulas using edge (e), length (l), width (w), height (h), and radius (r) are as follows:

CUBE	BOX	RIGHT CYLINDER	SPHERE

$$V = e^3 \qquad V = lwh \qquad V = \pi r^2 h \qquad V = \frac{4}{3}\pi r^3$$

Example 5

Find the volume of a cube that has an edge that is 5 3/4 inches long. What does the answer tell us about the cube?

Using the volume formula for a cube, we get: $V = e^3$

$$= \left(5\frac{3}{4}\right)^3 = \left(\frac{23}{4}\right)^3$$

$$= \frac{12{,}167}{64}$$

$$= 190\frac{7}{64} \text{ cu in.}$$

The answer tells us that the cube can be completely filled with 190 cubes and $\frac{7}{64}$ of a cube that have one inch edges.

Example 6

A right cylindrical water tank has an inside radius of 5 ft and inside height of 12.5 ft. If the tank is full, can the water be transferred to an empty spherical tank with a radius of 6 ft?

For the cylinder,

$$V = \pi r^2 h$$

$$V = (3.14)(5)^2(12.5)$$

$$V = 981.25 \text{ cu ft}$$

For the sphere,

$$V = \frac{4}{3}\pi r^3$$

$$V = \frac{4}{3}(3.14)(6)^3$$

$$V = \frac{2712.96}{3} = 904.32 \text{ cu ft}$$

Examining the volume of both tanks shows that all the water will not fit in the spherical tank.

Problem 1:   Find the surface area and volume of the box shown below.

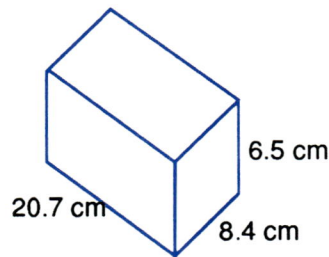

20.7 cm
6.5 cm
8.4 cm

Answers: $S = 726.06$ sq cm
$V = 1130.22$ cu cm

$S = 2lw + 2lh + 2wh$
$\quad = 2(20.7)(8.4) + 2(20.7)(6.5)$
$\quad\quad + 2(8.4)(6.5)$
$\quad = 726.06$ sq cm

$V = lwh$
$\quad = (20.7)(8.4)(6.5)$
$\quad = 1130.22$ cu cm

Problem 2:   Find the surface area and volume of a right cylinder with a diameter of 16 inches and a height of 10 inches.

Answers: $S = 904.32$ sq in.
$V = 2009.6$ cu in.

$r = \dfrac{D}{2} = \dfrac{16}{2} = 8$

$S = 2\pi r^2 + 2\pi rh$
$\quad = 2(3.14)(8^2) + 2(3.14)(8)(10)$
$\quad = 401.92 + 502.4$
$\quad = 904.32$ sq in.

$V = \pi r^2 h$
$\quad = 3.14(8^2)(10)$
$\quad = 2009.6$ cu in.

Problem 3:   A 20 foot length of water pipe with a diameter of 4 feet is filled with water. Since water weighs about 62.4 pounds per cubic foot, what is the weight of the water in the pipe.

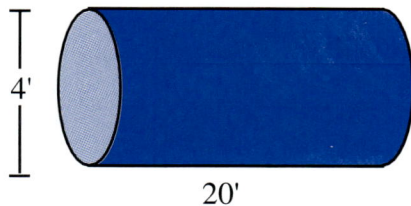

4'
20'

Answer: 15,674.88 lbs
Since the pipe is a cylinder, we get:

$V = \pi r^2 h$
$\quad = 3.14(2)^2(20)$
$\quad = 3.14(4)(20)$
$\quad = 251.2$ cu ft

$Wt = 251.2(62.4)$
$\quad = 15,674.88$ lbs

Problem 4:   A cement slab is 6 inches thick, 16 feet long, and 12 feet wide. How many cubic feet of cement does the slab contain?

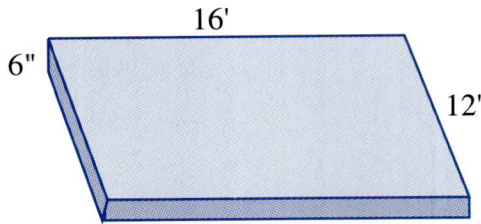

Answer:
The same unit (ft) should be used for the dimensions of the box. 6″ = 0.5 ft
$$V = lwh$$
$$= 16(12)(0.5)$$
$$= 192(0.5)$$
$$= 96 \text{ cu ft}$$

Problem 5:   The tanks (cube, cylinder, sphere) pictured below use 10 feet in its basic dimensions. Which of the three has the largest surface area?

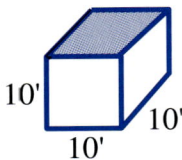

Answer: The cube

Cube:
$$S = 6e^2$$
$$= 6(10)^2$$
$$= 600 \text{ sq ft}$$

Cylinder:
$$S = 2\pi r^2 + 2\pi rh$$
$$= 2(3.14)(5)^2$$
$$+ 2(3.14)(5)(10)$$
$$= 471 \text{ sq ft}$$

Sphere:
$$S = 4\pi r^2$$
$$= 4(3.14)(5)^2$$
$$= 3.14 \text{ sq ft}$$

Problem 6:   Which of the three tanks in Problem 5 has the largest volume?

Answer: The cube

Cube:
$$V = e^3$$
$$= 10^3$$
$$= 1000 \text{ cu ft}$$

Cylinder:
$$V = \pi r^2 h$$
$$= 3.14(5)^2(10)$$
$$= 785 \text{ cu ft}$$

Sphere:
$$V = \tfrac{4}{3}\pi r^3$$
$$= \tfrac{4}{3}(3.14)(5)^3$$
$$\approx 523.33 \text{ cu ft}$$

Name _____ Date _____

Exercise 8.7 Set A

In problems 1–8, find the surface area and volume of each object.

1.

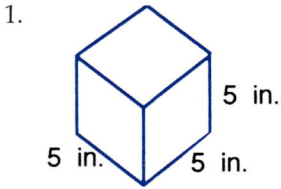

5 in.
5 in.   5 in.

2.

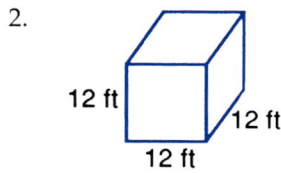

12 ft
12 ft
12 ft

1. _____

2. _____

3.

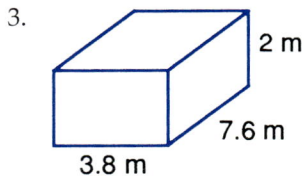

2 m
7.6 m
3.8 m

4.

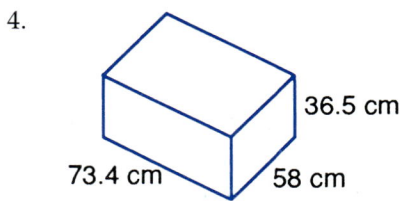

36.5 cm
73.4 cm   58 cm

3. _____

4. _____

5.

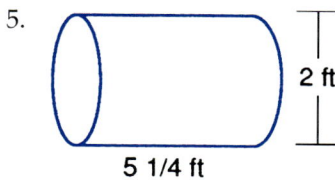

2 ft
5 1/4 ft

6.

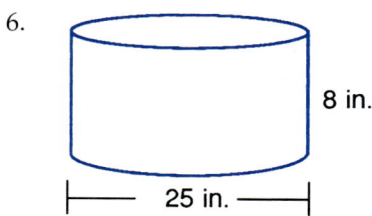

8 in.
25 in.

5. _____

6. _____

7.

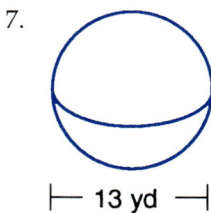

13 yd

8.

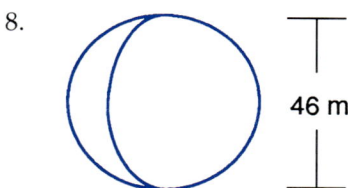

46 m

7. _____

8. _____

In problems 9–10, determine which tank holds more water.

9. A box with $w = 4.4$ ft, $l = 6.5$ ft, and $h = 3$ ft or a right cylinder with $r = 2.2$ ft and $h = 6.5$ ft.

9. _____

10. _____

10. A cube with $e = 8.6$ m or a sphere with $r = 5.4$ m.

In problems 11–12, use the fact that a cubic yard equals the volume of a cube with one yard edges,

11. to determine the number of cubic feet in a cubic yard.

11. _____

12. to determine the number of cubic inches in a cubic yard.

12. _____

Exercise 8.7 Set B

In problems 1–8, find the surface area and volume of each object.

1.

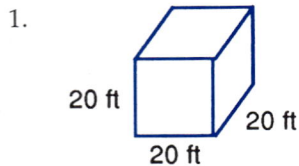

20 ft 20 ft 20 ft

2.

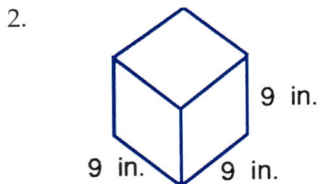

9 in. 9 in. 9 in.

1. _____

2. _____

3.

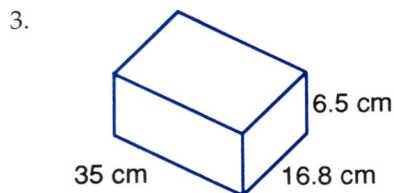

6.5 cm 35 cm 16.8 cm

4.

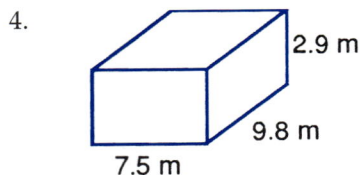

2.9 m 9.8 m 7.5 m

3. _____

4. _____

5.

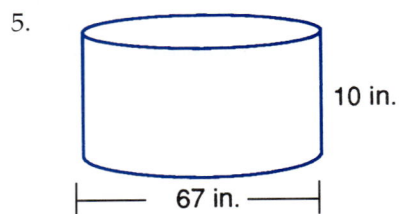

10 in. 67 in.

6.

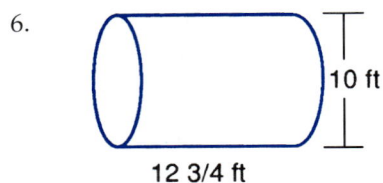

10 ft 12 3/4 ft

5. _____

6. _____

7.

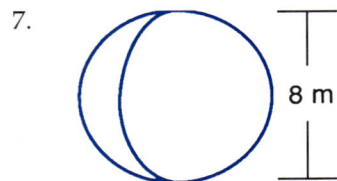

8 m

8.

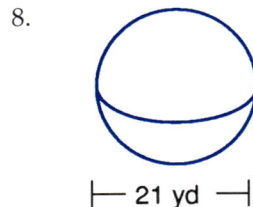

21 yd

7. _____

8. _____

In problems 9–10, determine which tank holds more water.

9. A box with $w = 3.5$ m, $l = 10.6$ m, and $h = 5$ m or a right cylinder with $r = 5.3$ m and $h = 2$ m.

9. _____

10. A cube with $e = 6.4$ ft or a sphere with $r = 3.9$ ft.

10. _____

In problems 11–12, use the fact that a cubic meter equals the volume of a cube with one meter edges,

11. to determine the number of cubic centimeters in a cubic meter.

11. _____

12. to determine the number of cubic millimeters in a cubic meter.

12. _____

8.8 The Pythagorean Theorem

Hypotenuse:

If you boil water in the Sierras, you'll have a high pot in use.

A study of geometry would not be complete without a look at one of the most famous facts of geometry, the **Pythagorean Theorem.** The Greek mathematician, Pythagoras (572–501 B.C.), is credited with proving that there is a relationship between the hypotenuse (longest side, opposite the 90° angle) and the legs (sides that make the 90° angle) of a right triangle. He showed that the areas of the squares drawn on each leg is equal to the area of the square drawn on the hypotenuse of the right triangle.

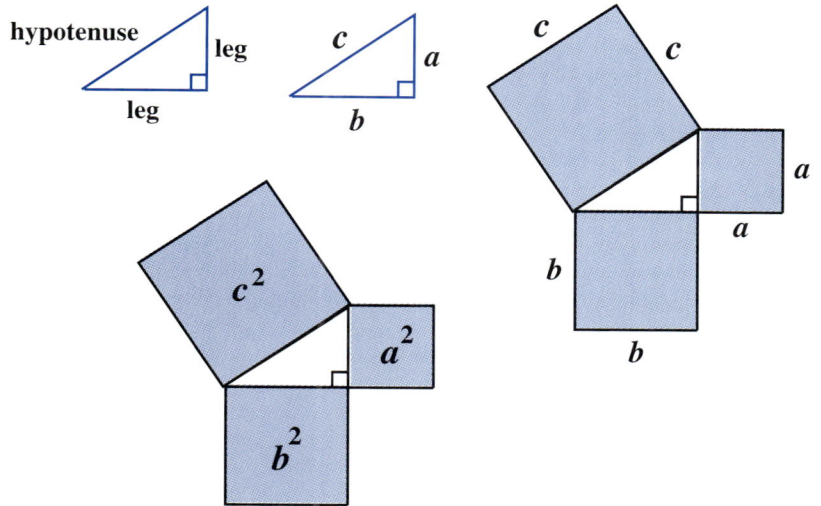

The relationship between the areas of the squares is usually stated in an algebraic form. In a right triangle, if the legs have lengths of *a* and *b* and the hypotenuse has a length of *c*, then

$$a^2 + b^2 = c^2$$

This formula can be used to find the length of a side of a right triangle when only two sides are known. For example, if the two legs of a right triangle are 3 and 4 respectively, how long is the hypotenuse of the right triangle?

In the formula, we can substitute 3 for *a* and 4 for *b* and leave *c* as an unknown amount. Solving this equation we get:

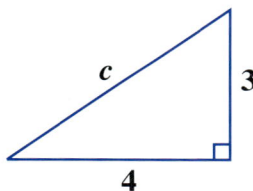

$a^2 + b^2 = c^2$ The Pythagorean Theorem
$3^2 + 4^2 = c^2$ replacing *a* with 3 and *b* with 4, $3^2 = 9$ and $4^2 = 16$
$9 + 16 = c^2$
$25 = c^2$
$5 = c$ since $5^2 = 25$.

$\left(\begin{array}{l}\text{Note: even though } (-5)^2 = 25,\\ c \neq -5 \text{ since the length of a}\\ \text{side of a triangle cannot be}\\ \text{negative.}\end{array}\right)$

In the last step of the previous equation, we concluded that $c = 5$ since $c^2 = 25$. Another way to get the positive solution is to conclude that if $c^2 = 25$, then $c = \sqrt{25} = 5$. In general, if

$$x^2 = n$$
$$x = \sqrt{n}$$

where x and n are positive.

For example, if

$$a^2 = 79$$
$$a = \sqrt{79}$$
$$a \approx 8.89$$

using a calculator and rounding off results to two decimal places.

Example 1

The hypotenuse of a right triangle is 13″ and one of its legs is 5″. How long is the other leg?

In the Pythagorean Theorem, let $c = 13$, $a = 5$, and solve for b.

$$a^2 + b^2 = c^2$$
$$5^2 + b^2 = 13^2 \qquad \text{letting } a = 5 \text{ and } c = 13.$$
$$25 + b^2 = 169 \qquad 5^2 = 25 \text{ and } 13^2 = 169.$$
$$\underline{-25 \qquad\quad -25} \qquad \text{subtracting from both sides.}$$
$$b^2 = 144$$
$$b = \sqrt{144}$$
$$= 12″ \qquad \text{taking the positive square root.}$$

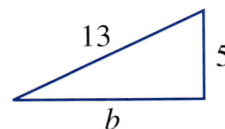

Problem 1: If both legs of a right triangle are 53′, how long is its hypotenuse?

Answer: 74.95′

$$a^2 + b^2 = c^2$$
$$53^2 + 53^2 = c^2$$
$$2809 + 2809 = c^2$$
$$5618 = c^2$$
$$\sqrt{5618} = c$$
$$74.95 \approx c$$

Problem 2: If the hypotenuse of a right triangle is 184.6 and one leg is 32.5. How long is the other leg?

Answer: 181.72

$$a^2 + b^2 = c^2$$
$$a^2 + 32.5^2 = 184.6^2$$
$$a^2 + 1056.25 = 34{,}077.16$$
$$a^2 = 33{,}020.91$$
$$a = \sqrt{33{,}020.91}$$
$$a \approx 181.72$$

Name _____   Date _____

Exercise 8.8 Set A

In problems 1–10, *a* and *b* are legs and *c* is the hypotenuse of a right triangle. You will need a calculator to find square roots.

1. $a = 6$, $b = 8$, find c.

1. _____

2. $a = 7$, $b = 24$, find c.

2. _____

3. $a = 9$, $c = 15$, find b.

3. _____

4. $a = 9$, $c = 41$, find b.

4. _____

5. $b = 3.9$, $c = 6.5$, find a.

5. _____

6. $b = 3.3$, $c = 6.5$, find a.

6. _____

7. $a = 8$, $b = 9$, find c.

7. _____

8. $a = 13$, $b = 13$, find c.

8. _____

9. $a = 24.3$, $c = 57.5$, find b.

9. _____

10. $b = 65.9$, $c = 84.4$, find a.

10. _____

In problems 11–13, find the value of x in each right triangle.

11.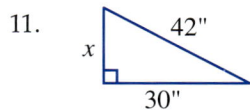

11. _____

12.

12. _____

13. _____

13.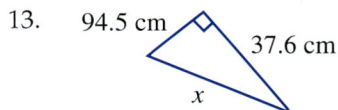

Exercise 8.8 Set B

In problems 1–10, a and b are legs and c is the hypotenuse of a right triangle. You will need a calculator to find square roots.

1. $a = 9$, $b = 12$, find c.

1. _____

2. $a = 8$, $b = 15$, find c.

2. _____

3. $a = 12$, $c = 20$, find b.

3. _____

4. $a = 12$, $c = 37$, find b.

4. _____

5. $b = 2.4$, $c = 5.1$, find a.

5. _____

6. $b = 2.4$, $c = 4.0$, find a.

6. _____

7. $a = 7$, $b = 8$, find c.

7. _____

8. $a = 17$, $b = 17$, find c.

8. _____

9. $a = 45.4$ $c = 92.6$, find b.

9. _____

10. $b = 32.7$, $c = 56.5$, find a.

10. _____

In problems 11–13, find the value of x in each right triangle.

11.

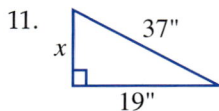

37"

x

19"

11. _____

12.

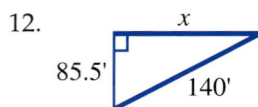

x

85.5'

140'

12. _____

13. 48.6 m

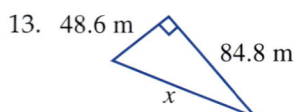

84.8 m

x

13. _____

8.9 Applications Involving Geometry

Analyze:
Don't believe her!
Anna lies!

In this section, we will investigate real-life applications involving perimeters, areas, volumes, and the Pythagorean Theorem.

Example 1

You are carpeting a room that is a rectangle measuring 12 ft by 15 ft. If the carpeting costs $24.99 a square yard and the pad costs $2.99 a square yard, how much will it cost for the carpet and the pad?

Analyze:

1. Since the carpet is being sold by the sq yd, convert the dimensions to yards by dividing by 3 (3 ft = 1 yd).
2. Determine the number of square yards needed by finding the area of the floor.
3. Find the cost of the carpet and pad by multiplying cost per sq yd by the number of square yards needed.
4. Find the total cost by adding the cost of carpet and pad.

Solve:

1. 12 ft by 15 ft = 4 yd by 5 yd

2. $A = lw$
   $= (4)(5) = 20$ sq yd

3. Carpet: $24.99(20) = $499.80
   Pad: $2.99(20) = $59.80

4. Total Cost:
   $499.80 + $59.80 = $559.60

Example 2

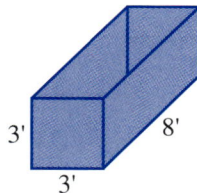

3'   8'

3'

The trough shown on the left is filled with water.
a) How many of gallons of water does it hold?
b) If the cows using the watering trough drink 32 gallons per day, in how many days will the trough be empty? (Note: 1 cu. ft ≈ 7.48 gal.)

Analyze:

1. To find the amount the trough holds, find its volume.

2. Convert the cu. ft to gal.

3. Since the cows drink 32 gallons per day, to find the number of days, divide the number of gallons in the trough by 32.

Solve:

1. $V = lwh$
   $= (3)(8)(3)$
   $= 72$ cu. ft

2. $72 \text{ cu. ft} \times \dfrac{7.48 \text{ gal}}{1 \text{ cu. ft}}$

   $= (72)(7.48) = 538.56$ gal

3. $538.56 \div 32 = 16.83$ days

   The trough will be empty in the 17th day.

Example 3

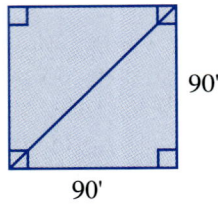

90'

90'

Consider a major league baseball diamond with 90 ft between bases. How long is the throw from homeplate to second base?

Analyze:

1. The triangle on the right side of the diamond is a right triangle so the Pythagorean Theorem applies with $a = b = 90$ and the hypotenuse unknown.

Solve:

1.
$$a^2 + b^2 = c^2$$
$$90^2 + 90^2 = c^2$$
$$8100 + 8100 = c^2$$
$$16{,}200 = c^2$$
$$\sqrt{16{,}200} = c$$
$$127.28 \text{ ft} \approx c$$

Example 4

The enamel used to paint a steel tank comes in one-gallon cans that cover 400 sq ft per gallon. How many full gallons of paint should you buy to paint a spherical tank with a 12 ft radius?

Analyze:

1. Find the surface area of the sphere.

2. Find the number of gallons needed by dividing the surface area by 400.

3. Since the paint comes in gallon cans, round off the amount to the next whole gallon.

Solve:

1. $S = 4\pi r^2$
$$= 4(3.14)(12)^2$$
$$= 1808.64 \text{ sq ft}$$

2. $1808.64 \div 400 = 4.5216$

3. $4.5216 \approx 5$ gallons

Example 5

A water tank is a right cylinder with an inside radius of 5 ft and an inside height of 12.5 ft. If the tank is full, find the weight of the water in the tank. (Note: water weighs 62.4 lbs per cu ft.)

Analyze:

1. We must first find the number of cubic feet in the tank by finding its volume.

2. Since each cubic foot of water weighs 62.4 lbs, we multiply the number of cubic feet of water in the tank by 62.4 to find the weight.

Solve:

1. $V = \pi r^2 h$
$$= 3.14(5)^2(12.5)$$
$$= 981.25 \text{ cu ft}$$

2. Weight $= 981.25(62.4)$
$$= 61{,}230 \text{ lbs}$$

Problem 1: You are painting the walls of a rectangular room that is 20 ft by 16 ft with 9 ft ceilings. If the paint comes in one-gallon cans that cover 350 sq ft and you don't subtract for windows or doors, how many gallons of paint should you buy?

Answer: 2 gallons

Area of walls to be painted:
Two walls are 9 by 20 and two walls are 9 by 16.

$$A = 2(9)(20) + 2(9)(16)$$
$$A = 648 \text{ sq ft}$$

Number of gallons:

$$648 \div 350 \approx 1.8514$$
$$\approx 2 \text{ gal}$$

Problem 2: A 16″ television means that the diagonal of the screen is 16 inches. If the one dimension of the screen is 10 inches, what is the other dimension?

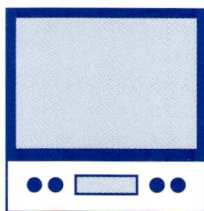

Answer: 12.5 in

The Pythagorean Theorem applies here ($c = 16$, $b = 10$).

$$a^2 + b^2 = c^2$$
$$a^2 + 10^2 = 16^2$$
$$a^2 + 100 = 256$$
$$a^2 = 156$$
$$a = \sqrt{156} \approx 12.5''$$

Problem 3: How much would it cost to fence-off a rectangular 56 ft by 70 ft area and plant the inside area with sod, if the fencing costs $3.95 a foot and the sod costs 49¢ a square foot?

Answer: $2916.20

Amount of fence needed:

$$P = 2l + 2w$$
$$= 2(56) + 2(70)$$
$$= 252 \text{ ft}$$

Amount of sod needed:

$$A = lw$$
$$= 56(70) = 3920 \text{ sq ft}$$

Total cost: (note: 49¢ = $0.49)

$$= 252(\$3.95) + 3920(\$0.49)$$
$$= \$995.40 + \$1920.80$$
$$= \$2916.20$$

Problem 4:

A right cylindrical oil tank has a radius of 5 ft and a height of 15 ft. A small hole at the bottom of the tank allows oil to leak out of the tank at a rate of 2.5 cu ft per day. At that rate, how long will it take for a full tank of oil to become empty?

Answer: 471 days

Volume of the tank:

$$V = \pi r^2 h$$
$$= 3.14(25)(15)$$
$$= 1177.5 \text{ cu. ft}$$

Number of days:

$$1177.5 \div 2.5 = 471$$

Problem 5:   The dimensions of a cement slab for a house are shown below. a) What is the square footage of the slab? b) If the slab is 6 inches thick, how many cubic feet of cement will the slab contain?

Answers: a) 2740 sq ft
                  b) 1370 cu. ft

The slab can be divided into three rectangles. Using, $A = lw$, we get:

$$A = (70)(30) + (20)(20) + (12)(20)$$
$$= 2740 \text{ sq ft}$$

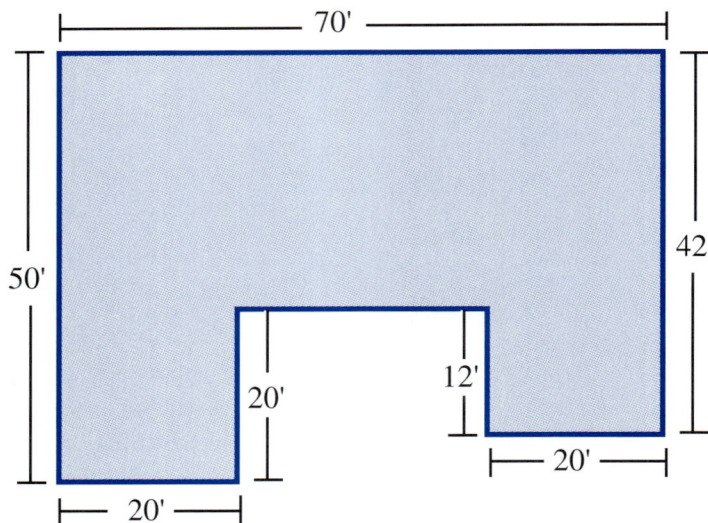

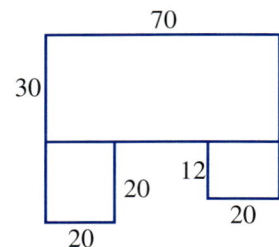

Find the volume ($V = lwh$) of the three rectangle sections using the above lengths and widths and a height of $6'' = 0.5$ ft.

$$V = (70)(30)(0.5) + (12)(20)(0.5)$$
$$+ (20)(20)(0.5) = 1370 \text{ cu. ft}$$

Name _____   Date _____

Exercise 8.9 Set A

1. If linoleum costs $11.99 a square yard, how much would it cost for the linoleum in a 9 ft by 15 ft kitchen?

1. _____

2. How much would it cost to carpet a 12' by 15' room if the complete cost for the carpet is $29.99 a square yard?

2. _____

3. You are building a dog run for your pedigree poodles on a rectangular 10' by 24' slab of cement. You are going to put a fence completely around the cement slab and cover the cement slab with Astro-Turf. If the fencing costs $5.19 a foot and the Astro-Turf costs $1.99 a square foot, what will the project cost you?

3. _____

4. A 32 ft guy wire is attached to a ring 20 ft up a vertical pole and anchored to a stake on level ground. How from the base of the pole is the stake placed?

4. _____

5. In softball the bases are 60 feet apart. How far is the throw from third base to first base?

5. _____

6. If mirror tile cost $1.59 a square foot, what is the minimum amount of one foot square tiles you would need and how much would it cost to tile a rectangular strip of wall that is 3.5' by 8'?

6. _____

7. An iron slab is 42 inches long, 12 inches wide, and 3 inches thick. If the iron weighs 490 pounds per cubic foot, find the weight of the slab.

7. _____

8. A solid lead bar is a right cylinder that has a height of 4 feet and a radius of 3 inches. If lead weighs 704 pounds per cubic foot, find the weight of the lead bar.

8. _____

9. A tank that is a sphere with a 9 foot radius is full of sea water. If sea water weighs 64 pounds per cubic foot, find the weight of the water in the tank.

9. _____

10. A tank that is a cube with 16 foot edges is full of gasoline. If gasoline weighs 42 pounds per cubic foot, find the weight of the gasoline in the tank.

10. _____

11. A sign for the city of Wells, Nevada, along Highway I-80, has a missing corner. Using the dimensions given, what percent of the sign is missing?

11. _____

12. A section of land, a square with sides one mile long, sold for $332,000. What is the cost per acre of this land? (Note: 1 acre = 43,560 sq ft)

12. _____

13. If "ready-mix" concrete sells for $56 a cubic yard, what would the concrete cost for a rectangular patio slab that is 15 feet long, 12 feet wide, and 4 inches thick? (Note: 27 cu ft = 1 cu yd)

13. _____

14. A treasure chest weighs 256 pounds and its dimensions are 3 ft by 2 ft by 1.5 ft. If the chest is full of gold, find the total weight of the chest and the gold. (Note: gold weighs approximately 1202 pounds per cubic foot.)

14. _____

15. A tank in the shape of a right cylinder has a height of 12′ and a radius of 10′. a) If a gallon of paint covers 400 sq ft, how many gallons of paint would be needed to paint the tank? b) How many gallons of water will the tank hold (1 cu ft ≈ 7.48 gal)? Give answers accurate to the nearest tenth.

15. _____

506

Exercise 8.9 Set B

1. How much would it cost to carpet a 9 ft by 12 ft room if the complete cost for the carpet is $23.65 a square yard?

1. _____

2. If Astro-Turf costs $12.56 a square yard, how much would it cost to cover a 24′ by 21′ area with Astro-Turf?

2. _____

3. You are enclosing a 46′ by 52′ rectangular play area with a fence that costs $5.12 a foot. If you also cover the area with three inches gravel that costs $0.25 per square foot of area, what is the total cost of the project?

3. _____

4. A Big Screen TV is advertised as a 56″ TV. This means that the diagonal of the screen is 56 inches. If one side of the screen measures 34 inches, how long is the other side?

4. _____

5. A rectangular field measures 850 meters by 200 meters. If instead of walking along the edge of the field, you walk along the diagonal from one corner to another, how many yards less do you walk?

5. _____

6. If carpet tiles cost $1.25 a square foot, how many one foot square tiles will you need and how much would it cost for enough tiles to carpet two 8′ by 10′ bedrooms?

6. _____

7. An iron slab is 3 ft long, 18 inches wide, and 4 inches thick. If the iron weighs 490 pounds per cubic foot, find the weight of the slab.

7. _____

8. How much would a lead ball weigh that has a diameter of 3 feet? (Note: lead weighs 704 pounds per cubic foot.)

8. _____

9. A tank that is a right cylinder with a radius of 20′ and a height of 15′ is full of gasoline. If gasoline weighs 42 pounds per cubic foot, find the weight of the gasoline in the tank.

9. _____

10. A tank that is a cube with 10 foot edges is full of sea water. If sea water weighs 64 pounds per cubic foot, find the weight of the water in the tank.

10. _____

11. A sign advertising a truck stop along a freeway has two missing panels. Using the dimensions given, what percent of the sign is missing?

11. _____

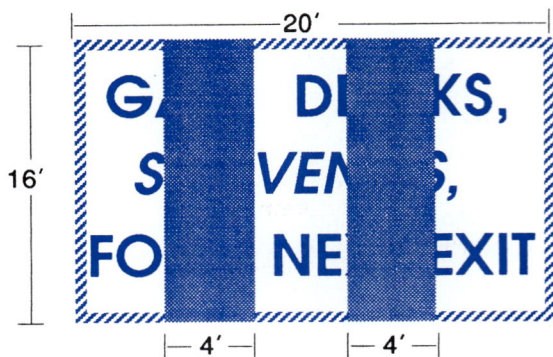

12. A township is a square area of land with sides six miles long. If a township sold for $6,535,000, what is the cost per acre of this land? (Note: 1 acre = 43,560 sq ft)

12. _____

13. If decorator rock sells for $59.95 a cubic yard, what would the rock cost to cover a rectangular area that is 54 feet long and 6 feet wide with 3 inches of rock?

13. _____

14. A treasure chest box with dimensions 3 ft by 2 ft by 1.5 ft. weighs 135 pounds. If the chest is full of silver, find the total weight of the chest and the silver. (Note: silver weighs 654 pound per cubic foot.)

14. _____

15. A spherical water tank has an inside radius of 9 feet and an outside radius of 9.25 feet. a) If a gallon of paint covers 300 sq ft, how many gallons of paint would be needed to paint the outside of the tank? b) How many gallons of water will the tank hold (1 cu ft ≈ 7.48 gal)? Round off answers to one decimal place.

15. _____

Chapter 8 Summary

Concepts   You may refer to the sections listed below to review how to do the following:

1. illustrate basic geometric objects—points, lines, planes, and line segments. (8.1)
2. distinguish between different types of angles. (8.2)
3. identify different kinds of triangles. (8.3)
4. identify different quadrilaterals and their properties. (8.4)
5. identify the different parts of a circle. (8.4)
6. find the sum of the angles (S) of a polygon with n sides using the formula $S = 180\ (n - 2)$. (8.5)
7. find each angle of regular polygons using **E.A.** = S/n where S = the sum of the angles and n = the number of sides. (8.5)
8. find perimeters and areas of common plane figures. (8.6)
9. find surface areas and volumes of common 3-dimensional objects. (8.7)
10. use the Pythagorean Theorem, $a^2 + b^2 = c^2$, to find sides of right triangles. (8.8)
11. solve applications involving geometry. (8.9)

Terminology   This chapter's important terms and their corresponding page numbers are as follows:

acute angle: an angle that measures between 0° and 90°. (464)
actue triangle: a triangle with three acute angles. (469)
angle: the figure formed by two rays and/or segments with the same end point. (463)
area: a measure of the number of square units that covers the interior of a closed plane figure. (483)
box: a 3-dimensional object with six rectangular faces meeting at eight vertices. (489)
chord: line segment with endpoints on a circle. (474)
circle: the set of points in a plane that are the same distance from a center point. (474)
circumference: the distance around a circle. (483)
complementary angles: two angles that have a sum of 90°. (464)
cube: a 3-dimensional object with six equal square faces. (489)
diameter: a chord that passes through the center of a circle. (474)
equilateral triangle: a triangle that has all sides equal. (469)
hexagon: a polygon with six sides. (477)
intersecting lines: two lines that cross each other at one point. (460)
isosceles triangle: a triangle that has two equal sides. (p. 469)
line segment: a part of a line consisting of two points and all the points between those points. (450)
midpoint: a point that divides a line segment into two equal parts. (450)
obtuse angle: an angle that measures between 90° and 180°. (464)
obtuse triangle: a triangle with one obtuse angle. (470)
octagon: a polygon with eight sides. (477)

parallel lines: lines in the same plane that never intersect. (460)

parallelogram: a quadrilateral with both pairs of sides parallel. (473)

pentagon: a polygon with five sides. (477)

perimeter: the measure of the outer boundary of a 2-dimensional closed figure. (483)

pi: ($\pi \approx 3.14$) the ratio of the circumference of a circle to the diameter of a circle. (483)

plane figure: a figure that is entirely contained in a plane. (473)

polygon: a closed plane figure formed by line segments that intersect each other only at their end points. (477)

Pythagorean Theorem: relationship between the legs, a and b, and the hypotenuse, c, of a right triangle which states: $a^2 + b^2 = c^2$ (497)

quadrilateral: a polygon with four sides. (473)

radius: a line segment connecting the center of a circle and a point on the circle. (474)

ray: part of a line that has one end point and extends in only one direction. (463)

rectangle: a quadrilateral with four right angles. (473)

regular polygon: a polygon with equal sides and angles. (477)

right angle: an angle that measures 90°. (469)

right cylinder: a 3-dimensional object with a circular top and bottom that are equal in area and at right angles to its middle surface. (489)

right triangle: a triangle with one right angle. (469)

scalene triangle: a triangle with each side having a different length. (464)

sphere: a 3-dimensional object consisting of all the points that are the same distance from a center point. (489)

square: a quadrilateral with equal sides and four right angles. (473)

straight angle: an angle that measures 180°. (464)

supplementary angles: two angles that have a sum of 180°. (464)

surface area: a measure of the number of square units that covers the outside of a 3-dimensional object. (490)

trapezoid: a quadrilateral with one pair of parallel sides. (473)

triangle: a polygon with three sides. (464)

volume: a measure of the number of cubes of a given size that fills a 3-dimensional object. (491)

Chapter 8 Crossword Puzzle

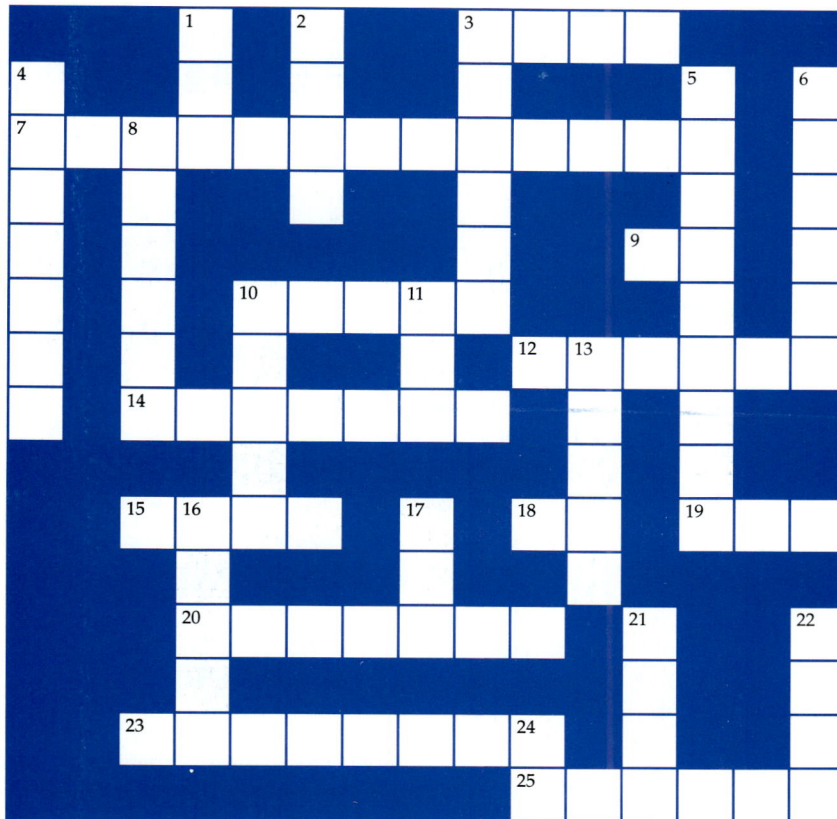

Across
3. Has 6 square faces
7. Perimeter of a circle
9. About 3.14
10. Less than 90°
12. Ball
14. Part of a line
15. Measured in square units
18. Abbreviation for 1/36 of a yard
19. Part of a line
20. Obtuse angles are _____ than 90°
23. 180° angle
25. Between 90° and 180°

Down
1. Part of a circle
2. Half-circle
3. Points the same distance from one point
4. Has 8 sides
5. Distance around a plane figure
6. Measured in cubic units
8. Half the diameter
10. Two rays with the same endpoint
11. Supplement of 170°
13. Represented by a parallelogram
16. 90° angle
17. Represents a point
21. The area of a 3′ by 5′ rectangle is 15 _____.
22. If the radius is 2.5, the diameter is _____.
24. Mistaken for two

MATH MAGIC VI

Magic Circles

Consider the circular pattern created by placing consecutive whole numbers starting with 1 in the diagram shown below. If sum of the numbers on any circle and the number at the center is the same as the sum of the numbers on each line through the circle, it is called a **magic circle.** A magic circle using the whole numbers from 1 to 9 is shown below.

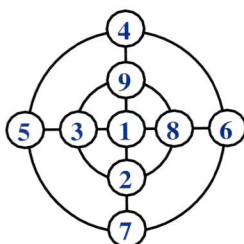

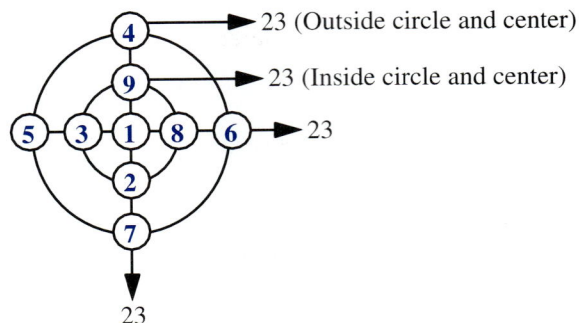

23 (Outside circle and center)

23 (Inside circle and center)

23

23

The sum of the numbers on each circle and the number in the center is the same as the sum of numbers on each line through the circle.

Recreations

1. Find the two other ways to create a magic circle using the whole numbers from 1 to 9. Each one has a different magic sum.

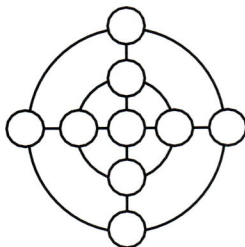

2. Place the whole numbers from 1 to 19 in the diagram to create a magic circle. Three magic sums are possible.

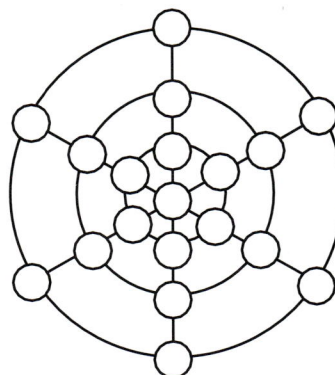

Chapter 8 Practice Test A

1. List all the line segments in the figure on the right.

   G   N

   A   Y

   1. _____

2. In the figure on the right, if I is the midpoint of $\overline{GY}$, and GY = 17, then how long is GI?

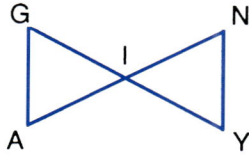

   2. _____

3. What kind of an angle is ∠GIN, if it measures 136°?

   3. _____

4. Find the complement and supplement of a 37° angle.

   4. _____

5. Sketch and label equilateral triangle, △KLS.

   5. _____

6. Sketch and label obtuse triangle, △CRS, with ∠S the obtuse angle.

   6. _____

7. Sketch and label parallelogram QFUZ, with ∠F an acute angle.

   7. _____

8. Sketch a regular hexagon and find the measure of each of its angles.

   8. _____

9. Find the circumference and area of a circle with a 37 cm diameter.

   9. _____

10. Find the perimeter and area of the figure on the right.

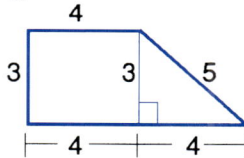

    4

    3   3   5

    ├── 4 ──┼── 4 ──┤

    10. _____

11. Find the surface area and volume of a sphere with a diameter of 8.6 ft.

    11. _____

12. The hypotenuse of a right triangle is 17 cm long. If one leg is 9 cm, how long is the other leg?

    12. _____

13. A box shaped tank with dimensions 5.2′ by 7.5′ by 6′ is filled with water. How many gallons of water does the tank hold? (Note: 1 cu ft ≈ 7.48 gal)

    13. _____

Chapter 8 Practice Test B

1. List all the line segments in the figure on the right.

2. In the figure on the right, if X is the midpoint of $\overline{ST}$, and SX = 19, then how long is ST?

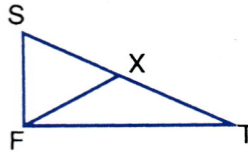

3. What kind of an angle is ∠SFT, if it measures 90°?

4. Find the complement and supplement of a 29° angle.

5. Sketch and label scalene triangle, △MQT, with MQ > QT.

6. Sketch and label acute triangle, △SLT.

7. Sketch and label trapezoid ACFG, with ∠C a right angle.

8. Sketch a regular octagon and find the measure of each of its angles.

9. Find the circumference and area of a circle with a 43 cm diameter.

10. Find the perimeter and area of the figure on the right.

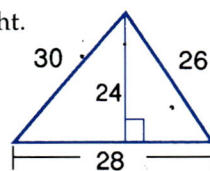

11. Find the surface area and volume of a cube with 8.6 ft edges.

12. The hypotenuse of a right triangle is 33 ft long. If one leg is 15 ft, how long is the other leg?

13. The height of a cylinder is 8 meters. If its radius increased from 3 meters to 3.1 meters and its height remained the same, what is the percent increase in the volume of the cylinder?

1. _____

2. _____

3. _____

4. _____

5. _____

6. _____

7. _____

8. _____

9. _____

10. _____

11. _____

12. _____

13. _____

Chapter 8 Supplementary Exercises

Section 8.1

In problems 1–10, draw and label a figure for each description.

1. $\overleftrightarrow{PR}$ containing point S.

2. Line n containing points A and B.

3. Plane E containing $\overleftrightarrow{AB}$.

4. Plane D containing segment $\overline{AB}$.

5. $\overleftrightarrow{TQ} \parallel \overleftrightarrow{SP}$

6. Lines t, s, r, with t ∥ s ∥ r.

7. $\overleftrightarrow{RT}$ intersecting $\overleftrightarrow{TQ}$.

8. Line m intersecting line n.

9. Line segment $\overline{FD}$ with midpoint X.

10. Line segment $\overline{GH}$ with midpoint K.

In problems 11–13, list all the line segments in each figure.

11.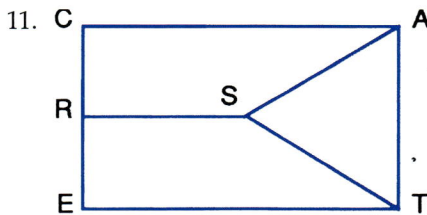

12.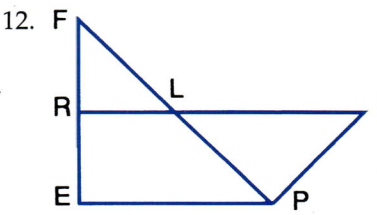

13.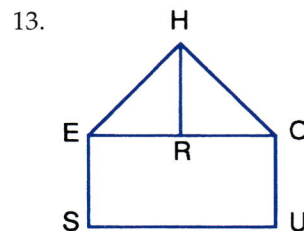

Section 8.2

In problems 1–10, draw and label a figure for each description.

1. Acute ∠COT.

2. Straight ∠GOT.

3. Right ∠DOT.

4. Obtuse ∠HOT.

5. ∠JOT with $\overleftrightarrow{PQ} \parallel \overleftrightarrow{OT}$.

6. ∠KOT with line m ∥ $\overleftrightarrow{OK}$.

7. Plane F containing ∠LOT.

8. Plane G containing ∠MOT and ∠NOT.

9. ∠POT with line t passing through point P.

10. ∠ROT with line t passing through point R.

In problems 11–18, find the complement and supplement of an angle with the given measure.

11. 35°

12. 65°

13. 70°

14. 45°

15. 17.5°

16. 52.3°

17. $78\frac{1}{4}°$

18. 80.7°

Section 8.3

Draw and label a figure for each description.

1. Acute △ABC.

2. Obtuse △ABD.

3. Right △ABE.

4. Scalene △ABF.

5. Equilateral △ABG.

6. Isosceles △ABH.

7. Line t intersecting side $\overline{AB}$ of isosceles △ABI.

8. Plane E containing right △ABJ with ∠J the right angle.

Section 8.4

In problems 1–10, draw and label a figure for each description.

1. Trapezoid FTBL.

2. Parallelogram BASE.

3. Rectangle BSKT.

4. Square GOLF.

5. A circle with radius $\overline{UN}$ and center at U.

6. A circle with diameter $\overline{US}$ and center at A.

7. Rectangle BELT with BE > EL.

8. Parallelogram SALT with SA < AL.

9. Trapezoid DION with DI = ON.

10. Trapezoid LANI with LA > NI.

In problems 11–19, refer to the circle below with center at point O.

11. List all radii.

12. List all diameters.

13. List all chords.

14. List all chords that are not diameters.

15. If RG = 18, OA = ?

16. If ON = $6\frac{1}{2}$, AE = ?

17. If AE = 75.6, RG = ?

18. If OA = 7.9, RG = ?

19. If RG = 16.7, EO = ?

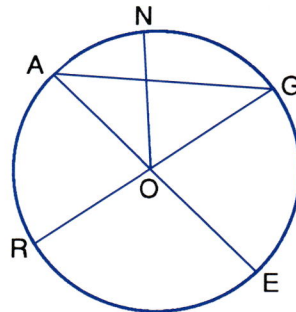

Section 8.5

In problems 1–4, make a sketch of each polygon.

1. Pentagon

2. Regular quadrilateral

3. Regular hexagon

4. Octagon

In problems 5–10, find the sum of the angles and each angle of the regular polygons described.

5. Regular pentagon

6. Regular 10-sided polygon

7. Regular octagon

8. Regular 20-sided polygon

9. Regular 13-sided polygon

10. Regular hexagon

Section 8.6

Find the perimeter and area of the plane figures described below.

1. A square with 10″ sides.

2. A square with 6″ sides.

3. A 5′ by 7′ rectangle.

4. A 3′ by 8′ rectangle.

5. A circle with a 4.6 cm radius.

6. A circle with a 7.8 cm diameter.

7. The triangle below:

8. The parallelogram below:

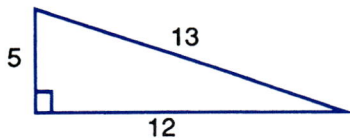

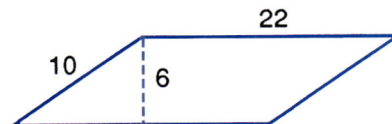

9. The circle below:

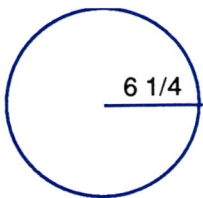

10. The triangle below:

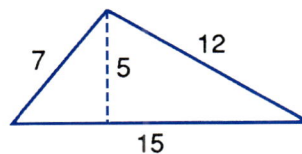

Section 8.7

Find the surface area and volume of each object described below:

1. Cube with 7 cm edges.

2. Cube with 2.5 ft edges.

3. Box with dimensions 1.5″ by 4.25″ by 12″.

4. Box with dimensions 5″ by 6″ by 20″.

5. Right cylinder with a height of 12 cm and a radius of 4.6 cm.

6. Right cylinder with a height of 44.5 cm and a radius of 10.4 cm.

7. Sphere with a 8.5 m radius.

8. Sphere with a 12 m radius.

9. Box with dimensions 2 feet by 3 feet by 6 inches.

10. Right cylinder with a 3 inch radius and a 4 foot height.

Section 8.8

If a and b are the legs and c is the hypotenuse of a right triangle, find the side that is not given.

1. $a = 8$ in. $b = 15$ in.

2. $a = 10$ ft $b = 24$ ft

3. $a = 15$ yd $c = 39$ yd

4. $a = 10$ m $c = 27$ m

5. $b = 33$ ft $c = 65$ ft

6. $b = 12$ km $c = 46$ km

7. $a = 7\frac{1}{2}$ mi $b = 19\frac{1}{4}$ mi

8. $b = 15.6$ cm $c = 84.5$ cm

9. $a = 125.8$ m $c = 277.7$ m

10. $a = 100$ ft $b = 100$ ft

Section 8.9

1. If the complete cost for carpeting a room is $39.95 a square yard, find the cost to carpet the room shown below:

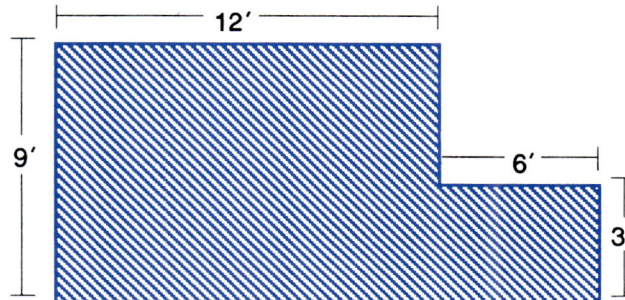

2. A water tank is a right cylinder with an inside radius of 10 ft, an outside radius of 10.2 ft, an inside height of 20 ft, and an outside height of 20.4 ft.
   a) To paint the outside of the tank, you use paint with a coverage of 375 sq ft per gallon. To the nearest tenth of a gallon, how many gallons of paint will be needed?
   b) Since a cubic foot of water is about 7.48 gallons, how many gallons of water will the tank hold?
   c) Since water weighs about 62.4 pounds per cubic foot, how heavy is the water in a full tank?

3. If Ready-Mix Concrete sells for $59.50 a cubic yard plus 7% sales tax and $35.00 for delivery, how much would it cost for the cement for the rectangular shaped region shown below?

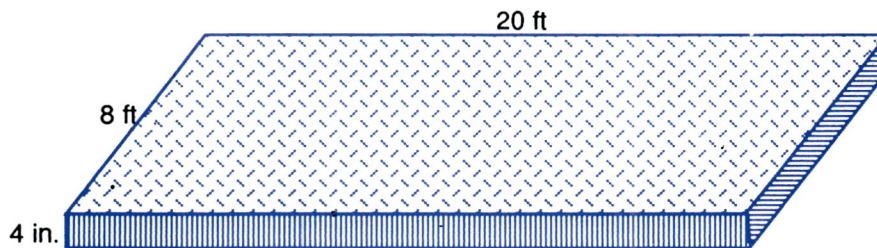

4. If the radius of a sphere increased from 4 meters to 4.5 meters, what is the percent increase in
   a) the surface area of the sphere?
   b) the volume of the sphere?

5. If the edge of a cube increased from 4 meters to 4.5 meters, what is the percent increase in
   a) the surface area of the cube?
   b) the volume of the cube?

6. A peewee league baseball diamond has bases that are 50 feet apart. How far is it from homeplate to second base in that baseball diamond?

7. On level ground, 200 feet of rope connects the top of a vertical pole to a point 18 feet away from the bottom of the pole. How tall is the pole?

Name _____ Date _____

Unit IV Exam

Chapters 7 and 8

1. If $x = 3$ and $y = 5$, then $3x - y + 16 = ?$

1. _____

In problems 2–7, perform the indicated operations.

2. $8 + (-17)$ 3. $16 - 24$

2. _____

3. _____

4. $-3 - (-7)$ 5. $(-5)(-9)$

4. _____

5. _____

6. $\dfrac{-125}{25}$ 7. $5(-8 - 2) + 7 - 2(3)$

6. _____

7. _____

In problems 8–9, solve for x.

8. $-13 = x - 3$ 9. $3x + 5 = 26$

8. _____

9. _____

10. $6x + 2x - x = -14$ 11. $2(x + 5) = 3(x - 1) + 9$

10. _____

11. _____

12. One-half a number, decreased by 4, is −10. What is the number? 12. _____

13. What is the name for a regular polygon with three sides? 13. _____

14. Sketch and label parallelogram ROXY, with ∠X being obtuse. 14. _____

15. Find the area and perimeter of a square that has 8 inch sides. 15. _____

16. Find the area and circumference of a circle with a diameter of 6 cm. 16. _____

17. The enamel used to paint a 12′ by 16′ by 8.5′ steel box costs $28.95 a gallon and has a coverage of 300 sq ft per gallon. a) How many full gallons of paint do you need to buy to paint the box? b) If there is 8% sales tax on the paint, how much would the paint cost? 17. _____

18. If the legs of a right triangle are 12.5″ and 30″, how long is the hypotenuse? 18. _____

19. If you deposit $2000 in a savings account that pays 3.65%, compounded daily, how much would be in the account after 10 years? 19. _____

Name _____ Date _____

Final Exam

Chapters 1 to 8

In problems 1–12, perform the indicated operations.

1. 4076×5000

2. $35,000 - 7,509$

3. $49,329 \div 87$

4. $9^2 - \sqrt{49} + 3 \times 6$

5. $6\dfrac{3}{8} \div 2\dfrac{1}{3}$

6. $\dfrac{3}{4} + \dfrac{5}{14} - \dfrac{1}{21}$

7. $85\dfrac{1}{2} - 31\dfrac{2}{3}$

8. 74.05×3.6

9. $3.6 + 0.185 + 91 + 3.26$

10. $19.723 \div 3.26$

11. 45% of 982

12. $3(-7) + (-8)$

13. Express $\dfrac{18}{37}$ as a decimal rounded to the thousandths place.

14. $16.52 is what percent of $472?

15. $5800 \text{ g} = \underline{?} \text{ kg}$

16. $14.5 \text{ m} = \underline{?} \text{ in.}$

1. _____

2. _____

3. _____

4. _____

5. _____

6. _____

7. _____

8. _____

9. _____

10. _____

11. _____

12. _____

13. _____

14. _____

15. _____

16. _____

In problems 17–20, solve for x.

17. $\dfrac{5}{8} = \dfrac{x}{140}$

18. $4x + 3 = 51$

19. $5x - 2x = 3 - 9$

20. $3(x + 5) = 2(4x - 3) + 1$

17. _____

18. _____

19. _____

20. _____

21. Your scores out of 100 points on chapter tests in the semester were 89, 95, 78, 82, 86, 93, 92, and 97. What are the mean and median of your test scores?

21. _____

22. You started the week with an $85.06 balance in your checking account. During the week you deposited $195.87 and wrote checks for $12.74, $38.56, $107.50, $20.00, and $7.65. What was the balance in your account at the end of the week?

22. _____

23. What would it cost to rent a truck, if you drive it 485 miles in two days and are charged $37.50 a day plus 19.6¢ a mile?

23. _____

24. What would the monthly payments be to pay off a loan of $775 in two years with a simple interest rate of 12% per year?

24. _____

25. A 15% discount is given on the purchase of a $784.00 item. If 5% sales tax is calculated on the discount price, what is the final cost of the item?

25. _____

26. Find the total cost of carpeting a 9′ by 12′ room, if the carpet with pad costs $24.95 a square yard, and a 6.5% sales tax and $75.00 installation fee are added.

26. _____

27. Find the number of gallons and weight of the water that is needed to fill a cylindrical tank that has a height of 30′ and a diameter of 20′. (Note: 1 cu ft of water weighs 62.4 lbs and contains 7.48 gallons.)

27. _____

28. If the distance between bases on a baseball diamond is 80 ft, how far is it from first base to third base?

28. _____

29. The sum of three consecutive whole numbers is 174. What are the numbers?

29. _____

30. Three less than twice my age is seventeen more than my age. How old am I?

30. _____

Answers

Unit I

Brain Buster
a. $524,288
b. $1,048,575

Chapter 1

Pretest

1. 602,067,005
2. forty-two thousand, one hundred seven
3. 543,000
4. 540,000
5. 1325
6. 97,763
7. 2492
8. 3,090,474
9. 23,560,000,000
10. 3,224,007,254
11. 8
12. 7
13. $5 \times 10^3 + 3 \times 10^2 + 0 \times 10 + 6 \times 1$
14. <
15. >
16. $60

Exercise 1.1

Set A

1. eight hundred fifty-two
2. four thousand, two hundred fifty-six
3. seventeen thousand, one hundred nine
4. three million, fifty-seven thousand, ten
5. fourteen million, one hundred thousand, seven hundred
6. nine hundred forty-six thousand, three
7. one billion, three hundred fifty-seven million, nine hundred twenty-six thousand, one hundred eighty-three
8. 745
9. 50,068
10. 105,006
11. 40,000,036
12. 5,007,238
13. 12,015,000,000
14. 89,000,000,089
15. 313,710,000
16. 712,000,422
17. 5 millions
18. 9 tens
19. 8 hundred thousands
20. 6 thousands
21. 7 ten thousands

Set B

1. nine hundred twenty-five
2. six thousand, one hundred seventy-two
3. thirteen thousand, four hundred two
4. six million, twenty-six thousand, fifty
5. seventeen million, two hundred thousand, four hundred
6. one hundred ninety-six thousand, two
7. four billion, three hundred seven million, nine hundred sixteen thousand, four hundred fifty-two
8. 916
9. 30,043
10. 207,004
11. 50,072,040

12. 4,006,385
13. 18,012,000,000
14. 79,000,000,035
15. 144,730,000
16. 913,000,553
17. 2 ten thousands
18. 8 hundred thousands
19. 1 million
20. 6 hundreds
21. 7 thousands

Exercise 1.2

Set A

* 1. 50
2. 80
3. 30
4. 510
5. 1470
6. 5900
* 7. 7000
8. 500
9. 900
10. 700
11. 14,700
12. 27,900
*13. 180,000
14. 1,538,300
15. 215,749,540
16. 215,749,500
*17. 215,750,000
18. 215,750,000
19. 215,700,000
20. 216,000,000
21. 220,000,000
22. 200,000,000

Set B

1. 70
2. 50
3. 70
4. 310
5. 2580
6. 4800
7. 4000
8. 700
9. 600
10. 900
11. 25,600
12. 37,600
13. 80,000
14. 4,356,500
15. 927,563,740
16. 927,563,700
17. 927,564,000
18. 927,560,000
19. 927,600,000
20. 928,000,000
21. 930,000,000
22. 900,000,000

*Selected Solutions from Set A

1.

$$53 \approx 50$$

tens place ⟶ digit to the right is less than 5

Round off to the lower multiple, 50.

7.

$$6997 \approx 7000$$

tens place ⟶ digit to the right is more than 5

Round off to the higher multiple, 7000.

13.

$$179,950 \approx 180,000$$

hundreds place ⟶ digit to the right is 5

Round off to the higher multiple by increasing the hundreds place by 1.

17.

$$215,749,538 \approx 215,750,000$$

thousands place ⟶ digit to the right is 5

Round off to the higher multiple by increasing the thousands place by 1.

Exercise 1.4

Set A

* 1. 68
 2. 88
* 3. 380
 4. 775
* 5. 6018
 6. 9304
* 7. 5898
 8. 2853
* 9. 467
 10. 5484
*11. 204
 12. 433
*13. 1746
 14. 584,757
*15. 9975
 16. 5,856,296
*17. 3574

Set B

 1. 77
 2. 59
 3. 773
 4. 292
 5. 5091
 6. 10,180
 7. 4596
 8. 2095
 9. 4555
 10. 1637
 11. 341
 12. 846
 13. 4866
 14. 327,702
 15. 7469
 16. 6,767,575
 17. 5203

*Selected Solutions from Set A

```
1.      45          3.      356
      +23                 + 24
      ───                 ────
       68                  380

       11
5.    5072          7.        1
     + 946                  426
     ─────                  5382
      6018                 +  90
                          ─────
                           5898

       11                      11
9.       5          11.        76
        76                   +128
       130                   ────
      +256                    204
      ────
       467

         1                     11
13.   1400          15.        52
         7                   9000
       322                    876
     +  17                     43
     ─────                  +   4
      1746                  ────
                            9975

       133
17.      18
        196
         45
       2463
        757
      +  95
      ─────
       3574
```

Exercise 1.6

Set A

* 1. 212
 2. 522
* 3. 702
 4. 776
* 5. 1626
 6. 2860
* 7. 965
 8. 3682
* 9. 11,412
 10. 23,424
*11. 107,282
 12. 193,480
*13. 10,304
 14. 975
*15. 140,400
 16. 529,718
*17. 9,907,800
 18. 141,913,863
*19. 28,608

Set B

 1. 243
 2. 148
 3. 603
 4. 696
 5. 1692
 6. 2456
 7. 1470
 8. 6132
 9. 11,216
 10. 52,236
 11. 170,632
 12. 601,192
 13. 7752
 14. 103,780
 15. 919,692
 16. 28,005,306
 17. 454,384
 18. 38,155,284
 19. 285,768

*Selected Solutions from Set A

```
          1                      7
1.       53          3.        78
       ×  4                   ×  9
       ────                   ────
        212                    702

          1                      41
5.      542          7.        193
       ×  3                   ×   5
       ────                   ─────
       1626                    965

        1 1                    3214
9.     5706          11.     15326
       ×   2                 ×    7
      ─────                 ──────
      11412                 107282

       232                     22
13.   2576          15.     23400
       ×   4                 ×   6
      ─────                 ──────
      10304                 140400

      136364
17.  1238475
     ×     8
     ───────
     9907800

       222
19.   4768          14304
     ×   3          ×   2
     ─────          ─────
     14304          28608
```

Exercise 1.7

Set A

* 1. 943
  2. 408
*3. 65,928
  4. 50,997
* 5. 21,571
  6. 42,252
* 7. 145,040
  8. 430,430
* 9. 8,097,408
  10. 11,337,844
*11. 290,928
  12. 232,468
*13. 10,524,046
  14. 31,316,615
*15. 5,361,845
  16. 252,793,536

Set B

  1. 946
  2. 1333
  3. 54,768
  4. 40,964
  5. 59,585
  6. 39,494
  7. 112,320
  8. 691,840
  9. 8,390,928
  10. 34,194,638
  11. 291,729
  12. 295,106
  13. 12,064,035
  14. 26,052,422
  15. 4,880,925
  16. 53,348,040

*Selected Solutions from Set A

```
1.        41
       ×  23
         123
          82
         943
```

```
3.       984
       ×  67
        6888
        5904
       65928
```

```
5.       407
       ×  53
        1221
        2035
       21571
```

```
7.       518
       ×  280
         000
        4144
        1036
      145040
```

```
9.     14256
       ×  568
       114048
        85536
        71280
      8097408
```

```
11.     5016
       ×   58
        40128
        25080
       290928
```

```
13.    74113
       ×  142
       148226
       296452
        74113
      10524046
```

```
15.     6515
       ×  823
        19545
        13030
        52120
      5361845
```

Exercise 1.8

Set A

* 1. 4270
  2. 4350
* 3. 32,576
  4. 60,525
* 5. 9,821,000
  6. 12,046,000
* 7. 280,000
  8. 300,000
* 9. 592,000,000
  10. 318,000,000
*11. 126,210
  12. 189,378
*13. 10,031,024
  14. 18,971,745
*15. 9,805,000
  16. 3,264,000,000
*17. 65,858,780
  18. 8,036,000,000

Set B

  1. 3640
  2. 2450
  3. 21,939
  4. 67,260
  5. 6,766,000
  6. 19,909,000
  7. 300,000
  8. 630,000
  9. 135,000,000
  10. 532,000,000
  11. 92,115
  12. 216,108
  13. 13,667,416
  14. 23,443,812
  15. 30,832,000
  16. 2,001,000,000
  17. 76,845,763
  18. 14,049,000,000

*Selected Solutions from Set A

```
1.        61
       ×  70
        4270
```

```
3.        64
       ×  509
         576
        3200
       32576
```

```
5.       427
       ×  23000
      1281000
          854
      9821000
```

```
7.       700
       ×  400
      280000
```

```
9.     74000
       ×  8000
      592000000
```

```
11.       42
       ×  3005
          210
        12600
       126210
```

```
13.     2504
       ×  4006
        15024
      1001600
      10031024
```

```
15.      185
       ×  53000
       555000
          925
      9805000
```

```
17.     2195
       ×  30004
         8780
      6585000
      65858780
```

Exercise 1.9

Set A

* 1. 9
  2. 49
  3. 144
  4. 225
* 5. 64
  6. 8
  7. 0
  8. 0
* 9. 1
  10. 1
  11. 32
  12. 243
  13. 1,000,000
  14. 10,000
*15. 1156
  16. $3 \times 10^2 + 5 \times 10 + 6 \times 1$
  17. $6 \times 10^3 + 0 \times 10^2$
      $+ 9 \times 10 + 8 \times 1$
  18. $3 \times 10^4 + 3 \times 10^3$
      $+ 6 \times 10^2 + 9 \times 10$
      $+ 0 \times 1$
  19. $4 \times 10^6 + 2 \times 10^5$
      $+ 6 \times 10^4 + 7 \times 10^3$
      $+ 9 \times 10^2 + 8 \times 10$
      $+ 3 \times 1$
  20. $2 \times 10^7 + 0 \times 10^6$
      $+ 6 \times 10^5 + 0 \times 10^4$
      $+ 7 \times 10^3 + 5 \times 10^2$
      $+ 1 \times 10 + 2 \times 1$

21. 2	22. 3
23. 5	24. 4
*25. 6	26. 7
27. 1	28. 8
29. 0	30. 15
*31. 10	32. 9
*33. =	34. <
35. =	36. >
*37. <	38. >

Set B

1. 16
2. 36
3. 169
4. 324
5. 125
6. 27
7. 0
8. 0
9. 1
10. 1
11. 243
12. 32
13. 100,000
14. 1000
15. 1849
16. $6 \times 10^2 + 1 \times 10 + 7 \times 1$
17. $7 \times 10^3 + 3 \times 10^2$
    $+ 0 \times 1 + 4 \times 1$
18. $4 \times 10^4 + 4 \times 10^3$
    $+ 2 \times 10^2 + 7 \times 10$
    $+ 5 \times 1$
19. $5 \times 10^6 + 1 \times 10^5$
    $+ 4 \times 10^4 + 3 \times 10^3$
    $+ 8 \times 10^2 + 7 \times 10$
    $+ 9 \times 1$
20. $4 \times 10^7 + 0 \times 10^6$
    $+ 0 \times 10^5 + 3 \times 10^4$
    $+ 4 \times 10^3 + 1 \times 10^2$
    $+ 2 \times 10 + 6 \times 1$

21. 4	22. 1
23. 6	24. 5
25. 7	26. 3
27. 0	28. 10
29. 14	30. 11
31. 9	32. 2
33. =	34. <
35. =	36. >
37. <	38. >

*Selected Solutions from Set A

1. $3^2 = 3 \times 3 = 9$
5. $4^3 = 4 \times 4 \times 4 = 64$
9. $1^4 = 1 \times 1 \times 1 \times 1 = 1$
15. $34^2 = 34 \times 34 = 1156$
25. 6, since $6 \times 6 = 36$
31. 10, since $10 \times 10 = 100$
33. $24 = 24$
37. $5 < 25$

Exercise 1.10

Set A

* 1. $102
  2. $504,500
* 3. 585 mi
  4. 12,000 sheets
* 5. 2190 cubes
  6. 336 pieces
* 7. 1649 sq ft
  8. 4248 pts.
* 9. 430 ft
  10. 5400 eggs
*11. $4875
  12. 16,000
*13. yes
  14. yes
  15. a) 103,680
      b) 172,800

Set B

1. $214
2. 435 cal
3. 10,048 invoices
4. 168 lb
5. 336 gal
6. 1152 peanuts
7. $427
8. 338 pts.
9. $520
10. 144 pens
11. $39
12. 187,500,000
13. no
14. yes
15. 8400

*Selected Solutions from Set A

1. Add the amounts.

   $35 + $48 + $19 = $102

3. Multiply the number of gallons by number of miles per gallon.

   $15 \times 39 = 585$ mi

5. Cubes per day: $2 \times 3 = 6$ cubes
   For 365 days: $365 \times 6 = 2190$ cubes

7. bedrooms: $3 \times 144 = 432$ sq ft
   master bdrm: $= 300$ sq ft
   bathrooms: $2 \times 56 = 112$ sq ft
   kitchen: $= 240$ sq ft
   living rm: $= 460$ sq ft
   hallway: $= 105$ sq ft
                total: 1649 sq ft

9. pipe: $24 \times 16 = 384$ ft
   joints: $23 \times 2 = \ 46$ ft
              total: 430 ft

11. general: $575 \times $5 = 2875
    reserved: $250 \times $8 = 2000
                 total: $4875

13. 35 pizzas at $16 each is
    $35 \times $16 = 560 and $560 is less than $629.

Chapter 1

Practice Test A

1. 254,030,107
2. three million, four hundred seven thousand, one hundred twenty-three
3. 753,000
4. 800,000
5. 4116
6. 86,385
7. 4614
8. 4,730,778
9. 39,032,000,000
10. 255,502,190
11. 81
12. 3
13. $1 \times 10^4 + 4 \times 10^3 + 0 \times 10^2 + 2 \times 10 + 7 \times 1$
14. <
15. =
16. 1048 lb

Chapter 1

Practice Test B

1. 1,025,306,517
2. six hundred seventy-eight thousand, three hundred nine
3. 1,257,380
4. 1,260,000
5. 1437
6. 94,041
7. 3824
8. 1,659,860
9. 19,040,000
10. 5,436,000,906
11. 64
12. 9
13. $2 \times 10^2 + 5 \times 10 + 9 \times 1$
14. =
15. >
16. 85°

Chapter 2

Pretest

1. 331
2. 66,604
3. 5053
4. 6
5. 5 R6
6. impossible
7. 53
8. 2063 R3
9. 295
10. 606 R20
11. 600
12. 9008
13. 97
14. $2 \times 2 \times 5 \times 7$
15. 91

Exercise 2.2

Set A		Set B	
* 1.	64	1.	33
2.	34	2.	23
* 3.	501	3.	805
4.	802	4.	702
* 5.	8842	5.	4764
6.	4464	6.	2762
* 7.	56	7.	35
8.	28	8.	18
* 9.	234	9.	369
10.	375	10.	469
*11.	1578	11.	2387
12.	1788	12.	3089
*13.	548	13.	438
14.	729	14.	828
*15.	3245	15.	2377
16.	4365	16.	4267
*17.	362	17.	4439
18.	1703	18.	5725
*19.	9552	19.	9191
20.	8008	20.	9009
*21.	749,257	21.	2,111,795

*Selected Solutions from Set A

1.
$$\begin{array}{r} 96 \\ -32 \\ \hline 64 \end{array}$$

3.
$$\begin{array}{r} 514 \\ -13 \\ \hline 501 \end{array}$$

5.
$$\begin{array}{r} 9876 \\ -1034 \\ \hline 8842 \end{array}$$

7.
$$\begin{array}{r} 7\,13 \\ 8\,\cancel{3} \\ -2\,7 \\ \hline 56 \end{array}$$

9.
$$\begin{array}{r} 2\;12 \\ 3\,\cancel{2}\,9 \\ -95 \\ \hline 234 \end{array}$$

11.
$$\begin{array}{r} 14\;15 \\ 3\;4\;5\,13 \\ 4\,\cancel{5}\,\cancel{6}\,\cancel{3} \\ -2985 \\ \hline 1578 \end{array}$$

13.
$$\begin{array}{r} 5\;9\;17 \\ \cancel{6}\,\cancel{0}\,\cancel{7} \\ -59 \\ \hline 548 \end{array}$$

15.
$$\begin{array}{r} 3\;9\;9\,13 \\ 4\,\cancel{0}\,\cancel{0}\,\cancel{3} \\ -758 \\ \hline 3245 \end{array}$$

17.
$$\begin{array}{r} 4\;4\;9\,10 \\ \cancel{3}\,\cancel{0}\,\cancel{0}\,\cancel{0} \\ -4638 \\ \hline 362 \end{array}$$

19.
$$\begin{array}{r} 5\,12 \\ 14\,\cancel{6}\,\cancel{2}\,5 \\ -5073 \\ \hline 9552 \end{array}$$

21.
$$\begin{array}{r} 8\;16\;\;7\,15 \\ 15\,\cancel{9}\,\cancel{6}\,3\,\cancel{8}\,\cancel{5} \\ -847128 \\ \hline 749257 \end{array}$$

Exercise 2.3

Set A		Set B	
1.	1	1.	4
2.	1	2.	2
3.	1	3.	5
4.	5	4.	4
5.	4	5.	9
6.	4	6.	6
7.	3	7.	9
8.	3	8.	2
9.	4	9.	6
10.	5	10.	5
11.	5	11.	6
12.	7	12.	6
13.	5	13.	5
14.	2	14.	4
15.	8	15.	8
16.	5	16.	3
17.	2	17.	8
18.	9	18.	4
19.	8	19.	7
20.	6	20.	2
21.	4	21.	8
22.	6	22.	8
23.	9	23.	2
24.	5	24.	6
25.	8	25.	7
26.	7	26.	9
27.	6	27.	5
28.	8	28.	6
29.	9	29.	8
30.	9	30.	7
31.	4	31.	9
32.	5	32.	7
33.	3	33.	7
34.	5	34.	5
35.	7	35.	7
36.	6	36.	1
37.	7	37.	6
38.	6	38.	9
39.	3	39.	6

Selected Solutions from Set A

40. $20 \xrightarrow{-4} 16 \xrightarrow{-4} 12 \xrightarrow{-4} 8 \xrightarrow{-4} 4 \xrightarrow{-4} 0$

Thus, $20 \div 4 = 5$

41. $18 \xrightarrow{-3} 15 \xrightarrow{-3} 12 \xrightarrow{-3} 9 \xrightarrow{-3} 6 \xrightarrow{-3} 3 \xrightarrow{-3} 0$

Thus, $3\overline{)18} = 6$

Exercise 2.4

Set A		Set B	
* 1.	6 R1	1.	4 R1
2.	5 R2	2.	6 R1
* 3.	9 R2	3.	9 R2
4.	7 R1	4.	7 R4
* 5.	impossible	5.	impossible
6.	8 R3	6.	8 R7
7.	6 R1	7.	8 R1
8.	impossible	8.	impossible
* 9.	7	9.	6
10.	9	10.	16
*11.	3 R6	11.	7 R3
12.	5 R5	12.	6 R6
*13.	6 R3	13.	9 R3
14.	8 R8	14.	7 R7
15.	2 R5	15.	4 R3
16.	8 R1	16.	5 R3
*17.	8 R2	17.	9 R3
18.	7 R1	18.	8 R3
*19.	7 R4	19.	9 R2
20.	2 R3	20.	7 R1
*21.	8 R3	21.	8 R6
22.	7 R4	22.	9 R1
*23.	4	23.	5
24.	8	24.	8

*Selected Solutions from Set A

1. $4\overline{)25}$ with quotient 6; $\underline{24}$; remainder 1

3. $5\overline{)47}$ with quotient 9; $\underline{45}$; remainder 2

5. It is impossible to divide by zero.

9. $7\overline{)49}$ with quotient 7; $\underline{49}$

11. $8\overline{)30}$ with quotient 3; $\underline{24}$; remainder 6

13. $5\overline{)33}$ with quotient 6; $\underline{30}$; remainder 3

17. $7\overline{)58}$ with quotient 8; $\underline{56}$; remainder 2

19. $7\overline{)53}$ with quotient 7; $\underline{49}$; remainder 4

21. $9\overline{)75}$ with quotient 8; $\underline{72}$; remainder 3

23. $9\overline{)36}$ with quotient 4; $\underline{36}$

Exercise 2.5

Set A

* 1. 243
  2. 332
  3. 24
  4. 24
* 5. 63
  6. 57
  7. 86 R3
  8. 84 R3
  9. 257
  10. 653
*11. 2457 R1
  12. 174 R5
*13. 4772 R1
  14. 3909 R2
*15. 6853
  16. 2457
*17. 51,249
  18. 68,792

Set B

  1. 341
  2. 232
  3. 13
  4. 23
  5. 54
  6. 84
  7. 61 R2
  8. 73 R3
  9. 542 R2
  10. 197 R2
  11. 243 R2
  12. 657 R1
  13. 3216 R1
  14. 2783 R1
  15. 2496
  16. 2468
  17. 24,583
  18. 57,842

*Selected Solutions from Set A

1.
```
    243
2) 486
   4
   8
   8
    6
    6
```

5.
```
    63
7) 441
   42
   21
   21
```

11.
```
    2457
3) 7372
   6
   13
   12
   17
   15
   22
   21
    1
```

13.
```
     4772
4) 19089
   16
   30
   28
   28
   28
    9
    8
    1
```

15.
```
     6853
7) 47971
   42
   59
   56
   37
   35
   21
   21
```

17.
```
      51249
9) 461241
   45
   11
    9
   22
   18
   44
   36
    81
    81
```

Exercise 2.6

Set A

* 1. 17
  2. 23
* 3. 53
  4. 36
* 5. 47 R6
  6. 61 R20
* 7. 65
  8. 65
* 9. 135 R12
  10. 86 R101
*11. 453
  12. 357
*13. 86 R218
  14. 47 R123
*15. 175
  16. 195

Set B

  1. 26
  2. 67
  3. 35
  4. 62
  5. 53 R11
  6. 26 R42
  7. 65
  8. 75
  9. 47 R205
  10. 74 R223
  11. 347
  12. 428
  13. 48 R324
  14. 72 R825
  15. 255
  16. 275

*Selected Solutions from Set A

1.
```
      17
23) 391
    23
    161
    161
```

3.
```
       53
47) 2491
    235
    141
    141
```

5.
```
       47
69) 3249
    276
    489
    483
      6
```

7.
```
        65
232) 15080
     1392
     1160
     1160
```

9.
```
        135
247) 33357
     247
     865
     741
     1247
     1235
       12
```

11.
```
         453
706) 319818
     2824
     3741
     3530
     2118
     2118
```

13.
```
          86
4125) 354968
      33000
      24968
      24750
        218
```

15.
```
           175
5806) 1016050
      5806
      43545
      40642
      29030
      29030
```

Exercise 2.7

Set A

* 1. 400
   2. 700
* 3. 250
   4. 250
* 5. 400
   6. 500
* 7. 503
   8. 206
* 9. 406 R40
  10. 304 R50
*11. 1002
  12. 1003
*13. 602 R50
  14. 703 R40
*15. 2030
  16. 3020

Set B

   1. 500
   2. 800
   3. 250
   4. 250
   5. 600
   6. 900
   7. 307
   8. 408
   9. 302 R37
  10. 406 R25
  11. 1007
  12. 1009
  13. 307 R20
  14. 205 R20
  15. 2004
  16. 3006

*Selected Solutions from Set A

$$1. \quad 6\overline{)2400} = 400$$
$$\underline{24}$$
$$0$$
$$\underline{0}$$
$$0$$
$$\underline{0}$$

$$3. \quad 24\overline{)6000} = 250$$
$$\underline{48}$$
$$120$$
$$\underline{120}$$
$$0$$
$$\underline{0}$$

$$5. \quad 70\overline{)28000} = 400$$
$$\underline{280}$$
$$0$$
$$\underline{0}$$
$$0$$
$$\underline{0}$$

$$7. \quad 43\overline{)21629} = 503$$
$$\underline{215}$$
$$129$$
$$\underline{129}$$

$$9. \quad 68\overline{)27648} = 406$$
$$\underline{272}$$
$$448$$
$$\underline{408}$$
$$40$$

$$11. \quad 23\overline{)23046} = 1002$$
$$\underline{23}$$
$$046$$
$$\underline{46}$$

$$13. \quad 503\overline{)302856} = 602$$
$$\underline{3018}$$
$$1056$$
$$\underline{1006}$$
$$50$$

$$15. \quad 345\overline{)700350} = 2030$$
$$\underline{690}$$
$$1035$$
$$\underline{1035}$$
$$0$$
$$\underline{0}$$

Exercise 2.8

Set A

* 1. 17
   2. 19
* 3. 32
   4. 54
* 5. 16
   6. 16
* 7. 36
   8. 25
   9. 1
  10. 12
*11. 162
  12. 75
*13. 31
  14. 25
  15. 16
  16. 19
*17. 597,000
  18. 4,970,000
*19. 23
  20. 30
  21. 56
  22. 136

Set B

   1. 20
   2. 44
   3. 56
   4. 72
   5. 16
   6. 49
   7. 81
   8. 64
   9. 62
  10. 78
  11. 50
  12. 567
  13. 19
  14. 16
  15. 14
  16. 17
  17. 39,800
  18. 7,995,000
  19. 28
  20. 62
  21. 52
  22. 70

*Selected Solutions from Set A

1. $5 + 3 \times 4 =$
   $5 + \quad 12 \quad =$
   17

3. $(5 + 3) \quad \times 4 =$
   $8 \quad \times 4 =$
   32

5. $24 \times 4 \div 6 =$
   $96 \quad \div 6 =$
   16

7. $24 \div 4 \times 6 =$
   $6 \quad \times 6 =$
   36

11. $(2 + 1)^4 \times (12 - 2 \times 5) =$
    $3^4 \quad \times (12 - 10) =$
    $81 \quad \times \quad 2 =$
    162

13. $\sqrt{100} + 3 \times \sqrt{49} =$
    $10 + 3 \times \quad 7 =$
    $10 + \quad 21 \quad =$
    31

17. $\sqrt{36} \times 10^5 - 3 \times 10^3 =$
    $6 \times 100{,}000 - 3 \times 1000 =$
    $600{,}000 \quad - 3000 =$
    $597{,}000$

19. $16 - 12 \div 4 \times 3 + 8 \times 2 =$
    $16 - \quad 3 \quad \times 3 + 8 \times 2 =$
    $16 - \quad\quad 9 \quad + \quad 16 =$
    $7 \quad\quad + \quad 16 =$
    23

Exercise 2.9

Set A

* 1. prime
2. prime
* 3. composite
4. composite
* 5. composite
6. composite
* 7. 2×3^2
8. $2^3 \times 3$
* 9. 2×23
10. 2×17
*11. $2 \times 3 \times 7$
12. $2 \times 3 \times 11$
13. $2^2 \times 5^3 \times 11$
14. $2^2 \times 5^3 \times 7$
*15. 3×5^2
16. 5×7^2
*17. $5^3 \times 11$
18. $5^3 \times 13$
19. $2^2 \times 3 \times 5 \times 11$
20. $2 \times 5^2 \times 13$
*21. $2 \times 3 \times 37$
22. $3^2 \times 43$
23. 7×19
24. 11×13

Set B

1. composite
2. prime
3. prime
4. composite
5. composite
6. composite
7. 2^4
8. 3^3
9. 2×29
10. 2×31
11. $2^2 \times 3^2$
12. $2^3 \times 5$
13. $2^3 \times 5^4$
14. 2×5^4
15. 2×7^2
16. 2×3^3
17. $5^2 \times 7 \times 11$
18. $3 \times 5^2 \times 7$
19. $2^3 \times 5 \times 13$
20. $2^2 \times 3 \times 5 \times 7$
21. $2 \times 3^2 \times 13$
22. $2 \times 3 \times 7 \times 41$
23. 11×19
24. 7×23

*Selected Solutions from Set A

1. No divisors except for 1 and itself.
3. 3 is a divisor.
5. 5 is a divisor.

7.
$$\begin{array}{r} 1 \\ 3\overline{)3} \\ 3\overline{)9} \\ 2\overline{)18} \\ 18 = 2 \times 3^2 \end{array}$$

9.
$$\begin{array}{r} 1 \\ 23\overline{)23} \\ 2\overline{)46} \\ 46 = 2 \times 23 \end{array}$$

11.
$$\begin{array}{r} 1 \\ 7\overline{)7} \\ 3\overline{)21} \\ 2\overline{)42} \\ 42 = 2 \times 3 \times 7 \end{array}$$

15.
$$\begin{array}{r} 1 \\ 3\overline{)3} \\ 5\overline{)15} \\ 5\overline{)75} \\ 75 = 3 \times 5^2 \end{array}$$

17.
$$\begin{array}{r} 1 \\ 11\overline{)11} \\ 5\overline{)55} \\ 5\overline{)275} \\ 5\overline{)1375} \\ 1375 = 5^3 \times 11 \end{array}$$

21.
$$\begin{array}{r} 1 \\ 37\overline{)37} \\ 3\overline{)111} \\ 2\overline{)222} \\ 222 = 2 \times 3 \times 37 \end{array}$$

Exercise 2.10

Set A

* 1. $949
2. 1148 mi
* 3. $150
4. 40 min
* 5. 168
6. 71 lb
* 7. $348
8. $85
* 9. $1616
10. 9 yrs; 13 yrs
*11. $188
12. 5700 lbs
13. 319,680
14. a) 17 b) 2 c) 15
15. $19,100

Set B

1. $61
2. 16 tickets
3. $1,058,414
4. $589
5. 23 pts.
6. 29 students
7. $93
8. $155,450
9. 443 mi
10. $604
11. 27 people
12. 1494 lb
13. 630,000
14. a) 220 yds
    b) 1320 yds
15. $456

*Selected Solutions from Set A

1. Subtract the discount from the original price.

   $1199 − 250 = $949

3. Divide total to be saved by the number of months.

   2 years = 24 months

   $3600 ÷ 24 = $150

5. Add the scores and divide by 3.

$$\begin{array}{r} 171 \\ 149 \\ +184 \\ \hline 504 \end{array} \qquad \begin{array}{r} 168 \\ 3\overline{)504} \end{array}$$

7. Number of overtime hours: $52 − 40 = 12$

   Regular pay: $6 × 40 = $240
   Overtime pay: $9 × 12 = $\underline{108}$
                    total: $348

9. Divide the yearly earnings by 12.

   $19,392 ÷ 12 = $1616 per month

11. Subtract costs from amount received and divide that amount into four parts.

    $787 − 35 = $752
    $752 ÷ 4 = $188

Chapter 2

Practice Test A

1. 225
2. 28,824
3. 30,416
4. 8
5. 8 R3
6. impossible
7. 69 R5
8. 2972
9. 657
10. 309 R5
11. 800
12. 30,030
13. 49
14. $2 \times 3 \times 5^3$
15. 163

Practice Test B

1. 521
2. 67,655
3. 5214
4. 5
5. 8 R1
6. impossible
7. 78 R1
8. 2063
9. 356
10. 409 R20
11. 800
12. 370
13. 56
14. $2^2 \times 3 \times 5 \times 11$
15. 106 boxes

Unit 1 Exam

1. five billion, twelve thousand, five hundred seventy-six
2. 3717
3. 83,259
4. 3,502,625
5. 174,320,000
6. 73
7. 4636
8. 45,643
9. 398
10. 82 R3
11. 3006
12. 76
13. $2^3 \times 5 \times 17$
14. $140
15. $164

Unit II

Brain Buster

approximately 31.7 years

Chapter 3

Pretest

1. 49
2. $3\frac{2}{3}$
3. $\frac{27}{50}$
4. $\frac{7}{10}$
5. $5\frac{16}{21}$
6. 185 people
7. $\frac{2}{3}$
8. $\frac{7}{16}$
9. $1\frac{29}{240}$
10. $\frac{7}{72}$
11. $\frac{8}{9}$
12. $6\frac{7}{15}$
13. $1\frac{13}{22}$
14. $\frac{8}{9}$, $\frac{7}{8}$, $\frac{2}{3}$
15. 12¢

Exercise 3.1

Set A

* 1. $\frac{9}{16}$
2. $\frac{7}{16}$
* 3. $\frac{4}{7}$
4. $\frac{3}{7}$
* 5. $\frac{3}{8}$
6. $\frac{5}{8}$
* 7. $\frac{17}{20}$, $\frac{3}{20}$
8. $\frac{3}{11}$, $\frac{8}{11}$
* 9. $\frac{17}{30}$, $\frac{13}{30}$
10. $\frac{63}{100}$

Set B

1. $\frac{3}{5}$
2. $\frac{2}{5}$
3. $\frac{5}{9}$
4. $\frac{4}{9}$
5. $\frac{3}{8}$
6. $\frac{5}{8}$
7. $\frac{19}{25}$, $\frac{6}{25}$
8. $\frac{5}{12}$, $\frac{7}{12}$
9. $\frac{23}{40}$, $\frac{17}{40}$
10. $\frac{11}{100}$

*11. $\dfrac{1}{5}$

11. $\dfrac{1}{8}$

*12. $\dfrac{1}{2}, \dfrac{3}{5}, \dfrac{15}{16}$

12. $\dfrac{1}{5}, \dfrac{2}{3}, \dfrac{5}{8}$

13. $\dfrac{9}{6}, \dfrac{8}{1}, \dfrac{7}{7}$

13. $\dfrac{9}{4}, \dfrac{7}{1}, \dfrac{3}{3}$

14. $\dfrac{7}{8}, \dfrac{3}{4}$

14. $\dfrac{17}{32}, \dfrac{3}{5}, \dfrac{1}{10}$

*15. $\dfrac{12}{7}, \dfrac{7}{3}, \dfrac{10}{1}, \dfrac{19}{19}$

15. $\dfrac{11}{8}, \dfrac{5}{1}, \dfrac{5}{5}$

*Selected Solutions from Set A

1. 9 out of 16 sections are shaded. It is $\dfrac{9}{16}$ shaded.

3. 4 out of 7 sections are shaded. It is $\dfrac{4}{7}$ shaded.

5. 3 out of 8 sections are shaded. It is $\dfrac{3}{8}$ shaded.

7. 17 out of 20 $= \dfrac{17}{20}$, 3 out of 20 $= \dfrac{3}{20}$

9. 17 out of 30 $= \dfrac{17}{30}$, 13 out of 30 $= \dfrac{13}{30}$

11. 1 out of 5 $= \dfrac{1}{5}$

12. Proper fractions have numerators that are smaller than their denominators. Thus, $\dfrac{1}{2}$, $\dfrac{3}{5}$, and $\dfrac{15}{16}$ are proper fractions.

15. In $\dfrac{12}{7}$, $\dfrac{7}{3}$, $\dfrac{10}{1}$, and $\dfrac{19}{19}$, the denominators are not larger then the numerators. Thus, they are improper fractions.

Exercise 3.2

Set A	Set B
* 1. 3	1. 5
2. 4	2. 2
3. 6	3. 12
4. 9	4. 8
* 5. 28	5. 28
6. 32	6. 24
* 7. 60	7. 24
8. 36	8. 35
9. 30	9. 63
10. 12	10. 60
*11. $\dfrac{1}{5}$	11. $\dfrac{1}{4}$
12. $\dfrac{1}{3}$	12. $\dfrac{1}{2}$
13. $\dfrac{5}{9}$	13. $\dfrac{2}{3}$
14. $\dfrac{2}{3}$	14. $\dfrac{3}{5}$
15. $\dfrac{7}{11}$	15. $\dfrac{9}{11}$

16. $\dfrac{9}{13}$

16. $\dfrac{7}{13}$

*17. $\dfrac{2}{3}$

17. $\dfrac{3}{4}$

18. $\dfrac{3}{8}$

18. $\dfrac{2}{5}$

19. $\dfrac{5}{12}$

19. $\dfrac{25}{36}$

20. $\dfrac{11}{15}$

20. $\dfrac{22}{45}$

21. $\dfrac{26}{147}$

21. $\dfrac{32}{105}$

22. $\dfrac{28}{117}$

22. $\dfrac{29}{138}$

*23. $\dfrac{3}{4}$

23. $\dfrac{47}{59}$

24. $\dfrac{13}{17}$

24. $\dfrac{37}{47}$

*25. $\dfrac{2}{5}$

25. $\dfrac{5}{6}$

26. $\dfrac{3}{4}$

26. $\dfrac{3}{4}$

*27. $\dfrac{4}{7}$

27. $\dfrac{3}{4}$

28. $\dfrac{6}{7}$

28. $\dfrac{29}{36}$

*Selected Solutions from Set A

1. $\dfrac{1}{2} \xrightarrow{\times 3} \dfrac{3}{6}$ (numerator $\times 3$, denominator $\times 3$)

5. $\dfrac{8}{7} \xrightarrow{\times 4} \dfrac{32}{28}$ (numerator $\times 4$, denominator $\times 4$)

7. $\dfrac{6}{5} \xrightarrow{\times 12} \dfrac{72}{60}$ (numerator $\times 12$, denominator $\times 12$)

11. $\dfrac{3}{15} \xrightarrow{\div 3} \dfrac{1}{5}$ (numerator $\div 3$, denominator $\div 3$)

17. $\dfrac{80}{120} \xrightarrow{\div 10} \dfrac{8}{12} \xrightarrow{\div 4} \dfrac{2}{3}$

23. $\dfrac{108}{144} \xrightarrow{\div 2} \dfrac{54}{72} \xrightarrow{\div 6} \dfrac{9}{12} \xrightarrow{\div 3} \dfrac{3}{4}$

25. $\dfrac{34}{85} \xrightarrow{\div 17} \dfrac{2}{5}$

27. $\dfrac{52}{91} \xrightarrow{\div 13} \dfrac{4}{7}$

Exercise 3.3

Set A	Set B
1. 8	1. 6
2. 7	2. 9
* 3. 5	3. 6
4. 4	4. 6
* 5. $5\frac{2}{3}$	5. $6\frac{1}{3}$
6. $4\frac{1}{6}$	6. $6\frac{1}{4}$
7. $1\frac{3}{7}$	7. $1\frac{5}{6}$
8. $1\frac{3}{8}$	8. $2\frac{2}{5}$
* 9. $7\frac{2}{5}$	9. $5\frac{2}{7}$
10. $9\frac{2}{5}$	10. $8\frac{2}{7}$
*11. $7\frac{13}{16}$	11. $7\frac{7}{19}$
12. $8\frac{4}{17}$	12. $11\frac{7}{13}$
13. $65\frac{2}{7}$	13. $78\frac{1}{7}$
14. $56\frac{4}{7}$	14. $84\frac{5}{7}$
15. $\frac{9}{1}$	15. $\frac{7}{1}$
16. $\frac{8}{1}$	16. $\frac{6}{1}$
*17. $\frac{3}{2}$	17. $\frac{5}{3}$
18. $\frac{8}{5}$	18. $\frac{7}{4}$
*19. $\frac{21}{8}$	19. $\frac{17}{6}$
20. $\frac{20}{7}$	20. $\frac{23}{8}$
21. $\frac{37}{4}$	21. $\frac{33}{4}$
22. $\frac{25}{3}$	22. $\frac{28}{3}$
*23. $\frac{75}{2}$	23. $\frac{49}{2}$
24. $\frac{313}{6}$	24. $\frac{231}{5}$
*25. $\frac{65}{6}$	25. $\frac{165}{8}$
26. $\frac{188}{9}$	26. $\frac{97}{9}$
*27. $\frac{871}{7}$	27. $\frac{996}{7}$
28. $\frac{629}{3}$	28. $\frac{859}{8}$
*29. $\frac{780}{17}$	29. $\frac{758}{19}$
30. $\frac{627}{32}$	30. $\frac{561}{32}$

Selected Solutions from Set A

3. $3\overline{)15}$ has quotient 5

5. $3\overline{)17}$ quotient 5, $\frac{15}{2}$ $= 5\frac{2}{3}$

9. $5\overline{)37}$ quotient 7, $\frac{35}{}$ $= 7\frac{2}{5}$

11. $16\overline{)125}$ quotient 7, $\frac{112}{}$ $= 7\frac{13}{16}$

17. $1 \overset{+}{\underset{\times}{\gtrless}} \frac{1}{2} \Rightarrow \frac{3}{2}$

19. $2 \overset{+}{\underset{\times}{\gtrless}} \frac{5}{8} \Rightarrow \frac{21}{8}$

23. $37 \overset{+}{\underset{\times}{\gtrless}} \frac{1}{2} \Rightarrow \frac{75}{2}$

25. $10 \overset{+}{\underset{\times}{\gtrless}} \frac{5}{6} \Rightarrow \frac{65}{6}$

27. $124 \overset{+}{\underset{\times}{\gtrless}} \frac{3}{7} \Rightarrow \frac{871}{7}$

29. $45 \overset{+}{\underset{\times}{\gtrless}} \frac{15}{17} \Rightarrow \frac{780}{17}$

Exercise 3.4

Set A	Set B
* 1. $\frac{3}{8}$	1. $\frac{3}{16}$
2. $\frac{2}{15}$	2. $\frac{1}{6}$
3. $\frac{35}{72}$	3. $\frac{30}{77}$
4. $\frac{63}{80}$	4. $\frac{21}{40}$
* 5. $\frac{3}{5}$	5. $\frac{4}{5}$
6. $\frac{2}{3}$	6. $\frac{3}{4}$
7. $3\frac{1}{3}$	7. $3\frac{3}{4}$
8. $2\frac{4}{7}$	8. $4\frac{2}{3}$
* 9. $\frac{5}{21}$	9. $\frac{7}{15}$
10. $\frac{5}{21}$	10. $\frac{5}{14}$
11. $1\frac{13}{42}$	11. $2\frac{8}{9}$
12. $1\frac{7}{15}$	12. $1\frac{5}{21}$
*13. $\frac{3}{28}$	13. $\frac{4}{15}$
14. $\frac{1}{6}$	14. $\frac{7}{15}$
*15. $\frac{1}{5}$	15. $\frac{1}{5}$
16. $\frac{1}{7}$	16. $\frac{1}{7}$
*17. $1\frac{5}{21}$	17. $\frac{22}{27}$

18. $1\frac{5}{28}$

19. $\frac{32}{105}$

20. $\frac{21}{40}$

*21. $\frac{2}{5}$

22. $\frac{1}{9}$

*23. $\frac{55}{126}$

24. $\frac{11}{12}$

25. $\frac{35}{576}$

26. $\frac{147}{2560}$

18. $\frac{14}{15}$

19. 1

20. $\frac{4}{75}$

21. $\frac{14}{135}$

22. $\frac{15}{56}$

23. $\frac{7}{72}$

24. $\frac{5}{84}$

25. $\frac{392}{405}$

26. $\frac{28}{405}$

*Selected Solutions from Set A

1. $\frac{1}{2} \times \frac{3}{4} = \frac{3}{8}$

5. $3 \times \frac{1}{5} = \frac{3}{5}$

9. $\frac{\cancel{6}^{1}}{7} \times \frac{5}{\cancel{9}_{3}} = \frac{5}{21}$

13. $\frac{\cancel{12}^{3}}{\cancel{35}_{7}} \times \frac{\cancel{5}^{1}}{\cancel{16}_{4}} = \frac{3}{28}$

15. $3 \times \frac{\cancel{4}^{1}}{\cancel{25}_{5}} \times \frac{\cancel{5}^{1}}{\cancel{12}_{3}} = \frac{3}{15} = \frac{1}{5}$

17. $\frac{13}{\cancel{35}_{7}} \times \frac{\cancel{14}^{2}}{\cancel{21}_{3}} \times \frac{\cancel{5}^{1}}{} = \frac{26}{21} = 1\frac{5}{21}$

21. $\frac{1}{\cancel{3}_{1}} \times \frac{\cancel{6}^{2}}{\cancel{13}_{1}} \times \frac{\cancel{39}^{3}}{15} = \frac{6}{15} = \frac{2}{5}$

23. $\frac{\cancel{20}^{5}}{\cancel{21}_{7}} \times \frac{\cancel{19}^{1}}{\cancel{36}_{9}} \times \frac{\cancel{33}^{11}}{\cancel{38}_{2}} = \frac{55}{126}$

Exercise 3.5

Set A

*1. $\frac{2}{3}$

2. $\frac{3}{4}$

*3. $1\frac{1}{9}$

4. $\frac{35}{36}$

*5. $\frac{10}{21}$

6. $\frac{28}{45}$

Set B

1. $\frac{5}{6}$

2. $\frac{3}{5}$

3. $1\frac{3}{25}$

4. $\frac{15}{16}$

5. $\frac{15}{28}$

6. $\frac{21}{44}$

7. $\frac{5}{7}$

8. $1\frac{1}{3}$

*9. $\frac{1}{6}$

10. $\frac{1}{10}$

11. 3

12. $\frac{1}{4}$

*13. $20\frac{1}{4}$

14. $11\frac{1}{5}$

*15. $\frac{11}{42}$

16. $\frac{5}{18}$

*17. $\frac{8}{9}$

18. $\frac{9}{20}$

19. $3\frac{1}{9}$

20. $1\frac{1}{2}$

7. $1\frac{1}{4}$

8. $\frac{3}{5}$

9. $\frac{1}{12}$

10. $\frac{1}{16}$

11. 5

12. 3

13. $13\frac{1}{3}$

14. $12\frac{3}{5}$

15. $\frac{5}{24}$

16. $\frac{7}{30}$

17. $2\frac{4}{9}$

18. $\frac{5}{12}$

19. $1\frac{1}{7}$

20. $\frac{1}{2}$

*Selected Solutions from Set A

1. $\frac{1}{3} \div \frac{1}{2} = \frac{1}{3} \times \frac{2}{1} = \frac{2}{3}$

3. $\frac{2}{3} \div \frac{3}{5} = \frac{2}{3} \times \frac{5}{3} = \frac{10}{9} = 1\frac{1}{9}$

5. $\frac{6}{9} \div \frac{7}{5} = \frac{\cancel{6}^{2}}{\cancel{9}_{3}} \times \frac{5}{7} = \frac{10}{21}$

9. $\frac{2}{3} \div 4 = \frac{2}{3} \div \frac{4}{1} = \frac{\cancel{2}^{1}}{3} \times \frac{1}{\cancel{4}_{2}} = \frac{1}{6}$

13. $18 \div \frac{8}{9} = \frac{\cancel{18}^{9}}{1} \times \frac{9}{\cancel{8}_{4}} = \frac{81}{4} = 20\frac{1}{4}$

15. $\frac{5}{18} \div \frac{35}{33} = \frac{\cancel{5}^{1}}{\cancel{18}_{6}} \times \frac{\cancel{33}^{11}}{\cancel{35}_{7}} = \frac{11}{42}$

17. $\frac{20}{42} \div \frac{15}{28} = \frac{\cancel{20}^{4}}{\cancel{42}_{3}} \times \frac{\cancel{28}^{2}}{\cancel{15}_{3}} = \frac{8}{9}$

Exercise 3.6

Set A

* 1. $4\frac{7}{12}$

2. $6\frac{3}{4}$

* 3. 86

4. $91\frac{1}{5}$

* 5. $109\frac{5}{7}$

6. 496

* 7. $1\frac{13}{63}$

8. $\frac{65}{76}$

* 9. $6\frac{5}{32}$

10. $2\frac{5}{32}$

*11. $\frac{2}{3}$

12. 6

Set B

1. $6\frac{5}{12}$

2. $12\frac{3}{4}$

3. 105

4. $66\frac{1}{4}$

5. $54\frac{6}{11}$

6. 100

7. $1\frac{21}{37}$

8. $\frac{25}{36}$

9. $8\frac{27}{32}$

10. $8\frac{1}{8}$

11. $\frac{6}{7}$

12. 12

*Selected Solutions from Set A

1. $2\frac{3}{4} \times 1\frac{2}{3} = \frac{11}{4} \times \frac{5}{3} = \frac{55}{12} = 4\frac{7}{12}$

3. $5\frac{3}{8} \times 16 = \frac{43}{\cancel{8}} \times \frac{\overset{2}{\cancel{16}}}{1} = \frac{86}{1} = 86$

5. $26\frac{2}{3} \times 4\frac{4}{35} = \frac{\overset{16}{\cancel{80}}}{\cancel{3}} \times \frac{\overset{48}{\cancel{144}}}{\cancel{35}} = \frac{768}{7} = 109\frac{5}{7}$

7. $7\frac{3}{5} \div 6\frac{3}{10} = \frac{38}{5} \div \frac{63}{10} = \frac{38}{\cancel{5}} \times \frac{\overset{2}{\cancel{10}}}{63}$

$= \frac{76}{63} = 1\frac{13}{63}$

9. $24\frac{5}{8} \div 4 = \frac{197}{8} \div \frac{4}{1} = \frac{197}{8} \times \frac{1}{4}$

$= \frac{197}{32} = 6\frac{5}{32}$

11. $5 \div 7\frac{1}{2} = \frac{5}{1} \div \frac{15}{2} = \frac{\overset{1}{\cancel{5}}}{1} \times \frac{2}{\underset{3}{\cancel{15}}} = \frac{2}{3}$

Exercise 3.7

Set A

* 1. $268\frac{1}{2}$

2. 147

* 3. 1708

4. $1578\frac{3}{4}$

* 5. $2\frac{13}{16}$

6. $3\frac{1}{3}$

* 7. $9\frac{5}{32}$

8. $16\frac{7}{10}$

* 9. 1839 voters

10. 6250 bulbs

*11. \$39
12. 628 students
*13. 219 pennies
14. 16 players

Set B

1. 13

2. $28\frac{1}{2}$

3. $380\frac{2}{3}$

4. 488

5. $18\frac{27}{32}$

6. $10\frac{5}{16}$

7. $53\frac{21}{32}$

8. $81\frac{9}{16}$

9. 930 students

10. $42\frac{2}{3}$ oz

11. 3562 students
12. \$39
13. 308 people
14. 171 workers

*Selected Solutions from Set A

1. $\frac{1}{2}$ of $537 = \frac{1}{2} \times \frac{537}{1} = 268\frac{1}{2}$

3. $\frac{2}{5}$ of $4270 = \frac{2}{\cancel{5}} \times \frac{\overset{854}{\cancel{4270}}}{1} = 1708$

5. $\frac{3}{8}$ of $7\frac{1}{2} = \frac{3}{8} \times \frac{15}{2} = \frac{45}{16} = 2\frac{13}{16}$

7. $\frac{1}{4}$ of $36\frac{5}{8} = \frac{1}{4} \times \frac{293}{8} = \frac{293}{32} = 9\frac{5}{32}$

9. Find $\frac{3}{4}$ of the total voters:

$\frac{3}{4}$ of $2452 = \frac{3}{\cancel{4}} \times \frac{\overset{613}{\cancel{2452}}}{1} = 1839$

11. Discount:
    1/4 of \$52 = 1/4 × \$52 = \$13
    Sale price: \$52− \$13 = \$39

13. Find the number of pennies:
    3/4 of 876 = 3/4 × 876 = 657
    2/3 are dated 1983 or later.
    2/3 of 657 = 2/3 × 657 = 438
    Number after 1983: 657 − 438 = 219

Exercise 3.8

Set A   **Set B**

* 1. $\frac{2}{7}$ 1. $\frac{2}{9}$

2. $\frac{2}{3}$ 2. $\frac{2}{5}$

* 3. $\frac{1}{9}$ 3. $\frac{1}{7}$

4. $\frac{2}{7}$ 4. $\frac{2}{9}$

* 5. $\frac{1}{2}$ 5. $\frac{1}{2}$

6. $\frac{1}{2}$ 6. $\frac{1}{2}$

* 7. $\frac{1}{9}$ 7. $\frac{1}{3}$

8. $\frac{2}{5}$ 8. $\frac{2}{9}$

* 9. 3   9. 5
10. 6   10. 4
*11. 3   11. 2

12. $3\frac{2}{3}$ 12. 2

*13. 1   13. 1
14. 1   14. 1

*15. $\frac{7}{16}$ 15. $\frac{9}{16}$

16. $\frac{9}{16}$ 16. $\frac{3}{4}$

*17. $1\frac{1}{6}$ 17. $\frac{31}{32}$

18. $\frac{15}{16}$ 18. $1\frac{1}{18}$

*Selected Solutions from Set A

1. $\frac{1}{7} + \frac{1}{7} = \frac{1+1}{7} = \frac{2}{7}$

3. $\frac{3}{9} - \frac{2}{9} = \frac{3-2}{9} = \frac{1}{9}$

5. $\frac{3}{8} + \frac{1}{8} = \frac{3+1}{8} = \frac{4}{8} = \frac{1}{2}$

7. $\frac{7}{18} - \frac{5}{18} = \frac{7-5}{18} = \frac{2}{18} = \frac{1}{9}$

9. $\frac{4}{3} + \frac{5}{3} = \frac{4+5}{3} = \frac{9}{3} = 3$

11. $\frac{19}{5} - \frac{4}{5} = \frac{19-4}{5} = \frac{15}{5} = 3$

13. $\frac{3}{8} + \frac{2}{8} + \frac{3}{8} = \frac{3+2+3}{8} = \frac{8}{8} = 1$

15. $\frac{11}{32} + \frac{5}{32} - \frac{2}{32} = \frac{11+5-2}{32} = \frac{14}{32} = \frac{7}{16}$

17. $\frac{25}{54} + \frac{21}{54} + \frac{17}{54} = \frac{25+21+17}{54}$

$= \frac{63}{54} = \frac{7}{6} = 1\frac{1}{6}$

Exercise 3.9

Set A   **Set B**

* 1. $\frac{3}{4}$ 1. $\frac{1}{2}$

2. $\frac{5}{6}$ 2. $\frac{3}{4}$

* 3. $\frac{1}{8}$ 3. $\frac{3}{8}$

4. $\frac{3}{8}$ 4. $\frac{5}{8}$

* 5. $\frac{5}{12}$ 5. $\frac{1}{12}$

6. $\frac{5}{12}$ 6. $\frac{1}{12}$

* 7. $\frac{9}{10}$ 7. $\frac{3}{4}$

8. $\frac{9}{10}$ 8. $\frac{3}{4}$

* 9. $\frac{1}{30}$ 9. $\frac{1}{20}$

10. $\frac{1}{40}$ 10. $\frac{7}{30}$

*11. 4   11. 3
12. 5   12. 4

*13. $1\frac{9}{32}$ 13. $\frac{29}{32}$

14. $\frac{27}{32}$ 14. $\frac{31}{32}$

*15. $2\frac{11}{12}$ 15. $1\frac{1}{4}$

16. $2\frac{5}{12}$ 16. $2\frac{3}{4}$

*Selected Solutions from Set A

1. $\frac{1}{2} = \frac{2}{4}$ 3. $\frac{3}{4} = \frac{6}{8}$
   $\underline{+\frac{1}{4} = \frac{1}{4}}$ $\underline{-\frac{5}{8} = \frac{5}{8}}$
   $\qquad \frac{3}{4}$ $\qquad \frac{1}{8}$

5. $\frac{3}{4} = \frac{9}{12}$ 7. $\frac{3}{20} = \frac{3}{20}$
   $\underline{-\frac{1}{3} = \frac{4}{12}}$ $\underline{+\frac{3}{4} = \frac{15}{20}}$
   $\qquad \frac{5}{12}$ $\qquad \frac{18}{20} = \frac{9}{10}$

9. $\dfrac{5}{6} = \dfrac{25}{30}$
$-\dfrac{4}{5} = \dfrac{24}{30}$
$\dfrac{1}{30}$

11. $\dfrac{7}{10} = \dfrac{7}{10}$
$+\dfrac{5}{2} = \dfrac{25}{10}$
$+\dfrac{4}{5} = \dfrac{8}{10}$
$\dfrac{40}{10} = 4$

13. $\dfrac{3}{8} = \dfrac{12}{32}$
$+\dfrac{15}{32} = \dfrac{15}{32}$
$+\dfrac{7}{16} = \dfrac{14}{32}$
$\dfrac{41}{32} = 1\dfrac{9}{32}$

15. $\dfrac{1}{4} = \dfrac{3}{12}$
$+\dfrac{3}{6} = \dfrac{6}{12}$
$+\dfrac{9}{2} = \dfrac{54}{12}$
$-\dfrac{7}{3} = \dfrac{28}{12}$
$\dfrac{35}{12} = 2\dfrac{11}{12}$

5. LCD = 36
$\dfrac{5}{18} = \dfrac{10}{36}$
$+\dfrac{1}{12} = \dfrac{3}{36}$
$\dfrac{13}{36}$

7. LCD = 72
$\dfrac{13}{18} = \dfrac{52}{72}$
$-\dfrac{11}{24} = \dfrac{33}{72}$
$\dfrac{19}{72}$

9. LCD = 252
$\dfrac{5}{42} = \dfrac{30}{252}$
$+\dfrac{7}{36} = \dfrac{49}{252}$
$+\dfrac{1}{21} = \dfrac{12}{252}$
$\dfrac{91}{252}$ 91 ÷7 →13, = , 252 ÷7 →36 → $\dfrac{13}{36}$

11. LCD = 960
$\dfrac{7}{64} = \dfrac{105}{960}$
$+\dfrac{11}{48} = \dfrac{220}{960}$
$-\dfrac{5}{40} = \dfrac{120}{960}$
$\dfrac{205}{960} = \dfrac{41}{192}$

LCD for Problem 9:
$42 = 2 \times 3 \times 7$
$36 = 2^2 \times 3^2$
$21 = 3 \times 7$
$LCD = 2^2 \times 3^2 \times 7 = 252$

Exercise 3.10

Set A	Set B
* 1. $\dfrac{7}{18}$	1. $\dfrac{19}{24}$
2. $\dfrac{13}{24}$	2. $\dfrac{11}{18}$
* 3. $\dfrac{1}{12}$	3. $\dfrac{13}{30}$
4. $\dfrac{11}{30}$	4. $\dfrac{1}{12}$
* 5. $\dfrac{13}{36}$	5. $\dfrac{23}{48}$
6. $\dfrac{25}{48}$	6. $\dfrac{23}{36}$
* 7. $\dfrac{19}{72}$	7. $\dfrac{83}{240}$
8. $\dfrac{101}{240}$	8. $\dfrac{23}{72}$
* 9. $\dfrac{13}{36}$	9. $\dfrac{7}{12}$
10. $\dfrac{55}{84}$	10. $\dfrac{127}{252}$
*11. $\dfrac{41}{192}$	11. $\dfrac{127}{960}$
12. $\dfrac{79}{252}$	12. $\dfrac{17}{84}$

*Selected Solutions from Set A

1. LCD = 18
$\dfrac{1}{6} = \dfrac{3}{18}$
$+\dfrac{2}{9} = \dfrac{4}{18}$
$\dfrac{7}{18}$

3. LCD = 60
$\dfrac{11}{20} = \dfrac{33}{60}$
$-\dfrac{7}{15} = \dfrac{28}{60}$
$\dfrac{5}{60} = \dfrac{1}{12}$

Exercise 3.11

Set A	Set B
* 1. 7	1. 8
2. $11\dfrac{3}{8}$	2. $14\dfrac{1}{2}$
* 3. $16\dfrac{7}{16}$	3. $16\dfrac{7}{16}$
4. $23\dfrac{1}{24}$	4. $14\dfrac{1}{18}$
5. $128\dfrac{23}{24}$	5. $106\dfrac{1}{24}$
6. $141\dfrac{67}{90}$	6. $136\dfrac{31}{42}$
* 7. $2\dfrac{3}{4}$	7. $2\dfrac{3}{4}$
8. $4\dfrac{1}{2}$	8. $2\dfrac{4}{7}$
* 9. $72\dfrac{5}{6}$	9. $62\dfrac{5}{6}$
10. $54\dfrac{13}{30}$	10. $114\dfrac{35}{54}$
*11. $4\dfrac{4}{9}$	11. $2\dfrac{2}{3}$
12. $5\dfrac{3}{7}$	12. $3\dfrac{4}{11}$

*Selected Solutions from Set A

1. $4\dfrac{5}{6} = \dfrac{29}{6}$

   $+2\dfrac{1}{6} = \dfrac{13}{6}$

   $\rule{3cm}{0.4pt}$

   $\dfrac{42}{6} = 7$

3. $9\dfrac{13}{16} = 9\dfrac{13}{16}$

   $+6\dfrac{5}{8} = 6\dfrac{10}{16}$

   $\rule{4cm}{0.4pt}$

   $15\dfrac{23}{16} = 15 + 1\dfrac{7}{16} = 16\dfrac{7}{16}$

7. $8\dfrac{5}{8} = \dfrac{69}{8}$

   $-5\dfrac{7}{8} = \dfrac{47}{8}$

   $\rule{4cm}{0.4pt}$

   $\dfrac{22}{8} = \dfrac{11}{4} = 2\dfrac{3}{4}$

11. $9 = 8\dfrac{9}{9}$

   $-4\dfrac{5}{9} = 4\dfrac{5}{9}$

   $\rule{3cm}{0.4pt}$

   $4\dfrac{4}{9}$

9. $94\dfrac{5}{14} = 94\dfrac{15}{42} = 93\dfrac{57}{42}$

   $-21\dfrac{11}{21} = -21\dfrac{22}{42} = -21\dfrac{22}{42}$

   $\rule{6cm}{0.4pt}$

   $72\dfrac{35}{42} = 72\dfrac{5}{6}$

Exercise 3.12

Set A

* 1. $1\dfrac{1}{8}$
2. $\dfrac{20}{21}$
3. $1\dfrac{1}{6}$
4. $1\dfrac{1}{4}$
* 5. $\dfrac{111}{122}$
6. $\dfrac{145}{194}$
7. $1\dfrac{4}{7}$
8. $1\dfrac{7}{13}$
* 9. $\dfrac{12}{17}$

Set B

1. $\dfrac{9}{10}$
2. $1\dfrac{1}{20}$
3. $2\dfrac{1}{2}$
4. $\dfrac{5}{6}$
5. $\dfrac{116}{195}$
6. $\dfrac{201}{308}$
7. $1\dfrac{5}{14}$
8. $4\dfrac{3}{5}$
9. $\dfrac{12}{17}$

10. $\dfrac{15}{22}$

*11. $\dfrac{61}{384}$

12. $\dfrac{41}{288}$

13. $2\dfrac{19}{34}$

14. $2\dfrac{2}{9}$

10. $\dfrac{15}{22}$

11. $\dfrac{19}{90}$

12. $\dfrac{55}{144}$

13. $12\dfrac{2}{7}$

14. $4\dfrac{16}{21}$

*Selected Solutions from Set A

1. $\dfrac{\frac{3}{4}}{\frac{2}{3}} = \dfrac{3}{4} \div \dfrac{2}{3} = \dfrac{3}{4} \times \dfrac{3}{2} = \dfrac{9}{8} = 1\dfrac{1}{8}$

5. $\dfrac{3\frac{7}{10}}{4\frac{1}{15}} = \dfrac{\frac{37}{10}}{\frac{61}{15}} = \dfrac{37}{10} \div \dfrac{61}{15}$

   $= \dfrac{37}{\underset{2}{\cancel{10}}} \times \dfrac{\overset{3}{\cancel{15}}}{61} = \dfrac{111}{122}$

9. $\dfrac{\frac{3}{8} + \frac{5}{8}}{\frac{2}{3} + \frac{3}{4}} = \dfrac{\frac{8}{8}}{\frac{8}{12} + \frac{9}{12}} = \dfrac{1}{\frac{17}{12}}$

   $= 1 \div \dfrac{17}{12} = 1 \times \dfrac{12}{17} = \dfrac{12}{17}$

11. $\dfrac{1\frac{5}{16} + 2\frac{1}{2}}{24} = \dfrac{\frac{21}{16} + \frac{5}{2}}{24}$

   $= \dfrac{\frac{21}{16} + \frac{40}{16}}{24} = \dfrac{\frac{61}{16}}{\frac{24}{1}}$

   $= \dfrac{61}{16} \div \dfrac{24}{1} = \dfrac{61}{16} \times \dfrac{1}{24} = \dfrac{61}{384}$

Exercise 3.13

Set A

* 1. =
2. =
3. >
4. >
* 5. <
6. <
* 7. <
8. >
* 9. $\dfrac{9}{16}, \dfrac{1}{2}, \dfrac{3}{8}$
10. $1\dfrac{2}{3}, 1\dfrac{3}{5}, 1\dfrac{1}{2}$

Set B

1. =
2. =
3. >
4. >
5. <
6. <
7. >
8. <
9. $\dfrac{5}{8}, \dfrac{1}{2}, \dfrac{7}{16}$
10. $1\dfrac{3}{4}, 1\dfrac{2}{3}, 1\dfrac{2}{5}$

*11. $\dfrac{3}{2}, \dfrac{5}{4}, \dfrac{4}{5}, \dfrac{2}{3}$ 11. $\dfrac{3}{2}, \dfrac{4}{3}, \dfrac{4}{5}, \dfrac{3}{4}$

12. $\dfrac{9}{4}, \dfrac{15}{7}, 2, \dfrac{11}{6}$ 12. $\dfrac{7}{3}, \dfrac{15}{7}, 2, \dfrac{11}{6}$

*13. $\dfrac{11}{12}, \dfrac{13}{15}, \dfrac{11}{18}$ 13. $\dfrac{7}{15}, \dfrac{5}{12}, \dfrac{7}{18}$

*Selected Solutions from Set A

1. LCD = 6; $\dfrac{1}{2} = \dfrac{3}{6}$

5. LCD = 42; $\dfrac{5}{6} = \dfrac{35}{42}, \dfrac{6}{7} = \dfrac{36}{42}$

   So, $\dfrac{5}{6} < \dfrac{6}{7}$

7. LCD = 12; $\dfrac{5}{4} = \dfrac{15}{12}, \dfrac{4}{3} = \dfrac{16}{12}$

   So, $\dfrac{5}{4} < \dfrac{4}{3}$

9. LCD = 16; $\dfrac{1}{2} = \dfrac{8}{16}, \dfrac{3}{8} = \dfrac{6}{16}, \dfrac{9}{16} = \dfrac{9}{16}$

   But $\dfrac{9}{16} > \dfrac{8}{16} > \dfrac{6}{16}$

   So, $\dfrac{9}{16} > \dfrac{1}{2} > \dfrac{3}{8}$

11. LCD = 60

    $\dfrac{5}{4} = \dfrac{75}{60}$ $\dfrac{3}{2} = \dfrac{90}{60}$

    $\dfrac{4}{5} = \dfrac{48}{60}$ $\dfrac{2}{3} = \dfrac{40}{60}$

    But $\dfrac{90}{60} > \dfrac{75}{60} > \dfrac{48}{60} > \dfrac{40}{60}$

    So, $\dfrac{3}{2} > \dfrac{5}{4} > \dfrac{4}{5} > \dfrac{2}{3}$

13. LCD = 180

    $\dfrac{11}{12} = \dfrac{165}{180}, \dfrac{13}{15} = \dfrac{156}{180}, \dfrac{11}{18} = \dfrac{110}{180}$

    But $\dfrac{165}{180} > \dfrac{156}{180} > \dfrac{110}{180}$

    So, $\dfrac{11}{12} > \dfrac{13}{15} > \dfrac{11}{18}$

Exercise 3.14

Set A   **Set B**

1. 97   1. $\dfrac{1}{4}$

2. $\dfrac{1}{4}$ inch bit   2. $\dfrac{4}{5}$

* 3. $\dfrac{1}{5}$ 3. $34\dfrac{3}{8}$ mi

4. $13\dfrac{1}{2}$ lb   4. 48 boards

* 5. 14   5. 154

6. 20 ft   6. $\dfrac{1}{8}$

* 7. $101\dfrac{3}{4}$ lb   7. $4\dfrac{1}{8}$ lb

8. $1\dfrac{4}{5}$ gal   8. $3\dfrac{1}{4}$ lb

9. $77\dfrac{5}{8}$ in.   9. $69\dfrac{1}{8}$ in.

10. 77 oz   10. 391¢ = \$3.91

*11. $30\dfrac{1}{2}$ mi   11. 15 bottles

12. $1\dfrac{1}{3}$ oz   12. 7

13. 36 min   13. 40 min

14. \$7900   14. \$26,115

*15. \$18   15. $32\dfrac{1}{2}$ hr

16. $2\dfrac{5}{8}$ lb   16. $410\dfrac{5}{8}$ ft

17. a) $1\dfrac{3}{4}$ b) $4\dfrac{1}{4}$ 17. a) $4\dfrac{1}{4}$ b) $6\dfrac{5}{6}$

18. 46,000,000 acres   18. 2625 men

19. $1\dfrac{4}{5}$ to $2\dfrac{3}{5}$ lb   19. a) $\dfrac{7}{30}$ b) 168 min

20. 35 lb   20. 1400 lb

*Selected Solutions from Set A

3. "No Shows:" $26{,}000 - 20{,}800 = 5200$

   Fraction: $\dfrac{5200}{26000} = \dfrac{52}{260} = \dfrac{1}{5}$

5. Divide the total length by $3\dfrac{1}{2}$.

   $49 \div 3\dfrac{1}{2} = 49 \div \dfrac{7}{2} = \overset{7}{\cancel{49}} \times \dfrac{2}{\cancel{7}} = 14$

7. Subtract the two weights.

   $236\dfrac{1}{2} - 134\dfrac{3}{4} = \dfrac{473}{2} - \dfrac{539}{4}$

   $= \dfrac{946}{4} - \dfrac{539}{4} = \dfrac{407}{4} = 101\dfrac{3}{4}$

11. Divide miles driven by total number of gallons used.

    $14\dfrac{1}{2} + 15\dfrac{1}{5} + 14\dfrac{1}{10} + 16\dfrac{1}{5} =$

    $14\dfrac{5}{10} + 15\dfrac{2}{10} + 14\dfrac{1}{10} + 16\dfrac{2}{10} = 60$ gal

    $1830 \div 60 = 30\dfrac{1}{2}$

15. Find the difference in the cost of each ad.

    $6\dfrac{3}{4} \times 8 - 4\dfrac{1}{2} \times 8 = \dfrac{27}{4} \times 8 - \dfrac{9}{2} \times 8$

    $= 54 - 36 = \$18$

Chapter 3

Practice Test A   ## Practice Test B

1. 54

2. $\dfrac{107}{6}$

3. $\dfrac{5}{9}$

4. $1\dfrac{1}{4}$

5. $5\dfrac{1}{24}$

6. $\dfrac{3}{4}$

7. $\dfrac{1}{3}$

8. $1\dfrac{17}{45}$

9. $\dfrac{11}{135}$

10. $\dfrac{5}{6}$

11. $6\dfrac{19}{30}$

12. $1\dfrac{1}{3}$

13. $\dfrac{4}{3}, \dfrac{7}{6}, \dfrac{8}{7}$

14. 21 games

15. 27¢

---

1. 41

2. $3\dfrac{2}{3}$

3. $\dfrac{15}{56}$

4. $\dfrac{3}{4}$

5. $9\dfrac{43}{54}$

6. $\dfrac{2}{5}$

7. $1\dfrac{1}{5}$

8. $1\dfrac{8}{63}$

9. $\dfrac{13}{30}$

10. $\dfrac{7}{8}$

11. $7\dfrac{17}{21}$

12. $1\dfrac{11}{52}$

13. $\dfrac{9}{11}, \dfrac{7}{9}, \dfrac{2}{3}$

14. 539 people

15. 12¢

Chapter 4

Pretest

1. twenty-seven and sixteen thousandths
2. 3,907.620
3. 708.3235
4. 764.713
5. 6158.025
6. 6.5
7. 3.1
8. 26,370,000
9. 0.002182

10. $\dfrac{31}{50}$

11. 3.0625
12. 0.5, 0.05, 0.049, 0.005

13. $14\dfrac{23}{45}$

14. $154.96
15. $783.52

Exercise 4.1

Set A

1. five tenths
2. seventeen hundredths
3. thirty-nine thousandths
4. five and seven ten-thousandths
5. sixteen and thirty-five hundredths
6. four hundred twenty-six and nine tenths
7. six and one thousand two hundred thirty-six ten-thousandths
8. 0.7
9. 0.12
10. 9.003
11. 45.0006
12. 100.16
13. 356.207
14. 5023.3517
15. 2,080,000.001086
16. 2 tenths
17. 5 thousandths
18. 4 ten-thousandths
19. 6 tens
20. 7 ones
21. 3 hundredths

Set B

1. seven tenths
2. twenty-nine hundredths
3. seventy-six thousandths
4. six and seven ten-thousandths
5. seventeen and eighty-two hundredths
6. four hundred twenty-nine and seven tenths
7. five and two thousand one hundred seventy-four ten-thousandths
8. 0.5
9. 0.16
10. 4.009
11. 61.0004
12. 1000.05
13. 999.609
14. 8011.1418
15. 3,004,000.000102
16. 4 hundredths
17. 6 thousandths
18. 1 hundred
19. 7 ten-thousandths
20. 2 tens
21. 3 tenths

Exercise 4.2

Set A

* 1. 36.7
2. 4.7
3. 125.5
4. 90.0
* 5. 9.0
6. 0.1
7. 18.72
8. 5.48
* 9. 792.04
10. 0.90
*11. 7.20
12. 1.02
*13. 562.018
14. 562.0185
15. 560
16. 600
17. 46.96
18. 46.964
19. 46.9635

Set B

1. 43.8
2. 116.8
3. 3.3
4. 10.0
5. 38.0
6. 0.3
7. 95.62
8. 0.37
9. 706.02
10. 7.70
11. 24.30
12. 100.03
13. 382.019
14. 382.0194
15. 400
16. 380
17. 52.70
18. 52.695
19. 52.6952

Selected Solutions from Set A

1.   36.72 ≈ 36.7
tenths ⤷ digit to the right
place   is less than 5
Round off by discarding the digits to the right of the
tenths place.

5.   8.95 ≈ 9.0
tenths ⤷ digit to the right
place   is 5
Round off by increasing the tenths place by 1 and
discarding the 5.

9.   792.038218 ≈ 792.04
hundredths ⤷ digit to the right
place   is more than 5
Round off by increasing the hundredths place by 1 and
discarding the 8218.

11.   7.195 ≈ 7.20
hundredths ⤷ digit to the right
place   is 5
Round off by increasing the hundredths place by 1 and
discarding the 5.

13.   562.01846 ≈ 562.018
thousandths ⤷ digit to the right
place   is less than 5
Round off by discarding the digits to the right of the 8.

Exercise 4.3

Set A

* 1. 320.54
2. 523.69
* 3. 0.246
4. 1.236
* 5. 145.88
6. 68.76
* 7. 893.81
8. 1.166
* 9. 153.023
10. 867.2907
*11. 908.1502
12. 6104.2023
*13. 1564.7699

Set B

1. 221.57
2. 193.63
3. 0.0856
4. 0.0878
5. 65.46
6. 89.46
7. 600.15
8. 1.055
9. 545.607
10. 770.7505
11. 148.8833
12. 2131.2073
13. 17330.121

*Selected Solutions from Set A

```
       1 2
1.  2827.04
       4.5
    + 29.
    320.54
```

```
        1
3.    0.05
      0.096
    + 0.1
      0.246
```

```
      11 2
5.   81.26
     43.99
     16.57
    + 4.06
    145.88
```

```
       11 1
7.   586.94
    +306.87
     893.81
```

```
       11
9.   12.6
     14.
   +126.423
    153.023
```

```
       121 1
11. 809.
      3.65
     19.0702
    +76.43
    908.1502
```

```
        22
13.   123.
      86.057
    1283.001
       4.7
    + 68.0119
    1564.7699
```

Exercise 4.4

Set A

* 1. 3.431
2. 9.24
* 3. 21.45
4. 12.14
* 5. 157.983
6. 278.965
* 7. 33.693
8. 18.382
* 9. 688.1852
10. 448.1926
*11. 717.5
12. 405.3
*13. 17.6876
14. 414.0247
*15. 1504.4
16. 4088.2716

Set B

1. 3.433
2. 31.63
3. 48.36
4. 38.23
5. 31.872
6. 104.683
7. 32.986
8. 30.867
9. 329.1972
10. 181.0751
11. 823.2
12. 405.24
13. 18.8765
14. 688.4824
15. 1712.85841
16. 1254.6

*Selected Solutions from Set A

1. 8.6 4 7
    −5.2 1 6
    3.4 3 1

3. 6 10
    4 7 7̶ 0̶
    −2 6.2 5
    2 1.4 5

5. 10 15
    2 0̶ 5̶ 9 9 10
    3̶ 7̶ 6̶ 0̶ 0̶ 0̶
    −1 5 8.0 1 7
    1 5 7.9 8 3

7. 4 1110
    3̶ 7̶ 0̶ 9 3
    −1 8.4 0 0
    3 3.6 9 3

9. 17
    6 7̶ 15
    7̶ 8̶ 5̶.1 8 5 2
    − 9 7.0 0 0 0
    6 8 8.1 8 5 2

11. 4 9 10
    7̶ 5̶ 0̶ 0̶
    − 3 2.5
    7 1 7.5

13. 8 12
    8 9̶ 2̶ 8 7 6
    −7 1.6 0 0 0
    1 7.6 8 7 6

15. 11
    2 1̶ 10
    1 5 3̶ 2̶ 0̶
    −   2 7.6
    1 5 0 4.4

Exercise 4.5

Set A	Set B
* 1. 43.11	1. 65.44
2. 108.75	2. 51.75
* 3. 57.368	3. 57.267
4. 30.906	4. 55.449
* 5. 1805.44	5. 686.72
6. 2417.76	6. 1443.05
* 7. 0.0500350	7. 0.075042
8. 0.140147	8. 0.315072
* 9. 65.36	9. 60.45
10. 0.0212	10. 0.0093
*11. 0.28076	11. 0.63672
12. 265.02	12. 309.452
*13. 299.20178	13. 103.32816
14. 7.6155	14. 8.876525

*Selected Solutions from Set A

1. 1 4.3 7
    ×   3
    4 3.1 1

3. 8.0 8
    × 7.1
    8 0 8
    5 6 5 6
    5 7.3 6 8

5. 6 9 4.4
    ×   2.6
    4 1 6 6 4
    1 3 8 8 8
    1 8 0 5.4 4

7. 2.0 0 1 4
    ×   .0 2 5
    1 0 0 0 7 0
    4 0 0 2 8
    .0 5 0 0 3 5 0

9. 1 6.3 4
    ×   4
    6 5.3 6

11. 7.0 1 9
    ×   .0 4
    .2 8 0 7 6

13. 1 4 8.3 4
    ×   2.0 1 7
    1 0 3 8 3 8
    1 4 8 3 4
    2 9 6 6 8 0
    2 9 9.2 0 1 7 8

Exercise 4.6

Set A	Set B
* 1. 12.6	1. 16.9
2. 13.7	2. 13.7
* 3. 8.14	3. 7.23
4. 9.31	4. 9.16
* 5. 74	5. 25
6. 95	6. 45
* 7. 0.0185	7. 0.0645
8. 0.0175	8. 0.0145
* 9. 0.004	9. 0.0085
10. 0.0035	10. 0.0085
*11. 6200	11. 4700
12. 8400	12. 9800
*13. 39	13. 63
14. 58	14. 78
*15. 0.34375	15. 0.40625
16. 0.21875	16. 0.4375

*Selected Solutions from Set A

1.
```
      12.6
  4) 50.4
     4
     10
      8
      2 4
      2 4
```

3.
```
          8.14
  7.2) 58.6,08
       57 6
        1 00
          72
          2 88
          2 88
```

5.
```
        74.
  0.65) 48.10,
        45 5
         2 60
         2 60
```

7.
```
        .0185
  84) 1.5540
      84
      714
      672
       420
       420
```

9.
```
          .004
  4.09) .01,636
        1 636
```

11.
```
          6200.
  .0034) 21.0800,
         20 4
          68
          68
           0
           0
           0
           0
```

13.
```
         39.
  6.24) 243.36,
        187 2
         56 16
         56 16
```

15.
```
        .34375
  3.2) 1.1,00000
       9 6
       1 40
       1 28
        120
         96
        240
        224
        160
        160
```

Exercise 4.7

Set A

* 1. 1.2
  2. 0.9
* 3. 8.4
  4. 6.5
* 5. 253.3
  6. 203.3
* 7. 1.41
  8. 1.45
* 9. 31.49
 10. 17.45
*11. 0.167
 12. 0.605
 13. 4.010
 14. 5.010

Set B

  1. 0.8
  2. 1.9
  3. 4.7
  4. 5.5
  5. 443.3
  6. 346.7
  7. 0.37
  8. 0.75
  9. 30.77
 10. 71.07
 11. 0.583
 12. 0.467
 13. 3.010
 14. 6.010

*Selected Solutions from Set A

1.
```
        1.21 ≈ 1.2
   7) 8.50
      7
      1 5
      1 4
        10
         7
```

3.
```
           8.35 ≈ 8.4
   .36) 3.00,60
         2 88
         12 6
         10 8
          1 80
          1 08
```

5. 253.33 ≈ 253.3
```
        25 3.33
   2.4) 608.0 00
        48
        128
        120
          8 0
          7 2
            8 0
            7 2
              80
              72
```

7. 1.405 ≈ 1.41
```
         1.405
   6) 8.430
      6
      2 4
      2 4
        30
        30
```

9. 31.487 ≈ 31.49
```
            31.487
   .289) 9.100,000
         8 67
         430
         289
         141 0
         115 6
          25 40
          23 12
           2 280
           2 023
```

11. 0.1666 ≈ 0.167
```
          .1666
   66) 11.0000
       6 6
       4 40
       3 96
         440
         396
         440
         396
```

Exercise 4.8

Set A

* 1. 4360
  2. 52,300
* 3. 952,340
  4. 212,436
* 5. 3906
  6. 4536
* 7. 312,700
  8. 4,173,000
* 9. 0.543
 10. 0.756
*11. 0.35
 12. 0.4
*13. 0.00529
 14. 0.00746
*15. 0.003765
 16. 0.0004087

Set B

  1. 817,000
  2. 6040
  3. 277,725
  4. 16,803,800
  5. 3888
  6. 3876
  7. 7,263,000
  8. 610,800
  9. 0.823
 10. 0.645
 11. 0.4
 12. 0.3
 13. 0.00472
 14. 0.00351
 15. 0.0005103
 16. 0.008274

*Selected Solutions from Set A

1.
```
    4.3 6¦
  ×   1¦0 0 0
    4 3 6¦0.0 0
```

3.
```
    4 7.6 1 7¦
  ×       2¦0 0 0 0
  9 5 2 3 4¦0.0 0 0
```

5.
```
    0.0 9 3¦
  ×   4 2¦0 0 0
    1 8 6¦0 0 0
    3 7 2 ¦
    3 9 0 6¦0 0 0
```

7.
```
    3.1 2 7¦
  ×     1¦0 0 0 0 0
  3 1 2 7¦0 0.0 0 0
```

9.
```
                .543
   100) 54.3 → 1) .543
```

11.
```
               .35
   2 000) 700 → 2) .70
```

13.
```
                           .00529
   370,000) 1957.3 → 37) .19573
                         185
                         107
                          74
                         333
                         333
```

15. $10^5 = 10 \times 10 \times 10 \times 10 \times 10 = 100,000$
```
                         .003765
   100,000) 376.5 → 1) .003765
```

Exercise 4.9

Set A	Set B
* 1. 0.6	1. 0.8
2. 0.5	2. 0.75
3. 0.625	3. 0.375
4. 0.0625	4. 0.3125
* 5. 1.28125	5. 1.21875
6. 1.15625	6. 1.09375
* 7. 0.545	7. 0.556
8. 0.833	8. 0.571
* 9. 1.857	9. 2.231
10. 2.444	10. 3.455
11. 23.667	11. 44.167
12. 37.778	12. 32.143

*13. $\dfrac{3}{5}$ 13. $\dfrac{1}{5}$

14. $\dfrac{2}{5}$ 14. $\dfrac{3}{5}$

*15. $\dfrac{31}{50}$ 15. $\dfrac{43}{50}$

16. $\dfrac{37}{50}$ 16. $\dfrac{49}{50}$

*17. $\dfrac{17}{400}$ 17. $\dfrac{3}{80}$

18. $\dfrac{19}{400}$ 18. $\dfrac{11}{400}$

*19. $4\dfrac{1}{1000}$ 19. $1\dfrac{7}{1000}$

20. $3\dfrac{9}{1000}$ 20. $2\dfrac{3}{1000}$

*Selected Solutions from Set A

1. $\dfrac{3}{5} = 5\overline{)\,\overset{.6}{3.0}}$
   $\underline{3\,0}$

5. $\dfrac{41}{32} = 32\overline{)\,\overset{1.28125}{41.00000}}$
   $\underline{32}$
   $9\,0$
   $\underline{6\,4}$
   $2\,60$
   $\underline{2\,56}$
   40
   $\underline{32}$
   80
   $\underline{64}$
   160
   $\underline{160}$

7. $0.5454 \approx 0.545$

$\dfrac{6}{11} = 11\overline{)\,\overset{.5454\ \approx\ .545}{6.0000}}$
   $\underline{5\,5}$
   50
   $\underline{44}$
   60
   $\underline{55}$
   50
   $\underline{44}$

9. $1\dfrac{6}{7} = \dfrac{13}{7}$

$1.8571 \approx 1.857$

$7\overline{)\,\overset{1.8571}{13.0000}}$
   $\underline{7}$
   $6\,0$
   $\underline{5\,6}$
   40
   $\underline{35}$
   50
   $\underline{49}$
   10
   $\underline{7}$

13. $0.6 = \dfrac{6}{10} = \dfrac{3}{5}$

15. $.62 = \dfrac{62}{100} = \dfrac{31}{50}$

17. $0.0425 = \dfrac{425}{10000}$

$= \dfrac{17}{400}$

19. $4.001 = 4\dfrac{1}{1000}$

Exercise 4.10

Set A	Set B
1. 0.6	1. 0.9
2. 0.75	2. 0.98
3. 2.076	3. 3.1205
4. 5.092	4. 12.706
* 5. 0.6	5. 0.7
6. 0.162	6. 0.129
* 7. 3.402	7. 3.507
8. 76.125	8. 84.306

* 9. $\dfrac{2}{3}$ 9. 0.4

10. $3\dfrac{1}{4}$ 10. $4\dfrac{1}{3}$

*11. $0.76 > 0.706 > 0.7$ 11. $0.37 > 0.307 > 0.3$
   $> 0.6 > 0.076$ $> 0.07 > 0.037$

12. $0.54 > 0.504 > 0.3\ 0.5$ 12. $0.901 > 0.9001 > 0.9$
   $> 0.4 > 0.054$ $> 0.19 > 0.091$

13. $3.12 > 3.102 > 2.3$ 13. $4.3 > 4.03 > 3.4003$
   $> 2.13 > 2$ $> 3.4 > 3.04$

14. $\dfrac{3}{4} > .7 > .65$ 14. $.82 > \dfrac{4}{5} > .755$
   $> \dfrac{3}{5} > .076$ $> \dfrac{5}{8} > .5$

*15. $1.8 > 1.625 > 1\dfrac{1}{2}$ 15. $2\dfrac{7}{8} > 2.78 > 2.7$
   $> 1\dfrac{1}{3} > 1.258$ $> 2\dfrac{2}{3} > 2.66$

*Selected Solutions from Set A

5. $.6 = .60$
       $.06 = .06$
   but $60 > 06$
   so, $.6 > .06$

7. $3.4002 = 3.4002$
       $3.402 = 3.4020$
   but $3.4020 > 3.4002$
   so, $3.402 > 3.4002$

9. $\dfrac{2}{3} = .666\ .\ .$ so $\dfrac{2}{3} > .66$

11. $0.76 = .760$
      $0.706 = .706$
      $0.7 = .700$
      $0.6 = .600$
   $0.076 = .076$
   so, $.76 > .706 > .7 > .6 > .076$

15. $1.8 = 1.800$
      $1.625 = 1.625$
      $1\dfrac{1}{2} = 1.500$
      $1\dfrac{1}{3} = 1.333$
   $1.258 = 1.258$
   so, $1.8 > 1.625 > 1\dfrac{1}{2} > 1\dfrac{1}{3} > 1.258$

Exercise 4.11

Set A
- * 1. 3.2
- 2. 12
- 3. 21
- 4. 11.7
- * 5. $5\frac{9}{20} = 5.45$
- 6. $15\frac{7}{9} \approx 15.78$
- 7. $\frac{7}{12} \approx 0.58$
- 8. $1\frac{13}{20} = 1.65$
- * 9. ≈ 13.34
- 10. 5.17
- 11. 12.25
- 12. 1608.25
- *13. $5\frac{1}{3} \approx 5.33$
- 14. $7\frac{1}{6} \approx 7.17$
- 15. 4.8
- 16. 93.75
- 17. 76
- 18. 11.375

Set B
- 1. 6.4
- 2. 15
- 3. 29.9
- 4. 11.7
- 5. $7\frac{1}{25} = 7.04$
- 6. $21\frac{1}{2} = 21.5$
- 7. $1\frac{2}{3} \approx 1.67$
- 8. $3\frac{3}{16} \approx 3.19$
- 9. 46.53
- 10. 20.59
- 11. 11.35
- 12. 2006.35
- 13. $11\frac{1}{3} \approx 11.33$
- 14. $7\frac{2}{3} \approx 7.67$
- 15. 12.5
- 16. 0.625
- 17. 87
- 18. 8.125

*Selected Solutions from Set A

1. $14.4 \div 4\frac{1}{2} = 4.5)\overline{14.4.0}$

$$\begin{array}{r} 3.2 \\ 4.5)\overline{14.4.0} \\ \underline{13\ 5} \\ 9\ 0 \\ \underline{9\ 0} \end{array}$$

5.
$$\left(1\frac{1}{2}\right)^2 + 2\frac{2}{3} \times 1.2 =$$
$$\left(\frac{3}{2} \times \frac{3}{2}\right) + 2\frac{2}{3} \times 1\frac{1}{5} =$$
$$\frac{9}{4} + \frac{8}{\overset{1}{\cancel{3}}} \times \frac{\overset{2}{\cancel{6}}}{5} = \frac{9}{4} + \frac{16}{5} =$$
$$\frac{45}{20} + \frac{64}{20} = \frac{109}{20} = 5\frac{9}{20} = 5.45$$

9.
$$\frac{1}{2} \times 3^3 - 5.3 \times .031 =$$
$$.5 \times 27 - 5.3 \times .031 =$$
$$13.5 - .1643 \approx 13.34$$

13.
$$\frac{1}{3} \times \sqrt{16} + 10 \div 2.5 =$$
$$\frac{1}{3} \times 4 + 10 \div 2\frac{1}{2} =$$
$$\frac{4}{3} + 10 \div \frac{5}{2} = \frac{4}{3} + \overset{2}{\cancel{10}} \times \frac{2}{\underset{1}{\cancel{5}}} =$$
$$\frac{4}{3} + \frac{4}{1} = \frac{4}{3} + \frac{12}{3} = \frac{16}{3} = 5\frac{1}{3} \approx 5.33$$

Exercise 4.12

Set A
- * 1. $117.98
- 2. $569.08
- * 3. the $62.95 tire
- 4. the 5.5 oz tube
- * 5. ≈ 28.16
- 6. 72 oz
- 7. $300.98
- 8. $\approx \$3.17$
- * 9. $5.44
- 10. ≈ 118.10
- *11. $1569.50
- 12. $169.50
- 13. 234 min or 3.9 hrs
- 14. $6601.16
- 15. 1163 cu ft, 8699.24 gal
- 16. 684
- 17. ≈ 9
- 18. ≈ 742.41 oz
- *19. ≈ 24.42 barrels
- 20. ≈ 163
- 21. Cost is more at $9.95 a month.

Set B
- 1. $141.06
- 2. $13.98
- 3. the 12.5 oz can
- 4. $589.68
- 5. ≈ 23.99 mpg
- 6. $0.14
- 7. $182.92
- 8. 1.625 in.
- 9. $14.69
- 10. $137.80
- 11. $250.60
- 12. $5.93
- 13. 94 min
- 14. $10,678.08
- 15. 1329 cu ft, 9940.92 gal
- 16. $171
- 17. ≈ 18
- 18. 3064.32 oz
- 19. ≈ 15.84 barrels
- 20. ≈ 17.1 pupils
- 21. Cost is more at $29 a month.

*Selected Solutions from Set A

1. Subtract the total of the checks from balance plus deposits.

checks:	$ 47.35	bal.:	$ 22.56
	10.00	dep:	+ 415.25
	239.50		437.81
	+ 22.98	checks:	− 319.83
	$319.83		$117.98

3. Determine the cost per 1000 miles of each tire. The one that costs less per 1000 miles is a better buy. Remember: "per" indicates division.
$62.95 ÷ 50 = 1.2590 ≈ $1.26
$57.50 ÷ 40 = 1.4375 ≈ $1.44

5. Divide number of miles driven (difference in odometer readings) by the number of gallons used.
39762.4 − 39247.1 = 515.3 miles
515.3 ÷ 18.3 ≈ 28.16 miles per gallon

9. Add the cost for the first 3 min. ($.85) and the cost for the next 27 min. (27 × $.17 = $4.59).
$4.59 + 0.85 = $5.44

11. Multiply the cost for each day
(2 × $2.15 = $4.30) by 365.
365 × $4.30 = $1569.50

19. Divide the number of barrels consumed by the number of people.
6,299,900,000 ÷ 258,000,000 ≈ 24.42 barrels

Chapter 4
Practice Test A

1. 407.007
2. 746.33
3. 321.4217
4. 38.004
5. 809.4572
6. 70.5
7. 11.15
8. 2,431,000
9. 0.0001911
10. $\dfrac{13}{500}$
11. 2.3125
12. 1.27, 1.2, 1.1027, 1.0127
13. $37\dfrac{17}{18} = 37.94$
14. $61.54
15. $18,887.10

Chapter 4
Practice Test B

1. eighty-four and fifty-six hundredths
2. 56.4
3. 944.5118
4. 38.042
5. 1270.2
6. 2.65
7. 7.22
8. 36,866,000
9. 0.000953
10. $\dfrac{19}{50}$
11. 5.375
12. 0.306, 0.3, 0.036, 0.0306
13. $52\dfrac{19}{27} \approx 52.7$
14. $6.73
15. $\approx$ $5654.17

Unit II Exam

1. $4\dfrac{2}{3}$
2. one hundred fifty-two and thirty-seven thousandths
3. 0.58
4. $\dfrac{7}{36}$
5. $1\dfrac{1}{2}$
6. $1\dfrac{13}{120}$
7. $7\dfrac{13}{15}$
8. $\dfrac{9}{10}$
9. 196.376
10. 260,400
11. 88.76
12. 14 students
13. $3\dfrac{5}{6}$ ft
14. $4237.44
15. 10, 518.75 sq in.

Unit III

Brain Buster

height $\approx$ 5.3 miles

Chapter 5
Pretest

1. $\dfrac{3}{5}$
2. 24
3. 195
4. $\approx$ 3.94
5. $\approx$ 8.76
6. 0.045; $\dfrac{9}{200}$
7. $\dfrac{57}{500}$; 11.4%
8. 44.7
9. $\approx$ $5.20
10. 16%
11. 75
12. $\approx$ $170.13
13. $1.82
14. $\approx$ 44.9%
15. $80.54

Note: Unless otherwise indicated in this unit, when the answers have more than three decimal digits, they will be rounded off to the nearest hundredth.

Exercise 5.1

Set A		Set B	
* 1.	$\dfrac{2}{3}$	1.	$\dfrac{9}{20}$
2.	$\dfrac{2}{1}$	2.	$\dfrac{9}{11}$
* 3.	$\dfrac{1}{3}$	3.	$\dfrac{11}{20}$
4.	$\dfrac{2}{3}$	4.	$\dfrac{1}{2}$
* 5.	$\dfrac{1}{4}$	5.	$\dfrac{8}{15}$
6.	$\dfrac{9}{11}$	6.	$\dfrac{1}{4}$
* 7.	$\dfrac{10}{7}$	7.	$\dfrac{3}{5}$
8.	$\dfrac{7}{10}$	8.	$\dfrac{5}{3}$
* 9.	$\dfrac{14}{45}$	9.	$\dfrac{1}{3}$
10.	$\dfrac{45}{79}$	10.	$\dfrac{15}{23}$

*11. $\dfrac{2}{5}$

12. $\dfrac{1}{12}$

*13. $\dfrac{4}{15}$

14. $\dfrac{91}{68}$

*15. $\dfrac{5}{14}$

16. $\dfrac{32}{1}$

*17. $\dfrac{3}{16}$

11. $\dfrac{2}{5}$

12. $\dfrac{1}{12}$

13. $\dfrac{1}{4}$

14. $\dfrac{4}{3}$

15. $\dfrac{42}{79}$

16. $\dfrac{64}{7}$

17. $\dfrac{1}{8}$

*Selected Solutions from Set A

1. 8 out of 12 = $\dfrac{8}{12} = \dfrac{2}{3}$

3. 4 out of 12 = $\dfrac{4}{12} = \dfrac{1}{3}$

5. The total number of balls is 12 + 10 + 18 = 40. Red balls to total = $\dfrac{10}{40} = \dfrac{1}{4}$.

7. 20 nickels = 100¢; 7 dimes = 70¢; $\dfrac{100}{70} = \dfrac{10}{7}$

9. 7 dimes = 70¢; 9 quarters = 225¢; $\dfrac{70}{225} = \dfrac{14}{45}$

11. 18:45 = $\dfrac{18}{45} = \dfrac{2}{5}$

13. 10 yd = 30 ft, so 8 ft to 10 yd = 8:30 = $\dfrac{8}{30} = \dfrac{4}{15}$

15. $\dfrac{3\frac{3}{4}}{10\frac{1}{2}} = \dfrac{\frac{15}{4}}{\frac{21}{2}} = \dfrac{15}{4} \div \dfrac{21}{2} = \dfrac{\cancel{15}^{5}}{\cancel{4}_{2}} \times \dfrac{\cancel{2}^{1}}{\cancel{21}_{7}} = \dfrac{5}{14}$

17. 3 yd = 108 in.

$\dfrac{20\frac{1}{4}}{108} = \dfrac{\frac{81}{4}}{\frac{108}{1}} = \dfrac{81}{4} \div \dfrac{108}{1} = \dfrac{\cancel{81}^{3}}{4} \times \dfrac{1}{\cancel{108}_{4}} = \dfrac{3}{16}$

Exercise 5.2

Set A	Set B
* 1. yes	1. no
2. yes	2. yes
* 3. yes	3. yes
4. yes	4. yes
* 5. no	5. no
6. no	6. no
* 7. 3	7. 2
8. 4	8. 3
* 9. 35	9. 48
10. 56	10. 63

*11. 120

12. 450

*13. 4

14. 13

*15. 42

16. 28

*17. 171

18. 40

11. 90

12. 60

13. 95

14. 91

15. 56

16. 20

17. 153

18. 39

*Selected Solutions from Set A

1. cross products are equal. $12 \times 14 = 168$ $21 \times 8 = 168$

3. cross products are equal. $57 \times 76 = 4332$ $38 \times 114 = 4332$

5. cross products are not equal. $73 \times 33 = 2409$ $53 \times 53 = 2809$

7. $\dfrac{N}{4} = \dfrac{6}{8}$

$8 \times N = 4 \times 6$

$\dfrac{8 \times N}{8} = \dfrac{24}{8}$

$N = 3$

9. $\dfrac{20}{N} = \dfrac{4}{7}$

$4 \times N = 20 \times 7$

$\dfrac{4 \times N}{4} = \dfrac{140}{4}$

$N = 35$

11. $\dfrac{18}{15} = \dfrac{N}{100}$

$15 \times N = 18 \times 100$

$\dfrac{15 \times N}{15} = \dfrac{1800}{15}$

$N = 120$

13. $\dfrac{65}{52} = \dfrac{5}{N}$

$65 \times N = 52 \times 5$

$\dfrac{65 \times N}{65} = \dfrac{260}{65}$

$N = 4$

15. $\dfrac{N}{18} = \dfrac{63}{27}$

$27 \times N = 18 \times 63$

$\dfrac{27 \times N}{27} = \dfrac{1134}{27}$

$N = 42$

17. $\dfrac{9}{14} = \dfrac{N}{266}$

$14 \times N = 9 \times 266$

$\dfrac{14 \times N}{14} = \dfrac{2394}{14}$

$N = 171$

Exercise 5.3

Set A	Set B
* 1. yes	1. yes
2. yes	2. yes
* 3. yes	3. yes
4. yes	4. yes
* 5. 1.12	5. 0.54
6. 1.35	6. 2.31
* 7. 11.2	7. ≈ 6.86
8. 15.75	8. ≈ 5.83
* 9. ≈ 2.47	9. ≈ 8.28
10. ≈ .30	10. ≈ 14.44
*11. ≈ 58.89	11. ≈ 38.18
12. ≈ 65.71	12. ≈ 40.77
*13. 76	13. 28
14. 18	14. 144
*15. 680	15. ≈ 228.07
16. ≈ 717.95	16. ≈ 220.93
17. $2\frac{1}{2}$ or 2.5	17. $\frac{1}{5}$ or 0.2
18. $3\frac{1}{2}$ or 3.5	18. $\frac{5}{18} \approx 0.28$

*Selected Solutions from Set A

1. cross products are equal.

$$2\frac{2}{3} \times \frac{3}{4} = 2$$

$$1\frac{1}{5} \times 1\frac{2}{3} = 2$$

3. cross products are equal. $1.4 \times 1.6 = 2.24$
$5.6 \times .4 = 2.24$

5. $\dfrac{A}{16} = \dfrac{7}{100}$

$100 \times A = 16 \times 7$

$\dfrac{100 \times A}{100} = \dfrac{112}{100}$

$A = 1.12$

7. $\dfrac{5}{8} = \dfrac{7}{N}$

$5 \times N = 8 \times 7$

$\dfrac{5 \times N}{5} = \dfrac{56}{5}$

$N = 11.2$

9. $\dfrac{Y}{.35} = \dfrac{1.2}{.17}$

$.17 \times Y = 1.2 \times .35$

$\dfrac{.17 \times Y}{.17} = \dfrac{.42}{.17}$

$Y \approx 2.47$

11. $\dfrac{5.3}{B} = \dfrac{9}{100}$

$9 \times B = 5.3 \times 100$

$\dfrac{9 \times B}{9} = \dfrac{530}{9}$

$B \approx 58.89$

13. $\dfrac{F}{\frac{1}{2}} = \dfrac{38}{\frac{1}{4}}$

$\dfrac{1}{4} \times F = \dfrac{1}{2} \times 38$

$\dfrac{\frac{1}{4} \times F}{\frac{1}{4}} = \dfrac{19}{\frac{1}{4}}$

$F = 76$

15. $\dfrac{17}{2.5} = \dfrac{P}{100}$

$2.5 \times P = 17 \times 100$

$\dfrac{2.5 \times P}{2.5} = \dfrac{1700}{2.5}$

$P = 680$

Exercise 5.4

Set A

* 1. 44.4 ft
  2. 35 ft
* 3. $20\frac{1}{4}$ mi
  4. ≈ 9.33 mi
* 5. ≈ 8.57 lb
  6. 17 gal
* 7. \$48,500
  8. ≈ 335.42 mi
* 9. ≈ 48.39 min
  10. \$7.00
  *11. $\approx \$5.30$
  12. $\approx \$5.38$
  13. 3,190,590
  14. $\approx \$0.28$
  15. ≈ 152 nd
  16. $2\frac{3}{4}$ laps
  *17. 36.57 oz
  18. 20 games
  *19. 1400, 4900 acres
  20. 2450 tickets

Set B

1. 123 ft or 41 yds
2. 63 women
3. 6 mi
4. ≈ 21.40 in
5. ≈ 4.67 oz
6. 474
7. $\approx \$20,824.07$
8. 44 qt jars
9. ≈ 37.13 gal
10. $\approx \$8.59$
11. $\approx \$4.98$
12. 792,000 ft
13. $\approx 67,241.38$ mi
14. 32,779,110
15. 8,782 nd
16. ≈ 14.29 miles
17. 1587, 3703 lbs
18. 9 people
19. 77 games
20. 2000 greens
21. 96 bits

*Selected Solutions from Set A

1. $\dfrac{\text{height}}{\text{shadow}} = \dfrac{\text{height}}{\text{shadow}}$

$\dfrac{6}{5} = \dfrac{H}{37}$

$5 \times H = 222$

$H = 44.4$

3. $\dfrac{\text{miles}}{\text{inches}} = \dfrac{\text{miles}}{\text{inches}}$

$\dfrac{27}{7} = \dfrac{M}{5\frac{1}{4}}$

$7 \times M = 141.75$

$M = 20.25$

5. $\dfrac{\text{lb}}{\text{sq ft}} = \dfrac{\text{lb}}{\text{sq ft}}$

$\dfrac{6}{1400} = \dfrac{L}{2000}$

$1400 \times L = 12000$

$L \approx 8.57$

7. $\dfrac{\text{tax}}{\text{price}} = \dfrac{\text{tax}}{\text{price}}$

$\dfrac{688}{40000} = \dfrac{834.20}{P}$

$688 \times P = 33,368,000$

$P = 48,500$

9. $\dfrac{\text{miles}}{\text{time}} = \dfrac{\text{miles}}{\text{time}}$

$\dfrac{6.2}{40} = \dfrac{7.5}{T}$

$6.2 \times T = 300$

$T \approx 48.39$

11. $\dfrac{\text{oz}}{\text{cost}} = \dfrac{\text{oz}}{\text{cost}}$

$\dfrac{12.5}{3.95} = \dfrac{16.76}{C}$

$12.5 \times C = 66.202$

$C \approx 5.30$

17. $\dfrac{\text{mix}}{\text{total}} = \dfrac{\text{mix}}{\text{total}}$

$\dfrac{2}{7} = \dfrac{M}{128}$

$7 \times M = 256$

$M \approx 36.57$

19. $\dfrac{\text{part}}{\text{total}} = \dfrac{\text{part}}{\text{total}}$

$\dfrac{2}{9} = \dfrac{P}{6300}$

$9 \times P = 12600$

$P = 1400$

other = 4900

Exercise 5.5

Set A

* 1. $\dfrac{17}{100}$
  2. $\dfrac{23}{100}$
* 3. $\dfrac{1}{20}$
  4. $\dfrac{3}{50}$
* 5. $\dfrac{21}{250}$
  6. $\dfrac{31}{500}$
* 7. $\dfrac{29}{300}$
  8. $\dfrac{47}{600}$
* 9. $1\frac{9}{25}$
  10. $2\frac{3}{20}$
  *11. $\dfrac{7}{16}$
  12. $\dfrac{109}{400}$

Set B

1. $\dfrac{19}{100}$
2. $\dfrac{31}{100}$
3. $\dfrac{2}{25}$
4. $\dfrac{1}{50}$
5. $\dfrac{19}{250}$
6. $\dfrac{6}{125}$
7. $\dfrac{19}{300}$
8. $\dfrac{11}{120}$
9. $2\frac{3}{25}$
10. $1\frac{13}{25}$
11. $\dfrac{229}{400}$
12. $\dfrac{351}{400}$

*13. 0.45
14. 0.58
*15. 0.05
16. 0.08
*17. 2.36
18. 1.89
*19. 0.265
20. 0.204
*21. 0.0825
22. 0.0975

13. 0.36
14. 0.45
15. 0.04
16. 0.03
17. 1.57
18. 1.39
19. 0.158
20. 0.163
21. 0.0475
22. 0.0625

*Selected Solutions from Set A

1. $17\% = \dfrac{17}{100}$

3. $5\% = \dfrac{5}{100} = \dfrac{1}{20}$

5. $8.4\% = .084 = \dfrac{84}{1000} = \dfrac{21}{250}$

7. $9\dfrac{2}{3}\% = \dfrac{9\frac{2}{3}}{100} = \dfrac{\frac{29}{3}}{\frac{100}{1}} = \dfrac{29}{3} \times \dfrac{1}{100} = \dfrac{29}{300}$

9. $136\% = \dfrac{136}{100} = 1\dfrac{36}{100} = 1\dfrac{9}{25}$

11. $43\dfrac{3}{4}\% = \dfrac{43\frac{3}{4}}{100} = \dfrac{\frac{175}{4}}{\frac{100}{1}} = \dfrac{\overset{7}{\cancel{175}}}{4} \times \dfrac{1}{\underset{4}{\cancel{100}}} = \dfrac{7}{16}$

13. $45\% = .45$

15. $5\% = .05$

17. $2\,36\% = 2.36$

19. $26.5\% = .265$

21. $8\dfrac{1}{4}\% = 8.25\% = .0825$

Exercise 5.6

Set A

* 1. 0.74; 74%
2. 0.12; 12%
* 3. $\dfrac{1}{50}$; 2%
4. $\dfrac{2}{25}$; 8%
* 5. $\dfrac{57}{1000}$; .057
6. $\dfrac{19}{1000}$; .019
* 7. 0.2; 20%
8. 0.7; 70%
* 9. $\dfrac{187}{400}$; 46.75%
10. $\dfrac{177}{400}$; 44.25%
*11. ≈ 2.17; ≈ 217%
12. ≈ 1.83; ≈ 183%

Set B

1. .26; 26%
2. .08; 8%
3. $\dfrac{1}{25}$; 4%
4. $\dfrac{3}{50}$; 6%
5. $\dfrac{61}{1000}$; .061
6. $\dfrac{43}{1000}$; .043
7. 0.6; 60%
8. 0.4; 40%
9. $\dfrac{19}{80}$; 23.75%
10. $\dfrac{97}{400}$; 24.25%
11. ≈ 1.67; ≈ 167%
12. ≈ 2.33; ≈ 233%

*13. $2\dfrac{3}{8}$; 237.5%
14. $1\dfrac{1}{40}$; 102.5%
15. $\dfrac{53}{800}$; .06625

13. $1\dfrac{1}{8}$; 112.5%
14. $2\dfrac{3}{40}$; 207.5%
15. $\dfrac{43}{800}$; .05375

*Selected Solutions from Set A

1. $\dfrac{37}{50} = 50)\overline{37.00}\quad .74 = .74 = 74\%$
$\qquad\qquad \underline{35\,0}$
$\qquad\qquad\ \ 2\,00$
$\qquad\qquad\ \ \underline{2\,00}$

3. $.02 = 2\% = \dfrac{2}{100} = \dfrac{1}{50}$

5. $5.7\% = .057 = \dfrac{57}{1000}$

7. $\dfrac{1}{5} = 5)\overline{1.0}\quad .2 = .20 = 20\%$
$\qquad\quad\ \underline{1\,0}$

9. $.4675 = \dfrac{4675}{10000} = \dfrac{187}{400}$
$.46\,75 = 46.75\%$

11. $2\dfrac{1}{6} = \dfrac{13}{6} = 6)\overline{13.000}\quad 2.166 = 2.17 = 217\%$
$\qquad\qquad\qquad\ \underline{12}$
$\qquad\qquad\qquad\ \ 1\,0$
$\qquad\qquad\qquad\quad \underline{6}$
$\qquad\qquad\qquad\quad 40$
$\qquad\qquad\qquad\quad \underline{36}$
$\qquad\qquad\qquad\quad 40$

13. $2.375 = 2\dfrac{375}{1000} = 2\dfrac{3}{8}$
$2.37\,5 = 237.5\%$

Exercise 5.7

Set A

* 1. 15
2. 39
* 3. 0.935
4. 1.062
* 5. ≈ $11.81
6. ≈ $17,100.78
* 7. 98.4
8. 135.1
* 9. $60.30
10. ≈ $670.97
*11. 4.715
12. ≈ 3.87
*13. ≈ $14.25
14. ≈ $52.80
*15. $80.85
16. $4062.50
*17. $1043.55
18. $90,141.60

Set B

1. 11
2. 26
3. 1.104
4. 0.552
5. ≈ $59,520.89
6. ≈ $25.97
7. 73
8. 116.9
9. ≈ $528.37
10. ≈ $61.38
11. 1.885
12. 5.67
13. ≈ $15.55
14. $35.90
15. ≈ $95.63
16. ≈ $14,642,78
17. $1447.25
18. $30.59 a share

*Selected Solutions from Set A

1. 30% of 50 = 0.30 × 50 = 15
3. 5% of 18.7 = 0.05 × 18.7 = 0.935
5. 0.8% of $1476.59 = 0.008 × $1476.59
   $\approx 11.81
7. 16.4% of 600 = 0.164 × 600 = 98.4
9. 78.32% of $76.99 = 0.7832 × $76.99
   $\approx 60.30
11. $5\frac{3}{4}$% of 82 = 0.0575 × 82 = 4.715
13. 75% of $189.98 = 0.075 × $189.95
    $\approx 14.25
15. $8\frac{1}{4}$ % of $980 = 0.0825 × $980
    $= 80.85
17. 15% of $6957 = 0.15 × $6957
    $= 1043.55

Exercise 5.8

Set A

* 1. 60%
  2. 80%
* 3. ≈ 33.33
  4. 45
* 5. 3
  6. 3.5
  7. 26%
  8. 21%
* 9. 225
  10. 187.5
  11. 47.36
  12. 125.13
*13. 360%
  14. 600%
*15. ≈ 423.53
  16. ≈ 385.71
*17. ≈ 8.03
  18. ≈ 3.17
  19. 120%

Set B

  1. 30%
  2. 40%
  3. 80
  4. 45
  5. 3.2
  6. 4.2
  7. 22%
  8. 24%
  9. ≈ 566.67
  10. 600
  11. 144.32
  12. 130.91
  13. 250%
  14. 640%
  15. ≈ 547.83
  16. ≈ 415.38
  17. ≈ 3.23
  18. ≈ 5.54
  19. 50%

*Selected Solutions from Set A

1. P is unknown
   $B = 15, A = 9$
   $$\frac{9}{15} = \frac{P}{100}$$
   $$\frac{15 \times P}{15} = \frac{900}{15}$$
   $$P = 60$$

5. A is unknown
   $P = 6, B = 50$
   $$\frac{A}{50} = \frac{6}{100}$$
   $$\frac{100 \times A}{100} = \frac{300}{100}$$
   $$A = 3$$

3. B is unknown
   $P = 60, A = 20$
   $$\frac{20}{B} = \frac{60}{100}$$
   $$\frac{60 \times B}{60} = \frac{2000}{60}$$
   $$B \approx 33.33$$

9. B is unknown
   $P = 8, A = 18$
   $$\frac{18}{B} = \frac{8}{100}$$
   $$\frac{8 \times B}{8} = \frac{1800}{8}$$
   $$B = 225$$

13. P is unknown
    $B = 17.5, B = 63$
    $$\frac{63}{17.5} = \frac{P}{100}$$
    $$\frac{17.5 \times P}{17.5} = \frac{6300}{17.5}$$
    $$P = 360$$

15. B is unknown
    $P = 5\frac{2}{3}, A = 24$
    $$\frac{24}{B} = \frac{5\frac{2}{3}}{100}$$
    $$\frac{5\frac{2}{3} \times B}{5\frac{2}{3}} = \frac{2400}{5\frac{2}{3}}$$
    $$B = \frac{2400}{\frac{17}{3}} \approx 423.53$$

17. A is unknown
    $P = 17.6, B = 45.6$
    $$\frac{A}{45.6} = \frac{17.6}{100}$$
    $$\frac{100 \times A}{100} = \frac{802.56}{100}$$
    $$A \approx 8.03$$

Exercise 5.9

Set A

* 1. $723.98
  2. $107.99
* 3. $671.84
  4. $1494.79
  5. $54,170.50
  6. $2587.50
* 7. 14,896 voters
  8. $26,160.82
* 9. $733.50
  10. 85%
  11. $322.92
  12. 70%
*13. 30%
  14. 15%
*15. 625 people
  16. 2630 people
  17. 6.25%
  18. ≈ 15.16%
  19. 1983
  20. ≈ 73.65%
  21. 0.32 oz

Set B

  1. $1042.51
  2. $475.29
  3. $67.31
  4. $2545.16
  5. $79,370.50
  6. $16,532.50
  7. 7755 voters
  8. $19,522.80
  9. $14,542.23
  10. 40%
  11. ≈ $452.09
  12. 67.5%
  13. 18%
  14. ≈ 6.86%
  15. 45 students
  16. 1200 bulbs
  17. 12%
  18. 624,352
  19.   Ford: ≈ 32.49% inc.
        Honda: ≈ 7.47% dec.
  20. 79.65%

*Selected Solutions from Set A

1. Add sales tax to original price.
   tax: $0.065 \times 679.79 \approx \$44.19$
   total: $\$679.79 + 44.19 = \$723.98$

3. Subtract discount ($0.12 \times \$763.45$) from the cost.
   $\$763.45 - \$91.61 = \$671.84$

7. Find 32% of 46,550.
   $0.32 \times 46,550 = 14,896$

9. Add raise (12.5% of 652) to original salary.
   $12.5\% \text{ of } 652 = 0.125 \times 652 = \$81.50$
   new salary $= 652 + 81.50 = \$733.50$

13. Amount of decrease $(200 - 140) = 60$.
    Base price is 200, percent unknown.
    $$\frac{60}{200} = \frac{P}{100}$$
    $$200 \times P = 6000$$
    $$P = 30$$

15. Restate the problem: <u>325</u> is <u>52%</u> of <u>what number</u>?
    $$\frac{325}{B} = \frac{52}{100}$$
    $$52 \times B = 32,500$$
    $$B = 625$$

Exercise 5.10

Set A	Set B
* 1. $150.00	1. $256.00
2. $336.00	2. $156.00
* 3. $630.00	3. $1980.00
4. $1000.00	4. $108.00
* 5. $3828.00	5. $3553.68
6. $7080.00	6. $6106.70
* 7. $2253.25	7. $998.50
8. $2135.36	8. $4865.78
* 9. $9720.00	9. 8346.00
10. $10,972.80	10. $11,692.80
*11. $24.79	11. $35.88
12. $273.68	12. $264.03
*13. $43.12	13. $62.82
14. $343.39	14. $249.34
15. $228.31	15. $227.30

*Selected Solutions from Set A

1. $I = P \times R \times T$
   $= 500 \times .15 \times 2 = \$150.00$

3. $I = P \times R \times T$
   $= 2000 \times .09 \times 3.5 = \$630.00$

5. $I = P \times R \times T$
   $= 7500 \times .1276 \times 4 = \$3828.00$

7. $T = 42$ months $= 3.5$ years
   $I = 4655 \times .1383 \times 3.5 \approx \$2253.25$

9. $T = 5$ years $= 60$ months
   $I = 10800 \times .015 \times 60 = \$9720.00$

11. Calculate interest:
    $I = 700 \times .175 \times 4 = \$490$
    Add interest to amount borrowed:
    $\$700 + 490 = \$1190.00$
    Divide total by 48 months:
    $\$1190 \div 48 \approx \$24.79$

13. Calculate amount after discount:
    $\$987.48 - (.25 \times 987.48) = \$740.61$
    Calculate amount after sales tax:
    $\$740.61 + (.065 \times 740.61) \approx \$788.75$
    Calculate interest:
    $I = 788.75 \times .156 \times 2 \approx \$246.09$
    Add interest to amount borrowed:
    $\$788.75 + 246.09 \approx \$1034.84$
    Divide total by 24 months:
    $\$1034.84 \div 24 \approx \$43.12$

Chapter 5

Practice Test A

1. $\frac{4}{15}$
2. 56
3. 700
4. ≈ 10.71
5. 62.5
6. $.064; \frac{8}{125}$
7. $\frac{33}{250}; 13.2\%$
8. 70.56
9. 60%
10. ≈ 271.43
11. ≈ 71.28
12. $68.11
13. $26\frac{2}{3}$ ft
14. $3077
15. $76.99

Chapter 5

Practice Test B

1. $\frac{10}{21}$
2. 35
3. 550
4. ≈ 10.52
5. 43.75
6. $.082; \frac{41}{500}$
7. $\frac{73}{500}; 14.6\%$
8. 20.76
9. 36%
10. ≈ 188.89
11. $\approx \$49.86$
12. $90.05
13. 38.7 oz
14. $564.90
15. $139.84

Chapter 6

Pretest

1. 4.075
2. 14,256 mi
3. 12.5 c
4. 56,000 oz
5. 1000 liters
6. 100 cg
7. 900 cm
8. 1.159 m
9. 57.6 mg
10. 127 cm
11. 67 kg
12. 8.48 gal
13. 65.56° C
14. mean: 4892, median: 4750
15. 120 yd

Exercise 6.1

Set A	Set B
* 1. 0.6 cm	1. $\frac{3}{16}$ in.
2. 2.8 cm	2. $1\frac{7}{16}$ in.
* 3. 4.5 cm	3. $2\frac{3}{8}$ in.
4. 5.6 cm	4. $3\frac{5}{8}$ in.
* 5. 7.2 cm	5. $4\frac{1}{4}$ in.
6. 9 cm	6. $5\frac{3}{4}$ in.
* 7. 30 mph	7. 102 lb
8. 37.5 mph	8. 116 lb
* 9. 52.5 mph	9. 134 lb
10. 60 mph	10. 146 lb
*11. 480 ml	11. 28°
12. 360 ml	12. 20°
*13. 240 ml	13. 12°
14. 120 ml	14. 3°

*Selected Solutions from Set A

1. basic interval: $1 \div 10 = 0.1$ cm
   A is 6 basic intervals above 0 cm.
   A measures 0.6 cm

3. C is 5 basic intervals above 4 cm
   3 measures $4 + 5 \times 0.1 = 4.5$ cm

5. E is 2 basic intervals above 7 cm
   E measures $7 + 2 \times 0.1 = 7.2$ cm

7. basic interval: $10 \div 4 = 2.5$ mph
   G is 2 basic intervals above 25 mph.
   G measures $25 + 2 \times 2.5 = 30$ mph

9. I is 3 basic intervals above 45 mph.
   I measures $45 + 3 \times 2.5 = 52.5$ mph

11. basic interval: $100 \div 5 = 20$ ml
    K is 4 basic intervals above 400 ml.
    K measures $400 + 4 \times 20 = 480$ ml

13. M is 2 basic intervals above 200 ml.
    M measures $200 + 2 \times 20 = 240$ ml

Exercise 6.2

Set A	Set B
* 1. 108 in.	1. 40 fl oz
2. 240 oz	2. 14 pt
* 3. 24 qt	3. $6\frac{3}{4}$ ft
4. 9 c	4. 6 lb
* 5. 37.8 ft	5. 9500 lb
6. 19.2 qt	6. 5385.6 in.
* 7. 4.76 T	7. 16.9 yd
8. 11.6 ft	8. $9\frac{3}{8}$ gal
* 9. 22,000 ft	9. 294 oz
10. $30\frac{2}{3}$ c	10. 332 in
*11. $1\frac{1}{12}$ lb	11. $3\frac{1}{4}$ yd
12. $1\frac{17}{32}$ ft	12. $3\frac{3}{8}$ c
13. 300 c	13. 2.3 T
14. 1.6 T	14. 92 c
*15. 112,000 oz	15. 976 oz
16. 21.15 qt	16. 1.025 gal
*17. 5456 yd	17. $9\frac{1}{8}$ qt
18. 2.41 mi	18. 86,400 oz

*Selected Solutions from Set A

1. $9 \, ft \times \dfrac{12 \text{ in.}}{1 \, ft} = \dfrac{9 \times 12 \text{ in.}}{1} = 108$ in.

3. $48 \, pt \times \dfrac{1 \text{ qt}}{2 \, pt} = \dfrac{48 \times 1 \text{ qt}}{2} = 24$ qt

5. $12.6 \, yd \times \dfrac{3 \text{ ft}}{1 \, yd} = \dfrac{12.6 \times 3 \text{ ft}}{1} = 37.8$ ft

7. $9516.8 \, lb \times \dfrac{1 \text{ T}}{2000 \, lb} = \dfrac{9516.8 \times 1 \text{ T}}{2000}$
   $= 4.76$ T

9. $4\frac{1}{6} \, mi \times \dfrac{5280 \text{ ft}}{1 \, mi} = \dfrac{4\frac{1}{6} \times 5280 \text{ ft}}{1}$
   $= 22,000$ ft

11. $17\frac{1}{3} \, oz \times \dfrac{1 \text{ lb}}{16 \, oz} = \dfrac{17\frac{1}{3} \times 1 \text{ lb}}{16} = 1\frac{1}{12}$ lb

15. $3\frac{1}{2} \, T \times \dfrac{2000 \text{ lb}}{1 \, T} = 7000$ lb
    $7000 \, lb \times \dfrac{16 \text{ oz}}{1 \, lb} = 112,000$ oz

17. $3.1 \, mi \times \dfrac{5280 \text{ ft}}{1 \, mi} = 16,368$ ft
    $16,368 \, ft \times \dfrac{1 \text{ yd}}{3 \, ft} = 5456$ yd

Exercise 6.3

Set A

* 1. kilometer
2. kiloliter
* 3. centigram
4. centimeter
* 5. milliliter
6. milligram
* 7. 1000 m
8. 1000 g
* 9. 0.01 liter
10. 0.01 m
*11. 0.001 g
12. 0.001 liter
*13. 100 cm
14. 100 cg
*15. 1000 ml
16. 1000 mm
*17. kg, g, cg
18. m, cm, mm
19. km, cm, mm
20. kl, cl, ml

Set B

1. kilogram
2. kilometer
3. centiliter
4. centigram
5. millimeter
6. milliliter
7. 1000 liters
8. 1000 m
9. 0.01 g
10. 0.01 liter
11. 0.001 m
12. 0.001 g
13. 100 cl
14. 100 cm
15. 1000 mg
16. 1000 ml
17. g, cg, mg
18. km, m, cm
19. kl, cl, ml
20. kg, cg, mg

*Selected Solutions from Set A

1. k means kilo; m means meter; so km means kilometer.

3. c means centi; g means gram; so cg means centigram.

5. m means milli; l means liter; so ml means milliliter.

7. k means kilo (1000); so 1 km = 1000 m.

9. c means centi (.01); so 1 cl = 0.01 liter.

11. m means milli (.001); so 1 mg = 0.001 g.

13. cm = $\frac{1}{100}$ m; so 1 m = 100 cm.

15. ml = $\frac{1}{1000}$ liter; so 1 liter = 1000 ml.

17. kg = 1000 g; cg = 0.01 g; so the order is kg, g, cg.

Exercise 6.4

Set A

* 1. 3000 g
2. 8000 liters
3. 52 liters
4. 71 m
* 5. 500 cm
6. 700 cg
* 7. 5 liters
8. 7 g
9. 4600 ml
10. 7300 mm
11. 1.697 m
12. 1.555 g
*13. 8900 mg
14. 7600 ml
15. 0.57 kl
16. 0.86 km
*17. 400 mm
18. 500 ml
*19. 0.76 cl
20. 0.83 cg
*21. 420,000 cg
22. 370,000 cm
*23. 0.0165 liter
24. 1.8 m

Set B

1. 4000 liters
2. 9000 g
3. 53 m
4. 41 liters
5. 900 cg
6. 200 cm
7. 3 g
8. 2 liters
9. 5900 mm
10. 2800 ml
11. 3.127 g
12. 2.095 m
13. 4300 ml
14. 5900 mg
15. 0.61 km
16. 0.23 kl
17. 700 ml
18. 600 mm
19. 0.29 cg
20. 0.32 cl
21. 410,000 cm
22. 640,000 cg
23. 0.28 g
24. 0.14 m

*Selected Solutions from Set A

1. $3 \, \cancel{kg} \times \dfrac{1000 \text{ g}}{1 \, \cancel{kg}} = 3000$ g

5. $5 \, \cancel{m} \times \dfrac{1 \text{ cm}}{.01 \, \cancel{m}} = 500$ cm

7. 5 000 ml = 5 liters (ml to liter is a 3 place movement to the left).

13. 8.9 g = 8900 mg (g to mg is a 3 place movement to the right).

17. 40 cm = 400 mm (cm to mm is a 1 place movement to the right).

19. 7.6 ml = .76 cl (ml to cl is a 1 place movement to the left).

21. 4.2 kg = 420,000 cg (kg to cg is a 5 place movement to the right).

23. $16.5 \, \cancel{ml} \times \dfrac{.001 \text{ liter}}{1 \, \cancel{ml}} = .0165$ liter

Exercise 6.5

Set A

* 1. 22.86 cm
  2. 8.48 qt
* 3. 15 kg
  4. 5 m
* 5. 157.6 in.
  6. 3178 g
* 7. 6 oz
  8. 30 km
  9. 975.15 in.
  10. 129.69 lb
*11. 67 kg
  12. ≈ 24.70 in.
*13. 1.76 oz
  14. ≈ 3.05 m
*15. ≈ 16,509 ml
  16. 2.835 cg
  17. 188.68 l
  18. 13.25 gal
  19. 1.863 mi
  20. ≈ 4,830,917.9 m
  21. ≈ 9.43 l
  22. 16.96 c

Set B

  1. 141.75 g
  2. 19.8 lb
  3. 15 m
  4. 30 kg
  5. 49.68 mi
  6. 5.3 qt
  7. 3.65 lb
  8. 3.45 liters
  9. ≈ 135.255 cm
  10. 168.19 lb
  11. ≈ 2.15 m
  12. ≈ 11.27 oz
  13. 54.82 m
  14. ≈ 3.66 liters
  15. 8.48 gal
  16. ≈ 377.36 ml
  17. ≈ 328.33 ft
  18. ≈ 30.46 m
  19. ≈ 11.11 mm
  20. 0.47 in.
  21. 98,500 in.
  22. 1.46 km

*Selected Solutions from Set A

1. $9 \text{ in.} \times \dfrac{2.54 \text{ cm}}{1 \text{ in.}} = 22.86 \text{ cm}$

3. $33 \text{ lb} \times \dfrac{1 \text{ kg}}{2.2 \text{ lb}} = 15 \text{ kg}$

5. $4 \text{ m} \times \dfrac{39.4 \text{ in.}}{1 \text{ m}} = 157.6 \text{ in.}$

7. $170.1 \text{ g} \times \dfrac{1 \text{ oz}}{28.35 \text{ g}} = 6 \text{ oz}$

11. $147.4 \text{ lb} \times \dfrac{1 \text{ kg}}{2.2 \text{ lb}} = 67 \text{ kg}$

13. Change kg to lb:

$0.5 \text{ kg} \times \dfrac{2.2 \text{ lb}}{1 \text{ kg}} = 0.11 \text{ lb}$

Change lb to oz:

$0.11 \text{ lb} \times \dfrac{16 \text{ oz}}{1 \text{ lb}} = 1.76 \text{ oz}$

15. Change fl oz to qt:

$560 \text{ fl oz} \times \dfrac{1 \text{ qt}}{32 \text{ fl oz}} = 17.5 \text{ qt}$

Change qt to liters:

$17.5 \text{ qt} \times \dfrac{1 \text{ liter}}{1.06 \text{ qt}} \approx 16.509 \text{ liters}$

Change liters to ml:
16.509 liters ≈ 16,509 ml

Exercise 6.6

Set A

* 1. 158° F
  2. 113° F
* 3. 40° C
  4. 10° C
* 5. 125.6° F
  6. 179.6° F
* 7. ≈ 176.67° C
  8. ≈ 37.78° C
* 9. 162.68° F
  10. 180.86° F
*11. 200° C
  12. They are = .
*13. 4° C

Set B

  1. 140° F
  2. 185° F
  3. 20° C
  4. 35° C
  5. 109.4° F
  6. 163.4° F
  7. ≈ 204.44° C
  8. 135° C
  9. 200.12° F
  10. 167.54° F
  11. 300° C
  12. They are = .
  13. 36° F

*Selected Solutions from Set A

1. $F = \dfrac{9}{5} \times 70 + 32$

$= 126 + 32 = 158°$

3. $C = \dfrac{5}{9} \times (104 - 32)$

$= \dfrac{5}{9} \times 72 = 40°$

5. $F = \dfrac{9}{5} \times 52 + 32$

$= 93.6 + 32 = 125.6°$

7. $C = \dfrac{5}{9} \times (350 - 32)$

$= \dfrac{5}{9} \times 318 \approx 176.67°$

9. $F = \dfrac{9}{5} \times 72.6 + 32$

$= 130.68 + 32 = 162.68°$

11. Change 200° C to °F:

$$F = \dfrac{9}{5} \times 200 + 32 = 392°$$

So 200° C is hotter than 390° F.

13. Change 39° F to °C:

$$C = \dfrac{5}{9} \times (39 - 32) \approx 3.89°$$

So 4° C is hotter than 39° F.

Exercise 6.7

Set A

1. 81°
2. 45°
* 3. 62.25°
4. ≈ 48.89%
* 5. ≈ 31.34%
6. 25–44
7. 14–17
8. 192,400,000
* 9. 174,200,000
*10. 33,800,000

Set B

1. 25′0″
2. 20′6″
3. 22′
4. 12%
5. ≈ 19.05%
6. Asia; 17,250,000 sq mi
7. Australia; 2,875,000 sq mi
8. 7,475,000 sq mi
9. 2,300,000 sq mi
10. 16,100,000 sq mi

*Selected Solutions from Set A

3. To find the average, add up the temperatures and divide by 12. 45 + 50 + 54 + 60 + 67 + 74 + 81 + 78 + 74 + 64 + 54 + 46 = 747, and 747 ÷ 12 = 62.25

5. Amount of decrease (67 − 46) = 21; base temp. = 67°; percent unknown.

$$\frac{A}{B} = \frac{P}{100} \qquad \frac{21}{67} = \frac{P}{100}$$
$$67 \times P = 2100$$
$$P \approx 31.34$$

9. The percent under 45 is 67%:

25–44:	31%
18–24:	10%
14–17:	6%
under 14:	20%
total:	67%

67% of 260,000,000
= .67 × 260,000,000
= 174,200,000

10. under 18: 26% of 260,000,000
= 0.26 × 260,000,000
= 67,600,000

over 64: 13% of 260,000,000
= 0.13 × 260,000,000
= 33,800,000

difference: 67,600,000
−33,800,000
33,800,000

Exercise 6.8

Set A

*1. mean ≈ 56.86
   median = 67
2. mean = 67
   median = 72
*3. mean ≈ 80.44%
   median = 83.9%
4. mean ≈ 150.03
   median = 151.7
*5. mean: 7,676,000
   median: 6,420,000
6. mean: 384.2 min
   median: 374 min
*7. mean: $100,684.60
   median: $94,780

Set B

1. mean ≈ 44.71
   median = 48
2. mean = 80
   median = 82
3. mean = 50.65
   median = 46.95
4. mean = 4.575
   median = 4.65
5. mean: 478.6
   median: 476
6. mean ≈ 81.91°
   median = 79°
7. mean ≈ 104,867
   median: 13,000

*Selected Solutions from Set A

1. mean = $\dfrac{80 + 68 + 30 + 67 + 70 + 21 + 62}{7}$
= 56.857143 ≈ 56.86
median: in increasing order the middle number is 67.

3. mean = $\dfrac{\text{sum of the percents}}{8} = \dfrac{643.5}{8}$
= 80.4375 ≈ 80.44
median: in increasing order the two middle numbers order are 78.6 and 89.2 and (78.6 + 89.2) ÷ 2 = 83.9.

5. mean = $\dfrac{\text{sum of the thefts per day}}{10} = \dfrac{1060}{10} = 106$
median: in increasing order the two middle amounts order are 75 and 77 and (75 + 77) ÷ 2 = 76.

7. mean = $\dfrac{\text{sum of the salaries}}{5} = \dfrac{\$503,423}{5}$
= $100,684.60
median: in increasing order the middle salary is $94,780.

Exercise 6.9

Set A

*1. 182 km

2. $\dfrac{7}{16}$ inch bit

*3. ≈ 102.67 ft/sec
4. metric ton
5. ≈ 15.30 yd/day
6. 1858.56 in./sec
*7. 97,656.25 mi
8. mean: 4.3 million
   median: 1.9 million
*9. 21.978 gal

10. a) 21.12 oz, 18.48 oz
    b) medium eggs
    c) $0.86
    d) ≈ $0.98

Set B

1. 137 km

2. 200 liters

3. ≈ 54.42 mph
4. the 5 ft woman
5. 6.4 mph
6. ≈ $1.17
7. ≈ 41.43 mi
8. mean: 1583 acres
   median: 659 acres
9. a) $70, ≈ $70
   b) ≈ $68.56
   c) June–July
10. a) 26.4 oz, 23.76 oz
    b) jumbo eggs
    c) ≈ $0.90
    d) ≈ $1.02

*Selected Solutions from Set A

1. Convert 182 km to miles.

$$82 \text{ km} \times \frac{0.621 \text{ mi}}{1 \text{ km}} = 113.022 \text{ mi}$$

Thus, 182 km is longer than 113 mi.

3. Since a cheetah runs 70 miles per hour, we need to convert 70 miles to feet and 1 hour to seconds to determine the feet run per second.

$$70 \text{ mi} \times \frac{5280 \text{ ft}}{1 \text{ mi}} = 369,600 \text{ ft}$$

$$1 \text{ hr} = 60 \text{ min} = 3600 \text{ sec}$$

Thus, $\dfrac{70 \text{ mi}}{1 \text{ hr}} = \dfrac{369,600 \text{ ft}}{3600 \text{ sec}} \approx 102.67 \text{ ft/sec}$

7. Each dollar bill is $6\dfrac{3}{16}$ in. or 6.1875 in, long. So one billion dollar bills would reach, $1,000,000,000 \times 6.1875 = 6,187,500,000$ in.

$$6,187,500,000 \text{ in.} \times \frac{1 \text{ ft}}{12 \text{ in.}} = 515,625,000 \text{ ft}$$

$$515,625,000 \text{ ft} \times \frac{1 \text{ mi}}{5280 \text{ ft}} = 97,656.25 \text{ mi}$$

9. The amount of soft drinks consumed is 38% of the 122.1 gallons, while the amount of milk consumed is 20% of the 122.1 gallons. The difference between these two amounts is what we must find.

38% of 122.1 − 20% of 122.1 =
   $0.38 \times 122.1 - 0.20 \times 122.1 =$
      $46.398 - 24.42 = 21.978$ gal

Chapter 6

Practice Test A

1. 2.05
2. 17,400 lb
3. 13.5 ft
4. 3 gal
5. 1000 g
6. 100 cm
7. 8000 mg
8. 1.697 liters
9. 82.4 mm
10. 3.105 mi
11. 40 in.
12. ≈ 1.41 oz
13. 440 yd
14. 40° C
15. mean: 22′
    median: ≈ 21.6′ (21′7″)

Unit III Exam

1. 49
2. ≈ 1.27
3. 0.45; $\dfrac{9}{20}$
4. 75%
5. 86.5
6. 158,400 in.
7. 5.6 g
8. ≈ 1415.09 ml

Chapter 6

Practice Test B

1. 3.25
2. 150 in.
3. 576 oz
4. 140 fl oz
5. 1000 m
6. 1000 ml
7. 500 cm
8. 1.555 g
9. 0.623 cm
10. 1970 in.
11. 8 km
12. ≈ 9.55 liters
13. 1000 kg
14. 113° F
15. mean: 62.25°
    median: 62°

9. 140° F
10. 30 oz
11. $4\dfrac{31}{32}$ in.
12. $30,720
13. 420 mi
14. 31.25%
15. $192.72

Unit IV

Brain Buster

27 triangles

Chapter 7

Pretest

1. 8
2. >
3. <
4. −7
5. −31
6. −12
7. −2
8. −42
9. 45
10. 11
11. 9

12. −22
13. 38
14. −189
15. $11x + 11$
16. −4
17. a. $2(x + 3)$
    b. $x - 4 = 3x$
18. 27, 28, 29
19. $635.24
20. $367.04

Exercise 7.1

Set A

* 1. 8
2. 6
* 3. 14
4. 2
* 5. 0
6. 0
* 7. 62
8. 46
* 9. 23.5
10. 38.6
*11. $11\frac{1}{4}$
12. 9
*13. 522

Set B

1. 4
2. 8
3. 4
4. 4
5. 0
6. 0
7. 60
8. 60
9. 44.25
10. 13
11. $\frac{1}{2}$
12. 14
13. 75

*Selected Solutions from Set A

1. $A + B - C$
$= 2 + 7 - 1$
$= 8$

3. $\dfrac{4B}{A}$
$= \dfrac{4 \cdot 7}{2} = 14$

5. $2BC - 7A$
$= 2 \cdot 7 \cdot 1 - 7 \cdot 2$
$= 14 - 14$
$= 0$

7. $A(3B + 5A)$
$= 2(3 \cdot 7 + 5 \cdot 2)$
$= 2(21 + 10)$
$= 2 \cdot 31 = 62$

9. $x\,y + \dfrac{z}{x} - \dfrac{y}{2}$

$= (1.2)(5) + \dfrac{24}{1.2} - \dfrac{5}{2}$

$= 6.0 + 20 - 2.5 = 26 - 2.5$
$= 23.5$

11. $M(3N - 2M)$

$= \dfrac{3}{4}\left(3 \cdot 5\frac{1}{2} - 2 \cdot \frac{3}{4}\right)$

$= \dfrac{3}{4}\left(3 \cdot \frac{11}{2} - \frac{6}{4}\right)$

$= \dfrac{3}{4}\left(\frac{33}{2} - \frac{3}{2}\right) = \dfrac{3}{4}\left(\frac{30}{2}\right)$

$= \dfrac{3}{4}(15) = \dfrac{45}{4} = 11\frac{1}{4}$

13. $3hf + h\left(\dfrac{h}{f} - 6\,g\right)$

$= 3 \cdot 15 \cdot \dfrac{2}{5} + 15\left(\dfrac{15}{\frac{2}{5}} - 6(.65)\right)$

$= 18 + 15\left(\dfrac{75}{2} - 3.9\right)$

$= 18 + 15(33.6) = 18 + 504 = 522$

Exercise 7.2

Set A

1. (number line)
2. (number line)
3. (number line)
4. (number line)
5. (number line)
6. >
* 7. >
8. >
* 9. >
10. <
*11. <
12. <
*13. <
14. >
*15. >
16. <
*17. <
18. >
19. <

Set B

1. (number line)
2. (number line)
3. (number line)
4. (number line)
5. (number line)
6. >
7. >
8. >
9. >
10. <
11. <
12. <
13. <
14. >
15. >
16. <
17. <
18. <
19. <

*Selected Solutions from Set A

7. $4 > 2$, since 4 is farther to the right on the number line.
9. $0 > -2$, since 0 is farther to the right on the number line.
11. $-7 < -2$, since -7 is farther to the left on the number line.
13. $-6 < -2$, since -6 is farther to the left on the number line.
15. $-7\frac{1}{2} > -7\frac{3}{4}$, since $-7\frac{1}{2}$ is farther to the right on the number line.
17. $-2.7 < -2.6$, since -2.7 is farther to the left on the number line.

Exercise 7.3

Set A

1. 12
2. 14
* 3. 3
4. 2
5. −4
6. −6
* 7. −10
8. −12
* 9. 2
10. 3
*11. −18
12. −18
13. −9
14. 4
15. 0
16. 0
*17. 38
18. 35
*19. −48
20. −50
21. −239
22. −281
23. −132
24. −262

Set B

1. 12
2. 14
3. 3
4. 1
5. −6
6. −8
7. −15
8. −14
9. 7
10. 11
11. −16
12. −17
13. −11
14. −10
15. 0
16. 0
17. 38
18. 54
19. −73
20. −38
21. −211
22. −314
23. −88
24. −133

*Selected Solutions from Set A

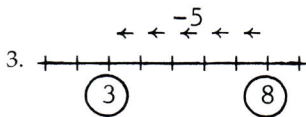

3.

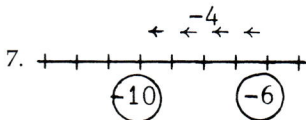

7.

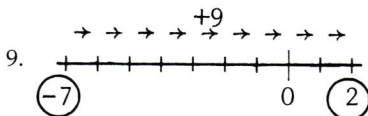

9.

11. $-3 + (-15) = -18$; both signs are the same, so add the number parts and use the "−" sign.
17. $75 + (-37) = 38$; signs are different, so subtract the number parts and use the sign of the larger number part—the "+" of 75.
19. $-124 + 76 = -48$; signs are different, so subtract the number parts and use the sign of the larger number part—the "−" of −124.

Exercise 7.4

Set A

1. 3
2. 5
* 3. −4
4. −5
* 5. −10
6. −12
* 7. 8
8. 10
* 9. −2
10. −5
*11. 0
12. 0
*13. 27
14. 14
*15. −8
16. −2
*17. −90
18. −93
*19. 166
20. 160
*21. −13
22. 69
*23. −53
24. −85

Set B

1. 3
2. 5
3. −6
4. −6
5. −13
6. −14
7. 9
8. 11
9. −2
10. −2
11. 0
12. 0
13. 16
14. 14
15. −4
16. −8
17. −92
18. −64
19. 145
20. 131
21. −4
22. 68
23. −93
24. −146

*Selected Solutions from Set A

3. $6 - 10 = 6 + (-10) = -4$
5. $-7 - 3 = -7 + (-3) = -10$
7. $5 - (-3) = 5 + 3 = 8$
9. $-7 - (-5) = -7 + 5 = -2$
11. $-7 - (-7) = -7 + 7 = 0$
13. $52 - 6 - 19 = 52 + (-6) + (-19)$
$\qquad = 46 + (-19) = 27$
15. $20 - 11 - 17 = 20 + (-11) + (-17)$
$\qquad = 9 + (-17) = -8$
17. $53 - 143 = 53 + (-143) = -90$
19. $72 - (-94) = 72 + 94 = 166$
21. $-51 - (-38) = -51 + 38 = -13$
23. $-125 - (-72) = -125 + 72 = -53$

Exercise 7.5

Set A
1. 15
2. 24
* 3. −21
4. −18
* 5. −32
6. −30
* 7. 48
8. 35
* 9. 72
10. 63
11. 4
12. 9
*13. −8
14. −6
*15. −7
16. −7
*17. 8
18. 4
19. 5
20. 6
21. −13
22. −12

Set B
1. 21
2. 24
3. −40
4. −27
5. −42
6. −63
7. 56
8. 36
9. 45
10. 32
11. 5
12. 4
13. −4
14. −5
15. −7
16. −6
17. 9
18. 6
19. 9
20. 7
21. −12
22. −15

*Selected Solutions from Set A

3. $3(-7) = -21$, since $(+) \cdot (-) = (-)$ and $3 \cdot 7 = 21$.
5. $-4 \cdot 8 = -32$, since $(-) \cdot (+) = (-)$ and $4 \cdot 8 = 32$.
7. $(-8)(-6) = +48$, since $(-) \cdot (-) = (+)$ and $8 \cdot 6 = 48$.
9. $-9 \cdot (-8) = +72$, since $(-) \cdot (-) = (+)$ and $9 \cdot 8 = 72$.

13. $\dfrac{-40}{5} = -8$, since the numbers have different signs and $\dfrac{40}{5} = 8$.

15. $\dfrac{56}{-8} = -7$, since the numbers have different signs and $\dfrac{56}{8} = 7$.

17. $\dfrac{-72}{-9} = +8$, since the numbers have the same signs and $\dfrac{72}{9} = 8$.

Exercise 7.6

Set A
* 1. 10
2. 26
* 3. −27
4. −26
* 5. −20
6. 18
* 7. −11
8. −13
* 9. −1
10. 6
*11. 2
12. 9
*13. 19
14. 2
*15. −2
16. 4
*17. $\dfrac{1}{4}$
18. $-\dfrac{1}{2}$
19. 5
20. 2

Set B
1. −6
2. 1
3. −28
4. −18
5. 14
6. −24
7. −10
8. −8
9. 8
10. 1
11. 0
12. −20
13. 17
14. 37
15. −3
16. 4
17. $-\dfrac{2}{5}$
18. $-\dfrac{2}{3}$
19. 3
20. −14

*Selected Solutions from Set A

1. $4^2 + (2)(-3) = 16 + (2)(-3)$
$\quad\quad = 16 + (-6) = 10$

3. $(-2)(6) - 3 \cdot 5 = -12 - 15$
$\quad\quad\quad = -12 + (-15) = -27$

5. $-5(-3 + 7) = -5(4) = -20$

7. $8 - \dfrac{8}{2} - 5 \cdot 3 = 8 - 4 - 15$
$\quad\quad\quad\quad = 8 + (-4) + (-15) = -11$

9. $-3 - (4 - 6) = -3 - (-2)$
$\quad\quad\quad = -3 + 2 = -1$

11. $(-5 + 2 \cdot 2)(7 - 9) = (-5 + 4)(7 - 9)$
$\quad\quad\quad\quad = (-1)(-2) = 2$

13. $5 + 2[3 - (-4)] = 5 + 2[3 + 4]$
$\quad\quad\quad\quad = 5 + 2 \cdot 7$
$\quad\quad\quad\quad = 5 + 14 = 19$

15. $\dfrac{-4 - 2(8 - 5)}{5} = \dfrac{-4 - 2(3)}{5}$
$\quad\quad = \dfrac{-4 - 6}{5} = \dfrac{-10}{5} = -2$

17. $\dfrac{8 + (-6)}{5 - (-3)} = \dfrac{2}{5 + 3} = \dfrac{2}{8} = \dfrac{1}{4}$

Exercise 7.7

Set A

* 1. $A = 2$
2. $B = 4$
* 3. $X = 11$
4. $Y = 11$
* 5. $P = 4$
6. $z = 3$
* 7. $r = 20$
8. $s = 18$
* 9. $t = -9$
10. $v = -8$
*11. $T = 2$
12. $N = 5$
*13. $y = 2$
14. $k = 3$
*15. $m = 0$
16. $n = 0$
*17. no
18. no
*19. yes
20. yes

Set B

1. $X = 4$
2. $Y = 5$
3. $C = 7$
4. $D = 10$
5. $r = 6$
6. $s = 6$
7. $t = 15$
8. $V = 8$
9. $A = -4$
10. $B = -6$
11. $R = 4$
12. $T = 3$
13. $n = 2$
14. $m = 3$
15. $Z = 0$
16. $r = 0$
17. no
18. no
19. yes
20. no

*Selected Solutions from Set A

1. $A + 3 = 5$; $A = 2$
   since $2 + 3 = 5$.

3. $X - 4 = 7$; $X = 11$
   since $11 - 4 = 7$.

5. $3P = 12$; $P = 4$
   since $3 \cdot 4 = 12$.

7. $\dfrac{r}{5} = 4$; $r = 20$

   since $\dfrac{20}{5} = 4$.

9. $-5 = t + 4$; $t = -9$
   since $-5 = -9 + 4$.

11. $-16 = -8T$; $T = 2$
    since $-16 = -8 \cdot 2$.

13. $3y + 2 = 8$; $y = 2$
    since $3 \cdot 2 + 2 = 8$.

15. $5 = 5 - 2m$; $m = 0$
    since $5 = 5 - 2 \cdot 0$.

17. No; $\dfrac{-3(-2)}{2} - 6 = 3 - 6 = -3$.

19. Yes; $5(-2) + (-7) = -10 + (-7) = -17$.

Exercise 7.8

Set A

* 1. $S = 2$
2. $S = 6$
* 3. $t = 12$
4. $t = 9$
* 5. $y = -4$
6. $y = -5$
* 7. $X = -2$
8. $x = -1$
* 9. $x = 13$
10. $X = 29$
*11. $K = 32$
12. $K = 42$
*13. $Z = -3$
14. $Z = -4$
*15. $p = 0.8$
16. $p = 2.1$
*17. $R = 12$
18. $R = 21$

*19. $A = \dfrac{2}{15}$

*20. $x = 1\dfrac{7}{15}$

Set B

1. $Z = 9$
2. $X = 8$
3. $K = 12$
4. $K = 10$
5. $X = -4$
6. $Z = -4$
7. $R = -3$
8. $R = -6$
9. $S = 19$
10. $S = 26$
11. $t = 31$
12. $t = 41$
13. $y = -3$
14. $y = -9$
15. $N = 1.9$
16. $N = 2.1$
17. $M = 8$
18. $M = 15$

19. $B = -\dfrac{1}{12}$

20. $x = 1\dfrac{5}{12}$

*Selected Solutions from Set A

1. $\begin{array}{rl} S + 7 = & 9 \\ -7 & -7 \\ \hline S = & 2 \end{array}$

3. $\begin{array}{rl} t - 7 = & 5 \\ +7 & +7 \\ \hline t = & 12 \end{array}$

5. $\begin{array}{rl} 1 = & y + 5 \\ -5 & -5 \\ \hline -4 = & y \end{array}$

7. $\begin{array}{rl} -6 = & X - 4 \\ +4 & +4 \\ \hline -\sigma 2 = & X \end{array}$

9. $\begin{array}{rl} x + 9 = & 22 \\ -9 = & -9 \\ \hline x = & 13 \end{array}$

11. $\begin{array}{rl} K - 15 = & 17 \\ +15 & +15 \\ \hline K = & 32 \end{array}$

13. $\begin{array}{rl} 12 = & Z + 15 \\ -15 & -15 \\ \hline -3 = & Z \end{array}$

15. $\begin{array}{rl} -2.5 + p = & -1.7 \\ +2.5 & +2.5 \\ \hline p = & 0.8 \end{array}$

17. $\begin{array}{rl} R - (-8) = & 20 \\ R + 8 = & 20 \\ -8 & -8 \\ \hline R = & 12 \end{array}$

19. $A + \dfrac{2}{3} = \dfrac{4}{5}$

    $\dfrac{-2}{3} \qquad -\dfrac{2}{3}$

    $A = \dfrac{4}{5} - \dfrac{2}{3} = \dfrac{12}{15} - \dfrac{10}{15}$

    $A = \dfrac{2}{15}$

Exercise 7.9

Set A

* 1. $m = 9$
  2. $m = 7$
* 3. $Z = -8$
  4. $X = -12$
* 5. $N = 35$
  6. $N = 24$
* 7. $R = 648$
  8. $R = 208$
* 9. $K = -8$
  10. $K = -8$
*11. $t = -32$
  12. $t = -36$
*13. $y = 15$
  14. $y = 14$
*15. $v = 7$
  16. $v = 6$
*17. $m = -6.5$
  18. $m = -3.5$
*19. $T = -936$
  20. $X = 31$

Set B

  1. $m = 8$
  2. $m = 7$
  3. $X = -8$
  4. $X = -7$
  5. $N = 21$
  6. $N = 36$
  7. $R = 63$
  8. $R = 48$
  9. $K = -6$
  10. $K = -9$
  11. $t = -27$
  12. $t = -55$
  13. $y = 13$
  14. $y = 14$
  15. $r = 9$
  16. $r = 8$
  17. $m = -2.5$
  18. $m = -4.5$
  19. $T = -897$
  20. $X = 31.2$

*Selected Solutions from Set A

1. $\dfrac{5m}{5} = \dfrac{45}{5}$
   $m = 9$

3. $\dfrac{-8Z}{-8} = \dfrac{64}{-8}$
   $Z = -8$

5. $5 \cdot \dfrac{N}{5} = 7 \cdot 5$
   $N = 35$

7. $-9 \cdot \dfrac{R}{-9} = -72(-9)$
   $R = 648$

9. $\dfrac{-48}{6} = \dfrac{6K}{6}$
   $-8 = K$

11. $-8 = \dfrac{1}{4} t$
    $4(-8) = 4 \cdot \dfrac{1}{4} t$
    $-32 = t$

13. $\dfrac{-90}{-6} = \dfrac{-6y}{-6}$
    $15 = y$

15. $\dfrac{85v}{85} = \dfrac{595}{85}$
    $v = 7$

17. $\dfrac{-3.2m}{-3.2} = \dfrac{20.8}{-3.2}$
    $m = 6.5$

19. $78 = \dfrac{T}{-12}$
    $(-12) \cdot 78 = \dfrac{T}{-12} \cdot (-12)$
    $-936 = T$

Exercise 7.10

Set A

* 1. $X = 2$
  2. $X = 4$
* 3. $y = -4$
  4. $y = -6$
* 5. $z = 3$
  6. $z = 5$
* 7. $K = 4$
  8. $K = 3$
* 9. $N = 12$
  10. $N = 16$
*11. $m = 42$
  12. $m = 28$
*13. $R = -20$
  14. $R = -54$
*15. $t = 84$
  16. $t = 36$
*17. $X = 36$
  18. $X = 27$
  19. $N = 7.7$
  20. $X = -36$

Set B

  1. $X = 6$
  2. $X = 5$
  3. $y = -6$
  4. $y = -8$
  5. $z = 2$
  6. $z = 3$
  7. $k = 2$
  8. $k = 1$
  9. $N = 8$
  10. $N = 25$
  11. $m = 24$
  12. $m = 24$
  13. $R = -18$
  14. $R = -35$
  15. $t = 80$
  16. $t = 45$
  17. $X = 48$
  18. $X = 20$
  19. $N = 6.5$
  20. $X = -48$

*Selected Solutions from Set A

1. $2X + 5 = 9$
   $\underline{ -5 \qquad -5}$
   $\dfrac{2X}{2} = \dfrac{4}{2}$
   $X = 2$

3. $40 = -8y + 8$
   $\underline{-8 \qquad\qquad -8}$
   $\dfrac{32}{-8} = \dfrac{-8y}{-8}$
   $-4 = y$

5. $-3 + 5z = 12$
   $\underline{+3 \qquad\quad +3}$
   $\dfrac{5z}{5} = \dfrac{15}{5}$
   $z = 3$

7. $-18 = -3K - 6$
   $\underline{+6 \qquad\quad +6}$
   $\dfrac{-12}{-3} = \dfrac{-3K}{-3}$
   $4 = K$

9. $\dfrac{N}{3} + 6 = 10$
   $\underline{\qquad -6 \quad -6}$
   $3 \cdot \dfrac{N}{3} = 4 \cdot 3$
   $N = 12$

11. $\dfrac{1}{6} m - 4 = 3$
    $\underline{+4 \qquad\quad +4}$
    $6 \cdot \dfrac{1}{6} m = 7 \cdot 6$
    $m = 42$

13. $-12 = \dfrac{R}{5} - 8$
    $\underline{+8 \qquad\quad +8}$
    $5 \cdot (-4) = \dfrac{R}{5} \cdot 5$
    $-20 = R$

15. $4 + \dfrac{t}{-7} = -8$
    $\underline{-4 \qquad\qquad -4}$
    $-7 \cdot \dfrac{t}{-7} = -12(-7)$
    $t = 84$

17. $4 \cdot \dfrac{3X}{4} = 27 \cdot 4$
    $\dfrac{3X}{3} = \dfrac{108}{3}$
    $X = 36$

Exercise 7.11

Set A

1. associative
2. commutative
3. distributive
4. distributive
5. commutative
6. $11x$
7. $4y$
8. $8m - 4$
* 9. 2
10. $-6x + 10$
*11. $2x + 6$
12. $q - 4$
*13. $2f - 19$
14. $-8x - 2y + 5$
*15. $9y + 7x - 9$
16. $4a - 2b - c$

Set B

1. associative
2. distributive
3. distributive
4. commutative
5. commutative
6. $5x$
7. $9y$
8. $6m - 9$
9. 5
10. $-10x - 2$
11. $3x + 7$
12. $2q - 6$
13. $2f - 14$
14. $-16x + 2y + 2$
15. $11y + 3x - 7$
16. $4a - 4b + c$

* Selected Solutions from Set A

9. $\quad -5p - 7 + 6p + 9 - p$
$= -5p + 6p - p - 7 + 9$
$= 0 - 7 + 9$
$= 2$

11. $\quad -4(x - 4) + 2(3x - 5)$
$= -4x + 16 + 6x - 10$
$= -4x + 6x + 16 - 10$
$= 2x + 6$

13. $\quad 4(f - 5) - (3f - 1) + f$
$= 4f - 20 - 3f + 1 + f$
$= 4f - 3f + f - 20 + 1$
$= 2f - 19$

15. $\quad 4y - 3x + 5(2x + y) - 9$
$= 4y - 3x + 10x + 5y - 9$
$= 4y + 5y - 3x + 10x - 9$
$= 9y + 7x - 9$

Exercise 7.12

Set A

* 1. 3
2. -3
* 3. -2
4. -2
5. 5
6. -4
* 7. -1
8. -7
9. 23
10. -16
*11. 0
12. 0
*13. 1
14. -1
*15. 3

Set B

1. 2
2. 3
3. 3
4. -1
5. 7
6. -9
7. -2
8. -7
9. 27
10. -18
11. 0
12. 0
13. -1
14. 1
15. -7

* Selected Solutions from Set A

1. $3x + 2x = 7 + 8$
$5x = 15$
$x = 3$

3. $4(2x - 1) = -20$
$8x - 4 = -20$
$8x = -16$
$x = -2$

7. $5 - 2x = 4x + 11$
$5 = 6x + 11$
$-6 = 6x$
$-1 = x$

11. $-6(2x + 1) + 8 = 4x + 2$
$-12x - 6 + 8 = 4x + 2$
$-12x + 2 = 4x + 2$
$-16x + 2 = 2$
$-16x = 0$
$x = 0$

13. $9 + 8x - 5x = 4(2x + 3) - 8$
$9 + 3x = 8x + 12 - 8$
$9 + 3x = 8x + 4$
$9 = 5x + 4$
$5 = 5x$
$1 = x$

15. $7 - (3x - 5) = 3(x + 1) - 3x$
$7 - 3x + 5 = 3x + 3 - 3x$
$12 - 3x = 3$
$-3x = -9$
$x = 3$

Exercise 7.13

Set A

1. $x + 6$
2. $3 + x$
3. $2x - 5$
4. $2x - 6$
5. $6x$
6. $9x$
7. $3x + 4$
8. $5x + 2$
9. $\dfrac{x}{7}$
10. $\dfrac{x}{4}$
11. $2x + 6 = 24$
12. $x - 2 = 16$
13. $2(x + 6) = 24$
14. $4x + 7 = -13$
15. $-7x - 5 = 86$
16. $3x - 10 = x + 6$
17. $2x + 3x + 4x = 90$
18. $3(x - 5) = -25 + 4$
19. $4(x + 3) = 48$
20. $2(x + 3) + x = x + 18$

Set B

1. $x + 2$
2. $8 + x$
3. $2x - 7$
4. $2x - 4$
5. $5x$
6. $3x$
7. $4x + 6$
8. $3x + 1$
9. $\dfrac{x}{9}$
10. $\dfrac{x}{2}$
11. $2x + 4 = 18$
12. $x - 5 = 12$
13. $2(x + 3) = 32$
14. $5x + 9 = 39$
15. $-6x - 5 = 67$
16. $3x - 4 = x + 12$
17. $2x + 3x + 5x = 90$
18. $4(x - 6) = -21 + 5$
19. $3(x + 4) = 18$
20. $2(x + 5) + x = x + 16$

Exercise 7.14

Set A

* 1. 9
2. 18
3. 6
4. −5
* 5. −13
6. 8
7. 10
8. −2
* 9. 9
10. 6
*11. 101, 102, 103
12. 42, 43, 44, 45
*13. 2008 for Pico,
    2578 for Mercer
14. wife − 129 lbs
    center − 266 lbs
*15. 19

Set B

1. 7
2. 17
3. 13
4. 6
5. −12
6. 8
7. 9
8. 2
9. 2
10. 3
11. 66, 67, 68
12. 54, 55, 56, 57
13. 262 for Ed
    318 for Alan
14. wife − 63"
    center − 88"
15. 23

* Selected Solutions from Set A

1. x = the number
   $2x + 6 = 24$
   $2x = 18$
   $x = 9$

5. x = the number
   $-7x - 5 = 86$
   $-7x = 91$
   $x = -13$

9. x = the number
   $4(x + 3) = 48$
   $4x + 12 = 48$
   $4x = 36$
   $x = 9$

11. x = the 1st whole number
   $x + 1$ = the 2nd whole number
   $x + 2$ = the 3rd whole number
   $x + x + 1 + x + 2 = 306$
   $3x + 3 = 306$
   $3x = 303$
   $x = 101$
   $x + 1 = 102$
   $x + 2 = 103$

13. x = # of votes for Pico
   $x + 570$ = # of votes for Mercer
   $x + x + 570 = 4586$
   $2x + 570 = 4586$
   $2x = 4016$
   $x = 2008$
   $x + 570 = 2578$

15. x = my age
   $3x + 2x = 7x - 38$
   $5x = 7x - 38$
   $-2x = -38$
   $x = 19$

Exercise 7.15

Set A
* 1. $1,100.27
  2. $1,344.82
* 3. $1,112.21
  4. $1,049.78
* 5. $12,044.34
  6. $36,576.71
* 7. $164.70
  8. $522.90

Set B
  1. $1,533.44
  2. $1,971.18
  3. $2,138.09
  4. $3,465.04
  5. $21,636.48
  6. $705,980.50
  7. $1,430.63
  8. $561.85

*Selected Solutions from Set A

1. A is unknown.
   $P = 750$, $r = 0.048 \div 12 = 0.004$,
   $n = 12 \times 8 = 96$

   $A = 750(1 + 0.004)^{96}$
   $A = 750(1.004)^{96}$
   $A = 750(1.467021)$
   $A = \$1,100.27$

3. P is unknown.
   $A = 1250$, $r = 0.0584 \div 365 = 0.00016$,
   $n = 365 \times 2 = 730$

   $1250 = P(1 + 0.00016)^{730}$
   $1250 = P(1.00016)^{730}$
   $1250 = P(1.123884)$
   $P = \$1,112.21$

5. S is unknown.
   $PMT = 75$, $r = 0.084 \div 12 = 0.007$,
   $n = 12 \times 9 = 108$

   $S = 75 \left[\dfrac{(1 + 0.007)^{108} - 1}{0.007} \right]$

   $S = 75 \left[\dfrac{2.124138 - 1}{0.007} \right]$

   $S = 75[160.591143]$
   $S = \$12,044.34$

7. PMT is unknown.
   $r = 0.156 \div 12 = 0.013$,
   $n = 12 \times 3 = 36$, S = 7500

   $7500 = PMT \left[\dfrac{(1 + 0.013)^{36} - 1}{0.013} \right]$

   $7500 = PMT \left[\dfrac{1.591989 - 1}{0.013} \right]$
   $7500 = PMT[45.537615]$
   $\$164.70 = PMT$

Chapter 7

Practice Test A
 1. 2
 2. <
 3. >
 4. −4
 5. −42
 6. −11
 7. 6
 8. −40
 9. −7
10. −6
11. $x = 24$
12. $x = 36$
13. $x = 38$
14. $x = 57$
15. $9x − 15$
16. $x = −2$
17. $4x = x + 12$
    $x = 4$
18. $5509.03

Chapter 7

Practice Test B
 1. 19
 2. >
 3. >
 4. 3
 5. −53
 6. −15
 7. 14
 8. −54
 9. 32
10. −32
11. $x = 26$
12. $x = 36$
13. $x = 39$
14. $x = −8$
15. $10x − 22$
16. $x = 2$
17. $x − 6 = 2x + 4$
    $x = −10$
18. $28,062.82

Chapter 8

Pretest

1. $\overline{AE}$, $\overline{BD}$, $\overline{AB}$, $\overline{AC}$, $\overline{BC}$, $\overline{ED}$, $\overline{DC}$, $\overline{EC}$
2. AB = 12.5
3. acute angle
4. supplement = 134°, complement = 44°
5.
6.
7.
8. Each angle is 108°.

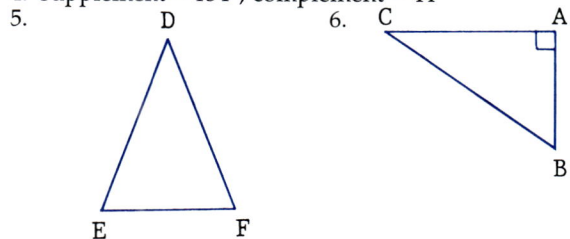

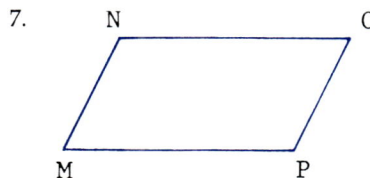

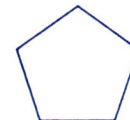

 9. $C = 78.5$ cm, $A = 490.625$ sq cm
10. $A = 28$, $P = 24$
11. $SA = 244.92$ sq cm; $V = 282.6$ cu cm
12. 26 in.
13. 7800 lbs

Exercise 8.1

Set A

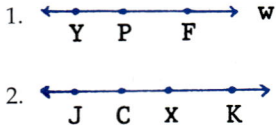

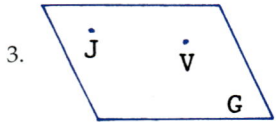

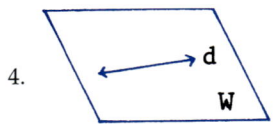

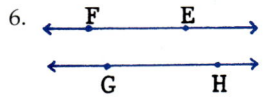

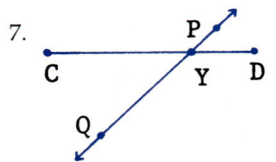

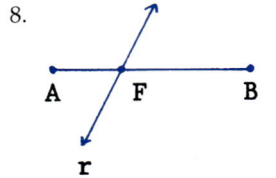

1. Y P F w
2. J C X K
3. J V G
4. d W
5. g h
6. F E / G H
7. P C Y D Q
8. A F B r
9. $\overline{MA}$, $\overline{MT}$, $\overline{MH}$, $\overline{AT}$, $\overline{AH}$, $\overline{TH}$
10. $\overline{SR}$, $\overline{SE}$, $\overline{RE}$, $\overline{SU}$, $\overline{SP}$, $\overline{UP}$, $\overline{RU}$, $\overline{EP}$
11. EA = 5, AS = 5, AY = 10
12. NI = 24, IC = 12, CE = 12

Set B

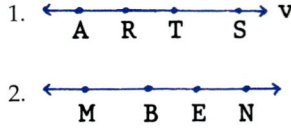

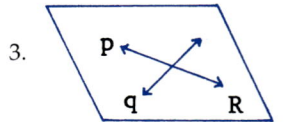

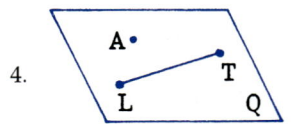

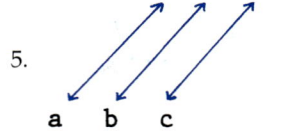

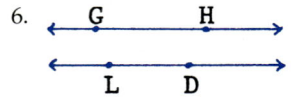

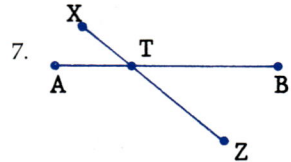

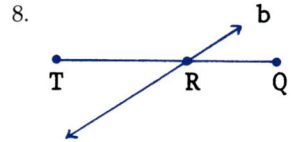

1. A R T S v
2. M B E N
3. P q R
4. A L T Q
5. a b c
6. G H / L D
7. X T A B Z
8. b T R Q
9. $\overline{GR}$, $\overline{RE}$, $\overline{AE}$, $\overline{GA}$, $\overline{GT}$, $\overline{GE}$, TE, RT, RA, TA
10. $\overline{LE}$, $\overline{LK}$, $\overline{EK}$, $\overline{LI}$, $\overline{IE}$, $\overline{IK}$
11. HO = 3, OP = 3, PE = 6
12. LU = 7, UC = 7, CK = 7

Exercise 8.2

Set A

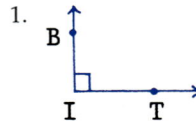

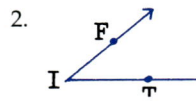

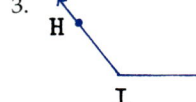

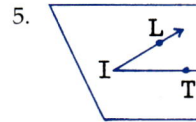

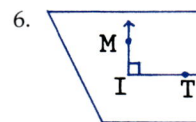

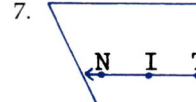

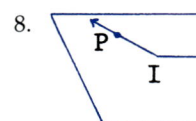

1. B I T
2. F I T
3. H I T
4. K I T
5. L I T F
6. M I T G
7. N I T H
8. P I T J
9. acute
10. obtuse
11. straight
12. right
13. comp.: 45° supp.: 135°
14. comp.: 30° supp.: 120°
15. comp.: $67\frac{1}{2}$ ° supp.: $157\frac{1}{2}$ °
16. comp.: 74.5° supp.: 164.5°
17. 150°
18. 30°

Set B

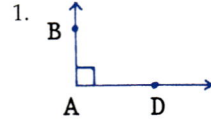

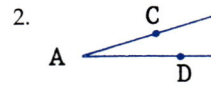

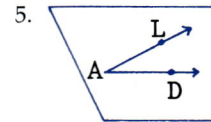

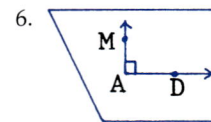

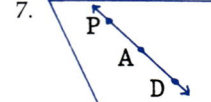

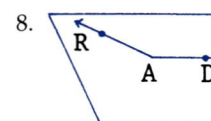

1. B A D
2. C A D
3. F A D
4. H A D
5. L A D H
6. M A D I
7. P A D J
8. R A D K
9. acute
10. obtuse
11. right
12. straight
13. comp.: 75° supp.: 165°
14. comp.: 60° supp.: 150°
15. comp.: $72\frac{1}{2}$ ° supp.: $162\frac{1}{2}$ °
16. comp.: 59.5° supp.: 149.5°
17. 165°
18. 30°

Exercise 8.3

Set A

1.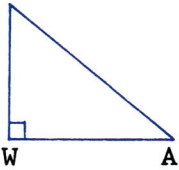

2.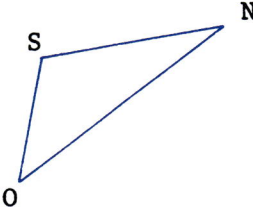

3.

4.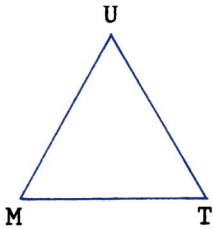

5. △FRA, △FAC, △ENC

6. △PAS, △PAN, △PNS, △PAI, △ANI

7. right
8. acute
9. obtuse
10. acute
11. isosceles
12. scalene
13. equilateral
14. isosceles

Set B

1.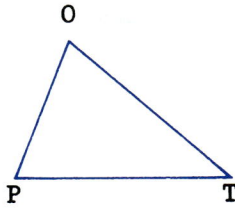

2.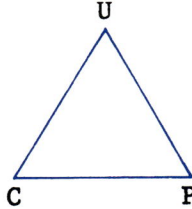

3.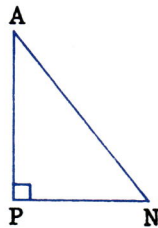

4.

5. △JSE, △JSN, △JSO, △JEN, △JEO, △JNO

6. △TSW, △TSO, △TWO, △TAZ, △TAK, △TZK

7. obtuse
8. right
9. right
10. acute
11. equilateral
12. isosceles
13. isosceles
14. scalene

Exercise 8.4

Set A

1.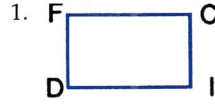

2.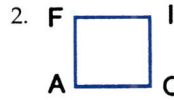

3.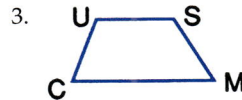

4.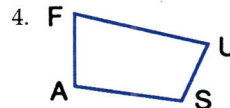

5.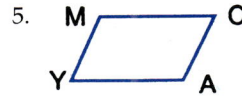

6.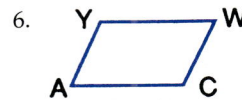

7.

8.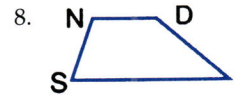

9.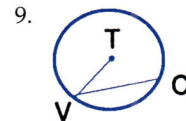

10.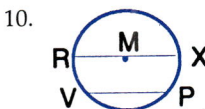

11. $\overline{ED}$, $\overline{EI}$, $\overline{EA}$, $\overline{EN}$

12. $\overline{DN}$

13. $\overline{DN}$, $\overline{IA}$
14. 4
15. 10
16. 6.5

Set B

1.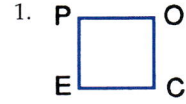

2.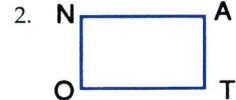

3.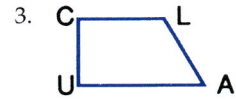

4.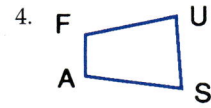

5.

6.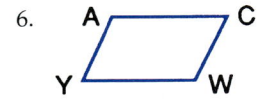

7.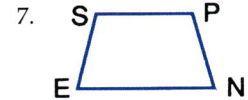

8.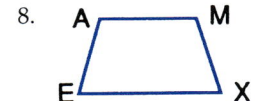

9.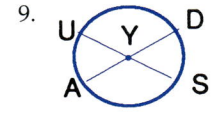

10.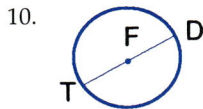

11. $\overline{AF}$, $\overline{AE}$, $\overline{AD}$

12. $\overline{FE}$

13. $\overline{FR}$, $\overline{FE}$
14. 5
15. 8
16. 12.5

Exercise 8.5

Set A

1.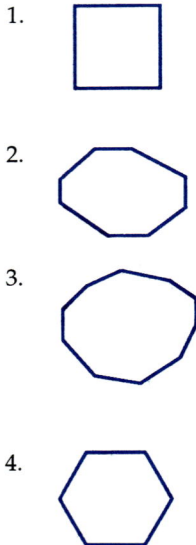

2.

3.

4.

* 5. 540°
   6. 720°
   7. 1260°
   8. 2340°
* 9. 1620°
  10. 2160°
  11. 60°
  12. 135°
*13. 144°
  14. 150°
*15. ≈152.31°
  16. 157.5°

Set B

1.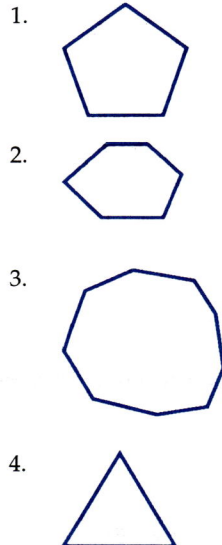

2.

3.

4.

   5. 180°
   6. 1080°
   7. 1440°
   8. 1800°
   9. 1980°
  10. 2520°
  11. 108°
  12. 120°
  13. 140°
  14. 160°
  15. ≈147.27°
  16. ≈154.29°

*Selected Solutions from Set A

5. A pentagon has 5 sides. Using $n = 5$ in the sum of the angles formula, we get the following:
$$S = 180(n - 2)$$
$$= 180(5 - 2) = 180(3) = 540°$$

9. Using $n = 11$ in the sum of the angles formula, we get the following:
$$S = 180(n - 2)$$
$$= 180(11 - 2) = 180(9) = 1620°$$

13. The sum of the angles of a 10-sided polygon is $S = 180(10 - 2) = 180(8) = 1440°$. To get the measure of each angle, divide the sum of the angles by the number of angles in the polygon. We get $1440 ÷ 10 = 144°$.

15. The sum of the angles of a 13-sided polygon is $S = 180(13 - 2) = 180(11) = 1980°$. To get the measure of each angle, divide the sum of the angles by the number of angles in the polygon. We get $1980 ÷ 13 ≈ 152.31°$.

Exercise 8.6

Set A

1. $P = 28$ ft
   $A = 45$ sq ft
2. $P = 22$ ft
   $A = 28$ sq ft
3. $P = 34$ in
   $A = 72.25$ sq in.
4. $P = 46$ in
   $A = 132.25$ sq in.
5. $C = 42.076$ cm
   $A ≈ 140.95$ sq cm
6. $C = 52.124$ cm
   $A ≈ 216.31$ sq cm
* 7. $P = 54$
   $A = 126$
8. $P = 60$
   $A = 120$
* 9. $P = 25$
   $A = 31.25$
10. $P = 20$
   $A = 19.5$
*11. $P = 17.99$
   $A ≈ 19.23$
12. $P = 12.85$
   $A ≈ 9.81$
13. $P = 18$
   $A = 15$
14. $P = 64$
   $A = 222$

Set B

1. $P = 26$ cm
   $A = 40$ sq cm
2. $P = 30$ cm
   $A = 54$ sq cm
3. $P = 25$ in
   $A ≈ 39.06$ sq in.
4. $P = 45$ in
   $A ≈ 126.56$ sq in.
5. $C = 79.756$ m
   $A ≈ 506.45$ sq m
6. $C = 97.968$ m
   $A ≈ 764.15$ sq m
7. $P = 24$
   $A = 24$
8. $P = 54$
   $A = 126$
9. $P = 9$
   $P = 3.6$
10. $P = 9.2$
   $A = 4.59$
11. $P = 32.13$
   $A = 63.585$
12. $P = 24.99$
   $A = 38.465$
13. $P = 44$
   $A = 112$
14. $P = 34$
   $A = 66$

*Selected Solutions from Set A

7. perimeter = sum of the sides = $13 + 20 + 21 = 54$
   area = $\frac{1}{2} bh = \frac{1}{2}(21)(12) = 126$

9. perimeter = sum of the sides
   $$= 6\frac{1}{4} + 6\frac{1}{4} + 6\frac{1}{4} + 6\frac{1}{4} = 25$$
   area = $bh = \left(6\frac{1}{4}\right)(5) = 6.25 \times 5 = 31.25$

11. circumference of the half-circle = $\frac{1}{2}(2\pi r) =$
    $$\frac{1}{2}(2)(3.14)(3.5) = 10.99$$
    perimeter = circumference of the half-circle + length of diameter = $10.99 + 7 = 17.99$
    area of the half-circle = $\frac{1}{2}(\pi r^2) = \frac{1}{2}(3.14)(3.5)^2$
    $$= \frac{1}{2}(38.465) = 19.2325 ≈ 19.23$$

Exercise 8.7

Set A

1. 150 sq in.
   125 cu in.
2. 864 sq ft
   1728 cu ft
* 3. 103.36 sq m
   57.76 cu m
4. 18,106.6 sq cm
   155,387.8 cu cm
* 5. 39.25 sq ft
   16.485 cu ft
6. 1609.25 sq in.
   3925 cu in
7. 530.66 sq yd
   1149.76 cu yd
8. 6644.24 sq m
   $\approx$ 50,939.17 cu m
9. The cylinder
*10. The sphere
*11. 27
12. 46,656

Set B

1. 2400 sq ft
   8000 cu ft
2. 486 sq in.
   729 cu in.
3. 1849.4 sq cm
   3822 cu cm
4. 247.34 sq m
   213.15 cu m
5. 9151.53 sq in.
   35,238.65 cu in.
6. 557.35 sq ft
   1000.875 cu ft
7. 200.96 sq m
   267.95 cu m
8. 1384.74 sq yd
   4846.59 cu yd
9. The box
10. The cube
11. 1,000,000
12. 1,000,000,000

*Selected Solutions from Set A

3. The surface area of the box:
$$S = 2lw + 2lh + 2wh$$
$$= 2(7.6)(3.8) + 2(7.6)(2) + 2(3.8)(2)$$
$$= 57.76 + 30.4 + 15.2 = 103.36 \text{ sq m}$$
The volume of the box:
$$V = lwh$$
$$= 7.6(3.8)(2) = 57.76 \text{ cu m}$$

5. Since the diameter is 2 ft, the radius is 1 ft. The surface area of the right cylinder:
$$S = 2\pi r^2 + 2\pi rh$$
$$= 2(3.14)(1)^2 + 2(3.14)(1)(5.25)$$
$$= 6.28 + 32.97 = 39.25 \text{ sq ft}$$
The volume of the right cylinder:
$$V = \pi r^2 h$$
$$= (3.14)(1)^2(5.25) = 16.485 \text{ cu ft}$$

10. We need to find the volume of each tank.
Cube: $V = e^3 = (8.6)^3 = 636.056$ cu ft
Sphere: $V = \dfrac{4\pi r^3}{3} = \dfrac{4(3.14)(5.4)^3}{3}$
$$= 659.24928 \approx 659.25 \text{ cu ft}$$
Thus, the spherical tank holds more water.

11. Since 1 yd = 3 ft, the cube has edges that measure 3 ft.
The volume of the cube is:
$$V = e^3 = (3)^3 = 27 \text{ cu ft}$$

Exercise 8.8

Set A

* 1. 10
2. 25
3. 12
4. 40
* 5. 5.2
6. 5.6
7. $\approx$ 12.04
8. $\approx$ 18.38
* 9. $\approx$ 52.11
10. $\approx$ 52.73
11. $\approx$ 29.39"
12. $\approx$ 131.92'
* 13. $\approx$ 101.71 cm

Set B

1. 15
2. 17
3. 16
4. 35
5. 4.5
6. 3.2
7. $\approx$ 10.63
8. $\approx$ 24.04
9. $\approx$ 80.71
10. $\approx$ 46.08
11. $\approx$ 31.75"
12. $\approx$ 110.86'
13. $\approx$ 97.74 m

* Selected Solutions from Set A

1. $c^2 = 6^2 + 8^2$
$c^2 = 36 + 64$
$c^2 = 100$
$c = \sqrt{100} = 10$

5. $a^2 + 3.9^2 = 6.5^2$
$a^2 + 15.21 = 42.25$
$a^2 = 27.04$
$a = \sqrt{27.04} = 5.2$

9. $24.3^2 + b^2 = 57.5^2$
$590.49 + b^2 = 3306.25$
$b^2 = 2715.76$
$b = \sqrt{2715.76} \approx 52.11$

13. $x^2 = 37.6^2 + 94.5^2$
$x^2 = 1413.76 + 8930.25$
$x^2 = 10,344.01$
$x = \sqrt{10,344.01} \approx 101.71$

Exercise 8.9

Set A

* 1. $179.85
  2. $599.80
  3. $830.52
  4. ≈ 24.98 ft
  5. ≈ 84.85 ft
  6. 28 tiles
     $44.52
* 7. 428.75 lb
  8. 552.64 lb
  9. 195,333.12 lb
  10. 172,032 lb
*11. 10%
  12. $518.75
  13. $124.44
  14. 11,074 lb
*15. a) ≈ 3.45 gal
     b) 28,184.64 gal

Set B

  1. $283.80
  2. $703.36
  3. $1601.52
  4. ≈ 44.5 in.
  5. ≈ 176.79 m
  6. 160 tiles
     $200.00
  7. 735 lb
  8. 9947.52 lb
  9. 791,280 lb
  10. 64,000 lb
  11. 40%
  12. $283.64
  13. $179.85
  14. 6021 lb
  15. a) ≈ 3.58 gal
     b) ≈ 22,829.56 gal

*Selected Solutions from Set A

1. Since the linoleum is being sold by the sq yd, convert the 9 ft by 15 ft dimensions to yards (9 ft = 3 yd and 15 ft = 5 yd). Thus, the area of the kitchen is $A = lw = 3 \times 5 = 15$ sq yd. At $11.99 a yd, the cost is $15(\$11.99) = \$179.85$.

7. Since the iron slab weighs 490 lb per cu ft, we need to find the number of cubic feet in the slab and multiply it by 490. Find the volume of slab by first changing the dimensions to ft:
   42 in. = 3.5 ft, 3 in = 0.25 ft, and 12 in = 1 ft.
   $V = lwh = 3.5(0.25)(1) = 0.875$ cu ft
   weight $= 490(0.875) = 428.75$ lb

11. The sign without a missing section is a rectangle with an area of $A = lw = 20(16) = 320$ sq ft. The missing section is a rectangle with an area of $A = lw = 8(4) = 32$ sq ft. Thus,
   the percent that is missing is $\dfrac{32}{320} = \dfrac{P}{100}$
   $$320P = 3200$$
   $$P = 10$$

15. a) Since the coverage of the paint is 400 sq ft per gallon, to find the amount of paint, find the surface area of the tank and divide by 400.
   $$\frac{S}{400} = \frac{2\pi r^2 + 2\pi rh}{400}$$
   $$= \frac{2(3.14)(100) + 2(3.14)(10)(12)}{400} \approx 3.45 \text{ gal}$$
   b) Since 1 cu ft ≈ 7.48 gal, find the volume of the tank in cubic feet and multiply by 7.48.
   $V = \pi r^2 h = 3.14(10)^2(12)$
   $V = 3768$ cu ft
   gallons: $3768(7.48) = 28{,}184.64$ gal

Chapter 8

Practice Test A

1. $\overline{AG}$, $\overline{GI}$, $\overline{IN}$, $\overline{NY}$, $\overline{YI}$, $\overline{IA}$, $\overline{GY}$, $\overline{AN}$
2. $GI = 8\frac{1}{2}$
3. obtuse angle
4. supplement = 143°, complement = 53°
5.

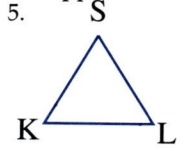

6.

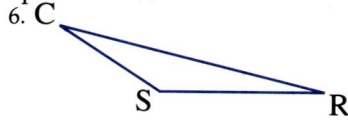

7.

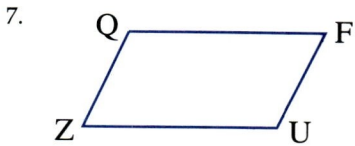

8. 120°

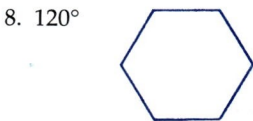

9. $C = 116.18$ cm, $A = 1074.665$ sq cm
10. $A = 18$, $P = 20$
11. $S \approx 232.23$ sq ft, $V \approx 332.87$ cu ft
12. ≈ 14.42 cm
13. 1750.32 gal

Chapter 8

Practice Test B

1. $\overline{SX}$, $\overline{ST}$, $\overline{XT}$, $\overline{SF}$, $\overline{FX}$, $\overline{FT}$
2. $ST = 38$
3. right angle
4. supplement = 151°, complement = 61°
5.

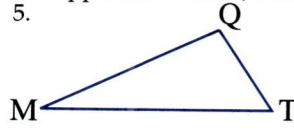

6.

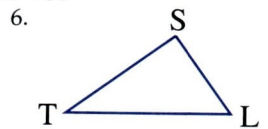

7.

8. 135°

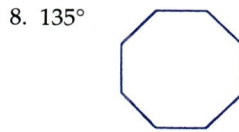

9. $C = 135.02$ cm, $A = 1451.465$ sq cm
10. $A = 336$, $P = 84$
11. $S = 443.76$ sq ft, $V = 636.056$ cu ft
12. ≈ 29.39 ft
13. 6.78%

Unit IV. Exam

1. 20
2. −9
3. −8
4. 4
5. 45
6. −5
7. −49
8. −10
9. 7
10. −2
11. 4
12. −12
13. equilateral triangle
14.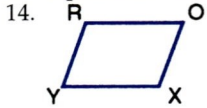

15. A = 64 sq in.
    P = 32 in.
16. A = 28.26 sq cm
    C = 18.84 cm
17. a) 3 gal
    b) $93.80
18. 32.5 in.
19. $2880.98

Final Exam

1. 20,380,000
2. 27,491
3. 567
4. 92
5. $2\frac{41}{56}$
6. $1\frac{5}{84}$
7. $53\frac{5}{6}$
8. 266.58
9. 98.045
10. 6.05
11. 441.9
12. −29
13. 0.486
14. 3.5%
15. 5.8 kg
16. 571 in. (rounded to the nearest inch)
17. 87.5
18. 12
19. −2
20. 4
21. mean = 89, median = 90.5
22. $94.48
23. $170.06
24. $40.04
25. $699.72
26. $393.86
27. 70,461.6 gal; 587,808 lb
28. ≈ 113.14 ft
29. 57, 58, 59
30. 20 yrs old

Answers Crossword Puzzles

Chapter 1

Across
1. THREE
2. TEN
4. VALUE
7. EXPONENT
8. ODD
9. SIX
12. ROOT
15. ADDEND
18. ONE
20. EIGHT
21. FACTORS
22. SQUARE
23. MULT
24. NUMBER
25. THREE

Down
1. TENS
3. NINE
5. ADD
6. POWER
7. EXPANDED FORM
10. FOUR
11. BASE
13. PLACE VALUE
14. TWO
16. DIGIT
17. PLACE
19. PRODUCT
22. SUM

Chapter 2

Across
4. SIX
7. FOUR
8. SUBTRACT
10. DIVISOR
11. ORDER
14. SIX
15. TOP
17. DIFFERENCE
20. NINE
21. AVERAGE
23. TEN
24. REMAINDER

Down
1. QUOTIENT
2. TWO
3. YES
4. SUB
5. FACTORING
6. PRIME
9. COMPOSITE
10. DIVIDEND
12. DIV
13. MINUEND
16. ONE
18. SEVEN
19. CAT
22. RAM

Chapter 3

Across
1. CANCELING
5. FIVE
6. ADD
9. THREE
11. DENOMINATOR
13. ONE
16. IMPROPER
17. DENOMINATOR
20. RECIPROCAL
21. PER

Down
1. COMPLEX
2. NO
3. LCD
4. NEW
5. FOUR
7. PROPER
8. FRACTION
9. TWO
10. MIXED
12. REAR
14. NUMERATOR
18. ONE
19. SIX

Chapter 4

Across
2. SHOP
4. HUNDREDTHS
7. TWO
8. EVEN
9. ONE
10. TENTHS
13. EIGHT
14. TWO
15. DIGIT
16. PLACE
18. TEN
20. SEVEN
22. NINE
24. NINE
25. TWO THREE

Down
1. THREE
3. PRODUCT
5. EIGHT
6. THOUSANDTHS
7. TWO
10. TWO
11. NUMBER
12. SIXTY
16. POINT
17. TEN ONE
19. TEN
21. NINE
23. TWO

Chapter 5

Across
4. INTEREST
6. LOW
8. ONE
9. FIVE
10. PERCENT
11. FOUR
13. RATE
14. ONES
15. TWO
19. SEVEN
20. CROSS PRODUCTS
22. EVEN
23. SIX

Down
1. TIME
2. PRINCIPAL
3. TWO
5. TENTHS
6. LEFT
7. TENTHS
10. PROPORTION
12. HUNDREDTHS
16. ONE
18. THREE
21. SIX

Chapter 6

Across
1. TWO
3. GAL
5. YARD
8. CENTI
9. THREE
10. LINE
12. BAR
13. AVE
15. PERCENT
16. DECA
18. METER
19. LESS
20. MEDIAN
21. SIX
22. MI
23. FIVE
26. LEAST
28. EVEN
29. UNIT FRACTION

Down
2. ONE
4. LITER
6. AVERAGE
7. KILO
8. CIRCLE
11. TENTHS
12. BAD
14. GRAM
16. DUE
17. MEAN
20. MILLI
21. SEVEN
24. IN
25. NINE
27. QT

Chapter 7

Across

3. SEVENTY-ONE
6. LESS
8. FIVE
9. EQUATION
12. MORE THAN
14. ROAD
15. CUP
18. VARIABLE
20. FT
22. NEGATIVE
23. FORTY
25. NINETEEN
26. ZERO

Down

1. ALGEBRAIC
2. IS
4. ONE
5. EVEN
7. SIGNED
8. FOUR
10. ADD
11. NUMBER LINE
13. GREATER
15. CM
16. POSITIVE
17. LETTERS
19. IN
21. KG
24. TEN

Chapter 8

Across

3. CUBE
7. CIRCUMFERENCE
9. PI
10. ACUTE
12. SPHERE
14. SEGMENT
15. AREA
18. IN
19. RAY
20. GREATER
23. STRAIGHT
25. OBTUSE

Down

1. ARC
2. SEMI
3. CIRCLE
4. OCTAGON
5. PERIMETER
6. VOLUME
8. RADIUS
10. ANGLE
11. TEN
13. PLANE
16. RIGHT
17. DOT
21. SQ FT
22. FIVE
24. TO

Index

DEVTUTOR

MAC Version 1996*

The *DEVTUTOR* software for a Macintosh Computer gives drill, practice, and tutoring on the majors topics found in the *MATH FOR COLLEGE STUDENTS*, 5th ed, by Ronald Staszkow. The software is coordinated with the text and uses explanations that are found in the text. The *DEVTUTOR* interactive programs give the one-on-one help you may need to understand basic mathematics. The programs have been adapted to the MAC environment from the programs used for many years in the Ohlone College Mathematics Learning Center. The *DEVTUTOR* software package contains the following 33 programs found on three 3.5" floppy disks.

MATH1A	Reading & Rounding Off Whole Numbers	MATH5A	Solving Proportions
MATH1B	Basic Facts in Addition & Multiplication	MATH5B	Changing Percents, Decimals, Fractions
MATH1C	Advanced Work: Addition & Multiplication	MATH5C	Percentage Problems
MATH1D	Applications: Addition & Multiplication	MATH5D	Applications: Proportions and Percents
MATH2A	Basic Facts in Subtraction & Division	MATH6A	Measurement Conversions
MATH2B	Advanced Work: Subtraction & Division	MATH6B	Reading Statistical Graphs
MATH2C	The Order of Operations	MATH6C	Applications: Measurement & Statistics
MATH2D	Applications: Subtraction & Division	MATH7A	Operating With Signed Numbers
MATH3A	Reducing Fractions	MATH7B	Solving Equations
MATH3B	Multiplying and Dividing Fractions	MATH7C	Equations and Word Problems
MATH3C	Finding the Least Common Denominator	MATH8A	Lines, Angles, and Polygons
MATH3D	Adding & Subtracting Fractions	MATH8B	Perimeters and Areas
MATH3E	Working with Mixed Numbers	MATH8C	Surface Areas, Volumes, Pythagorean Th.
MATH3F	Applications: Fractions	FINAL1	Practice Exam: Chapters 1 - 4
MATH4A	Rounding Off Decimals	FINAL2	Practice Exam: Chapters 5 - 6
MATH4B	Changing Between Fractions & Decimals	FINAL3	Practice Exam: Chapters 7 - 8
MATH4C	Applications: Decimal		

Before you can run the programs, you need to make a new folder on the hard disk drive called DEVTUTOR and you must copy the *DEVTUTOR* programs into that folder.

Making the new folder called DEVTUTOR.
1. Turn on computer system.
2. Use the mouse pointer to click on File Menu and drag pointer to New Folder.
3. Release clicker. (*An **Untitled** folder will be created and highlighted on the Hard Drive*)
4. Type the word, DEVTUTOR, press the return key, and the name of the Untitled folder will be changed to DEVTUTOR.

Copying the *DEVTUTOR* programs into the *DEVTUTOR* folder.
1. Insert Disk 1 into the floppy drive..
2. Double click on the Disc 1 with the mouse pointer.
3. Use the mouse pointer to click on the Edit Menu and drag pointer to Select All.
4. Release clicker. (*All programs on Disk 1 should be highlighted.*)
5. Use the mouse pointer to click on any of the highlighted programs and drag the programs into the DEVTUTOR folder on the hard drive.

(Repeat steps 1-5 for Disk 2 and Disk 3.)

Running the *DEVTUTOR* programs.
(*Note: all programs from the three disks must be in the* DEVTUTOR *folder.*)
1. Turn on computer system.
2. Use the mouse pointer to double click on DEVTUTOR folder.
3. Double click on the TUTOR application.
4. Follow the on screen instructions to run desired programs.

---

*To receive a Mac version of the DEVTUTOR, contact Kendall/Hunt Publishing Company.

DEVTUTOR

IBM Version 1996

The *DEVTUTOR* software for an IBM PC/compatible gives drill, practice, and tutoring on the major topics found in the *MATH FOR COLLEGE STUDENTS*, 5th ed, by Ronald Staszkow. The software is coordinated with the text and uses explanations that are found in the text. The *DEVTUTOR* interactive programs give the one-on-one help you may need to understand basic mathematics. The programs have been adapted to the IBM environment from the programs used for many years in the Ohlone College Mathematics Learning Center. The *DEVTUTOR* software package contains the following 33 programs found on one 3.5" floppy disk.

MATH1A	Reading & Rounding Off Whole Numbers	MATH5A	Solving Proportions
MATH1B	Basic Facts in Addition & Multiplication	MATH5B	Changing Percents, Decimals, Fractions
MATH1C	Advanced Work: Addition & Multiplication	MATH5C	Percentage Problems
MATH1D	Applications: Addition & Multiplication	MATH5D	Applications: Proportions and Percents
MATH2A	Basic Facts in Subtraction & Division	MATH6A	Measurement Conversions
MATH2B	Advanced Work: Subtraction & Division	MATH6B	Reading Graphs
MATH2C	The Order of Operations	MATH6C	Applications: Measurement & Statistics
MATH2D	Applications: Subtraction & Division	MATH7A	Operating With Signed Numbers
MATH3A	Reducing Fractions	MATH7B	Solving Equations
MATH3B	Multiplying and Dividing Fractions	MATH7C	Equations and Word Problems
MATH3C	Finding the Least Common Denominator	MATH8A	Lines, Angles, and Polygons
MATH3D	Adding & Subtracting Fractions	MATH8B	Perimeters and Areas
MATH3E	Working with Mixed Numbers	MATH8C	Surface Areas, Volumes, Pythagorean Thm.
MATH3F	Applications: Fractions	FINAL1	Practice Exam: Chapters 1–4
MATH4A	Rounding Off Decimals	FINAL2	Practice Exam: Chapters 5–6
MATH4B	Changing Between Fractions & Decimals	FINAL3	Practice Exam: Chapters 7–8
MATH4C	Applications: Decimals		

Running *DEVTUTOR* from a 3.5" floppy disk drive (A:)*

1. Boot computer system and exit to DOS.
2. At A> prompt, insert 3.5" *DEVTUTOR* Disk into Drive A.
3. Type: TUTOR (*and press Enter key*)
4. Follow the on-screen directions to run the desired programs.

Using *DEVTUTOR* on a hard disk drive (C:)*

Before you can run the programs from a hard disk drive, you need to install the program onto the hard drive. The install program on the floppy disk creates a directory called DEVTUTOR and copies the *DEVTUTOR* programs into that directory.

Installing *DEVTUTOR* onto a hard drive (C:) from a 3.5" floppy disk drive.

1. Boot computer system and exit to DOS.
2. At A> prompt, insert DEVTUTOR Disk into drive (A:),
   type: INSTALL (*and press Enter key*)

Running *DEVTUTOR* from a hard disk drive (C:).

1. Boot computer system and exit to DOS.
2. At C> prompt, type: CD\DEVTUTOR (*and press Enter key*)
3. Type: TUTOR (*and press Enter key*)
4. Follow the on-screen directions to run desired programs.

---

* *The directions assume the hard disk drive is at the* **C>** *prompt and the floppy disk drive is at the* **A>** *prompt.*